THE OPENGL EXTENSIONS GUIDE

THE OPENGL®
EXTENSIONS GUIDE

Eric Lengyel

CHARLES RIVER MEDIA, INC.
Hingham, Massachusetts

Editor: David Pallai
Production: Publishers' Design and Production Services
Cover Design: The Printed Image

CHARLES RIVER MEDIA, INC.
10 Downer Avenue
Hingham, Massachusetts 02043
781-740-0400
781-740-8816 (FAX)
info@charlesriver.com
www.charlesriver.com

This book is printed on acid-free paper.

Eric Lengyel. *The OpenGL Extensions Guide.*
ISBN: 1-58450-294-0

Library of Congress Cataloging-in-Publication Data

Lengyel, Eric.
   The OpenGL extensions guide / Eric Lengyel.
      p.   cm.
   ISBN 1-58450-294-0 (Hardback : alk. paper)
   1. Computer graphics. 2. OpenGL. 3. Computer games—Programming. I. Title.
   T385.L43 2003
   006.6'869—dc21
                          2003008206
Printed in the United States of America
03 7 6 5 4 3 2 First Edition

CHARLES RIVER MEDIA titles are available for site license or bulk purchase by institutions, user groups, corporations, etc. For additional information, please contact the Special Sales Department at 781-740-0400.

CONTENTS

PREFACE

Although the base OpenGL library provides a great deal of functionality, 3D graphics hardware capabilities advance rapidly, and new rendering features often become available that are not accessible through OpenGL's conventional interface. Fortunately, OpenGL was designed to be extensible. Hardware vendors are able to define an *OpenGL extension* that exposes functionality not present in the base library.

After the first release of OpenGL, it was realized that some much-needed base functionality was missing. Extensions were created to fill in the gaps, and many of these were later incorporated into OpenGL version 1.1. This book describes a multitude of OpenGL extensions that were created *after* the release of OpenGL 1.1, including some that have been promoted to core features in OpenGL versions 1.2, 1.3, and 1.4.

Book Organization

The OpenGL Extensions Guide is divided into chapters covering groups of extensions that pertain to the same general area of functionality. This book assumes that the reader is already familiar with the (unextended) OpenGL library and the 3D rendering pipeline. The first chapter describes the OpenGL extension mechanism and the methods of accessing an extension's capabilities on different platforms. The remainder of the book describes the extensions themselves and is organized into the chapters listed in the following table.

Chapter	*Topics*
Chapter 2—Blending	Frame-buffer color and alpha blending operations
Chapter 3—Texture Environment	Texture environment application, multitexturing
Chapter 4—Texture Mapping	Cube and 3D texturing, texture wrap modes, texture objects
Chapter 5—Texture Compression	Texture compression, S3TC
Chapter 6—Fragment Shading	Advanced fixed-function fragment shading
Chapter 7—Vertex Blending	Vertex weighting and blending
Chapter 8—Array Management	Efficient vertex array usage
Chapter 9—Synchronization	Synchronization with the GPU
Chapter 10—Lighting	Lighting, secondary color

Chapter	*Topics*
Chapter 11—Fog	Fog coordinates, fog distance
Chapter 12—Stencil Operations	Stencil wrap modes, two-sided stenciling
Chapter 13—Shadow Mapping	Depth textures, shadow mapping
Chapter 14—Occlusion Culling	Occlusion culling, occlusion querying
Chapter 15—Point Rendering	Point parameters, point sprites
Chapter 16—Pixel Formats	Color formats, packed pixels, depth-stencil format
Chapter 17—Miscellaneous	Miscellaneous extensions
Chapter 18—Vertex Programs	ARB and NV vertex programs
Chapter 19—Fragment Programs	ARB and NV fragment programs

The coverage of each extension begins with a table containing four entries having the following meanings.

- **OpenGL version required.** This specifies the oldest version of OpenGL required by the extension. This book assumes that all extensions at least require OpenGL 1.1.

- **Dependencies.** This lists any other extensions that are required by the extension. Extensions required by transitivity are not listed.

- **Promotions.** This indicates whether the extension has been integrated into OpenGL as a core feature and lists any previously used names for the extension.

- **Related extensions.** This lists any related extensions and describes any noteworthy interactions with other extensions.

The area devoted to each extension is divided into a discussion section and one or two reference sections named "New Functions" and "Extended Functions." The "New Functions" section provides a detailed description of the new functions defined by an extension, and the "Extended Functions" section describes how existing OpenGL functions are augmented or modified by the extension. If an extension defines no new functions, then the "New Functions" section is omitted.

Style Conventions

A number of typefaces are used throughout this book to denote different types of text.

- Extension names, source code, and pseudocode are written in a plain monospace font. For example, `GL_EXT_blend_subtract`.

- Function names are written in a bold monospace font. For example, **`glBlendEquationEXT`**.

- Function parameter names are written in italic. For example, *pname*.

- Enumerants are written in a plain monospace font. For example, GL_BLEND_
EQUATION_EXT.

Many OpenGL functions have several variants that take different numbers of parameters or different parameter types. This book uses a compact notation to refer to all variants of a function using a single name, and when doing so often treats the set of functions as a single entity. Braces (**{}**) are used to denote a sequence from which one item is chosen from a sequence, and brackets (**[]**) are used to denote that its contents appear in some variants, but not others. As an example, there are four variants of the function used to specify a fog coordinate:

- **glFogCoordfEXT**
- **glFogCoorddEXT**
- **glFogCoordfvEXT**
- **glFogCoorddvEXT**

The text would generally refer to this set of functions as **glFogCoord{fd}[v]EXT**. The letters **f** and **d** appended to the function name stand for "float" and "double," and represent the type of parameter accepted by the function. Functions that accept unsigned integer types require a two-letter suffix that begins with **u**. For instance, a variant of the **glSecondaryColor3{bsifdubusui}[v]EXT** function may use one of the following parameter type suffixes:

- **b**—GLbyte
- **s**—GLshort
- **i**—GLint
- **f**—GLfloat
- **d**—GLdouble
- **ub**—GLubyte
- **us**—GLushort
- **ui**—GLuint

When the **v** suffix is present, it indicates that the function takes a pointer to its parameters instead of taking the values directly. Functions whose names have a number preceding the type identifier take the number of parameters specified by that number. For example, the variants of the **glMultiTexCoord{1234}{sifd}[v]ARB** function take 1, 2, 3, or 4 parameters of type GLshort, GLint, GLfloat, or GLdouble.

## CHAPTER 1

ABOUT OPENGL EXTENSIONS

An OpenGL extension usually begins its life as a mechanism for accessing 3D graphics rendering features offered by a single hardware vendor. The vendor defines new tokens and functions that serve as the interface to the features that are being exposed by the extension. An extension offered by a single hardware vendor is called a *vendor-specific* extension and may be available for a limited set of hardware configurations. If two or more vendors agree to expose the same features using the same extension, the extension is called a *multivendor* extension. Over time, a vendor-specific or multivendor extension may prove its worth to the OpenGL Architecture Review Board (ARB), who may decide to promote it to an *ARB-approved* extension. The ARB may also decide to integrate an extension into OpenGL as a core feature.

Specific naming conventions are implemented to avoid collisions between token and function names appearing in extensions offered by different hardware vendors. The name of an extension takes the form:

    GL_XYZ_extension_name

where XYZ is an abbreviation for the particular vendor who created the extension. New tokens and functions defined by the extension are suffixed with the same abbreviation. A token name takes the form GL_NEW_TOKEN_XYZ, and a function name takes the form **glNewFunctionXYZ**. A multivendor extension uses the abbreviation EXT instead of its own vendor-specific abbreviation, and an ARB-approved extension uses the abbreviation ARB. The following list summarizes the abbreviations used by extensions covered in this book.

- ARB—An extension approved by the Architecture Review Board
- EXT—An extension agreed upon by multiple vendors
- NV—A proprietary extension of NVIDIA Corporation
- ATI—A proprietary extension of ATI Technologies, Inc.
- APPLE—A proprietary extension of Apple Computer, Inc.
- SGIS—A specialized extension defined by Silicon Graphics, Inc.
- HP—A proprietary extension of Hewlett-Packard Company

Silicon Graphics maintains a Web site known as the OpenGL Extension Registry at *http://oss.sgi.com/projects/ogl-sample/registry/*. The extension registry contains the official specifications for almost every OpenGL extension in existence. These specifications provide the definitions of the token values and function prototypes introduced by each extension. Platform-dependent header files containing the token and function definitions are also provided on the Web site.

Detecting Extensions

Before an extension is utilized, an application must be sure that it is supported by the OpenGL implementation. An OpenGL implementation provides an *extension string* that contains the names of all the extensions it supports. The extensions string is retrieved by calling the **glGetString** function with *name* parameter GL_EXTENSIONS, as shown in the following line of code.

```
const GLubyte *extensions = glGetString(GL_EXTENSIONS);
```

Applications should make no assumptions about the length of the extensions string, because it can be quite long and will grow with future hardware and driver releases.

The extensions string contains a sequence of extension names separated by spaces. The names of the extensions themselves never contain a space character. An application determines that an extension is supported by searching the extensions string for the exact name of the particular extension it wishes to use. If an extension is supported by the implementation, then all of the new tokens and functions defined by the extension are available.

Using Extensions

An OpenGL extension might or might not define new functions. If no new functions are defined, then an application may simply use any newly defined tokens in the appropriate places. Of course, the token values themselves must be defined somewhere, and these can be either extracted from an extension's specification or included by using an existing header file.

Before an application can call a function defined by an extension, it must retrieve the function's address from the implementation. Subsequent access to the function is achieved by assigning the function's address to a variable having a pointer-to-function type. The method for retrieving function pointers varies among different platforms. Here, we describe the procedure for retrieving function pointers under Windows and under MacOS X.

WINDOWS

On the Windows platform, a pointer to a function defined in an OpenGL extension is retrieved by calling the **wglGetProcAddress** function. The following code demonstrates how an application would retrieve a pointer to the **glBlendColorEXT** function defined by the GL_EXT_blend_color extension.

```
typedef void (APIENTRY *PFNGLBLENDCOLORPROC)
        (GLclampf red, GLclampf green,
         GLclampf blue, GLclampf alpha);

    PFNGLBLENDCOLORPROC glBlendColorEXT = (PFNGLBLENDCOLORPROC)
        wglGetProcAddress("glBlendColorEXT");
```

The APIENTRY identifier in the type definition of the function pointer specifies the correct calling convention for OpenGL functions. Once the function address has been assigned to the variable glBlendColorEXT, it may be called using the same syntax as a normal function. The following line of code sets the blend color to green.

```
    glBlendColorEXT(0.0F, 1.0F, 0.0F, 1.0F);
```

The **wglGetProcAddress** function should only be called after an OpenGL context has been established, and any function pointers returned should only be used with the context that was current at the time **wglGetProcAddress** was called. Different function addresses may be returned for different contexts.

MacOS X

On the MacOS X platform, retrieving function addresses is more complicated. An application must obtain a reference to the bundle containing the OpenGL library and then query it for function pointers. The necessary code for performing these tasks is shown in Listing 1.1.

LISTING 1.1   This code defines three functions that are used when retrieving pointers to functions defined by extensions on MacOS X. The **GetOpenGLBundle** function returns a reference to the OpenGL bundle. A function pointer is retrieved by calling the **GetBundleProcAddress** function with this bundle reference and the name of the function. The **ReleaseBundle** function releases the reference to the OpenGL bundle.

```
    CFBundleRef GetOpenGLBundle(void)
    {
        SInt16 frameworksVRefNum;
        SInt32 frameworksDirID;

        // Return value
        CFBundleRef bundle = 0;

        // Find the Frameworks folder
        if (FindFolder(kSystemDomain, kFrameworksFolderType,
            kDontCreateFolder, &frameworksVRefNum,
            &frameworksDirID) == noErr)
```

```
        {
            FSSpec  spec;
            FSRef   ref;

            // Locate the OpenGL framework
            if (FSMakeFSSpec(frameworksVRefNum,
                frameworksDirID, "\pOpenGL.framework",
                &spec) == noErr)
            {
                FSpMakeFSRef(&spec, &ref);
                CFURLRef url = CFURLCreateFromFSRef
                    (kCFAllocatorDefault, &ref);
                if (url)
                {
                    // Grab a reference to the OpenGL bundle
                    CFBundleRef bundle = CFBundleCreate
                        (kCFAllocatorDefault, url);
                    CFRelease(url);
                }
            }
        }

        return (bundle);
    }

    void *GetBundleProcAddress(CFBundleRef bundle,
        const char *name)
    {
        CFStringRef string =
            CFStringCreateWithCString(kCFAllocatorDefault,
            name, kCFStringEncodingMacRoman);
        void *address = CFBundleGetFunctionPointerForName
            (bundle, string);
        CFRelease(string);
        return (address);
    }

    void ReleaseBundle(CFBundleRef bundle)
    {
        if (bundle) CFRelease(bundle);
    }
```

Using the **GetBundleProcAddress** function defined in Listing 1.1, a pointer to the **glBlendColorEXT** function is retrieved using the following code.

```
    typedef void (*BlendColorProcType)
        (GLclampf red, GLclampf green,
```

```
        GLclampf blue, GLclampf alpha);

    CFBundle bundle = GetOpenGLBundle();

    BlendColorProcType glBlendColorEXT =
        (BlendColorProcType)
        GetBundleProcAddress(bundle, "glBlendColorEXT");

    ReleaseBundle(bundle);
```

Any other function pointers needed by the application would also be retrieved between the calls to **GetOpenGLBundle** and **ReleaseBundle**. Once the function address has been assigned to the variable glBlendColorEXT, it may be called using the same syntax as a normal function.

BLENDING

IN THIS CHAPTER

2.1 GL_EXT_blend_color

OpenGL version required	OpenGL 1.1
Dependencies	—
Promotions	Promoted to a core feature in OpenGL 1.4
Related extensions	—

DISCUSSION

In addition to zero, one, and several factors derived from the source and destination colors, a constant color may be used in the blending equation when the GL_EXT_blend_color extension is available. The constant color is specified using the **glBlendColorEXT** function

```
void glBlendColorEXT(GLclampf red,
                     GLclampf green,
                     GLclampf blue,
                     GLclampf alpha);
```

The color specified by the *red*, *green*, *blue*, and *alpha* parameters is used in the blending equation by specifying one of the enumerants listed in Table 2.1.1 as the *sfactor* or *dfactor* parameter of the **glBlendFunc** function.

TABLE 2.1.1   These values can be passed to the **glBlendFunc** function for both the *sfactor* and *dfactor* parameters. The values K_R, K_G, K_B, and K_A, represent the red, green, blue, and alpha components of the constant color.

Enumerant	Blending factor
GL_CONSTANT_COLOR_EXT	(K_R,K_G,K_B,K_A)
GL_ONE_MINUS_CONSTANT_COLOR_EXT	$(1-K_R,1-K_G,1-K_B,1-K_A)$
GL_CONSTANT_ALPHA_EXT	(K_A,K_A,K_A,K_A)
GL_ONE_MINUS_CONSTANT_ALPHA_EXT	$(1-K_A,1-K_A,1-K_A,1-K_A)$

The components of the constant color are clamped to the range [0,1]. The initial value of the constant color is (0,0,0,0). The current value of the constant color can be retrieved by calling the **glGetFloatv** function with *pname* parameter GL_BLEND_COLOR_EXT.

USEFUL TIPS

How can I use the constant blending color to perform certain conventional blending operations for RGB and alpha channels separately?

Specifying a constant color of (1,1,1,0) enables the configuration of any blending equation for which an RGB channel should be multiplied by one and the associated alpha channel should be multiplied by zero, or vice versa. For example:

1. Making the function call

   glBlendFunc(GL_ONE, GL_CONSTANT_COLOR_EXT);

   causes the blending equation to add the source and destination RGB values, but it replaces the alpha values with the source alpha.

2. Making the function call

   glBlendFunc(GL_DST_ALPHA, GL_CONSTANT_COLOR_EXT);

   causes the blending equation to multiply the source RGB values by the destination alpha, but it multiplies the source and destination alpha values together.

NEW FUNCTIONS

■ **glBlendColorEXT**—Specify the constant blending color.

Prototype

```
void glBlendColorEXT(GLclampf red,
                     GLclampf green,
                     GLclampf blue,
                     GLclampf alpha);
```

Parameters

red, green, blue   Specify new red, green, and blue values for the constant blending color. These are clamped to the range [0,1].

alpha   Specifies a new alpha value for the constant blending color. This is clamped to the range [0,1].

Description

The **glBlendColorEXT** function sets the constant blending color used when one of the values listed in Table 2.1.1 is passed to the **glBlendFunc** function. The initial value of the constant color is (0,0,0,0).

Special Considerations

glBlendColorEXT may not be called between calls to **glBegin** and **glEnd**.

Get Functions

glGetFloatv with *pname* parameter GL_BLEND_COLOR_EXT

Errors

GL_INVALID_OPERATION is generated if **glBlendColorEXT** is called between calls to **glBegin** and **glEnd**.

EXTENDED FUNCTIONS

■ **glBlendFunc**—Extended to support constant color blend factors.

Prototype

```
void glBlendFunc(GLenum sfactor, GLenum dfactor);
```

Extended Parameters

sfactor   Specifies the blending factor by which source colors are multiplied in the blending equation. This parameter may be any of the values listed in Table 2.1.1.

dfactor   Specifies the blending factor by which destination colors are multiplied in the blending equation. This parameter may be any of the values listed in Table 2.1.1.

Description

The **glBlendFunc** function is extended so that the values listed in Table 2.1.1 are accepted for the *sfactor* and *dfactor* parameters in addition to the normally accepted values.

■ **glBlendFuncSeparateEXT**—Extended to support constant color blend factors.

Prototype

    void **glBlendFuncSeparateEXT**(GLenum *sfactorRGB*, GLenum *dfactorRGB*,
        GLenum *sfactorAlpha*, GLenum *dfactorAlpha*);

Extended Parameters

sfactorRGB   Specifies the blending factor by which source color red, green, and blue components are multiplied in the blending equation. This parameter may be any of the values listed in Table 2.1.1.

dfactorRGB   Specifies the blending factor by which destination color red, green, and blue components are multiplied in the blending equation. This parameter may be any of the values listed in Table 2.1.1.

sfactorAlpha   Specifies the blending factor by which the source color alpha component is multiplied in the blending equation. This parameter may be any of the values listed in Table 2.1.1.

dfactorAlpha   Specifies the blending factor by which the destination color alpha component is multiplied in the blending equation. This parameter may be any of the values listed in Table 2.1.1.

Description

The **glBlendFuncSeparateEXT** function is extended so that the values listed in Table 2.1.1 are accepted for the *sfactorRGB*, *dfactorRGB*, *sfactorAlpha*, and *dfactorAlpha* parameters, in addition to the normally accepted values.

■ **glGetFloatv**—Extended to support retrieval of the constant blending color.

Prototype

    void **glGetFloatv**(GLenum *pname*, GLfloat *params*);

Extended Parameters

pname   Specifies the symbolic name of the parameter to return. May be GL_BLEND_COLOR_EXT.

Description

The **glGetFloatv** function is used to retrieve the constant blending color. When the *pname* parameter is GL_BLEND_COLOR_EXT, the four-component constant blending color is returned in the array specified by the *params* parameter.

2.2   GL_EXT_blend_minmax

OpenGL version required	OpenGL 1.1
Dependencies	—
Promotions	Promoted to a core feature in OpenGL 1.4
Related extensions	GL_EXT_blend_subtract

DISCUSSION

Calling the source color **S** and the destination color **D**, the conventional blending equation calculates a color **C** given by

$$C = f_S S + f_D D \,, \tag{2.2.1}$$

where f_S and f_D are the source and destination blending factors specified using the **glBlendFunc** function. The GL_EXT_blend_minmax extension provides two new blending equations that perform componentwise minimum or maximum operations.

The current blending equation is specified using the **glBlendEquationEXT** function:

```
void glBlendEquationEXT(GLenum mode);
```

Calling **glBlendEquationEXT** with *mode* parameter GL_MIN_EXT changes the blending equation to

$$C = \big(\min(S_R, D_R), \min(S_G, D_G), \min(S_B, D_B), \min(S_A, D_A)\big). \tag{2.2.2}$$

Calling **glBlendEquationEXT** with *mode* parameter GL_MAX_EXT changes the blending equation to

$$C = \big(\max(S_R, D_R), \max(S_G, D_G), \max(S_B, D_B), \max(S_A, D_A)\big). \tag{2.2.3}$$

When the blending equation is configured to perform the minimum or maximum operation, the source and destination factors passed to the **glBlendFunc** function are ignored.

The conventional blending equation is restored by passing GL_FUNC_ADD_EXT to the **glBlendEquationEXT** function. This is the initial blending equation. The current blending equation can be retrieved by calling the **glGetIntegerv** function with *pname* parameter GL_BLEND_EQUATION_EXT.

NEW FUNCTIONS

■ **glBlendEquationEXT**—Select the blending equation.

Prototype

    void **glBlendEquationEXT**(GLenum *mode*);

Parameters

mode Specifies the blending equation mode. The following values are accepted: GL_FUNC_ADD_EXT, GL_MIN_EXT, or GL_MAX_EXT.

Description

The **glBlendEquationEXT** function sets the current blending equation. The *mode* parameter may be one of the following values:

GL_FUNC_ADD_EXT
  Sets the blending equation to the conventional sum given by Equation (2.2.1).

GL_MIN_EXT
  Sets the blending equation to the minimum operation given by Equation (2.2.2).

GL_MAX_EXT
  Sets the blending equation to the maximum operation given by Equation (2.2.3).

Special Considerations

glBlendEquationEXT may not be called between calls to **glBegin** and **glEnd**.

The **glBlendEquationEXT** function is also defined by the GL_EXT_blend_subtract extension.

Get Functions

glGetIntegerv with *pname* parameter GL_BLEND_EQUATION_EXT

Errors

GL_INVALID_ENUM is generated if *mode* is not an accepted value.

GL_INVALID_OPERATION is generated if **glBlendEquationEXT** is called between calls to **glBegin** and **glEnd**.

EXTENDED FUNCTIONS

■ **glGetIntegerv**—Extended to support retrieval of the blending equation.

Prototype

    void **glGetIntegerv**(GLenum *pname*, GLint **params*);

Extended Parameters

pname   Specifies the symbolic name of the parameter to return. May be GL_
                   BLEND_EQUATION_EXT.

Description

The **glGetIntegerv** function is used to retrieve the blending equation. When the *pname* parameter is GL_BLEND_EQUATION_EXT, the blending equation is returned in the location specified by the *params* parameter.

2.3   GL_EXT_blend_subtract

OpenGL version required	OpenGL 1.1
Dependencies	—
Promotions	Promoted to a core feature in OpenGL 1.4
Related extensions	GL_EXT_blend_minmax

DISCUSSION

Calling the source color **S** and the destination color **D**, the conventional blending equation calculates a color **C** given by

$$C = f_S S + f_D D, \tag{2.3.1}$$

where f_S and f_D are the source and destination blending factors specified using the **glBlend-Func** function. The GL_EXT_blend_subtract extension provides two new blending equations that perform componentwise subtraction.

The current blending equation is specified using the **glBlendEquationEXT** function

    void **glBlendEquationEXT**(GLenum *mode*);

Calling **glBlendEquationEXT** with *mode* parameter GL_FUNC_SUBTRACT_EXT changes the blending equation to

$$C = f_S S - f_D D. \tag{2.3.2}$$

Calling **glBlendEquationEXT** with *mode* parameter GL_FUNC_REVERSE_SUBTRACT_EXT changes the blending equation to

$$C = f_D D - f_S S. \tag{2.3.3}$$

When the blending equation involves subtraction, the components of the color **C** are always clamped to zero.

The conventional blending equation is restored by passing GL_FUNC_ADD_EXT to the **glBlendEquationEXT** function. This is the initial blending equation. The current blending equation can be retrieved by calling the **glGetIntegerv** function with *pname* parameter GL_BLEND_EQUATION_EXT.

NEW FUNCTIONS

■ **glBlendEquationEXT**—Select the blending equation.

Prototype

   void **glBlendEquationEXT**(GLenum *mode*);

Parameters

mode   Specifies the blending equation mode. The following values are accepted: GL_FUNC_ADD_EXT, GL_FUNC_SUBTRACT_EXT, or GL_FUNC_REVERSE_ SUBTRACT_EXT.

Description

The **glBlendEquationEXT** function sets the current blending equation. The *mode* parameter may be one of the following values:

GL_FUNC_ADD_EXT

Sets the blending equation to the conventional sum given by Equation (2.3.1).

GL_FUNC_SUBTRACT_EXT

Sets the blending equation to the subtraction of the destination term from the source term as shown in Equation (2.3.2).

GL_FUNC_REVERSE_SUBTRACT_EXT

Sets the blending equation to the subtraction of the source term from the destination term as shown in Equation (2.3.3).

Special Considerations

glBlendEquationEXT may not be called between calls to **glBegin** and **glEnd**.

The **glBlendEquationEXT** function is also defined by the GL_EXT_blend_minmax extension.

Get Functions

glGetIntegerv with *pname* parameter GL_BLEND_EQUATION_EXT

Errors

GL_INVALID_ENUM is generated if *mode* is not an accepted value.

GL_INVALID_OPERATION is generated if **glBlendEquationEXT** is called between calls to **glBegin** and **glEnd**.

EXTENDED FUNCTIONS

■ **glGetIntegerv**—Extended to support retrieval of the blending equation.

Prototype

    void **glGetIntegerv**(GLenum *pname*, GLint **params*);

Extended Parameters

pname   Specifies the symbolic name of the parameter to return. May be GL_BLEND_EQUATION_EXT.

Description

The **glGetIntegerv** function is used to retrieve the blending equation. When the *pname* parameter is GL_BLEND_EQUATION_EXT, the blending equation is returned in the location specified by the *params* parameter.

2.4   GL_EXT_blend_func_separate

OpenGL version required	OpenGL 1.1
Dependencies	—
Promotions	—
Related extensions	—

DISCUSSION

The conventional blending equation applies the same operation to both the RGB and alpha channels of the source and destination colors. The GL_EXT_blend_func_separate extension allows two sets of blending factors to be selected that affect the RGB channels and alpha channel separately.

Separate blending factors are specified using the **glBlendFuncSeparateEXT** function

    void **glBlendFuncSeparateEXT**(GLenum *sfactorRGB*,
                                    GLenum *dfactorRGB*,
                                    GLenum *sfactorAlpha*,
                                    GLenum *dfactorAlpha*);

This function accepts a pair of blending factors that are applied to the red, green, and blue channels, and a second pair of blending factors that are applied to the alpha channel. The values that can be passed to **glBlendFuncSeparateEXT** are listed in Table 2.4.1 with the corresponding RGB factor and alpha factor.

When the GL_EXT_blend_func_separate extension is available, the conventional blending equation becomes

$$C_{R,G,B} = c_S S_{R,G,B} + c_D D_{R,G,B}$$
$$C_A = a_S S_A + a_D D_A,$$

(2.4.1)

where **S** and **D** are the source and destination colors, c_S and c_D are the source and destination blending factors for the RGB color channels, and a_S and a_D are the source and destination blending factors for the alpha channel. Calling **glBlendFunc** has the effect of setting both c_S and a_S to the value corresponding to the *sfactor* parameter, and setting both c_D and a_D to the value corresponding to the *dfactor* parameter.

The initial value of both source factors is one, and the initial value of both destination factors is zero. The current values of the blending factors can be retrieved by calling **glGetIntegerv** with the arguments GL_BLEND_SRC_RGB_EXT, GL_BLEND_DST_RGB_EXT, GL_BLEND_SRC_ALPHA_EXT, and GL_BLEND_DST_ALPHA_EXT.

TABLE 2.4.1   These values can be passed to the **glBlendFuncSeparateEXT** function for the same source and destination parameters for which they are accepted by the **glBlendFunc** function. The values S_R, S_G, S_B, and S_A represent the red, green, blue, and alpha components of the source color, the values D_R, D_G, D_B, and D_A represent the components of the destination color, and the values K_R, K_G, K_B, and K_A represent the components of the constant blending color provided by the GL_EXT_blend_color extension.

Enumerant	RGB Blending Factor	Alpha Blending Factor
GL_ZERO	$(0,0,0)$	0
GL_ONE	$(1,1,1)$	1
GL_SRC_COLOR	(S_R,S_G,S_B)	S_A
GL_ONE_MINUS_SRC_COLOR	$(1-S_R,1-S_G,1-S_B)$	$1-S_A$
GL_DST_COLOR	(D_R,D_G,D_B)	D_A
GL_ONE_MINUS_DST_COLOR	$(1-D_R,1-D_G,1-D_B)$	$1-D_A$
GL_SRC_ALPHA	(S_A,S_A,S_A)	S_A
GL_ONE_MINUS_SRC_ALPHA	$(1-S_A,1-S_A,1-S_A)$	$1-S_A$
GL_DST_ALPHA	(D_A,D_A,D_A)	D_A
GL_ONE_MINUS_DST_ALPHA	$(1-D_A,1-D_A,1-D_A)$	$1-D_A$
GL_CONSTANT_COLOR_EXT	(K_R,K_G,K_B)	K_A
GL_ONE_MINUS_CONSTANT_COLOR_EXT	$(1-K_R,1-K_G,1-K_B)$	$1-K_A$
GL_CONSTANT_ALPHA_EXT	(K_A,K_A,K_A)	K_A
GL_ONE_MINUS_CONSTANT_ALPHA_EXT	$(1-K_A,1-K_A,1-K_A)$	$1-K_A$
GL_SRC_ALPHA_SATURATE	(f,f,f) $f=\min(S_A,1-D_A)$	1

NEW FUNCTIONS

■ **glBlendFuncSeparateEXT**—Specify blend functions for color and alpha channels.

Prototype

```
void glBlendFuncSeparateEXT(GLenum sfactorRGB,
                            GLenum dfactorRGB,
                            GLenum sfactorAlpha,
                            GLenum dfactorAlpha);
```

Parameters

sfactorRGB   Specifies the source blending factor for the red, green, and blue components of the blending equation. Accepts the same values that are accepted by the *sfactor* parameter of the **glBlendFunc** function. The initial value is GL_ONE.

dfactorRGB   Specifies the destination blending factor for the red, green, and blue components of the blending equation. Accepts the same values that are accepted by the *dfactor* parameter of the **glBlendFunc** function. The initial value is GL_ZERO.

sfactorAlpha   Specifies the source blending factor for the alpha component of the blending equation. Accepts the same values that are accepted by the *sfactor* parameter of the **glBlendFunc** function. The initial value is GL_ONE.

dfactorAlpha   Specifies the destination blending factor for the alpha component of the blending equation. Accepts the same values that are accepted by the *dfactor* parameter of the **glBlendFunc** function. The initial value is GL_ZERO.

Description

The **glBlendFuncSeparateEXT** function sets the current source and destination blending factors for the RGB color channels and the alpha channel separately. These factors are applied as shown in Equation (2.4.1) to evaluate the blending equation.

Special Considerations

glBlendFuncSeparateEXT may not be called between calls to **glBegin** and **glEnd**.

Get Functions

glGetIntegerv with *pname* parameter GL_BLEND_SRC_RGB_EXT

glGetIntegerv with *pname* parameter GL_BLEND_DST_RGB_EXT

glGetIntegerv with *pname* parameter GL_BLEND_SRC_ALPHA_EXT

glGetIntegerv with *pname* parameter GL_BLEND_DST_ALPHA_EXT

Errors

GL_INVALID_ENUM is generated if any of *sfactorRGB*, *dfactorRGB*, *sfactorAlpha*, or *dfactorAlpha* is not an accepted value.

GL_INVALID_OPERATION is generated if **glBlendEquationEXT** is called between calls to **glBegin** and **glEnd**.

EXTENDED FUNCTIONS

■ **glGetIntegerv**—Extended to support retrieval of separate RGB and alpha blending factors.

Prototype

        void **glGetIntegerv**(GLenum *pname*, GLint **params*);

Extended Parameters

pname   Specifies the symbolic name of the parameter to return. May be GL_BLEND_SRC_RGB_EXT, GL_BLEND_DST_RGB_EXT, GL_BLEND_SRC_ALPHA_EXT, or GL_BLEND_DST_ALPHA_EXT.

Description

The **glGetIntegerv** function is used to retrieve the source and destination blending factors for separate RGB and alpha channels. The *pname* parameter may be one of the following values:

GL_BLEND_SRC_RGB_EXT
                   The source blending factor for the red, green, and blue channels is returned.

GL_BLEND_DST_RGB_EXT
                   The destination blending factor for the red, green, and blue channels is returned.

GL_BLEND_SRC_ALPHA_EXT
                   The source blending factor for the alpha channel is returned.

GL_BLEND_DST_ALPHA_EXT
                   The destination blending factor for the alpha channel is returned.

2.5   GL_NV_blend_square

OpenGL version required	OpenGL 1.1
Dependencies	—
Promotions	Promoted to a core feature in OpenGL 1.4
Related extensions	—

DISCUSSION

The GL_NV_blend_square extension allows the values GL_SRC_COLOR and GL_ONE_ MINUS_SRC_COLOR to be specified as the *sfactor* parameter, and allows the values GL_ DST_COLOR and GL_ONE_MINUS_DST_COLOR to be specified as the *dfactor* parameter of the **glBlendFunc** function. This enables blending equations in which the square of the source color or destination color appears.

EXTENDED FUNCTIONS

■ **glBlendFunc**—Extended to support constant color blend factors.

Prototype

```
void glBlendFunc(GLenum sfactor, GLenum dfactor);
```

Extended Parameters

sfactor Specifies the blending factor by which source colors are multiplied in the blending equation. May be GL_SRC_COLOR or GL_ONE_MINUS_SRC_COLOR.

dfactor Specifies the blending factor by which destination colors are multiplied in the blending equation. May be GL_DST_COLOR or GL_ONE_MINUS_DST_ COLOR.

Description

The **glBlendFunc** is extended to accept a source blending factor based on the source color and a destination blending factor based on the destination color.

■ **glBlendFuncSeparateEXT**—Extended to support constant color blend factors.

Prototype

```
void glBlendFuncSeparateEXT(GLenum sfactorRGB, GLenum dfactorRGB,
    GLenum sfactorAlpha, GLenum dfactorAlpha);
```

Extended Parameters

sfactorRGB Specifies the blending factor by which the source color red, green, and blue components are multiplied in the blending equation. May be GL_SRC_COLOR or GL_ONE_MINUS_SRC_COLOR.

dfactorRGB	Specifies the blending factor by which the destination color red, green, and blue components are multiplied in the blending equation. May be `GL_DST_COLOR` or `GL_ONE_MINUS_DST_COLOR`.
sfactorAlpha	Specifies the blending factor by which the source color alpha component is multiplied in the blending equation. May be `GL_SRC_COLOR` or `GL_ONE_MINUS_SRC_COLOR`.
dfactorAlpha	Specifies the blending factor by which the destination color alpha component is multiplied in the blending equation. May be `GL_DST_COLOR` or `GL_ONE_MINUS_DST_COLOR`.

Description

The **glBlendFuncSeparateEXT** is extended to accept source blending factors based on the source color and destination blending factors based on the destination color.

TEXTURE ENVIRONMENT

IN THIS CHAPTER

3.1   GL_ARB_multitexture

OpenGL version required	OpenGL 1.1
Dependencies	—
Promotions	Promoted to a core feature in OpenGL 1.3
Related extensions	—

DISCUSSION

The GL_ARB_multitexture extension expands the texture application portion of the OpenGL rendering pipeline into two or more stages, allowing multiple texture maps to be applied in a single rendering pass. All of the state data and processing power required to support each individual texturing stage is collectively referred to as a *texture unit*. Any implementation supporting the GL_ARB_multitexture extension is required to support at least two texture units, each having its own set of texture-related states. The actual number of available texture units is retrieved by calling **glGetIntegerv** with *pname* parameter GL_MAX_TEXTURE_UNITS_ARB.

Because the functions that modify or query states pertaining to texture images, texture environment, and texture coordinate generation do not accept a parameter that indicates which texture unit to affect, the notion of an active texture unit is introduced by the GL_ARB_multitexture extension. Calling the **glActiveTextureARB** function

> void **glActiveTextureARB**(GLenum *texture*);

selects the currently active texture unit. The *texture* parameter must be GL_TEXTURE*i*_ARB, where *i* is in the range 0 to GL_MAX_TEXTURE_UNITS_ARB − 1. The initial value is GL_TEXTURE0_ARB. Any subsequent calls to the list of functions in Table 3.1.1 are then directed to the active texture unit.

TABLE 3.1.1   Functions Directed to the Active Texture Unit

glTexImage1D
glTexImage2D
glTexImage3DEXT
glTexSubImage1D
glTexSubImage2D
glTexSubImage3DEXT
glCopyTexImage1D
glCopyTexImage2D
glCopyTexSubImage1D
glCopyTexSubImage2D
glCopyTexSubImage3DEXT
glBindTexture
glGetTexImage
glTexParameter{if}[v]
glGetTexParameter{if}v
glGetTexLevelParameter{if}v
glTexEnv{if}[v]
glGetTexEnv{if}v
glTexGen{ifd}[v]
glGetTexGen{ifd}v

Additionally, each texture unit possesses its own texture matrix stack. The maximum depth of the texture matrix stack, retrieved by calling the **glGetIntegerv** function with *pname* parameter GL_MAX_TEXTURE_STACK_DEPTH, is required to be the same for every texture unit. When the matrix mode is GL_TEXTURE, calls to the functions listed in Table 3.1.2 affect the texture matrix stack corresponding to the active texture unit.

TABLE 3.1.2   Functions Affecting the Texture Matrix Stack Corresponding to the Active Texture Unit

`glLoadIdentity`
`glLoadMatrix{fd}`
`glMultMatrix{fd}`
`glLoadTransposeMatrix{fd}ARB`
`glMultTransposeMatrix{fd}ARB`
`glPushMatrix`
`glPopMatrix`
`glRotate{fd}`
`glTranslate{fd}`
`glScale{fd}`
`glFrustum`
`glOrtho`

When using the **glEnable**, **glDisable**, **glIsEnabled**, or any of the **glGet** functions to access texture-related state with an argument from the list in Table 3.1.3, the action affects the active texture unit.

TABLE 3.1.3   Arguments Affecting the Active Texture Unit

GL_TEXTURE_1D
GL_TEXTURE_2D
GL_TEXTURE_3D_EXT
GL_TEXTURE_CUBE_MAP_ARB
GL_TEXTURE_RECTANGLE_NV
GL_TEXTURE_1D_BINDING
GL_TEXTURE_2D_BINDING
GL_TEXTURE_3D_BINDING_EXT
GL_TEXTURE_BINDING_CUBE_MAP_ARB
GL_TEXTURE_BINDING_RECTANGLE_NV
GL_TEXTURE_GEN_S
GL_TEXTURE_GEN_T
GL_TEXTURE_GEN_R
GL_TEXTURE_GEN_Q
GL_TEXTURE_MATRIX
GL_TEXTURE_MATRIX_STACK_DEPTH

The currently active texture unit can be retrieved by calling the **glGetIntegerv** function with *pname* parameter GL_ACTIVE_TEXTURE_ARB.

When texturing is enabled for multiple texture units, the corresponding texture environments are applied to the incoming fragment color in succession. For texture unit 0, the incoming fragment color is the primary color. For all other texture units, the incoming fragment color is the result of the previous texture unit's texture environment application. If texturing is disabled for a particular texture unit, but is enabled for a subsequent texture unit, then the fragment color is passed through the disabled unit, unaltered.

State pertaining to texture coordinate arrays is considered client-side state. A separate active texture unit is maintained by OpenGL for client-side state and is selected using the **glClientActiveTextureARB** function:

> void **glClientActiveTextureARB**(GLenum *texture*);

Texture coordinate arrays are enabled or disabled for each texture unit by first calling the **glClientActiveTextureARB** function to select the texture unit and then calling the **glEnableClientState** or **glDisableClientState** function with *array* parameter GL_TEXTURE_COORD_ARRAY. The texture coordinate array is specified for the current client active texture unit by calling the usual **glTexCoordPointer** function. When using the **glEnableClientState**, **glDisableClientState**, **glIsEnabled**, or any of the **glGet** functions to access state related to texture coordinate arrays with an argument from the list in Table 3.1.4, the action affects the client active texture unit.

TABLE 3.1.4   Arguments Affecting the Client Active Texture Unit

GL_TEXTURE_COORD_ARRAY
GL_TEXTURE_COORD_ARRAY_SIZE
GL_TEXTURE_COORD_ARRAY_TYPE
GL_TEXTURE_COORD_ARRAY_STRIDE
GL_TEXTURE_COORD_ARRAY_POINTER

The currently active client texture unit can be retrieved by calling the **glGetIntegerv** function with *pname* parameter GL_CLIENT_ACTIVE_TEXTURE_ARB.

The current texture coordinates corresponding to a particular texture unit are specified using the **glMultiTexCoord{1234}{sifd}[v]ARB** function. This function does take a parameter that indicates which texture unit to affect, so it does not depend on the currently active texture unit. The **glTexCoord{1234}{sifd}[v]** function may still be called, and doing so is equivalent to calling the **glMultiTexCoord{1234}{sifd}[v]ARB** function with the *texture* parameter set to GL_TEXTURE0_ARB, regardless of the currently active texture unit.

Texture coordinates corresponding to texture units other than GL_TEXTURE0_ARB cannot be generated by evaluators and are not returned in feedback mode.

NEW FUNCTIONS

■ **glActiveTextureARB**—Select the active texture unit.

Prototype

    void **glActiveTextureARB**(GLenum *texture*);

Parameters

texture Specifies the current texture unit. Must be GL_TEXTURE*i*_ARB, where *i* is in the range 0 to GL_MAX_TEXTURE_UNITS_ARB − 1. The initial value is GL_TEXTURE0_ARB.

Description

The **glActiveTextureARB** function selects the texture unit to which subsequent commands pertaining to texture images, texture environment, texture coordinate generation, and the texture matrix stack are directed.

Get Functions

glGetIntegerv with *pname* parameter GL_ACTIVE_TEXTURE_ARB

Errors

GL_INVALID_ENUM is generated if *texture* is not an accepted value.

■ **glClientActiveTextureARB**—Select the active texture coordinate array unit.

Prototype

    void **glClientActiveTextureARB**(GLenum *texture*);

Parameters

texture Specifies the current texture unit for texture coordinate arrays. Must be GL_TEXTURE*i*_ARB, where *i* is in the range 0 to GL_MAX_TEXTURE_UNITS_ARB − 1. The initial value is GL_TEXTURE0_ARB.

Description

The **glClientActiveTextureARB** function selects the texture unit to which subsequent commands pertaining to texture coordinate arrays are directed.

Get Functions

glGetIntegerv with *pname* parameter GL_CLIENT_ACTIVE_TEXTURE_ARB

Errors

GL_INVALID_ENUM is generated if *texture* is not an accepted value.

■ **glMultiTexCoord{1234}{sifd}[v]ARB**—Set the current texture coordinates for a particular texture unit.

Prototypes

```
void glMultiTexCoord1sARB(GLenum texture,
                          GLshort s);
void glMultiTexCoord1iARB(GLenum texture,
                          GLint s);
void glMultiTexCoord1fARB(GLenum texture,
                          GLfloat s);
void glMultiTexCoord1dARB(GLenum texture,
                          GLdouble s);
void glMultiTexCoord2sARB(GLenum texture,
                          GLshort s,
                          GLshort t);
void glMultiTexCoord2iARB(GLenum texture,
                          GLint s,
                          GLint t);
void glMultiTexCoord2fARB(GLenum texture,
                          GLfloat s,
                          GLfloat t);
void glMultiTexCoord2dARB(GLenum texture,
                          GLdouble s,
                          GLdouble t);
void glMultiTexCoord3sARB(GLenum texture,
                          GLshort s,
                          GLshort t,
                          GLshort r);
void glMultiTexCoord3iARB(GLenum texture,
                          GLint s,
                          GLint t,
                          GLint r);
void glMultiTexCoord3fARB(GLenum texture,
                          GLfloat s,
                          GLfloat t,
                          GLfloat r);
void glMultiTexCoord3dARB(GLenum texture,
                          GLdouble s,
                          GLdouble t,
                          GLdouble r);
void glMultiTexCoord4sARB(GLenum texture,
                          GLshort s,
                          GLshort t,
                          GLshort r,
                          GLshort q);
void glMultiTexCoord4iARB(GLenum texture,
                          GLint s,
                          GLint t,
                          GLint r,
                          GLint q);
```

```
void glMultiTexCoord4fARB(GLenum texture,
                          GLfloat s,
                          GLfloat t,
                          GLfloat r,
                          GLfloat q);
void glMultiTexCoord4dARB(GLenum texture,
                          GLdouble s,
                          GLdouble t,
                          GLdouble r,
                          GLdouble q);
```

Parameters

texture   Specifies the texture unit for which texture coordinates are being set. Must be GL_TEXTURE*i*_ARB, where *i* is in the range 0 to GL_MAX_ TEXTURE_UNITS_ARB − 1.

s, t, r, q   Specify the new current texture coordinates.

Prototypes

```
void glMultiTexCoord1svARB(GLenum texture,
                           const GLshort *coords);
void glMultiTexCoord1ivARB(GLenum texture,
                           const GLint *coords);
void glMultiTexCoord1fvARB(GLenum texture,
                           const GLfloat *coords);
void glMultiTexCoord1dvARB(GLenum texture,
                           const GLdouble *coords);
void glMultiTexCoord2svARB(GLenum texture,
                           const GLshort *coords);
void glMultiTexCoord2ivARB(GLenum texture,
                           const GLint *coords);
void glMultiTexCoord2fvARB(GLenum texture,
                           const GLfloat *coords);
void glMultiTexCoord2dvARB(GLenum texture,
                           const GLdouble *coords);
void glMultiTexCoord3svARB(GLenum texture,
                           const GLshort *coords);
void glMultiTexCoord3ivARB(GLenum texture,
                           const GLint *coords);
void glMultiTexCoord3fvARB(GLenum texture,
                           const GLfloat *coords);
void glMultiTexCoord3dvARB(GLenum texture,
                           const GLdouble *coords);
void glMultiTexCoord4svARB(GLenum texture,
                           const GLshort *coords);
void glMultiTexCoord4ivARB(GLenum texture,
                           const GLint *coords);
```

```
    void glMultiTexCoord4fvARB(GLenum texture,
                               const GLfloat *coords);
    void glMultiTexCoord4dvARB(GLenum texture,
                               const GLdouble *coords);
```

Parameters

texture   Specifies the texture unit for which texture coordinates are being set. Must be GL_TEXTURE*i*_ARB, where *i* is in the range 0 to GL_MAX_TEXTURE_UNITS_ARB − 1.

coords   Specifies a pointer to an array containing the new current texture coordinates.

Description

The **glMultiTexCoord{1234}{sifd}[v]ARB** function sets the current texture coordinates for the texture unit indicated by the *texture* parameter. If fewer than four coordinates are specified, then the *t*, *r*, and *q* coordinates are implied to be 0, 0, and 1, respectively. Hence, calling the **glMultiTexCoord1{sifd}[v]ARB** function sets the current texture coordinates to $\langle s,0,0,1\rangle$, calling the **glMultiTexCoord2{sifd}[v]ARB** function sets the current texture coordinates to $\langle s,t,0,1\rangle$, and calling the **glMultiTexCoord3{sifd}[v]ARB** function sets the current texture coordinates to $\langle s,t,r,1\rangle$. Initially, the values for *s*, *t*, *r*, and *q* are $\langle 0,0,0,1\rangle$ for every texture unit.

Special Considerations

The current texture coordinates for any texture unit can be updated at any time. In particular, **glMultiTexCoord{1234}{sifd}[v]ARB** can be called between calls to **glBegin** and **glEnd**.

Get Functions

glGet with *pname* parameter GL_CURRENT_TEXTURE_COORDS

EXTENDED FUNCTIONS

■ **glGetIntegerv**—Extended to support retrieval of the active texture unit and the maximum number of texture units.

Prototype

```
    void glGetIntegerv(GLenum pname, GLint *params);
```

Extended Parameters

pname   Specifies the symbolic name of the parameter to return. May be GL_ACTIVE_TEXTURE_ARB, GL_CLIENT_ACTIVE_TEXTURE_ARB, or GL_MAX_TEXTURE_UNITS_ARB.

Description

The **glGetIntegerv** function can be used to retrieve state related to multitexturing. The *pname* parameter may be one of the following values:

GL_ACTIVE_TEXTURE_ARB

> The symbolic constant representing the currently active texture unit is returned in *params*. This corresponds to the value most recently set with the **glActiveTextureARB** function. The initial value is GL_TEXTURE0_ARB.

GL_CLIENT_ACTIVE_TEXTURE_ARB

> The symbolic constant representing the currently active client texture unit is returned in *params*. This corresponds to the value most recently set with the **glClientActiveTextureARB** function. The initial value is GL_TEXTURE0_ARB.

GL_MAX_TEXTURE_UNITS_ARB

> The maximum number of textures units is returned in *params*. This is always at least 2.

3.2   GL_ARB_texture_env_add

OpenGL version required	OpenGL 1.1
Dependencies	—
Promotions	Promoted to a core feature in OpenGL 1.3 Previously GL_EXT_texture_env_add
Related extensions	—

DISCUSSION

The GL_ARB_texture_env_add extension allows the GL_ADD texture function to be specified in the texture environment in addition to GL_MODULATE, GL_DECAL, GL_BLEND, and GL_REPLACE. When the texture function is GL_ADD, application of the texture environment adds the texture color to the incoming fragment color and clamps the result to 1. The alpha component is handled differently and depends on the base internal format of the texture map. Table 3.2.1 lists the exact operations performed.

TABLE 3.2.1   These are the operations performed by the GL_ADD texture function when the texture map has one of the listed base internal formats. The color **F** is the incoming fragment color, **T** is the filtered texel color, and **E** is the color output by the texture environment. The subscripts R, G, B, A, L, and I represent the red, green, blue, alpha, luminance, and intensity components, respectively.

Base Internal Format	**GL_ADD** *Texture Function*
GL_ALPHA	$E_R = F_R$
	$E_G = F_G$
	$E_B = F_B$
	$E_A = F_A T_A$
GL_LUMINANCE 1	$E_R = \min(F_R + T_L, 1)$
	$E_G = \min(F_G + T_L, 1)$
	$E_B = \min(F_B + T_L, 1)$
	$E_A = F_A$
GL_LUMINANCE_ALPHA 2	$E_R = \min(F_R + T_L, 1)$
	$E_G = \min(F_G + T_L, 1)$
	$E_B = \min(F_B + T_L, 1)$
	$E_A = F_A T_A$
GL_INTENSITY	$E_R = \min(F_R + T_I, 1)$
	$E_G = \min(F_G + T_I, 1)$
	$E_B = \min(F_B + T_I, 1)$
	$E_A = \min(F_A + T_I, 1)$
GL_RGB 3	$E_R = \min(F_R + T_R, 1)$
	$E_G = \min(F_G + T_G, 1)$
	$E_B = \min(F_B + T_B, 1)$
	$E_A = F_A$
GL_RGBA 4	$E_R = \min(F_R + T_R, 1)$
	$E_G = \min(F_G + T_G, 1)$
	$E_B = \min(F_B + T_B, 1)$
	$E_A = F_A T_A$

EXTENDED FUNCTIONS

■ **glTexEnvi**—Extended to support the GL_ADD texture environment mode.

Prototype

void **glTexEnvi**(GLenum *target*, GLenum *pname*, GLint *param*);

Extended Parameters

param   When the *pname* parameter is GL_TEXTURE_ENV_MODE, this may be GL_ADD.

Description

The **glTexEnvi** function is used to set the texture environment mode for the currently active texture unit. The texture environment mode is set to addition by specifying GL_ADD for the *param* parameter.

3.3   GL_ARB_texture_env_combine

OpenGL version required	OpenGL 1.1
Dependencies	—
Promotions	Promoted to a core feature in OpenGL 1.3 Previously GL_EXT_texture_env_combine
Related extensions	GL_ARB_texture_env_crossbar GL_ARB_texture_env_dot3 GL_NV_texture_env_combine4

DISCUSSION

The conventional texture environment provides a limited number of operations that can be performed by each texture unit. The GL_ARB_texture_env_combine extension adds a new texture environment mode, GL_COMBINE_ARB, that provides the six operations listed in Table 3.3.1. Furthermore, RGB and alpha texture functions are decoupled, allowing different operations to be performed independently on the color and alpha portions of the incoming fragment. The arguments a_0, a_1, and a_2 are derived from the four color inputs listed in Table 3.3.2. Each color input can be remapped using one of the four mappings listed in Table 3.3.3 to produce the actual operands used in the color and alpha portions of the texture environment operations. Finally, the output of the texture function for each texture unit may be scaled by 1, 2, or 4.

TABLE 3.3.1   The Operations that are Available When the Texture Environment Mode is `GL_COMBINE_ARB`

Operation	Result
`GL_REPLACE`	a_0
`GL_MODULATE`	$a_0 a_1$
`GL_ADD`	$a_0 + a_1$
`GL_ADD_SIGNED_ARB`	$a_0 + a_1 - \frac{1}{2}$
`GL_SUBTRACT_ARB`	$a_0 - a_1$
`GL_INTERPOLATE_ARB`	$a_0 a_2 + a_1 (1 - a_2)$

TABLE 3.3.2   The Inputs that May be Used in Each of the Operations Listed in Table 3.3.1

Input	Description
`GL_PRIMARY_COLOR_ARB`	The primary color of the incoming fragment
`GL_TEXTURE`	The filtered texel color
`GL_CONSTANT_ARB`	The texture environment constant color
`GL_PREVIOUS_ARB`	The output color from the previous texture environment. For texture unit 0, this is equivalent to the primary color.

TABLE 3.3.3   The Mappings that May be Applied to Each Color Input **C** Listed in Table 3.3.2

Mapping	Color Operand	Alpha Operand
`GL_SRC_COLOR`	(C_R, C_G, C_B)	Not accepted
`GL_ONE_MINUS_SRC_COLOR`	$(1 - C_R, 1 - C_G, 1 - C_B)$	Not accepted
`GL_SRC_ALPHA`	(C_A, C_A, C_A)	
`GL_ONE_MINUS_SRC_ALPHA`	$(1 - C_A, 1 - C_A, 1 - C_A)$	

The texture environment operations to be performed on the RGB and alpha portions of the incoming fragment color are established by calling the **`glTexEnv{if}[v]`** function, specifying `GL_COMBINE_RGB_ARB` or `GL_COMBINE_ALPHA_ARB` for the *pname* parameter, and one of the operations listed in Table 3.3.1 for the *params* parameter. The initial value of the RGB and alpha operations is `GL_MODULATE`.

The inputs to the RGB and alpha portions of texture environment operations are specified by calling the **`glTexEnv{if}[v]`** function with the *pname* parameter set to `GL_SOURCE`*n*`_RGB_ARB` or `GL_SOURCE`*n*`_ALPHA_ARB`, where $0 \le n \le 2$. The *params* parameter then specifies one of the input colors listed in Table 3.3.2.

The mappings that are applied to the RGB and alpha portions of the inputs to the texture environment operations are specified by calling the **glTexEnv{if}[v]** function with the *pname* parameter set to GL_OPERAND*n*_RGB_ARB or GL_OPERAND*n*_ALPHA_ARB, where $0 \leq n \leq 2$. The *params* parameter then specifies one of the mappings listed in Table 3.3.3. When specifying mappings for the alpha portion of the operation, only GL_SRC_ALPHA and GL_ONE_MINUS_SRC_ALPHA are accepted by the *params* parameter.

The initial values of the source inputs and operand mappings for the texture environment operations are listed in Table 3.3.4.

TABLE 3.3.4 Initial Values for the Source Inputs and Operand Mappings

Operand State	*Initial Value*
GL_SOURCE0_RGB_ARB	GL_TEXTURE
GL_SOURCE1_RGB_ARB	GL_PREVIOUS_ARB
GL_SOURCE2_RGB_ARB	GL_CONSTANT_ARB
GL_SOURCE0_ALPHA_ARB	GL_TEXTURE
GL_SOURCE1_ALPHA_ARB	GL_PREVIOUS_ARB
GL_SOURCE2_ALPHA_ARB	GL_CONSTANT_ARB
GL_OPERAND0_RGB_ARB	GL_SRC_COLOR
GL_OPERAND1_RGB_ARB	GL_SRC_COLOR
GL_OPERAND2_RGB_ARB	GL_SRC_ALPHA
GL_OPERAND0_ALPHA_ARB	GL_SRC_ALPHA
GL_OPERAND1_ALPHA_ARB	GL_SRC_ALPHA
GL_OPERAND2_ALPHA_ARB	GL_SRC_ALPHA

The scale factor for the RGB and alpha portions of the texture environment operations is specified by calling the **glTexEnv{if}[v]** function with the *pname* parameter set to GL_RGB_SCALE_ARB or GL_ALPHA_SCALE. The *params* parameter then specifies the scale factor, which must be 1, 2, or 4. The initial value of both the RGB and alpha scale factor is 1.

EXTENDED FUNCTIONS

■ **glTexEnv{if}**—Extended to support specification of texture environment combiner settings.

Prototypes

```
void glTexEnvi(GLenum target, GLenum pname, GLint param);
void glTexEnvf(GLenum target, GLenum pname, GLfloat param);
```

Extended Parameters

pname   Specifies the symbolic name of a texture environment parameter. When the target parameter is GL_TEXTURE_ENV, this may be GL_COMBINE_ RGB_ARB, GL_COMBINE_ALPHA_ARB, GL_SOURCE*n*_RGB_ARB, GL_ SOURCE*n*_ALPHA_ARB, GL_OPERAND*n*_RGB_ARB, GL_OPERAND*n*_ALPHA_ ARB, GL_RGB_SCALE_ARB, or GL_ALPHA_SCALE, where $0 \leq n \leq 2$.

param   Specifies a texture environment parameter value. The values accepted for each value of the *pname* parameter are listed in Description.

Description

Texture environment combiner settings are specified using the **glTexEnvi** function. The *pname* parameter may be one of the following values. The values accepted by the *param* parameter depend on the value of the *pname* parameter and are described below.

GL_TEXTURE_ENV_MODE

The *param* parameter specifies the texture environment mode. This may be GL_COMBINE_ARB.

GL_COMBINE_RGB_ARB, GL_COMBINE_ALPHA_ARB

The *param* parameter specifies the texture operation to perform and may be any of the values listed in Table 3.3.1. The initial value is GL_ MODULATE.

GL_SOURCE*n*_RGB_ARB, GL_SOURCE*n*_ALPHA_ARB

The *param* parameter specifies the input source for operand *n* and may be any of the values listed in Table 3.3.2. The initial values are given in Table 3.3.4.

GL_OPERAND*n*_RGB_ARB

The *param* parameter specifies the input mapping for the RGB portion of operand *n* and may be any of the values listed in Table 3.3.3. The initial values are given in Table 3.3.4.

GL_OPERAND*n*_ALPHA_ARB

The *param* parameter specifies the input mapping for the alpha portion of operand *n* and may be GL_SRC_ALPHA or GL_ONE_MINUS_SRC_ALPHA. The initial values are given in Table 3.3.4.

GL_RGB_SCALE_ARB, GL_ALPHA_SCALE

The *param* parameter specifies the scale for the entire texture operation and may be 1.0, 2.0, or 4.0. The initial value is 1.0.

3.4 **GL_ARB_texture_env_crossbar**

OpenGL version required	OpenGL 1.1
Dependencies	Requires GL_ARB_texture_env_combine
Promotions	Promoted to a core feature in OpenGL 1.4
Related extensions	—

DISCUSSION

For each texture unit, the GL_ARB_texture_env_combine extension allows only the filtered texel color that is actually bound to the texture unit to be used as an input to the texture function. The GL_ARB_texture_env_crossbar extension allows the filtered texel color from any enabled texture map to be used as an input. When the **glTexEnv{if}[v]** function is called with the *pname* parameter set to GL_SOURCEn_RGB_ARB or GL_SOURCEn_ALPHA_ARB, where $0 \leq n \leq 2$, the values GL_TEXTUREi_ARB may now be specified for the *params* parameter, where i is less than the number of available texture units. For texture unit k, specifying GL_TEXTURE for the *params* parameter is equivalent to specifying GL_TEXTUREk_ARB.

If an input to the texture environment function for a particular texture unit references a texture unit for which texturing is disabled or to which no valid texture object is bound, then the result of the texture environment is undefined.

EXTENDED FUNCTIONS

■ **glTexEnvi**—Extended to allow any texture color to be specified as the input to the texture environment combiner operation for each texture unit.

Prototype

    void **glTexEnvi**(GLenum *target*, GLenum *pname*, GLint *param*);

Extended Parameters

param   Specifies a texture environment parameter value. When the *pname* parameter is GL_SOURCEn_RGB_ARB or GL_SOURCEn_ALPHA_ARB, where $0 \leq n \leq 2$, this may be GL_TEXTUREi_ARB, where i is in the range 0 to GL_MAX_TEXTURE_UNITS_ARB − 1.

Description

When specifying the texture environment combiner input for a particular operand, the *param* parameter may be any of the values listed in Table 3.3.2 (allowed by the GL_ARB_texture_env_combine extension) or may be GL_TEXTUREi_ARB, where i is in the range 0 to GL_MAX_TEXTURE_UNITS_ARB − 1. Specifying GL_TEXTUREi_ARB causes the color associated with texture unit i to be used as the input. Specifying GL_TEXTURE causes the color associated with the currently active texture unit to be used as the input.

3.5   GL_ARB_texture_env_dot3

OpenGL version required	OpenGL 1.1
Dependencies	Requires GL_ARB_texture_env_combine
Promotions	Promoted to a core feature in OpenGL 1.3
Related extensions	—

DISCUSSION

The GL_ARB_texture_env_dot3 extension provides two new operations that compute a dot product between two RGB-encoded vectors and replicate the result into either the red, green, and blue channels, or all four color channels of the texture environment result. When the **glTexEnv{if}[v]** function is called with the *pname* parameter set to GL_COMBINE_RGB_ARB and the *params* parameter set to GL_DOT3_RGB_ARB or GL_DOT3_RGBA_ARB, a dot product d between the source input colors a_0 and a_1 is calculated as follows.

$$
\begin{aligned}
d \;=\; & 4\!\left(\left(a_0\right)_R - \tfrac{1}{2}\right)\!\left(\left(a_1\right)_R - \tfrac{1}{2}\right) \\
+ \; & 4\!\left(\left(a_0\right)_G - \tfrac{1}{2}\right)\!\left(\left(a_1\right)_G - \tfrac{1}{2}\right) \\
+ \; & 4\!\left(\left(a_0\right)_B - \tfrac{1}{2}\right)\!\left(\left(a_1\right)_B - \tfrac{1}{2}\right)
\end{aligned}
\qquad (3.5.1)
$$

The dot product d is scaled by the value of GL_RGB_SCALE_ARB for the associated texture environment.

If the GL_DOT3_RGB_ARB operation is used, then the alpha component of the result is calculated normally using the independent operation specified with GL_COMBINE_ALPHA_ARB. However, if the GL_DOT3_RGBA_ARB operation is used, then the alpha component of the result is the dot product d scaled by the RGB scaling factor. In this case, the operation specified with GL_COMBINE_ALPHA_ARB and the scale factor specified with GL_ALPHA_SCALE are ignored.

EXTENDED FUNCTIONS

■ **glTexEnvi**—Extended to support the dot product texture environment operation.

Prototype

    void **glTexEnvi**(GLenum *target*, GLenum *pname*, GLint *param*);

Extended Parameters

param   Specifies a texture environment parameter value. When the *pname* parameter is GL_COMBINE_RGB_ARB, this may be GL_DOT3_RGB_ARB or GL_DOT3_RGBA_ARB.

Description

The dot product operation is specified for the currently active texture environment by calling the **glTexEnvi** function with *pname* parameter GL_COMBINE_RGB_ARB and specifying GL_DOT3_RGB_ARB or GL_DOT3_RGBA_ARB for the *param* parameter.

3.6   GL_NV_texture_env_combine4

OpenGL version required	OpenGL 1.1
Dependencies	Requires GL_ARB_texture_env_combine
Promotions	—
Related extensions	This extension modifies GL_ARB_texture_env_combine in such that any of the inputs listed in Table 3.6.2 are valid sources to the operations performed when the texture environment mode is GL_COMBINE_ARB.

DISCUSSION

The GL_NV_texture_env_combine4 extension augments the functionality provided by the GL_ARB_texture_env_combine extension by adding a new texture environment mode, GL_COMBINE4_NV, that provides the two operations listed in Table 3.6.1. The arguments a_0, a_1, a_2, and a_3 are derived from the larger number of color inputs listed in Table 3.6.2. As with the GL_ARB_texture_env_combine extension, these color inputs can each be remapped using one of the four mappings listed in Table 3.3.3.

TABLE 3.6.1   The Operations that are Available When the Texture Environment Mode is GL_COMBINE4_NV

Operation	*Result*
GL_ADD	$a_0 a_1 + a_2 a_3$
GL_ADD_SIGNED_ARB	$a_0 a_1 + a_2 a_3$

TABLE 3.6.2   The Inputs that May be Used in Each of the Operations Listed in Table 3.6.1

Input	*Description*
GL_ZERO	The value zero.
GL_PRIMARY_COLOR_ARB	The primary color of the incoming fragment.
GL_TEXTURE	The filtered texel color corresponding to the current texture unit.

(continues)

TABLE 3.6.2 *Continued*

Input	Description
GL_CONSTANT_ARB	The texture environment constant color.
GL_PREVIOUS_ARB	The output color from the previous texture environment. For texture unit 0, this is equivalent to the primary color.
GL_TEXTUREi_ARB	The filtered texel color from the *i*th texture unit.

The texture environment operations to be performed on the RGB and alpha portions of the incoming fragment color are established just as they are using the GL_ARB_texture_env_combine extension, except that GL_SOURCE3_RGB_NV, GL_SOURCE3_ALPHA_NV, GL_OPERAND3_RGB_NV, and GL_OPERAND3_ALPHA_NV are now accepted by the *pname* parameter of the **glTexEnv{if}[v]** function. The initial values of these operand states are listed in Table 3.6.3.

TABLE 3.6.3 Initial Values for the Source Inputs and Operand Mappings Introduced by the GL_NV_texture_env_combine4 Extension

Operand State	Initial Value
GL_SOURCE3_RGB_NV	GL_ZERO
GL_SOURCE3_ALPHA_NV	GL_ZERO
GL_OPERAND3_RGB_NV	GL_ONE_MINUS_SRC_COLOR
GL_OPERAND3_ALPHA_NV	GL_ONE_MINUS_SRC_ALPHA

As with the GL_ARB_texture_env_combine extension, the results of any operation listed in Table 3.6.1 are scaled by the values of GL_RGB_SCALE_ARB and GL_ALPHA_SCALE.

EXTENDED FUNCTIONS

■ **glTexEnvi**—Extended to support specification of texture environment combiner settings.

Prototype

    void **glTexEnvi**(GLenum *target*, GLenum *pname*, GLint *param*);

Extended Parameters

pname   Specifies the symbolic name of a texture environment parameter. When the target parameter is GL_TEXTURE_ENV, this may be GL_SOURCE3_RGB_NV, GL_SOURCE3_ALPHA_NV, GL_OPERAND3_RGB_NV, or GL_

OPERAND3_ALPHA_NV, in addition to the values accepted under the GL_ARB_texture_env_combine extension.

param   Specifies a texture environment parameter value. The values accepted for each value of the *pname* parameter are listed below.

Description

Texture environment combiner settings are specified using the **glTexEnvi** function. The *pname* parameter may be one of the following values. The values accepted by the *param* parameter depend on the value of the *pname* parameter and are described below.

GL_TEXTURE_ENV_MODE
          The *param* parameter specifies the texture environment mode. This may be GL_COMBINE4_NV.

GL_SOURCE*n*_RGB_ARB, GL_SOURCE*n*_ALPHA_ARB
          The *param* parameter specifies the input source for operand *n* and may be any of the values listed in Table 3.6.2. The initial values are given in Table 3.3.4.

GL_SOURCE3_RGB_NV, GL_SOURCE3_ALPHA_NV
          The *param* parameter specifies the input source for operand 3 and may be any of the values listed in Table 3.6.2. The initial value is GL_ZERO.

GL_OPERAND3_RGB_NV
          The *param* parameter specifies the input mapping for the RGB portion of operand 3 and may be any of the values listed in Table 3.3.3. The initial values is GL_ONE_MINUS_SRC_COLOR.

GL_OPERAND3_ALPHA_NV
          The *param* parameter specifies the input mapping for the alpha portion of operand 3 and may be GL_SRC_ALPHA or GL_ONE_MINUS_SRC_ALPHA. The initial values is GL_ONE_MINUS_SRC_ALPHA.

3.7   GL_EXT_texture_lod_bias

OpenGL version required	OpenGL 1.1
Dependencies	—
Promotions	Promoted to a core feature in OpenGL 1.4
Related extensions	GL_SGIS_texture_lod

DISCUSSION

The GL_EXT_texture_lod_bias extension provides a way to bias the Level of Detail (LOD) selected during texture rasterization by a constant amount. A LOD bias is associated with each texture unit and can be used to achieve a variety of effects, such as depth-of-field blurring and simple image processing. Using a small, positive LOD bias can also improve overall scene rendering performance by promoting the selection of lower resolution mipmaps.

The LOD bias is specified for the currently active texture unit by calling the **glTex-Env{if}[v]** function with the *target* parameter set to GL_TEXTURE_FILTER_CONTROL_EXT and the *pname* parameter set to GL_TEXTURE_LOD_BIAS_EXT. The *param* parameter specifies the LOD bias, which may be positive or negative and need not be an integer. The value of the LOD bias parameter is clamped to the range $[-b_{max}, b_{max}]$, where b_{max} is the value returned by the **glGetFloatv** function with *pname* parameter GL_MAX_TEXTURE_LOD_BIAS_EXT, which must be at least 4.0.

Let $s(x,y)$ be the function that maps window-space coordinates x and y to the texture coordinate s within a primitive, let $t(x,y)$ be the function that maps x and y to the texture coordinate t, and let $r(x,y)$ be the function that maps x and y to the texture coordinate r. Let n, m, and l be the base-2 logarithms of the width, height, and depth of the texture map, and define $u(x,y) = 2^n s(x,y)$, $v(x,y) = 2^m t(x,y)$, and $w(x,y) = 2^l r(x,y)$. For one-dimensional textures, assume $v(x,y) \equiv 0$; and for one- or two-dimensional textures, assume $w(x,y) \equiv 0$. The level-of-detail parameter λ is calculated using the following formula, where b is the value of the LOD bias.

$$\rho_x = \sqrt{\left(\frac{\partial u}{\partial x}\right)^2 + \left(\frac{\partial v}{\partial x}\right)^2 + \left(\frac{\partial w}{\partial x}\right)^2}$$

$$\rho_y = \sqrt{\left(\frac{\partial u}{\partial y}\right)^2 + \left(\frac{\partial v}{\partial y}\right)^2 + \left(\frac{\partial w}{\partial y}\right)^2}$$

$$\lambda = \log_2\left[\max(\rho_x, \rho_y)\right] + b \tag{3.7.1}$$

The value of λ is clamped to the range $[0,q]$, where $q = \max\{n,m,l\}$.

USEFUL TIPS

How do I perform an unsharp mask operation using the LOD bias?

An unsharp mask operation can be performed by calculating the value

$$2\mathbf{T}_0 - \mathbf{T}_b,$$

where $\mathbf{T}_0$ represents a sample from a texture map using an unbiased level of detail, and $\mathbf{T}_b$ represents a sample from the same texture map using a bias $b \geq 1$. The texture map, with a complete set of mipmaps, should be bound to both texture units 0 and 1, and the LOD bias should be set to zero for texture unit 0 and b for texture unit 1.

EXTENDED FUNCTIONS

■ **glTexEnvf**—Extended to support texture LOD bias.

Prototype

```
void glTexEnvf(GLenum target, GLenum pname, GLfloat param);
```

Extended Parameters

target   Specifies a texture environment. May be GL_TEXTURE_FILTER_ CONTROL_EXT.

pname   Specifies the symbolic name of a texture environment parameter. When the *target* parameter is GL_TEXTURE_FILTER_CONTROL_EXT, this may be GL_TEXTURE_LOD_BIAS_EXT.

Description

The texture LOD bias for the currently active texture unit is set by calling the **glTexEnvf** function with *target* parameter GL_TEXTURE_FILTER_CONTROL_EXT and *pname* parameter GL_TEXTURE_LOD_BIAS_EXT. The *param* parameter then specifies the texture LOD bias and must be in the range $[-b, b]$, where b is the value of GL_MAX_TEXTURE_ LOD_BIAS_EXT.

■ **glGetTexEnvfv**—Extended to allow retrieval of the texture LOD bias.

Prototype

```
void glGetTexEnvfv(GLenum target, GLenum pname, GLfloat *params);
```

Extended Parameters

target   Specifies a texture environment. May be GL_TEXTURE_FILTER_ CONTROL_EXT.

pname   Specifies the symbolic name of a texture environment parameter to retrieve. When the *target* parameter is GL_TEXTURE_FILTER_CONTROL_EXT, this may be GL_TEXTURE_LOD_BIAS_EXT.

Description

The texture LOD bias for the currently active texture unit is retrieved by calling the **glGetTexEnvfv** function with *target* parameter GL_TEXTURE_FILTER_CONTROL_EXT and *pname* parameter GL_TEXTURE_LOD_BIAS_EXT.

■ **glGetFloatv**—Extended to allow retrieval of the maximum supported LOD bias.

Prototype

```
void glGetFloatv(GLenum pname, GLfloat *params);
```

Extended Parameters

pname   Specifies the parameter to be returned. May be GL_MAX_TEXTURE_
                 LOD_BIAS_EXT.

Description

The maximum supported LOD bias is retrieved by calling the **glGetFloatv** function with
pname parameter GL_MAX_TEXTURE_LOD_BIAS_EXT. This value is always at least 4.0.

TEXTURE MAPPING

IN THIS CHAPTER

4.1 GL_ARB_texture_cube_map

OpenGL version required	OpenGL 1.1
Dependencies	—
Promotions	Promoted to a core feature in OpenGL 1.3 Previously GL_EXT_texture_cube_map
Related extensions	—

DISCUSSION

The `GL_ARB_texture_cube_map` extension defines a texturing mode in which six 2D texture images corresponding to the six faces of a cube are accessed using 3D texture coordinates. The many applications of cube texture maps include environment mapping and omnidirectional image projection. This extension also defines special texture coordinate generation modes that are commonly used in conjunction with texture cube mapping.

Cube Texturing

The six 2D images that make up a cube texture map are referred to as the positive and negative x, y, and z faces. As shown in Figure 4.1.1, the 3D texture coordinates $\langle s,t,r \rangle$ are interpreted as a direction vector emanating from the center of the cube and pointing toward the texel to be sampled.

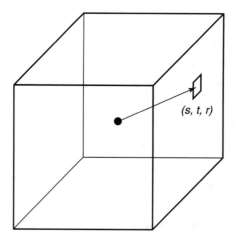

(s, t, r)

FIGURE 4.1.1   A cube texture map consists of six components that correspond to the six faces of a cube. Three-dimensional texture coordinates are treated as a ray emanating from the center of the cube and intersecting one of the cube's faces.

Which face to sample is determined by the sign of the coordinate having the largest absolute value. The other two coordinates are divided by the largest coordinate and remapped to the range [0,1] using the formulas listed in Table 4.1.1 to produce 2D texture coordinates $\langle s',t' \rangle$. These coordinates are then used to sample the 2D image corresponding to the selected face of the cube texture map. Figure 4.1.2 shows the orientation of the s' and t' axes relative to each of the six cube faces.

TABLE 4.1.1 Formulas Used to Calculate the 2D Texture Coordinates $\langle s',t'\rangle$ Given 3D Texture Coordinates $\langle s,t,r\rangle$ and the Face Corresponding to the Coordinate Having the Largest Absolute Value

Face	s'	t'
Positive x	$\dfrac{1}{2} - \dfrac{r}{2s}$	$\dfrac{1}{2} - \dfrac{t}{2s}$
Negative x	$\dfrac{1}{2} - \dfrac{r}{2s}$	$\dfrac{1}{2} + \dfrac{t}{2s}$
Positive y	$\dfrac{1}{2} + \dfrac{s}{2t}$	$\dfrac{1}{2} + \dfrac{r}{2t}$
Negative y	$\dfrac{1}{2} - \dfrac{s}{2t}$	$\dfrac{1}{2} - \dfrac{t}{2t}$
Positive z	$\dfrac{1}{2} + \dfrac{s}{2r}$	$\dfrac{1}{2} - \dfrac{t}{2r}$
Negative z	$\dfrac{1}{2} + \dfrac{s}{2r}$	$\dfrac{1}{2} + \dfrac{t}{2r}$

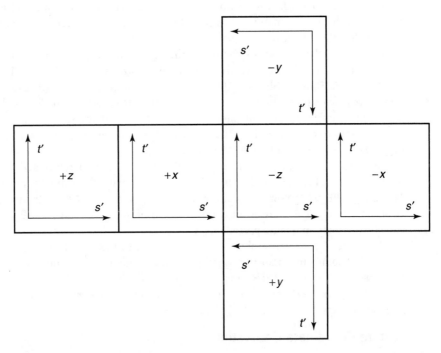

FIGURE 4.1.2 Orientation of the 2D texture coordinate s' and t' axes relative to the six faces of a cube texture map.

Cube Texture Map Management

A cube texture map is created by using the **glBindTexture** function to bind an unused texture name to the target GL_TEXTURE_CUBE_MAP_ARB. Once a cube texture map is bound, the six images necessary to construct a complete cube map are loaded by calling the **glTexImage2D** function with the *target* parameter set to one of the following values.

GL_TEXTURE_CUBE_MAP_POSITIVE_X_ARB

GL_TEXTURE_CUBE_MAP_NEGATIVE_X_ARB

GL_TEXTURE_CUBE_MAP_POSITIVE_Y_ARB

GL_TEXTURE_CUBE_MAP_NEGATIVE_Y_ARB

GL_TEXTURE_CUBE_MAP_POSITIVE_Z_ARB

GL_TEXTURE_CUBE_MAP_NEGATIVE_Z_ARB

For each face of a cube texture map, the *width* and *height* parameters passed to **glTexImage2D** must be equal (i.e., the cube faces must be square). The maximum width and height of a texture cube map face image can be determined by calling the **glGetIntegerv** function with *pname* parameter GL_MAX_CUBE_MAP_TEXTURE_SIZE_ARB.

A cube texture map is considered complete when images for all six faces have been specified for mipmap level 0, or when images have been specified for all mipmap levels for all six faces. If a cube texture map is incomplete because one or more required images have not been loaded, then the texture target is implicitly disabled.

A proxy mechanism exists for determining whether an implementation is capable of supporting a cube texture map of a given size and format. Passing the value GL_PROXY_TEXTURE_CUBE_MAP_ARB into the *target* parameter of the **glTexImage2D** function causes the texture state to be calculated for the proxy target as if all six cube map faces had been specified. If an implementation cannot support the size and format specified, then any state returned by the **glGetTexLevelParameter{if}v** function for the target GL_PROXY_TEXTURE_CUBE_MAP_ARB will be 0.

Cube texture mapping is enabled and disabled for the currently active texture unit by calling the **glEnable** and **glDisable** functions with the *cap* parameter set to GL_TEXTURE_CUBE_MAP_ARB. If any of the texture targets GL_TEXTURE_1D, GL_TEXTURE_2D, or GL_TEXTURE_3D_EXT are enabled at the same time as GL_TEXTURE_CUBE_MAP_ARB, then cube texture mapping takes precedence.

The name of the texture object currently bound to the cube texture target can be retrieved by calling the **glGetIntegerv** function with *pname* parameter GL_TEXTURE_BINDING_CUBE_MAP_ARB. The image for a particular face of a cube texture is retrieved by calling the **glGetTexImage** function with the *target* parameter set to one of the six cube map face targets.

Texture Coordinate Generation

Two new texture coordinate generation modes often used with cube texture maps are defined by the GL_ARB_texture_cube_map extension. The first copies the eye-space normal vector into the $\langle s,t,r \rangle$ texture coordinates, and the second calculates the eye-space reflection of the view direction about the normal vector.

Normal vector texture coordinate generation is accomplished by calling the **glTex-Gen{ifd}** function with the *coord* parameter set to GL_S, GL_T, or GL_R, and the *param* parameter set to GL_NORMAL_MAP_ARB. The *x*, *y*, and *z* coordinates of the eye-space normal vector are copied into the *s*, *t*, and *r* coordinates of the texture coordinate set, respectively.

Reflection vector texture coordinate generation is accomplished by calling the **glTex-Gen{ifd}** function with the *coord* parameter set to GL_S, GL_T, or GL_R, and the *param* parameter set to GL_REFLECTION_MAP_ARB. The eye-space reflection vector **R** is calculated using the formula

$$\mathbf{R} = \mathbf{V} - 2(\mathbf{N} \cdot \mathbf{V})\mathbf{N}, \qquad (4.1.1)$$

where **N** is the eye-space normal vector and **V** is the unit vector pointing from the origin to the vertex position in eye space. The values R_x, R_y, and R_z are assigned to the *s*, *t*, and *r* coordinates of the texture coordinate set, respectively.

It is possible to enable normal vector or reflection vector texture coordinate generation for fewer than three coordinates, but doing so is of questionable utility. Attempting to call the **glTexGen{ifd}** function with the *coord* parameter set to GL_Q and the *param* parameter set to GL_NORMAL_MAP_ARB or GL_REFLECTION_MAP_ARB is not legal and generates a GL_INVALID_ENUM error.

EXTENDED FUNCTIONS

■ **glEnable, glDisable, glIsEnabled**—Extended to enable/disable cube texture maps.

Prototypes

```
void glEnable(GLenum cap);
void glDisable(GLenum cap);
GLboolean glIsEnabled(GLenum cap);
```

Extended Parameters

cap   Specifies a GL capability. To enable or disable cube texture mapping for the currently active texture unit, or to query whether cube texture mapping is enabled, this should be GL_TEXTURE_CUBE_MAP_ARB.

Description

Cube texture mapping is enabled and disabled for the currently active texture unit by passing the value GL_TEXTURE_CUBE_MAP_ARB to the **glEnable** and **glDisable** functions.

Calling the **glIsEnabled** function with the parameter GL_TEXTURE_CUBE_MAP_ARB returns a value indicating whether cube texture mapping is enabled for the currently active texture unit. Initially, cube texture mapping is disabled for all texture units.

- **glBindTexture**—Extended to support cube texture maps.

Prototype

> void **glBindTexture**(GLenum *target*, GLuint *texture*);

Extended Parameters

target　　　　Specifies the target to which the texture is bound. May be GL_TEXTURE_CUBE_MAP_ARB.

Description

A texture object is bound to the cube texture map target by calling the **glBindTexture** function with *target* parameter GL_TEXTURE_CUBE_MAP_ARB.

- **glTexImage2D**—Extended to support cube texture maps.

Prototype

> void **glTexImage2D**(GLenum *target*, GLint *level*, GLint *internalFormat*,
>   GLsizei *width*, GLsizei *height*, GLint *border*, GLenum *format*,
>   GLenum *type*, const GLvoid **pixels*);

Extended Parameters

target　　　　Specifies the target texture. May be GL_PROXY_TEXTURE_CUBE_MAP_ARB or one of the six cube face targets GL_TEXTURE_CUBE_MAP_POSITIVE_X_ARB, GL_TEXTURE_CUBE_MAP_NEGATIVE_X_ARB, GL_TEXTURE_CUBE_MAP_POSITIVE_Y_ARB, GL_TEXTURE_CUBE_MAP_NEGATIVE_Y_ARB, GL_TEXTURE_CUBE_MAP_POSITIVE_Z_ARB, or GL_TEXTURE_CUBE_MAP_NEGATIVE_Z_ARB.

Description

A cube texture map face is loaded from memory by calling the **glTexImage2D** function with *target* parameter GL_TEXTURE_CUBE_MAP_POSITIVE_*k*_ARB or GL_TEXTURE_CUBE_MAP_NEGATIVE_*k*_ARB, where *k* represents X, Y, or Z. When specifying faces of a cube texture map, the *width* and *height* parameters must be equal. Otherwise, the error GL_ILLEGAL_VALUE is generated.

If the *target* parameter is GL_PROXY_TEXTURE_CUBE_MAP_ARB, then the texture state for all six faces of the proxy target is calculated using the same parameters. If an implementation cannot support the size and format specified, then any state returned by the **glGetTexLevelParameter{if}v** function for the target GL_PROXY_TEXTURE_CUBE_MAP_ARB will be 0.

- **glCopyTexImage2D**—Extended to support cube texture maps.

Prototype

> void **glCopyTexImage2D**(GLenum *target*, GLint *level*, GLenum *internalFormat*,
>   GLint *x*, GLint *y*, GLsizei *width*, GLsizei *height*, GLint *border*);

Extended Parameters

target   Specifies the target texture. May be one of the six cube face targets
                      GL_TEXTURE_CUBE_MAP_POSITIVE_X_ARB, GL_TEXTURE_CUBE_MAP_
                      NEGATIVE_X_ARB, GL_TEXTURE_CUBE_MAP_POSITIVE_Y_ARB, GL_
                      TEXTURE_CUBE_MAP_NEGATIVE_Y_ARB,   GL_TEXTURE_CUBE_MAP_
                      POSITIVE_Z_ARB, or GL_TEXTURE_CUBE_MAP_NEGATIVE_Z_ARB.

Description

The pixel data for a cube texture map face can be copied from the current GL_READ_BUFFER
by calling the **glCopyTexImage2D** function with *target* parameter GL_TEXTURE_
CUBE_MAP_POSITIVE_*k*_ARB or GL_TEXTURE_CUBE_MAP_NEGATIVE_*k*_ARB, where *k* represents X, Y, or Z. When specifying faces of a cube texture map, the *width* and *height* parameters must be equal. Otherwise, the error GL_ILLEGAL_VALUE is generated.

■ **glTexSubImage2D**, **glCopyTexSubImage2D**—Extended to support cube texture maps.

Prototypes

    void **glTexSubImage2D**(GLenum *target*, GLint *level*, GLint *xoffset*,
        GLint *yoffset*, GLsizei *width*, GLsizei *height*, GLenum *format*,
        GLenum *type*, const GLvoid **pixels*);
    void **glCopyTexSubImage2D**(GLenum *target*, GLint *level*, GLint *xoffset*,
        GLint *yoffset*, GLint *x*, GLint *y*, GLsizei *width*, GLsizei *height*);

Extended Parameters

target   Specifies the target texture. May be one of the six cube face targets
                      GL_TEXTURE_CUBE_MAP_POSITIVE_X_ARB, GL_TEXTURE_CUBE_MAP_
                      NEGATIVE_X_ARB, GL_TEXTURE_CUBE_MAP_POSITIVE_Y_ARB, GL_
                      TEXTURE_CUBE_MAP_NEGATIVE_Y_ARB,   GL_TEXTURE_CUBE_MAP_
                      POSITIVE_Z_ARB, or GL_TEXTURE_CUBE_MAP_NEGATIVE_Z_ARB.

Description

A subimage of a cube texture map face is loaded from memory or copied from the current
GL_READ_BUFFER by calling the **glTexSubImage2D** or **glCopyTexSubImage2D** function,
respectively, with *target* parameter GL_TEXTURE_CUBE_MAP_POSITIVE_*k*_ARB or GL_
TEXTURE_CUBE_MAP_NEGATIVE_*k*_ARB, where *k* represents X, Y, or Z.

■ **glGetTexImage**—Extended to allow retrieval of cube texture map images.

Prototypes

    void **glGetTexImage**(GLenum *target*, GLint *level*, GLenum *format*,
        GLenum *type*, GLvoid **pixels*);

Extended Parameters

target   Specifies the target texture. May be one of the six cube face targets
                      GL_TEXTURE_CUBE_MAP_POSITIVE_X_ARB, GL_TEXTURE_CUBE_MAP_
                      NEGATIVE_X_ARB, GL_TEXTURE_CUBE_MAP_POSITIVE_Y_ARB, GL_

TEXTURE_CUBE_MAP_NEGATIVE_Y_ARB, GL_TEXTURE_CUBE_MAP_ POSITIVE_Z_ARB, or GL_TEXTURE_CUBE_MAP_NEGATIVE_Z_ARB.

Description

The pixel data corresponding to a particular mipmap level of a cube texture map face is retrieved by calling the **glGetTexImage** function. When a pixel image is stored in memory, the current packing parameters (specified using the **glPixelStorei** function) are applied.

■ **glTexParameter{if}[v]**—Extended to support cube texture maps.

Prototypes

```
void glTexParameteri(GLenum target, GLenum pname, GLint param);
void glTexParameterf(GLenum target, GLenum pname, GLfloat param);
void glTexParameteriv(GLenum target, GLenum pname,
    const GLint *params);
void glTexParameterfv(GLenum target, GLenum pname,
    const GLfloat *params);
```

Extended Parameters

target   Specifies the target texture. May be GL_TEXTURE_CUBE_MAP_ARB.

Description

Texture parameters for the currently bound cube texture map are specified by calling the **glTexParameter{if}[v]** function with *target* parameter GL_TEXTURE_CUBE_MAP_ARB.

■ **glGetTexParameter{if}v**—Extended to support cube texture maps.

Prototypes

```
void glGetTexParameteriv(GLenum target, GLenum pname,
    GLint *params);
void glGetTexParameterfv(GLenum target, GLenum pname,
    GLfloat *params);
```

Extended Parameters

target   Specifies the target texture. May be GL_TEXTURE_CUBE_MAP_ARB.

Description

Texture parameters for the currently bound cube texture map are retrieved by calling the **glGetTexParameter{if}v** function with *target* parameter GL_TEXTURE_CUBE_MAP_ARB.

■ **glGetTexLevelParameter{if}v**—Extended to support cube texture maps.

Prototypes

```
void glGetTexLevelParameteriv(GLenum target, GLint level,
    GLenum pname, GLint *params);
```

```
void glGetTexLevelParameterfv(GLenum target, GLint level,
    GLenum pname, GLfloat *params);
```

Extended Parameters

target   Specifies the target texture. May be GL_PROXY_TEXTURE_CUBE_MAP_ARB
                  or one of the six cube face targets GL_TEXTURE_CUBE_MAP_POSITIVE_
                  X_ARB, GL_TEXTURE_CUBE_MAP_NEGATIVE_X_ARB, GL_TEXTURE_CUBE_
                  MAP_POSITIVE_Y_ARB,   GL_TEXTURE_CUBE_MAP_NEGATIVE_Y_ARB,
                  GL_TEXTURE_CUBE_MAP_POSITIVE_Z_ARB, or GL_TEXTURE_CUBE_
                  MAP_NEGATIVE_Z_ARB.

Description

Texture parameters corresponding to a specific level of detail of a specific face for the currently
bound cube texture map are retrieved by calling the **glGetTexLevelParameter{if}v** function
with *target* parameter GL_TEXTURE_CUBE_MAP_POSITIVE_*k*_ARB or GL_TEXTURE_
CUBE_MAP_NEGATIVE_*k*_ARB, where *k* represents X, Y, or Z.

Texture parameters for the proxy cube texture map target are queried by calling the **glGet-
TexLevelParameter{if}v** function with *target* parameter GL_PROXY_TEXTURE_
CUBE_MAP_ARB.

■ **glTexGeni**—Extended to support normal vector and reflection vector texture coordinate generation.

Prototypes

```
void glTexGeni(GLenum coord, GLenum pname, GLint param);
```

Extended Parameters

param   Specifies a texture coordinate generation parameter. When the *pname*
                 parameter is GL_TEXTURE_GEN_MODE, this may be GL_NORMAL_MAP_ARB
                 or GL_REFLECTION_MAP_ARB.

Description

Normal vector and reflection vector texture coordinate generation are specified by calling
the **glTexGeni** function. For each texture coordinate *s*, *t*, or *r* whose texture coordinate
generation mode is GL_NORMAL_MAP_ARB, the corresponding *x*, *y*, or *z* coordinate of the
normal vector is copied. For each texture coordinate *s*, *t*, or *r* whose texture coordinate generation mode is GL_RELFECTION_MAP_ARB, the corresponding *x*, *y*, or *z* coordinate of the
reflected eye vector is calculated.

■ **glGetIntegerv**—Extended to allow retrieval of cube texture map state.

Prototypes

```
void glGetIntegerv(GLenum pname, GLint *params);
```

Extended Parameters

pname   Specifies the parameter to be returned. May be GL_MAX_CUBE_MAP_
                        TEXTURE_SIZE_ARB or GL_TEXTURE_BINDING_CUBE_MAP_ARB.

Description

Various state values related to cube texture mapping can be retrieved by calling the **glGet-
Integerv** function. The *pname* parameter may be one of the following values.

GL_MAX_CUBE_MAP_TEXTURE_SIZE_ARB
                        The maximum size of a cube texture map face is returned. Any cube tex-
                        ture map whose faces have widths and heights of this size or smaller is
                        guaranteed to be supported by the implementation.

GL_TEXTURE_BINDING_CUBE_MAP_ARB
                        The name of the texture map bound to the GL_TEXTURE_CUBE_MAP_ARB
                        texture target for the currently active texture unit is returned. The initial
                        value is 0.

4.2   GL_EXT_texture3D

OpenGL version required	OpenGL 1.1
Dependencies	—
Promotions	Promoted to a core feature in OpenGL 1.2
Related extensions	—

DISCUSSION

The GL_EXT_texture3D extension provides the ability to sample three-dimensional textures using three-dimensional texture coordinates. A 3D texture map can be used to encode
an arbitrary light attenuation function. Three-dimensional texturing is also useful for applications needing to render volumetric data.

A 3D texture map is created by using the **glBindTexture** function to bind an unused
texture name to the target GL_TEXTURE_3D_EXT. A single 3D texture image or an array of
3D texture mipmaps can then be loaded using the **glTexImage3DEXT** function,

```
void glTexImage3DEXT(GLenum target,
                     GLint level,
                     GLenum internalFormat,
                     GLsizei width,
                     GLsizei height,
                     GLsizei depth,
                     GLint border,
                     GLenum format,
```

```
                        GLenum type,
                        const GLvoid *pixels);
```

with *target* parameter GL_TEXTURE_3D_EXT. The *width*, *height*, and *depth* parameters specify the dimensions of the texture image, and the remainder of the parameters have the same meaning as they do for the **glTexImage1D** and **glTexImage2D** functions. The maximum width, height, and depth of a 3D texture map can be determined by calling the **glGet-Integerv** function with *pname* parameter GL_MAX_3D_TEXTURE_SIZE_EXT.

A subregion of a 3D texture map can be redefined by calling the **glTexSubImage3DEXT** function,

```
        void glTexSubImage3DEXT(GLenum target,
                                GLint level,
                                GLint xoffset,
                                GLint yoffset,
                                GLint zoffset,
                                GLsizei width,
                                GLsizei height,
                                GLsizei depth,
                                GLenum format,
                                GLenum type,
                                const GLvoid *pixels);
```

with *target* parameter GL_TEXTURE_3D_EXT. The *width*, *height*, and *depth* parameters specify the dimensions of the texture subimage, the *xoffset*, *yoffset*, and *zoffset* parameters specify the position within the texture image at which the subimage is loaded, and the remainder of the parameters have the same meaning as they do for the **glTexSubImage1D** and **glTexSubImage2D** functions.

A two-dimensional subregion of a 3D texture map may be copied from the current read buffer by calling the **glCopyTexSubImage3DEXT** function,

```
        void glCopyTexSubImage3DEXT(GLenum target,
                                    GLint level,
                                    GLint xoffset,
                                    GLint yoffset,
                                    GLint zoffset,
                                    GLint x,
                                    GLint y,
                                    GLsizei width,
                                    GLsizei height);
```

with *target* parameter GL_TEXTURE_3D_EXT. The *xoffset*, *yoffset*, and *zoffset* parameters specify the position within the texture image to which the subimage is copied, and the remainder of the parameters have the same meaning as they do for the **glCopyTexImage2D** function.

When a 3D texture image is read from client memory, the current unpacking state is considered. The value of GL_UNPACK_IMAGE_HEIGHT_EXT specifies the number of complete rows in each rectangular 2D slice of a 3D texture image. (Recall that each row has a length given by the GL_UNPACK_ROW_LENGTH state.) The value of GL_UNPACK_SKIP_ IMAGES_EXT specifies the number of complete 2D image slices to skip at the beginning of the region of memory being unpacked.

The wrap mode for the *r* texture coordinate can be set by passing the value GL_TEX- TURE_WRAP_R_EXT into the *pname* parameter of the **glTexParameter{if}[v]** function. The same wrap modes that are supported for the *s* and *t* coordinates are supported for the *r* coordinate.

A proxy mechanism exists for determining whether an implementation is capable of supporting a 3D texture map of a given size and format. Passing the value GL_ PROXY_TEXTURE_3D_EXT into the *target* parameter of the **glTexImage3DEXT** function causes the texture state to be calculated for the proxy target. If an implementation cannot support the size and format specified, then any state returned by the **glGetTexLevel- Parameter{if}v** function for the target GL_PROXY_TEXTURE_3D_EXT will be 0.

Three-dimensional texture mapping is enabled and disabled for the currently active tex- ture unit by calling the **glEnable** and **glDisable** functions with the *cap* parameter set to GL_TEXTURE_3D_EXT. If either of the texture targets GL_TEXTURE_1D or GL_TEXTURE_2D are enabled at the same time as GL_TEXTURE_3D_EXT, then 3D texture mapping takes precedence.

The name of the texture object currently bound to the 3D texture target can be retrieved by calling the **glGetIntegerv** function with *pname* parameter GL_TEXTURE_3D_ BINDING_EXT. The image for a 3D texture is retrieved by calling the **glGetTexImage** func- tion with the *target* parameter set to GL_TEXTURE_3D_EXT.

NEW FUNCTIONS

■ **glTexImage3DEXT**—Specify a three-dimensional texture image.

Prototype

```
void glTexImage3DEXT(GLenum target,
                     GLint level,
                     GLenum internalFormat,
                     GLsizei width,
                     GLsizei height,
                     GLsizei depth,
                     GLint border,
                     GLenum format,
                     GLenum type,
                     const GLvoid *pixels);
```

Parameters

target   Specifies the target texture. Must be GL_TEXTURE_3D_EXT or GL_PROXY_TEXTURE_3D_EXT.

level   Specifies the level-of-detail number. Level 0 is the base image level. Level *n* is the *n*th mipmap reduction image.

internalFormat	Specifies the number of color components in the texture. Accepted values are the same as those accepted by the *internalFormat* parameter of the **glTexImage1D** and **glTexImage2D** functions.
width	Specifies the width of the texture image. Must be $2^n + 2(border)$ for some nonnegative integer n.
height	Specifies the height of the texture image. Must be $2^m + 2(border)$ for some nonnegative integer m.
depth	Specifies the depth of the texture image. Must be $2^l + 2(border)$ for some nonnegative integer l.
border	Specifies the width of the border. Must be either 0 or 1.
format	Specifies the format of the pixel data. Accepted values are the same as those accepted by the *format* parameter of the **glTexImage1D** and **glTexImage2D** functions.
type	Specifies the data type of the pixel data. Accepted values are the same as those accepted by the *type* parameter of the **glTexImage1D** and **glTexImage2D** functions.
pixels	Specifies a pointer to the image data in memory.

Description

The **glTexImage3DEXT** function defines a three-dimensional texture map. The *width*, *height*, and *depth* parameters specify the size of the texture image, and the *border* parameter specifies the width of the border.

If the *target* parameter is GL_PROXY_TEXTURE_3D_EXT, no data is read from client memory at *pixels*, but the texture state is recalculated and checked against the implementation's capabilities. If the requested texture size exceeds the implementation's limits, then all of the texture image state is set to 0 and no error is generated. The **glGetTexLevelParameter{if}v** function can then be called to determine whether the texture image could be accommodated.

If the *target* parameter is GL_TEXTURE_3D_EXT, then the texture image data is read from *pixels* using the unpacking state set with the **glPixelStore{if}** function. The values of GL_UNPACK_SKIP_IMAGES_EXT and GL_UNPACK_IMAGE_HEIGHT_EXT are applied in addition to the unpacking state used for two-dimensional images.

The first element in the image pointed to by *pixels* represents the texel corresponding to the least values of *s*, *t*, and *r* texture coordinates. Subsequent elements progress first in the positive *s*-direction to form a complete row. Rows then progress in the positive *t*-direction to form two-dimensional images. Finally, images progress in the positive *r*-direction to form the complete three-dimensional texture.

Special Considerations

glPixelStore{if} and **glPixelTransfer{if}** modes affect the texture image. **glTexImage3DEXT** may not be called between calls to **glBegin** and **glEnd**.

Get Functions

glGetTexImage with *target* parameter GL_TEXTURE_3D_EXT

glIsEnabled with *cap* parameter GL_TEXTURE_3D_EXT

Errors

GL_INVALID_ENUM is generated if *target* is not GL_TEXTURE_3D_EXT or GL_PROXY_ TEXTURE_3D_EXT.

GL_INVALID_VALUE is generated if *level* is less than 0.

GL_INVALID_VALUE may be generated if *level* is greater than $\log_2 max$, where *max* is the returned value of GL_MAX_3D_TEXTURE_SIZE_EXT.

GL_INVALID_VALUE is generated if *internalFormat* is not an accepted value.

GL_INVALID_VALUE is generated if *width*, *height*, or *depth* is less than 0 or greater than 2 + GL_MAX_3D_TEXTURE_SIZE_EXT, or if any cannot be represented as $2^k + 2(border)$ for some nonnegative integer value of k.

GL_INVALID_VALUE is generated if *border* is not 0 or 1.

GL_INVALID_ENUM is generated if *format* is not an accepted value.

GL_INVALID_ENUM is generated if *type* is not an accepted value.

GL_INVALID_ENUM is generated if *type* is GL_BITMAP and *format* is not GL_COLOR_INDEX.

GL_INVALID_OPERATION is generated if **glTexImage3DEXT** is called between calls to **glBegin** and **glEnd**.

■ **glTexSubImage3DEXT**—Specify a three-dimensional texture subimage.

Prototype

```
void glTexSubImage3DEXT(GLenum target,
                        GLint level,
                        GLint xoffset,
                        GLint yoffset,
                        GLint zoffset,
                        GLsizei width,
                        GLsizei height,
                        GLsizei depth,
                        GLenum format,
                        GLenum type,
                        const GLvoid *pixels);
```

Parameters

target   Specifies the target texture. Must be GL_TEXTURE_3D_EXT.

level   Specifies the level-of-detail number. Level 0 is the base image level. Level *n* is the *n*th mipmap reduction image.

xoffset	Specifies a texel offset in the *x*-direction within the texture array.
yoffset	Specifies a texel offset in the *y*-direction within the texture array.
zoffset	Specifies a texel offset in the *z*-direction within the texture array.
width	Specifies the width of the texture subimage.
height	Specifies the height of the texture subimage.
depth	Specifies the depth of the texture subimage.
format	Specifies the format of the pixel data. Accepted values are the same as those accepted by the *format* parameter of the **glTexSubImage1D** and **glTexSubImage2D** functions.
type	Specifies the data type of the pixel data. Accepted values are the same as those accepted by the *type* parameter of the **glTexSubImage1D** and **glTexSubImage2D** functions.
pixels	Specifies a pointer to the subimage data in memory.

Description

The **glTexSubImage3DEXT** function redefines a contiguous subregion of an existing three-dimensional texture image. The texels pointed to by the *pixels* parameter replace the texels in the existing image having *x* coordinates in the range *xoffset* to *xoffset* + *width* − 1, *y* coordinates in the range *yoffset* to *yoffset* + *height* − 1, and *z* coordinates in the range *zoffset* to *zoffset* + *depth* − 1. This region must be completely contained within the original texture image for the mipmap level given by the *level* parameter.

The image data read from *pixels* is affected by the unpacking state set using the **glPixelStore{if}** function. The values of GL_UNPACK_SKIP_IMAGES_EXT and GL_UNPACK_IMAGE_HEIGHT_EXT are applied, in addition to the unpacking state used for two-dimensional images.

If any of the *width*, *height*, or *depth* parameters is 0, no error is generated, but the call to **glTexSubImage3DEXT** has no effect.

Special Considerations

glPixelStore{if} and **glPixelTransfer{if}** modes affect the texture image.

glTexSubImage3DEXT may not be called between calls to **glBegin** and **glEnd**.

Get Functions

glGetTexImage with *target* parameter GL_TEXTURE_3D_EXT

glIsEnabled with *cap* parameter GL_TEXTURE_3D_EXT

Errors

GL_INVALID_OPERATION is generated if the texture array has not been defined by a previous call to the **glTexImage3DEXT** function.

GL_INVALID_ENUM is generated if *target* is not GL_TEXTURE_3D_EXT.

GL_INVALID_VALUE is generated if *level* is less than 0.

GL_INVALID_VALUE may be generated if *level* is greater than $\log_2 max$, where *max* is the returned value of GL_MAX_3D_TEXTURE_SIZE_EXT.

GL_INVALID_VALUE is generated if $xoffset < -b$, $xoffset + width > w - b$, $yoffset < -b$, $yoffset + height > h - b$, $zoffset < -b$, or $zoffset + depth > d - b$, where b is the border width of the texture image being modified, and w, h, and d are the values of GL_TEXTURE_WIDTH, GL_TEXTURE_HEGHT, and GL_TEXTURE_DEPTH_EXT (which include twice the border width), respectively.

GL_INVALID_VALUE is generated if *width*, *height*, or *depth* is less than 0.

GL_INVALID_ENUM is generated if *format* is not an accepted value.

GL_INVALID_ENUM is generated if *type* is not an accepted value.

GL_INVALID_ENUM is generated if *type* is GL_BITMAP and *format* is not GL_COLOR_INDEX.

GL_INVALID_OPERATION is generated if **glTexSubImage3DEXT** is called between calls to **glBegin** and **glEnd**.

■ **glCopyTexSubImage3DEXT**—Specify a three-dimensional texture subimage.

Prototype

```
void glCopyTexSubImage3DEXT(GLenum target,
                            GLint level,
                            GLint xoffset,
                            GLint yoffset,
                            GLint zoffset,
                            GLint x,
                            GLint y,
                            GLsizei width,
                            GLsizei height);
```

Parameters

target	Specifies the target texture. Must be GL_TEXTURE_3D_EXT.
level	Specifies the level-of-detail number. Level 0 is the base image level. Level *n* is the *n*th mipmap reduction image.
xoffset	Specifies a texel offset in the *x*-direction within the texture array.
yoffset	Specifies a texel offset in the *y*-direction within the texture array.
zoffset	Specifies a texel offset in the *z*-direction within the texture array.
x, y	Specify the window coordinates of the lower left corner of the rectangular region of pixels to be copied.
width	Specifies the width of the texture subimage.
height	Specifies the height of the texture subimage.

Description

The **glCopyTexSubImage3DEXT** function replaces a two-dimensional region of an existing three-dimensional texture with pixels read from the current GL_READ_BUFFER. Texels are read from the screen-aligned pixel rectangle having the lower left corner (x,y), the width given by the *width* parameter, and the height given by the *height* parameter. These texels replace the texels in the existing image having x coordinates in the range *xoffset* to *xoffset* + *width* − 1, y coordinates in the range *yoffset* to *yoffset* + *height* − 1, and z coordinates in the range *zoffset* to *zoffset* + *depth* − 1. This region must be completely contained within the original texture image for the mipmap level given by the *level* parameter.

If either of the *width* or *height* parameters is 0, no error is generated, but the call to **glCopy-TexSubImage3DEXT** has no effect.

If the rectangle specified by the *x*, *y*, *width*, and *height* parameters extends beyond the boundary of the current read buffer, then the texels read from outside the valid region are undefined.

Special Considerations

glPixelTransfer{if} modes affect the texture image.

glCopyTexSubImage3DEXT may not be called between calls to **glBegin** and **glEnd**.

Get Functions

glGetTexImage with *target* parameter GL_TEXTURE_3D_EXT

glIsEnabled with *cap* parameter GL_TEXTURE_3D_EXT

Errors

GL_INVALID_OPERATION is generated if the texture array has not been defined by a previous call to the **glTexImage3DEXT** function.

GL_INVALID_ENUM is generated if *target* is not GL_TEXTURE_3D_EXT.

GL_INVALID_VALUE is generated if *level* is less than 0.

GL_INVALID_VALUE may be generated if *level* is greater than $\log_2 max$, where *max* is the returned value of GL_MAX_3D_TEXTURE_SIZE_EXT.

GL_INVALID_VALUE is generated if *xoffset* < −*b*, *xoffset* + *width* > *w* − *b*, *yoffset* < −*b*, *yoffset* + *height* > *h* − *b*, *zoffset* < −*b*, or *zoffset* + 1 > *d* − *b*, where *b* is the border width of the texture image being modified, and *w*, *h*, and *d* are the values of GL_TEXTURE_WIDTH, GL_TEX-TURE_HEGHT, and GL_TEXTURE_DEPTH_EXT (which include twice the border width), respectively.

GL_INVALID_OPERATION is generated if **glCopyTexSubImage3DEXT** is called between calls to **glBegin** and **glEnd**.

EXTENDED FUNCTIONS

■ **glEnable, glDisable, glIsEnabled**—Extended to enable/disable 3D texture maps.

Prototypes

```
void glEnable(GLenum cap);
void glDisable(GLenum cap);
GLboolean glIsEnabled(GLenum cap);
```

Extended Parameters

cap   Specifies a GL capability. To enable or disable 3D texture mapping for the currently active texture unit or to query whether 3D texture mapping is enabled, this should be GL_TEXTURE_3D_EXT.

Description

3D texture mapping is enabled and disabled for the currently active texture unit by passing the value GL_TEXTURE_3D_EXT to the **glEnable** and **glDisable** functions. Calling the **glIsEnabled** function with the parameter GL_TEXTURE_3D_EXT returns a value indicating whether 3D texture mapping is enabled for the currently active texture unit. Initially, 3D texture mapping is disabled for all texture units.

■ **glBindTexture**—Extended to support 3D texture maps.

Prototype

```
void glBindTexture(GLenum target, GLuint texture);
```

Extended Parameters

target   Specifies the target to which the texture is bound. May be GL_TEXTURE_3D_EXT.

Description

A texture object is bound to the 3D texture map target by calling the **glBindTexture** function with *target* parameter GL_TEXTURE_3D_EXT.

■ **glGetTexImage**—Extended to allow retrieval of 3D texture map images.

Prototype

```
void glGetTexImage(GLenum target, GLint level, GLenum format,
    GLenum type, GLvoid *pixels);
```

Extended Parameters

target   Specifies the target texture. May be GL_TEXTURE_3D_EXT.

Description

The pixel data corresponding to a particular mipmap level of a 3D texture map is retrieved by calling the **glGetTexImage** function. When a pixel image is stored in memory, the current packing parameters (specified using the **glPixelStorei** function) are applied.

- **glTexParameter{if}[v]**—Extended to support 3D texture maps.

Prototypes

```
void glTexParameteri(GLenum target, GLenum pname, GLint param);
void glTexParameterf(GLenum target, GLenum pname, GLfloat param);
void glTexParameteriv(GLenum target, GLenum pname,
    const GLint *params);
void glTexParameterfv(GLenum target, GLenum pname,
    const GLfloat *params);
```

Extended Parameters

target   Specifies the target texture. May be GL_TEXTURE_3D_EXT.

pname   Specifies the symbolic name of a texture parameter. May be
                 GL_TEXTURE_WRAP_R_EXT.

Description

Texture parameters for the currently bound 3D texture map are specified by calling the **glTexParameter{if}[v]** function with *target* parameter GL_TEXTURE_3D_EXT. If the *pname* parameter is GL_TEXTURE_WRAP_R_EXT, then the *param* or *params* parameter specifies the wrap mode for the *r* texture coordinate.

- **glGetTexParameter{if}v**—Extended to support 3D texture maps.

Prototypes

```
void glGetTexParameteriv(GLenum target, GLenum pname,
    GLint *params);
void glGetTexParameterfv(GLenum target, GLenum pname,
    GLfloat *params);
```

Extended Parameters

target   Specifies the target texture. May be GL_TEXTURE_3D_EXT.

pname   Specifies the symbolic name of the texture parameter to return. May be
                 GL_TEXTURE_WRAP_R_EXT.

Description

Texture parameters for the currently bound 3D texture map are retrieved by calling the **glGetTexParameter{if}v** function with *target* parameter GL_TEXTURE_CUBE_MAP_ARB.

If the *pname* parameter is GL_TEXTURE_WRAP_R_EXT, then the current wrap mode for the *r* texture coordinate is returned.

■ **glGetTexLevelParameter{if}v**—Extended to support 3D texture maps.

Prototypes

```
void glGetTexLevelParameteriv(GLenum target, GLint level,
    GLenum pname, GLint *params);
void glGetTexLevelParameterfv(GLenum target, GLint level,
    GLenum pname, GLfloat *params);
```

Extended Parameters

target   Specifies the target texture. May be GL_TEXTURE_3D_EXT or GL_PROXY_TEXTURE_3D_EXT.

pname   Specifies the symbolic name of the texture parameter to return. May be GL_TEXTURE_DEPTH_EXT.

Description

Texture parameters corresponding to a specific level of detail for the currently bound 3D texture map are retrieved by calling the **glGetTexLevelParameter{if}v** function with *target* parameter GL_TEXTURE_3D_EXT. If the *pname* parameter is GL_TEXTURE_DEPTH_EXT, then the depth of the texture image for the level of detail specified by the *level* parameter is returned.

Texture parameters for the proxy 3D texture map target are queried by calling the **glGetTexLevelParameter{if}v** function with *target* parameter GL_PROXY_TEXTURE_3D_EXT.

■ **glPixelStorei**—Extended to support packing and unpacking parameters for 3D texture maps.

Prototype

```
void glPixelStorei(GLenum pname, GLint param);
```

Extended Parameters

pname   Specifies the symbolic name of the packing or unpacking parameter to set. May be GL_PACK_IMAGE_HEIGHT_EXT, GL_PACK_SKIP_IMAGES_EXT, GL_UNPACK_IMAGE_HEIGHT_EXT, or GL_UNPACK_SKIP_IMAGES_EXT.

Description

Packing parameters used when writing 3D texture map pixel data to memory and unpacking parameters used when reading 3D texture map pixel data from memory are specified by calling the **glPixelStorei** function. In addition to the packing and unpacking parameters applied to 2D pixel maps, the *pname* parameter may specify one of the following values that are applied to 3D pixel maps.

GL_PACK_IMAGE_HEIGHT_EXT

The *param* parameter specifies the number of rows in each two-dimensional image of a 3D texture map when packing pixel data in memory. The size of each row is controlled by the value of the GL_PACK_ROW_LENGTH parameter.

GL_PACK_SKIP_IMAGES_EXT

The *param* parameter specifies the number of complete two-dimensional images to skip when packing pixel data in memory. This is provided as a convenience and could be functionally duplicated by incrementing the pointer passed to the **glGetTexImage** function. The number of rows and pixels corresponding to the values of GL_PACK_SKIP_ROWS and GL_PACK_SKIP_PIXELS are skipped, in addition to the number of images specified by the value of GL_PACK_SKIP_IMAGES_EXT.

GL_UNPACK_IMAGE_HEIGHT_EXT

The *param* parameter specifies the number of rows in each two-dimensional image of a 3D texture map when unpacking pixel data from memory. The size of each row is controlled by the value of the GL_UNPACK_ROW_LENGTH parameter.

GL_UNPACK_SKIP_IMAGES_EXT

The *param* parameter specifies the number of complete two-dimensional images to skip when unpacking pixel data from memory. This is provided as a convenience and could be functionally duplicated by incrementing the pointer passed to the **glTexImage3DEXT** function and related functions used to load texture images. The number of rows and pixels corresponding to the values of GL_UNPACK_SKIP_ROWS and GL_UNPACK_SKIP_PIXELS are skipped, in addition to the number of images specified by the value of GL_UNPACK_SKIP_IMAGES_EXT.

■ **glGetIntegerv**—Extended to allow retrieval of 3D texture map state and related packing state.

Prototypes

```
void glGetIntegerv(GLenum pname, GLint *params);
```

Extended Parameters

pname   Specifies the parameter to be returned. May be one of the values listed below.

Description

Various state values related to 3D texture mapping can be retrieved by calling the **glGetIntegerv** function. The *pname* parameter may be one of the following values.

`GL_MAX_3D_TEXTURE_SIZE_EXT`

> The maximum value for the *width*, *height*, or *depth* of a 3D texture map is returned. Any 3D texture map having dimensions of this size or smaller is guaranteed to be supported by the implementation.

`GL_TEXTURE_3D_BINDING_EXT`

> The name of the texture map bound to the `GL_TEXTURE_3D_EXT` texture target for the currently active texture unit is returned. The initial value is 0.

`GL_PACK_IMAGE_HEIGHT_EXT`

> The number of rows in each two-dimensional image of a 3D texture map used when packing pixel data in memory is returned. The initial value is 0, indicating that the number of rows is equal to the *height* of the texture map.

`GL_PACK_SKIP_IMAGES_EXT`

> The number of complete two-dimensional images of a 3D texture map skipped when packing pixel data in memory is returned. The initial value is 0.

`GL_UNPACK_IMAGE_HEIGHT_EXT`

> The number of rows in each two-dimensional image of a 3D texture map used when unpacking pixel data from memory is returned. The initial value is 0, indicating that the number of rows is equal to the height of the texture map.

`GL_UNPACK_SKIP_IMAGES_EXT`

> The number of complete two-dimensional images of a 3D texture map skipped when unpacking pixel data from memory is returned. The initial value is 0.

4.3   GL_NV_texture_rectangle

OpenGL version required	OpenGL 1.1
Dependencies	—
Promotions	—
Related extensions	—

DISCUSSION

OpenGL requires that textures have power-of-two dimensions with an optional one-pixel thick border. The `GL_NV_texture_rectangle` extension defines a new texture target that allows a 2D texture map to possess non-power-of-two dimensions. We call a texture having non-power-of-two dimensions a "rectangle" texture map to distinguish it from an ordinary 2D texture map.

There are several limitations imposed on rectangle textures due to their non-power-of-two nature. The following list summarizes the differences between rectangle textures and 2D textures.

- Rectangle textures may not use mipmap filtering. Only the level 0 image may be specified for a rectangle texture map. The minification filter used with a rectangle texture map must be GL_NEAREST or GL_LINEAR.

- Rectangle textures may not use repeating wrap modes. The wrap mode for the *s* or *t* texture coordinate must be GL_CLAMP, GL_CLAMP_TO_EDGE_EXT, or GL_CLAMP_TO_BORDER_ARB.

- Rectangle textures do not support one-pixel borders. The size of the border specified when an rectangular image is loaded must be 0.

- Color palettes are not supported for rectangle textures. The format of a rectangle texture cannot be GL_COLOR_INDEX.

- Texture coordinates are not normalized when accessing a rectangle texture. A 2D texture map is accessed using *s* and *t* texture coordinates in the range [0,1], but a rectangle texture map having width *w* and height *h* is accessed using an *s* texture coordinate in the range [0,*w*] and a *t* texture coordinate in the range [0,*h*].

Rectangle texture mapping is enabled and disabled by calling the **glEnable** and **glDisable** functions with *cap* parameter GL_TEXTURE_RECTANGLE_NV. If multiple texture targets are enabled, rectangle textures have higher priority than 2D textures but lower priority than 3D textures. The complete order of texture target precedence is as follows:

1. GL_TEXTURE_1D
2. GL_TEXTURE_2D
3. GL_TEXTURE_RECTANGLE_NV
4. GL_TEXTURE_3D_EXT
5. GL_TEXTURE_CUBE_MAP_ARB

The highest-numbered enabled texture target for a particular texture unit is the target used for texturing.

A texture object is bound to the rectangle texture target by calling the **glBindTexture** function with the *target* parameter set to GL_TEXTURE_RECTANGLE_NV. When an unused texture name is bound to the rectangle target for the first time, a texture object is created for that name and is associated with the rectangle target. The name of the texture object currently bound to the rectangle texture target can be retrieved by calling the **glGetIntegerv** function with *pname* parameter GL_TEXTURE_BINDING_RECTANGLE_NV.

An image for the currently bound rectangle texture is loaded by calling the **glTexImage2D** function with the *target* parameter set to GL_TEXTURE_RECTANGLE_NV. Since mipmaps and borders are not supported for rectangle textures, the *level* and *border* parameters must be 0. The *width* and *height* parameters are no longer restricted to powers of two, but must be less than the value returned by **glGetIntegerv** with *pname* parameter GL_MAX_RECTANGLE_TEXTURE_SIZE_NV, which must be at least 64. Since rectangle textures do not support color palettes, the *format* parameter may not be GL_COLOR_INDEX.

A subimage for the currently bound rectangle texture can be redefined by calling the **glTexSubImage2D** function with the *target* parameter set to GL_TEXTURE_RECTANGLE_NV. The *level* parameter must be 0, and the *format* parameter cannot be GL_COLOR_INDEX.

An image for a rectangle texture can also be read from the current read buffer by calling the **glCopyTexImage2D** or **glCopyTexSubImage2D** functions with the *target* parameter set to GL_TEXTURE_RECTANGLE_NV. The *level* parameter passed to either function must be 0, and the *border* parameter passed to the **glCopyTexImage2D** function must be 0.

The image for a rectangle texture is retrieved by calling the **glGetTexImage** function with the *target* parameter set to GL_TEXTURE_RECTANGLE_NV. The *level* parameter must be 0. Likewise, when retrieving texture parameter values for the GL_TEXTURE_RECTANGLE_NV target using the **glGetTexLevelParameter{if}v** function, the *level* parameter must be 0.

A proxy mechanism exists for determining whether an implementation is capable of supporting a rectangle texture of a given size and format. Passing the value GL_PROXY_TEXTURE_RECTANGLE_NV into the *target* parameter of the **glTexImage2D** function causes the texture state to be calculated for the proxy target. If an implementation cannot support the size and format specified, then any state returned by the **glGetTexLevelParameter{if}v** function for the target GL_PROXY_TEXTURE_RECTANGLE_NV will be 0.

The wrap mode specified by the **glTexParameter{if}[v]** function for the *s* and *t* texture coordinates must be GL_CLAMP, GL_CLAMP_TO_EDGE_EXT, or GL_CLAMP_TO_BORDER_ARB. The initial value for both texture coordinates is GL_CLAMP_TO_EDGE_EXT. Table 4.3.1 lists the ranges to which the *s* and *t* texture coordinates are clamped for each wrap mode.

TABLE 4.3.1   Ranges to Which the *s* and *t* Texture Coordinates are Clamped for a Rectangle Texture Map Having Width *w* and Height *h*

Wrap Mode	Clamp Range for s	Clamp Range for t
GL_CLAMP	$[0, w]$	$[0, h]$
GL_CLAMP_TO_EDGE_EXT	$[\frac{1}{2}, w - \frac{1}{2}]$	$[\frac{1}{2}, h - \frac{1}{2}]$
GL_CLAMP_TO_BORDER_ARB	$[-\frac{1}{2}, w + \frac{1}{2}]$	$[-\frac{1}{2}, h + \frac{1}{2}]$

EXTENDED FUNCTIONS

- **glEnable, glDisable, glIsEnabled**—Extended to enable/disable rectangle texture maps.

Prototypes

```
void glEnable(GLenum cap);
void glDisable(GLenum cap);
GLboolean glIsEnabled(GLenum cap);
```

Extended Parameters

cap   Specifies a GL capability. To enable or disable rectangle texture mapping for the currently active texture unit, or to query whether rectangle texture mapping is enabled, this should be GL_TEXTURE_RECTANGLE_NV.

Description

Rectangle texture mapping is enabled and disabled for the currently active texture unit by passing the value GL_TEXTURE_RECTANGLE_NV to the **glEnable** and **glDisable** functions. Calling the **glIsEnabled** function with the parameter GL_TEXTURE_RECTANGLE_NV returns a value indicating whether rectangle texture mapping is enabled for the currently active texture unit. Initially, rectangle texture mapping is disabled for all texture units.

■ **glBindTexture**—Extended to support rectangle texture maps.

Prototype

```
void glBindTexture(GLenum target, GLuint texture);
```

Extended Parameters

target   Specifies the target to which the texture is bound. May be GL_TEXTURE_RECTANGLE_NV.

Description

A texture object is bound to the rectangle texture map target by calling the **glBindTexture** function with *target* parameter GL_TEXTURE_RECTANGLE_NV.

■ **glTexImage2D**—Extended to support rectangle texture maps.

Prototype

```
void glTexImage2D(GLenum target, GLint level, GLint internalFormat,
    GLsizei width, GLsizei height, GLint border, GLenum format,
    GLenum type, const GLvoid *pixels);
```

Extended Parameters

target   Specifies the target texture. May be GL_TEXTURE_RECTANGLE_NV or GL_PROXY_TEXTURE_RECTANGLE_NV.

Description

A rectangle texture map is loaded from memory by calling the **glTexImage2D** function with *target* parameter GL_TEXTURE_RECTANGLE_NV.

If the *target* parameter is GL_PROXY_TEXTURE_RECTANGLE_NV, then the texture state for the proxy target is calculated. If an implementation cannot support the size and format specified, then any state returned by the **glGetTexLevelParameter{if}v** function for the target GL_PROXY_TEXTURE_RECTANGLE_NV will be 0.

■ **glCopyTexImage2D**—Extended to support rectangle texture maps.

Prototypes

> void **glCopyTexImage2D**(GLenum *target*, GLint *level*, GLenum *internalFormat*, GLint *x*, GLint *y*, GLsizei *width*, GLsizei *height*, GLint *border*);

Extended Parameters

target   Specifies the target texture. May be GL_TEXTURE_RECTANGLE_NV.

Description

The pixel data for a rectangle texture map can be copied from the current GL_READ_BUFFER by calling the **glCopyTexImage2D** function with *target* parameter GL_TEXTURE_RECTANGLE_NV.

■ **glTexSubImage2D**, **glCopyTexSubImage2D**—Extended to support rectangle texture maps.

Prototypes

> void **glTexSubImage2D**(GLenum *target*, GLint *level*, GLint *xoffset*, GLint *yoffset*, GLsizei *width*, GLsizei *height*, GLenum *format*, GLenum *type*, const GLvoid **pixels*);
> void **glCopyTexSubImage2D**(GLenum *target*, GLint *level*, GLint *xoffset*, GLint *yoffset*, GLint *x*, GLint *y*, GLsizei *width*, GLsizei *height*);

Extended Parameters

target   Specifies the target texture. May be GL_TEXTURE_RECTANGLE_NV.

Description

A subimage of a rectangle texture map face is loaded from memory or copied from the current GL_READ_BUFFER by calling the **glTexSubImage2D** or **glCopyTexSubImage2D** function, respectively, with *target* parameter GL_TEXTURE_RECTANGLE_NV.

■ **glGetTexImage**—Extended to allow retrieval of rectangle texture map images.

Prototypes

> void **glGetTexImage**(GLenum *target*, GLint *level*, GLenum *format*, GLenum *type*, GLvoid **pixels*);

Extended Parameters

target   Specifies the target texture. May be GL_TEXTURE_RECTANGLE_NV.

Description

The pixel data for a rectangle texture map is retrieved by calling the **glGetTexImage** function. For a rectangle texture map, the *level* parameter must be 0, or the error GL_INVALID_VALUE is generated. When a pixel image is stored in memory, the current packing parameters (specified using the **glPixelStorei** function) are applied.

■ **glTexParameter{if}[v]**—Extended to support rectangle texture maps.

Prototypes

```
void glTexParameteri(GLenum target, GLenum pname, GLint param);
void glTexParameterf(GLenum target, GLenum pname, GLfloat param);
void glTexParameteriv(GLenum target, GLenum pname,
    const GLint *params);
void glTexParameterfv(GLenum target, GLenum pname,
    const GLfloat *params);
```

Extended Parameters

target   Specifies the target texture. May be GL_TEXTURE_RECTANGLE_NV.

Description

Texture parameters for the currently bound rectangle texture map are specified by calling the **glTexParameter{if}[v]** function with *target* parameter GL_TEXTURE_RECTANGLE_NV.

■ **glGetTexParameter{if}v**—Extended to support rectangle texture maps.

Prototypes

```
void glGetTexParameteriv(GLenum target, GLenum pname,
    GLint *params);
void glGetTexParameterfv(GLenum target, GLenum pname,
    GLfloat *params);
```

Extended Parameters

target   Specifies the target texture. May be GL_TEXTURE_RECTANGLE_NV.

Description

Texture parameters for the currently bound rectangle texture map are retrieved by calling the **glGetTexParameter{if}v** function with *target* parameter GL_TEXTURE_RECTANGLE_NV.

■ **glGetTexLevelParameter{if}v**—Extended to support rectangle texture maps.

Prototypes

```
void glGetTexLevelParameteriv(GLenum target, GLint level,
    GLenum pname, GLint *params);
void glGetTexLevelParameterfv(GLenum target, GLint level,
    GLenum pname, GLfloat *params);
```

Extended Parameters

target   Specifies the target texture. May be GL_TEXTURE_RECTANGLE_NV or
                        GL_PROXY_TEXTURE_RECTANGLE_NV.

Description

Texture parameters corresponding to the pixel image for the currently bound rectangle texture map are retrieved by calling the **glGetTexLevelParameter{if}v** function with *target* parameter GL_TEXTURE_RECTANGLE_NV. For rectangle texture maps, the *level* parameter must be 0, or the error GL_INVALID_VALUE is generated.

Texture parameters for the proxy rectangle texture map target are queried by calling the **glGetTexLevelParameter{if}v** function with *target* parameter GL_PROXY_TEXTURE_RECTANGLE_NV.

■ **glGetIntegerv**—Extended to allow retrieval of rectangle texture map state.

Prototypes

```
void glGetIntegerv(GLenum pname, GLint *params);
```

Extended Parameters

pname   Specifies the parameter to be returned. May be GL_MAX_RECTANGLE_
                        TEXTURE_SIZE_NV or GL_TEXTURE_BINDING_RECTANGLE_NV.

Description

Various state values related to rectangle texture mapping can be retrieved by calling the **glGetIntegerv** function. The *pname* parameter may be one of the following values:

GL_MAX_RECTANGLE_TEXTURE_SIZE
                        The maximum size of a rectangle texture map is returned. Any rectangle texture map having dimensions of this size or smaller is guaranteed to be supported by the implementation.

GL_TEXTURE_BINDING_RECTANGLE_NV
                        The name of the texture map bound to the GL_TEXTURE_RECTANGLE_NV texture target for the currently active texture unit is returned. The initial value is 0.

4.4   GL_EXT_texture_edge_clamp

OpenGL version required	OpenGL 1.1
Dependencies	—
Promotions	Promoted to a core feature in OpenGL 1.2
Related extensions	GL_ARB_texture_border_clamp GL_ARB_texture_mirrored_repeat GL_ATI_texture_mirror_once

DISCUSSION

The GL_CLAMP wrap mode clamps texture coordinates to the range [0,1]. If the minification filter mode is not GL_NEAREST, then border texels (for a texture map containing a border) or the constant border color may be sampled when a texture coordinate is near 0 or 1, because the filtering box straddles the texture map boundary. The result is that sampled colors along the edge of a texture map are a mixture of image texel colors and the border color, possibly an undesired effect. The GL_EXT_texture_edge_clamp extension adds a new wrap mode, GL_CLAMP_TO_EDGE_EXT, that clamps texture coordinates to a range coinciding with the centers of the edge texels of a texture map at each mipmap level. This effectively prevents border texels or the constant border color from ever being sampled.

Edge clamping for the *s*, *t*, or *r* texture coordinate is specified by calling the **glTexParameter{if}[v]** function with the *pname* parameter set to GL_TEXTURE_WRAP_S, GL_TEXTURE_WRAP_T, or GL_TEXTURE_WRAP_R_EXT, respectively, and the *param* parameter set to GL_CLAMP_TO_EDGE_EXT. As shown in Figure 4.4.1, clamping to edge texels for a particular texture coordinate causes the coordinate to be clamped to the range

$$\left[\frac{1}{2n}, 1 - \frac{1}{2n} \right],$$

where *n* is the size of the texture map in the direction corresponding to the clamped coordinate.

EXTENDED FUNCTIONS

■ **glTexParameteri**—Extended to support the edge clamp wrap mode.

Prototype

```
void glTexParameteri(GLenum target, GLenum pname, GLint param);
```

Extended Parameters

param	Specifies the value of a texture parameter. When the *pname* parameter is GL_TEXTURE_WRAP_S, GL_TEXTURE_WRAP_T, or GL_TEXTURE_WRAP_R_EXT, this may be GL_CLAMP_TO_EDGE_EXT.

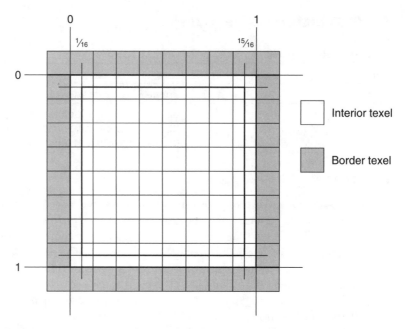

FIGURE 4.4.1 An 8 × 8 texture image and the clamping ranges for the GL_CLAMP and GL_CLAMP_TO_EDGE_EXT wrap modes. Coordinates are clamped to the range [0,1] when the wrap mode is GL_CLAMP, and coordinates are clamped to the range $\left[\frac{1}{16}, \frac{15}{16}\right]$ when the wrap mode is GL_CLAMP_TO_EDGE_EXT.

Description

The wrap mode for the texture target specified by the *target* parameter and the texture coordinate specified by the *pname* parameter is set to GL_CLAMP_TO_EDGE_EXT by calling the **glTexParameteri** function.

4.5 GL_ARB_texture_border_clamp

OpenGL version required	OpenGL 1.1
Dependencies	—
Promotions	Promoted to a core feature in OpenGL 1.3
Related extensions	GL_EXT_texture_edge_clamp GL_ARB_texture_mirrored_repeat GL_ATI_texture_mirror_once

DISCUSSION

The GL_CLAMP wrap mode clamps texture coordinates to the range [0,1]. If the minification filter mode is not GL_NEAREST, then border texels (for a texture map containing a border) or the constant border color may be sampled when a texture coordinate is near 0 or 1, because the filtering box straddles the texture map boundary. The result is that sampled colors along the edge of a texture map are a mixture of image texel colors and the border color, possibly an undesired effect. The GL_ARB_texture_border_clamp extension adds a new wrap mode, GL_CLAMP_TO_BORDER_ARB, that clamps texture coordinates to a range coinciding with the centers of the border texels of a texture map at each mipmap level. This effectively ensures that only border texels are sampled when texture coordinates are clamped.

Border clamping for the *s*, *t*, or *r* texture coordinate is specified by calling the **glTexParameter{if}[v]** function with the *pname* parameter set to GL_TEXTURE_WRAP_S, GL_TEXTURE_WRAP_T, or GL_TEXTURE_WRAP_R_EXT, respectively, and the *param* parameter set to GL_CLAMP_TO_BORDER_ARB. As shown in Figure 4.5.1, clamping to border texels for a particular texture coordinate causes the coordinate to be clamped to the range

$$\left[-\frac{1}{2n}, 1+\frac{1}{2n} \right],$$

where *n* is the size of the texture map in the direction corresponding to the clamped coordinate.

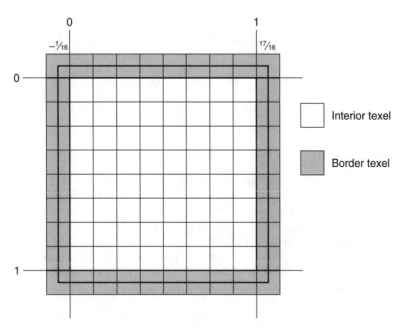

FIGURE 4.5.1   An 8 × 8 texture image and the clamping ranges for the GL_CLAMP and GL_CLAMP_TO_BORDER_ARB wrap modes. Coordinates are clamped to the range [0,1] when the wrap mode is GL_CLAMP, and coordinates are clamped to the range $[-\frac{1}{16}, \frac{17}{16}]$ when the wrap mode is GL_CLAMP_TO_BORDER_ARB.

EXTENDED FUNCTIONS

■ **glTexParameteri**—Extended to support the border clamp wrap mode.

Prototype

void **glTexParameteri**(GLenum *target*, GLenum *pname*, GLint *param*);

Extended Parameters

param   Specifies the value of a texture parameter. When the *pname* parameter is
                   GL_TEXTURE_WRAP_S, GL_TEXTURE_WRAP_T, or GL_TEXTURE_WRAP_
                   R_EXT, this may be GL_CLAMP_TO_BORDER_ARB.

Description

The wrap mode for the texture target specified by the *target* parameter and the texture coordinate specified by the *pname* parameter is set to GL_CLAMP_TO_BORDER_EXT by calling
the **glTexParameteri** function.

4.6   GL_ARB_texture_mirrored_repeat

OpenGL version required	OpenGL 1.1
Dependencies	—
Promotions	Promoted to a core feature in OpenGL 1.4
Related extensions	GL_EXT_texture_edge_clamp
	GL_ARB_texture_border_clamp
	GL_ATI_texture_mirror_once

DISCUSSION

The GL_ARB_texture_mirrored_repeat extension adds a new wrap mode that removes
the need to store redundant information in texture maps that are symmetric in one or
more directions. When the wrap mode is set to GL_MIRRORED_REPEAT_ARB, a texture
image is repeated in such a way that every odd repetition is a mirror image.

The mirrored repeat wrap mode is specified for the *s*, *t*, or *r* texture coordinate by calling the **glTexParameter{if}[v]** function with the *pname* parameter set to GL_TEXTURE_
WRAP_S, GL_TEXTURE_WRAP_T, or GL_TEXTURE_WRAP_R_EXT, respectively, and the *param*
parameter set to GL_MIRRORED_REPEAT_ARB. When the wrap mode for a particular texture
coordinate *f'* is set to GL_MIRRORED_REPEAT_ARB, a new texture coordinate is calculated
using the rule

$$f' = \begin{cases} f - \lfloor f \rfloor, & \text{if } \lfloor f \rfloor \text{ is even;} \\ 1 - (f - \lfloor f \rfloor), & \text{if } \lfloor f \rfloor \text{ is odd.} \end{cases} \qquad (4.6.1)$$

The coordinate f' is then clamped to the range

$$\left[\frac{1}{2n}, 1 - \frac{1}{2n}\right],$$

where n is the size of the texture map in the direction corresponding to f.

EXTENDED FUNCTIONS

■ **glTexParameteri**—Extended to support the mirrored repeat wrap mode.

Prototype

void **glTexParameteri**(GLenum *target*, GLenum *pname*, GLint *param*);

Extended Parameters

param   Specifies the value of a texture parameter. When the *pname* parameter is GL_TEXTURE_WRAP_S, GL_TEXTURE_WRAP_T, or GL_TEXTURE_WRAP_R_EXT, this may be GL_MIRRORED_REPEAT_ARB.

Description

The wrap mode for the texture target specified by the *target* parameter and the texture coordinate specified by the *pname* parameter is set to GL_MIRRORED_REPEAT_ARB by calling the **glTexParameteri** function. The mirrored repeat wrap mode is not supported by the GL_TEXTURE_RECTANGLE_NV texture target.

4.7   GL_ATI_texture_mirror_once

OpenGL version required	OpenGL 1.1
Dependencies	—
Promotions	—
Related extensions	GL_EXT_texture_edge_clamp
	GL_ARB_texture_border_clamp
	GL_ARB_texture_mirrored_repeat

DISCUSSION

The GL_ATI_texture_mirror_once extension adds a new wrap mode that removes the need to store redundant information in texture maps that are symmetric in one or more directions. When the wrap mode is set to GL_MIRROR_CLAMP_ATI or GL_MIRROR_CLAMP_TO_EDGE_ATI, the absolute value of a texture coordinate is evaluated before clamping, mirroring the texture image for coordinates in the range [−1,0].

The mirror once wrap modes are specified for the *s*, *t*, or *r* texture coordinate by calling the **glTexParameter{if}[v]** function with the *pname* parameter set to GL_TEXTURE_ WRAP_S, GL_TEXTURE_WRAP_T, or GL_TEXTURE_WRAP_R_EXT, respectively, and the *param* parameter set to GL_MIRROR_CLAMP_ATI or GL_MIRROR_CLAMP_TO_EDGE_ATI. When the wrap mode for a particular texture coordinate *f* is set to GL_MIRROR_CLAMP_ATI, the absolute value $|f|$ is evaluated and clamped to the range [0,1]. When the wrap mode is GL_ MIRROR_CLAMP_TO_EDGE_ATI, the absolute value $|f|$ is evaluated and clamped to the range

$$\left[\frac{1}{2n}, 1 - \frac{1}{2n}\right],$$

where *n* is the size of the texture map in the direction corresponding to *f*.

EXTENDED FUNCTIONS

■ **glTexParameteri**—Extended to support the mirror once wrap modes.

Prototype

void **glTexParameteri**(GLenum *target*, GLenum *pname*, GLint *param*);

Extended Parameters

param   Specifies the value of a texture parameter. When the *pname* parameter is GL_TEXTURE_WRAP_S, GL_TEXTURE_WRAP_T, or GL_TEXTURE_WRAP_R_ EXT, this may be GL_MIRROR_CLAMP_ATI or GL_MIRROR_CLAMP_TO_ EDGE_ATI.

Description

The wrap mode for the texture target specified by the *target* parameter and the texture coordinate specified by the *pname* parameter is set to GL_MIRROR_CLAMP_ATI or GL_MIRROR_ CLAMP_TO_EDGE_ATI by calling the **glTexParameteri** function. The mirror once wrap modes are not supported by the GL_TEXTURE_RECTANGLE_NV texture target.

4.8   GL_EXT_texture_filter_anisotropic

OpenGL version required	OpenGL 1.1
Dependencies	—
Promotions	—
Related extensions	—

DISCUSSION

During rasterization, the area within a texture map applied to a polygon that is oriented at an oblique to the camera may be stretched far more in one of the *s* and *t* directions than the other, as shown in Figure 4.8.1. The conventional minification filtering modes do not account for different rates of change in the texture coordinates relative to the *x* and *y* window-space directions, but instead only consider the maximum of the two values. The `GL_EXT_texture_filter_anisotropic` extension provides a mechanism for increasing the number of texture samples in the direction of the greater rate of change in texture coordinates to produce higher quality images.

FIGURE 4.8.1 Texture coordinates may have different rates of change relative to the *x* and *y* window-space directions, resulting in poor mipmap selection and different texture-space sampling frequencies.

Anisotropic texture filtering is controlled by calling the **glTexParameter{if}[v]** function with the *target* parameter set to GL_TEXTURE_2D and the *pname* parameter set to GL_TEXTURE_MAX_ANISOTROPY_EXT. The *param* parameter specifies the maximum anisotropic filtering to apply. This value is clamped to the implementation-dependent maximum value returned by the **glGetFloatv** function with *pname* parameter GL_MAX_TEXTURE_MAX_ANISOTROPY_EXT. The default value is 1.0 and corresponds to conventional isotropic filtering.

When anisotropic filtering is enabled, multiple samples of a texture map are taken, whereas one sample would be taken for isotropic filtering. Let *s(x,y)* be the function that maps window-space coordinates *x* and *y* to the texture coordinate *s* within a primitive, and let *t(x,y)* be the function that maps *x* and *y* to the texture coordinate *t*. Let *n* and *m* be the base-2 logarithms of the width and height of the texture map, and define $u(x,y) = 2^n s(x,y)$ and $v(x,y) = 2^m t(x,y)$. For isotropic filtering, the level-of-detail parameter λ can be calculated using the following formula:

$$\rho_x = \sqrt{\left(\frac{\partial u}{\partial x}\right)^2 + \left(\frac{\partial v}{\partial x}\right)^2}$$

$$\rho_y = \sqrt{\left(\frac{\partial u}{\partial y}\right)^2 + \left(\frac{\partial v}{\partial y}\right)^2}$$

$$\lambda = \log_2\left[\max\left(\rho_x, \rho_y\right)\right] \tag{4.8.1}$$

For anisotropic filtering, the value of λ can be calculated by first determining the number of samples N that should be taken in the direction of greater change in the functions $u(x,y)$ and $v(x,y)$. Setting $\rho_{\max} = \max(\rho_x, \rho_y)$ and $\rho_{\min} = \min(\rho_x, \rho_y)$, we have

$$N = \min\left(\left\lceil \frac{\rho_{\max}}{\rho_{\min}} \right\rceil, a_{\max}\right)$$

$$\lambda = \log_2 \frac{\rho_{\max}}{N} \qquad (4.8.2)$$

where $a_{\max}$ is the maximum anisotropy passed to the **glTexParameter{if}[v]** function. The value of λ selects the mipmap. If $\rho_x > \rho_y$, then N samples are taken in the s-direction for every one sample taken in the t direction. If $\rho_x \leq \rho_y$, then N samples are taken in the t direction for every one sample taken in the s direction.

EXTENDED FUNCTIONS

■ **glTexParameterf**—Extended to support anisotropic filtering parameters.

Prototype

```
void glTexParameterf(GLenum target, GLenum pname, GLfloat param);
```

Extended Parameters

pname   Specifies the symbolic name of a texture parameter. May be GL_TEXTURE_MAX_ANISOTROPY_EXT.

Description

The maximum anisotropy applied during filtering for a particular texture is specified by calling the **glTexParameterf** function. When the *pname* parameter is GL_TEXTURE_MAX_ANISOTROPY_EXT, the *param* parameter specifies the maximum anisotropy for the currently bound texture map.

■ **glGetTexParameterfv**—Extended to allow retrieval of anisotropic filtering parameters.

Prototype

```
void glGetTexParameterfv(GLenum target, GLenum pname,
    GLfloat *params);
```

Extended Parameters

pname   Specifies the symbolic name of the texture parameter to return. May be GL_TEXTURE_MAX_ANISOTROPY_EXT.

Description

The maximum anisotropy applied to the currently bound texture map is retrieved by calling the **glGetTexParameterfv** function with *pname* parameter GL_TEXTURE_MAX_ ANISOTROPY_EXT.

- **glGetIntegerv**—Extended to allow retrieval of the maximum supported anisotropy value.

Prototype

```
void glGetIntegerv(GLenum pname, GLint *params);
```

Extended Parameters

pname   Specifies the parameter to be returned. May be GL_MAX_TEXTURE_MAX_ ANISOTROPY_EXT.

Description

The maximum value of maximum anisotropy supported by an implementation is retrieved by calling the **glGetIntegerv** function with *pname* parameter GL_MAX_TEXTURE_MAX_ ANISOTROPY_EXT. This value is always at least 2.0.

4.9   GL_SGIS_texture_lod

OpenGL version required	OpenGL 1.1
Dependencies	—
Promotions	Promoted to a core feature in OpenGL 1.2
Related extensions	—

DISCUSSION

The GL_SGIS_texture_lod extension provides control over the range of detail levels selected for a texture map and provides a way to use only a contiguous subset of the texture's mipmap array. This functionality is useful for applications that wish to progressively load mipmap levels while continuing to render using initially lower resolutions.

The base detail level and maximum detail level for the currently bound texture are specified by calling the **glTexParameter{if}[v]** function with the *pname* parameter set to GL_TEXTURE_BASE_LEVEL_SGIS or GL_TEXTURE_MAX_LEVEL_SGIS. The maximum detail level may not be less than the base detail level, or the mipmap array is considered incomplete, and it is as if texturing was disabled for the corresponding texture target. The base detail level must be nonnegative and specifies the first image in the mipmap array that can be sampled.

Let n, m, and l be the base-2 logarithms of the width, height, and depth of the base-level image of a texture map ($m = 0$ for 1D textures, and $l = 0$ for both 1D and 2D textures). Define $p = \max\{n,m,l\} + level_{base}$, where $level_{base}$ is the base detail level, and define $q = \min\{p, level_{max}\}$, where $level_{max}$ is the maximum detail level. Detail levels $level_{base}$ through q must be specified in order for a texture's mipmap array to be considered complete. Detail levels outside the range $[level_{base}, level_{max}]$ are prevented from being sampled.

The minimum and maximum level-of-detail (LOD) values for the currently bound texture are specified by calling the **glTexParameter{if}[v]** function with the *pname* parameter set to GL_TEXTURE_MIN_LOD_SGIS or GL_TEXTURE_MAX_LOD_SGIS.

The LOD parameter λ is calculated using the dimensions of the base-level texture image. Let $s(x,y)$ be the function that maps window-space coordinates x and y to the texture coordinate s within a primitive, let $t(x,y)$ be the function that maps x and y to the texture coordinate t, and let $r(x,y)$ be the function that maps x and y to the texture coordinate r. Define $u(x,y) = 2^n s(x,y)$, $v(x,y) = 2^m t(x,y)$, and $w(x,y) = 2^l r(x,y)$, where n, m, and l be the base-2 logarithms of the width, height, and depth of the base-level image of a texture map, as before. The LOD parameter λ is calculated using the following formula:

$$\rho_x = \sqrt{\left(\frac{\partial u}{\partial x}\right)^2 + \left(\frac{\partial v}{\partial x}\right)^2 + \left(\frac{\partial w}{\partial x}\right)^2}$$

$$\rho_y = \sqrt{\left(\frac{\partial u}{\partial y}\right)^2 + \left(\frac{\partial v}{\partial y}\right)^2 + \left(\frac{\partial w}{\partial y}\right)^2}$$

$$\lambda = \log_2\left[\max(\rho_x, \rho_y)\right] + b \tag{4.9.1}$$

(If the GL_EXT_texture_lod_bias extension is supported, the value of b is the LOD bias; otherwise, $b \equiv 0$.) The value of λ is then clamped to the range $[\lambda_{min}, \lambda_{max}]$, where λ_{min} and λ_{max} correspond to the values specified for GL_TEXTURE_MIN_LOD_SGIS and GL_TEXTURE_MAX_LOD_SGIS. After λ is clamped, the value of $level_{base}$ is added to select mipmaps.

EXTENDED FUNCTIONS

■ **glTexParameterf**—Extended to support texture LOD parameters.

Prototype

```
void glTexParameterf(GLenum target, GLenum pname, GLfloat param);
```

Extended Parameters

pname   Specifies the symbolic name of a texture parameter. May be GL_TEXTURE_MIN_LOD_SGIS, GL_TEXTURE_MAX_LOD_SGIS, GL_TEXTURE_BASE_LEVEL_SGIS, or GL_TEXTURE_MAX_LEVEL_SGIS.

Description

Texture LOD parameters are specified for a particular texture target by calling the **glTexParameterf** function. The *pname* parameter may be one of the following values.

GL_TEXTURE_MIN_LOD_SGIS

> The *param* parameter specifies the minimum value to which the texture LOD is clamped.

GL_TEXTURE_MAX_LOD_SGIS

> The *param* parameter specifies the maximum value to which the texture LOD is clamped.

GL_TEXTURE_BASE_LEVEL_SGIS

> The *param* parameter specifies the base level that is added to the clamped LOD for the texture.

GL_TEXTURE_MAX_LEVEL_SGIS

> The *param* parameter specifies the maximum detail level that is sampled during texel filtering.

■ **glGetTexParameterfv**—Extended to allow retrieval of texture LOD parameters.

Prototype

    void **glGetTexParameterfv**(GLenum *target*, GLenum *pname*,
        GLfloat *params*);

Extended Parameters

pname   Specifies the symbolic name of the texture parameter to return. May be GL_TEXTURE_MIN_LOD_SGIS, GL_TEXTURE_MAX_LOD_SGIS, GL_TEXTURE_BASE_LEVEL_SGIS, or GL_TEXTURE_MAX_LEVEL_SGIS.

Description

Texture LOD parameters are retrieved for a particular texture target by calling the **glTexParameterfv** function. The *pname* parameter may be one of the following values:

GL_TEXTURE_MIN_LOD_SGIS

> The minimum value to which the texture LOD is clamped is returned.

GL_TEXTURE_MAX_LOD_SGIS

> The maximum value to which the texture LOD is clamped is returned.

GL_TEXTURE_BASE_LEVEL_SGIS

> The base level that is added to the clamped LOD for the texture is returned.

GL_TEXTURE_MAX_LEVEL_SGIS

> The maximum detail level that is sampled during texel filtering is returned.

4.10   GL_SGIS_generate_mipmap

OpenGL version required	OpenGL 1.1
Dependencies	—
Promotions	Promoted to a core feature in OpenGL 1.4
Related extensions	—

DISCUSSION

The GL_SGIS_generate_mipmap extension provides the ability to automatically generate all mipmap levels for a texture map when the base-level image is modified.

Automatic mipmap generation is enabled or disabled for the currently bound texture object by calling the **glTexParameter{if}[v]** function with the *pname* parameter set to GL_GENERATE_MIPMAP_SGIS and the *param* parameter set to GL_TRUE or GL_FALSE. Once enabled, any updates to the base-level texture image cause the lower resolution mipmap images to be recalculated, replacing any previous contents. When mipmap generation is enabled, the mipmap array is considered complete when the base-level image is specified.

The recommended method for calculating mipmap images is by using a simple 2×2 box filter. Some implementations may provide more than one algorithm for calculating mipmap images, which may offer higher quality resolution reduction at a possible performance cost. The **glHint** function with the *target* parameter set to GL_GENERATE_MIPMAP_HINT_SGIS can be used to select the fastest or highest quality algorithm by passing the values GL_FASTEST or GL_NICEST into the *mode* parameter, respectively. The initial value of the mipmap generation hint is GL_DONT_CARE.

If the GL_SGIS_texture_lod extension is supported, then updates to the detail level given by the current value of GL_TEXTURE_BASE_LEVEL_SGIS for a texture trigger the recalculation of the mipmap array.

EXTENDED FUNCTIONS

- **glTexParameteri**—Extended to support automatic mipmap generation.

Prototype

    void **glTexParameteri**(GLenum *target*, GLenum *pname*, GLint *param*);

Extended Parameters

pname   Specifies the symbolic name of a texture parameter. May be
               GL_GENERATE_MIPMAP_SGIS.

Description

Automatic mipmap generation is turned on and off for a particular texture map by calling the **glTexParameteri** function. When the *pname* parameter is GL_GENERATE_MIPMAP_SGIS, specifying the value GL_TRUE enables automatic mipmap generation, and specifying the value GL_FALSE disables it.

■ **glGetTexParameteriv**—Extended to allow retrieval of automatic mipmap generation parameters.

Prototype

    void **glGetTexParameteri**(GLenum *target*, GLenum *pname*, GLint **params*);

Extended Parameters

pname   Specifies the symbolic name of the texture parameter to return. May be GL_GENERATE_MIPMAP_SGIS.

Description

Whether automatic mipmap generation is turned on for a particular texture map can be determined by calling the **glGetTexParameteriv** function with *pname* parameter GL_GENERATE_MIPMAP_SGIS. The value returned in the *params* parameter is GL_TRUE or GL_FALSE.

■ **glHint**—Extended to allow specification of a mipmap generation hint.

Prototype

    void **glHint**(GLenum *target*, GLenum *mode*);

Extended Parameters

target   Specifies a symbolic constant representing the behavior to modify. May be GL_GENERATE_MIPMAP_HINT_SGIS.

Description

A hint indicating whether the fastest or highest quality mipmap generation algorithm should be used by an implementation can be specified by calling the **glHint** function with *target* parameter GL_GENERATE_MIPMAP_HINT_SGIS. When the *mode* parameter is GL_FASTEST, an implementation will select the fastest method for generating mipmaps at a possible cost in quality. When the *mode* parameter is GL_NICEST, an implementation will select the highest quality method for generating mipmaps at a possible cost in speed. The initial value is GL_DONT_CARE.

■ **glGetIntegerv**—Extended to allow retrieval of the mipmap generation hint.

Prototype

    void **glGetIntegerv**(GLenum *pname*, GLint **params*);

Extended Parameters

pname   Specifies the parameter to be returned. May be GL_GENERATE_MIPMAP_HINT_SGIS.

Description

The current value of the mipmap generation hint can be retrieved by calling the **glGetIntegerv** function with *pname* parameter GL_GENERATE_MIPMAP_HINT_SGIS.

4.11   GL_NV_texture_expand_normal

OpenGL version required	OpenGL 1.1
Dependencies	—
Promotions	—
Related extensions	—

DISCUSSION

The GL_NV_texture_expand_normal extension provides a per-texture remapping mode that can perform a linear mapping from the range [0,1] to the range [−1,1] for each of a texture map's unsigned color components.

The unsigned component remapping mode for the currently bound texture is specified by calling the **glTexParameter{if}[v]** function with *pname* parameter GL_TEXTURE_UNSIGNED_REMAP_MODE_NV. The *param* parameter then specifies the remapping mode and can be GL_NONE or GL_EXPAND_NORMAL_NV. The initial value, GL_NONE, causes no remapping to take place. Specifying the value GL_EXPAND_NORMAL_NV causes any unsigned color component c to be remapped according to the formula $c' = 2c - 1$.

The unsigned remapping mode is not applied to signed texture components, such as those existing in a texture having the GL_SIGNED_RGBA_NV format. If a texture map contains a mixture of signed and unsigned components, as is the case when using the GL_SIGNED_RGB_UNSIGNED_ALPHA_NV format, the signed components are not remapped, but the unsigned components are remapped according to the value of GL_TEXTURE_UNSIGNED_REMAP_MODE_NV.

EXTENDED FUNCTIONS

■ **glTexParameteri**—Extended to allow specification of an unsigned component remapping mode.

Prototype

```
void glTexParameteri(GLenum target, GLenum pname, GLint param);
```

Extended Parameters

pname   Specifies the symbolic name of a texture parameter. May be GL_TEXTURE_UNSIGNED_REMAP_MODE_NV.

param   Specifies the value of the texture parameter. When *pname* is GL_TEXTURE_UNSIGNED_REMAP_MODE_NV, this may be GL_NONE or GL_EXPAND_NORMAL_NV. The initial value is GL_NONE.

Description

The remapping mode for the unsigned components of a texture map is specified by calling the **glTexParameteri** function with *pname* parameter GL_TEXTURE_UNSIGNED_REMAP_ MODE_NV. Initially, the remapping mode is GL_NONE, meaning that no remapping takes place. If the remapping mode is set to GL_EXPAND_NORMAL_NV, then unsigned components are linearly mapped from the range [0,1] to the range [−1,1].

■ **glGetTexParameteriv**—Extended to allow retrieval of the current unsigned component remapping mode.

Prototype

```
void glGetTexParameteriv(GLenum target, GLenum pname,
    GLint *params);
```

Extended Parameters

pname   Specifies the symbolic name of a texture parameter. May be GL_ TEXTURE_UNSIGNED_REMAP_MODE_NV.

Description

The current state of the unsigned component remapping mode is retrieved by calling the **glGetTexParameteriv** function with *pname* parameter GL_TEXTURE_UNSIGNED_REMAP_ MODE_NV.

TEXTURE COMPRESSION

IN THIS CHAPTER

5.1   GL_ARB_texture_compression

OpenGL version required	OpenGL 1.1
Dependencies	—
Promotions	Promoted to a core feature in OpenGL 1.3
Related extensions	`GL_EXT_texture_compression_s3tc` `GL_NV_texture_compression_vtc`

DISCUSSION

The `GL_ARB_texture_compression` extension provides a general framework for working with compressed texture formats. Using compressed textures can reduce memory requirements and can increase rendering performance on hardware that natively supports particular compression formats. Many texture compression formats exist, but the `GL_ARB_texture_compression` extension does not define or require any of these formats. Instead, it is intended to serve as a basis upon which further extensions are built to support specific texture compression formats.

The general framework established by the `GL_ARB_texture_compression` extension provides the following functionality:

- Generic compressed internal texture formats that can be specified when loading a texture image to indicate to the driver that it should select an appropriate compression format and use it as its internal storage format;

- The ability to retrieve texture images in compressed form so that they can be stored and later reloaded without having to recompress; and

- A mechanism for retrieving the texture compression formats supported by the implementation.

Compressing Texture Images

A texture image is compressed by calling one of the **glTexImage1D**, **glTexImage2D**, or **glTexImage3DEXT** functions, and specifying a compressed format as the *internalFormat* parameter. The GL_ARB_texture_compression extension provides six symbolic constants that correspond to generic compressed internal formats. Symbolic constants corresponding to specific compression formats are defined by other extensions, such as the GL_EXT_texture_compression_s3tc extension described in Section 5.2.

When one of the constants GL_COMPRESSED_ALPHA_ARB, GL_COMPRESSED_LUMINANCE_ARB, GL_COMPRESSED_LUMINANCE_ALPHA_ARB, GL_COMPRESSED_INTENSITY_ARB, GL_COMPRESSED_RGB_ARB, or GL_COMPRESSED_RGBA_ARB is specified as the *internalFormat* parameter of the **glTexImage1D**, **glTexImage2D**, or **glTexImage3DEXT** function, the implementation attempts to compress the texture image specified by the *pixels* parameter using the most suitable texture compression format available. If no compression format would be appropriate for the image data, then the image remains uncompressed, and it is as if the corresponding base internal format listed in Table 5.1.1 were specified as the *internalFormat* parameter.

TABLE 5.1.1 Base internal formats corresponding to the generic compressed internal formats. The compressed internal format is replaced by the base internal format when the driver is unable to compress a texture image.

Compressed Format	Base Format
GL_COMPRESSED_ALPHA_ARB	GL_ALPHA
GL_COMPRESSED_LUMINANCE_ARB	GL_LUMINANCE
GL_COMPRESSED_LUMINANCE_ALPHA_ARB	GL_LUMINANCE_ALPHA
GL_COMPRESSED_INTENSITY_ARB	GL_INTENSITY
GL_COMPRESSED_RGB_ARB	GL_RGB
GL_COMPRESSED_RGBA_ARB	GL_RGBA

Specific compressed internal formats defined by other extensions may impose restrictions on a texture image that is to be compressed. If one of the **glTexImage1D**, **glTexImage2D**, or **glTexImage3DEXT** functions is called with a specific compressed internal format specified as the *internalFormat* parameter, and the implementation cannot compress the image because certain restrictions are not satisfied, then the implementation replaces the specified internal format with the corresponding base internal format and does not compress the image.

Whether the texture image was successfully compressed can be determined by calling the `glGetTexLevelParameter{if}v` function with *pname* parameter `GL_TEXTURE_COMPRESSED_ARB`. If the image is compressed, then the value returned in the *params* parameter is `GL_TRUE`. If the implementation had to fall back to a base internal format, then the returned value is `GL_FALSE`. To determine whether an image would be compressed by the implementation without actually performing the compression, the targets `GL_PROXY_TEXTURE_1D`, `GL_PROXY_TEXTURE_2D`, and `GL_PROXY_TEXTURE_3D_EXT` may be passed into the *target* parameter of the `glTexImage1D`, `glTexImage2D`, and `glTexImage3DEXT` functions, respectively. Querying the value of `GL_TEXTURE_COMPRESSED_ARB` for the same proxy target reveals whether the implementation supports compression of the texture image having the specified dimensions, border width, and internal format.

When a texture image is compressed using one of the six generic compressed internal formats, the actual internal format chosen by the implementation can be retrieved by calling the `glGetTexLevelParameter{if}v` function with *pname* parameter `GL_TEXTURE_INTERNAL_FORMAT`. The returned symbolic constant is never one of the generic compressed internal formats, but instead a specific format that is supported by the implementation.

Different levels of quality may be available to an implementation when compressing texture images. A hint may be specified by calling the **glHint** function with *target* parameter `GL_TEXTURE_COMPRESSION_HINT_ARB` to inform the implementation whether the fastest or highest quality compression method should be used. Generally, the texture compression hint should be set to `GL_FASTEST` when textures are being compressed on the fly as they are uploaded to the implementation. If a texture image is being compressed with the intent of retrieving the compressed data and storing it for future use, then the texture compression hint should be set to `GL_NICEST`.

The specific internal compressed texture formats support by an implementation can be retrieved by calling the **glGetIntegerv** function. The number of compressed formats is returned when the *pname* parameter is `GL_NUM_COMPRESSED_TEXTURE_FORMATS_ARB`. This value can be used to allocate a buffer to receive the symbolic constants corresponding to each of the supported formats. These constants are retrieved by specifying `GL_COMPRESSED_TEXTURE_FORMATS_ARB` for the *pname* parameter. Each symbolic constant represents a supported internal compressed texture format that may be passed to the *internalFormat* parameter of the **glTexImage1D**, **glTexImage2D**, or **glTexImage3DEXT** function. Any supported formats that carry unusual restrictions are *not* returned in this array so that an application may use the compression formats without having to know about any restrictions that are specific to a particular compression algorithm.

Retrieving Compressed Images

The data corresponding to a compressed texture image can be retrieved by calling the **glGetCompressedTexImageARB** function,

```
void glGetCompressedTexImageARB(GLenum target,
                                GLint level,
                                GLvoid *data);
```

This function can only be called for compressed texture images. If it is called for an uncompressed image, the error GL_INVALID_OPERATION is generated. The region of memory specified by the *data* parameter must be large enough to accommodate the entire compressed image. The actual size of the compressed data corresponding to a texture image can be retrieved by calling the **glGetTexLevelParameter{if}v** function with *pname* parameter GL_TEXTURE_COMPRESSED_IMAGE_SIZE_ARB.

Once the compressed data corresponding to a texture image has been retrieved, it can be saved and later reloaded in compressed form by calling one of the **glCompressedTexImage1DARB**, **glCompressedTexImage2DARB**, or **glCompressedTexImage3DARB** functions. The size of the compressed data and the internal format of the image, both retrieved using the **glGetTexLevelParameter{if}v** function, should also be saved and later passed to the *imageSize* and *internalFormat* parameters, respectively, when the texture image is reloaded.

Loading Compressed Texture Images

When texture image data is available in compressed form, either because it was previously retrieved using the **glGetCompressedTexImageARB** function or the data format corresponding to a particular compression algorithm is known, it can be directly loaded by calling one of the **glCompressedTexImage1DARB**, **glCompressedTexImage2DARB**, or **glCompressedTexImage3DARB** functions.

```
void glCompressedTexImage1DARB(GLenum target,
                               GLint level,
                               GLenum internalFormat,
                               GLsizei width,
                               GLint border,
                               GLsizei imageSize,
                               const GLvoid *data);

void glCompressedTexImage2DARB(GLenum target,
                               GLint level,
                               GLenum internalFormat,
                               GLsizei width,
                               GLsizei height,
                               GLint border,
                               GLsizei imageSize,
                               const GLvoid *data);

void glCompressedTexImage3DARB(GLenum target,
                               GLint level,
                               GLenum internalFormat,
                               GLsizei width,
```

```
GLsizei height,
GLsizei depth,
GLint border,
GLsizei imageSize,
const GLvoid *data);
```

This avoids compression overhead at the time that a texture image is loaded and allows a texture image to be stored using less space.

When compressed image data is loaded, the value of the *internalFormat* parameter passed to the **glCompressedTexImage1DARB**, **glCompressedTexImage2DARB**, or **glCompressedTexImage3DARB** function must be a symbolic constant defined by another extension that exposes a specific texture compression format. The six generic compression formats are not accepted, and if specified, they generate a GL_INVALID_ENUM error. If the specified internal format is different from that used to encode the image specified by the *data* parameter, then the results are undefined. If the value of the *imageSize* parameter is not consistent with the appropriate size of the compressed image using the particular texture compression algorithm specified by the *internalFormat* parameter, then GL_INVALID_VALUE is generated.

Some compressed internal formats defined by other extensions may impose restrictions on the texture image. For instance, a particular compression algorithm may operate only on two-dimensional textures or may require that the texture border width is zero. If a call is made to one of the **glCompressedTexImage1DARB**, **glCompressedTexImage2DARB**, or **glCompressedTexImage3DARB** functions with parameter values that violate any such restrictions, then the error GL_INVALID_OPERATION is generated.

A call to **glCompressedTexImage1DARB**, **glCompressedTexImage2DARB**, or **glCompressedTexImage3DARB** is guaranteed to succeed if the following conditions are met:

- The *data* parameter points to a compressed image returned by the **glGetCompressedTexImageARB** function.

- The *target* and *level* parameters match those passed to the **glGetCompressedTexImageARB** function when the compressed image was retrieved.

- The *width, height, depth, border, internalFormat*, and *imageSize* parameters match the values of GL_TEXTURE_WIDTH, GL_TEXTURE_HEIGHT, GL_TEXTURE_DEPTH_EXT, GL_TEXTURE_BORDER, GL_TEXTURE_INTERNAL_FORMAT, and GL_TEXTURE_ COMPRESSED_IMAGE_SIZE_ARB, respectively, for the image corresponding to the *level* parameter for the texture object bound at the time that the **glGetCompressedTex-ImageARB** function was called.

Updating Texture Subimages

The **glTexSubImage1D**, **glTexSubImage2D**, and **glTexSubImage3DEXT** functions may be used to update a rectangular subimage of a texture that is internally stored in a compressed format. However, complications arise when modifying a compressed image. For instance, a texture image may need to be decompressed, have part of its image replaced with the new data, and then be recompressed. For lossy compression algorithms, it is not guaranteed that pixels outside the updated rectangle are unmodified after such a procedure. Therefore, the usage of the subimage specification functions is heavily restricted to the point that they are practical only for respecifying the entire texture image. Using the **glTexSubImage1D**, **glTexSubImage2D**, and **glTexSubImage3DEXT** functions for this purpose still has the advantage that memory reallocations may be avoided.

When one of the **glTexSubImage1D**, **glTexSubImage2D**, and **glTexSubImage3DEXT** functions is called to update a compressed texture image, the *xoffset*, *yoffset*, and *zoffset* parameters must be $-b$, where b is the width of the texture's border. Otherwise, the error **GL_INVALID_OPERATION** is generated. This means that any updated subimage of a compressed texture must be aligned to the lower left corner of the whole image. The new image data is compressed using the previously specified internal format for the texture, and any pixels lying outside of the updated rectangle become undefined. Extensions defining specific texture compression formats may relax these restrictions if they are able to edit compressed images in a lossless manner.

Three new functions, **glCompressedTexSubImage1DARB**, **glCompressedTexSubImage2DARB**, and **glCompressedTexSubImage3DARB**, are added by the GL_ARB_texture_compression extension to allow respecification of a compressed texture image using previously compressed data:

```
void glCompressedTexSubImage1DARB(GLenum target,
                                  GLint level,
                                  GLint xoffset,
                                  GLsizei width,
                                  GLenum format,
                                  GLsizei imageSize,
                                  const GLvoid *data);

void glCompressedTexSubImage2DARB(GLenum target,
                                  GLint level,
                                  GLint xoffset,
                                  GLint yoffset,
                                  GLsizei width,
                                  GLsizei height,
                                  GLenum format,
                                  GLsizei imageSize,
                                  const GLvoid *data);

void glCompressedTexSubImage3DARB(GLenum target,
                                  GLint level,
                                  GLint xoffset,
                                  GLint yoffset,
                                  GLint zoffset,
                                  GLsizei width,
                                  GLsizei height,
```

```
GLsizei depth,
GLenum format,
GLsizei imageSize,
const GLvoid *data);
```

These functions carry greater restrictions than the **glTexSubImage1D**, **glTexSubImage2D**, and **glTexSubImage3DEXT** functions. The *xoffset*, *yoffset*, and *zoffset* parameters must be −*b*, where *b* is the width of the texture's border. Furthermore, the *width*, *height*, and *depth* parameters must match the width, height, and depth of the texture being modified. That is, the entire image must be respecified. Conversion between different compressed formats is not supported in general, so the *format* parameter must match the internal format of the texture image being modified. Failing to meet these restrictions results in the generation of the error GL_INVALID_OPERATION. Again, extensions defining specific texture compression formats may relax these restrictions.

A call to **glCompressedTexSubImage1DARB**, **glCompressedTexSubImage2DARB**, or **glCompressedTexSubImage3DARB** is guaranteed to succeed if the following conditions are met:

- The *data* parameter points to a compressed image returned by the **glGetCompressed-TexImageARB** function.

- The *target* and *level* parameters match those passed to the **glGetCompressed-TexImageARB** function when the compressed image was retrieved.

- The *width*, *height*, *depth*, *border*, *format*, and *imageSize* parameters match the values of GL_TEXTURE_WIDTH, GL_TEXTURE_HEIGHT, GL_TEXTURE_DEPTH_EXT, GL_TEXTURE_BORDER, GL_TEXTURE_INTERNAL_FORMAT, and GL_TEXTURE_COMPRESSED_IMAGE_SIZE_ARB, respectively, for the image corresponding to the *level* parameter for the texture object bound at the time that the **glGet-CompressedTexImageARB** function was called.

- The *xoffset*, *yoffset*, and *zoffset* parameters are all −*b*, where *b* is the value of GL_TEXTURE_BORDER for the image corresponding to the *level* parameter for the currently bound texture object.

- The *width*, *height*, *depth*, and *format* parameters match the values of GL_TEXTURE_WIDTH, GL_TEXTURE_HEIGHT, GL_TEXTURE_DEPTH_EXT, and GL_TEXTURE_INTERNAL_FORMAT, respectively, for the image corresponding to the *level* parameter for the currently bound texture object.

NEW FUNCTIONS

- **glCompressedTexImage1DARB**—Specify a one-dimensional compressed texture image.

Prototype

```
void glCompressedTexImage1DARB(GLenum target,
                               GLint level,
                               GLenum internalFormat,
```

```
GLsizei width,
GLint border,
GLsizei imageSize,
const GLvoid *data);
```

Parameters

target	Specifies the target texture. Must be GL_TEXTURE_1D.
level	Specifies the level-of-detail number. Level 0 is the base image level. Level *n* is the *n*th mipmap reduction image.
internalFormat	Specifies the compression format used by the texture image data. This parameter must be an enumerant defined by an extension implementing a specific texture compression format.
width	Specifies the width of the texture image. Must be $2^n + 2(border)$ for some nonnegative integer *n*.
border	Specifies the width of the border. Must be either 0 or 1.
imageSize	Specifies the size of the compressed image data in bytes.
data	Specifies a pointer to the compressed image data in memory.

Description

The **glCompressedTexImage1DARB** function specifies a one-dimensional texture image using previously compressed data. The *target*, *level*, *width*, and *border* parameters have the same meanings as they do for the **glTexImage1D** function.

The *internalFormat* parameter specifies the compression format used by the texture image data pointed to by the *data* parameter. The value of the *internalFormat* parameter may not be one of the six generic compression formats, but instead must be an enumerant corresponding to a specific format defined by another extension.

The *imageSize* parameter specifies the size of the compressed data. This value must be consistent with the correct size of the data corresponding to the compressed image being loaded. The image size for a texture image previously compressed using the **glTexImage1D** function with a compressed internal format can be retrieved by calling the **glGet-TexLevelParameter{if}v** function with *pname* parameter GL_TEXTURE_COMPRESSED_IMAGE_SIZE_ARB.

Special Considerations

The unpacking parameters specified by the **glPixelStore{if}** function are ignored when specifying a compressed texture image.

Get Functions

glGetCompressedTexImageARB with *target* parameter GL_TEXTURE_1D.

Errors

GL_INVALID_ENUM is generated if *internalFormat* is any of the six generic compression formats (e.g., GL_COMPRESSED_RGB_ARB).

GL_INVALID_OPERATION is generated if any of the parameter combinations are not supported by the specific compression format.

GL_INVALID_VALUE is generated if *imageSize* is not consistent with the format, dimensions, and contents of the specified image.

GL_INVALID_ENUM is generated if *target* is not GL_TEXTURE_1D.

GL_INVALID_VALUE is generated if *level* is less than 0.

GL_INVALID_VALUE may be generated if *level* is greater than $\log_2 max$, where *max* is the returned value of GL_MAX_TEXTURE_SIZE.

GL_INVALID_VALUE is generated if *width* is less than 0 or greater than 2 + GL_MAX_TEXTURE_SIZE, or if it cannot be represented as $2^k + 2(border)$ for some nonnegative integer value of k.

GL_INVALID_VALUE is generated if *border* is not 0 or 1.

GL_INVALID_OPERATION is generated if **glCompressedTexImage1DARB** is called between calls to **glBegin** and **glEnd**.

■ **glCompressedTexImage2DARB**—Specify a two-dimensional compressed texture image.

Prototype

```
void glCompressedTexImage2DARB(GLenum target,
                               GLint level,
                               GLenum internalFormat,
                               GLsizei width,
                               GLsizei height,
                               GLint border,
                               GLsizei imageSize,
                               const GLvoid *data);
```

Parameters

target	Specifies the target texture. Accepted values are GL_TEXTURE_2D and the six cube map targets (e.g., GL_TEXTURE_CUBE_MAP_POSITIVE_X_ARB).
level	Specifies the level-of-detail number. Level 0 is the base image level. Level *n* is the *n*th mipmap reduction image.
internalFormat	Specifies the compression format used by the texture image data. This parameter must be an enumerant defined by an extension implementing a specific texture compression format.

width	Specifies the width of the texture image. Must be $2^n + 2(border)$ for some nonnegative integer n.
height	Specifies the height of the texture image. Must be $2^m + 2(border)$ for some nonnegative integer m.
border	Specifies the width of the border. Must be either 0 or 1.
imageSize	Specifies the size of the compressed image data in bytes.
data	Specifies a pointer to the compressed image data in memory.

Description

The **glCompressedTexImage2DARB** function specifies a two-dimensional texture image using previously compressed data. The *target, level, width, height,* and *border* parameters have the same meanings as they do for the **glTexImage2D** function.

The *internalFormat* parameter specifies the compression format used by the texture image data pointed to by the *data* parameter. The value of the *internalFormat* parameter may not be one of the six generic compression formats, but instead must be an enumerant corresponding to a specific format defined by another extension.

The *imageSize* parameter specifies the size of the compressed data. This value must be consistent with the correct size of the data corresponding to the compressed image being loaded. The image size for a texture image previously compressed using the **glTexImage2D** function with a compressed internal format can be retrieved by calling the **glGet-TexLevelParameter{if}v** function with *pname* parameter GL_TEXTURE_COMPRESSED_IMAGE_SIZE_ARB.

Special Considerations

The unpacking parameters specified by the **glPixelStore{if}** function are ignored when specifying a compressed texture image.

Get Functions

glGetCompressedTexImageARB with *target* parameter GL_TEXTURE_2D or any of the six cube map targets (e.g., GL_TEXTURE_CUBE_MAP_POSITIVE_X_ARB).

Errors

GL_INVALID_ENUM is generated if *internalFormat* is any of the six generic compression formats (e.g., GL_COMPRESSED_RGB_ARB).

GL_INVALID_OPERATION is generated if any of the parameter combinations are not supported by the specific compression format.

GL_INVALID_VALUE is generated if *imageSize* is not consistent with the format, dimensions, and contents of the specified image.

GL_INVALID_ENUM is generated if *target* is not an accepted value.

GL_INVALID_VALUE is generated if *level* is less than 0.

GL_INVALID_VALUE may be generated if *level* is greater than $\log_2 max$, where *max* is the returned value of GL_MAX_TEXTURE_SIZE.

GL_INVALID_VALUE is generated if *width* or *height* is less than 0 or greater than 2 + GL_MAX_TEXTURE_SIZE, or if either cannot be represented as $2^k + 2(border)$ for some nonnegative integer value of *k*.

GL_INVALID_VALUE is generated if *border* is not 0 or 1.

GL_INVALID_OPERATION is generated if **glCompressedTexImage2DARB** is called between calls to **glBegin** and **glEnd**.

■ **glCompressedTexImage3DARB**—Specify a three-dimensional compressed texture image.

Prototype

```
void glCompressedTexImage3DARB(GLenum target,
                               GLint level,
                               GLenum internalFormat,
                               GLsizei width,
                               GLsizei height,
                               GLsizei depth,
                               GLint border,
                               GLsizei imageSize,
                               const GLvoid *data);
```

Parameters

target	Specifies the target texture. Must be GL_TEXTURE_3D_EXT.
level	Specifies the level-of-detail number. Level 0 is the base image level. Level *n* is the *n*th mipmap reduction image.
internalFormat	Specifies the compression format used by the texture image data. This parameter must be an enumerant defined by an extension implementing a specific texture compression format.
width	Specifies the width of the texture image. Must be $2^n + 2(border)$ for some nonnegative integer *n*.
height	Specifies the height of the texture image. Must be $2^m + 2(border)$ for some nonnegative integer *m*.
depth	Specifies the depth of the texture image. Must be $2^l + 2(border)$ for some nonnegative integer *l*.
border	Specifies the width of the border. Must be either 0 or 1.
imageSize	Specifies the size of the compressed image data in bytes.
data	Specifies a pointer to the compressed image data in memory.

Description

The **glCompressedTexImage3DARB** function specifies a three-dimensional texture image using previously compressed data. The *target*, *level*, *width*, *height*, *depth*, and *border* parameters have the same meanings as they do for the **glTexImage3DEXT** function.

The *internalFormat* parameter specifies the compression format used by the texture image data pointed to by the *data* parameter. The value of the *internalFormat* parameter may not be one of the six generic compression formats, but instead must be an enumerant corresponding to a specific format defined by another extension.

The *imageSize* parameter specifies the size of the compressed data. This value must be consistent with the correct size of the data corresponding to the compressed image being loaded. The image size for a texture image previously compressed using the **glTexImage3DEXT** function with a compressed internal format can be retrieved by calling the **glGetTexLevelParameter{if}v** function with *pname* parameter GL_TEXTURE_COMPRESSED_IMAGE_SIZE_ARB.

Special Considerations

The unpacking parameters specified by the **glPixelStore{if}** function are ignored when specifying a compressed texture image.

Get Functions

glGetCompressedTexImageARB with *target* parameter GL_TEXTURE_3D_EXT.

Errors

GL_INVALID_ENUM is generated if *internalFormat* is any of the six generic compression formats (e.g., GL_COMPRESSED_RGB_ARB).

GL_INVALID_OPERATION is generated if any of the parameter combinations are not supported by the specific compression format.

GL_INVALID_VALUE is generated if *imageSize* is not consistent with the format, dimensions, and contents of the specified image.

GL_INVALID_ENUM is generated if *target* is not GL_TEXTURE_3D_EXT.

GL_INVALID_VALUE is generated if *level* is less than 0.

GL_INVALID_VALUE may be generated if *level* is greater than $\log_2 max$, where *max* is the returned value of GL_MAX_3D_TEXTURE_SIZE_EXT.

GL_INVALID_VALUE is generated if *width*, *height*, or *depth* is less than 0 or greater than 2 + GL_MAX_3D_TEXTURE_SIZE_EXT, or if any cannot be represented as $2^k + 2(border)$ for some nonnegative integer value of k.

GL_INVALID_VALUE is generated if *border* is not 0 or 1.

GL_INVALID_OPERATION is generated if **glCompressedTexImage3DARB** is called between calls to **glBegin** and **glEnd**.

■ **glCompressedTexSubImage1DARB**—Specify a one-dimensional compressed texture subimage.

Prototype

```
void glCompressedTexSubImage1DARB(GLenum target,
                                  GLint level,
                                  GLint xoffset,
                                  GLsizei width,
                                  GLenum format,
                                  GLsizei imageSize,
                                  const GLvoid *data);
```

Parameters

target	Specifies the target texture. Must be GL_TEXTURE_1D.
level	Specifies the level-of-detail number. Level 0 is the base image level. Level n is the nth mipmap reduction image.
xoffset	Specifies a texel offset in the x-direction within the texture array.
width	Specifies the width of the texture subimage.
format	Specifies the compression format used by the texture image data. This parameter must be an enumerant defined by an extension implementing a specific texture compression format.
imageSize	Specifies the size of the compressed subimage data in bytes.
data	Specifies a pointer to the compressed subimage data in memory.

Description

The **glCompressedTexSubImage1DARB** function specifies a one-dimensional texture subimage using previously compressed data. The *target*, *level*, *xoffset*, and *width* parameters have the same meanings as they do for the **glTexSubImage1D** function.

The *format* parameter specifies the compression format used by the texture image data pointed to by the *data* parameter. The value of the *format* parameter must match the internal format used by the texture image being updated and may not be one of the six generic compression formats.

The *imageSize* parameter specifies the size of the compressed data. This value must be consistent with the correct size of the data corresponding to the compressed image being loaded. The image size for a texture image previously compressed using the **glTexImage1D** function with a compressed internal format can be retrieved by calling the **glGet-TexLevelParameter{if}v** function with *pname* parameter GL_TEXTURE_COMPRESSED_IMAGE_SIZE_ARB.

Restrictions are placed on the region that can be updated using the **glCompressedTex-SubImage1DARB** function. Specifically, the value of the *xoffset* parameter must be $-b$, where *b* is the border width for the texture image being updated, and the value of the *width* parameter must be equal to the width of the texture image being updated.

Special Considerations

The unpacking parameters specified by the **glPixelStore{if}** function are ignored when specifying a compressed texture image.

Get Functions

glGetCompressedTexImageARB with *target* parameter GL_TEXTURE_1D.

Errors

GL_INVALID_ENUM is generated if *format* is any of the six generic compression formats (e.g., GL_COMPRESSED_RGB_ARB).

GL_INVALID_OPERATION is generated if *format* does not match the internal format of the texture image being modified.

GL_INVALID_OPERATION is generated if any of the parameter combinations are not supported by the specific compression format.

GL_INVALID_VALUE is generated if *imageSize* is not consistent with the format, dimensions, and contents of the specified subimage.

GL_INVALID_ENUM is generated if *target* is not GL_TEXTURE_1D.

GL_INVALID_VALUE is generated if *level* is less than 0.

GL_INVALID_VALUE may be generated if *level* is greater than $\log_2 max$, where *max* is the returned value of GL_MAX_TEXTURE_SIZE.

GL_INVALID_VALUE is generated if $xoffset < -b$ or $xoffset + width > w - b$, where *b* is the border width of the texture image being modified, and *w* is the value of GL_TEXTURE_WIDTH (which includes twice the border width).

GL_INVALID_VALUE is generated if *width* is less than 0.

GL_INVALID_OPERATION is generated if **glCompressedTexSubImage1DARB** is called between calls to **glBegin** and **glEnd**.

■ **glCompressedTexSubImage2DARB**—Specify a two-dimensional compressed texture subimage.

Prototype

```
void glCompressedTexSubImage2DARB(GLenum target,
                                  GLint level,
                                  GLint xoffset,
                                  GLint yoffset,
```

```
GLsizei width,
GLsizei height,
GLenum format,
GLsizei imageSize,
const GLvoid *data);
```

Parameters

target   Specifies the target texture. Accepted values are GL_TEXTURE_2D and the six cube map targets (e.g., GL_TEXTURE_CUBE_MAP_POSITIVE_X_ARB).

level   Specifies the level-of-detail number. Level 0 is the base image level. Level *n* is the *n*th mipmap reduction image.

xoffset   Specifies a texel offset in the *x*-direction within the texture array.

yoffset   Specifies a texel offset in the *y*-direction within the texture array.

width   Specifies the width of the texture subimage.

height   Specifies the height of the texture subimage.

format   Specifies the compression format used by the texture image data. This parameter must be an enumerant defined by an extension implementing a specific texture compression format.

imageSize   Specifies the size of the compressed subimage data in bytes.

data   Specifies a pointer to the compressed subimage data in memory.

Description

The **glCompressedTexSubImage2DARB** function specifies a two-dimensional texture subimage using previously compressed data. The *target*, *level*, *xoffset*, *yoffset*, *width*, and *height* parameters have the same meanings as they do for the **glTexSubImage2D** function.

The *format* parameter specifies the compression format used by the texture image data pointed to by the *data* parameter. The value of the *format* parameter must match the internal format used by the texture image being updated and may not be one of the six generic compression formats.

The *imageSize* parameter specifies the size of the compressed data. This value must be consistent with the correct size of the data corresponding to the compressed image being loaded. The image size for a texture image previously compressed using the **glTexImage2D** function with a compressed internal format can be retrieved by calling the **glGetTexLevelParameter{if}v** function with *pname* parameter GL_TEXTURE_ COMPRESSED_IMAGE_SIZE_ARB.

Restrictions are placed on the region that can be updated using the **glCompressedTexSubImage2DARB** function. Specifically, the values of the *xoffset* and *yoffset* parameters must be $-b$, where b is the border width for the texture image being updated, and the values of the *width* and *height* parameters must be equal to the width and height of the texture image being updated.

Special Considerations

The unpacking parameters specified by the **glPixelStore{if}** function are ignored when specifying a compressed texture image.

Get Functions

glGetCompressedTexImageARB with *target* parameter GL_TEXTURE_2D or any of the six cube map targets (e.g., GL_TEXTURE_CUBE_MAP_POSITIVE_X_ARB).

Errors

GL_INVALID_ENUM is generated if *format* is any of the six generic compression formats (e.g., GL_COMPRESSED_RGB_ARB).

GL_INVALID_OPERATION is generated if *format* does not match the internal format of the texture image being modified.

GL_INVALID_OPERATION is generated if any of the parameter combinations are not supported by the specific compression format.

GL_INVALID_VALUE is generated if *imageSize* is not consistent with the format, dimensions, and contents of the specified subimage.

GL_INVALID_ENUM is generated if *target* is not an accepted value.

GL_INVALID_VALUE is generated if *level* is less than 0.

GL_INVALID_VALUE may be generated if *level* is greater than $\log_2 max$, where *max* is the returned value of GL_MAX_TEXTURE_SIZE.

GL_INVALID_VALUE is generated if $xoffset < -b$, $xoffset + width > w - b$, $yoffset < -b$, or $yoffset + heigth > h - b$, where b is the border width of the texture image being modified, and w and h are the values of GL_TEXTURE_WIDTH and GL_TEXTURE_HEGHT (which include twice the border width), respectively.

GL_INVALID_VALUE is generated if *width* or *height* is less than 0.

GL_INVALID_OPERATION is generated if **glCompressedTexSubImage2DARB** is called between calls to **glBegin** and **glEnd**.

■ **glCompressedTexSubImage3DARB**—Specify a three-dimensional compressed texture subimage.

Prototype

```
void glCompressedTexSubImage3DARB(GLenum target,
                                  GLint level,
                                  GLint xoffset,
                                  GLint yoffset,
                                  GLint zoffset,
                                  GLsizei width,
                                  GLsizei height,
```

```
GLsizei depth,
GLenum format,
GLsizei imageSize,
const GLvoid *data);
```

Parameters

target	Specifies the target texture. Must be GL_TEXTURE_3D_EXT.
level	Specifies the level-of-detail number. Level 0 is the base image level. Level n is the nth mipmap reduction image.
xoffset	Specifies a texel offset in the x-direction within the texture array.
yoffset	Specifies a texel offset in the y-direction within the texture array.
zoffset	Specifies a texel offset in the z-direction within the texture array.
width	Specifies the width of the texture subimage.
height	Specifies the height of the texture subimage.
depth	Specifies the depth of the texture subimage.
format	Specifies the compression format used by the texture image data. This parameter must be an enumerant defined by an extension implementing a specific texture compression format.
imageSize	Specifies the size of the compressed subimage data in bytes.
data	Specifies a pointer to the compressed subimage data in memory.

Description

The **glCompressedTexSubImage3DARB** function specifies a three-dimensional texture subimage using previously compressed data. The *target, level, xoffset, yoffset, zoffset, width, height,* and *depth* parameters have the same meanings as they do for the **glTexSubImage3DEXT** function.

The *format* parameter specifies the compression format used by the texture image data pointed to by the *data* parameter. The value of the *format* parameter must match the internal format used by the texture image being updated and may not be one of the six generic compression formats.

The *imageSize* parameter specifies the size of the compressed data. This value must be consistent with the correct size of the data corresponding to the compressed image being loaded. The image size for a texture image previously compressed using the **glTexImage3DEXT** function with a compressed internal format can be retrieved by calling the **glGetTexLevelParameter{if}v** function with *pname* parameter GL_TEXTURE_ COMPRESSED_IMAGE_SIZE_ARB.

Restrictions are placed on the region that can be updated using the **glCompressedTexSubImage3DARB** function. Specifically, the values of the *xoffset, yoffset,* and *zoffset* parameters must be $-b$, where b is the border width for the texture image being updated, and the values of the *width*, *height*, and *depth* parameters must be equal to the width, height, and depth of the texture image being updated.

Special Considerations

The unpacking parameters specified by the **glPixelStore{if}** function are ignored when specifying a compressed texture image.

Get Functions

glGetCompressedTexImageARB with *target* parameter GL_TEXTURE_3D_EXT.

Errors

GL_INVALID_ENUM is generated if *format* is any of the six generic compression formats (e.g., GL_COMPRESSED_RGB_ARB).

GL_INVALID_OPERATION is generated if *format* does not match the internal format of the texture image being modified.

GL_INVALID_OPERATION is generated if any of the parameter combinations are not supported by the specific compression format.

GL_INVALID_VALUE is generated if *imageSize* is not consistent with the format, dimensions, and contents of the specified subimage.

GL_INVALID_ENUM is generated if *target* is not an accepted value.

GL_INVALID_VALUE is generated if *level* is less than 0.

GL_INVALID_VALUE may be generated if *level* is greater than $\log_2 max$, where *max* is the returned value of GL_MAX_3D_TEXTURE_SIZE_EXT.

GL_INVALID_VALUE is generated if $xoffset < -b$, $xoffset + width > w - b$, $yoffset < -b$, $yoffset + heigth > h - b$, or $zoffset + depth > d - b$, where b is the border width of the texture image being modified, and w, h, and d are the values of GL_TEXTURE_WIDTH, GL_TEXTURE_HEGHT, and GL_TEXTURE_DEPTH_EXT (which include twice the border width), respectively.

GL_INVALID_VALUE is generated if *width*, *height*, or *depth* is less than 0.

GL_INVALID_OPERATION is generated if **glCompressedTexSubImage3DARB** is called between calls to **glBegin** and **glEnd**.

■ **glGetCompressedTexImageARB**—Return a compressed texture image.

Prototype

```
void glGetCompressedTexImageARB(GLenum target,
                                GLint level,
                                GLvoid *data);
```

Parameters

target   Specifies which compressed texture is to be obtained. Must be GL_
TEXTURE_1D, GL_TEXTURE_2D, GL_TEXTURE_3D_EXT, or one of the six
cube map targets (e.g., GL_TEXTURE_CUBE_MAP_POSITIVE_X_ARB).

level   Specifies the level-of-detail number of the desired image. Level 0 is the
base image level. Level *n* is the *n*th mipmap reduction image.

data   Specifies a pointer to a region of memory that receives the compressed
image data.

Description

The **glGetCompressedTexImageARB** function is used to retrieve the data corresponding to
a compressed texture image. The *target* and *level* parameters have the same meanings as they
do for the **glGetTexImage** function.

The *data* parameter points to a region of memory that receives the compressed texture
image data. The required size of this memory region can be determined by calling the
glGetTexLevelParameter{if}v with *pname* parameter GL_TEXTURE_COMPRESSED_
IMAGE_SIZE_ARB.

Special Considerations

The packing parameters specified by the **glPixelStore{if}** function are ignored when retrieving a compressed texture image.

Get Functions

glGetTexLevelParameter{if}v with *pname* parameter GL_TEXTURE_COMPRESSED_
IMAGE_SIZE_ARB.

glGetTexLevelParameter{if}v with *pname* parameter GL_TEXTURE_COMPRESSED_ARB.

Errors

GL_INVALID_VALUE is generated if *level* is less than 0 or greater than the maximum allowable value.

GL_INVALID_OPERATION is generated if **glGetCompressedTexImageARB** is called for an
uncompressed texture image.

EXTENDED FUNCTIONS

■ **glTexImage1D, glTexImage2D, glTexImage3DEXT, glCopyTexImage1D,
glCopyTexImage2D**— Extended to allow compressed internal formats.

Prototypes

```
void glTexImage1D(GLenum target, GLint level, GLint internalFormat,
    GLsizei width, GLint border, GLenum format, GLenum type,
    const GLvoid *pixels);
```

```
void glTexImage2D(GLenum target, GLint level, GLint internalFormat,
    GLsizei width, GLsizei height, GLint border, GLenum format,
    GLenum type, const GLvoid *pixels);
void glTexImage3DEXT(GLenum target, GLint level, GLenum internalFormat,
    GLsizei width, GLsizei height, GLsizei depth, GLint border,
    GLenum format, GLenum type, const GLvoid *pixels);
void glCopyTexImage1D(GLenum target, GLint level, GLenum internalFormat,
    GLint x, GLint y, GLsizei width, GLint border);
void glCopyTexImage2D(GLenum target, GLint level, GLenum internalFormat,
    GLint x, GLint y, GLsizei width, GLsizei height, GLint border);
```

Extended Parameters

internalFormat   Specifies the internal format of the texture. May be
                            GL_COMPRESSED_ALPHA_ARB, GL_COMPRESSED_LUMINANCE_ARB,
                            GL_COMPRESSED_LUMINANCE_ALPHA_ARB, GL_COMPRESSED_
                            INTENSITY_ARB, GL_COMPRESSED_RGB_ARB, or GL_COMPRESSED_
                            RGBA_ARB.

Description

The functions that specify texture images are extended to accept the six generic compressed formats for the *internalFormat* parameter. When one of these formats is specified, the implementation attempts to compress the specified image using the most suitable compression algorithm available. If the implementation cannot compress the image, then the corresponding base internal format listed in Table 5.1.1 is used instead, and the image is loaded in uncompressed form.

Whether the texture image was successfully compressed can be determined by calling the **glGetTexLevelParameter{if}v** function with *pname* parameter GL_TEXTURE_COMPRESSED_ARB.

Specifying a proxy texture target as the *target* parameter of one of the **glTexImage1D**, **glTexImage2D**, or **glTexImage3DEXT** functions allows an application to determine whether a texture image would be compressed without actually loading (and possibly compressing) the image.

■ **glGetTexLevelParameteriv**—Extended to allow retrieval of compressed texture parameters.

Prototype

```
void glGetTexLevelParameteriv(GLenum target, GLint level,
    GLenum pname, GLint *params);
```

Extended Parameters

pname   Specifies the symbolic name of the texture parameter to return. May be
                         GL_TEXTURE_COMPRESSED_ARB or GL_TEXTURE_COMPRESSED_IMAGE_
                         SIZE_ARB.

Description

The **glGetTexLevelParameteriv** function is used to retrieve parameters pertaining to a
compressed texture image. The *pname* parameter may be one of the following values:

GL_TEXTURE_COMPRESSED_ARB

                         A Boolean value is returned indicating whether the texture image is com-
                         pressed.

GL_TEXTURE_COMPRESSED_IMAGE_SIZE_ARB

                         The size of the compressed image data is returned. This value can later be
                         passed to the *imageSize* parameter of the **glGetCompressedTex-
                         ImageARB** function. If this parameter is queried for an uncompressed
                         texture image, the error GL_INVALID_OPERATION is generated.

■ **glHint**—Extended to allow specification of a texture compression hint.

Prototype

        void **glHint**(GLenum *target*, GLenum *mode*);

Extended Parameters

target   Specifies a symbolic constant representing the behavior to modify. May
                         be GL_TEXTURE_COMPRESSION_HINT_ARB.

Description

The **glHint** function can be used to inform an implementation that the fastest or highest
quality method for compressing a texture image should be used when a choice exists. Specifying GL_FASTEST as the *mode* parameter causes the implementation to choose the fastest
compression method at a possible loss of quality. Specifying GL_NICEST as the *mode* parameter causes the implementation to choose the highest quality compression method at a
possible performance penalty.

■ **glGetIntegerv**—Extended to allow retrieval of compressed texture state.

Prototype

        void **glGetIntegerv**(GLenum *pname*, GLint **params*);

Extended Parameters

pname   Specifies the parameter to be returned. May be one of the values listed in
                         Description.

Description

Various state values related to compressed textures can be retrieved by calling the **glGet-Integerv** function. The *pname* parameter may be one of the following values:

GL_NUM_COMPRESSED_TEXTURE_FORMATS_ARB

>   The number of compressed texture formats supported by the implementation is returned.

GL_COMPRESSED_TEXTURE_FORMATS_ARB

>   The symbolic constants representing the compressed texture formats supported by the implementation are returned in the array pointed to by the *params* parameter. The number of constants returned is determined by retrieving the value of GL_NUM_COMPRESSED_TEXTURE_FORMATS_ARB.

GL_TEXTURE_COMPRESSION_HINT_ARB

>   The value of the texture compression hint is returned.

5.2   GL_EXT_texture_compression_s3tc

OpenGL version required	OpenGL 1.1
Dependencies	Requires GL_ARB_texture_compression
Promotions	—
Related extensions	GL_NV_texture_compression_vtc

DISCUSSION

The GL_EXT_texture_compression_s3tc extension builds upon the GL_ARB_texture_compression extension by adding S3TC texture compression capabilities. S3TC texture compression is designed to compress every 4 × 4 block of pixels within a two-dimensional image, independently. The amount of space required to encode each 4 × 4 block is either a fixed 8 bytes or 16 bytes, depending on the particular format chosen. For RGBA images occupying 32 bits per pixel, this results in fixed compression ratios of 8:1 or 4:1.

The GL_EXT_texture_compression_s3tc extension defines the four new internal texture compression formats that are listed in Table 5.2.1. The symbolic constants associated with each format may be passed to the *internalFormat* parameter of the **glTexImage2D**, **glCopyTexImage2D**, and **glCompressedTexImage2DARB** functions.

Because images compressed using the S3TC algorithm are easily modified along boundaries that are multiples of four pixels, the restrictions given under the GL_ARB_texture_compression extension for texture subimage specification are relaxed for S3TC texture formats. If the *xoffset*, *yoffset*, *width*, and *height* parameters passed to the **glTexSubImage2D** or **glCompressedTexSubImage2D** functions are all multiples of four, then the texture subimage can be successfully modified, assuming all other requirements are met.

S3TC texture compression supports only two-dimensional textures. If any of the internal formats listed in Table 5.2.1 are specified for one-dimensional or three-dimensional tex-

TABLE 5.2.1   The Four Texture Compression Formats Defined by the `GL_EXT_texture_compression_s3tc` Extension

Compression Format	Description
`GL_COMPRESSED_RGB_S3TC_DXT1_EXT`	Every 4 × 4 block of pixels is encoded using 8 bytes. RGB data is stored as weighted averages of two 16-bit color values. The alpha channel is always 1.0 (completely opaque).
`GL_COMPRESSED_RGBA_S3TC_DXT1_EXT`	Every 4 × 4 block of pixels is encoded using 8 bytes. RGB data is stored as weighted averages of two 16-bit color values. The alpha value for each pixel is either 0.0 (completely transparent) or 1.0 (completely opaque).
`GL_COMPRESSED_RGBA_S3TC_DXT3_EXT`	Every 4 × 4 block of pixels is encoded using 16 bytes. RGB data is stored as weighted averages of two 16-bit color values. The alpha channel is stored using a fixed 4 bits per pixel.
`GL_COMPRESSED_RGBA_S3TC_DXT5_EXT`	Every 4 × 4 block of pixels is encoded using 16 bytes. RGB data is stored as weighted averages of two 16-bit color values. The alpha channel is stored as weighted averages of two 8-bit alpha values.

tures, the error `GL_INVALID_ENUM` is generated. Additionally, S3TC texture compression does not support texture images with borders. If a nonzero border width is specified in conjunction with an S3TC internal format, the error `GL_INVALID_OPERATION` is generated.

EXTENDED FUNCTIONS

■ **glTexImage2D**, **glCopyTexImage2D**, **glCompressedTexImage2DARB**—Extended to support S3TC texture compression.

Prototypes

```
void glTexImage2D(GLenum target, GLint level, GLint internalFormat,
    GLsizei width, GLsizei height, GLint border, GLenum format,
    GLenum type, const GLvoid *pixels);
void glCopyTexImage2D(GLenum target, GLint level, GLenum internalFormat,
    GLint x, GLint y, GLsizei width, GLsizei height, GLint border);
void glCompressedTexImage2DARB(GLenum target, GLint level,
    GLenum internalFormat, GLsizei width, GLsizei height, GLint border,
    GLsizei imageSize, const GLvoid *data);
```

Extended Parameters

internalFormat   Specifies the internal format in which the pixel data is stored. May be GL_COMPRESSED_RGB_S3TC_DXT1_EXT, GL_COMPRESSED_RGBA_S3TC_DXT1_EXT, GL_COMPRESSED_RGBA_S3TC_DXT3_EXT, or GL_COMPRESSED_RGBA_S3TC_DXT5_EXT.

Description

The functions used to specify two-dimensional texture images accept the symbolic constants corresponding to the S3TC texture compression formats as the *internalFormat* parameter. Since S3TC formats do not support textures with borders, the value of the *border* parameter must be zero.

■ **glCompressedTexSubImage2DARB**—Extended to support S3TC texture compression.

Prototype

```
void glCompressedTexSubImage2DARB(GLenum target, GLint level,
    GLint xoffset, GLint yoffset, GLsizei width, GLsizei height,
    GLenum format, GLsizei imageSize, const GLvoid *data);
```

Extended Parameters

format   Specifies the format of the pixel data pointed to by the *data* parameter. May be GL_COMPRESSED_RGB_S3TC_DXT1_EXT, GL_COMPRESSED_RGBA_S3TC_DXT1_EXT, GL_COMPRESSED_RGBA_S3TC_DXT3_EXT, or GL_COMPRESSED_RGBA_S3TC_DXT5_EXT.

Description

The **glCompressedTexSubImage2DARB** function may be called to update a subimage of a texture that has been compressed using the S3TC compression algorithm. The *format* parameter may be one of the symbolic constants corresponding to the S3TC texture compression formats and must match the internal format of the texture image being modified. S3TC texture compression supports subimage modifications to rectangles whose boundaries are all multiples of four pixels. If the values of *xoffset*, *yoffset*, *width*, and *height* are multiples of four, and all other requirements are met, then the corresponding texture subimage is successfully updated without affecting the remainder of the image.

5.3   GL_NV_texture_compression_vtc

OpenGL version required	OpenGL 1.1
Dependencies	Requires GL_EXT_texture_compression_s3tc
Promotions	—
Related extensions	—

Discussion

The GL_NV_texture_compression_vtc extension adds support for S3TC texture compression to three-dimensional textures. When applied to three-dimensional texture images, the S3TC compression algorithm operates on $4 \times 4 \times 4$ blocks of pixels within which the two-dimensional S3TC algorithm is applied to each $4 \times 4 \times 1$ two-dimensional subblock. The results are the same compression ratios obtained by using S3TC texture compression for two-dimension textures. When the GL_NV_texture_compression_vtc extension is available, the symbolic constants listed in Table 5.2.1 may be passed to the *internalFormat* parameter of the **glTexImage3DEXT** and **glCompressedTexImage3DARB** functions.

Because images compressed using the S3TC algorithm are easily modified along boundaries that are multiples of four pixels, the restrictions given under the GL_ARB_texture_compression extension for texture subimage specification are relaxed for S3TC texture formats. If the *xoffset*, *yoffset*, *zoffset*, *width*, *height*, and *depth* parameters passed to the **glTexSubImage3D** or **glCompressedTexSubImage3D** functions are all multiples of four, then the texture subimage can be successfully modified, assuming all other requirements are met.

S3TC texture compression does not support one-dimensional textures. If any of the internal formats listed in Table 5.2.1 are specified for one-dimensional textures, the error GL_INVALID_ENUM is generated. Additionally, S3TC texture compression does not support texture images with borders. If a nonzero border width is specified in conjunction with an S3TC internal format, the error GL_INVALID_OPERATION is generated.

Extended Functions

■ **glTexImage3DEXT**, **glCompressedTexImage3DARB**—Extended to support VTC texture compression.

Prototypes

```
void glTexImage3DEXT(GLenum target, GLint level, GLenum internalFormat,
    GLsizei width, GLsizei height, GLsizei depth, GLint border,
    GLenum format, GLenum type, const GLvoid *pixels);
void glCompressedTexImage3DARB(GLenum target, GLint level,
    GLenum internalFormat,GLsizei width,GLsizei height, GLsizei depth,
    GLint border, GLsizei imageSize, const GLvoid *data);
```

Extended Parameters

internalFormat Specifies the internal format in which the pixel data is stored. May be GL_COMPRESSED_RGB_S3TC_DXT1_EXT, GL_COMPRESSED_RGBA_S3TC_DXT1_EXT, GL_COMPRESSED_RGBA_S3TC_DXT3_EXT, or GL_COMPRESSED_RGBA_S3TC_DXT5_EXT.

Description

The functions used to specify three-dimensional texture images accept the symbolic constants corresponding to the S3TC texture compression formats as the *internalFormat* parameter. Since S3TC formats do not support textures with borders, the value of the *border* parameter must be zero.

■ **glCompressedTexSubImage3DARB**—Extended to support VTC texture compression.

Prototype

```
void glCompressedTexSubImage3DARB(GLenum target, GLint level,
    GLint xoffset, GLint yoffset, GLint zoffset, GLsizei width,
    GLsizei height, GLsizei depth, GLenum format, GLsizei imageSize,
    const GLvoid *data);
```

Extended Parameters

format   Specifies the format of the pixel data pointed to by the *data* parameter. May be GL_COMPRESSED_RGB_S3TC_DXT1_EXT, GL_COMPRESSED_RGBA_S3TC_DXT1_EXT, GL_COMPRESSED_RGBA_S3TC_DXT3_EXT, or GL_COMPRESSED_RGBA_S3TC_DXT5_EXT.

Description

The **glCompressedTexSubImage3DARB** function may be called to update a subimage of a texture that has been compressed using the S3TC compression algorithm. The *format* parameter may be one of the symbolic constants corresponding to the S3TC texture compression formats and must match the internal format of the texture image being modified. S3TC texture compression supports subimage modifications to rectangles whose boundaries are all multiples of four pixels. If the values of *xoffset, yoffset, zoffset, width, height,* and *depth* are multiples of four, and all other requirements are met, then the corresponding texture subimage is successfully updated without affecting the remainder of the image.

CHAPTER **6**

FRAGMENT SHADING

IN THIS CHAPTER

6.1   GL_NV_register_combiners

OpenGL version required	OpenGL 1.1
Dependencies	Requires `GL_ARB_multitexture`
Promotions	—
Related extensions	`GL_NV_register_combiners2`

DISCUSSION

The `GL_NV_register_combiners` extension provides a powerful fragment coloring environment that replaces the conventional texture environment application, the color sum operation, and the fog-blending operation. In the register combiners setting, one or more general combiner stages are executed, and then a special final combiner stage determines the fragment color. A set of registers that includes the primary and secondary color, the texture color corresponding to each texture unit, the fog color, and two constant colors is used as the inputs and outputs for each stage. Inputs can be modified using one of several remapping modes, and outputs can be scaled and biased. All computations are carried out in the [−1,1] range.

Register Combiner Operation

Register combiners are enabled and disabled by calling the **glEnable** and **glDisable** functions with *cap* parameter GL_REGISTER_COMBINERS_NV. When register combiners are enabled, the texture environment operations, the color sum operation, and the fog-blending operation are ignored. All state pertaining to these operations is independently maintained, however, and is not affected by register combiner settings. Register combiners operate by executing one or more general combiner stages followed by a final combiner stage. The number of general combiner stages executed is specified by calling the **glCombinerParameteriNV** function,

```
void glCombinerParameteriNV(GLenum pname,
                            GLint param);
```

with *pname* parameter GL_NUM_GENERAL_COMBINERS_NV. At least one general combiner stage must always be executed, and the maximum number of general combiner stages available can be queried by calling the **glGetIntegerv** function with *pname* parameter GL_MAX_GENERAL_COMBINERS_NV.

Each general combiner stage performs calculations independently for RGB and alpha color components, and generates three outputs for each portion. The final combiner stage performs a single calculation for the RGB portion and simply copies an existing alpha value to the final fragment color. The register set available as inputs and outputs to each stage is summarized in Table 6.1.1. Each register consists of four components representing the red, green, blue, and alpha color components.

TABLE 6.1.1   Registers available as inputs and outputs for each general combiner stage, and as inputs to the final combiner stage. Registers that are read-only may not be used as outputs in the general combiner stages.

Register	Type	Description
GL_ZERO	Read-only	The constant color (0,0,0,0). This register may not be used as an output.
GL_CONSTANT_COLOR0_NV	Read-only	A user-defined constant color. This register may not be used as an output.
GL_CONSTANT_COLOR1_NV	Read-only	A user-defined constant color. This register may not be used as an output.
GL_PRIMARY_COLOR_NV	Read/Write	The interpolated primary color.
GL_SECONDARY_COLOR_NV	Read/Write	The interpolated secondary color. The alpha component is initially undefined.
GL_TEXTURE*i*_ARB	Read/Write	The texture color corresponding to texture unit *i*, where *i* is in the range 0 to GL_MAX_TEXTURE_UNITS_ARB $-$ 1. If no texture color is fetched for texture unit *i*, then the initial contents of this register is undefined.

TABLE 6.1.1   *Continued*

Register	Type	Description
GL_FOG	Read-only	The RGB components contain the fog color, and the alpha component contains the fragment's fog factor. The alpha component may be used as an input only in the final combiner stage. This register may not be used as an output.
GL_SPARE0_NV	Read/Write	A general purpose read/write register. In the first general combiner stage, the alpha component is set equal to the alpha component of the GL_TEXTURE0_ARB register. The RGB portion of this register is initially undefined.
GL_SPARE1_NV	Read/Write	A general purpose read/write register. The contents of this register are initially undefined.

The user-defined constant colors GL_CONSTANT_COLOR0_NV and GL_CONSTANT_ COLOR1_NV are specified by calling the **glCombinerParameter{if}vNV** function,

```
void glCombinerParameterivNV(GLenum pname,
                             const GLint *params);

void glCombinerParameterfvNV(GLenum pname,
                             const GLfloat *params);
```

The *pname* parameter specifies which constant color to set, and must be GL_CONSTANT_COLOR0_NV or GL_CONSTANT_COLOR1_NV. The *params* parameter points to an array containing the red, green, blue, and alpha components of the new constant color value. The current value of a constant color is retrieved by calling the **glGetFloatv** function. The GL_NV_register_combiners extension supports only two constant colors for the entire register combiner environment, but the GL_NV_register_combiners2 extension provides an additional pair of constant colors for each general combiner stage.

General Combiner Stages

The RGB and alpha portions of each general combiner stage both accept four inputs—labeled variables *A*, *B*, *C*, and *D*—and both generate three results. The registers assigned to the input variables are specified by calling the **glCombinerInputNV** function,

```
void glCombinerInputNV(GLenum stage,
                       GLenum portion,
                       GLenum variable,
                       GLenum input,
                       GLenum mapping,
                       GLenum componentUsage);
```

The *stage* parameter accepts symbolic constant GL_COMBINER*i*_NV, where *i* indicates the index of the general combiner stage. The *portion* parameter may be GL_RGB or GL_ALPHA and specifies whether the variable input is being set for the RGB or alpha portion of the general combiner stage. The *variable* parameter indicates which variable is being set and may be GL_VARIABLE_A_NV, GL_VARIABLE_B_NV, GL_VARIABLE_C_NV, or GL_VARIABLE_D_NV. The *input* parameter names the register that is assigned to the variable and may be any of the registers listed in Table 6.1.1.

The *mapping* parameter specifies how the color components in the input register should be transformed before being assigned to the input variable. Table 6.1.2 lists the available mapping modes. Using various input mapping modes with the input register GL_ZERO can generate additional constant values. For example, applying the GL_UNSIGNED_INVERT_NV mapping mode to the GL_ZERO register produces a value of 1.0, and applying the GL_HALF_BIAS_NEGATE_NV mapping mode produces a value of 0.5.

TABLE 6.1.2   Input mapping modes. Each mapping transforms an input *x* into the value *x'* using the given formula.

Input mapping	Definition
GL_UNSIGNED_IDENTITY_NV	$x' = \max(0, x)$
GL_UNSIGNED_INVERT_NV	$x' = 1 - \min(\max(0, x), 1)$
GL_EXPAND_NORMAL_NV	$x' = 2\max(0, x) - 1$
GL_EXPAND_NEGATE_NV	$x' = -2\max(0, x) + 1$
GL_HALF_BIAS_NORMAL_NV	$x' = \max(0, x) - \frac{1}{2}$
GL_HALF_BIAS_NEGATE_NV	$x' = -\max(0, x) + \frac{1}{2}$
GL_SIGNED_IDENTITY_NV	$x' = x$
GL_SIGNED_NEGATE_NV	$x' = -x$

Finally, the *componentUsage* parameter indicates which color channels should be read from the input register. If the *portion* parameter is GL_RGB, then the *componentUsage* parameter may be GL_RGB or GL_ALPHA. In the case that *componentUsage* is GL_RGB, the red, green, and blue components of the input register are remapped and directly assigned to the red, green, and blue components of the combiner variable. If *componentUsage* is GL_ALPHA, then the alpha component of the input register is remapped and replicated to all three components of the combiner variable. If the *portion* parameter is GL_ALPHA, then the *componentUsage* parameter may be GL_ALPHA or GL_BLUE. These values indicate whether the alpha component or the blue component of the input register is remapped and assigned to the combiner variable.

Note that the alpha component of the GL_FOG register cannot be read by the RGB portion or alpha portion of the general combiner stages. The alpha component of the GL_FOG register contains the fragment's fog factor and is available only in the final combiner stage.

As illustrated in Figure 6.1.1, the RGB portion of each general combiner stage performs three calculations using the variables A, B, C, and D. The first calculation produces either the componentwise product AB or the dot product $A{\cdot}B$, and the second calculation produces either the componentwise product CD or the dot product $C{\cdot}D$. If both of the first two calculations do not select the dot product, then a third calculation produces either the sum $AB + CD$ or performs a special 'mux' operation given by

$$AB\,\mathrm{mux}\,CD = \begin{cases} AB, & \text{if spare0.alpha} < 0.5; \\ CD, & \text{if spare0.alpha} \geq 0.5. \end{cases} \tag{6.1.1}$$

The mux operation produces the product AB if the value in the alpha component of the GL_SPARE0_NV register is less than 0.5 and produces the product CD otherwise.

The alpha portion of each general combiner stage also performs the same three calculations that are performed by the RGB portion, except that no dot products can be produced. As illustrated in Figure 6.1.2, the alpha portion always produces the scalar products AB and CD. A third calculation also always produces either the sum $AB + CD$ or performs the mux operation given by Equation (6.1.1).

The output registers to which the three results produced by the RGB and alpha portions of each general combiner stage are assigned are specified by calling the **glCombiner-OutputNV** function,

```
void glCombinerOutputNV(GLenum stage,
                        GLenum portion,
                        GLenum abOutput,
                        GLenum cdOutput,
                        GLenum sumOutput,
                        GLenum scale,
                        GLenum bias,
                        GLboolean abDotProduct,
                        GLboolean cdDotProduct,
                        GLboolean muxSum);
```

The *stage* parameter accepts symbolic constant GL_COMBINER*i*_NV, where i indicates the index of the general combiner stage. The *portion* parameter may be GL_RGB or GL_ALPHA and specifies whether the output registers are being set for the RGB or alpha portion of the general combiner stage.

The *abOutput* parameter specifies the output register that receives the product AB or the dot product $A{\cdot}B$, the *cdOutput* parameter specifies the output register that receives the product CD or the dot product $C{\cdot}D$, and the *sumOutput* parameter specifies the output register that receives the sum $AB + CD$ or the result of the mux operation. The three output parameters must name unique registers, or the error GL_INVALID_OPERATION is generated.

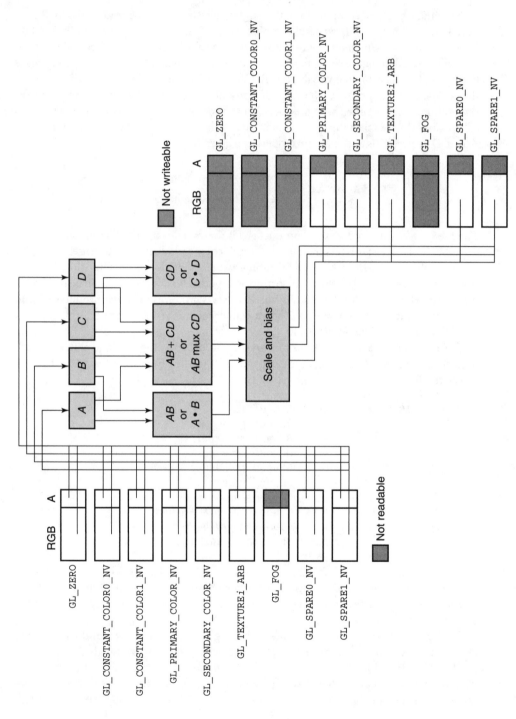

FIGURE 6.1.1 Operation of the RGB portion of each general combiner stage.

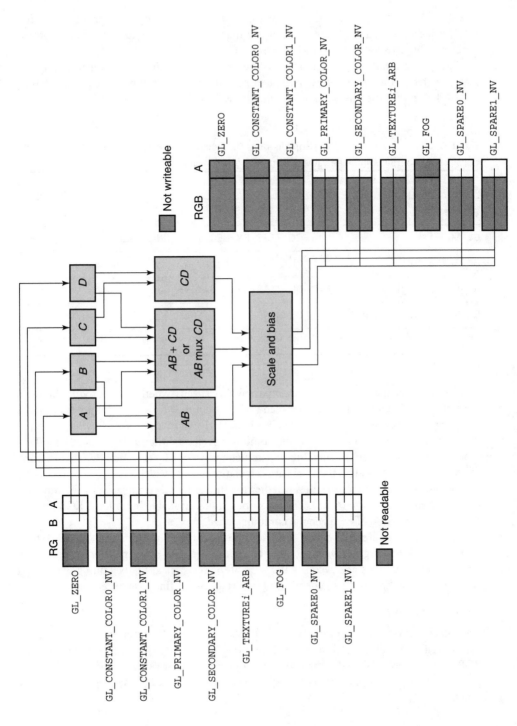

FIGURE 6.1.2   Operation of the alpha portion of each general combiner stage.

The special constant GL_DISCARD_NV may also be specified as any of the three output registers; it indicates that the corresponding calculation is unwanted and should be ignored. Specifying GL_DISCARD_NV for multiple outputs is allowed.

The *scale* and *bias* parameters specify how the outputs should be transformed before being written to the output registers. The same scale and bias is applied to all three output values. Table 6.1.3 lists the possible combinations of scale and bias values.

TABLE 6.1.3   Legal scale and bias combinations for general combiner stage outputs. Each pair transforms an output x into the value x' using the given formula.

Scale	Bias	Operation
GL_NONE	GL_NONE	$x' = x$
GL_NONE	GL_BIAS_BY_NEGATIVE_ONE_HALF_NV	$x' = x - \frac{1}{2}$
GL_SCALE_BY_TWO_NV	GL_NONE	$x' = 2x$
GL_SCALE_BY_TWO_NV	GL_BIAS_BY_NEGATIVE_ONE_HALF_NV	$x' = 2x - \frac{1}{2}$
GL_SCALE_BY_FOUR_NV	GL_NONE	$x' = 4x$
GL_SCALE_BY_ONE_HALF_NV	GL_NONE	$x' = \frac{1}{2}x$

The *abDotProduct* and *cdDotProduct* parameters specify whether the product between variables A and B and the product between variables C and D should be dot products. If the *portion* parameter is GL_ALPHA, then both *abDotProduct* and *cdDotProduct* must be GL_FALSE. For the RGB portion of the combiner stage, if either *abDotProduct* or *cdDotProduct* is GL_TRUE, then the *sumOutput* parameter must be GL_DISCARD_NV. That is, if any dot products are calculated, then the sum calculation is not available.

The *muxSum* parameter specifies whether the sum $AB + CD$ is replaced by the mux operation given by Equation (6.1.1). The mux operation is available in both the RGB portion and the alpha portion of each general combiner stage.

Output registers are not written until all input registers have been read, so it is safe to output a result to a register that is used as an input. The state of the registers at the end of one general combiner stage becomes the state of the registers at the beginning of the next stage, which is either another general combiner stage or the final combiner stage.

Final Combiner Stage

After all enabled general combiner stages have been executed, the final combiner stage generates the RGBA color that is assigned to the fragment. The final combiner stage has six RGB input variables labeled A through F and one alpha input variable labeled G. The registers assigned to the input variables are specified by calling the **glFinalCombinerInputNV** function,

```
void glFinalCombinerInputNV(GLenum variable,
                            GLenum input,
                            GLenum mapping,
                            GLenum componentUsage);
```

The *variable* parameter indicates which variable is being set and may be GL_VARIABLE_*k*_NV, where *k* ranges from A to G. The *input* parameter names the register that is assigned to the variable and may be any of the registers listed in Table 6.1.1. For variables *A*, *B*, *C*, and *D*, the special input GL_E_TIMES_F_NV is accepted and indicates that the product of the variables *E* and *F* should be assigned to the input variable. For variables *B*, *C*, and *D*, the special input GL_SPARE0_PLUS_SECONDARY_COLOR_NV is accepted, and indicates that the sum of the unmodified RGB components of the GL_SPARE0_NV and GL_SECONDARY_COLOR_NV registers should be assigned to the input variable. This sum may optionally be clamped to the range [0,1] before it is remapped and assigned to the input variable. The clamping mechanism is controlled by calling the **glCombinerParameteriNV** function with *pname* parameter GL_COLOR_SUM_CLAMP_NV.

The *mapping* parameter specifies how the color components in the input register should be transformed before being assigned to the input variable. In the final combiner stage, only the mapping modes GL_UNSIGNED_IDENTITY_NV and GL_UNSIGNED_INVERT_NV may be specified.

The *componentUsage* parameter indicates which color channels should be read from the input register. For variables *A* through *F*, the value of *componentUsage* may be GL_RGB or GL_ALPHA, and these have the same meanings as they do in the general combiner stages. If the *input* parameter specifies either of the special inputs GL_E_TIMES_F_NV or GL_SPARE0_PLUS_SECONDARY_COLOR_NV, then the *componentUsage* parameter must be GL_RGB. For variable *G*, the value of *componentUsage* may be GL_ALPHA or GL_BLUE.

As illustrated in Figure 6.1.3, the final combiner stage performs a single calculation that produces the RGB portion of the fragment color. The red, green, and blue components of the fragment color are assigned the quantity $AB + (1 - A)C + D$, and the alpha component of the fragment color is assigned the value of the *G* variable. All components are clamped to the range [0,1].

The initial state of the register combiner stages mimics the conventional OpenGL color-sum and fog-blending operations, but ignores all textures. Initially, one general combiner stage is enabled, and the initial values of its input variables are listed in Table 6.1.4. The *AB* and *CD* products are discarded, and the *AB* + *CD* sum is written to the register GL_SPARE0_NV. Table 6.1.5 lists the initial values for the input variables to the final combiner stage.

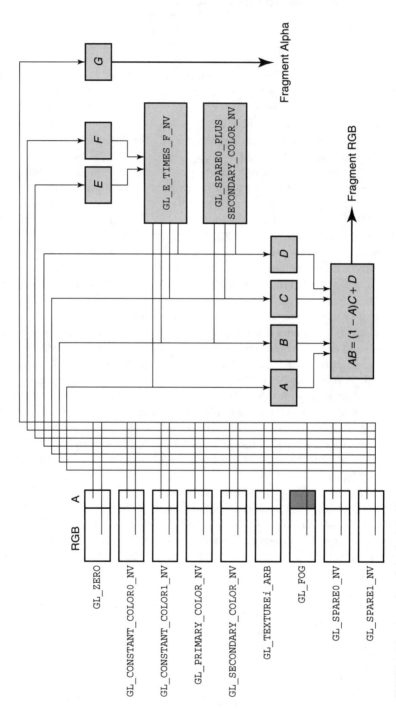

FIGURE 6.1.3 Operation of the final combiner stage.

TABLE 6.1.4   Initial Input Values for General Combiner Stage 0

Portion	Variable	Input	Mapping	Component Usage
GL_RGB	GL_VARIABLE_A_NV	GL_PRIMARY_COLOR_NV	GL_UNSIGNED_IDENTITY_NV	GL_RGB
GL_RGB	GL_VARIABLE_B_NV	GL_ZERO	GL_UNSIGNED_INVERT_NV	GL_RGB
GL_RGB	GL_VARIABLE_C_NV	GL_ZERO	GL_UNSIGNED_IDENTITY_NV	GL_RGB
GL_RGB	GL_VARIABLE_D_NV	GL_ZERO	GL_UNSIGNED_IDENTITY_NV	GL_RGB
GL_ALPHA	GL_VARIABLE_A_NV	GL_PRIMARY_COLOR_NV	GL_UNSIGNED_IDENTITY_NV	GL_ALPHA
GL_ALPHA	GL_VARIABLE_B_NV	GL_ZERO	GL_UNSIGNED_INVERT_NV	GL_ALPHA
GL_ALPHA	GL_VARIABLE_C_NV	GL_ZERO	GL_UNSIGNED_IDENTITY_NV	GL_ALPHA
GL_ALPHA	GL_VARIABLE_D_NV	GL_ZERO	GL_UNSIGNED_IDENTITY_NV	GL_ALPHA

TABLE 6.1.5   Initial Input Values for the Final Combiner Stage

Variable	Input	Mapping	Component Usage
GL_VARIABLE_A_NV	GL_FOG	GL_UNSIGNED_IDENTITY_NV	GL_ALPHA
GL_VARIABLE_B_NV	GL_SPAREO_PLUS_SECONDARY_COLOR_NV	GL_UNSIGNED_IDENTITY_NV	GL_RGB
GL_VARIABLE_C_NV	GL_FOG	GL_UNSIGNED_IDENTITY_NV	GL_RGB
GL_VARIABLE_D_NV	GL_ZERO	GL_UNSIGNED_IDENTITY_NV	GL_RGB
GL_VARIABLE_E_NV	GL_ZERO	GL_UNSIGNED_IDENTITY_NV	GL_RGB
GL_VARIABLE_F_NV	GL_ZERO	GL_UNSIGNED_IDENTITY_NV	GL_RGB
GL_VARIABLE_G_NV	GL_SPAREO_NV	GL_UNSIGNED_IDENTITY_NV	GL_ALPHA

NEW FUNCTIONS

■ **glCombinerParameter{if}[v]NV**—Specify a combiner parameter.

Prototypes

```
void glCombinerParameteriNV(GLenum pname, GLint param);
void glCombinerParameterfNV(GLenum pname, GLfloat param);
```

Parameters

pname   Specifies the symbolic name of a single-valued combiner parameter. The *pname* parameter can be GL_NUM_GENERAL_COMBINERS_NV or GL_COLOR_SUM_CLAMP_NV.

param   Specifies the value of the combiner parameter corresponding to the *pname* parameter.

Prototypes

```
void glCombinerParameterivNV(GLenum pname, const GLint *params);
void glCombinerParameterfvNV(GLenum pname, const GLfloat *params);
```

Parameters

pname   Specifies the symbolic name of a combiner parameter. The *pname* parameter can be one of the following: GL_NUM_GENERAL_COMBINERS_NV, GL_COLOR_SUM_CLAMP_NV, GL_CONSTANT_COLOR0_NV, or GL_CON-STANT_COLOR1_NV.

params   Specifies a pointer to an array where the value or values of a combiner parameter corresponding to the *pname* parameter are stored.

Description

The **glCombinerParameter{if}[v]NV** function is used to specify register combiner parameters. The *pname* parameter indicates what parameter to set and may be one of the following values.

GL_NUM_GENERAL_COMBINERS_NV

The *param* parameter specifies the number of general combiner stages that should be executed. This value must be at least 1 and no greater than GL_MAX_GENERAL_COMBINERS_NV. The initial value is 1.

GL_COLOR_SUM_CLAMP_NV

The *param* parameter specifies a Boolean value indicating whether the GL_SPARE0_PLUS_SECONDARY_COLOR_NV input to the final combiner is clamped to the range [0,1]. The initial value is GL_TRUE.

GL_CONSTANT_COLOR0_NV

The *params* parameter points to an array containing the red, green, blue, and alpha components of constant color 0. The initial value is (0,0,0,0).

GL_CONSTANT_COLOR1_NV

The *params* parameter points to an array containing the red, green, blue, and alpha components of constant color 1. The initial value is (0,0,0,0).

Get Functions

glGetIntegerv with *pname* parameter GL_NUM_GENERAL_COMBINERS_NV

glGetBooleanv with *pname* parameter GL_COLOR_SUM_CLAMP_NV

glGetFloatv with *pname* parameter GL_CONSTANT_COLOR0_NV

glGetFloatv with *pname* parameter GL_CONSTANT_COLOR1_NV

Errors

GL_INVALID_VALUE is generated if *pname* is GL_NUM_GENERAL_COMBINERS_NV and *param* is less than 1 or greater than GL_MAX_GENERAL_COMBINERS_NV.

■ **glCombinerInputNV**—Specify a general combiner input.

Prototype

```
void glCombinerInputNV(GLenum stage,
                       GLenum portion,
                       GLenum variable,
                       GLenum input,
                       GLenum mapping,
                       GLenum componentUsage);
```

Parameters

stage   Specifies which general combiner stage to affect. Must be GL_
                   COMBINERi_NV, where i is in the range 0 to GL_MAX_GENERAL_
                   COMBINERS_NV $- 1$.

portion   Specifies whether the color portion or alpha portion of the general
                   combiner stage is affected. Must be GL_RGB or GL_ALPHA.

variable   Specifies which general combiner variable to affect. Must be
                   GL_VARIABLE_A_NV, GL_VARIABLE_B_NV, GL_VARIABLE_C_NV, or
                   GL_VARIABLE_D_NV.

input   Specifies the input register for the general combiner stage, portion,
                   and variable given by the *stage*, *portion*, and *variable* parameters, re-
                   spectively. The *input* parameter can be one of the following: GL_ZERO,
                   GL_CONSTANT_COLOR0_NV, GL_CONSTANT_COLOR1_NV, GL_PRIMARY_
                   COLOR_NV, GL_SECONDARY_COLOR_NV, GL_SPARE0_NV, GL_SPARE1_
                   NV, or GL_TEXTUREi_NV, where i is in the range 0 to GL_MAX_
                   TEXTURE_UNITS_ARB $- 1$.

                   If the value of the *portion* parameter is GL_RGB, then the *input* para-
                   meter can also be GL_FOG.

mapping   Specifies the mapping that is applied to the input given by the *input*
                   parameter. The *mapping* parameter can be one of the following:
                   GL_UNSIGNED_IDENTITY_NV,   GL_UNSIGNED_INVERT_NV,   GL_
                   EXPAND_NORMAL_NV,   GL_EXPAND_NEGATE_NV,   GL_HALF_BIAS_
                   NORMAL_NV, GL_HALF_BIAS_NEGATE_NV, GL_SIGNED_IDENTITY_NV,
                   or GL_SIGNED_NEGATE_NV.

componentUsage   Specifies which components of the input register are used in the gen-
                   eral combiner stage.

If the value of the *portion* parameter is GL_RGB, then the *component-Usage* parameter can be GL_RGB or GL_ALPHA.

If the value of the *portion* parameter is GL_ALPHA, then the *component-Usage* parameter can be GL_ALPHA or GL_BLUE.

Description

The **glCombinerInputNV** function is used to set an input register for the general combiner stage specified by the *stage* parameter. The *portion* parameter indicates whether the input register is being set for the RGB or alpha portion of the general combiner stage, and the *variable* parameter indicates whether the input is being set for the *A*, *B*, *C*, or *D* input variable. The input register assigned to the indicated variable is specified by the *input* parameter, and this input undergoes the mapping specified by the *mapping* parameter. The components of the input register used as the general combiner stage variable are specified by the *componentUsage* parameter.

Get Functions

glGetCombinerInputParameter{if}vNV

Errors

GL_INVALID_OPERATION is generated if *portion* is GL_RGB and *componentUsage* is GL_BLUE.

GL_INVALID_OPERATION is generated if *portion* is GL_ALPHA and *componentUsage* is GL_RGB.

GL_INVALID_OPERATION is generated if *portion* is GL_ALPHA and *input* is GL_FOG.

■ **glCombinerOutputNV**—Specify general combiner outputs.

Prototype

```
void glCombinerOutputNV(GLenum stage,
                        GLenum portion,
                        GLenum abOutput,
                        GLenum cdOutput,
                        GLenum sumOutput,
                        GLenum scale,
                        GLenum bias,
                        GLboolean abDotProduct,
                        GLboolean cdDotProduct,
                        GLboolean muxSum);
```

Parameters

stage   Specifies which general combiner stage to affect. Must be GL_COMBINER*i*_NV, where *i* is in the range 0 to GL_MAX_GENERAL_COMBINERS_NV − 1.

portion   Specifies whether the color portion or alpha portion of the general combiner stage is affected. Must be GL_RGB or GL_ALPHA.

abOutput   Specifies the output register for the *AB* product of the general combiner stage and portions given by the *stage* and *portion* parameters. The *abOutput* parameter can be one of the following: GL_DISCARD_NV, GL_PRIMARY_COLOR_NV, GL_SECONDARY_COLOR_NV, GL_SPARE0_NV, GL_SPARE1_NV, or GL_TEXTURE*i*_NV, where *i* is in the range 0 to GL_MAX_TEXTURE_UNITS_ARB − 1. The initial value is GL_DISCARD_NV.

cdOutput   Specifies the output register for the *CD* product of the general combiner stage and portions given by the *stage* and *portion* parameters. The *cdOutput* parameter can be one of the following: GL_DISCARD_NV, GL_PRIMARY_COLOR_NV, GL_SECONDARY_COLOR_NV, GL_SPARE0_NV, GL_SPARE1_NV, or GL_TEXTURE*i*_NV, where *i* is in the range 0 to GL_MAX_TEXTURE_UNITS_ARB − 1. The initial value is GL_DISCARD_NV.

sumOutput   Specifies the output register for the *AB* + *CD* sum of the general combiner stage and portions given by the *stage* and *portion* parameters. The *cdOutput* parameter can be one of the following: GL_DISCARD_NV, GL_PRIMARY_COLOR_NV, GL_SECONDARY_COLOR_NV, GL_SPARE0_NV, GL_SPARE1_NV, or GL_TEXTURE*i*_NV, where *i* is in the range 0 to GL_MAX_TEXTURE_UNITS_ARB − 1. The initial value is GL_SPARE0_NV.

                 If either the *abDotProduct* or *cdDotProduct* parameter is GL_TRUE, then the *sumOutput* parameter must be GL_DISCARD_NV.

scale   Specifies the scale factor for the general combiner stage and portions given by the *stage* and *portion* parameters. The *scale* parameter can be one of the following: GL_NONE, GL_SCALE_BY_TWO_NV, GL_SCALE_BY_FOUR_NV, or GL_SCALE_BY_ONE_HALF_NV. The initial value is GL_NONE.

bias   Specifies the bias for the general combiner stage and portions given by the *stage* and *portion* parameters. The *bias* parameter can be GL_NONE or GL_BIAS_BY_NEGATIVE_ONE_HALF_NV. The initial value is GL_NONE.

                 If the *scale* parameter is GL_SCALE_BY_ONE_HALF_NV or GL_SCALE_BY_FOUR_NV, then the *bias* parameter must be GL_NONE.

abDotProduct   Specifies a Boolean value indicating whether the general combiner stage's *AB* product should be a dot product. The initial value is GL_FALSE.

                 If the *portion* parameter is GL_ALPHA, then the *abDotProduct* parameter must be GL_FALSE.

cdDotProduct   Specifies a Boolean value indicating whether the general combiner stage's *CD* product should be a dot product. The initial value is GL_FALSE.

                 If the *portion* parameter is GL_ALPHA, then the *cdDotProduct* parameter must be GL_FALSE.

muxSum	Specifies a Boolean value indicating whether the general combiner stage's $AB + CD$ sum should perform the mux operation. The initial value is GL_FALSE.

Description

The **glCombinerOutputNV** function is used to set the output registers for the general combiner stage specified by the *stage* parameter. The *portion* parameter indicates whether the output registers are being set for the RGB or alpha portion of the general combiner stage. The *abOutput* and *cdOutput* parameters specify which registers should receive the products *AB* and *CD*, and the *sumOutput* parameter specifies which register should receive the sum $AB + CD$. If either of the products *AB* or *CD* is a dot product, as indicated by the *abDotProduct* and *cdDotProduct* parameters, then the *sumOutput* parameter must be GL_DISCARD_NV. The *muxSum* parameter indicates whether the sum $AB + CD$ should be replaced by the mux operation given by Equation (6.1.1). All three outputs are scaled and biased by the values specified by the *scale* and *bias* parameters. Any of the output registers specified by the *abOutput*, *cdOutput*, and *sumOutput* parameters may be GL_DISCARD_NV, in which case the corresponding calculation is ignored.

Get Functions

glGetCombinerOutputParameter{if}vNV

Errors

GL_INVALID_VALUE is generated if *portion* is GL_ALPHA and *abDotProduct* is not GL_FALSE, or *cdDotProduct* is not GL_FALSE.

GL_INVALID_OPERATION is generated if *sumOutput* is not GL_DISCARD_NV, and either *abDotProduct* is not GL_FALSE or *cdDotProduct* is not GL_FALSE.

GL_INVALID_OPERATION is generated if *bias* is GL_BIAS_BY_NEGATIVE_ONE_HALF_NV, and *scale* is either GL_SCALE_BY_ONE_HALF_NV or GL_SCALE_BY_FOUR_NV.

GL_INVALID_OPERATION is generated if any values of *abOutput*, *cdOutput*, and *sumOutput* that are not GL_DISCARD_NV do not all name unique registers.

■ **glFinalCombinerInputNV**—Specify a final combiner input.

Prototype

```
void glFinalCombinerInputNV(GLenum variable,
                            GLenum input,
                            GLenum mapping,
                            GLenum componentUsage);
```

Parameters

variable	Specifies which final combiner variable to affect. The *variable* parameter can be one of the following: GL_VARIABLE_A_NV, GL_VARIABLE_B_NV,

GL_VARIABLE_C_NV, GL_VARIABLE_D_NV, GL_VARIABLE_E_NV, GL_
VARIABLE_F_NV, or GL_VARIABLE_G_NV.

input Specifies the input register. The *input* parameter can be one of the following: GL_ZERO, GL_CONSTANT_COLOR0_NV, GL_CONSTANT_COLOR1_
NV, GL_FOG, GL_PRIMARY_COLOR_NV, GL_SECONDARY_COLOR_NV,
GL_SPARE0_NV, GL_SPARE1_NV, or GL_TEXTURE*i*_NV, where *i* is in the
range 0 to GL_MAX_TEXTURE_UNITS_ARB − 1.

If the *variable* parameter is GL_VARIABLE_A_NV, GL_VARIABLE_B_NV,
GL_VARIABLE_C_NV, or GL_VARIABLE_D_NV, then the *input* parameter
can also be GL_E_TIMES_F_NV.

If the *variable* parameter is GL_VARIABLE_B_NV, GL_VARIABLE_C_NV, or
GL_VARIABLE_D_NV, then the *input* parameter can also be
GL_SPARE0_PLUS_SECONDARY_COLOR_NV.

mapping Specifies the mapping that is applied to the input given by the *input*
parameter. The *mapping* parameter can be GL_UNSIGNED_IDENTITY_NV
or GL_UNSIGNED_INVERT_NV.

componentUsage Specifies which components of the input register are used in the final
combiner stage.

If the value of the *input* parameter is either GL_E_TIMES_F_NV or
GL_SPARE0_PLUS_SECONDARY_COLOR_NV, then the *componentUsage*
parameter must be GL_RGB. Otherwise, if the value of the *variable* parameter is not GL_VARIABLE_G_NV, then the *componentUsage* parameter
can be GL_RGB or GL_ALPHA.

If the value of the *variable* parameter is GL_VARIABLE_G_NV, then the
componentUsage parameter can be GL_ALPHA or GL_BLUE.

Description

The **glFinalCombinerInputNV** function is used to set an input register for the final combiner stage. The *portion* parameter indicates whether the input register is being set for the
RGB or alpha portion of the final combiner stage, and the *variable* parameter indicates
whether the input is being set for the *A*, *B*, *C*, *D*, *E*, *F*, or *G* input variable. The input register assigned to the indicated variable is specified by the *input* parameter, and this input undergoes the mapping specified by the *mapping* parameter. The components of the input
register used as the final combiner stage variable are specified by the *componentUsage*
parameter.

Get Functions

glGetFinalCombinerInputParameter{if}vNV

Errors

GL_INVALID_OPERATION is generated if *variable* is any of GL_VARIABLE_E_NV, GL_
VARIABLE_F_NV, or GL_VARIABLE_G_NV and *input* is GL_E_TIMES_F_NV.

GL_INVALID_OPERATION is generated if *variable* is any of GL_VARIABLE_A_NV, GL_VARIABLE_E_NV, GL_VARIABLE_F_NV, or GL_VARIABLE_G_NV and *input* is GL_SPAREO_PLUS_SECONDARY_COLOR_NV.

GL_INVALID_OPERATION is generated if *variable* is GL_VARIABLE_G_NV and *componentUsage* is GL_RGB.

GL_INVALID_OPERATION is generated if *variable* is not GL_VARIABLE_G_NV and *componentUsage* is GL_BLUE.

GL_INVALID_OPERATION is generated if *input* is either GL_E_TIMES_F_NV or GL_SPAREO_PLUS_SECONDARY_COLOR_NV, and *componentUsage* is either GL_ALPHA or GL_BLUE.

■ **glGetCombinerInputParameter{if}vNV**—Return a general combiner input parameter.

Prototypes

```
void glGetCombinerInputParameterivNV(GLenum stage,
                                     GLenum portion,
                                     GLenum variable,
                                     GLenum pname,
                                     GLint *params);
void glGetCombinerInputParameterfvNV(GLenum stage,
                                     GLenum portion,
                                     GLenum variable,
                                     GLenum pname,
                                     GLfloat *params);
```

Parameters

stage   Specifies which general combiner stage to query. Must be GL_COMBINER*i*_NV, where *i* is in the range 0 to GL_MAX_GENERAL_COMBINERS_NV − 1.

portion   Specifies whether the color portion or alpha portion of the general combiner stage is queried. Must be GL_RGB or GL_ALPHA.

variable   Specifies which general combiner variable to query. Must be GL_VARIABLE_A_NV, GL_VARIABLE_B_NV, GL_VARIABLE_C_NV, or GL_VARIABLE_D_NV.

pname   Specifies the symbolic name of a general combiner input parameter. Must be GL_COMBINER_INPUT_NV, GL_COMBINER_MAPPING_NV, or GL_COMBINER_COMPONENT_USAGE_NV.

params   Specifies a pointer to an array that receives the value of the general combiner input parameter corresponding to the *pname* parameter.

Description

The **glGetCombinerInputParameter{if}vNV** function is used to retrieve a combiner input parameter for the general combiner stage specified by the *stage* parameter. The *por-*

tion parameter indicates whether the returned parameter corresponds to the RGB or alpha portion of the general combiner stage, and the *variable* parameter indicates whether the returned parameter corresponds to the *A, B, C,* or *D* input variable. The *pname* parameter specifies which parameter to return and may be one of the following values:

GL_COMBINER_INPUT_NV

        The input register corresponding to the specified portion and variable for the general combiner stage is returned.

GL_COMBINER_MAPPING_NV

        The input mapping corresponding to the specified portion and variable for the general combiner stage is returned.

GL_COMBINER_COMPONENT_USAGE_NV

        The component usage corresponding to the specified portion and variable for the general combiner stage is returned.

■ **glGetCombinerOutputParameter{if}vNV**—Return a general combiner output parameter.

Prototypes

```
void glGetCombinerOutputParameterivNV(GLenum stage,
                                      GLenum portion,
                                      GLenum pname,
                                      GLint *params);
void glGetCombinerOutputParameterfvNV(GLenum stage,
                                      GLenum portion,
                                      GLenum pname,
                                      GLfloat *params);
```

Parameters

stage   Specifies which general combiner stage to query. Must be GL_COMBINER*i*_NV, where *i* is in the range 0 to GL_MAX_GENERAL_COMBINERS_NV − 1.

portion   Specifies whether the color portion or alpha portion of the general combiner stage is queried. Must be GL_RGB or GL_ALPHA.

pname   Specifies the symbolic name of a general combiner output parameter. The *pname* parameter can be one of the following: GL_COMBINER_AB_OUTPUT_NV, GL_COMBINER_CD_OUTPUT_NV, GL_COMBINER_SUM_OUTPUT_NV, GL_COMBINER_SCALE_NV, GL_COMBINER_BIAS_NV, GL_COMBINER_AB_DOT_PRODUCT_NV, GL_COMBINER_CD_DOT_PRODUCT_NV, or GL_COMBINER_MUX_SUM_NV.

params   Specifies a pointer to an array that receives the value of the general combiner output parameter corresponding to the *pname* parameter.

Description

The **glGetCombinerOutputParameter{if}vNV** function is used to retrieve a combiner output parameter for the general combiner stage specified by the *stage* parameter. The *portion* parameter indicates whether the returned parameter corresponds to the RGB or alpha portion of the general combiner stage. The *pname* parameter specifies which parameter to return and may be one of the following values:

GL_COMBINER_AB_OUTPUT_NV

> The output register for the product *AB* corresponding to the specified portion of the general combiner stage is returned.

GL_COMBINER_CD_OUTPUT_NV

> The output register for the product *CD* corresponding to the specified portion of the general combiner stage is returned.

GL_COMBINER_SUM_OUTPUT_NV

> The output register for the sum *AB* + *CD* corresponding to the specified portion of the general combiner stage is returned.

GL_COMBINER_SCALE_NV

> The scale value applied to the three outputs corresponding to the specified portion of the general combiner stage is returned.

GL_COMBINER_BIAS_NV

> The bias value applied to the three outputs corresponding to the specified portion of the general combiner stage is returned.

GL_COMBINER_AB_DOT_PRODUCT_NV

> A Boolean value indicating whether the *AB* product is a dot product is returned. This is always GL_FALSE for the alpha portion of the general combiner stage.

GL_COMBINER_CD_DOT_PRODUCT_NV

> A Boolean value indicating whether the *CD* product is a dot product is returned. This is always GL_FALSE for the alpha portion of the general combiner stage.

GL_COMBINER_MUX_SUM_NV

> A Boolean value indicating whether the sum *AB* + *CD* is replaced by the mux operation for the specified portion of the general combiner stage is returned.

■ **glGetFinalCombinerInputParameter{if}vNV**—Return a final combiner input parameter.

Prototypes

```
void glGetFinalCombinerInputParameterivNV(GLenum variable,
                                          GLenum pname,
                                          GLint *params);
```

```
void glGetFinalCombinerInputParameterfvNV(GLenum variable,
                                          GLenum pname,
                                          GLfloat *params);
```

Parameters

variable Specifies which general combiner variable to query. The *variable* parameter can be one of the following: GL_VARIABLE_A_NV, GL_VARIABLE_B_NV, GL_VARIABLE_C_NV, GL_VARIABLE_D_NV, GL_VARIABLE_E_NV, GL_VARIABLE_F_NV, or GL_VARIABLE_G_NV.

pname Specifies the symbolic name of a final combiner input parameter. Must be GL_COMBINER_INPUT_NV, GL_COMBINER_MAPPING_NV, or GL_COMBINER_COMPONENT_USAGE_NV.

params Specifies a pointer to an array that receives the value of the final combiner input parameter corresponding to the *pname* parameter.

Description

The **glGetFinalCombinerInputParameter{if}vNV** function is used to retrieve a combiner input parameter for the final combiner stage. The *variable* parameter indicates whether the returned parameter corresponds to the *A*, *B*, *C*, *D*, *E*, *F*, or *G* input variable. The *pname* parameter specifies which parameter to return and may be one of the following values:

GL_COMBINER_INPUT_NV
  The input register corresponding to the specified variable for the final combiner stage is returned.

GL_COMBINER_MAPPING_NV
  The input mapping corresponding to the specified variable for the final combiner stage is returned.

GL_COMBINER_COMPONENT_USAGE_NV
  The component usage corresponding to the specified variable for the final combiner stage is returned.

EXTENDED FUNCTIONS

■ **glEnable**, **glDisable**, **glIsEnabled**—Extended to enable/disable register combiners.

Prototypes

```
void glEnable(GLenum cap);
void glDisable(GLenum cap);
GLboolean glIsEnabled(GLenum cap);
```

Extended Parameters

cap   Specifies a GL capability. To enable or disable register combiners, or to query whether register combiners are enabled, this should be GL_REGISTER_COMBINERS_ NV.

Description

Register combiners are enabled and disabled by passing the value GL_REGISTER_COMBIN- ERS_NV to the **glEnable** and **glDisable** functions. Calling the **glIsEnabled** function with the parameter GL_REGISTER_COMBINERS_NV returns a value indicating whether register combiners are enabled.

- **glGetIntegerv**—Extended to allow retrieval of register combiner state.

Prototype

```
void glGetIntegerv(GLenum pname, GLint *params);
```

Extended Parameters

pname   Specifies the parameter to be returned. May be one of the values listed in Description.

Description

Various state values related to register combiners can be retrieved by calling the **glGet- Integerv** function. The *pname* parameter may be one of the following values:

GL_MAX_GENERAL_COMBINERS_NV

The maximum number of general combiner stages supported by the implementation is returned. This value is always at least 2.

GL_NUM_GENERAL_COMBINERS_NV

The current number of general combiner stages in use is returned.

- **glGetBooleanv**—Extended to allow retrieval of the color sum clamp state.

Prototype

```
void glGetBooleanv(GLenum pname, GLboolean *params);
```

Extended Parameters

pname   Specifies the parameter to be returned. May be GL_COLOR_SUM_CLAMP_NV.

Description

The **glGetBooleanv** function can be used to retrieve the current value of the color sum clamp parameter.

■ **glGetFloatv**—Extended to allow retrieval of register combiner constant colors.

Prototype

```
void glGetFloatv(GLenum pname, GLfloat *params);
```

Extended Parameters

pname   Specifies the parameter to be returned. May be GL_CONSTANT_COLOR0_NV or GL_CONSTANT_COLOR1_NV.

Description

The **glGetFloatv** function can be used to retrieve the current values of the register combiner constant colors. Four values—the red, green, blue, and alpha components of the specified constant color—are returned in the array pointed to by the *params* parameter.

6.2   GL_NV_register_combiners2

OpenGL version required	OpenGL 1.1
Dependencies	Requires GL_NV_register_combiners2
Promotions	—
Related extensions	—

DISCUSSION

The GL_NV_register_combiners extension provides two constant color registers that can be accessed in any general combiner stage or in the final combiner stage. Many applications require more than two constant colors for advanced fragment-shading operations, so the GL_NV_register_combiners2 extension provides a mode in which separate pairs of constant colors are available in each general combiner stage. This amounts to a total of $2n + 2$ constant colors, where n is the maximum number of general combiner stages supported by the implementation.

The per-stage constant color mode is enabled and disabled by calling the **glEnable** and **glDisable** functions with *cap* parameter GL_PER_STAGE_CONSTANTS_NV. When per-stage constants are enabled, the GL_CONSTANT_COLOR0_NV and GL_CONSTANT_COLOR1_NV registers represent the per-stage constant colors when used as inputs in the general combiner stages. The values to which these registers are initialized for each stage are specified by calling the **glCombinerStageParameterfvNV** function,

```
void glCombinerStageParameterfvNV(GLenum stage,
                                  GLenum pname,
                                  const GLfloat *params);
```

The *stage* parameter specifies the general combiner stage for which the constant color is being set and must be GL_COMBINER*i*_NV, where *i* is in the range 0 to GL_MAX_

GENERAL_COMBINERS − 1. The *pname* parameter specifies which constant color to set and must be GL_CONSTANT_COLORO_NV or GL_CONSTANT_COLOR1_NV. The *params* parameter points to an array containing the red, green, blue, and alpha components of the new constant color value. The current value of a per-stage constant color is retrieved by calling the **glGetCombinerStageParameterfvNV** function,

```
void glGetCombinerStageParameterfvNV(GLenum stage,
                                     GLenum pname,
                                     GLfloat *params);
```

The four components of the constant color corresponding to the *stage* and *pname* parameters are returned in the array pointed to by the *params* parameter.

When per-stage constants are disabled, the GL_CONSTANT_COLORO_NV and GL_CONSTANT_COLOR1_NV registers represent the global constant colors, which are specified by calling the **glCombinerParameter{if}vNV** function, in every general combiner stage. The per-stage constant colors are not accessible in the general combiner stages. This provides backward compatibility with the GL_NV_register_combiner extension.

The global constant colors are assigned to the GL_CONSTANT_COLORO_NV and GL_CONSTANT_COLOR1_NV registers in the final combiner stage regardless of whether per-stage constants are enabled. When per-stage constants are enabled, the global constant colors can be regarded as the final stage constant colors, since that is the only stage in which they can be accessed.

NEW FUNCTIONS

■ **glCombinerStageParameterfvNV**—Specify a general combiner stage parameter.

Prototype

```
void glCombinerStageParameterfvNV(GLenum stage,
                                  GLenum pname,
                                  const GLfloat *params);
```

Parameters

stage   Specifies which general combiner stage to affect. Must be GL_COMBINER*i*_NV, where *i* is in the range 0 to GL_MAX_GENERAL_COMBINERS_NV − 1.

pname   Specifies the symbolic name of a combiner stage parameter. Must be GL_CONSTANT_COLORO_NV or GL_CONSTANT_COLOR1_NV.

params   Specifies a pointer to an array where the values of the general combiner stage parameter corresponding to the *pname* parameter are stored.

Description

The **glCombinerStageParameterfvNV** function is used to set the constant colors corresponding to the general combiner stage specified by the *stage* parameter. The *pname* parameter specifies which constant color is to be set, and the *params* parameter points to an array containing the new red, green, blue, and alpha components of the constant color.

Special Considerations

The per-stage constant colors are ignored if GL_PER_STAGE_CONSTANTS_NV is disabled. When per-stage constant colors are disabled, globally available constant colors are set by calling the **glCombinerParameter{if}[v]NV** function.

Get Functions

glGetCombinerStageParameterfvNV

- **glGetCombinerStageParameterfvNV**—Return a general combiner stage parameter.

Prototype

```
void glGetCombinerStageParameterfvNV(GLenum stage,
                                     GLenum pname,
                                     GLfloat *params);
```

Parameters

stage   Specifies which general combiner stage to query. Must be GL_COMBINER*i*_NV, where *i* is in the range 0 to GL_MAX_GENERAL_COMBINERS_NV − 1.

pname   Specifies the symbolic name of a combiner stage parameter. Must be GL_CONSTANT_COLOR0_NV or GL_CONSTANT_COLOR1_NV.

params   Specifies a pointer to an array that receives the value of the general combiner stage parameter corresponding to the *pname* parameter.

Description

The **glGetCombinerStageParameterfvNV** function is used to retrieve the constant colors corresponding to the general combiner stage specified by the *stage* parameter. The *pname* parameter specifies which constant color to retrieve. The red, green, blue, and alpha components are returned in the array pointed to by the *params* parameter.

EXTENDED FUNCTIONS

- **glEnable, glDisable, glIsEnabled**—Extended to enable/disable per-stage register combiner constant colors.

Prototypes

```
void glEnable(GLenum cap);
void glDisable(GLenum cap);
GLboolean glIsEnabled(GLenum cap);
```

Extended Parameters

cap   Specifies a GL capability. To enable or disable per-stage constant colors, or to query whether per-stage constant colors are enabled, this should be GL_PER_STAGE_CONSTANTS_NV.

Description

Per-stage constant colors are enabled and disabled by passing the value GL_PER_STAGE_CONSTANTS_NV to the **glEnable** and **glDisable** functions. Calling the **glIsEnabled** function with the parameter GL_PER_STAGE_CONSTANTS_NV returns a value indicating whether per-stage constant colors are enabled.

6.3   GL_NV_texture_shader

OpenGL version required	OpenGL 1.1
Dependencies	Requires GL_ARB_multitexture
	Requires GL_ARB_texture_cube_map
	Requires at least four texture units
Promotions	—
Related extensions	GL_NV_texture_shader2
	GL_NV_texture_shader3

DISCUSSION

Unextended OpenGL accesses texture maps by selecting the texture target of highest priority (e.g., GL_TEXTURE_1D, GL_TEXTURE_2D, GL_TEXTURE_RECTANGLE_NV, GL_TEXTURE_3D_EXT, or GL_TEXTURE_CUBE_MAP_ARB) that is enabled for a particular texture unit and fetching a sample by directly applying the texture unit's associated texture coordinates. The GL_NV_texture_shader extension adds considerable functionality that allows computations to be performed at each fragment before a texture map is sampled, and these computations may depend on the result of a previous texture fetch.

When texture shaders are enabled, each texture unit can be assigned one of 21 fixed texture shader operations. This set of operations includes the conventional 1D, 2D, rectangle, and cube map texture fetches (3D textures are support by the GL_NV_texture_shader2 extension), as well as programs that perform various calculations using results from previous stages. Additionally, some operations can have side effects, such as replacing the depth of the fragment or culling the fragment altogether.

Texture Formats

To better facilitate various texture shader operations, two new texture formats are introduced. The first is a two-component, high-precision format called HILO ("high-low") that is intended to be used with dot product shader operations. The components of a HILO texture image, referred to as HI and LO, can be both signed or both unsigned. The second format is an offset group that includes signed DS and DT values that are intended to be used to offset s and t texture coordinates. Offset groups may also include unsigned magnitude (MAG) and vibrance (VIB) components to form three- or four-component texture images. Table 6.3.1 summarizes the new texture formats and lists the symbolic constants that are accepted by the *format* parameter of the **glTexImage1D**, **glTexImage2D**, **glTexSubImage1D**, and **glTexSubImage2D** functions.

TABLE 6.3.1 New texture formats defined by the GL_NV_texture_shader extension. HI and LO components may be signed or unsigned. DS and DT components are always signed. MAG and VIB components are always unsigned.

Texture Format	*First Component*	*Second Component*	*Third Component*	*Fourth Component*
GL_HILO_NV	HI	LO	—	—
GL_DSDT_NV	DS	DT	—	—
GL_DSDT_MAG_NV	DS	DT	MAG	—
GL_DSDT_MAG_VIB_NV	DS	DT	MAG	VIB

HILO and offset group formats apply only to texture maps and cannot be used with the **glDrawPixels**, **glReadPixels**, **glCopyTexImage1D**, and **glCopyTexImage2D** functions. Attempting to do so generates the error GL_INVALID_OPERATION.

HILO and offset group texture formats cannot be converted to RGBA color and are stored internally by an implementation as HILO or offset group images. The *internalFormat* parameter passed to the **glTexImage1D** or **glTexImage2D** function must match the format of the image being loaded. Table 6.3.2 lists the internal formats that may be specified for each particular external format listed in Table 6.3.1.

TABLE 6.3.2 New internal texture formats defined by the GL_NV_texture_shader extension. Each internal format may be specified only for the matching external format when loading texture images. Sized internal formats specify how many bits should be used to store each component. Bit counts preceded by S represent signed components, and bit counts preceded by U represent unsigned components. The vibrance (VIB) external component becomes intensity (I), internally.

Internal Format	*Base Internal Format*	*Required External Format*	*HI Bits*	*LO Bits*	*DS Bits*	*DT Bits*	*MAG Bits*	*I Bits*
GL_HILO_NV	GL_HILO_NV	GL_HILO_NV	—	—	—	—	—	—
GL_HILO16_NV	GL_HILO_NV	GL_HILO_NV	U16	U16	—	—	—	—
GL_SIGNED_HILO_NV	GL_HILO_NV	GL_HILO_NV	—	—	—	—	—	—

(continues)

TABLE 6.3.2 *Continued*

Internal Format	Base Internal Format	Required External Format	HI Bits	LO Bits	DS Bits	DT Bits	MAG Bits	I Bits
GL_SIGNED_ HILO16_NV	GL_HILO_NV	GL_HILO_NV	S16	S16	—	—	—	—
GL_DSDT_NV	GL_DSDT_NV	GL_DSDT_NV	—	—	—	—	—	—
GL_DSDT8_NV	GL_DSDT_NV	GL_DSDT_NV	—	—	S8	S8	—	—
GL_DSDT_ MAG_NV	GL_DSDT_MAG_ NV	GL_DSDT_MAG_NV	—	—	—	—	—	—
GL_DSDT8_ MAG8_NV	GL_DSDT_MAG_ NV	GL_DSDT_MAG_NV	—	—	S8	S8	U8	—
GL_DSDT_MAG_ INTENSITY_NV	GL_DSDT_MAG_ INTENSITY_NV	GL_DSDT_MAG_ VIB_NV	—	—	—	—	—	—
GL_DSDT8_MAG8_ INTENSITY8_NV	GL_DSDT_MAG_ INTENSITY_NV	GL_DSDT_MAG_ VIB_NV	—	—	S8	S8	U8	U8

HI, LO, DS, DT, MAG, and VIB texture image components have separate scale and bias values that may be used to modify a texture image as it is transferred to OpenGL. The **glPixelTransferf** function may be called with *pname* parameter GL_*k*_SCALE_NV or GL_*k*_BIAS_NV, where *k* is HI, LO, DS, DT, MAGNITUDE, or VIBRANCE, to set the scale and bias applied to each component. Initially, all scale values are set to 1.0, and all bias values are set to 0.0. The vibrance component is stored internally by an implementation as intensity. The reason it has a different name externally is to allow it to have an independent pixel transfer operation, since none exists for intensity.

When a texture image having the format GL_DSDT_MAG_VIB_NV is loaded, the *type* parameter of the **glTexImage1D** or **glTexImage2D** function may be one of the packed pixel types GL_UNSIGNED_INT_S8_S8_8_8_NV or GL_UNSIGNED_INT_8_8_S8_S8_REV_NV. These types indicate that the DS and DT components contain signed data, and the MAG and VIB components contain unsigned data in client memory. The GL_UNSIGNED_ INT_8_8_S8_S8_REV_NV type indicates that the components are stored in the order VIB, MAG, DT, DS. Without these packed pixel types, specifying GL_UNSIGNED_BYTE for the *type* parameter would prevent the DS and DT components from attaining negative values, and specifying GL_BYTE for the *type* parameter would only allow half the number of values to be specified for the MAG and VIB components, since they are clamped to 0.

The GL_NV_texture_shader extension also defines signed internal formats that correspond to the conventional OpenGL formats. Table 6.3.3 lists values that are accepted by the *internalFormat* parameter of the **glTexImage1D**, **glTexImage2D**, **glCopyTexImage1D**, and **glCopyTexImage2D** functions. Unextended OpenGL clamps component values to the range [0,1] when texture images are loaded; but when a signed internal format is specified, any signed components are clamped to the range [−1,1]. (This applies to signed HILO components and DS/DT offset components, as well.)

TABLE 6.3.3 Signed internal formats defined by the GL_NV_texture_shader extension. Sized internal formats specify how many bits should be used to store each component. Bit counts preceded by S represent signed components, and bit counts preceded by U represent unsigned components.

Internal Format	Base Internal Format	R Bits	G Bits	B Bits	A Bits	L Bits	I Bits
GL_SIGNED_RGBA_NV	GL_RGBA	—	—	—	—	—	—
GL_SIGNED_RGBA8_NV	GL_RGBA	S8	S8	S8	S8	—	—
GL_SIGNED_RGB_NV	GL_RGB	—	—	—	—	—	—
GL_SIGNED_RGB8_NV	GL_RGB	S8	S8	S8	—	—	—
GL_SIGNED_LUMINANCE_NV	GL_LUMINANCE	—	—	—	—	—	—
GL_SIGNED_LUMINANCE8_NV	GL_LUMINANCE	—	—	—	—	S8	—
GL_SIGNED_LUMINANCE_ ALPHA_NV	GL_LUMINANCE_ALPHA	—	—	—	—	—	—
GL_SIGNED_LUMINANCE8_ ALPHA8_NV	GL_LUMINANCE_ALPHA	—	—	—	S8	S8	—
GL_SIGNED_ALPHA_NV	GL_ALPHA	—	—	—	—	—	—
GL_SIGNED_ALPHA8_NV	GL_ALPHA	—	—	—	S8	—	—
GL_SIGNED_INTENSITY_NV	GL_INTENSITY	—	—	—	—	—	—
GL_SIGNED_INTENSITY8_NV	GL_INTENSITY	—	—	—	—	—	S8
GL_SIGNED_RGB_ UNSIGNED_ALPHA_NV	GL_RGBA	—	—	—	—	—	—
GL_SIGNED_RGB8_ UNSIGNED_ALPHA8_NV	GL_RGBA	S8	S8	S8	U8	—	—

In unextended OpenGL, a texture border color can be specified by calling the **glTexParameterfv** function with *pname* parameter GL_TEXTURE_BORDER_COLOR. The four components of this color are clamped to the range [0,1]. To accommodate texture images that may contain component values outside this range, the new token GL_TEXTURE_BORDER_VALUES_NV is defined and may be passed to the *pname* parameter of the **glTexParameterfv** function to specify unclamped border texel components. Four floating-point components are specified by the *params* parameter and are stored as the texture border color. The only difference between specifying border values instead of a border color is that no clamping occurs. For HILO texture images, the first two components of the texture border values are interpreted as HI and LO components, and the last two components are ignored. For offset group texture images, the four components of the texture border values are interpreted as DS, DT, MAG, and VIB in that order. Calling the **glGetTexParameterfv** function to retrieve either the texture border color (with *pname* parameter GL_TEXTURE_BORDER_COLOR) or the texture border values (with *pname* parameter GL_TEXTURE_BORDER_VALUES_NV) returns the same four values for both queries.

Texture Shader Operations

Texture shaders are enabled and disabled by calling the **glEnable** and **glDisable** functions with *cap* parameter GL_TEXTURE_SHADER_NV. When texture shaders are enabled, the enable state of each texture target is ignored, and a series of texture shader stages, one per texture unit, is executed. Each stage performs one of the texture shader operations listed in Table 6.3.4 and generates two results. First, an ordinary RGBA color result is generated, and this becomes the color associated with the corresponding texture unit in the texture environment or in the register combiner setting. Second, a separate texture shader result is generated that may be used in subsequent texture shader operations. The texture shader result may be an RGBA color, a HILO pair, an offset group, a floating-point scalar, or an invalid result. Table 6.3.5 summarizes the RGBA results and texture shader results for all of the texture shader operations.

TABLE 6.3.4   Texture Shader Operations and the Stages in Which They May be Specified

Texture Shader Operation	*Stage 0*	*Stage 1*	*Stage 2*	*Stage 3*
GL_NONE	•	•	•	•
GL_TEXTURE_1D	•	•	•	•
GL_TEXTURE_2D	•	•	•	•
GL_TEXTURE_RECTANGLE_NV	•	•	•	•
GL_TEXTURE_CUBE_MAP_ARB	•	•	•	•
GL_PASS_THROUGH_NV	•	•	•	•
GL_CULL_FRAGMENT_NV	•	•	•	•
GL_OFFSET_TEXTURE_2D_NV		•	•	•
GL_OFFSET_TEXTURE_2D_SCALE_NV		•	•	•
GL_OFFSET_TEXTURE_RECTANGLE_NV		•	•	•
GL_OFFSET_TEXTURE_RECTANGLE_SCALE_NV		•	•	•
GL_DEPENDENT_AR_TEXTURE_2D_NV		•	•	•
GL_DEPENDENT_GB_TEXTURE_2D_NV		•	•	•
GL_DOT_PRODUCT_NV		•	•	•
GL_DOT_PRODUCT_TEXTURE_2D_NV			•	•
GL_DOT_PRODUCT_TEXTURE_RECTANGLE_NV			•	•
GL_DOT_PRODUCT_TEXTURE_CUBE_MAP_NV				•
GL_DOT_PRODUCT_REFLECT_CUBE_MAP_NV				•
GL_DOT_PRODUCT_CONST_EYE_REFLECT_CUBE_MAP_NV				•
GL_DOT_PRODUCT_DIFFUSE_CUBE_MAP_NV			•	
GL_DOT_PRODUCT_DEPTH_REPLACE_NV			•	•

TABLE 6.3.5   Texture Shader Result Types

Texture Shader Operation	Shader Stage Result Type	Shader Stage Result Value	Texture Unit RGBA Color Result
GL_NONE	Invalid	Invalid	(0,0,0,0)
GL_TEXTURE_1D	Matches 1D target	Filtered texel	Filtered texel if RGBA, else (0,0,0,0)
GL_TEXTURE_2D	Matches 2D target	Filtered texel	Filtered texel if RGBA, else (0,0,0,0)
GL_TEXTURE_RECTANGLE_NV	Matches rectangle target	Filtered texel	Filtered texel if RGBA, else (0,0,0,0)
GL_TEXTURE_CUBE_MAP_ARB	Matches cube map target	Filtered texel	Filtered texel if RGBA, else (0,0,0,0)
GL_PASS_THROUGH_NV	RGBA	(s,t,r,q), clamped to [0,1]	(s,t,r,q), clamped to [0,1]
GL_CULL_FRAGMENT_NV	Invalid	Invalid	(0,0,0,0)
GL_OFFSET_TEXTURE_2D_NV	Matches 2D target	Filtered texel	Filtered texel if RGBA, else (0,0,0,0)
GL_OFFSET_TEXTURE_2D_SCALE_NV	RGBA	Filtered texel	Scaled filtered texel
GL_OFFSET_TEXTURE_RECTANGLE_NV	Matches rectangle target	Filtered texel	Filtered texel if RGBA, else (0,0,0,0)
GL_OFFSET_TEXTURE_RECTANGLE_SCALE_NV	RGBA	Filtered texel	Scaled filtered texel
GL_DEPENDENT_AR_TEXTURE_2D_NV	Matches 2D target	Filtered texel	Filtered texel if RGBA, else (0,0,0,0)
GL_DEPENDENT_GB_TEXTURE_2D_NV	Matches 2D target	Filtered texel	Filtered texel if RGBA, else (0,0,0,0)
GL_DOT_PRODUCT_NV	Floating-point scalar	Dot product	(0,0,0,0)
GL_DOT_PRODUCT_TEXTURE_2D_NV	Matches 2D target	Filtered texel	Filtered texel if RGBA, else (0,0,0,0)

(continues)

TABLE 6.3.5   *Continued*

Texture Shader Operation	Shader Stage Result Type	Shader Stage Result Value	Texture Unit RGBA Color Result
GL_DOT_PRODUCT_ TEXTURE_RECTANGLE_NV	Matches rectangle target	Filtered texel	Filtered texel if RGBA, else (0,0,0,0)
GL_DOT_PRODUCT_ TEXTURE_CUBE_MAP_NV	Matches cube map target	Filtered texel	Filtered texel if RGBA, else (0,0,0,0)
GL_DOT_PRODUCT_ REFLECT_CUBE_MAP_NV	Matches cube map target	Filtered texel	Filtered texel if RGBA, else (0,0,0,0)
GL_DOT_PRODUCT_CONST_EYE_ REFLECT_CUBE_MAP_NV	Matches cube map target	Filtered texel	Filtered texel if RGBA, else (0,0,0,0)
GL_DOT_PRODUCT_ DIFFUSE_CUBE_MAP_NV	Matches cube map target	Filtered texel	Filtered texel if RGBA, else (0,0,0,0)
GL_DOT_PRODUCT_ DEPTH_REPLACE_NV	Invalid	Invalid	(0,0,0,0)

A texture shader operation is specified for a particular stage by calling the **glTexEnvi** function with *target* parameter GL_TEXTURE_SHADER_NV and *pname* parameter GL_ SHADER_OPERATION_NV. The *param* parameter then specifies one of the operations listed in Table 6.3.4. Many operations require the texture shader result of a previous texture shader stage. In these cases, the previous stage from which the texture shader result is used is specified by calling the **glTexEnvi** function with *pname* parameter GL_PREVIOUS_ TEXTURE_INPUT_NV. The previous texture input names a texture stage GL_TEXTURE*i*_ARB, where *i* is less than the index of the texture unit for which the previous texture input is being specified. Texture shader stage interdependencies are summarized in Table 6.3.6.

Many texture shader operations require that previous shader stages perform certain operations, or that the texture maps accessed adhere to certain format restrictions. An internal value is maintained that represents the consistency of each texture shader stage, telling whether all of the requirements of the stage's operation have been met. The consistency flag can be retrieved by calling the **glGetTexEnviv** function with *pname* parameter GL_SHADER_CONSISTENT_NV. If the shader stage is consistent, then the value GL_TRUE is returned in the *params* parameter; otherwise, GL_FALSE is returned. If a texture shader stage is not consistent, then it operates as though its shader operation is GL_NONE.

The effects of the 21 available shader operations are described below.

None
The GL_NONE texture shader operation always generates the RGBA result (0,0,0,0), ignoring all texture maps and the texture coordinates corresponding to the associated texture unit.

TABLE 6.3.6   Texture shader stage interdependencies. For the shader operation specified for stage i, any operations listed for stages $i - 2$, $i - 1$, or $i + 1$ must be performed. Also, any texture shader result type requirements listed for the stage corresponding to the previous texture input must be met. Otherwise, texture shader stage i is not consistent. RGBA and HILO formats for textures used as a previous input must not have mixed signs.

Texture Shader Operation For Stage i	Stage $i - 2$ Shader Operation	Stage $i - 1$ Shader Operation	Stage $i + 1$ Shader Operation	Previous Texture Input Result Types
GL_NONE	—	—	—	—
GL_TEXTURE_1D	—	—	—	—
GL_TEXTURE_2D	—	—	—	—
GL_TEXTURE_RECTANGLE_NV	—	—	—	—
GL_TEXTURE_CUBE_MAP_ARB	—	—	—	—
GL_PASS_THROUGH_NV	—	—	—	—
GL_CULL_FRAGMENT_NV	—	—	—	—
GL_OFFSET_TEXTURE_2D_NV	—	—	—	DSDT DSDT_MAG DSDT_MAG_ INTENSITY
GL_OFFSET_TEXTURE_ 2D_SCALE_NV	—	—	—	DSDT_MAG DSDT_MAG_ INTENSITY
GL_OFFSET_TEXTURE_ RECTANGLE_NV	—	—	—	DSDT DSDT_MAG DSDT_MAG_ INTENSITY
GL_OFFSET_TEXTURE_ RECTANGLE_SCALE_NV	—	—	—	DSDT_MAG DSDT_MAG_ INTENSITY
GL_DEPENDENT_AR_ TEXTURE_2D_NV	—	—	—	Unsigned RGBA

(continues)

TABLE 6.3.6   *Continued*

Texture Shader Operation For Stage i	Stage i − 2 Shader Operation	Stage i − 1 Shader Operation	Stage i + 1 Shader Operation	Previous Texture Input Result Types
GL_DEPENDENT_GB_TEXTURE_2D_NV	—	—	—	Unsigned RGBA
GL_DOT_PRODUCT_NV	—	—	—	RGBA HILO
GL_DOT_PRODUCT_TEXTURE_2D_NV	—	GL_DOT_PRODUCT_NV	—	RGBA HILO
GL_DOT_PRODUCT_TEXTURE_RECTANGLE_NV	—	GL_DOT_PRODUCT_NV	—	RGBA HILO
GL_DOT_PRODUCT_TEXTURE_CUBE_MAP_NV	GL_DOT_PRODUCT_NV	GL_DOT_PRODUCT_NV	—	RGBA HILO
GL_DOT_PRODUCT_REFLECT_CUBE_MAP_NV	GL_DOT_PRODUCT_NV	GL_DOT_PRODUCT_DIFFUSE_CUBE_MAP_NV	—	RGBA HILO
GL_DOT_PRODUCT_CONST_EYE_REFLECT_CUBE_MAP_NV	GL_DOT_PRODUCT_NV	GL_DOT_PRODUCT_DIFFUSE_CUBE_MAP_NV	—	RGBA HILO
GL_DOT_PRODUCT_DIFFUSE_CUBE_MAP_NV	—	GL_DOT_PRODUCT_NV	GL_DOT_PRODUCT_REFLECT_CUBE_MAP_NV GL_DOT_PRODUCT_CONST_EYE_REFLECT_CUBE_MAP_NV	RGBA HILO
GL_DOT_PRODUCT_DEPTH_REPLACE_NV	—	GL_DOT_PRODUCT_NV	—	RGBA HILO

The texture shader result is invalid. GL_NONE is the initial operation assigned to each texture unit. Setting a stage's texture shader operation to GL_NONE is the most efficient way to disable a texture unit when texture shaders are enabled.

1D Projective Texturing

The GL_TEXTURE_1D texture shader operation accesses the texture unit's 1D texture target using the coordinate s/q. This is equivalent to conventional texturing when the 1D texture target is the highest priority target enabled. The result of the texture access becomes both the RGBA result and texture shader result.

2D Projective Texturing

The GL_TEXTURE_2D texture shader operation accesses the texture unit's 2D texture target using the coordinates $\langle s/q, t/q \rangle$. This is equivalent to conventional texturing when the 2D texture target is the highest priority target enabled. The result of the texture access becomes both the RGBA result and texture shader result.

Rectangle Projective Texturing

The GL_TEXTURE_RECTANGLE_NV texture shader operation accesses the texture unit's rectangle texture target using the coordinates $\langle s/q, t/q \rangle$. This is equivalent to conventional texturing when the rectangle texture target is the highest priority target enabled. The result of the texture access becomes both the RGBA result and texture shader result.

Cube Map Texturing

The GL_TEXTURE_CUBE_MAP_ARB texture shader operation accesses the texture unit's cube map texture target using the coordinates $\langle s,t,r \rangle$. This is equivalent to conventional texturing when the cube map texture target is the highest priority target enabled. The result of the texture access becomes both the RGBA result and texture shader result.

Pass Through

The GL_PASS_THROUGH_NV texture shader operation converts the texture coordinates $\langle s,t,r,q \rangle$ directly into a color value (r,g,b,a) without accessing any texture maps. The red, green, blue, and alpha components of the resulting color are clamped to the range $[0,1]$. Both the RGBA result and the texture shader result are assigned the clamped color value.

Cull Fragment

The GL_CULL_FRAGMENT_NV texture shader operation compares each of the texture coordinates s, t, r, and q to zero without accessing any texture maps. Each texture coordinate has an associated cull mode that is either GL_LESS or GL_GEQUAL. These cull modes are set by calling the **glTexEnviv** function with *pname* parameter GL_CULL_MODES_NV. If the cull mode is GL_GEQUAL (the initial value), then the value of the texture coordinate must be greater than or equal to zero for the cull test to pass. If the cull mode corresponding to a texture coordinate is GL_LESS, then the value of the texture coordinate must be less than zero for the cull test to pass. If the cull test fails for any of the four texture coordinates, then the fragment is discarded. The RGBA result is always $(0,0,0,0)$, and the texture shader result is invalid.

Offset Texture 2D

The GL_OFFSET_TEXTURE_2D_NV texture shader operation uses the texture shader result of a previous stage to perturb the texture coordinates $\langle s,t \rangle$ associated with the current stage before accessing the texture unit's 2D texture target. (No projective division by q is performed.) The perturbed texture coordinates $\langle s',t' \rangle$ are calculated using Equation (6.3.1),

$$\begin{bmatrix} s' \\ t' \end{bmatrix} = \begin{bmatrix} s \\ t \end{bmatrix} + \begin{bmatrix} a_1 & a_3 \\ a_2 & a_4 \end{bmatrix} \begin{bmatrix} ds \\ dt \end{bmatrix}, \tag{6.3.1}$$

where the values ds and dt are offset values fetched in the previous texture shader stage specified by the value of GL_PREVIOUS_TEXTURE_INPUT_NV, and the quantities a_1, a_2, a_3, and a_4 are the four entries of the texture unit's texture offset matrix. The texture offset matrix is specified by calling the **glTexEnvfv** function with *pname* parameter GL_OFFSET_TEXTURE_MATRIX_NV and is initially the 2×2 identity matrix. The texture unit's 2D texture target is accessed using the texture coordinates $\langle s',t' \rangle$, and the result of the texture access becomes both the RGBA result and texture shader result.

Offset Texture 2D and Scale

The GL_OFFSET_TEXTURE_2D_SCALE_NV texture shader operation calculates texture coordinates $\langle s',t' \rangle$ using Equation (6.3.1) just as the GL_OFFSET_TEXTURE_2D_NV operations does. The texture unit's 2D texture target is accessed using the texture coordinates $\langle s',t' \rangle$, and the result of the texture access becomes the texture shader result. The same result also becomes the RGBA result, but after the RGB portion of the color is scaled by a factor derived from the magnitude component of the previous texture stage's result according to the following equation:

$$\begin{aligned} r' &= r(ms+b) \\ g' &= g(ms+b) \\ b' &= b(ms+b) \\ a' &= a \end{aligned} \tag{6.3.2}$$

The value m is the magnitude value fetched in the previous texture shader stage specified by the value of GL_PREVIOUS_TEXTURE_INPUT_NV, and the quantities s and b are the texture unit's offset texture scale and bias values, respectively. The offset texture scale and bias values are specified by calling the **glTexEnvf** function with *pname* parameter GL_OFFSET_TEXTURE_SCALE_NV or GL_OFFSET_TEXTURE_BIAS_NV and are initially 1.0 and 0.0, respectively. The scaled color components r', g', and b' are clamped to the range [0,1] and assigned to the stage's RGBA result.

Offset Texture Rectangle

The GL_OFFSET_TEXTURE_RECTANGLE_NV texture shader operation performs the same function as the GL_OFFSET_TEXTURE_2D_NV operation, except that the rectangle texture target is accessed instead of the 2D texture target.

Offset Texture Rectangle and Scale

The `GL_OFFSET_TEXTURE_RECTANGLE_SCALE_NV` texture shader operation performs the same function as the `GL_OFFSET_TEXTURE_2D_SCALE_NV` operation, except that the rectangle texture target is accessed instead of the 2D texture target.

Dependent Alpha-Red Texturing

The `GL_DEPENDENT_AR_TEXTURE_2D_NV` texture shader operation accesses the texture unit's 2D texture target using the coordinates $\langle a,r \rangle$, where a and r are the alpha and red components of the color fetched in the previous texture shader stage specified by the value of `GL_PREVIOUS_TEXTURE_INPUT_NV`. The result of the texture access becomes both the RGBA result and texture shader result.

Dependent Green-Blue Texturing

The `GL_DEPENDENT_GB_TEXTURE_2D_NV` texture shader operation accesses the texture unit's 2D texture target using the coordinates $\langle g,b \rangle$, where g and b are the green and blue components of the color fetched in the previous texture shader stage specified by the value of `GL_PREVIOUS_TEXTURE_INPUT_NV`. The result of the texture access becomes both the RGBA result and texture shader result.

Dot Product

The `GL_DOT_PRODUCT_NV` texture shader operation calculates a 3D dot product between the texture coordinates $\langle s,t,r \rangle$ and the result of a previous texture shader stage, and produces a floating-point shader result. The RGBA result is always $(0,0,0,0)$.

The exact dot product calculation depends on the type of the previous texture shader stage's result, which can be an RGBA color or a HILO pair. If the previous stage's result is an RGBA color for which all four components are signed, then the dot product d is given by

$$d = \langle s,t,r \rangle \cdot \left(R,G,B \right), \tag{6.3.3}$$

where R, G, and B are the red, green, and blue components of the color. If the previous stage's result is an RGBA color for which all four components are unsigned, then the dot product depends on the unsigned remapping mode corresponding to the current shader stage. The unsigned dot product remapping mode is specified by calling the **glTexEnvi** function with *pname* parameter `GL_RGBA_UNSIGNED_DOT_PRODUCT_MAPPING_NV`. The *param* parameter specifies either `GL_UNSIGNED_IDENTITY_NV` (the initial value) or `GL_EXPAND_NORMAL_NV`. If the unsigned dot product remapping mode is set to `GL_UNSIGNED_IDENTITY_NV`, then the dot product d is calculated using Equation (6.3.3). If the unsigned dot product remapping mode is set to `GL_EXPAND_NORMAL_NV`, then the dot product d is calculated using the equation

$$d = \langle s,t,r \rangle \cdot \left(2R-1, 2G-1, 2B-1 \right). \tag{6.3.4}$$

If the previous stage's result is a HILO pair having unsigned components, then the dot product d is given by

$$d = \langle s,t,r \rangle \cdot \langle H,L,1 \rangle, \tag{6.3.5}$$

where H and L are the HI and LO components of the shader result. If the previous stage's result is a HILO pair having signed components, then the dot product d is given by

$$d = \langle s,t,r \rangle \cdot \left\langle H,L,\sqrt{\max\left(0,1-H^2-L^2\right)} \right\rangle. \tag{6.3.6}$$

This allows the HI and LO components to specify the x and y coordinates of a vector that is assumed to lie in the positive z hemisphere and have unit length.

Dot Product Texture 2D

The GL_DOT_PRODUCT_TEXTURE_2D_NV texture shader operation calculates a dot product in exactly the same manner as the GL_DOT_PRODUCT_NV operation. The GL_DOT_PROD-UCT_TEXTURE_2D_NV operation must be immediately preceded by an additional GL_DOT_PRODUCT_NV operation. The results of the two dot products are combined to form texture coordinates $\langle s,t \rangle$, where s is the result of the preceding stage's dot product, and t is the result of the current stage's dot product. These coordinates are then used to access the texture unit's 2D texture target. The result of the texture access becomes both the RGBA result and texture shader result.

Dot Product Texture Rectangle

The GL_DOT_PRODUCT_TEXTURE_RECTANGLE_NV texture shader operation calculates a dot product in exactly the same manner as the GL_DOT_PRODUCT_NV operation. The GL_DOT_PRODUCT_TEXTURE_RECTANGLE_NV operation must be immediately preceded by an additional GL_DOT_PRODUCT_NV operation. The results of the two dot products are combined to form texture coordinates $\langle s,t \rangle$, where s is the result of the preceding stage's dot product, and t is the result of the current stage's dot product. These coordinates are then used to access the texture unit's rectangle texture target. The result of the texture access becomes both the RGBA result and texture shader result.

Dot Product Texture Cube Map

The GL_DOT_PRODUCT_TEXTURE_CUBE_MAP_NV texture shader operation calculates a dot product in exactly the same manner as the GL_DOT_PRODUCT_NV operation. The GL_DOT_PRODUCT_TEXTURE_CUBE_MAP_NV operation must be immediately preceded by two additional GL_DOT_PRODUCT_NV operations. The results of the three dot products are combined to form texture coordinates $\langle s,t,r \rangle$, where s is the result of the first of the three stage's dot products, t is the result of the preceding stage's dot product, and r is the result of the current stage's dot product. These coordinates are then used to access the texture unit's cube map texture target. The result of the texture access becomes both the RGBA result and texture shader result.

Dot Product Reflect Cube Map

The GL_DOT_PRODUCT_REFLECT_CUBE_MAP_NV texture shader operation calculates a dot product and combines it with two preceding dot products to form a 3D normal vector **N**. The GL_DOT_PRODUCT_REFLECT_CUBE_MAP_NV operation must be immediately preceded by two additional GL_DOT_PRODUCT_NV operations or by a GL_DOT_PRODUCT_NV operation followed by a GL_DOT_PRODUCT_DIFFUSE_CUBE_MAP_NV operation. The results of the three dot products are combined to form the vector $\langle N_x, N_y, N_z \rangle$, where N_x is the result of the first of the three stage's dot products, N_y is the result of the preceding stage's dot product, and N_z is the result of the current stage's dot product. An eye vector $\mathbf{E} = \langle E_x, E_y, E_z \rangle$ is assembled using the q texture coordinates associated with the three dot product stages. E_x is given by the q coordinate of the first of the three stages, E_y is given by the q coordinate of the preceding stage, and E_z is given by the q coordinate of the current stage. A 3D reflection vector **R** is calculated using the equation

$$R = 2\frac{\mathbf{N} \cdot \mathbf{E}}{\mathbf{N} \cdot \mathbf{N}} \mathbf{N} - \mathbf{E}. \tag{6.3.7}$$

The coordinates $\langle R_x, R_y, R_z \rangle$ are then used to access the texture unit's cube map texture target. The result of the texture access becomes both the RGBA result and texture shader result. (See the environment-mapped bump mapping application in the Useful Tips section for an example using the GL_DOT_PRODUCT_REFLECT_CUBE_MAP_NV operation.)

Dot Product Constant Eye Reflect Cube Map

The GL_DOT_PRODUCT_CONST_EYE_REFLECT_CUBE_MAP_NV texture shader operation calculates the third dot product in a three-stage sequence in the same manner as the GL_DOT_PRODUCT_REFLECT_CUBE_MAP_NV operation. The difference is that the eye vector **E** is not assembled from the q coordinates of the three stages involved, but is instead given by the constant eye vector associated with the current stage. The constant eye vector is specified by calling the **glTexEnvfv** function with *pname* parameter GL_CONST_EYE_NV.

Dot Product Diffuse Cube Map

The GL_DOT_PRODUCT_DIFFUSE_CUBE_MAP_NV texture shader operation may be the second operation performed in a three-stage sequence beginning with a GL_DOT_PRODUCT_NV operation and ending with a GL_DOT_PRODUCT_REFLECT_CUBE_MAP_NV or GL_DOT_PRODUCT_CONST_EYE_REFLECT_CUBE_MAP_NV operation. The GL_DOT_PRODUCT_DIFFUSE_CUBE_MAP_NV operation calculates a dot product in exactly the same manner as the GL_DOT_PRODUCT_NV operation. It then uses the coordinates $\langle N_x, N_y, N_z \rangle$ resulting from the three dot products (with one occurring in the following stage) to access the texture unit's cube map texture target. The result of the texture access becomes both the RGBA result and texture shader result.

Dot Product Depth Replace

The GL_DOT_PRODUCT_DEPTH_REPLACE_NV texture shader operation calculates a dot product in exactly the same manner as the GL_DOT_PRODUCT_NV operation. The GL_DOT_PRODUCT_DEPTH_REPLACE_NV operation must be immediately preceded by an additional

GL_DOT_PRODUCT_NV operation. The results of the two dot products are then combined to calculate a new fragment depth z using the equation

$$z = \frac{d_0}{d_1}, \tag{6.3.8}$$

where d_0 is the dot product result of the preceding stage, and d_1 is the dot product result of the current stage. The fragment's depth in window coordinates (where depth values normally fall in the range [0,1]) is replaced by the value of z. If z falls outside the near and far depth range values (set using the **glDepthRange** function), then the fragment is discarded. The RGBA result is always (0,0,0,0), and the texture shader result is invalid. At most, one texture shader stage may use the GL_DOT_PRODUCT_DEPTH_REPLACE_NV operation.

TEXTURE ENVIRONMENT

In many cases, a texture shader stage does not produce a useful RGBA color result, but instead produces a texture shader result that is used in a subsequent stage. An application may indicate that it wishes to ignore the RGBA result for any texture unit by specifying a texture environment mode of GL_NONE by calling the **glTexEnvi** function with *target* parameter GL_TEXTURE_ENV and *pname* parameter GL_TEXTURE_ENV_MODE. When the texture environment mode is GL_NONE, the incoming color is passed through to the next texture unit, unaltered.

When texture shaders are enabled and the texture shader operation for a particular texture unit is GL_NONE, GL_CULL_FRAGMENT_NV, GL_DOT_PRODUCT_NV, or GL_DOT_PRODUCT_DEPTH_REPLACE_NV, the texture environment always operates as if its mode is GL_NONE.

If the base internal format of the texture accessed by a particular texture unit is GL_HILO_NV, GL_DSDT_NV, or GL_DSDT_MAG_NV, then the texture environment always operates as if its mode is GL_NONE, regardless of whether texture shaders are enabled. If the base internal format of the texture accessed is GL_DSDT_MAG_INTENSITY_NV, then the texture environment for the corresponding texture unit operates as if the base internal format is GL_INTENSITY.

Because RGBA color components may be signed, its possible that the blending factors used in some of the texture environment functions could fall outside the range [0,1] and that the sum of two components could fall outside the range [−1,1]. To prevent this, the GL_DECAL, GL_BLEND, and GL_ADD texture environment functions are redefined according to the rules listed in Table 6.3.7.

TABLE 6.3.7 The calculations performed by the texture environment functions GL_DECAL, GL_BLEND, and GL_ADD when the texture map has one of the listed base internal formats, and the GL_NV_texture_shader extension is present. The color **F** is the incoming fragment color, **T** is the filtered texel color, **C** is the texture environment constant color, and **E** is the color output by the texture environment. The subscripts R, G, B, A, L, and I represent the red, green, blue, alpha, luminance, and intensity components, respectively. Primed components are clamped to 0 so that they are always nonnegative. The *clamp* function clamps to the range $[-1,1]$.

Base Internal Format	GL_DECAL	GL_BLEND	GL_ADD
GL_ALPHA	$E_R = F_R$	$E_R = F_R$	$E_R = F_R$
	$E_G = F_G$	$E_G = F_G$	$E_G = F_G$
	$E_B = F_B$	$E_B = F_B$	$E_B = F_B$
	$E_A = F_A$	$E_A = F_A T_A$	$E_A = F_A T_A$
GL_LUMINANCE 1	$E_R = F_R$	$E_R = F_R(1-T'_L)+C_R T'_L$	$E_R = clamp(F_R + T_L)$
	$E_G = F_G$	$E_G = F_G(1-T'_L)+C_G T'_L$	$E_G = clamp(F_G + T_L)$
	$E_B = F_B$	$E_B = F_B(1-T'_L)+C_B T'_L$	$E_B = clamp(F_B + T_L)$
	$E_A = F_A$	$E_A = F_A$	$E_A = F_A$
GL_LUMINANCE_ ALPHA 2	$E_R = F_R$	$E_R = F_R(1-T'_L)+C_R T'_L$	$E_R = clamp(F_R + T_L)$
	$E_G = F_G$	$E_G = F_G(1-T'_L)+C_G T'_L$	$E_G = clamp(F_G + T_L)$
	$E_B = F_B$	$E_B = F_B(1-T'_L)+C_B T'_L$	$E_B = clamp(F_B + T_L)$
	$E_A = F_A$	$E_A = F_A T_A$	$E_A = F_A T_A$
GL_INTENSITY	$E_R = F_R$	$E_R = F_R(1-T'_I)+C_R T'_I$	$E_R = clamp(F_R + T_I)$
	$E_G = F_G$	$E_G = F_G(1-T'_I)+C_G T'_I$	$E_G = clamp(F_G + T_I)$
	$E_B = F_B$	$E_B = F_B(1-T'_I)+C_B T'_I$	$E_B = clamp(F_B + T_I)$
	$E_A = F_A$	$E_A = F_A T_I$	$E_A = clamp(F_A + T_I)$
GL_RGB 3	$E_R = T_R$	$E_R = F_R(1-T'_R)+C_R T'_R$	$E_R = clamp(F_R + T_R)$
	$E_G = T_G$	$E_G = F_G(1-T'_G)+C_G T'_G$	$E_G = clamp(F_G + T_G)$
	$E_B = T_B$	$E_B = F_B(1-T'_B)+C_B T'_B$	$E_B = clamp(F_B + T_B)$
	$E_A = F_A$	$E_A = F_A$	$E_A = F_A$
GL_RGBA 4	$E_R = F_R(1-T'_A)+T_R T'_A$	$E_R = F_R(1-T'_R)+C_R T'_R$	$E_R = clamp(F_R + T_R)$
	$E_G = F_G(1-T'_A)+T_G T'_A$	$E_G = F_G(1-T'_G)+C_G T'_G$	$E_G = clamp(F_G + T_G)$
	$E_B = F_B(1-T'_A)+T_B T'_A$	$E_B = F_B(1-T'_B)+C_B T'_B$	$E_B = clamp(F_B + T_B)$
	$E_A = F_A$	$E_A = F_A T_A$	$E_A = F_A T_A$

USEFUL TIPS

How do I use texture shaders to perform environment-mapped bump mapping?

Environment-mapped bump mapping is performed by calculating the reflection of the direction to the camera at each fragment and using the resulting vector to fetch a sample from a cube texture map containing an image of the environment. This environment cube map is typically stored in world space so that it can be generated without any dependency on a particular model's local coordinate system.

The reflection vector calculation depends on the normal vector fetched from the bump map at each fragment. Since samples from the bump map are stored in tangent space, we must transform them into world space before the texture shader can determine the appropriate reflection vector. This is accomplished by calculating a 3×3 transformation matrix at each vertex that maps tangent space to world space and storing its rows in three sets of texture coordinates. Three dot products are evaluated in the texture shader stages to perform the matrix-vector multiply needed to transform the normal vector into world space for each fragment.

Let $\mathbf{M}$ be the 3×3 matrix that transforms 3D vectors from model space to world space. Typically, the normal vector $\mathbf{N}$, the tangent vector $\mathbf{T}$, and the binormal vector $\mathbf{B}$ (where $\mathbf{B} = \pm \mathbf{N} \times \mathbf{T}$) are available in model space at each vertex. The matrix $\mathbf{W}$ that transforms 3D vectors from tangent space to world space is given by

$$\mathbf{W} = \mathbf{M} \begin{bmatrix} T_x & B_x & N_x \\ T_y & B_y & N_y \\ T_z & B_z & N_z \end{bmatrix}. \tag{6.3.9}$$

The rows of the matrix $\mathbf{W}$ are stored in the s, t, and r texture coordinates for texture units 1, 2, and 3, respectively, for each vertex. As shown in Table 6.3.8, dot products are performed in these texture shader stages in order to transform the normal vector fetched in stage 0 into world space.

When reflecting the direction to camera $\mathbf{E}$ (the eye vector) across the world-space normal vector at each fragment, we may choose to use either a direction to camera calculated at each vertex or a constant direction to camera. The GL_DOT_PRODUCT_REFLECT_ CUBE_MAP_NV texture shader operation assembles the x, y, and z coordinates of the 3D eye vector from the q texture coordinates corresponding to texture units 1, 2, and 3, respectively. These components of the eye vector must be calculated in world space at each vertex and are obtained by evaluating the equation

$$\mathbf{E} = \mathbf{M}(\mathbf{C} - \mathbf{V}), \tag{6.3.10}$$

where $\mathbf{C}$ is the model-space camera position and $\mathbf{V}$ is the model-space vertex position. The vector $\mathbf{E}$ does not need to be normalized since its reflection is used to sample a cube texture map for which vector length is irrelevant. As an alternative to calculating the eye vector at each vertex, a constant eye vector may be used by specifying the texture shader operation GL_DOT_PRODUCT_CONST_EYE_REFLECT_CUBE_MAP_NV for stage 3. In this case, the eye vector **E** is given by the value of GL_CONST_EYE_NV for texture unit 3.

The world-space normal vector calculated in stages 1, 2, and 3 may optionally be used to fetch a sample from a diffuse cube texture map in stage 2. If the texture shader operation for stage 2 is GL_DOT_PRODUCT_DIFFUSE_CUBE_MAP_NV, then the transformed normal vector is used to access the cube map bound to texture unit 2. The result of the cube map fetches in stages 2 and 3 can be added in the texture environment or in register combiners. If no diffuse cube map fetch is desired, then the texture shader operation for stage 2 should be set to GL_DOT_PRODUCT_NV.

TABLE 6.3.8   Texture maps, texture shader operations, previous texture inputs, and texture coordinate values used to perform environment-mapped bump mapping. Stage 2 differs in the two cases that (a) a diffuse lighting cube map is used, and (b) only the environment cube map is used. Stage 3 differs in the two cases that (1) the eye vector is calculated at each vertex, and (2) the eye vector is constant. The matrix **W** is the 3×3 matrix that transforms normal vectors from tangent space to world space, and the vector **E** is the world-space direction to the camera.

Stage	Texture Map	Shader Operation	Previous Texture Input	Texture Coordinates
0	Bump map	GL_TEXTURE_2D	—	Ordinary 2D texture coordinates
1	None	GL_DOT_PRODUCT_NV	GL_TEXTURE0_ARB	
2	(a) Diffuse lighting cube map (b) None	(a) GL_DOT_PRODUCT_DIFFUSE_CUBE_MAP_NV (b) GL_DOT_PRODUCT_NV	GL_TEXTURE0_ARB	
3	Environment cube map	(1) GL_DOT_PRODUCT_REFLECT_CUBE_MAP_NV (2) GL_DOT_PRODUCT_CONST_EYE_REFLECT_CUBE_MAP_NV	GL_TEXTURE0_ARB	

How do I use texture shaders to render bump-mapped specular reflection?

When rendering bump-mapped specular reflection, the normal vector **N** used for each fragment is typically fetched from a texture map (the bump map), and a tangent-space halfway vector **H** is interpolated among values calculated at each vertex. Even though the halfway vector may be unit length at each vertex, it is invariably shortened during interpolation yielding an undesirable darkening of the specular reflection within a polygon's interior.

A solution to this problem is to construct a two-dimensional texture map that is accessed by setting $s = \mathbf{N} \cdot \mathbf{H}$ and $t = \mathbf{H} \cdot \mathbf{H}$. The pixels in the texture map itself store the specular reflection intensity values $\left[(\mathbf{N} \cdot \mathbf{H}) / \sqrt{\mathbf{H} \cdot \mathbf{H}} \right]^r$, where r is an arbitrarily chosen specular exponent. By precomputing the specular intensities for values of $\mathbf{N} \cdot \mathbf{H}$ and $\mathbf{H} \cdot \mathbf{H}$ in the range $[0,1]$, we reduce the normalization of $\mathbf{H}$ and computation of the specular reflection intensity to a single texture fetch during rasterization.

The values of $\mathbf{N} \cdot \mathbf{H}$ and $\mathbf{H} \cdot \mathbf{H}$ are calculated by performing two dot product operations in the texture shader stages. The exact texture shader operations used for each texture shader stage are summarized in Table 6.3.9. The dot product $\mathbf{N} \cdot \mathbf{H}$ is calculated in Stage 2, and the dot product $\mathbf{H} \cdot \mathbf{H}$ is calculated in Stage 3. The two dot products are combined to perform a 2D texture fetch to obtain the specular reflection intensity.

TABLE 6.3.9 Texture maps, texture shader operations, previous texture inputs, and texture coordinate values used to perform bump-mapped specular reflection. The value of GL_RGBA_UNSIGNED_DOT_PRODUCT_MAPPING_NV for stages 2 and 3 should be set to GL_EXPAND_NORMAL_NV.

Stage	Texture Map	Shader Operation	Previous Texture Input	Texture Coordinates
0	Bump map	GL_TEXTURE_2D	—	Ordinary 2D texture coordinates
1	None	GL_PASS_THROUGH_NV	—	Halfway vector **H** with components stored in the range [0,1]
2	None	GL_DOT_PRODUCT_NV	GL_TEXTURE0_ARB	Halfway vector **H** with components stored in the range [−1,1]
3	Specular intensity map	GL_DOT_PRODUCT_TEXTURE_2D_NV	GL_TEXTURE1_ARB	Halfway vector **H** with components stored in the range [−1,1]

EXTENDED FUNCTIONS

■ **glEnable, glDisable, glIsEnabled**—Extended to enable/disable texture shaders.

Prototypes

```
void glEnable(GLenum cap);
void glDisable(GLenum cap);
GLboolean glIsEnabled(GLenum cap);
```

Extended Parameters

cap   Specifies a GL capability. To enable or disable texture shaders, or to query whether texture shaders are enabled, this should be GL_TEXTURE_SHADER_NV.

Description

Texture shaders are enabled and disabled by calling the **glEnable** and **glDisable** functions. Calling the **glIsEnabled** function with the parameter GL_TEXTURE_SHADER_NV returns a value indicating whether texture shaders are enabled.

■ **glTexEnv{if}**—Extended to allow specification of texture shader state.

Prototypes

```
void glTexEnvi(GLenum target, GLenum pname, GLint param);
void glTexEnvf(GLenum target, GLenum pname, GLfloat param);
```

Extended Parameters

target   Specifies a texture environment. When texture shader state is being specified, this should be GL_TEXTURE_SHADER_NV.

pname   Specifies the symbolic name of a texture environment parameter. When *target* is GL_TEXTURE_SHADER_NV, this may be one of the values listed in Description.

param   Specifies the value of the texture environment parameter. Accepted values depend on the value of the *pname* parameter and are listed in Description.

Description

The **glTexEnv{if}** function is used to specify single-valued texture shader parameters. The *target* parameter must be set to GL_TEXTURE_SHADER_NV when specifying texture shader parameters, and the *pname* parameter may be one of the following values:

GL_SHADER_OPERATION_NV

The *param* parameter specifies the texture shader operation for the currently active texture unit. Accepted values are listed in Table 6.3.4. The initial value is GL_NONE.

GL_PREVIOUS_TEXTURE_INPUT_NV

The *param* parameter specifies the previous texture input for the currently active texture unit. The *param* parameter must be GL_TEXTURE*i*_ARB, where *i* is less than the index of the currently active texture unit. The initial value is GL_TEXTURE0_ARB.

GL_RGBA_UNSIGNED_DOT_PRODUCT_MAPPING_NV

The *param* parameter specifies the dot product mapping mode applied to unsigned RGBA texture components for the currently active texture unit. Accepted values are GL_UNSIGNED_IDENTITY_NV and GL_EXPAND_NORMAL_NV. If *param* is GL_UNSIGNED_IDENTITY_NV, then unsigned color components are not altered before the dot product operation. If *param* is GL_EXPAND_NORMAL_NV, then unsigned color components are expanded to the range [−1,1] before the dot product operation. The initial value is GL_UNSIGNED_IDENTITY_NV.

`GL_OFFSET_TEXTURE_SCALE_NV`

The *param* parameter specifies the offset texture scale for the currently active texture unit. The initial value is 1.0.

`GL_OFFSET_TEXTURE_BIAS_NV`

The *param* parameter specifies the offset texture bias for the currently active texture unit. The initial value is 0.0.

Errors

`GL_INVALID_OPERATION` is generated if *pname* is `GL_SHADER_OPERATION_NV`, and *param* specifies a texture shader operation that cannot be assigned to the active texture unit.

`GL_INVALID_OPERATION` is generated if *pname* is `GL_PREVIOUS_TEXTURE_INPUT_NV`, and *param* specifies a texture unit greater than or equal to the index of the active texture unit.

■ **glTexEnviv**—Extended to allow specification of texture shader state.

Prototype

```
void glTexEnviv(GLenum target, GLenum pname, const GLint *params);
```

Extended Parameters

target   Specifies a texture environment. When texture shader state is being specified, this should be `GL_TEXTURE_SHADER_NV`.

pname   Specifies the symbolic name of a texture environment parameter. When *target* is `GL_TEXTURE_SHADER_NV`, this may be `GL_CULL_MODES_NV`.

params   Specifies a pointer to an array containing the value of the texture environment parameter. When *pname* is `GL_CULL_MODES_NV`, this should point to an array of four values that are either `GL_LESS` or `GL_GEQUAL`.

Description

The **glTexEnviv** function is used to specify the fragment cull modes for the currently active texture unit. When *pname* is `GL_CULL_MODES_NV`, the *params* parameter points to an array containing four values that correspond to the culling mode for the *s*, *t*, *r*, and *q* texture coordinates. Each of the four values may be `GL_LESS` or `GL_GEQUAL`. The initial value is `GL_GEQUAL` for all four texture coordinates.

■ **glTexEnvfv**—Extended to allow specification of texture shader state.

Prototype

```
void glTexEnvfv(GLenum target, GLenum pname, const GLfloat *params);
```

Extended Parameters

target   Specifies a texture environment. When texture shader state is being specified, this should be `GL_TEXTURE_SHADER_NV`.

pname   Specifies the symbolic name of a texture environment parameter. When *target* is GL_TEXTURE_SHADER_NV, this may be GL_OFFSET_TEXTURE_MATRIX_NV or GL_CONST_EYE_NV.

params   Specifies a pointer to an array containing the value of the texture environment parameter. The meaning of the values in the array depend on the value of the *pname* parameter (see Description).

Description

The **glTexEnvfv** function is used to specify multiple-component texture shader parameters. When *target* is GL_TEXTURE_SHADER_NV, the *pname* parameter may be one of the following values:

GL_OFFSET_TEXTURE_MATRIX_NV

The *params* parameter points to an array containing the four entries of the 2×2 offset texture matrix in column-major order. The initial value is the identity matrix

$$\begin{bmatrix} 1 & 0 \\ 0 & 1 \end{bmatrix}.$$

GL_CONST_EYE_NV

The *params* parameter points to an array containing the three components of the constant eye position. The initial value is $\langle 0,0,-1 \rangle$.

■ **glGetTexEnv{if}v**—Extended to allow retrieval of texture shader state.

Prototypes

```
void glGetTexEnviv(GLenum target, GLenum pname, GLint *params);
void glGetTexEnvfv(GLenum target, GLenum pname, GLfloat *params);
```

Extended Parameters

target   Specifies a texture environment. When texture shader state is being retrieved, this should be GL_TEXTURE_SHADER_NV.

pname   Specifies the symbolic name of a texture environment parameter to return. When *target* is GL_TEXTURE_SHADER_NV, this may be one of the values listed in Description.

Description

The **glGetTexEnv{if}v** function is used to retrieved texture shader state for the currently active texture unit. When *target* is GL_TEXTURE_SHADER_NV, the *pname* parameter may be one of the following values:

GL_SHADER_OPERATION_NV

The texture shader operation is returned.

GL_PREVIOUS_TEXTURE_INPUT_NV
> The previous texture input is returned.

GL_RGBA_UNSIGNED_DOT_PRODUCT_MAPPING_NV
> The mapping mode applied to unsigned RGBA components before a dot product operation is returned.

GL_OFFSET_TEXTURE_SCALE_NV
> The offset texture scale is returned.

GL_OFFSET_TEXTURE_BIAS_NV
> The offset texture bias is returned.

GL_OFFSET_TEXTURE_MATRIX_NV
> The four entries of the offset texture matrix are returned in column-major order.

GL_CONST_EYE_NV
> The three components of the constant eye position are returned.

GL_SHADER_CONSISTENT_NV
> A Boolean value indicating whether the texture shader stage is consistent is returned.

■ **glTexImage1D**, **glTexImage2D**—Extended to support new texture formats.

Prototypes

> void **glTexImage1D**(GLenum *target*, GLint *level*, GLint *internalFormat*,
>   GLsizei *width*, GLint *border*, GLenum *format*, GLenum *type*,
>   const GLvoid **pixels*);
> void **glTexImage2D**(GLenum *target*, GLint *level*, GLint *internalFormat*,
>   GLsizei *width*, GLsizei *height*, GLint *border*, GLenum *format*,
>   GLenum *type*, const GLvoid **pixels*);

Extended Parameters

internalFormat   Specifies the internal format in which the texture image is stored. Accepted values are listed in Tables 6.3.2 and 6.3.3.

format   Specifies the component format of the texture image pointed to by the *pixels* parameter. May be GL_HILO_NV, GL_DSDT_NV, GL_DSDT_MAG_NV, or GL_DSDT_MAG_VIB_NV.

type   Specifies the data type of the texture image pointed to by the *pixels* parameter. If the *format* parameter is GL_DSDT_MAG_VIB_NV, this may be GL_UNSIGNED_INT_S8_S8_8_8_NV or GL_UNSIGNED_INT_8_8_S8_S8_REV_NV.

Description

The **glTexImage1D** and **glTexImage2D** functions can be used to load texture images having formats defined by the GL_NV_texture_shader extension. The internal format specified by the *internalFormat* parameter must have a base format that matches the image format specified by the *format* parameter.

Errors

GL_INVALID_OPERATION is generated if *format* is GL_HILO_NV, and *internalFormat* is not GL_HILO_NV, GL_HILO16_NV, GL_SIGNED_HILO_NV, or GL_SIGNED_HILO16_NV; or if *internalFormat* is GL_HILO_NV, GL_HILO16_NV, GL_SIGNED_HILO_NV, or GL_SIGNED_ HILO16_NV, and *format* is not GL_HILO_NV.

GL_INVALID_OPERATION is generated if *format* is GL_DSDT_NV, and *internalFormat* is not GL_DSDT_NV or GL_DSDT8_NV; or if *internalFormat* is GL_DSDT_NV or GL_DSDT8_NV, and *format* is not GL_DSDT_NV.

GL_INVALID_OPERATION is generated if *format* is GL_DSDT_MAG_NV, and *internalFormat* is not GL_DSDT_MAG_NV or GL_DSDT8_MAG8_NV; or if *internalFormat* is GL_DSDT_MAG_NV or GL_DSDT8_MAG8_NV, and *format* is not GL_DSDT_MAG_NV.

GL_INVALID_OPERATION is generated if *format* is GL_DSDT_MAG_VIB_NV, and *internalFormat* is not GL_DSDT_MAG_INTENSITY_NV or GL_DSDT8_MAG8_INTENSITY8_NV; or if *internalFormat* is GL_DSDT_MAG_INTENSITY_NV or GL_DSDT8_MAG8_INTENSITY8_NV, and *format* is not GL_DSDT_MAG_VIB_NV.

GL_INVALID_OPERATION is generated if *type* is GL_UNSIGNED_INT_S8_S8_8_8_NV or GL_UNSIGNED_INT_8_8_S8_S8_REV_NV, and *format* is not GL_DSDT_MAG_VIB_NV.

■ **glTexSubImage1D**, **glTexSubImage2D**—Extended to support new texture formats.

Prototypes

```
void glTexSubImage1D(GLenum target, GLint level, GLint xoffset,
    GLsizei width, GLenum format, GLenum type, const GLvoid *pixels);
void glTexSubImage2D(GLenum target, GLint level, GLint xoffset,
    GLint yoffset, GLsizei width, GLsizei height, GLenum format,
    GLenum type, const GLvoid *pixels);
```

Extended Parameters

format   Specifies the component format of the texture image pointed to by the *pixels* parameter. May be GL_HILO_NV, GL_DSDT_NV, GL_DSDT_MAG_NV, or GL_DSDT_MAG_VIB_NV.

type   Specifies the data type of the texture image pointed to by the *pixels* parameter. If the *format* parameter is GL_DSDT_MAG_VIB_NV, this may be GL_UNSIGNED_INT_S8_S8_8_8_NV or GL_UNSIGNED_INT_ 8_8_S8_S8_REV_NV.

Description

The **glTexSubImage1D** and **glTexSubImage2D** functions can be used to load texture subimages having formats defined by the GL_NV_texture_shader extension. The *format* parameter must match the base internal format of the texture.

Errors

GL_INVALID_OPERATION is generated if the texture's base internal format is GL_HILO_NV, and *format* is not GL_HILO_NV.

GL_INVALID_OPERATION is generated if the texture's base internal format is GL_DSDT_NV, and *format* is not GL_DSDT_NV.

GL_INVALID_OPERATION is generated if the texture's base internal format is GL_DSDT_MAG_NV, and *format* is not GL_DSDT_MAG_NV.

GL_INVALID_OPERATION is generated if the texture's base internal format is GL_DSDT_MAG_INTENSITY_NV, and *format* is not GL_DSDT_MAG_VIB_NV.

■ **glCopyTexImage1D, glCopyTexImage2D**—Extended to support new texture formats.

Prototypes

```
void glCopyTexImage1D(GLenum target, GLint level, GLenum internalFormat,
    GLint x, GLint y, GLsizei width, GLint border);
void glCopyTexImage2D(GLenum target, GLint level, GLenum internalFormat,
    GLint x, GLint y, GLsizei width, GLsizei height, GLint border);
```

Extended Parameters

internalFormat   Specifies the internal format in which the texture image is stored. This may be one of the values listed in Table 6.3.3.

Description

The **glCopyTexImage1D** and **glCopyTexImage2D** functions can be used to copy texture images from the current read buffer and store them using internal formats defined by the GL_NV_texture_shader extension.

■ **glGetTexImage**—Extended to support new texture formats.

Prototype

```
void glGetTexImage(GLenum target, GLint level, GLenum format,
    GLenum type, GLvoid *pixels);
```

Extended Parameters

format   Specifies the format in which to return the texture image. May be GL_HILO_NV, GL_DSDT_NV, GL_DSDT_MAG_NV, or GL_DSDT_MAG_VIB_NV.

type   Specifies the data type of the returned texture image. If the *format* parameter is GL_DSDT_MAG_VIB_NV, this may be GL_UNSIGNED_INT_S8_S8_8_8_NV or GL_UNSIGNED_INT_8_8_S8_S8_REV_NV.

Description

The **glGetTexImage** function can be used to retrieve texture images that are stored in one of the formats defined by the GL_NV_texture_shader extension. The value of the *format* parameter must match the internal format of the texture image being retrieved.

Errors

GL_INVALID_OPERATION is generated if *format* is a color format, and the internal format of the texture is not a color format.

GL_INVALID_OPERATION is generated if *format* is GL_HILO_NV, and the base internal format of the texture is not GL_HILO_NV.

GL_INVALID_OPERATION is generated if *format* is GL_DSDT_NV, and the base internal format of the texture is not GL_DSDT_NV.

GL_INVALID_OPERATION is generated if *format* is GL_DSDT_MAG_NV, and the base internal format of the texture is not GL_DSDT_MAG_NV.

GL_INVALID_OPERATION is generated if *format* is GL_DSDT_MAG_VIB_NV, and the base internal format of the texture is not GL_DSDT_MAG_INTENSITY_NV.

GL_INVALID_OPERATION is generated if *type* is GL_UNSIGNED_INT_S8_S8_8_8_NV or GL_UNSIGNED_INT_8_8_S8_S8_REV_NV, and *format* is not GL_DSDT_MAG_VIB_NV.

■ **glTexParameterfv**—Extended to allow specification of unclamped texture border values.

Prototype

```
void glTexParameterfv(GLenum target, GLenum pname,
    const GLfloat *params);
```

Extended Parameters

pname   Specifies the symbolic name of a texture parameter. May be GL_TEXTURE_BORDER_VALUES_NV.

Description

The **glTexParameterfv** function is used to specify texture border values. When the *pname* parameter is GL_TEXTURE_BORDER_VALUES_NV, the *params* parameter points to an array containing the four texture border values. These values are not clamped to the range [0,1]. The texture border values are equivalent to the texture border color components, and the same values are returned by the **glGetTexParameterfv** function whether the *pname* parameter is GL_TEXTURE_BORDER_VALUES_NV or GL_TEXTURE_BORDER_COLOR.

■ **glGetTexParameterfv**—Extended to allow retrieval of the texture border values.

Prototype

```
void glGetTexParameterfv(GLenum target, GLenum pname,
    GLfloat *params);
```

Extended Parameters

pname   Specifies the symbolic name of the texture parameter to return. May be GL_TEXTURE_BORDER_VALUES_NV.

Description

The **glGetTexParameterfv** function can be used to retrieve the texture border values. When the *pname* parameter is GL_TEXTURE_BORDER_VALUES_NV, the four texture border values are returned in the array pointed to by the *params* parameter. The texture border values are equivalent to the texture border color components, and the same values are returned by the **glGetTexParameterfv** function whether the *pname* parameter is GL_TEXTURE_BORDER_VALUES_NV or GL_TEXTURE_BORDER_COLOR.

■ **glGetTexLevelParameteriv**—Extended to allow retrieval of internal component sizes of new texture formats.

Prototype

```
void glGetTexLevelParameteriv(GLenum target, GLint level,
    GLenum pname, GLint *params);
```

Extended Parameters

pname   Specifies the symbolic name of the texture parameter to return. May be GL_TEXTURE_HI_SIZE_NV, GL_TEXTURE_LO_SIZE_NV, GL_TEXTURE_DS_SIZE_NV, GL_TEXTURE_DT_SIZE_NV, or GL_TEXTURE_MAG_SIZE_NV.

Description

The **glGetTexLevelParameteriv** function can be used to retrieve the internal component sizes of texture images stored in formats defined by the GL_NV_texture_shader extension. The *pname* parameter specifies which component size to return in the *params* parameter. The initial values are 0.

■ **glPixelTransferf**—Extended to allow specification of scale and bias values for new texture image component types.

Prototype

```
void glPixelTransferf(GLenum pname, GLfloat param);
```

Extended Parameters

pname   Specifies the symbolic name of a pixel transfer parameter. May be GL_HI_SCALE_NV, GL_HI_BIAS_NV, GL_LO_SCALE_NV, GL_LO_BIAS_

NV, GL_DS_SCALE_NV, GL_DS_BIAS_NV, GL_DT_SCALE_NV, GL_DT_
BIAS_NV, GL_MAGNITUDE_SCALE_NV, GL_MAGNITUDE_BIAS_NV, GL_
VIBRANCE_SCALE_NV, or GL_VIBRANCE_BIAS_NV.

Description

The **glPixelTransferf** function is used to specify scale and bias parameters that are applied when texture images having component types defined by the GL_NV_texture_shader extension are loaded. The *pname* parameter specifies a component type, and whether the scale or bias value is to be set. The initial scale values are 1.0, and the initial bias values are 0.0.

■ **glGetFloatv**—Extended to allow retrieval of scale and bias values for new texture image component types.

Prototype

   void **glGetFloatv**(GLenum *pname*, GLfloat *params*);

Extended Parameters

pname   Specifies the parameter to be returned. May be GL_HI_SCALE_NV,
                     GL_HI_BIAS_NV, GL_LO_SCALE_NV, GL_LO_BIAS_NV, GL_DS_SCALE_
                     NV, GL_DS_BIAS_NV, GL_DT_SCALE_NV, GL_DT_BIAS_NV,
                     GL_MAGNITUDE_SCALE_NV, GL_MAGNITUDE_BIAS_NV, GL_VIBRANCE_
                     SCALE_NV, or GL_VIBRANCE_BIAS_NV.

Description

The **glGetFloatv** function can be used to retrieve scale and bias parameters that are applied when texture images having component types defined by the GL_NV_texture_shader extension are loaded. The *pname* parameter specifies a component type and whether the scale or bias value is to be returned.

6.4   GL_NV_texture_shader2

OpenGL version required	OpenGL 1.1
Dependencies	Requires GL_NV_texture_shader
	Requires GL_EXT_texture3D
Promotions	—
Related extensions	GL_NV_texture_shader3

DISCUSSION

The GL_NV_texture_shader2 extension adds support for 3D textures to the texture shader functionality defined by the GL_NV_texture_shader extension. Two new texture shader operations are defined. The first performs a projective 3D texture access and is equivalent to conventional 3D texturing. The second combines the results of three dot product operations to form the texture coordinates used to perform a 3D texture access.

Texture Shader Operations

Each texture shader stage performs one of the operations listed in Table 6.3.4, defined by the GL_NV_texture_shader extension, or one of the new operations listed in Table 6.4.1. Table 6.4.2 summarizes the RGBA results and texture shader results for the additional texture shader operations defined by the GL_NV_texture_shader2 extension.

TABLE 6.4.1   Additional Texture Shader Operations and the Stages in Which They May be Specified

Texture Shader Operation	Stage 0	Stage 1	Stage 2	Stage 3
GL_TEXTURE_3D_EXT	•	•	•	•
GL_DOT_PRODUCT_TEXTURE_3D_NV				•

TABLE 6.4.2   Texture Shader Result Types

Texture Shader Operation	Shader Stage Result Type	Shader Stage Result Value	Texture Unit RGBA Color Result
GL_TEXTURE_3D_EXT	Matches 3D target	Filtered texel	Filtered texel if RGBA, else (0,0,0,0)
GL_DOT_PRODUCT_TEXTURE_3D_NV	Matches 2D target	Filtered texel	Filtered texel if RGBA, else (0,0,0,0)

Many operations require the texture shader result of a previous texture shader stage. The previous texture input (specified by calling the **glTexEnvi** function with *pname* parameter GL_PREVIOUS_TEXTURE_INPUT_NV) names a texture stage GL_TEXTURE*i*_ARB, where *i* is less than the index of the texture unit for which the previous texture input is being specified. Texture shader stage interdependencies for the new operations defined by the GL_NV_texture_shader2 extension are summarized in Table 6.4.3.

TABLE 6.4.3 Texture shader stage interdependencies. For the shader operation specified for stage *i*, any operations listed for stages *i* − 2, *i* − 1, or *i* + 1 must be performed. Also, any texture shader result type requirements listed for the stage corresponding to the previous texture input must be met. Otherwise, texture shader stage *i* is not consistent. RGBA and HILO formats for textures used as a previous input must not have mixed signs.

Texture Shader Operation for Stage i	Stage i - 2 Shader Operation	Stage i - 1 Shader Operation	Stage i + 1 Shader Operation	Previous Texture Input Result Types
GL_TEXTURE_3D_EXT	—	—	—	—
GL_DOT_PRODUCT_ TEXTURE_3D_NV	GL_DOT_ PRODUCT_NV	GL_DOT_ PRODUCT_NV	—	RGBA HILO

The effects of the new texture shader operations defined by the GL_NV_texture_ shader2 extension are described below.

3D Projective Texturing
The GL_TEXTURE_3D_EXT texture shader operation accesses the texture unit's 3D texture target using the coordinates ⟨*s*/*q*,*t*/*q*,*r*/*q*⟩. This is equivalent to conventional texturing when the 3D texture target is the highest priority target enabled. The result of the texture access becomes both the RGBA result and the texture shader result.

Dot Product Texture 3D
The GL_DOT_PRODUCT_TEXTURE_3D_NV texture shader operation calculates a dot product in exactly the same manner as the GL_DOT_PRODUCT_NV operation. The GL_DOT_PRODUCT_ TEXTURE_3D_NV operation must be immediately preceded by two additional GL_DOT_ PRODUCT_NV operations. The results of the three dot products are combined to form texture coordinates ⟨*s*,*t*,*r*⟩, where *s* is the result of the first of the three stage's dot products, *t* is the result of the preceding stage's dot product, and *r* is the result of the current stage's dot product. These coordinates are then used to access the texture unit's 3D texture target. The result of the texture access becomes both the RGBA result and texture shader result.

EXTENDED FUNCTIONS

■ **glTexEnvi**—Extended to allow specification of new texture shader operations.

Prototype
    void **glTexEnvi**(GLenum *target*, GLenum *pname*, GLint *param*);

Extended Parameters
param   Specifies the value of the texture parameter. When *target* is GL_ TEXTURE_SHADER_NV and *pname* is GL_SHADER_OPERATION_NV, this may be GL_TEXTURE_3D_EXT or GL_DOT_PRODUCT_TEXTURE_3D_NV.

Description

The **glTexEnvi** function is used to specify texture shader operations defined by the GL_NV_texture_shader2 extension. When the *target* parameter is GL_TEXTURE_SHADER_ NV and the *pname* parameter is GL_SHADER_OPERATION_NV, the *params* parameter specifies the texture shader operation for the currently active texture unit. The initial value is GL_NONE.

■ **glTexImage3DEXT**—Extended to support new texture formats.

Prototype

> void **glTexImage3DEXT**(GLenum *target*, GLint *level*, GLenum *internalFormat*,
>   GLsizei *width*, GLsizei *height*, GLsizei *depth*, GLint *border*,
>   GLenum *format*, GLenum *type*, const GLvoid **pixels*);

Extended Parameters

internalFormat   Specifies the internal format in which the texture image is stored. Accepted values are listed in Tables 6.3.2 and 6.3.3.

format   Specifies the component format of the texture image pointed to by the *pixels* parameter. May be GL_HILO_NV, GL_DSDT_NV, GL_DSDT_MAG_NV, or GL_DSDT_MAG_VIB_NV.

type   Specifies the data type of the texture image pointed to by the *pixels* parameter. If the *format* parameter is GL_DSDT_MAG_VIB_NV, this may be GL_UNSIGNED_INT_S8_S8_8_8_NV or GL_UNSIGNED_INT_ 8_8_S8_S8_REV_NV.

Description

The **glTexImage3DEXT** function can be used to load texture images having formats defined by the GL_NV_texture_shader extension. The internal format specified by the *internal-Format* parameter must have a base format that matches the image format specified by the *format* parameter.

Errors

GL_INVALID_OPERATION is generated if *format* is GL_HILO_NV, and *internalFormat* is not GL_HILO_NV, GL_HILO16_NV, GL_SIGNED_HILO_NV, or GL_SIGNED_HILO16_NV; or if *internalFormat* is GL_HILO_NV, GL_HILO16_NV, GL_SIGNED_HILO_NV, or GL_SIGNED_ HILO16_NV, and *format* is not GL_HILO_NV.

GL_INVALID_OPERATION is generated if *format* is GL_DSDT_NV, and *internalFormat* is not GL_DSDT_NV or GL_DSDT8_NV; or if *internalFormat* is GL_DSDT_NV or GL_DSDT8_NV, and *format* is not GL_DSDT_NV.

GL_INVALID_OPERATION is generated if *format* is GL_DSDT_MAG_NV, and *internalFormat* is not GL_DSDT_MAG_NV or GL_DSDT8_MAG8_NV; or if *internalFormat* is GL_DSDT_MAG_NV or GL_DSDT8_MAG8_NV, and *format* is not GL_DSDT_MAG_NV.

GL_INVALID_OPERATION is generated if *format* is GL_DSDT_MAG_VIB_NV, and *internalFormat* is not GL_DSDT_MAG_INTENSITY_NV or GL_DSDT8_MAG8_INTENSITY8_NV; or if *internalFormat* is GL_DSDT_MAG_INTENSITY_NV or GL_DSDT8_MAG8_INTENSITY8_NV, and *format* is not GL_DSDT_MAG_VIB_NV.

GL_INVALID_OPERATION is generated if *type* is GL_UNSIGNED_INT_S8_S8_8_8_NV or GL_UNSIGNED_INT_8_8_S8_S8_REV_NV, and *format* is not GL_DSDT_MAG_VIB_NV.

■ **glTexSubImage3DEXT**—Extended to support new texture formats.

Prototype

```
void glTexSubImage3DEXT(GLenum target, GLint level, GLint xoffset,
    GLint yoffset, GLint zoffset, GLsizei width, GLsizei height,
    GLsizei depth, GLenum format, GLenum type, const GLvoid *pixels);
```

Extended Parameters

format   Specifies the component format of the texture image pointed to by the *pixels* parameter. May be GL_HILO_NV, GL_DSDT_NV, GL_DSDT_MAG_NV, or GL_DSDT_MAG_VIB_NV.

type   Specifies the data type of the texture image pointed to by the *pixels* parameter. If the *format* parameter is GL_DSDT_MAG_VIB_NV, this may be GL_UNSIGNED_INT_S8_S8_8_8_NV or GL_UNSIGNED_INT_8_8_S8_S8_REV_NV.

Description

The **glTexSubImage3DEXT** function can be used to load texture subimages having formats defined by the GL_NV_texture_shader extension. The *format* parameter must match the base internal format of the texture.

Errors

GL_INVALID_OPERATION is generated if the texture's base internal format is GL_HILO_NV and *format* is not GL_HILO_NV.

GL_INVALID_OPERATION is generated if the texture's base internal format is GL_DSDT_NV and *format* is not GL_DSDT_NV.

GL_INVALID_OPERATION is generated if the texture's base internal format is GL_DSDT_MAG_NV and *format* is not GL_DSDT_MAG_NV.

GL_INVALID_OPERATION is generated if the texture's base internal format is GL_DSDT_MAG_INTENSITY_NV and *format* is not GL_DSDT_MAG_VIB_NV.

6.5   GL_NV_texture_shader3

OpenGL version required	OpenGL 1.1
Dependencies	Requires GL_NV_texture_shader2
Promotions	—
Related extensions	—

DISCUSSION

The GL_NV_texture_shader3 extension expands the functionality provided by the GL_NV_texture_shader and GL_NV_texture_shader2 extensions by adding 14 new texture shader operations that include projective offset texturing, offset texturing using a HILO result to perturb texture coordinates, dependent HILO and RGB texturing, and three dot product operations. The GL_NV_texture_shader3 extension also defines eight-bit-per-component internal HILO texture formats and a new unsigned RGBA dot product remapping mode that forces the blue component to a value of one.

Texture Formats

New internal formats, GL_HILO8_NV and GL_SIGNED_HILO8_NV, are defined by the GL_NV_texture_shader3 extension and store a HILO texture image internally using eight bits per component. These internal formats are accepted by the *internalFormat* parameter of the **glTexImage1D**, **glTexImage2D**, and **glTexImage3DEXT** functions when the *format* parameter is GL_HILO_NV. Table 6.5.1 lists all of the internal formats in which a HILO texture image may be stored.

TABLE 6.5.1   Internal texture formats in which a HILO texture image may be stored, including new formats defined by the GL_NV_texture_shader3 extension. Each internal format may be specified only for the GL_HILO_NV external format when loading texture images. Sized internal formats specify how many bits should be used to store each component. Bit counts preceded by S represent signed components, and bit counts preceded by U represent unsigned components.

Internal Format	*Base Internal Format*	*Required External Format*	*HI Bits*	*LO Bits*	*DS Bits*	*DT Bits*	*MAG Bits*	*I Bits*
GL_HILO_NV	GL_HILO_NV	GL_HILO_NV	—	—	—	—	—	—
GL_HILO8_NV	GL_HILO_NV	GL_HILO_NV	U8	U8	—	—	—	—
GL_HILO16_NV	GL_HILO_NV	GL_HILO_NV	U16	U16	—	—	—	—
GL_SIGNED_HILO_NV	GL_HILO_NV	GL_HILO_NV	—	—	—	—	—	—
GL_SIGNED_HILO8_NV	GL_HILO_NV	GL_HILO_NV	S8	S8	—	—	—	—
GL_SIGNED_HILO16_NV	GL_HILO_NV	GL_HILO_NV	S16	S16	—	—	—	—

Texture Shader Operations

Each texture shader stage performs one of the operations listed in Table 6.3.4 defined by the GL_NV_texture_shader extension, one of the operations listed in Table 6.4.1 defined by the GL_NV_texture_shader2 extension, or one of the new operations listed in Table 6.5.2. Table 6.5.3 summarizes the RGBA results and texture shader results for the additional texture shader operations defined by the GL_NV_texture_shader3 extension.

TABLE 6.5.2   Additional Texture Shader Operations and the Stages in Which They May be Specified

Texture Shader Operation	Stage 0	Stage 1	Stage 2	Stage 3
GL_OFFSET_PROJECTIVE_TEXTURE_2D_NV		•	•	•
GL_OFFSET_PROJECTIVE_TEXTURE_2D_SCALE_NV		•	•	•
GL_OFFSET_PROJECTIVE_TEXTURE_RECTANGLE_NV		•	•	•
GL_OFFSET_PROJECTIVE_TEXTURE_RECTANGLE_SCALE_NV		•	•	•
GL_OFFSET_HILO_TEXTURE_2D_NV		•	•	•
GL_OFFSET_HILO_TEXTURE_RECTANGLE_NV		•	•	•
GL_OFFSET_HILO_PROJECTIVE_TEXTURE_2D_NV		•	•	•
GL_OFFSET_HILO_PROJECTIVE_TEXTURE_RECTANGLE_NV		•	•	•
GL_DEPENDENT_HILO_TEXTURE_2D_NV		•	•	•
GL_DEPENDENT_RGB_TEXTURE_3D_NV		•	•	•
GL_DEPENDENT_RGB_TEXTURE_CUBE_MAP_NV		•	•	•
GL_DOT_PRODUCT_TEXTURE_1D_NV		•	•	•
GL_DOT_PRODUCT_PASS_THROUGH_NV		•	•	•
GL_DOT_PRODUCT_AFFINE_DEPTH_REPLACE_NV		•	•	•

TABLE 6.5.3   Texture Shader Result Types

Texture Shader Operation	Shader Stage Result Type	Shader Stage Result Value	Texture Unit RGBA Color Result
GL_OFFSET_PROJECTIVE_TEXTURE_2D_NV	Matches 2D target	Filtered texel	Filtered texel if RGBA, else (0,0,0,0)
GL_OFFSET_PROJECTIVE_TEXTURE_2D_SCALE_NV	RGBA	Filtered texel	Scaled filtered texel

(continues)

TABLE 6.5.3   *Continued*

Texture Shader Operation	Shader Stage Result Type	Shader Stage Result Value	Texture Unit RGBA Color Result
`GL_OFFSET_PROJECTIVE_TEXTURE_RECTANGLE_NV`	Matches rectangle target	Filtered texel	Filtered texel if RGBA, else (0,0,0,0)
`GL_OFFSET_PROJECTIVE_TEXTURE_RECTANGLE_SCALE_NV`	RGBA	Filtered texel	Scaled filtered texel
`GL_OFFSET_HILO_TEXTURE_2D_NV`	Matches 2D target	Filtered texel	Filtered texel if RGBA, else (0,0,0,0)
`GL_OFFSET_HILO_TEXTURE_RECTANGLE_NV`	Matches rectangle target	Filtered texel	Filtered texel if RGBA, else (0,0,0,0)
`GL_OFFSET_HILO_PROJECTIVE_TEXTURE_2D_NV`	Matches 2D target	Filtered texel	Filtered texel if RGBA, else (0,0,0,0)
`GL_OFFSET_HILO_PROJECTIVE_TEXTURE_RECTANGLE_NV`	Matches rectangle target	Filtered texel	Filtered texel if RGBA, else (0,0,0,0)
`GL_DEPENDENT_HILO_TEXTURE_2D_NV`	Matches 2D target	Filtered texel	Filtered texel if RGBA, else (0,0,0,0)
`GL_DEPENDENT_RGB_TEXTURE_3D_NV`	Matches 3D target	Filtered texel	Filtered texel if RGBA, else (0,0,0,0)
`GL_DEPENDENT_RGB_TEXTURE_CUBE_MAP_NV`	Matches cube map target	Filtered texel	Filtered texel if RGBA, else (0,0,0,0)
`GL_DOT_PRODUCT_TEXTURE_1D_NV`	Matches 1D target	Filtered texel	Filtered texel if RGBA, else (0,0,0,0)
`GL_DOT_PRODUCT_PASS_THROUGH_NV`	RGBA	(d,d,d,d)	(d,d,d,d)
`GL_DOT_PRODUCT_AFFINE_DEPTH_REPLACE_NV`	Invalid	Invalid	(0,0,0,0)

Many operations require the texture shader result of a previous texture shader stage. The previous texture input (specified by calling the **glTexEnvi** function with *pname* parameter `GL_PREVIOUS_TEXTURE_INPUT_NV`) names a texture stage `GL_TEXTUREi_ARB`, where *i* is less than the index of the texture unit for which the previous texture input is being specified. Texture shader stage interdependencies for the new operations defined by the GL_NV_texture_shader3 extension are summarized in Table 6.5.4.

TABLE 6.5.4 Texture shader stage interdependencies. For the shader operation specified for stage *i*, any operations listed for stages *i* − 2, *i* − 1, or *i* + 1 must be performed. Also, any texture shader result type requirements listed for the stage corresponding to the previous texture input must be met. Otherwise, texture shader stage *i* is not consistent. RGBA and HILO formats for textures used as a previous input must not have mixed signs.

Texture Shader Operation for Stage i	*Stage i − 2 Shader Operation*	*Stage i − 1 Shader Operation*	*Stage i + 1 Shader Operation*	*Previous Texture Input Result Types*
GL_OFFSET_PROJECTIVE_ TEXTURE_2D_NV	−	−	−	DSDT DSDT_MAG DSDT_MAG_INTENSITY
GL_OFFSET_PROJECTIVE_ TEXTURE_2D_SCALE_NV	−	−	−	DSDT_MAG DSDT_MAG_INTENSITY
GL_OFFSET_PROJECTIVE_ TEXTURE_RECTANGLE_NV	−	−	−	DSDT DSDT_MAG DSDT_MAG_INTENSITY
GL_OFFSET_PROJECTIVE_ TEXTURE_RECTANGLE_SCALE_NV	−	−	−	DSDT_MAG DSDT_MAG_INTENSITY
GL_OFFSET_HILO_ TEXTURE_2D_NV	−	−	−	HILO
GL_OFFSET_HILO_ TEXTURE_RECTANGLE_NV	−	−	−	HILO
GL_OFFSET_HILO_PROJECTIVE_ TEXTURE_2D_NV	−	−	−	HILO
GL_OFFSET_HILO_PROJECTIVE_ TEXTURE_RECTANGLE_NV	−	−	−	HILO
GL_DEPENDENT_HILO_ TEXTURE_2D_NV	−	−	−	HILO
GL_DEPENDENT_RGB_ TEXTURE_3D_NV	−	−	−	Unsigned RGBA
GL_DEPENDENT_RGB_ TEXTURE_CUBE_MAP_NV	−	−	−	Unsigned RGBA
GL_DOT_PRODUCT_ TEXTURE_1D_NV	−	−	−	RGBA HILO

(continues)

TABLE 6.5.4 *Continued*

Texture Shader Operation for Stage i	*Stage i − 2 Shader Operation*	*Stage i − 1 Shader Operation*	*Stage i + 1 Shader Operation*	*Previous Texture Input Result Types*
GL_DOT_PRODUCT_ PASS_THROUGH_NV	−	−	−	RGBA HILO
GL_DOT_PRODUCT_AFFINE_ DEPTH_REPLACE_NV	−	−	−	RGBA HILO

The effects of the new texture shader operations defined by the GL_NV_texture_shader3 extension are described below.

Offset Projective Texture 2D

The GL_OFFSET_PROJECTIVE_TEXTURE_2D_NV texture shader operation is similar to the GL_OFFSET_TEXTURE_2D_NV operation, except that it performs the division by q before perturbing the texture coordinates $\langle s/q, t/q \rangle$ associated with the current stage. The perturbed texture coordinates $\langle s', t' \rangle$ are calculated using the equation

$$\begin{bmatrix} s' \\ t' \end{bmatrix} = \begin{bmatrix} s/q \\ t/q \end{bmatrix} + \begin{bmatrix} a_1 & a_3 \\ a_2 & a_4 \end{bmatrix} \begin{bmatrix} ds \\ dt \end{bmatrix}, \tag{6.5.1}$$

where the values ds and dt are offset values fetched in the previous texture shader stage specified by the value of GL_PREVIOUS_TEXTURE_INPUT_NV, and the quantities a_1, a_2, a_3, and a_4 are the four entries of the texture unit's texture offset matrix. The texture unit's 2D texture target is accessed using the texture coordinates $\langle s', t' \rangle$, and the result of the texture access becomes both the RGBA result and texture shader result.

Offset Projective Texture 2D and Scale

The GL_OFFSET_PROJECTIVE_TEXTURE_2D_SCALE_NV texture shader operation is similar to the GL_OFFSET_TEXTURE_2D_SCALE_NV operation, except that it uses Equation (6.5.1) to calculate the texture coordinates $\langle s', t' \rangle$, performing the division by q. The texture unit's 2D texture target is accessed using the texture coordinates $\langle s', t' \rangle$, and the result of the texture access becomes the texture shader result. The same result also becomes the RGBA result, but after the RGB portion of the color is scaled by a factor derived from the magnitude component of the previous texture stage's result according to Equation (6.3.2). The scaled color components r', g', and b' are clamped to the range [1,0] and assigned to the stage's RGBA result.

Offset Projective Texture Rectangle

The `GL_OFFSET_PROJECTIVE_TEXTURE_RECTANGLE_NV` texture shader operation performs the same function as the `GL_OFFSET_PROJECTIVE_TEXTURE_2D_NV` operation, except that the rectangle texture target is accessed instead of the 2D texture target.

Offset Projective Texture Rectangle and Scale

The `GL_OFFSET_PROJECTIVE_TEXTURE_RECTANGLE_SCALE_NV` texture shader operation performs the same function as the `GL_OFFSET_PROJECTIVE_TEXTURE_2D_SCALE_NV` operation, except that the rectangle texture target is accessed instead of the 2D texture target.

Offset HILO Texture 2D

The `GL_OFFSET_HILO_TEXTURE_2D_NV` texture shader operation performs the same function as the `GL_OFFSET_TEXTURE_2D_NV` operation, except that the values of ds and dt, fetched in a previous stage, must be components of a HILO texture.

Offset HILO Texture Rectangle

The `GL_OFFSET_HILO_TEXTURE_RECTANGLE_NV` texture shader operation performs the same function as the `GL_OFFSET_HILO_TEXTURE_2D_NV` operation, except that the rectangle texture target is accessed instead of the 2D texture target.

Offset HILO Projective Texture 2D

The `GL_OFFSET_HILO_PROJECTIVE_TEXTURE_2D_NV` texture shader operation performs the same function as the `GL_OFFSET_HILO_TEXTURE_2D_NV` operation, except that the values of ds and dt, fetched in a previous stage, must be components of a HILO texture.

Offset HILO Projective Texture Rectangle

The `GL_OFFSET_HILO_PROJECTIVE_TEXTURE_RECTANGLE_NV` texture shader operation performs the same function as the `GL_OFFSET_HILO_PROJECTIVE_TEXTURE_2D_NV` operation, except that the rectangle texture target is accessed instead of the 2D texture target.

Dependent HILO Texturing

The `GL_DEPENDENT_HILO_TEXTURE_2D_NV` texture shader operation accesses the texture unit's 2D texture target using the coordinates $\langle H,L \rangle$, where H and L are the HI and LO components of the HILO pair fetched in the previous texture shader stage specified by the value of `GL_PREVIOUS_TEXTURE_INPUT_NV`. The result of the texture access becomes both the RGBA result and texture shader result.

Dependent RGB 3D Texturing

The `GL_DEPENDENT_RGB_TEXTURE_3D_NV` texture shader operation accesses the texture unit's 3D texture target using the coordinates $\langle r,g,b \rangle$, where r, g, and b are the red, green, and blue components of the color fetched in the previous texture shader stage specified by the value of `GL_PREVIOUS_TEXTURE_INPUT_NV`. The result of the texture access becomes both the RGBA result and texture shader result.

Dependent RGB Cube Map Texturing

The GL_DEPENDENT_RGB_TEXTURE_CUBE_MAP_NV texture shader operation accesses the texture unit's cube map texture target using the coordinates $\langle r,g,b \rangle$, where r, g, and b are the red, green, and blue components of the color fetched in the previous texture shader stage specified by the value of GL_PREVIOUS_TEXTURE_INPUT_NV. The result of the texture access becomes both the RGBA result and texture shader result.

Dot Product Texture 1D

The GL_DOT_PRODUCT_TEXTURE_1D_NV texture shader operation calculates a 3D dot product d between the texture coordinates $\langle s,t,r \rangle$ and the result of a previous texture shader stage. The value d is then used as the s texture coordinate, with which the texture unit's 1D texture target is accessed. The result of the texture access becomes both the RGBA result and texture shader result.

The exact dot product calculation depends on the type of the previous texture shader stage's result, which can be an RGBA color or a HILO pair. If the previous stage's result is an RGBA color for which all four components are signed, or if the previous stage's result is a HILO pair, then the dot product d is given by Equations (6.3.3) and (6.3.5), respectively. If the previous stage's result is an RGBA color for which all four components are unsigned, then the dot product depends on the unsigned remapping mode corresponding to the current shader stage. If the unsigned dot product remapping mode is set to GL_UN-SIGNED_IDENTITY_NV, then the dot product d is calculated using Equation (6.3.3). If the unsigned dot product remapping mode is set to GL_EXPAND_NORMAL_NV, then the dot product d is calculated using Equation (6.3.4). If the unsigned dot product remapping mode is set to GL_FORCE_BLUE_TO_ONE_NV, then the dot product d is calculated using the equation

$$d = \langle s,t,r \rangle \cdot \langle R,G,1 \rangle, \tag{6.5.2}$$

where R and G are the red and green components of the color.

Dot Product Pass Through

The GL_DOT_PRODUCT_PASS_THROUGH_NV texture shader operation calculates a dot product in exactly the same manner as the GL_DOT_PRODUCT_TEXTURE_1D_NV operation, but it does not access any textures. Instead, the value d of the dot product is clamped to the range [0,1] and replicated to form an RGBA color (d,d,d,d). This color becomes both the RGBA result and texture shader result.

Dot Product Affine Depth Replace

The GL_DOT_PRODUCT_AFFINE_DEPTH_REPLACE_NV texture shader operation calculates a dot product in exactly the same manner as the GL_DOT_PRODUCT_TEXTURE_1D_NV operation, but it does not access any textures. Instead, the value d of the dot product replaces the fragment's depth in window coordinates (where depth values normally fall in the range [0,1]). If d falls outside the near and far depth range values (set using the **glDepthRange** function), then the fragment is discarded. The RGBA result is always (0,0,0,0), and the texture shader result is invalid. At most, one texture shader stage may use either one of the operations GL_DOT_PRODUCT_DEPTH_REPLACE_NV or GL_DOT_PRODUCT_AFFINE_DEPTH_REPLACE_NV.

EXTENDED FUNCTIONS

■ **glTexEnvi**—Extended to allow specification of texture shader state.

Prototype

    void **glTexEnvi**(GLenum *target*, GLenum *pname*, GLint *param*);

Extended Parameters

param   Specifies the value of the texture parameter. The new values described below are accepted when the *pname* parameter is GL_SHADER_OPERATION_NV or GL_RGBA_UNSIGNED_DOT_PRODUCT_MAPPING_NV.

Description

The **glTexEnvi** function is used to specify texture shader state defined by the GL_NV_texture_shader3 extension. When the *target* parameter is GL_TEXTURE_SHADER_NV, the *pname* parameter may be one of the following values:

GL_SHADER_OPERATION_NV

The *param* parameter specifies the texture shader operation for the currently active texture unit. Accepted values are listed in Tables 6.3.4, 6.4.1, and 6.5.2. The initial value is GL_NONE.

GL_RGBA_UNSIGNED_DOT_PRODUCT_MAPPING_NV

The *param* parameter specifies the dot product mapping mode applied to unsigned RGBA texture components for the currently active texture unit. Specifying GL_FORCE_BLUE_TO_ONE_NV forces the blue component to 1.0 and leaves the unsigned values of the red and green components unchanged. The initial value is GL_UNSIGNED_IDENTITY_NV.

■ **glTexImage1D**, **glTexImage2D**, **glTexImage3DEXT**—Extended to support new internal texture formats.

Prototypes

    void **glTexImage1D**(GLenum *target*, GLint *level*, GLint *internalFormat*,
        GLsizei *width*, GLint *border*, GLenum *format*, GLenum *type*,
        const GLvoid **pixels*);
    void **glTexImage2D**(GLenum *target*, GLint *level*, GLint *internalFormat*,
        GLsizei *width*, GLsizei *height*, GLint *border*, GLenum *format*,
        GLenum *type*, const GLvoid **pixels*);

```
void glTexImage3DEXT(GLenum target, GLint level, GLenum internalFormat,
    GLsizei width, GLsizei height, GLsizei depth, GLint border,
    GLenum format, GLenum type, const GLvoid *pixels);
```

Extended Parameters

internalFormat   Specifies the internal format in which the texture image is stored. May be GL_HILO8_NV or GL_SIGNED_HILO8_NV.

Description

The **glTexImage1D, glTexImage2D,** and **glTexImage3DEXT** functions can be used to load texture images using internal formats defined by the GL_NV_texture_shader3 extension. The internal format specified by the *internalFormat* parameter must have a base format that matches the image format specified by the *format* parameter.

Errors

GL_INVALID_OPERATION is generated if *internalFormat* is GL_HILO8_NV or GL_SIGNED_HILO8_NV, and format is not GL_HILO_NV.

6.6   GL_ATI_fragment_shader

OpenGL version required	OpenGL 1.1
Dependencies	Requires GL_ARB_multitexture
Promotions	—
Related extensions	—

DISCUSSION

The GL_ATI_fragment_shader extension provides a powerful fragment-coloring instruction set that replaces the conventional texture environment application. When fragment shaders are enabled, instructions stored in a fragment shader object are executed for each fragment during rasterization. A fragment shader object may specify one or two 'passes' consisting of a sequence of texture-fetching instructions followed by a sequence of arithmetic instructions. A two-pass fragment shader may use results calculated in the first pass as the texture coordinates used to perform dependent texture fetches in the second pass.

Fragment Shader Management

Fragment shaders follow the named object convention that is used elsewhere in OpenGL for such things as texture objects and program objects. Previously unused names for fragment shader objects are allocated by calling the **glGenFragmentShadersATI** function,

```
GLuint glGenFragmentShadersATI(GLuint range);
```

This function returns the first name in a contiguous sequence of names having a length specified by the *range* parameter. After **glGenFragmentShadersATI** returns, the names generated are marked as used, but the associated fragment shader objects are not actually created until the first time a new name is passed to the **glBindFragmentShaderATI** function. Fragment shader objects are deleted, and the associated names are freed by calling the **glDeleteFragmentShaderATI** function,

> void **glDeleteFragmentShaderATI**(GLuint *id*);

The fragment shader corresponding to the name specified by the *id* parameter is deleted. If *id* does not name an existing fragment shader object, then the call to **glDelete-FragmentShaderATI** has no effect.

Fragment shaders are enabled and disabled by calling the **glEnable** and **glDisable** functions with *cap* parameter GL_FRAGMENT_SHADER_ATI. A fragment shader object is bound as the current fragment shader by calling the **glBindFragmentShaderATI** function,

> void **glBindFragmentShaderATI**(GLuint *id*);

When fragment shaders are enabled, the currently bound fragment shader object specified by the *id* parameter determines the sequence of instructions that are executed for each rendered fragment.

The instructions executed by a particular fragment shader are specified by first making the fragment shader object current using the **glBindFragmentShaderATI** function. Instruction specification is then begun by calling the **glBeginFragmentShaderATI** function,

> void **glBeginFragmentShaderATI**(void);

Instruction specification continues until a call is made to the **glEndFragmentShaderATI** function,

> void **glEndFragmentShaderATI**(void);

During fragment shader specification, any calls to the **glPassTexCoordATI**, **glSampleMapATI**, **glColorFragmentOp{123}ATI**, **glAlphaFragmentOp{123}ATI**, or **glSetFragmentShaderConstantATI** functions are compiled into the current fragment shader object.

Texture Coordinate Routing

A single fragment shader pass begins with up to six texture coordinate routing instructions that may be used to initialize a set of six fragment shader registers named GL_REG_*i*_ATI, where $0 \leq i \leq 5$. Each fragment shader register consists of four components representing the red, green, and blue color components, and an alpha component. The texture coordinate routing instructions can either pass texture coordinates directly into a fragment shader register or sample a texture map using a particular texture coordinate set and store the fetched color in a fragment shader register. After texture coordinates are routed to the registers, a shader pass executes a sequence of up to eight color instructions and eight alpha instructions. A fragment shader may consist of one or two passes and may use results calculated in the first pass to access textures in the second pass.

Texture coordinates are passed directly into a fragment shader register by calling the **glPassTexCoordATI** function,

> void **glPassTexCoordATI**(GLuint *dst*,
> GLuint *coord*,
> GLenum *swizzle*);

The *dst* parameter names the destination register and must be one of the constants GL_REG_*i*_ATI, where $0 \le i \le 5$. The *coord* parameter specifies which texture coordinate set to pass through to the destination register and can be one of the constants GL_TEXTURE*i*_ARB, where *i* is in the range 0 to GL_MAX_TEXTURE_UNITS_ARB − 1. In the second pass of a two-pass fragment shader, the *coord* parameter can also be GL_REG_*i*_ATI in order to pass the result of a calculation from the first pass to the second pass. Without calls to the **glPassTexCoordATI** function, the contents of the registers at the end of the first pass are not preserved at the beginning of the second pass.

When texture coordinates are passed directly into a fragment shader register, only the red, green, and blue components of the destination register are written. The alpha component is undefined. The *swizzle* parameter may be one of the values listed in Table 6.6.1 and indicates whether the *s*, *t*, and *r* coordinates, or the *s*, *t*, and *q* coordinates are passed through. Additionally, the *swizzle* parameter may indicate that a projection is performed in which the *s* and *t* coordinates are divided by the *r* or *q* coordinate. In the second pass of a two-pass fragment shader, only the swizzle modes GL_SWIZZLE_STR_ATI and GL_SWIZZLE_STR_DR_ATI may be specified.

TABLE 6.6.1 Swizzle modes accepted by the **glPassTexCoordATI** and **glSampleMapATI** functions. Coordinates labeled * are undefined.

Swizzle Mode	Coordinates Used by 1D and 2D Texture Fetches and by glPassTexCoordATI	Coordinates Used by 3D and Cube Map Texture Fetches
GL_SWIZZLE_STR_ATI	$\langle s,t,r,* \rangle$	$\langle s,t,r,* \rangle$
GL_SWIZZLE_STQ_ATI	$\langle s,t,q,* \rangle$	$\langle s,t,q,* \rangle$
GL_SWIZZLE_STR_DR_ATI	$\langle s/r,t/r,1/r,* \rangle$	$\langle *,*,*,* \rangle$
GL_SWIZZLE_STQ_DQ_ATI	$\langle s/q,t/q,1/q,* \rangle$	$\langle *,*,*,* \rangle$

A texture map is sampled by calling the **glSampleMapATI** function,

> void **glSampleMapATI**(GLuint *dst*,
> GLuint *interp*,
> GLenum *swizzle*);

The *dst* parameter names the destination register that receives the color fetched from the texture map and must be one of the constants GL_REG_*i*_ATI, where $0 \leq i \leq 5$. The texture unit accessed has the same index as the destination register, so specifying GL_REG_*k*_ATI as the destination register causes the highest priority texture target enabled for texture unit k to be accessed. The *interp* parameter specifies the texture coordinate set with which the texture map is accessed and can be one of the constants GL_TEXTURE*i*_ARB, where *i* is in the range 0 to GL_MAX_TEXTURE_UNITS_ARB − 1. In the second pass of a two-pass fragment shader, the *interp* parameter can also be GL_REG_*i*_ATI in order to utilize the result of a calculation from the first pass to perform a dependent texture access. Distinct registers may be specified as the *dst* and *interp* parameters.

The *swizzle* parameter may be one of the values listed in Table 6.6.1 and indicates whether the *s*, *t*, and *r* coordinates, or the *s*, *t*, and *q* coordinates are used to access the texture map. Additionally, the *swizzle* parameter may indicate that a projection is performed in which the *s* and *t* coordinates are divided by the *r* or *q* coordinate. It is not possible to perform a projective 3D texture access. In the second pass of a two-pass fragment shader, only the swizzle modes GL_SWIZZLE_STR_ATI and GL_SWIZZLE_STR_DR_ATI may be specified.

Fragment Shader Instructions

After texture coordinates have been routed to fragment shader registers and texture maps have been sampled, a fragment shader may execute up to eight color instructions and eight alpha paired instructions. Each instruction takes between one and three arguments that are drawn from the register set listed in Table 6.6.2. The registers GL_PRIMARY_COLOR_ARB and GL_SECONDARY_INTERPOLATOR_ATI, representing the primary and secondary colors, cannot be accessed during the first pass of a two-pass fragment shader.

TABLE 6.6.2   Fragment Shader Registers

Register	Description
GL_ZERO	The constant value (0,0,0,0).
GL_ONE	The constant value (1,1,1,1).
GL_REG_*i*_ATI	Fragment shader register *i*, where $0 \leq i \leq 5$.
GL_CON_*i*_ATI	Constant register *i*, where $0 \leq i \leq 7$.
GL_PRIMARY_COLOR_ARB	The interpolated primary color.
GL_SECONDARY_INTERPOLATOR_ATI	The interpolated secondary color. The alpha component is inaccessible.

The set of fragment shader instructions is listed in Table 6.6.3. The exact operations performed by each instruction are detailed in Table 6.6.4.

TABLE 6.6.3   Fragment Shader Instructions

Instruction	Arguments	Description
GL_MOV_ATI	1	Move
GL_ADD_ATI	2	Add
GL_SUB_ATI	2	Subtract
GL_MUL_ATI	2	Multiply
GL_MAD_ATI	3	Multiply-add
GL_LERP_ATI	3	Linear interpolation
GL_CND_ATI	3	Conditional select, compare to one half
GL_CND0_ATI	3	Conditional select, compare to zero
GL_DOT3_ATI	2	3D dot product
GL_DOT4_ATI	2	4D dot product
GL_DOT2_ADD_ATI	3	2D dot product and add scalar

TABLE 6.6.4   Fragment shader operations. The variable d represents the destination register, and the variables $a1$, $a2$, and $a3$ represent the first, second, and third input arguments. The subscripts R, G, B, and A represent the red, green, blue, and alpha components.

Instruction	Color Operation	Alpha Operation
GL_MOV_ATI	$d_R = a1_R$ $d_G = a1_G$ $d_B = a1_B$	$d_A = a1_A$
GL_ADD_ATI	$d_R = a1_R + a2_R$ $d_G = a1_G + a2_G$ $d_B = a1_B + a2_B$	$d_A = a1_A + a2_A$
GL_SUB_ATI	$d_R = a1_R - a2_R$ $d_G = a1_G - a2_G$ $d_B = a1_B - a2_B$	$d_A = a1_A - a2_A$
GL_MUL_ATI	$d_R = a1_R a2_R$ $d_G = a1_G a2_G$ $d_B = a1_B a2_B$	$d_A = a1_A a2_A$
GL_MAD_ATI	$d_R = a1_R a2_R + a3_R$ $d_G = a1_G a2_G + a3_G$ $d_B = a1_B a2_B + a3_B$	$d_A = a1_A a2_A + a3_A$

TABLE 6.6.4   *Continued*

Instruction	Color Operation	Alpha Operation
GL_LERP_ATI	$d_R = a1_R\,a2_R + (1 - a1_R)a3_R$ $d_G = a1_G\,a2_G + (1 - a1_G)a3_G$ $d_B = a1_B\,a2_B + (1 - a1_B)a3_B$	$d_A = a1_A\,a2_A + (1 - a1_A)a3_A$
GL_CND_ATI	$d_R = \begin{cases} a1_R, & \text{if } a3_R > \frac{1}{2} \\ a2_R, & \text{if } a3_R \le \frac{1}{2} \end{cases}$ $d_G = \begin{cases} a1_G, & \text{if } a3_G > \frac{1}{2} \\ a2_G, & \text{if } a3_G \le \frac{1}{2} \end{cases}$ $d_B = \begin{cases} a1_B, & \text{if } a3_B > \frac{1}{2} \\ a2_B, & \text{if } a3_B \le \frac{1}{2} \end{cases}$	$d_A = \begin{cases} a1_A, & \text{if } a3_A > \frac{1}{2} \\ a2_A, & \text{if } a3_A \le \frac{1}{2} \end{cases}$
GL_CND0_ATI	$d_R = \begin{cases} a1_R, & \text{if } a3_R \ge 0 \\ a2_R, & \text{if } a3_R < 0 \end{cases}$ $d_G = \begin{cases} a1_G, & \text{if } a3_G \ge 0 \\ a2_G, & \text{if } a3_G < 0 \end{cases}$ $d_B = \begin{cases} a1_B, & \text{if } a3_B \ge 0 \\ a2_B, & \text{if } a3_R < 0 \end{cases}$	$d_A = \begin{cases} a1_A, & \text{if } a3_A \ge 0 \\ a2_A, & \text{if } a3_A < 0 \end{cases}$
GL_DOT3_ATI	$d_R = a1_R\,a2_R + a1_G\,a2_G + a1_B\,a2_B$ $d_G = a1_R\,a2_R + a1_G\,a2_G + a1_B\,a2_B$ $d_B = a1_R\,a2_R + a1_G\,a2_G + a1_B\,a2_B$	$d_A = a1_R\,a2_R + a1_G\,a2_G + a1_B\,a2_B$
GL_DOT4_ATI	$d_R = a1_R\,a2_R + a1_G\,a2_G$ $\quad + a1_B\,a2_B + a1_A\,a2_A$ $d_G = a1_R\,a2_R + a1_G\,a2_G$ $\quad + a1_B\,a2_B + a1_A\,a2_A$ $d_B = a1_R\,a2_R + a1_G\,a2_G$ $\quad + a1_B\,a2_B + a1_A\,a2_A$	$d_A = a1_R\,a2_R + a1_G\,a2_G$ $\quad + a1_B\,a2_B + a1_A\,a2_A$
GL_DOT2_ADD_ATI	$d_R = a1_R\,a2_R + a1_G\,a2_G + a3_B$ $d_G = a1_R\,a2_R + a1_G\,a2_G + a3_B$ $d_B = a1_R\,a2_R + a1_G\,a2_G + a3_B$	$d_A = a1_R\,a2_R + a1_G\,a2_G + a3_B$

The function called to specify a fragment shader instruction is determined by the number of arguments taken by the instruction. A fragment shader color instruction taking a single argument is specified by calling the **glColorFragmentOp1ATI** function, an instruction taking two arguments is specified by calling the **glColorFragmentOp2ATI** function, and an instruction taking three arguments is specified by calling the **glColorFragmentOp3ATI** function,

```
void glColorFragmentOp{123}ATI(GLenum op,
                               GLuint dst,
                               GLuint dstMask,
                               GLuint dstMod,
                               GLuint arg1,
                               GLuint arg1Rep,
                               GLuint arg1Mod,
                               // glColorFragmentOp{23}ATI
                               GLuint arg2,
                               GLuint arg2Rep,
                               GLuint arg2Mod,
                               // glColorFragmentOp3ATI
                               GLuint arg3,
                               GLuint arg3Rep,
                               GLuint arg3Mod);
```

The *op* parameter specifies the operation to perform and may be any one of the instructions listed in Table 6.6.3, taking the number of arguments corresponding to the function called.

The *dst* parameter specifies the destination register and must be GL_REG_*i*_ATI, where $0 \leq i \leq 5$. The *dstMask* parameter specifies which color components of the destination register are written. A value of GL_NONE indicates that all three of the red, green, and blue components are written. To prevent one or more components of the destination register from being modified, a value consisting of a bitwise OR among the constants GL_RED_BIT_ATI, GL_GREEN_BIT_ATI, and GL_BLUE_BIT_ATI may be specified. For example, passing GL_RED_BIT_ATI | GL_GREEN_BIT_ATI as the *dstMask* parameter causes the red and green components to be updated, but leaves the blue component unchanged.

The *dstMod* parameter specifies a transformation to apply to the result of the operation before it is written to the destination register. A value of GL_NONE indicates that no transformation is applied, and other values specify a scale and optional clamp to the range [0,1]. All possible values of the *dstMod* parameter are listed in Table 6.6.5.

TABLE 6.6.5 Destination modifier flags. The operation listed is applied to each component x of the result that is written to the destination register to produce a quantity. The *clamp* function clamps its argument to the range [0,1].

Flags	Operation
GL_NONE	$x' = x$
GL_2X_BIT_ATI	$x' = 1 - x$
GL_4X_BIT_ATI	$x' = 4x$
GL_8X_BIT_ATI	$x' = 8x$

TABLE 6.6.5   *Continued*

Flags	Operation
GL_HALF_BIT_ATI	$x' = \frac{1}{2}x$
GL_QUARTER_BIT_ATI	$x' = \frac{1}{4}x$
GL_EIGHTH_BIT_ATI	$x' = \frac{1}{8}x$
GL_2X_BIT_ATI | GL_SATURATE_BIT_ATI	$x' = clamp$
GL_4X_BIT_ATI | GL_SATURATE_BIT_ATI	$x' = clamp(4x)$
GL_8X_BIT_ATI | GL_SATURATE_BIT_ATI	$x' = clamp(8x)$
GL_HALF_BIT_ATI | GL_SATURATE_BIT_ATI	$x' = clamp(\frac{1}{2}x)$
GL_QUARTER_BIT_ATI | GL_SATURATE_BIT_ATI	$x' = clamp(\frac{1}{4}x)$
GL_EIGHTH_BIT_ATI | GL_SATURATE_BIT_ATI	$x' = clamp(\frac{1}{8}x)$

The *arg1*, *arg2*, and *arg3* parameters specify the input registers for the operation's first, second, and third arguments. The inputs may be any of the registers listed in Table 6.6.2, with the exception that GL_PRIMARY_COLOR_ARB and GL_SECONDARY_INTERPOLATOR_ATI may not be specified in the first pass of a two-pass fragment shader. All three of the red, green, and blue components of each input register may be utilized, or a single component of the input register may be replicated to all three channels as specified by the *arg1Rep*, *arg2Rep*, and *arg3Rep* parameters. A value of GL_NONE indicates that no replication is performed, and the red, green, and blue components within the operation utilize the red, green, and blue components of the input register. A value of GL_RED, GL_GREEN, GL_BLUE, or GL_ALPHA indicates that the corresponding component of the input register is replicated to all three of the red, green, and blue components utilized by the operation. If the alpha component is replicated, then the corresponding input register cannot be GL_SEC-ONDARY_INTERPOLATOR_ATI.

The *arg1Mod*, *arg2Mod*, and *arg3Mod* parameters specify bitfields that control an input mapping that is applied to each argument. A value of GL_NONE indicates that no mapping is performed. The bits GL_COMP_BIT_ATI, GL_BIAS_BIT_ATI, GL_SCALE_BIT_ATI, and GL_NEGATE_BIT_ATI may be ORed together to indicate that the operations listed in Table 6.6.6 are to be applied. Any combination of these bits is legal, and the order in which the operations is applied corresponds to the order in which they are listed in the table. If all four bits are specified, the input mapping operation is given by

$$x' = -2\left[(1-x) - \frac{1}{2}\right].$$ (6.6.1)

TABLE 6.6.6   Input argument modifier flags. For each bit that is set in the *arg{123}Mod* parameter, the component value *x* is transformed into *x'* by the corresponding operation.

Flag	Operation
GL_NONE	$x' = x$
GL_COMP_BIT_ATI	$x' = 1 - x$
GL_BIAS_BIT_ATI	$x' = x - \frac{1}{2}$
GL_SCALE_BIT_ATI	$x' = 2x$
GL_NEGATE_BIT_ATI	$x' = -x$

If the *op* parameter of the **glColorFragmentOp2ATI** function is GL_DOT4_ATI, then the color instruction must be immediately followed by an alpha instruction taking the same parameters, because an alpha instruction must be implicitly generated to copy the result into the alpha channel of the destination register.

The same instructions that may be executed for RGB colors can also be executed for the alpha component. A fragment shader alpha instruction taking a single argument is specified by calling the **glAlphaFragmentOp1ATI** function, an instruction taking two arguments is specified by calling the **glALphaFragmentOp2ATI** function, and an instruction taking three arguments is specified by calling the **glAlphaFragmentOp3ATI** function,

```
void glAlphaFragmentOp{123}ATI(GLenum op,
                               GLuint dst,
                               GLuint dstMod,
                               GLuint arg1,
                               GLuint arg1Rep,
                               GLuint arg1Mod,
                               // glAlphaFragmentOp{23}ATI
                               GLuint arg2,
                               GLuint arg2Rep,
                               GLuint arg2Mod,
                               // glAlphaFragmentOp3ATI
                               GLuint arg3,
                               GLuint arg3Rep,
                               GLuint arg3Mod);
```

As with the **glColorFragmentOp{123}ATI** function, the *op* parameter specifies one of the instructions listed in Table 6.6.3, the *dst* parameter names a destination register, and the *dstMod* parameter specifies one of the destination modifier values listed in Table 6.6.5. There is no *dstMask* parameter, since the **glAlphaFragmentOp{123}ATI** function always writes only to the alpha component of the destination register.

The *arg1*, *arg2*, and *arg3* parameters specify the input registers for the operation's first, second, and third arguments. The inputs may be any of the registers listed in Table 6.6.2, with the exception that GL_PRIMARY_COLOR_ARB and GL_SECONDARY_INTERPOLATOR_ATI may not be specified in the first pass of a two-pass fragment shader. Any single component may be extracted from each input register. The *arg1Rep*, *arg2Rep*, and *arg3Rep* parameters specify which component is utilized by the operation. A value of GL_NONE or GL_ALPHA indicates that the alpha component is used, and a value of GL_RED, GL_GREEN, or GL_BLUE indicates that the red, green, or blue component is used. For any input argument that is GL_SECONDARY_INTERPOLATOR_ATI, the alpha component may not be utilized.

The *arg1Mod*, *arg2Mod*, and *arg3Mod* parameters specify bitfields that control an input mapping that is applied to each argument, as with the **glColorFragmentOp{123}ATI** function. A value of GL_NONE indicates that no mapping is performed.

If the *op* parameter of the **glAlphaFragmentOp{23}ATI** function is GL_DOT3_ATI, GL_DOT4_ATI, or GL_DOT2_ADD_ATI, then the alpha instruction must immediately follow a color instruction that performs the same operation. In these cases, the parameters to the alpha instruction are ignored, but they should match those passed to the color instruction, and the scalar result of the color instruction is copied to the alpha channel of the destination register.

Constant Colors

The color and alpha fragment shader instructions may specify a constant color as any one of their input arguments by naming one of the registers GL_CON_*i*_ATI, where $0 \leq i \leq 7$. A constant color is specified by calling the **glSetFragmentShaderConstantATI** function,

```
void glSetFragmentShaderConstantATI(GLuint dst,
                                    const GLfloat *value);
```

The *dst* parameter specifies which of the eight constant color registers to set and must be one of the constants GL_CON_*i*_ATI. The *value* parameter points to an array containing the red, green, blue, and alpha components of the new value of the constant color.

The **glSetFragmentShaderConstantATI** function may be called during fragment shader specification (between calls to **glBeginFragmentShaderATI** and **glEndFragment-ShaderATI**) or outside of a fragment shader specification block. When **glSet-FragmentShaderConstantATI** is called during the specification of a fragment shader, it sets the fragment shader's local value for the constant color. The local value is used whenever the fragment shader is currently bound. When **glSetFragmentShaderConstantATI** is called outside of a fragment shader specification block, it sets the global value of a constant color. Any fragment shaders that do not locally set a value for a constant color use the global value.

NEW FUNCTIONS

■ **glGenFragmentShadersATI**—Generate a contiguous set of fragment shader names.

Prototype

```
GLuint glGenFragmentShadersATI(GLuint range);
```

Parameters

range   Specifies the number of contiguous fragment shader names to be generated.

Description

The **glGenFragmentShadersATI** function returns the first name in a contiguous series of *range* fragment shader names. If the return value is *n*, then the names in the range *n* to *n range* – 1 are reserved with respect to fragment shader name generation. None of these names represent an existing fragment shader object, however, until the first time they are passed to the **glBindFragmentShaderATI** function.

If a contiguous range of names of the size specified by the *range* parameter could not be allocated, then the value 0 is returned.

Fragment shader objects are deleted, and the associated names are freed by calling the **glDeleteFragmentShaderATI** function.

Special Considerations

glGenFragmentShadersATI may not be called between calls to **glBeginFragmentShaderATI** and **glEndFragmentShaderATI**.

Errors

GL_INVALID_VALUE is generated if *range* is 0.

GL_INVALID_OPERATION is generated if **glGenFragmentShadersATI** is called between calls to **glBeginFragmentShaderATI** and **glEndFragmentShaderATI**.

■ **glDeleteFragmentShaderATI**—Delete a named fragment shader.

Prototype

    void **glDeleteFragmentShaderATI**(GLuint *id*);

Parameters

id   Specifies the name of the fragment shader to be deleted.

Description

The **glDeleteFragmentShaderATI** function deletes the fragment shader object whose name is specified by the *id* parameter. When a fragment shader object is deleted, it becomes nonexistent, and its name becomes unused. Deleted fragment shader names may subsequently be returned by the **glGenFragmentShadersATI** function. If the *id* parameter specifies an unused fragment shader name, then the **glDeleteFragmentShaderATI** function has no effect.

Special Considerations

glDeleteFragmentShaderATI may not be called between calls to **glBeginFragmentShaderATI** and **glEndFragmentShaderATI**.

Errors

GL_INVALID_OPERATION is generated if **glDeleteFragmentShaderATI** is called between calls to **glBeginFragmentShaderATI** and **glEndFragmentShaderATI**.

■ **glBindFragmentShaderATI**—Bind a named fragment shader.

Prototype

> void **glBindFragmentShaderATI**(GLuint *id*);

Parameters

id   Specifies the name of a fragment shader.

Description

The **glBindFragmentShaderATI** function sets the current fragment shader that is invoked for each rasterized fragment. If a previously nonexistent fragment shader is bound, then it becomes existent at the time that **glBindFragmentShaderATI** is called and is initially undefined.

Special Considerations

glBindFragmentShaderATI may not be called between calls to **glBeginFragment-ShaderATI** and **glEndFragmentShaderATI**.

Errors

GL_INVALID_OPERATION is generated if **glBindFragmentShaderATI** is called between calls to **glBeginFragmentShaderATI** and **glEndFragmentShaderATI**.

■ **glBeginFragmentShaderATI**—Begin fragment shader specification.

Prototype

> void **glBeginFragmentShaderATI**(void);

Description

The **glBeginFragmentShaderATI** function begins specification of the current fragment shader object. Subsequent calls to the **glPassTexCoordATI**, **glSampleMapATI**, **glColor-FragmentOp{123}ATI**, **glAlphaFragmentOp{123}ATI**, and **glSetFragmentShader-ConstantATI** functions are compiled into the fragment shader. Fragment shader specification is ended by calling the **glEndFragmentShaderATI** function.

Special Considerations

glBeginFragmentShaderATI may not be called between calls to **glBeginFrag-mentShaderATI** and **glEndFragmentShaderATI**.

Errors

GL_INVALID_OPERATION is generated if **glDeleteFragmentShaderATI** is called between calls to **glBeginFragmentShaderATI** and **glEndFragmentShaderATI**.

■ **glEndFragmentShaderATI**—End fragment shader specification.

Prototype

```
void glEndFragmentShaderATI(void);
```

Description

The **glEndFragmentShaderATI** function ends specification of a fragment shader object. Subsequent calls to the **glPassTexCoordATI**, **glSampleMapATI**, **glColorFragmentOp{123}ATI** and **glAlphaFragmentOp{123}ATI** functions are illegal until another fragment shader specification is begun by a call to the **glBeginFragmentShaderATI** function.

Errors

GL_INVALID_OPERATION is generated if **glEndFragmentShaderATI** is called without a previous call to **glBeginFragmentShaderATI**.

GL_INVALID_OPERATION is generated if a two-pass fragment shader was specified since the previous call to **glBeginFragmentShaderATI**, and the *arg{123}* parameter passed to any of the **glColorFragmentOp{123}ATI** or **glAlphaFragmentOp{123}ATI** calls in the first pass of the fragment shader was GL_PRIMARY_COLOR_ARB or GL_SECONDARY_INTERPOLATOR_ATI. In the case that this error is generated, the call to **glEndFragmentShaderATI** still closes the fragment shader specification begun with a call to **glBeginFragmentShaderATI**.

■ **glPassTexCoordATI**—Indicate that texture coordinates should be passed into a fragment shader register.

Prototype

```
void glPassTexCoordATI(GLuint dst,
                       GLuint coord,
                       GLenum swizzle);
```

Parameters

dst   Specifies a destination register. Must be GL_REG_*i*_ATI (where $0 \leq i \leq 5$).

coord   Specifies the source of the coordinates to pass through. The *coord* parameter can be GL_TEXTURE*i*_ARB, where *i* is in the range 0 to GL_MAX_TEXTURE_UNITS_ARB − 1.

              In the second pass of a two-pass fragment shader, the *coord* parameter can also be GL_REG_*i*_ATI (where $0 \leq i \leq 5$).

swizzle   Specifies the coordinate swizzle to be applied. Must be GL_SWIZZLE_STR_ATI, GL_SWIZZLE_STQ_ATI, GL_SWIZZLE_STR_DR_ATI, or GL_SWIZZLE_STQ_DQ_ATI.

              In the second pass of a two-pass fragment shader, the swizzle parameter cannot be GL_SWIZZLE_STQ_ATI or GL_SWIZZLE_STQ_DQ_ATI.

Description

The **glPassTexCoordATI** function indicates that a texture coordinate set is passed directly to the fragment shader register specified by the *dst* parameter. **glPassTexCoordATI** may only be called between calls to **glBeginFragmentShaderATI** and **glEndFragment-ShaderATI**. No immediate action is taken, but the operation is compiled into the fragment shader currently being specified.

In the first pass of a fragment shader, the *coord* parameter must specify a set of interpolated texture coordinates. The *swizzle* parameter specifies whether the *r* or *q* coordinate is passed through and whether a division by this coordinate takes place, as shown in Table 6.6.1.

In the second pass of a two-pass fragment shader, the *coord* parameter may also specify a fragment shader register, which is interpreted as a texture coordinate set $\langle s,t,r,q \rangle$. In the second pass, the *swizzle* parameter must specify that the *r* coordinate is passed through. The alpha component of any register written in the first pass is not accessible in the second pass.

The alpha component of the destination register specified by the *dst* parameter is always undefined after texture coordinates are passed through.

The **glPassTexCoordATI** function begins a pass when it is the first in a sequence of calls to the **glPassTexCoordATI** and **glSampleMapATI** functions. A fragment shader may have at most two passes.

Special Considerations

glPassTexCoordATI may only be called between calls to **glBeginFragmentShaderATI** and **glEndFragmentShaderATI**.

Errors

GL_INVALID_OPERATION is generated if **glPassTexCoordATI** is called outside calls to **glBeginFragmentShaderATI** and **glEndFragmentShaderATI**.

GL_INVALID_OPERATION is generated if **glPassTexCoordATI** is called after two passes have already been specified.

GL_INVALID_OPERATION is generated if the *dst* parameter specifies the same destination register for more than one call to **glPassTexCoordATI** or **glSampleMapATI** in the same pass.

GL_INVALID_OPERATION is generated if *coord* is GL_REG_*i*_ATI in the first pass of the fragment shader.

GL_INVALID_OPERATION is generated if *swizzle* is GL_SWIZZLE_STQ_ATI or GL_SWIZZLE_STQ_DQ_ATI in the second pass of a two-pass fragment shader.

GL_INVALID_OPERATION is generated if *coord* is equal to the *coord* parameter passed to a previous call to **glPassTexCoordATI** in the same pass, and *swizzle* does not specify the same three coordinates as the corresponding *swizzle* parameter passed to the previous call.

GL_INVALID_OPERATION is generated if *coord* is equal to the *interp* parameter passed to a previous call to **glSampleMapATI** in the same pass, and *swizzle* does not specify the same three coordinates as the corresponding *swizzle* parameter passed to the previous call.

GL_INVALID_ENUM is generated if *dst* or *coord* is not an accepted value.

■ **glSampleMapATI**—Indicate that a texture map should be sampled.

Prototype

```
void glSampleMapATI(GLuint dst,
                    GLuint interp,
                    GLenum swizzle);
```

Parameters

dst   Specifies a destination register that corresponds to the texture unit to be sampled. Must be GL_REG_*i*_ATI (where $0 \leq i \leq 5$).

interp   Specifies an interpolator to be used as the texture coordinate source. The *interp* parameter can be GL_TEXTURE*i*_ARB, where *i* is in the range 0 to GL_MAX_TEXTURE_UNITS_ARB $- 1$.

In the second pass of a two-pass fragment shader, the *interp* parameter can also be GL_REG_*i*_ATI (where $0 \leq i \leq 5$).

swizzle   Specifies the coordinate swizzle to be applied. Must be GL_SWIZZLE_STR_ATI, GL_SWIZZLE_STQ_ATI, GL_SWIZZLE_STR_DR_ATI, or GL_SWIZZLE_STQ_DQ_ATI.

In the second pass of a two-pass fragment shader, the swizzle parameter cannot be GL_SWIZZLE_STQ_ATI or GL_SWIZZLE_STQ_DQ_ATI.

Description

The **glSampleMapATI** function indicates that a texture map is sampled, and the result is stored in the fragment shader register specified by the *dst* parameter. **glSampleMapATI** may only be called between calls to **glBeginFragmentShaderATI** and **glEndFragment-ShaderATI**. No immediate action is taken, but the operation is compiled into the fragment shader currently being specified.

The texture map sampled corresponds to the index of the destination register. If the value of the *dst* parameter is GL_REG_*n*_ATI, then the texture map bound to texture unit *n* is sampled.

In the first pass of a fragment shader, the *interp* parameter must specify a set of interpolated texture coordinates. The *swizzle* parameter specifies whether the *r* or *q* coordinate is used and whether a division by this coordinate takes place, as shown in Table 6.6.1.

In the second pass of a two-pass fragment shader, the *interp* parameter may also specify a fragment shader register, which is interpreted as a texture coordinate set $\langle s,t,r,q \rangle$. Specifying a fragment shader register causes a dependent texture fetch to be performed. In the second pass, the *swizzle* parameter must specify that the *r* coordinate is used. The alpha component of any register written in the first pass is not accessible in the second pass.

The **glSampleMapATI** function begins a pass when it is the first in a sequence of calls to the **glSampleMapATI** and **glPassTexCoordATI** functions. A fragment shader may have at most two passes.

Special Considerations

glSampleMapATI may only be called between calls to **glBeginFragmentShaderATI** and **glEndFragmentShaderATI**.

Errors

GL_INVALID_OPERATION is generated if **glSampleMapATI** is called outside calls to **glBeginFragmentShaderATI** and **glEndFragmentShaderATI**.

GL_INVALID_OPERATION is generated if **glSampleMapATI** is called after two passes have already been specified.

GL_INVALID_OPERATION is generated if the *dst* parameter specifies the same destination register for more than one call to **glPassTexCoordATI** or **glSampleMapATI** in the same pass.

GL_INVALID_OPERATION is generated if *coord* is GL_REG_*i*_ATI in the first pass of the fragment shader.

GL_INVALID_OPERATION is generated if *swizzle* is GL_SWIZZLE_STQ_ATI or GL_SWIZZLE_STQ_DQ_ATI in the second pass of a two-pass fragment shader.

GL_INVALID_OPERATION is generated if *interp* is equal to the *coord* parameter passed to a previous call to **glPassTexCoordATI** in the same pass, and *swizzle* does not specify the same three coordinates as the corresponding *swizzle* parameter passed to the previous call.

GL_INVALID_OPERATION is generated if *interp* is equal to the *interp* parameter passed to a previous call to **glSampleMapATI** in the same pass, and *swizzle* does not specify the same three coordinates as the corresponding *swizzle* parameter passed to the previous call.

GL_INVALID_ENUM is generated if *dst* or *interp* is not an accepted value.

■ **glColorFragmentOp{123}ATI**—Specify a fragment shader color operation.

Prototypes

```
void glColorFragmentOp1ATI(GLenum op,
                           GLuint dst,
                           GLuint dstMask,
                           GLuint dstMod,
                           GLuint arg1,
                           GLuint arg1Rep,
                           GLuint arg1Mod);
```

```
void glColorFragmentOp2ATI(GLenum op,
                           GLuint dst,
                           GLuint dstMask,
                           GLuint dstMod,
                           GLuint arg1,
                           GLuint arg1Rep,
                           GLuint arg1Mod,
                           GLuint arg2,
                           GLuint arg2Rep,
                           GLuint arg2Mod);
void glColorFragmentOp3ATI(GLenum op,
                           GLuint dst,
                           GLuint dstMask,
                           GLuint dstMod,
                           GLuint arg1,
                           GLuint arg1Rep,
                           GLuint arg1Mod,
                           GLuint arg2,
                           GLuint arg2Rep,
                           GLuint arg2Mod,
                           GLuint arg3,
                           GLuint arg3Rep,
                           GLuint arg3Mod);
```

Parameters

op   Specifies the operation to perform.

For the **glColorFragmentOp1ATI** function, the *op* parameter must be GL_MOV_ATI.

For the **glColorFragmentOp2ATI** function, the *op* parameter can be one of the following: GL_ADD_ATI, GL_MUL_ATI, GL_SUB_ATI, GL_DOT3_ATI, or GL_DOT4_ATI.

For the **glColorFragmentOp3ATI** function, the *op* parameter can be one of the following: GL_MAD_ATI, GL_LERP_ATI, GL_CND_ATI, GL_CND0_ATI, or GL_DOT2_ADD_ATI.

dst   Specifies a destination register. Must be GL_REG_*i*_ATI (where $0 \leq i \leq 5$).

dstMask   Specifies a mask that controls what color components of the destination register are written. The *dstMask* parameter can be GL_NONE or a bitwise, OR of one or more of the values GL_RED_BIT_ATI, GL_GREEN_BIT_ATI, and GL_BLUE_BIT_ATI.

dstMod   Specifies a modifier to be applied to the destination register. The *dstMod* parameter can be GL_NONE or exactly one of the values GL_2X_BIT_ATI, GL_4X_BIT_ATI, GL_8X_BIT_ATI, GL_HALF_BIT_ATI, GL_QUARTER_BIT_ATI, or GL_EIGHTH_BIT_ATI. If the *dstMod* parameter is not

GL_NONE, then it can also be bitwise ORed with the value GL_SATURATE_
BIT_ATI.

arg{123}   Specifies the first, second, or third argument to the fragment shader operation. The *arg{123}* parameter can be one of the following: GL_REG_
*i*_ATI (where $0 \le i \le 5$), GL_CON_*i*_ATI (where $0 \le i \le 7$), GL_ZERO, or
GL_ONE.

On the last pass of the fragment shader, the *arg{123}* parameter can also
be GL_PRIMARY_COLOR_ARB or GL_SECONDARY_INTERPOLATOR_ATI.

arg{123}Rep   Specifies component replication for the first, second, or third argument
to the fragment shader operation. The *arg{123}Rep* parameter can be
GL_NONE or one of the values GL_RED, GL_GREEN, GL_BLUE, or
GL_ALPHA.

If *arg{123}* is GL_SECONDARY_INTERPOLATOR_ATI, then the corresponding *arg{123}Rep* cannot be GL_ALPHA.

If *op* is GL_DOT4_ATI and *arg{123}* is GL_SECONDARY_INTERPOLATOR_
ATI, then the corresponding *arg{123}Rep* cannot be GL_NONE or
GL_ALPHA.

arg{123}Mod   Specifies input modifiers for the first, second, or third argument to the
fragment shader operation. The *arg{123}Mod* parameter can be GL_NONE
or a bitwise OR of one or more of the values GL_2X_BIT_ATI,
GL_COMP_BIT_ATI, GL_NEGATE_BIT_ATI, and GL_BIAS_BIT_ATI.

Description

The **glColorFragmentOp{123}ATI** function indicates that the color operation specified by
the *op* parameter is performed, and the result is stored in the fragment shader register specified by the *dst* parameter. **glColorFragmentOp{123}ATI** may only be called between calls
to **glBeginFragmentShaderATI** and **glEndFragmentShaderATI**. No immediate action is
taken, but the operation is compiled into the fragment shader currently being specified.

If the *dstMask* parameter is GL_NONE, then all three of the red, green, and blue components
of the destination register are written; otherwise, only the components whose corresponding bit is set in the mask are written. The *dstMod* parameter specifies how the result of the
operation is transformed before it is written to the destination register. Possible destination
modifier values are listed in Table 6.6.5.

The *arg1*, *arg2*, and *arg3* parameters specify the input arguments to the fragment shader
color operation. Input arguments may be any of the registers listed in Table 6.6.2, with the
exception that at most two distinct constant registers may be used as arguments in a single
operation. Also, the primary color and secondary color may not be used as input arguments
in the first pass of a two-pass fragment shader.

The *arg1Rep*, *arg2Rep*, and *arg3Rep* parameters specify whether a single component of the
input argument is replicated to all three of the red, green, and blue components. If

arg{123}Rep is GL_NONE, then the red, green, and blue components are read directly; but if *arg{123}Rep* is GL_RED, GL_GREEN, GL_BLUE, or GL_ALPHA, then the corresponding color component is replicated to all three components of the input argument.

The *arg1Mod*, *arg2Mod*, and *arg3Mod* parameters specify the transformation that is applied to each input argument as it is read. Input argument modifier flags are listed in Table 6.6.6 and may be ORed together to produce all possible input transformations.

At most, eight color operations may be specified for each pass of a fragment shader.

Special Considerations

glColorFragmentOp{123}ATI may only be called between calls to **glBeginFragment-ShaderATI** and **glEndFragmentShaderATI**.

Errors

GL_INVALID_OPERATION is generated if **glColorFragmentOp{123}ATI** is called outside calls to **glBeginFragmentShaderATI** and **glEndFragmentShaderATI**.

GL_INVALID_OPERATION is generated if more than eight instructions have been specified in a single pass.

GL_INVALID_OPERATION is generated if all three arguments passed to **glColorFragment-Op3ATI** specify unique constant registers.

GL_INVALID_OPERATION is generated if *arg{123}* is GL_SECONDARY_INTERPOLATOR_ATI, and the corresponding *arg{123}Rep* is GL_ALPHA.

GL_INVALID_OPERATION is generated if *op* is GL_DOT4_ATI, *arg{123}* is GL_SECONDARY_INTERPOLATOR_ATI, and the corresponding *arg{123}Rep* is GL_NONE or GL_ALPHA.

GL_INVALID_ENUM is generated if *dst* or *arg{123}* is not an accepted value.

GL_INVALID_ENUM is generated if *dstMod* contains multiple, mutually exclusive bits.

■ **glAlphaFragmentOp{123}ATI**—Specify a fragment shader alpha operation.

Prototypes

```
void glAlphaFragmentOp1ATI(GLenum op,
                           GLuint dst,
                           GLuint dstMod,
                           GLuint arg1,
                           GLuint arg1Rep,
                           GLuint arg1Mod);
void glAlphaFragmentOp2ATI(GLenum op,
                           GLuint dst,
                           GLuint dstMod,
                           GLuint arg1,
                           GLuint arg1Rep,
```

```
                             GLuint arg1Mod,
                             GLuint arg2,
                             GLuint arg2Rep,
                             GLuint arg2Mod);
        void glAlphaFragmentOp3ATI(GLenum op,
                             GLuint dst,
                             GLuint dstMod,
                             GLuint arg1,
                             GLuint arg1Rep,
                             GLuint arg1Mod,
                             GLuint arg2,
                             GLuint arg2Rep,
                             GLuint arg2Mod,
                             GLuint arg3,
                             GLuint arg3Rep,
                             GLuint arg3Mod);
```

Parameters

op

Specifies the operation to perform.

For the **glAlphaFragmentOp1ATI** function, the *op* parameter must be GL_MOV_ATI.

For the **glAlphaFragmentOp2ATI** function, the *op* parameter can be one of the following: GL_ADD_ATI, GL_MUL_ATI, GL_SUB_ATI, GL_DOT3_ATI, or GL_DOT4_ATI.

For the **glAlphaFragmentOp3ATI** function, the *op* parameter can be one of the following: GL_MAD_ATI, GL_LERP_ATI, GL_CND_ATI, GL_CND0_ATI, or GL_DOT2_ADD_ATI.

dst

Specifies a destination register. Must be GL_REG_*i*_ATI (where $0 \le i \le 5$).

dstMod

Specifies a modifier to be applied to the destination register. The *dstMod* parameter can be GL_NONE or exactly one of the values GL_2X_BIT_ATI, GL_4X_BIT_ATI, GL_8X_BIT_ATI, GL_HALF_BIT_ATI, GL_QUARTER_BIT_ATI, or GL_EIGHTH_BIT_ATI. If the *dstMod* parameter is not GL_NONE, then it can also be bitwise ORed with the value GL_SATURATE_BIT_ATI.

arg{123}

Specifies the first, second, or third argument to the fragment shader operation. The *arg{123}* parameter can be one of the following: GL_REG_*i*_ATI (where $0 \le i \le 5$), GL_CON_*i*_ATI (where $0 \le i \le 7$), GL_ZERO, or GL_ONE.

On the last pass of the fragment shader, the *arg{123}* parameter can also be GL_PRIMARY_COLOR_ARB or GL_SECONDARY_INTERPOLATOR_ATI.

arg{123}Rep

Specifies component replication for the first, second, or third argument to the fragment shader operation. The *arg{123}Rep* parameter can be GL_NONE or one of the values GL_RED, GL_GREEN, GL_BLUE, or GL_ALPHA.

If *arg{123}* is GL_SECONDARY_INTERPOLATOR_ATI, then the corresponding *arg{123}Rep* cannot be GL_NONE or GL_ALPHA.

arg{123}Mod   Specifies input modifiers for the first, second, or third argument to the fragment shader operation. The *arg{123}Mod* parameter can be GL_NONE or a bitwise OR of one or more of the values GL_2X_BIT_ATI, GL_COMP_BIT_ATI, GL_NEGATE_BIT_ATI, and GL_BIAS_BIT_ATI.

Description

The **glAlphaFragmentOp{123}ATI** function indicates that the alpha operation specified by the *op* parameter is performed, and the result is stored in the fragment shader register specified by the *dst* parameter. **glAlphaFragmentOp{123}ATI** may only be called between calls to **glBeginFragmentShaderATI** and **glEndFragmentShaderATI**. No immediate action is taken, but the operation is compiled into the fragment shader currently being specified.

The *dstMod* parameter specifies how the result of the operation is transformed before it is written to the destination register. Possible destination modifier values are listed in Table 6.6.5.

The *arg1*, *arg2*, and *arg3* parameters specify the input arguments to the fragment shader alpha operation. Input arguments may be any of the registers listed in Table 6.6.2, with the exception that at most two distinct constant registers may be used as arguments in a single operation. Also, the primary color and secondary color may not be used as input arguments in the first pass of a two-pass fragment shader.

The *arg1Rep*, *arg2Rep*, and *arg3Rep* parameters specify which component of the input argument is read. If *arg{123}Rep* is GL_NONE or GL_ALPHA, then the alpha component is read. If *arg{123}Rep* is GL_RED, GL_GREEN, or GL_BLUE, then the red, green, or blue color component is read. The alpha component of the GL_SECONDARY_INTERPOLATOR_ATI register may not be read.

The *arg1Mod*, *arg2Mod*, and *arg3Mod* parameters specify the transformation that is applied to each input argument as it is read. Input argument modifier flags are listed in Table 6.6.6 and may be ORed together to produce all possible input transformations.

At most, eight alpha operations may be specified for each pass of a fragment shader.

Special Considerations

glAlphaFragmentOp{123}ATI may only be called between calls to **glBeginFragment-ShaderATI** and **glEndFragmentShaderATI**.

Errors

GL_INVALID_OPERATION is generated if **glAlphaFragmentOp{123}ATI** is called outside calls to **glBeginFragmentShaderATI** and **glEndFragmentShaderATI**.

GL_INVALID_OPERATION is generated if more than eight instructions have been specified in a single pass.

GL_INVALID_OPERATION is generated if all three arguments passed to **glAlphaFragment-Op3ATI** specify unique constant registers.

GL_INVALID_OPERATION is generated if *arg{123}* is GL_SECONDARY_INTERPOLATOR_ATI, and the corresponding *arg{123}Rep* is GL_NONE or GL_ALPHA.

GL_INVALID_OPERATION is generated if *op* is GL_DOT3_ATI, GL_DOT4_ATI, or GL_DOT2_ADD_ATI, and there was no matching call to **glColorFragmentOp{23}ATI** immediately preceding that had the same parameters.

GL_INVALID_OPERATION is generated if *op* is not GL_DOT4_ATI, and the *op* parameter to the immediately preceding call to **glColorFragmentOp3ATI** is GL_DOT4_ATI.

GL_INVALID_ENUM is generated if *dst* or *arg{123}* is not an accepted value.

GL_INVALID_ENUM is generated if *dstMod* contains multiple, mutually exclusive bits.

■ **glSetFragmentShaderConstantATI**—Specify a fragment shader constant color.

Prototype

```
void glSetFragmentShaderConstantATI(GLuint dst,
                                    const GLfloat *value);
```

Parameters

dst   Specifies a constant color register. Must be GL_CON_*i*_ATI (where $0 \leq i \leq 7$).

value   Specifies a pointer to an array of four values representing the red, green, blue, and alpha components of the constant color.

Description

The **glSetFragmentShaderConstantATI** function sets the value of the constant color register specified by the *dst* parameter. The *value* parameter points to an array containing the red, green, blue, and alpha components of the constant color.

The **glSetFragmentShaderConstantATI** function may be called during fragment shader specification (between calls to **glBeginFragmentShaderATI** and **glEndFragmentShaderATI**) or outside of a fragment shader specification block. When **glSetFragmentShaderConstantATI** is called during the specification of a fragment shader, it sets the fragment shader's local value for the constant color. The local value it used whenever the fragment shader is currently bound. When **glSetFragmentShaderConstantATI** is called outside of a fragment shader specification block, it sets the global value of a constant color. Any fragment shaders that do not locally set a value for a constant color use the global value.

Special Considerations

The color components specified by the *value* parameter must be in the range [0,1]. No clamping is performed, and values outside this range become undefined during fragment shader execution.

Errors

GL_INVALID_ENUM is generated if *dst* is not an accepted value.

EXTENDED FUNCTIONS

■ **glEnable, glDisable, glIsEnabled**—Extended to enable/disable fragment shaders.

Prototypes

```
void glEnable(GLenum cap);
void glDisable(GLenum cap);
GLboolean glIsEnabled(GLenum cap);
```

Extended Parameters

cap   Specifies a GL capability. To enable or disable fragment shaders, or to query whether fragment shaders are enabled, this should be GL_FRAGMENT_SHADER_ATI.

Description

Fragment shaders are enabled and disabled by calling the **glEnable** and **glDisable** functions. Calling the **glIsEnabled** function with the parameter GL_FRAGMENT_SHADER_ATI returns a value indicating whether fragment shaders are enabled.

VERTEX BLENDING

IN THIS CHAPTER

7.1   GL_EXT_vertex_weighting

OpenGL version required	OpenGL 1.1
Dependencies	—
Promotions	—
Related extensions	—

DISCUSSION

The GL_EXT_vertex_weighting extension provides a simple vertex blending mechanism. A second modelview matrix and the notion of a current vertex weight are introduced. When vertex weighting is enabled, eye-space vertex positions are calculated by transforming model-space vertex positions by both modelview matrices and then adding the results using a weighted sum. Eye-space normal vectors are calculated in a similar fashion, except that the inverse transpose of the modelview matrices are applied.

Vertex weighting is enabled and disabled by calling the **glEnable** and **glDisable** functions with *cap* parameter GL_VERTEX_WEIGHTING_EXT. When vertex weighting is enabled, vertex positions and normal vectors are transformed using two modelview matrices. Each modelview matrix is manipulated by calling the **glMatrixMode** function with *mode* parameter GL_MODELVIEW0_EXT or GL_MODELVIEW1_EXT. Subsequent calls to matrix functions apply to the first or second modelview matrix stack, respectively. Modelview matrix 0 is equivalent to the conventional modelview matrix, and the constant GL_MODELVIEW0_EXT is equivalent to GL_MODELVIEW.

The vertex weight is implemented as a new vertex attribute whose current value is specified using the **glVertexWeightf[v]EXT** function. There is only one weight w per vertex. The second weight is always $1 - w$. The **glVertexWeightf[v]EXT** function is useful for specifying per-vertex weights one at a time within a block delimited by calls to **glBegin** and **glEnd**. The current vertex weight is retrieved by calling the **glGetFLoatv** function with *pname* parameter GL_CURRENT_VERTEX_WEIGHT_EXT.

Vertex weights may also be specified as an array. A vertex weight array is specified by calling the **glVertexWeightPointerEXT** function,

```
void glVertexWeightPointerEXT(GLint size,
                              GLenum type,
                              GLsizei stride,
                              const GLvoid *pointer);
```

The *size* parameter specifies the number of weights per vertex and must always be 1. (This parameter exists to allow for future extensions that may allow multiple weights per vertex.) The *type* parameter specifies the data type of the elements in the array and must be the only supported value, GL_FLOAT. The *stride* parameter specifies the byte offset from one vertex weight to the next. As with all other arrays, a stride value of 0 indicates that the vertex weights are tightly packed in the array. The *pointer* parameter specifies the location where the vertex weight array begins in memory.

The current parameters pertaining to the vertex weight array are retrieved by calling the **glGetIntegerv** function with *pname* parameter GL_VERTEX_WEIGHT_ARRAY_SIZE_EXT, GL_VERTEX_WEIGHT_ARRAY_TYPE_EXT, or GL_VERTEX_WEIGHT_ARRAY_STRIDE_EXT. The current pointer to the vertex weight array is retrieved by calling the **glGetPointerv** function with *pname* parameter GL_VERTEX_WEIGHT_ARRAY_POINTER_EXT.

The vertex weight array is enabled and disabled by calling the **glEnableClientState** and **glDisableClientState** functions with *array* parameter GL_VERTEX_WEIGHT_ ARRAY_EXT. The vertex weight array is initially disabled.

When vertex weighting is enabled, two 4D homogeneous eye-space vertex positions, $\mathbf{E}_0$ and $\mathbf{E}_1$, are calculated using the formulas $\mathbf{E}_0 = \mathbf{M}_0\mathbf{V}$ and $\mathbf{E}_1 = \mathbf{M}_1\mathbf{V}$, where $\mathbf{M}_0$ and $\mathbf{M}_1$ are the two modelview matrices, and $\mathbf{V}$ is the 4D model-space vertex position. The final eye-space vertex position $\mathbf{V}_{\text{eye}}$ is then obtained as follows:

$$\mathbf{V}_{\text{eye}} = \begin{bmatrix} w(\mathbf{E}_0)_x + (1-w)(\mathbf{E}_1)_x \\ w(\mathbf{E}_0)_y + (1-w)(\mathbf{E}_1)_y \\ w(\mathbf{E}_0)_z + (1-w)(\mathbf{E}_1)_z \\ (\mathbf{E}_0)_w \end{bmatrix} \qquad (7.1.1)$$

The x, y, and z coordinates of the final eye-space vertex position are the weighted sums of the corresponding coordinates of $\mathbf{E}_0$ and $\mathbf{E}_1$, but the w coordinate of the final eye-space vertex position is always a copy of the w coordinate of the model-space vertex position after transformation by the single modelview matrix $\mathbf{M}_0$.

When vertex weighting is enabled, the 3D eye-space normal vector $\mathbf{N}_{eye}$ is calculated using the formula

$$\mathbf{N}_{eye} = f\left[w\left(\mathbf{M}_0^{-1}\right)^{\mathrm{T}}\mathbf{N} + (1-w)\left(\mathbf{M}_1^{-1}\right)^{\mathrm{T}}\mathbf{N}\right],\qquad(7.1.2)$$

where $\mathbf{N}$ is the 3D model-space normal vector, and f is the optional rescaling factor applied by the GL_EXT_rescale_normal extension (see Chapter 10, Section 10.3). If GL_NORMAL-IZE is enabled, then the vector $\mathbf{N}_{eye}$ is normalized after the weighted sum is calculated.

NEW FUNCTIONS

■ **glVertexWeightf[v]EXT**—Set the current vertex weight.

Prototype

```
void glVertexWeightfEXT(GLfloat weight);
```

Parameters

weight   Specifies the new current vertex weight.

Prototype

```
void glVertexWeightfvEXT(const GLfloat *weight);
```

Parameters

weight   Specifies a pointer to the new current vertex weight.

Description

The **glVertexWeightf[v]EXT** function sets the current vertex weight to the value specified by the *weight* parameter. When vertex weighting is enabled, the current vertex weight is used to blend the two eye-space vertex positions and normal vectors produced after transformation by the two modelview matrices.

Special Considerations

The current vertex weight can be updated at any time. In particular, **glVertex-Weightf[v]EXT** can be called between calls to **glBegin** and **glEnd**.

Get Functions

glGetFloatv with *pname* parameter GL_CURRENT_VERTEX_WEIGHT_EXT

■ **glVertexWeightPointerEXT**—Define an array of vertex weights.

Prototype

```
void glVertexWeightPointerEXT(GLint size,
                              GLenum type,
```

```
                    GLsizei stride,
                    const GLvoid *pointer);
```

Parameters

size	Specifies the number of weights per vertex. Must be 1.
type	Specifies the data type of each weight in the array. Must be GL_FLOAT.
stride	Specifies the byte offset between consecutive weights. A value of 0 indicates that the weights are tightly packed in the array.
pointer	Specifies a pointer to the first weight in the array.

Description

The **glVertexWeightPointerEXT** function specifies the location and data format of the vertex weight array. The *size* parameter specifies the number of weights per vertex and must always be 1. The *type* parameter specifies the data type of each vertex weight in the array and must always be GL_FLOAT. The *stride* parameter specifies the byte offset from one vertex weight to the next, and the *pointer* parameter specifies the location of the vertex weight array in memory.

The vertex weight array is enabled and disabled by calling the **glEnableClientState** and **glDisableClientState** functions with *array* parameter GL_VERTEX_WEIGHT_ARRAY_ EXT. Initially, the vertex weight array is disabled.

Special Considerations

The **glVertexWeightPointerEXT** function may not be called between calls to **glBegin** and **glEnd**, but an error may not be generated if it is. In this case, the operation is undefined.

Vertex weight array parameters are client-side state, and are saved and restored using the **glPushClientAttrib** and **glPopClientAttrib** functions.

Get Functions

glGetIntegerv with *pname* parameter GL_VERTEX_WEIGHT_ARRAY_SIZE_EXT

glGetIntegerv with *pname* parameter GL_VERTEX_WEIGHT_ARRAY_TYPE_EXT

glGetIntegerv with *pname* parameter GL_VERTEX_WEIGHT_ARRAY_STRIDE_EXT

glGetPointerv with *pname* parameter GL_VERTEX_WEIGHT_ARRAY_POINTER_EXT

Errors

GL_INVALID_VALUE is generated if *size* is not 1.

GL_INVALID_ENUM is generated if *type* is not GL_FLOAT.

GL_INVALID_VALUE is generated if *stride* is negative.

EXTENDED FUNCTIONS

■ **glEnable, glDisable**—Extended to enable/disable vertex weighting.

Prototypes

```
void glEnable(GLenum cap);
void glDisable(GLenum cap);
```

Extended Parameters

cap   Specifies a GL capability. To enable or disable vertex weighting, this should be GL_VERTEX_WEIGHTING_EXT.

Description

Vertex weighting is enabled and disabled by calling the **glEnable** and **glDisable** functions. When vertex weighting is enabled, vertex positions and normal vectors are transformed by both modelview matrices and added using a weighted sum.

■ **glEnableClientState, glDisableClientState**—Extended to enable/disable the vertex weight array.

Prototypes

```
void glEnableClientState(GLenum array);
void glDisableClientState(GLenum array);
```

Extended Parameters

array   Specifies an array to enable or disable. May be GL_VERTEX_WEIGHT_ARRAY_EXT.

Description

The **glEnableClientState** and **glDisableClientState** functions enable or disable arrays stored in client space. The vertex weight array is enabled or disabled by passing the value GL_VERTEX_WEIGHT_ARRAY_EXT to the *array* parameter.

■ **glIsEnabled**—Extended to return whether vertex weighting or the vertex weight array is enabled.

Prototype

```
GLboolean glIsEnabled(GLenum cap);
```

Extended Parameters

cap   Specifies an OpenGL capability. May be GL_VERTEX_WEIGHTING_EXT or GL_VERTEX_WEIGHT_ARRAY_EXT.

Description

The **glIsEnabled** function can be called to determine whether vertex weighting functionality is enabled. The *cap* parameter may be one of the following values:

GL_VERTEX_WEIGHTING_EXT

> The return value indicates whether vertex weighting is enabled.

GL_VERTEX_WEIGHT_ARRAY_EXT

> The return value indicates whether the vertex weight array is enabled.

■ **glMatrixMode**—Extended to support two modelview matrices.

Prototype

    void **glMatrixMode**(GLenum *mode*);

Extended Parameters

mode   Specifies the matrix stack to which subsequent matrix operations apply. May be GL_MODELVIEW0_EXT or GL_MODELVIEW1_EXT. The value GL_MODELVIEW0_EXT is equivalent to GL_MODELVIEW.

Description

The **glMatrixMode** function sets the current matrix mode. The second modelview matrix stack is made current by specifying GL_MODELVIEW1_EXT as the *mode* parameter.

■ **glGetFloatv**—Extended to retrieve vertex weighting state.

Prototype

    void **glGetFloatv**(GLenum *pname*, GLfloat *params*);

Extended Parameters

pname   Specifies the parameter to be returned. May be one of the values listed in Description.

Description

The **glGetFloatv** function can be used to retrieve various states related to vertex weighting. The *pname* parameter may be one of the following values:

GL_CURRENT_VERTEX_WEIGHT_EXT

> The current vertex weight is returned at the memory location specified by the *params* parameter.

GL_MODELVIEW0_MATRIX_EXT

> The 16 entries of modelview matrix 0 are returned in the array pointed to by the *params* parameter and are stored in column-major order. Modelview matrix 0 is equivalent to the conventional modelview matrix.

GL_MODELVIEW1_MATRIX_EXT

> The 16 entries of modelview matrix 1 are returned in the array pointed to by the *params* parameter and are stored in column-major order.

■ **glGetIntegerv**—Extended to retrieve vertex weighting state.

Prototype

> void **glGetIntegerv**(GLenum *pname*, GLint **params*);

Extended Parameters

pname   Specifies the parameter to be returned. May be one of the values listed in Description.

Description

The **glGetIntegerv** function can be used to retrieve various states related to vertex weighting. The *pname* parameter may be one of the following values:

GL_VERTEX_WEIGHT_ARRAY_SIZE_EXT

> The number of weights used by each element of the vertex weight array is returned. This value is always 1.

GL_VERTEX_WEIGHT_ARRAY_TYPE_EXT

> The data type of the vertex weight array is returned. This value is always GL_FLOAT.

GL_VERTEX_WEIGHT_ARRAY_STRIDE_EXT

> The stride of the vertex weight array is returned. The initial value is 0.

GL_MODELVIEW0_STACK_DEPTH_EXT

> The number of matrices on modelview matrix stack 0 is returned. The initial value is 1. Modelview matrix stack 0 is equivalent to the conventional modelview matrix stack.

GL_MODELVIEW1_STACK_DEPTH_EXT

> The number of matrices on modelview matrix stack 1 is returned. The initial value is 1.

■ **glGetPointerv**—Extended to retrieve the vertex weight array pointer.

Prototype

> void **glGetPointerv**(GLenum *pname*, GLvoid ***pointer*);

Extended Parameters

pname   Specifies the array pointer to be returned. May be GL_VERTEX_WEIGHT_ ARRAY_POINTER_EXT.

Description

The **glGetPointerv** function can be used to retrieve the pointer to the vertex weight array that was previously specified using the **glVertexWeightPointerEXT** function. When the *pname* parameter is GL_VERTEX_WEIGHT_ARRAY_POINTER_EXT, the pointer to the vertex weight array is returned in the *pointer* parameter. The initial value is a null pointer.

7.2   GL_ARB_vertex_blend

OpenGL version required	OpenGL 1.1
Dependencies	—
Promotions	—
Related extensions	GL_ATI_vertex_streams

DISCUSSION

The GL_ARB_vertex_blend extension provides generalized vertex weighting functionality. An implementation supplies two or more vertex blending units that each has its own modelview matrix and an associated weight value. An eye-space vertex position is calculated by transforming the model-space vertex position by multiple modelview matrices and then performing a weighted sum. Eye-space normal vectors are calculated in a similar fashion, except that the inverse transpose of the modelview matrices are applied.

Vertex blending is enabled and disabled by calling the **glEnable** and **glDisable** functions with *cap* parameter GL_VERTEX_BLEND_ARB. When vertex blending is enabled, vertex positions and normal vectors are transformed using the number of active vertex blending units set by calling the **glVertexBlendARB** function,

```
void glVertexBlendARB(GLint count);
```

The *count* parameter specifies the number of active vertex units and must be at least 1. The maximum number of vertex units supported by an implementation is retrieved by calling the **glGetIntegerv** function with *pname* parameter GL_MAX_VERTEX_UNITS_ARB.

Each vertex-blending unit has its own modelview matrix. The modelview matrix for vertex unit *i* is manipulated by calling the **glMatrixMode** function with *mode* parameter GL_MODELVIEW*i*_ARB. Subsequent calls to matrix functions apply to the modelview matrix stack for vertex unit *i*. Each vertex unit is required to support the same matrix stack depth as the conventional modelview matrix stack. The modelview matrix stack for vertex unit 0 is equivalent to the conventional modelview matrix stack.

Each vertex blending unit also has an associated weight value. The vertex weights are implemented as a new vertex attribute whose current value is specified using the **glWeight{bsifdubusui}vARB** function. The state representing the current weights is a vector whose size is equal to GL_MAX_VERTEX_UNITS_ARB. The number of weights specified may be anywhere from one to the maximum number of vertex units, and any weights not explicitly specified are set to zero. The **glWeight{bsifdubusui}vARB** function is useful for specifying per-vertex weight vectors one at a time within a block delimited by calls to **glBegin** and **glEnd**. The current weight vector is retrieved by calling the **glGet** function with *pname* parameter GL_CURRENT_WEIGHT_ARB.

Vertex weight vectors may also be specified as an array. A weight array is specified by calling the **glWeightPointerEXT** function,

```
void glWeightPointerARB(GLint size,
                        GLenum type,
                        GLsizei stride,
                        const GLvoid *pointer);
```

The *size* parameter specifies the number of weights per vertex and must be in the range 1 to GL_MAX_VERTEX_UNITS_ARB. The *type* parameter specifies the data type of elements in the array, and the *stride* parameter specifies the byte offset from the beginning of one weight vector to the next. As with all other arrays, a stride value of 0 indicates that the weight vectors are tightly packed in the array. The *pointer* parameter specifies the location where the weight array begins in memory.

The current parameters pertaining to the weight array are retrieved by calling the **glGetIntegerv** function with *pname* parameter GL_WEIGHT_ARRAY_SIZE_ARB, GL_WEIGHT_ARRAY_TYPE_ARB, or GL_WEIGHT_ARRAY_STRIDE_ARB. The current pointer to the weight array is retrieved by calling the **glGetPointerv** function with *pname* parameter GL_WEIGHT_ARRAY_POINTER_ARB.

The weight array is enabled and disabled by calling the **glEnableClientState** and **glDisableClientState** functions with *array* parameter GL_WEIGHT_ARRAY_ARB. The weight array is initially disabled.

The GL_ARB_vertex_blend extension provides a mechanism through which the last weight corresponding to each vertex may be automatically calculated by choosing a value that causes all of the weights for the vertex to sum to unity. This mode is enabled and disabled by calling the **glEnable** and **glDisable** functions with *cap* parameter GL_WEIGHT_SUM_UNITY_ARB. When enabled, a call to the **glWeight{bsifdubusui}vARB** function implicitly calculates the weight w_{size} whose index is equal to the *size* parameter using the formula

$$w_{size} = 1 - \sum_{i=0}^{size-1} w_i, \qquad (7.2.1)$$

where w_i is the weight corresponding to vertex unit i. If the weight array is enabled and a drawing command that uses arrays is issued, then Equation (7.2.1) is applied to each weight vector in the array at the time that drawing occurs. When GL_WEIGHT_SUM_UNITY_ARB is enabled, the size parameter passed to the **glWeight{bsifdubusui}vARB** and **glWeightPointerARB** functions cannot be GL_MAX_VERTEX_UNITS_ARB.

When vertex blending is enabled, the 4D homogeneous eye-space vertex position $\mathbf{V}_{eye}$ is calculated using the formula

$$V_{eye} = \sum_{i=0}^{n-1} w_i M_i V, \qquad (7.2.2)$$

where n is the number of active vertex units specified by calling the **glVertexBlendARB** function, w_i and M_i are the weight and modelview matrix corresponding to vertex unit i, and V is the 4D model-space vertex position. The 3D eye-space normal vector N_{eye} is calculated using the formula

$$N_{eye} = f \sum_{i=0}^{n-1} w_i \left(M_i^{-1}\right)^T N, \qquad (7.2.3)$$

where N is the 3D model-space normal vector, and f is the optional rescaling factor applied by the `GL_EXT_rescale_normal` extension (see Chapter 10, Section 10.3). If `GL_NORMALIZE` is enabled, then the vector N_{eye} is normalized after the weighted sum is calculated.

NEW FUNCTIONS

■ **glVertexBlendARB**—Set the number of active vertex units.

Prototype

```
void glVertexBlendARB(GLint count);
```

Parameters

count   Specifies the number of active vertex units. Must be in the range 1 to `GL_MAX_VERTEX_UNITS_ARB`.

Description

The **glVertexBlendARB** function sets the number of active vertex units that are used to blend transformed vertices to the number specified by the *count* parameter. The initial value is 1.

Get Functions

glGetIntegerv with *pname* parameter `GL_ACTIVE_VERTEX_UNITS_ARB`

Errors

`GL_INVALID_VALUE` is generated if *count* is greater than `GL_MAX_VERTEX_UNITS_ARB`.

■ **glWeight{bsifdubusui}vARB**—Set the current vertex weights.

Prototypes

```
void glWeightbvARB(GLint size,
                   const GLbyte *weights);
void glWeightsvARB(GLint size,
                   const GLshort *weights);
```

```
void glWeightivARB(GLint size,
                   const GLint *weights);
void glWeightfvARB(GLint size,
                   const GLfloat *weights);
void glWeightdvARB(GLint size,
                   const GLdouble *weights);
void glWeightubvARB(GLint size,
                    const GLubyte *weights);
void glWeightusvARB(GLint size,
                    const GLushort *weights);
void glWeightuivARB(GLint size,
                    const GLuint *weights);
```

Parameters

size   Specifies the number of weights. Must be in the range 1 to GL_MAX_
              VERTEX_UNITS_ARB. If GL_WEIGHT_SUM_UNITY_ARB is enabled, *size*
              cannot be GL_MAX_VERTEX_UNITS_ARB.

weights   Specifies a pointer to an array containing the weights.

Description

The **glWeight{bsifdubusui}vARB** function sets the current weight vector. The *size* parameter specifies how many weights are being specified in the array pointed to by the *weights* parameter. If *size* is less than GL_MAX_VERTEX_UNITS_ARB, then the unspecified weights are set to 0.0. If GL_WEIGHT_SUM_UNITY_ARB is enabled, then the weight having index *size* is calculated using Equation (7.2.1).

Get Functions

glGet with *pname* parameter GL_CURRENT_WEIGHT_ARB

Errors

GL_INVALID_VALUE is generated if *size* is not in the range 1 to GL_MAX_VERTEX_
UNITS_ARB, or if GL_WEIGHT_SUM_UNITY_ARB is enabled and *size* is greater than GL_MAX_
VERTEX_UNITS_ARB − 1.

■ **glWeightPointerARB**—Specify vertex weight array.

Prototype

```
void glWeightPointerARB(GLint size,
                        GLenum type,
                        GLsizei stride,
                        const GLvoid *pointer);
```

Parameters

size   Specifies the number of weights per vertex. Must be in the range 1 to
              GL_MAX_VERTEX_UNITS_ARB. If GL_WEIGHT_SUM_UNITY_ARB is enabled, *size* cannot be GL_MAX_VERTEX_UNITS_ARB.

type	Specifies the data type of each weight in the array. The symbolic constants GL_BYTE, GL_UNSIGNED_BYTE, GL_SHORT, GL_UNSIGNED_SHORT, GL_INT, GL_UNSIGNED_INT, GL_FLOAT, and GL_DOUBLE are accepted.
stride	Specifies the byte offset between the first weights corresponding to consecutive vertices. A value of 0 indicates that the weight vectors are tightly packed in the array.
pointer	Specifies a pointer to the first weight in the array.

Description

The **glWeightPointerARB** function specifies the location and data format of the weight array. The *size* parameter specifies the number of weights per vertex and must be in the range 1 to GL_MAX_VERTEX_UNITS_ARB. The *type* parameter specifies the data type of each weight in the array, and the *stride* parameter specifies the byte offset from one weight vector to the next. The *pointer* parameter specifies the location of the weight array in memory.

If GL_WEIGHT_SUM_UNITY_ARB is enabled, then the weight having index *size* is calculated using Equation (7.2.1) at the time that each weight array element is used for drawing.

The weight array is enabled and disabled by calling the **glEnableClientState** and **glDisableClientState** functions with *array* parameter GL_WEIGHT_ARRAY_ARB. Initially, the weight array is disabled.

Special Considerations

The **glWeightPointerARB** function may not be called between calls to **glBegin** and **glEnd**, but an error may not be generated if it is. In this case, the operation is undefined.

Weight array parameters are client-side state and are saved and restored using the **glPushClientAttrib** and **glPopClientAttrib** functions.

Get Functions

glGetIntegerv with *pname* parameter GL_WEIGHT_ARRAY_SIZE_ARB

glGetIntegerv with *pname* parameter GL_WEIGHT_ARRAY_TYPE_ARB

glGetIntegerv with *pname* parameter GL_WEIGHT_ARRAY_STRIDE_ARB

glGetPointerv with *pname* parameter GL_WEIGHT_ARRAY_POINTER_ARB

Errors

GL_INVALID_VALUE is generated if *size* is not in the range 1 to GL_MAX_VERTEX_UNITS_ARB, or if GL_WEIGHT_SUM_UNITY_ARB is enabled and *size* is greater than GL_MAX_VERTEX_UNITS_ARB − 1.

GL_INVALID_ENUM is generated if *type* is not an accepted value.

GL_INVALID_VALUE is generated if *stride* is negative.

EXTENDED FUNCTIONS

■ **glEnable, glDisable**—Extended to enable/disable vertex blending capabilities.

Prototypes

```
void glEnable(GLenum cap);
void glDisable(GLenum cap);
```

Extended Parameters

cap   Specifies a GL capability. May be GL_VERTEX_BLEND_ARB or GL_WEIGHT_SUM_UNITY_ARB.

Description

Vertex blending capabilities are enabled and disabled by calling the **glEnable** and **glDisable** functions. The *cap* parameter may be one of the following values:

GL_VERTEX_BLEND_ARB

    Vertex blending is enabled or disabled. When vertex blending is enabled, vertex positions and normal vectors are transformed by multiple modelview matrices and added using a weighted sum.

GL_WEIGHT_SUM_UNITY_ARB

    Automatic calculation of the final vertex weight is enabled or disabled. The final vertex weight is chosen so that the sum of all the weights is 1.0.

■ **glEnableClientState, glDisableClientState**—Extended to enable/disable the weight array.

Prototypes

```
void glEnableClientState(GLenum array);
void glDisableClientState(GLenum array);
```

Extended Parameters

array   Specifies an array to enable or disable. May be GL_WEIGHT_ARRAY_ARB.

Description

The **glEnableClientState** and **glDisableClientState** functions enable or disable arrays stored in client space. The weight array is enabled or disabled by passing the value GL_WEIGHT_ARRAY_ARB to the *array* parameter.

■ **glIsEnabled**—Extended to return whether vertex blending capabilities are enabled.

Prototype

```
GLboolean glIsEnabled(GLenum cap);
```

Extended Parameters

cap   Specifies an OpenGL capability. May be one of the values listed in Description.

Description

The **glIsEnabled** function can be called to determine whether vertex blending capabilities are enabled. The *cap* parameter may be one of the following values:

GL_VERTEX_BLEND_ARB

The return value indicates whether vertex blending is enabled.

GL_WEIGHT_SUM_UNITY_ARB

The return value indicates whether automatic final weight calculation is enabled.

GL_WEIGHT_ARRAY_ARB

The return value indicates whether the weight array is enabled.

■ **glMatrixMode**—Extended to support multiple vertex units.

Prototype

    void **glMatrixMode**(GLenum *mode*);

Extended Parameters

mode   Specifies the matrix stack to which subsequent matrix operations apply. May be GL_MODELVIEW*i*_ARB, where *i* is in the range 0 to GL_MAX_VERTEX_UNITS_ARB – 1. The value GL_MODELVIEW0_ARB is equivalent to GL_MODELVIEW.

Description

The **glMatrixMode** function sets the current matrix mode. Specifying GL_MODELVIEW*i*_ARB as the *mode* parameter makes modelview matrix *i* the current matrix stack.

■ **glGetFloatv**—Extended to retrieve vertex blending state.

Prototype

    void **glGetFloatv**(GLenum *pname*, GLfloat **params*);

Extended Parameters

pname   Specifies the parameter to be returned. May be one of the values listed in Description.

Description

The **glGetFloatv** function can be used to retrieve various states related to vertex weighting. The *pname* parameter may be one of the following values:

GL_CURRENT_WEIGHT_ARB

> The current weight vector is returned in the array pointed to by the *params* parameter. The number of weights returned is GL_MAX_ VERTEX_UNITS_ARB.

GL_MODELVIEW*i*_ARB

> The 16 entries of modelview matrix *i* are returned in the array pointed to by the *params* parameter and are stored in column-major order. Modelview matrix 0 is equivalent to the conventional modelview matrix.

■ **glGetIntegerv**—Extended to retrieve vertex blending state.

Prototype

    void **glGetIntegerv**(GLenum *pname*, GLint **params*);

Extended Parameters

pname   Specifies the parameter to be returned. May be one of the values listed in Description.

Description

The **glGetIntegerv** function can be used to retrieve various states related to vertex blending. The *pname* parameter may be one of the following values:

GL_WEIGHT_ARRAY_SIZE_ARB

> The number of weights used by each element of the weight array is returned.

GL_WEIGHT_ARRAY_TYPE_ARB

> The data type of the weight array is returned. The initial value is GL_FLOAT.

GL_WEIGHT_ARRAY_STRIDE_ARB

> The stride of the weight array is returned. The initial value is 0.

GL_MAX_VERTEX_UNITS_ARB

> The maximum number of vertex units is returned. This is always at least 2.

■ **glGetPointerv**—Extended to retrieve the weight array pointer.

Prototype

    void **glGetPointerv**(GLenum *pname*, GLvoid ***pointer*);

Extended Parameters

pname   Specifies the array pointer to be returned. May be GL_ARRAY_POINTER_ ARB.

Description

The **glGetPointerv** function can be used to retrieve the pointer to the weight array that was previously specified using the **glWeightPointerARB** function. When the *pname* parameter is GL_ARRAY_POINTER_ARB, the pointer to the weight array is returned in the *pointer* parameter. The initial value is a null pointer.

7.3   GL_ATI_vertex_streams

OpenGL version required	OpenGL 1.1
Dependencies	Requires GL_ARB_vertex_blend
Promotions	—
Related extensions	—

DISCUSSION

The GL_ATI_vertex_streams extension expands the number of vertex coordinate sets and normal coordinate sets so that multiple sources of vertex and normal data may be used by the GL_ARB_vertex_blend extension. Each new pair of auxiliary vertex coordinates and normal coordinates is referred to as a *vertex stream*. Any implementation supporting the GL_ATI_vertex_streams extension is required to support at least two streams. The actual number of available vertex streams is retrieved by calling **glGetIntegerv** with *pname* parameter GL_MAX_VERTEX_STREAMS_ATI.

Specification of vertex and normal coordinates follows the convention established by the GL_ARB_multitexture extension. New entry points exist for the immediate specification of a vertex stream's current vertex and normal coordinates. The notion of a currently active vertex stream is introduced to accommodate arrays of vertex and normal coordinates. Calling the **glClientActiveStreamATI** function,

```
void glClientActiveVertexStreamATI(GLenum stream);
```

selects the currently active vertex stream. The *stream* parameter must be GL_VERTEX_STREAM*i*_ATI, where *i* is in the range 0 to GL_MAX_VERTEX_STREAMS_ATI − 1. The initial value is GL_VERTEX_STREAM0_ATI.

Vertex and normal arrays are enabled or disabled for each vertex stream by first calling the **glClientActiveVertexStreamATI** function to select the vertex stream and then calling the **glEnableClientState** or **glDisableClientState** function with *array* parameter GL_VERTEX_ARRAY or GL_NORMAL_ARRAY. The vertex and normal arrays are specified for the current client active vertex stream by calling the usual **glVertexPointer** and **glNormalPointer** functions. When using the **glEnableClientState**, **glDisable-ClientState**, **glIsEnabled**, or any of the **glGet** functions to access state related to vertex and normal arrays with an argument from the following list, the action affects the client active vertex stream.

```
GL_VERTEX_ARRAY
GL_VERTEX_ARRAY_SIZE
GL_VERTEX_ARRAY_TYPE
GL_VERTEX_ARRAY_STRIDE
GL_VERTEX_ARRAY_POINTER
GL_NORMAL_ARRAY
GL_NORMAL_ARRAY_TYPE
GL_NORMAL_ARRAY_STRIDE
GL_NORMAL_ARRAY_POINTER
```

The current vertex and normal coordinates corresponding to a particular vertex stream are specified using the **glVertexStream{1234}{sifd}[v]ATI** and **glNormalStream3-{bsifd}[v]ATI** functions. These functions each take a parameter that indicates which vertex stream to affect, so they do not depend on the currently active vertex stream. The **glVertex{1234}{sifd}[v]** and **glNormal3{bsifd}[v]** functions may still be called, and doing so is equivalent to calling the **glVertexStream{1234}{sifd}[v]ATI** or **glNormalStream3{bsifd}[v]ATI** function with the *stream* parameter set to GL_VERTEX_STREAMO_ATI, regardless of the currently active vertex stream.

Multiple vertex streams exist so that separate vertex and normal coordinates may be fed into different vertex units established by the GL_ARB_vertex_blend extension. Initially, each vertex unit consumes vertices and normals from GL_VERTEX_STREAMO_ATI, which is equivalent to taking them from the conventional vertex and normal states. A different vertex stream may be fed into a vertex unit by calling the **glVertexBlendEnviATI** function,

```
void glVertexBlendEnviATI(GLenum pname,
                          GLint param);
```

with *pname* parameter GL_VERTEX_SOURCE_ATI. The *param* parameter must be GL_VERTEX_STREAMi_ATI, where i is in the range 0 to GL_MAX_VERTEX_STREAMS − 1. The vertex blend unit affected is whichever one corresponds to the current matrix mode at the time that **glVertexBlendEnviATI** is called. When the matrix mode is GL_MODELVIEWk_ARB, the stream used as the vertex and normal source for vertex blend unit k is set.

When vertex blending is enabled, the 4D homogeneous eye-space vertex position $\mathbf{V}_{eye}$ is calculated using the formula

$$\mathbf{V}_{eye} = \sum_{i=0}^{n-1} w_i \mathbf{M}_i \mathbf{V}_{stream(i)}, \tag{7.3.1}$$

where n is the number of active vertex units, w_i and $\mathbf{M}_i$ are the weight and modelview matrix corresponding to vertex unit i, and $\mathbf{V}_{stream(i)}$ is the 4D model-space vertex position taken from the vertex stream associated with vertex unit i by the **glVertexBlendEnviATI** function. The 3D eye-space normal vector $\mathbf{N}_{eye}$ is calculated using the formula

$$\mathbf{N}_{eye} = f\sum_{i=0}^{n-1} w_i\left(\mathbf{M}_i^{-1}\right)^{\mathrm{T}}\mathbf{N}_{stream(i)},\qquad (7.3.2)$$

where $\mathbf{N}_{stream(i)}$ is the 3D model-space normal vector taken from the vertex stream associated with vertex unit i, and f is the optional rescaling factor applied by the GL_EXT_rescale_normal extension (see Chapter 10, Section 10.3). If GL_NORMALIZE is enabled, then the vector $\mathbf{N}_{eye}$ is normalized after the weighted sum is calculated.

Vertex and normal coordinates corresponding to vertex streams other than GL_VERTEX_STREAMO_ATI cannot be generated by evaluators and are not returned in feedback mode.

NEW FUNCTIONS

■ **glClientActiveVertexStreamATI**—Select the active vertex stream.

Prototype

void **glClientActiveVertexStreamATI**(GLenum *stream*);

Parameters

stream   Specifies the current vertex stream. Must be GL_VERTEX_STREAM*i*_ATI, where i is in the range 0 to GL_MAX_VERTEX_STREAMS_ATI − 1. The initial value is GL_VERTEX_STREAMO_ATI.

Description

The **glClientActiveVertexStreamATI** function selects the vertex stream to which subsequent commands pertaining to vertex arrays and normal arrays are directed.

Errors

GL_INVALID_ENUM is generated if *stream* is not an accepted value.

■ **glVertexBlendEnv{if}ATI**—Set a vertex blend parameter.

Prototypes

void **glVertexBlendEnviATI**(GLenum *pname*,
                             GLint *param*);
void **glVertexBlendEnvfATI**(GLenum *pname*,
                             GLfloat *param*);

Parameters

pname   Specifies a vertex blending parameter. Must be GL_VERTEX_SOURCE_ATI.

param   Specifies the value of the vertex blending parameter. Must be GL_VERTEX_STREAM*i*_ATI, where i is in the range 0 to GL_MAX_VERTEX_STREAMS_ATI − 1.

Description

The **glVertexBlendEnv{if}ATI** function is used to set the vertex stream source for a particular vertex blending unit. The vertex blending unit for which the stream is set corresponds to the current matrix mode. When the matrix mode is GL_MODELVIEWk_ARB, then the vertex stream specified by the *param* parameter is fed into vertex unit k.

■ **glVertexStream{1234}{sifd}[v]ATI**—Set the current vertex coordinates for a particular vertex stream.

Prototypes

```
void glVertexStream1sATI(GLenum stream,
                         GLshort x);
void glVertexStream1iATI(GLenum stream,
                         GLint x);
void glVertexStream1fATI(GLenum stream,
                         GLfloat x);
void glVertexStream1dATI(GLenum stream,
                         GLdouble x);
void glVertexStream2sATI(GLenum stream,
                         GLshort x,
                         GLshort y);
void glVertexStream2iATI(GLenum stream,
                         GLint x,
                         GLint y);
void glVertexStream2fATI(GLenum stream,
                         GLfloat x,
                         GLfloat y);
void glVertexStream2dATI(GLenum stream,
                         GLdouble x,
                         GLdouble y);
void glVertexStream3sATI(GLenum stream,
                         GLshort x,
                         GLshort y,
                         GLshort z);
void glVertexStream3iATI(GLenum stream,
                         GLint x,
                         GLint y,
                         GLint z);
void glVertexStream3fATI(GLenum stream,
                         GLfloat x,
                         GLfloat y,
                         GLfloat z);
void glVertexStream3dATI(GLenum stream,
                         GLdouble x,
                         GLdouble y,
                         GLdouble z);
```

```
void glVertexStream4sATI(GLenum stream,
                         GLshort x,
                         GLshort y,
                         GLshort z,
                         GLshort w);
void glVertexStream4iATI(GLenum stream,
                         GLint x,
                         GLint y,
                         GLint z,
                         GLint w);
void glVertexStream4fATI(GLenum stream,
                         GLfloat x,
                         GLfloat y,
                         GLfloat z,
                         GLfloat w);
void glVertexStream4dATI(GLenum stream,
                         GLdouble x,
                         GLdouble y,
                         GLdouble z,
                         GLdouble w);
```

Parameters

stream   Specifies the vertex stream for which the vertex coordinates are being set. Must be `GL_VERTEX_STREAM`i`_ATI`, where i is in the range 0 to `GL_MAX_VERTEX_STREAMS_ATI` − 1.

x, y, z, w   Specify the new current vertex coordinates.

Prototypes

```
void glVertexStream1svATI(GLenum stream,
                          const GLshort *coords);
void glVertexStream1ivATI(GLenum stream,
                          const GLint *coords);
void glVertexStream1fvATI(GLenum stream,
                          const GLfloat *coords);
void glVertexStream1dvATI(GLenum stream,
                          const GLdouble *coords);
void glVertexStream2svATI(GLenum stream,
                          const GLshort *coords);
void glVertexStream2ivATI(GLenum stream,
                          const GLint *coords);
void glVertexStream2fvATI(GLenum stream,
                          const GLfloat *coords);
void glVertexStream2dvATI(GLenum stream,
                          const GLdouble *coords);
void glVertexStream3svATI(GLenum stream,
                          const GLshort *coords);
```

```
void glVertexStream3ivATI(GLenum stream,
                          const GLint *coords);
void glVertexStream3fvATI(GLenum stream,
                          const GLfloat *coords);
void glVertexStream3dvATI(GLenum stream,
                          const GLdouble *coords);
void glVertexStream4svATI(GLenum stream,
                          const GLshort *coords);
void glVertexStream4ivATI(GLenum stream,
                          const GLint *coords);
void glVertexStream4fvATI(GLenum stream,
                          const GLfloat *coords);
void glVertexStream4dvATI(GLenum stream,
                          const GLdouble *coords);
```

Parameters

stream   Specifies the vertex stream for which the vertex coordinates are being set. Must be `GL_VERTEX_STREAM`*i*`_ATI`, where *i* is in the range 0 to `GL_MAX_VERTEX_STREAMS_ATI` − 1.

coords   Specifies a pointer to an array containing the new current vertex coordinates.

Description

The `glVertexStream{1234}{sifd}[v]ATI` function sets the current vertex coordinates for the vertex stream indicated by the *stream* parameter.

If fewer than four coordinates are specified, then the *y*, *z*, and *w* coordinates are implied to be 0, 0, and 1, respectively. Hence, calling the `glVertexStream1{sifd}[v]ATI` function sets the current texture coordinates to $\langle x,0,0,1 \rangle$, calling the `glVertexStream2-{sifd}[v]ATI` function sets the current texture coordinates to $\langle x,y,0,1 \rangle$, and calling the `glVertexStream3{sifd}[v]ATI` function sets the current texture coordinates to $\langle x,y,z,1 \rangle$.

Initially, the values for *x*, *y*, *z*, and *w* are $\langle 0,0,0,1 \rangle$ for every vertex stream.

Special Considerations

The current vertex coordinates for any vertex stream can be updated at any time. In particular, `glVertexStream{1234}{sifd}[v]ATI` can be called between calls to `glBegin` and `glEnd`.

Errors

`GL_INVALID_ENUM` is generated if *stream* is not an accepted value.

■ `glNormalStream3{bsifd}[v]ATI`—Set the current normal coordinates for a particular vertex stream.

Prototypes

```
void glNormalStream3bATI(GLenum stream,
                         GLbyte x,
```

```
                              GLbyte y,
                              GLbyte z);
     void glNormalStream3sATI(GLenum stream,
                              GLshort x,
                              GLshort y,
                              GLshort z);
     void glNormalStream3iATI(GLenum stream,
                              GLint x,
                              GLint y,
                              GLint z);
     void glNormalStream3fATI(GLenum stream,
                              GLfloat x,
                              GLfloat y,
                              GLfloat z);
     void glNormalStream3dATI(GLenum stream,
                              GLdouble x,
                              GLdouble y,
                              GLdouble z);
```

Parameters

stream   Specifies the vertex stream for which the vertex coordinates are being set. Must be GL_VERTEX_STREAM*i*_ATI, where *i* is in the range 0 to GL_MAX_VERTEX_STREAMS_ATI − 1.

x, y, z   Specify the new current normal coordinates.

Prototypes

```
     void glNormalStream3bvATI(GLenum stream,
                               const GLbyte *coords);
     void glNormalStream3svATI(GLenum stream,
                               const GLshort *coords);
     void glNormalStream3ivATI(GLenum stream,
                               const GLint *coords);
     void glNormalStream3fvATI(GLenum stream,
                               const GLfloat *coords);
     void glNormalStream3dvATI(GLenum stream,
                               const GLdouble *coords);
```

Parameters

stream   Specifies the vertex stream for which the vertex coordinates are being set. Must be GL_VERTEX_STREAM*i*_ATI, where *i* is in the range 0 to GL_MAX_VERTEX_STREAMS_ATI − 1.

coords   Specifies a pointer to an array containing the new current normal coordinates.

Description

The **glNormalStream3{bsifd}[v]ATI** function sets the current normal coordinates for the vertex stream indicated by the *stream* parameter.

Initially, the values for *x*, *y*, and *z* are ⟨0,0,1⟩ for every vertex stream.

Special Considerations

The current normal coordinates for any vertex stream can be updated at any time. In particular, **glNormalStream3{bsifd}[v]ATI** can be called between calls to **glBegin** and **glEnd**.

Get Functions

glGet with *pname* parameter GL_CURRENT_NORMAL

Errors

GL_INVALID_ENUM is generated if *stream* is not an accepted value.

EXTENDED FUNCTIONS

■ **glGetIntegerv**—Extended to retrieve the maximum number of vertex streams.

Prototype

```
void glGetIntegerv(GLenum pname, GLint *params);
```

Extended Parameters

pname   Specifies the symbolic name of the parameter to return. May be GL_MAX_VERTEX_STREAMS_ATI.

Description

Calling the **glGetIntegerv** function with *pname* parameter GL_MAX_VERTEX_STREAMS_ATI can be used to retrieve the maximum number of vertex streams. This is always at least 2.

CHAPTER **8**

ARRAY MANAGEMENT

In This Chapter

8.1   GL_EXT_draw_range_elements

OpenGL version required	OpenGL 1.1
Dependencies	—
Promotions	Promoted to a core feature in OpenGL 1.2
Related extensions	—

Discussion

The `glDrawElements` function provides a mechanism through which indexed primitives are rendered. It accepts an index array upon which no range restriction is imposed, so an implementation must be prepared to handle any possible index value. This can necessitate preprocessing steps that can result in suboptimal performance, so the GL_EXT_draw_range_elements extension adds a new function that provides the same functionality as `glDrawElements`, but also specifies the bounds of the index values.

An indexed primitive can be rendered by calling the **glDrawRangeElementsEXT** function,

```
void glDrawRangeElementsEXT(GLenum mode,
                            GLuint start,
                            GLuint end,
                            GLsizei count,
                            GLenum type,
                            const GLvoid *indices);
```

whose *mode*, *count*, *type*, and *indices* parameters have the same meanings as they do for the **glDrawElements** function. The *start* and *end* parameters specify the minimum and maximum values, inclusive, of the elements in the index array. If any values in the index array fall outside this range, an error may not be generated, but the behavior is undefined.

An implementation is able to advertise the maximum number of vertices and maximum number of indices that should be used in conjunction with the **glDrawRangeElementsEXT** function in order to achieve optimal performance. Calling the **glGetIntegerv** function with *pname* parameter GL_MAX_ELEMENTS_VERTICES_EXT returns the maximum value that *end* − *start* + 1 should attain, and calling **glGetIntegerv** with *pname* parameter GL_MAX_ELEMENTS_INDICES_EXT returns the maximum value that should be passed to the *count* parameter of **glDrawRangeElementsEXT**. Exceeding these suggested limits is allowable, but it may result in lower performance. In any case, an application can expect the **glDrawRangeElementsEXT** function to perform at least as well as the **glDrawElements** function.

New Functions

■ **glDrawRangeElementsEXT**—Render indexed primitives from restricted array data.

Prototype

```
void glDrawRangeElementsEXT(GLenum mode,
                            GLuint start,
                            GLuint end,
                            GLsizei count,
                            GLenum type,
                            const GLvoid *indices);
```

Parameters

mode	Specifies what kind of primitives to render. Accepts the same values as the *mode* parameter of the **glDrawElements** function.
start	Specifies the minimum index that appears in the array pointed to by the *indices* parameter.
end	Specifies the maximum index that appears in the array pointed to by the *indices* parameter.

ttp3ttp

353333

count	Specifies the number of elements in the array pointed to by the *indices* parameter that are to be rendered.
type	Specifies the data type of the values in the array pointed to by the *indices* parameter. Must be GL_UNSIGNED_BYTE, GL_UNSIGNED_SHORT, or GL_UNSIGNED_INT.
indices	Specifies a pointer to the location in memory where the index array is stored.

Description

The **glDrawRangeElementsEXT** function performs the same function as the **glDrawElements** function, but also allows the application to specify the range of values that appear in the index array. The *start* and *end* parameters specify the minimum and maximum values, inclusive, that appear in the array pointed to by the *indices* parameter. If any values in the index array fall outside this range, an error may not be generated, but the behavior is undefined.

Special Considerations

Optimal performance may not be achieved if the *count* parameter specifies a value greater than GL_MAX_ELEMENTS_INDICES_EXT, or if the range specified by the *start* and *end* parameters exceeds GL_MAX_ELEMENTS_VERTICES_EXT. However, applications can expect that the performance of the **glDrawRangeElementsEXT** function will always be at least as good as the **glDrawElements** function.

Errors

GL_INVALID_ENUM is generated if *mode* is not an accepted value.

GL_INVALID_VALUE is generated if *end* is less than *start*.

GL_INVALID_VALUE is generated if *count* is negative.

GL_INVALID_OPERATION is generated if **glDrawRangeElementsEXT** is called between calls to **glBegin** and **glEnd**.

EXTENDED FUNCTIONS

■ **glGetIntegerv**—Extended to allow retrieval of suggested maximum vertex and index counts.

Prototype

```
void glGetIntegerv(GLenum pname, GLint *params);
```

Extended Parameters

pname	Specifies the parameter to be returned. May be one of the values listed in Description.

Description

The **glGetIntegerv** function can be used to retrieve an implementation's suggested maximum vertex count and index count to be used when drawing indexed primitives. The *pname* parameter may be one of the following values:

GL_MAX_ELEMENTS_VERTICES_EXT

> The maximum number of vertices that should be rendered with a single call to the **glDrawRangeElementsEXT** function is returned.

GL_MAX_ELEMENTS_INDICES_EXT

> The maximum number of indices that should be passed to the **gl-DrawRangeElementsEXT** function is returned.

8.2   GL_EXT_multi_draw_arrays

OpenGL version required	OpenGL 1.1
Dependencies	—
Promotions	—
Related extensions	—

DISCUSSION

The GL_EXT_multi_draw_arrays extension provides two functions that allow multiple sets of primitives to be rendered using the same array data.

Calling the **glMultiDrawArraysEXT** function,

```
void glMultiDrawArraysEXT(GLenum mode,
                          const GLint *first,
                          const GLsizei *count,
                          GLsizei primcount);
```

is equivalent to the following code.

```
for (int i = 0; i < primcount; i++)
{
    if (count[i] > 0)
        glDrawArrays(mode, first[i], count[i]);
}
```

The *first* and *count* parameters of the **glMultiDrawArraysEXT** function specify arrays from which the starting index and number of array indices are read for each set of primitives that is rendered.

Calling the **glMultiDrawElementsEXT** function,

```
void glMultiDrawElementsEXT(GLenum mode,
                            const GLsizei *count,
```

```
                                  GLenum type,
                                  const GLvoid **indices,
                                  GLsizei primcount);
```

is equivalent to the following code.

```
for (int i = 0; i < primcount; i++)
{
    if (count[i] > 0)
        glDrawElements(mode, count[i], type, indices[i]);
}
```

The *count* and *indices* parameters of the **glMultiDrawElementsEXT** function specify arrays from which the number of elements and the pointer to the index array are read for each set of primitives that is rendered.

NEW FUNCTIONS

- **glMultiDrawArraysEXT**—Render multiple sets of primitives from array data.

Prototype

```
void glMultiDrawArraysEXT(GLenum mode,
                          const GLint *first,
                          const GLsizei *count,
                          GLsizei primcount);
```

Parameters

mode   Specifies what kind of primitives to render. Accepts the same values as the *mode* parameter of the **glDrawArrays** function.

first   Specifies an array of size *primcount* containing the starting index for each set of primitives to be rendered.

count   Specifies an array of size *primcount* containing the number of indices to render for each set of primitives.

primcount   Specifies the number of sets of primitives to render.

Description

The **glMultiDrawArraysEXT** function renders multiple sets of primitives by performing the equivalent of a call to the **glDrawArrays** function the number of times specified by the *primcount* parameter. The *i*th set of primitives is rendered using the *i*th values in the arrays pointed to by the *first* and *count* parameters.

Errors

GL_INVALID_ENUM is generated if *mode* is not an accepted value.

GL_INVALID_VALUE is generated if *primcount* is negative.

GL_INVALID_OPERATION is generated if **glMultiDrawArraysEXT** is called between calls to **glBegin** and **glEnd**.

■ **glMultiDrawElementsEXT**—Render multiple sets of indexed primitives from array data.

Prototype

```
void glMultiDrawElementsEXT(GLenum mode,
                            const GLsizei *count,
                            GLenum type,
                            const GLvoid **indices,
                            GLsizei primcount);
```

Parameters

mode   Specifies what kind of primitives to render. Accepts the same values as the *mode* parameter of the **glDrawElements** function.

count   Specifies an array of size *primcount* containing the number of elements to render for each set of primitives.

type   Specifies the data type of the values in the array pointed to by the *indices* parameter. Must be GL_UNSIGNED_BYTE, GL_UNSIGNED_SHORT, or GL_UNSIGNED_INT.

indices   Specifies an array of size *primcount* containing the index array pointer for each set of primitives to be rendered.

primcount   Specifies the number of sets of primitives to render.

Description

The **glMultiDrawElementsEXT** function renders multiple sets of primitives by performing the equivalent of a call to the **glDrawElements** function the number of times specified by the *primcount* parameter. The *i*th set of primitives is rendered using the *i*th values in the arrays pointed to by the *count* and *indices* parameters.

Errors

GL_INVALID_ENUM is generated if *mode* is not an accepted value.

GL_INVALID_VALUE is generated if *primcount* is negative.

GL_INVALID_OPERATION is generated if **glMultiDrawElementsEXT** is called between calls to **glBegin** and **glEnd**.

8.3   GL_ATI_element_array

OpenGL version required	OpenGL 1.1
Dependencies	—
Promotions	—
Related extensions	—

DISCUSSION

The GL_ATI_element_array extension provides a mechanism that allows an application to specify an element index array. Replacements for the **glDrawElements** and **gl-DrawRangeElementsEXT** functions are also defined, and draw primitives using the current element array.

The element index array is specified by calling the **glElementPointerATI** function,

```
void glElementPointerATI(GLenum type,
                         const GLvoid *pointer);
```

The *type* parameter specifies the data type of each index in the array and may be GL_UNSIGNED_BYTE, GL_UNSIGNED_SHORT, or GL_UNSIGNED_INT. The *pointer* parameter specifies the location where the element array begins in memory.

Before drawing can take place using the element array, it must be enabled. The element array is enabled and disabled by calling the **glEnableClientState** and **glDisable-ClientState** functions with *array* parameter GL_ELEMENT_ARRAY_ATI. When the element array is enabled, primitives may be drawn by calling the **glDrawElementArrayATI** function,

```
void glDrawElementArrayATI(GLenum mode,
                           GLsizei count);
```

The *mode* and *count* parameters have the same meanings as they do for the **glDraw-Elements** function. The current data type and pointer corresponding to the element array are used to render *count* elements. Primitives may also be rendered using the **glDrawRangeElementArrayATI** function,

```
void glDrawRangeElementArrayATI(GLenum mode,
                                GLuint start,
                                GLuint end,
                                GLsizei count);
```

The *mode*, *start*, *end*, and *count* parameters have the same meanings as they do for the **glDrawRangeElementsEXT** function. The current data type and pointer corresponding to the element array are used to render *count* elements whose indexes must fall in the range defined by the *start* and *end* parameters.

NEW FUNCTIONS

■ **glElementPointerATI**—Define an array of index data.

Prototype

```
void glElementPointerATI(GLenum type,
                         const GLvoid *pointer);
```

Parameters

type   Specifies the data type of the values in the array. Must be GL_UNSIGNED_BYTE, GL_UNSIGNED_SHORT, or GL_UNSIGNED_INT.

pointer   Specifies a pointer to the element array.

Description

The **glElementPointerATI** function specifies the location and data type of the element array. The *type* parameter specifies the data type of each index in the array, and the *pointer* parameter specifies a pointer to the first index in memory.

The element array is enabled and disabled by calling the **glEnableClientState** and **glDisableClientState** functions with *array* parameter GL_ELEMENT_ARRAY_ATI. Initially, the element array is disabled.

Special Considerations

Unlike other array specification commands, the **glElementPointerATI** does not take a *stride* parameter. Element indices must be packed tightly together in memory.

Get Functions

glGetIntegerv with *pname* parameter GL_ELEMENT_ARRAY_TYPE_ATI

glGetPointerv with *pname* parameter GL_ELEMENT_ARRAY_POINTER_ATI

Errors

GL_INVALID_ENUM is generated if *type* is not an accepted value.

■ **glDrawElementArrayATI**—Render primitives using the element array.

Prototype

```
void glDrawElementArrayATI(GLenum mode,
                           GLsizei count);
```

Parameters

mode   Specifies what kind of primitives to render. Accepts the same values as the *mode* parameter of the **glDrawElements** function.

count   Specifies the number of elements to be rendered.

Description

The **glDrawElementArrayATI** function performs the same operation as the **glDrawElements** function, using same values for the *mode* and *count* parameters, but obtains element indices from the current element array.

Errors

GL_INVALID_ENUM is generated if *mode* is not an accepted value.

GL_INVALID_VALUE is generated if *count* is negative.

GL_INVALID_OPERATION is generated if **glDrawElementArrayATI** is called, and the element array is disabled.

■ **glDrawRangeElementArrayATI**—Render primitives using the element array with a restricted range of indices.

Prototype

```
void glDrawRangeElementArrayATI(GLenum mode,
                                GLuint start,
                                GLuint end,
                                GLsizei count);
```

Parameters

mode	Specifies what kind of primitives to render. Accepts the same values as the *mode* parameter of the **glDrawElements** function.
start	Specifies the minimum index that appears in the element array.
end	Specifies the maximum index that appears in the element array.
count	Specifies the number of elements to be rendered.

Description

The **glDrawRangeElementArrayATI** function performs the same operation as the **glDrawRangeElementsEXT** function, using same values for the *mode, start, end*, and *count* parameters, but obtains element indices from the current element array.

Errors

GL_INVALID_ENUM is generated if *mode* is not an accepted value.

GL_INVALID_VALUE is generated if *end* is less than *start*.

GL_INVALID_VALUE is generated if *count* is negative.

GL_INVALID_OPERATION is generated if **glDrawRangeElementArrayATI** is called, and the element array is disabled.

EXTENDED FUNCTIONS

■ **glEnableClientState, glDisableClientState**—Extended to enable/disable the element array.

Prototypes

```
void glEnableClientState(GLenum array);
void glDisableClientState(GLenum array);
```

Extended Parameters

array   Specifies an array to enable or disable. May be GL_ELEMENT_ARRAY_ATI.

Description

The **glEnableClientState** and **glDisableClientState** functions enable or disable arrays stored in client space. The element array is enabled or disabled by passing the value GL_ELEMENT_ARRAY_ATI to the *array* parameter.

■ **glIsEnabled**—Extended to return whether the element array is enabled.

Prototype

```
GLboolean glIsEnabled(GLenum cap);
```

Extended Parameters

cap   Specifies an OpenGL capability. May be GL_ELEMENT_ARRAY_ATI.

Description

Whether the element array is enabled is determined by calling the **glIsEnabled** function with *cap* parameter GL_ELEMENT_ARRAY_ATI.

■ **glGetIntegerv**—Extended to allow retrieval of element array state.

Prototype

```
void glGetIntegerv(GLenum pname, GLint *params);
```

Extended Parameters

pname   Specifies the parameter to be returned. May be GL_ELEMENT_ARRAY_ TYPE_ATI.

Description

The **glGetIntegerv** function can be used to retrieve state related to the element array that was previously specified using the **glElementPointerATI** function. If the *pname* parameter is GL_ELEMENT_ARRAY_TYPE_ATI, then the data type of the element array is returned. The initial value is GL_UNSIGNED_INT.

■ **glGetPointerv**—Extended to allow retrieval of the element array pointer.

Prototype

```
void glGetPointerv(GLenum pname, GLvoid **pointer);
```

Extended Parameters

pname   Specifies the array pointer to be returned. May be GL_ELEMENT_ARRAY_
                   POINTER_ATI.

Description

The **glGetPointerv** function can be used to retrieve the pointer to the element array that was previously specified using the **glElementPointerATI** function. When the *pname* parameter is GL_ELEMENT_ARRAY_POINTER_ATI, the pointer to the element array is returned in the *pointer* parameter. The initial value is a null pointer.

8.4   GL_APPLE_element_array

OpenGL version required	OpenGL 1.1
Dependencies	—
Promotions	—
Related extensions	—

DISCUSSION

The GL_APPLE_element_array extension provides a mechanism that allows an application to specify an element index array. Replacements for the **glDrawElements** and **glDrawRangeElementsEXT** functions are also defined, and draw primitives using the current element array.

The element index array is specified by calling the **glElementPointerAPPLE** function,

```
void glElementPointerAPPLE(GLenum type,
                           const GLvoid *pointer);
```

The *type* parameter specifies the data type of each index in the array and may be GL_UNSIGNED_BYTE, GL_UNSIGNED_SHORT, or GL_UNSIGNED_INT. The *pointer* parameter specifies the location where the element array begins in memory.

Before drawing can take place using the element array, it must be enabled. The element array is enabled and disabled by calling the **glEnableClientState** and **glDisableClientState** functions with *array* parameter GL_ELEMENT_ARRAY_APPLE. When the element array is enabled, primitives may be drawn by calling the **glDrawElementArrayAPPLE** function,

```
void glDrawElementArrayAPPLE(GLenum mode,
                             GLint first,
                             GLsizei count);
```

The *mode* and *count* parameters have the same meanings as they do for the **glDrawElements** function. The current data type and pointer corresponding to the element array are used to render *count* elements, starting with the index specified by the *first* parameter. Primitives may also be rendered using the **glDrawRangeElementArrayAPPLE** function,

```
void glDrawRangeElementArrayAPPLE(GLenum mode,
                                  GLuint start,
                                  GLuint end,
                                  GLint first,
                                  GLsizei count);
```

The *mode, start, end,* and *count* parameters have the same meanings as they do for the **glDrawRangeElementsEXT** function. The current data type and pointer corresponding to the element array are used to render *count* elements, starting with the index specified by the *first* parameter, whose indices must fall in the range defined by the *start* and *end* parameters.

Multiple sets of primitives may also be rendered using the element array. Calling the **glMultiDrawElementArrayAPPLE** function,

```
void glMultiDrawElementArrayAPPLE(GLenum mode,
                                  const GLint *first,
                                  const GLsizei *count,
                                  GLsizei primcount);
```

is equivalent to the following code.

```
for (int i = 0; i < primcount; i++)
{
    glDrawElementArrayAPPLE(mode, first[i], count[i]);
}
```

The *first* and *count* parameters of the **glMultiDrawElementArrayAPPLE** function specify arrays from which the starting index and number of elements are read for each set of primitives that is rendered.

Calling the **glMultiDrawRangeElementArrayAPPLE** function,

```
void glMultiDrawRangeElementArrayAPPLE(GLenum mode,
                                       GLuint start,
                                       GLuint end,
                                       const GLint *first,
                                       const GLsizei *count,
                                       GLsizei primcount);
```

is equivalent to the following code.

```
for (int i = 0; i < primcount; i++)
{
    if ((first[i] > 0) && (count[i] > 0))
        glDrawRangeElementArrayAPPLE(mode, start, end,
            first[i], count[i]);
}
```

The *first* and *count* parameters of the **glMultiDrawRangeElementArrayAPPLE** function specify arrays from which the starting index and number of elements are read for each set of primitives that is rendered.

NEW FUNCTIONS

■ **glElementPointerAPPLE**—Define an array of index data.

Prototype

```
void glElementPointerAPPLE(GLenum type,
                          const GLvoid *pointer);
```

Parameters

type   Specifies the data type of the values in the array. Must be GL_UNSIGNED_
           BYTE, GL_UNSIGNED_SHORT, or GL_UNSIGNED_INT.

pointer   Specifies a pointer to the element array.

Description

The **glElementPointerAPPLE** function specifies the location and data type of the element array. The *type* parameter specifies the data type of each index in the array, and the *pointer* parameter specifies a pointer to the first index in memory.

The element array is enabled and disabled by calling the **glEnableClientState** and **glDisableClientState** functions with *array* parameter GL_ELEMENT_ARRAY_APPLE. Initially, the element array is disabled.

Get Functions

glGetIntegerv with *pname* parameter GL_ELEMENT_ARRAY_TYPE_APPLE

glGetPointerv with *pname* parameter GL_ELEMENT_ARRAY_POINTER_APPLE

Errors

GL_INVALID_ENUM is generated if *type* is not an accepted value.

■ **glDrawElementArrayAPPLE**—Render primitives using the element array.

Prototype

```
void glDrawElementArrayAPPLE(GLenum mode,
                             GLint first,
                             GLsizei count);
```

Parameters

mode   Specifies what kind of primitives to render. Accepts the same values as the *mode* parameter of the **glDrawElements** function.

first   Specifies the index of the first element to be rendered.

count   Specifies the number of elements to be rendered.

Description

The **glDrawElementArrayAPPLE** function performs the same operation as the **glDrawElements** function, using the same values for the *mode* and *count* parameters, but obtains element indices from the current element array, starting with the index specified by the *first* parameter.

Errors

GL_INVALID_ENUM is generated if *mode* is not an accepted value.

GL_INVALID_VALUE is generated if *first* or *count* is negative.

GL_INVALID_OPERATION is generated if **glDrawElementArrayAPPLE** is called, and the element array is disabled.

■ **glDrawRangeElementArrayAPPLE**—Render primitives using the element array with a restricted range of indices.

Prototype

```
void glDrawRangeElementArrayAPPLE(GLenum mode,
                                  GLuint start,
                                  GLuint end,
                                  GLint first,
                                  GLsizei count);
```

Parameters

mode   Specifies what kind of primitives to render. Accepts the same values as the *mode* parameter of the **glDrawElements** function.

start   Specifies the minimum index that appears in the element array.

end   Specifies the maximum index that appears in the element array.

first   Specifies the index of the first element to be rendered.

count   Specifies the number of elements to be rendered.

Description

The **glDrawRangeElementArrayAPPLE** function performs the same operation as the **glDrawRangeElementsEXT** function using same values for the *mode*, *start*, *end*, and *count* parameters, but obtains element indices from the current element array, starting with the index specified by the *first* parameter.

Errors

GL_INVALID_ENUM is generated if *mode* is not an accepted value.

GL_INVALID_VALUE is generated if *end* is less than *start*.

GL_INVALID_VALUE is generated if *first* or *count* is negative.

GL_INVALID_OPERATION is generated if **glDrawRangeElementArrayAPPLE** is called, and the element array is disabled.

■ **glMultiDrawElementArrayAPPLE**—Render multiple primitives using the element array.

Prototype

```
void glMultiDrawElementArrayAPPLE(GLenum mode,
                                  const GLint *first,
                                  const GLsizei *count,
                                  GLsizei primcount);
```

Parameters

mode	Specifies what kind of primitives to render. Accepts the same values as the *mode* parameter of the **glDrawElements** function.
first	Specifies an array of size *primcount* containing the starting index for each set of primitives to be rendered.
count	Specifies an array of size *primcount* containing the number of elements to render for each set of primitives.
primcount	Specifies the number of sets of primitives to render.

Description

The **glMultiDrawElementArrayAPPLE** function renders multiple sets of primitives by performing the equivalent of a call to the **glDrawElementArrayAPPLE** function the number of times specified by the *primcount* parameter. The *i*th set of primitives is rendered using the *i*th values in the arrays pointed to by the *first* and *count* parameters.

Errors

GL_INVALID_ENUM is generated if *mode* is not an accepted value.

GL_INVALID_VALUE is generated if *primcount* is negative.

GL_INVALID_OPERATION is generated if **glMultiDrawElementArrayAPPLE** is called, and the element array is disabled.

■ **glMultiDrawRangeElementArrayAPPLE**—Render multiple primitives using the element array with a restricted range of indices.

Prototype

```
void glMultiDrawRangeElementArrayAPPLE(GLenum mode,
                                       GLuint start,
                                       GLuint end,
                                       const GLint *first,
                                       const GLsizei *count,
                                       GLsizei primcount);
```

Parameters

mode	Specifies what kind of primitives to render. Accepts the same values as the *mode* parameter of the **glDrawElements** function.
start	Specifies the minimum index that appears in the element array.
end	Specifies the maximum index that appears in the element array.
first	Specifies an array of size *primcount* containing the starting index for each set of primitives to be rendered.
count	Specifies an array of size *primcount* containing the number of elements to render for each set of primitives.
primcount	Specifies the number of sets of primitives to render.

Description

The **glMultiDrawRangeElementArrayAPPLE** function renders multiple sets of primitives by performing the equivalent of a call to the **glDrawRangeElementArrayAPPLE** function the number of times specified by the *primcount* parameter. The *i*th set of primitives is rendered using the *i*th values in the arrays pointed to by the *first* and *count* parameters.

Errors

GL_INVALID_ENUM is generated if *mode* is not an accepted value.

GL_INVALID_VALUE is generated if *end* is less than *start*.

GL_INVALID_VALUE is generated if *primcount* is negative.

GL_INVALID_OPERATION is generated if **glMultiDrawRangeElementArrayAPPLE** is called, and the element array is disabled.

EXTENDED FUNCTIONS

■ **glEnableClientState**, **glDisableClientState**—Extended to enable/disable the element array.

Prototypes

```
void glEnableClientState(GLenum array);
void glDisableClientState(GLenum array);
```

Extended Parameters

array   Specifies an array to enable or disable. May be GL_ELEMENT_ARRAY_
                 APPLE.

Description

The **glEnableClientState** and **glDisableClientState** functions enable or disable arrays stored in client space. The element array is enabled or disabled by passing the value GL_ELEMENT_ARRAY_APPLE to the *array* parameter.

■ **glIsEnabled**—Extended to return whether the element array is enabled.

Prototype

```
GLboolean glIsEnabled(GLenum cap);
```

Extended Parameters

cap   Specifies an OpenGL capability. May be GL_ELEMENT_ARRAY_APPLE.

Description

Whether the element array is enabled is determined by calling the **glIsEnabled** function with *cap* parameter GL_ELEMENT_ARRAY_APPLE.

■ **glGetIntegerv**—Extended to allow retrieval of element array state.

Prototype

```
void glGetIntegerv(GLenum pname, GLint *params);
```

Extended Parameters

pname   Specifies the parameter to be returned. May be GL_ELEMENT_ARRAY_
                 TYPE_APPLE.

Description

The **glGetIntegerv** function can be used to retrieve state related to the element array that was previously specified using the **glElementPointerAPPLE** function. If the *pname* parameter is GL_ELEMENT_ARRAY_TYPE_APPLE, then the data type of the element array is returned. The initial value is GL_UNSIGNED_INT.

■ **glGetPointerv**—Extended to allow retrieval of the element array pointer.

Prototype

```
void glGetPointerv(GLenum pname, GLvoid **pointer);
```

Extended Parameters

pname   Specifies the array pointer to be returned. May be GL_ELEMENT_ARRAY_
                 POINTER_APPLE.

Description

The **glGetPointerv** function can be used to retrieve the pointer to the element array that was previously specified using the **glElementPointerAPPLE** function. When the *pname* parameter is GL_ELEMENT_ARRAY_POINTER_APPLE, the pointer to the element array is returned in the *pointer* parameter. The initial value is a null pointer.

8.5   GL_EXT_compiled_vertex_array

OpenGL version required	OpenGL 1.1
Dependencies	—
Promotions	—
Related extensions	—

DISCUSSION

The GL_EXT_compiled_vertex_array extension provides a mechanism through which a range of vertex array data can be locked in order to give an implementation the opportunity to compile the data into a more efficient format or move it to fast memory for more efficient access. A performance gain could be realized by applications that render multiple primitives using the same vertex array data.

A range of vertex array data is locked by calling the **glLockArraysEXT** function,

```
void glLockArraysEXT(GLint first,
                     GLsizei count);
```

The *first* parameter specifies the starting index of the range for which data in all enabled vertex arrays is locked. The *count* parameter specifies how many elements of each array are locked. When the vertex array data is locked, the implementation is free to assume that the data in the arrays will not be changed by the application. If the application does change the data, the modifications may not be reflected in any drawing commands that occur while the arrays are locked. If any drawing operation accesses an array element outside the locked range, then the result is undefined.

Vertex array data is unlocked by calling the **glUnlockArraysEXT** function,

```
void glUnlockArraysEXT(void);
```

Subsequent changes to the vertex array data are recognized by the implementation. Calls to **glLockArraysEXT** and **glUnlockArraysEXT** may not be nested, and a call to **glUnlockArraysEXT** must be preceded by an unbalanced call to **glLockArraysEXT**.

NEW FUNCTIONS

■ **glLockArraysEXT**—Lock vertex arrays.

Prototype

```
void glLockArraysEXT(GLint first,
                     GLsizei count);
```

Parameters

first   Specifies the starting index of the range of array elements to lock.

count   Specifies the number of array elements to lock.

Description

The **glLockArraysEXT** function locks the data contained in all enabled vertex arrays starting at the index specified by the *first* parameter. The *count* parameter specifies the number of elements in each vertex array to lock.

When arrays are locked, changes to vertex data in the locked range may not be reflected in subsequent drawing operations until the **glUnlockArraysEXT** function is called. Also, if any drawing operation accesses an array element outside the locked range, then the result is undefined.

Get Functions

glGetIntegerv with *pname* parameter GL_ARRAY_ELEMENT_LOCK_FIRST_EXT

glGetIntegerv with *pname* parameter GL_ARRAY_ELEMENT_LOCK_COUNT_EXT

Errors

GL_INVALID_VALUE is generated if *first* is negative.

GL_INVALID_VALUE is generated if *count* is negative or zero.

GL_INVALID_OPERATION is generated if **glLockArraysEXT** is called after a previous call to **glLockArraysEXT**, but with no previous matching call to **glUnlockArraysEXT**.

GL_INVALID_OPERATION is generated if **glLockArraysEXT** is called between calls to **glBegin** and **glEnd**.

■ **glUnlockArraysEXT**—Unlock vertex arrays.

Prototype

```
void glUnlockArraysEXT(void);
```

Description

The **glUnlockArraysEXT** function unlocks the vertex array data that was previously locked using the **glLockArraysEXT** function.

Errors

GL_INVALID_OPERATION is generated if **glUnlockArraysEXT** is called without a previous matching call to **glLockArraysEXT**.

GL_INVALID_OPERATION is generated if **glUnlockArraysEXT** is called between calls to **glBegin** and **glEnd**.

EXTENDED FUNCTIONS

■ **glGetIntegerv**—Extended to allow retrieval of array locking parameters.

Prototype

```
void glGetIntegerv(GLenum pname, GLint *params);
```

Extended Parameters

pname   Specifies the parameter to be returned. May be one of the values listed in Description.

Description

The **glGetIntegerv** function can be used to retrieve array locking parameters. The *pname* parameter may be one of the following values:

GL_ARRAY_ELEMENT_LOCK_FIRST_EXT
        The index of the first array element locked is returned.

GL_ARRAY_ELEMENT_LOCK_COUNT_EXT
        The number of array elements locked is returned.

8.6   GL_NV_vertex_array_range

OpenGL version required	OpenGL 1.1
Dependencies	—
Promotions	—
Related extensions	GL_NV_vertex_array_range2 GL_NV_fence

DISCUSSION

Unextended OpenGL is required to finish reading array data before drawing commands return control to an application. Furthermore, array element indices are ordinarily unbounded and may reference any location in the client address space. For both of these reasons, implementations are generally forced to either copy vertex data when a rendering command is issued or directly feed all of the vertex data to the GPU (referred to as *pushing*) before returning control to the application. The purpose of the GL_NV_vertex_array_ range extension is to allow GPUs to asynchronously read vertex data from client memory (referred to as *pulling*) after a rendering command has returned control to the application. This usually results in significant performance gains, but at the price of memory coherency issues that must be handled by the application.

The region of memory from which a GPU may pull vertex data is called the *vertex array range*. The vertex array range is established by calling the **glVertexArrayRangeNV** function,

```
void glVertexArrayRangeNV(GLsizei length,
                          GLvoid *pointer);
```

The *pointer* parameter specifies a pointer to a region of memory having size specified by the *length* parameter. Once established, the vertex array range is enabled and disabled by calling the **glEnableClientState** and **glDisableClientState** functions with *pname* parameter GL_VERTEX_ARRAY_RANGE_NV.

It is possible that the implementation is not able to establish a vertex array range, or that it is unable to pull vertex data from client memory while certain state is enabled or disabled. The vertex array range is either valid or invalid, and this state can be retrieved by calling the **glGetIntegerv** function with *pname* parameter GL_VERTEX_ARRAY_RANGE_VALID_NV. The vertex array range is valid only if the following conditions are satisfied:

- GL_VERTEX_ARRAY_RANGE_NV is enabled.

- GL_VERTEX_ARRAY or GL_VERTEX_ATTRIB_ARRAY0_NV is enabled.

- The vertex array range has been established by calling the **glVertexArrayRangeNV** function with a nonzero length and non-null pointer.

- An implementation-dependent validity check based on the pointer alignment, size, and underlying memory type of the vertex array range has succeeded.

- An implementation-dependent validity check based on the vertex array pointer alignments, strides, sizes, and types has succeeded.

- Other implementation-dependent validity checks based on additional OpenGL state have succeeded.

When the vertex array range is enabled and valid, vertex data must be placed in the region of memory designated by the **glVertexArrayRangeNV** function where the GPU can access it. Rendering commands may return before all (or any) of the vertex data has been read from the vertex array range by the GPU, so changes to the vertex data after a draw function is called may have undesirable results. The GL_NV_fence extension (see Chapter 9, Section 9.1) is typically used to determine whether the GPU has finished reading the vertex data referenced by a particular rendering command, but an explicit synchronization can be provoked by calling the **glFlushVertexArrayRangeNV** function,

```
void glFlushVertexArrayRangeNV(void);
```

The **glFlushVertexArrayRangeNV** function waits until all rendering commands accessing the vertex array range have completed and then ensures that any previous changes made to the data in the vertex array range are visible to the GPU.

In addition to the explicit synchronization triggered by the **glFlushVertex-ArrayRangeNV** function, an implicit vertex array range flush occurs when any of the following actions take place:

- The **glFinish** function returns.
- The **glVertexArrayRangeNV** function returns.
- The **glEnableClientState** or **glDisableClientState** function called with *array* parameter GL_VERTEX_ARRAY_RANGE_NV returns.
- Another OpenGL context is made current.

When the vertex array range is enabled, any array element accessed whose data does not lie in the region of memory established as the vertex array range causes an undefined vertex to be generated. Also, there may be a limit on the maximum array element index that can be used when the vertex array range is enabled, and exceeding this limit may generate an undefined vertex. The maximum array element index supported by the implementation is retrieved by calling the **glGetIntegerv** function with *pname* parameter GL_MAX_VERTEX_ARRAY_RANGE_ELEMENT_NV.

The GL_NV_vertex_array_range extension provides two window-system-dependent functions that are intended to be used to allocate memory for a vertex array range. The **wglAllocateMemoryNV** function,

```
GLvoid *wglAllocateMemoryNV(GLsizei size,
                            GLfloat readFrequency,
                            GLfloat writeFrequency,
                            GLfloat priority);
```

returns a pointer to a region of memory whose size is specified by the *size* parameter. The *readFrequency*, *writeFrequency*, and *priority* parameters are hints having values in the range 0.0 to 1.0, which inform the implementation about how the application intends to use the memory. If a low value is specified for the read frequency or write frequency, it indicates that the memory will not be read or written very often. High values indicate that the memory will be read or written a lot. The implementation can take these values into account when choosing what type of memory to allocate. The *priority* parameter specifies a general priority value for the memory allocated and may be used as an additional factor when choosing the memory type. Memory allocated by the **wglAllocateMemoryNV** function is released by calling the **wglFreeMemoryNV** function,

```
void wglFreeMemoryNV(GLvoid *pointer);
```

The **wglAllocateMemoryNV** and **wglFreeMemoryNV** functions do not depend on any OpenGL context and may be called at any time.

NEW FUNCTIONS

■ `glVertexArrayRangeNV`—Specify the vertex array range.

Prototype

```
void glVertexArrayRangeNV(GLsizei length,
                          GLvoid *pointer);
```

Parameters

length   Specifies the length of the vertex array range, in bytes.

pointer   Specifies a pointer to the beginning of the vertex array range.

Description

The `glVertexArrayRangeNV` function establishes the vertex array range according to the values of the *length* and *pointer* parameters. If the vertex array range could not be established for system-dependent reasons, then the vertex array range is not valid. Whether the vertex array range is valid can be determined by calling the `glGetIntegerv` function with *pname* parameter GL_VERTEX_ARRAY_RANGE_VALID_NV.

If the *length* parameter is 0 or the *pointer* parameter is null, then any previously established vertex array range is released, and no vertex array range exists upon return. This should always be done before memory used by the vertex array range is released.

Get Functions

`glGetIntegerv` with *pname* parameter GL_VERTEX_ARRAY_RANGE_LENGTH_NV

`glGetIntegerv` with *pname* parameter GL_VERTEX_ARRAY_RANGE_VALID_NV

`glGetPointerv` with *pname* parameter GL_VERTEX_ARRAY_RANGE_POINTER_NV

Errors

GL_INVALID_OPERATION is generated if **glVertexArrayRangeNV** is called between calls to **glBegin** and **glEnd**.

■ `glFlushVertexArrayRangeNV`—Flush the vertex array range.

Prototype

```
void glFlushVertexArrayRangeNV(void);
```

Description

The **glFlushVertexArrayRangeNV** function performs an explicit synchronization, after which any drawing commands are guaranteed to access the most recently written data in the vertex array range.

Errors

GL_INVALID_OPERATION is generated if **glFlushVertexArrayRangeNV** is called between calls to **glBegin** and **glEnd**.

■ **wglAllocateMemoryNV**—Allocate memory for vertex array range.

Prototype

```
GLvoid *wglAllocateMemoryNV(GLsizei size,
                            GLfloat readFrequency,
                            GLfloat writeFrequency,
                            GLfloat priority);
```

Parameters

size   Specifies the size of the range of memory to allocate, in bytes.

readFrequency   Specifies a read frequency hint in the range 0.0 to 1.0. A value of 0.0 means that the application intends to rarely or never read from the memory allocated. A value of 1.0 means that the application intends to read from the memory frequently.

writeFrequency   Specifies a write frequency hint in the range 0.0 to 1.0. A value of 0.0 means that the application intends to rarely write (perhaps only once) to the memory allocated. A value of 1.0 means that the application intends to write to the memory frequently.

priority   Specifies a priority hint in the range 0.0 to 1.0. Higher values indicate that more efficiently accessible memory should be allocated relative to other types of resources, such as texture memory.

Description

The **wglAllocateMemoryNV** function is intended to be used to allocate memory for a vertex array range. The *readFrequency*, *writeFrequency*, and *priority* parameters specify usage hints that may be used by an implementation in whatever way it wishes to determine where to allocate the memory. If a region of size specified by the *size* parameter could be allocated, a valid pointer to the beginning of the range is returned. If the allocation fails, a null pointer is returned, and no error is generated.

The memory allocated by the **wglAllocateMemoryNV** function should be released using the **wglFreeMemoryNV** function.

Special Considerations

The **wglAllocateMemoryNV** function does not depend on an OpenGL context and may be called when no such context is active.

■ **wglFreeMemoryNV**—Free memory for vertex array range.

Prototype

```
void wglFreeMemoryNV(GLvoid *pointer);
```

Parameters

pointer   Specifies a pointer to a region of memory that was previously allocated using the **wglAllocateMemoryNV** function.

Description

The **wglFreeMemoryNV** function releases the memory that was previously allocated with the **wglAllocateMemoryNV** function. The *pointer* parameter should specify a pointer that was returned by the **wglAllocateMemoryNV** function and has not previously been freed. An attempt to free a pointer that does not correspond to memory allocated by the **wglAllocate-MemoryNV** function is ignored without generating an error.

Special Considerations

The **wglFreeMemoryNV** function does not depend on an OpenGL context and may be called when no such context is active.

EXTENDED FUNCTIONS

■ **glEnableClientState, glDisableClientState**—Extended to enable/disable the vertex array range.

Prototypes

```
void glEnableClientState(GLenum array);
void glDisableClientState(GLenum array);
```

Extended Parameters

array   Specifies an array to enable or disable. May be GL_VERTEX_ARRAY_
                   RANGE_NV.

Description

The **glEnableClientState** and **glDisableClientState** functions are used to enable or disable client array state. The vertex array range is enabled or disabled by passing the value GL_VERTEX_ARRAY_RANGE_NV to the *array* parameter.

■ **glIsEnabled**—Extended to return whether the vertex array range is enabled.

Prototype

```
GLboolean glIsEnabled(GLenum cap);
```

Extended Parameters

cap   Specifies an OpenGL capability. May be GL_VERTEX_ARRAY_RANGE_NV.

Description

Whether the vertex array range is enabled is determined by calling the **glIsEnabled** function with *cap* parameter GL_VERTEX_ARRAY_RANGE_NV.

■ **glGetIntegerv**—Extended to allow retrieval of vertex array range state.

Prototype

```
void glGetIntegerv(GLenum pname, GLint *params);
```

Extended Parameters

pname   Specifies the parameter to be returned. May be one of the values listed in Description.

Description

The **glGetIntegerv** function can be used to retrieve state related to the vertex array range. The *pname* parameter may be one of the following values:

GL_VERTEX_ARRAY_RANGE_LENGTH_NV

The length of the vertex array range is returned. The initial value is 0.

GL_VERTEX_ARRAY_RANGE_VALID_NV

A Boolean value indicating whether the vertex array range is valid is returned. The initial value is GL_FALSE.

GL_MAX_VERTEX_ARRAY_RANGE_ELEMENT_NV

The maximum index of any array element accessed inside the vertex array range supported by the implementation is returned. This is always at least 65535.

■ **glGetPointerv**—Extended to allow retrieval of the vertex array range pointer.

Prototype

```
void glGetPointerv(GLenum pname, GLvoid **pointer);
```

Extended Parameters

pname   Specifies the array pointer to be returned. May be GL_VERTEX_ARRAY_ RANGE_POINTER_NV.

Description

The **glGetPointerv** function can be used to retrieve the pointer to the vertex array range that was previously specified using the **glVertexArrayRangeNV** function. When the *pname* parameter is GL_VERTEX_ARRAY_RANGE_POINTER_NV, the pointer to the vertex array range is returned in the *pointer* parameter. The initial value is a null pointer.

8.7   GL_NV_vertex_array_range2

OpenGL version required	OpenGL 1.1
Dependencies	Requires GL_NV_vertex_array_range
Promotions	—
Related extensions	—

DISCUSSION

The GL_NV_vertex_array_range extension performs an implicit synchronization operation when the vertex array range is enabled or disabled. This can severely impact performance in applications that wish to mix rendering commands that access static data stored in the vertex array range and rendering commands that access dynamic vertex data stored outside the vertex array range. The GL_NV_vertex_array_range2 extension provides a way to enable and disable the vertex array range without performing the synchronization.

The vertex array range can be enabled and disabled by calling the **glEnable-ClientState** and **glDisableClientState** functions with *array* parameter GL_VERTEX_ARRAY_RANGE_NV. Doing either causes an implicit vertex array range flush that synchronizes access to the vertex array range between the CPU and GPU. The GL_NV_vertex_array_range2 extension allows an application to call the **glEnableClientState** or **glDisableClientState** function with *array* parameter GL_VERTEX_ARRAY_RANGE_WITHOUT_FLUSH_NV to enable or disable the vertex array range without performing a vertex array range flush. The effect is otherwise identical to using the constant GL_VERTEX_ARRAY_RANGE_NV. An application still queries **glGetIntegerv** with *pname* parameter GL_VERTEX_ARRAY_RANGE_NV to determine whether the vertex array range is enabled.

EXTENDED FUNCTIONS

- **glEnableClientState, glDisableClientState**—Extended to enable/disable the vertex array range without performing an implicit flush.

Prototypes

```
void glEnableClientState(GLenum array);
void glDisableClientState(GLenum array);
```

Extended Parameters

array   Specifies an array to enable or disable. May be GL_VERTEX_ARRAY_RANGE_WITHOUT_FLUSH_NV.

Description

The **glEnableClientState** and **glDisableClientState** functions are used to enable or disable client array state. The vertex array range is enabled or disabled by passing the value GL_VERTEX_ARRAY_RANGE_NV to the *array* parameter, but this causes an implicit flush that may impact performance. The vertex array range may be enabled and disabled without causing an implicit flush by passing the value GL_VERTEX_ARRAY_RANGE_WITHOUT_FLUSH_NV to the *array* parameter.

8.8 GL_APPLE_vertex_array_range

OpenGL version required	OpenGL 1.1
Dependencies	—
Promotions	—
Related extensions	GL_APPLE_fence

DISCUSSION

Unextended OpenGL is required to finish reading array data before drawing commands return control to an application. Furthermore, array element indices are ordinarily unbounded and may reference any location in the client address space. For both of these reasons, implementations are generally forced to either copy vertex data when a rendering command is issued or directly feed all of the vertex data to the GPU (referred to as *pushing*) before returning control to the application. The purpose of the GL_APPLE_vertex_ array_range extension is to allow GPUs to asynchronously read vertex data from client memory (referred to as *pulling*) after a rendering command has returned control to the application. This usually results in significant performance gains, but at the price of memory coherency issues that must be handled by the application.

The region of memory from which a GPU may pull vertex data is called the *vertex array range*. The vertex array range is established by calling the **glVertexArrayRangeAPPLE** function,

```
void glVertexArrayRangeAPPLE(GLsizei length,
                             GLvoid *pointer);
```

The *pointer* parameter specifies a pointer to a region of memory having a size specified by the *length* parameter. Once established, the vertex array range is enabled and disabled by calling the **glEnableClientState** and **glDisableClientState** functions with *pname* parameter GL_VERTEX_ARRAY_RANGE_APPLE.

When the vertex array range is enabled, vertex data must be placed in the region of memory designated by the **glVertexArrayRangeAPPLE** function, where the GPU can access it. Rendering commands may return before all (or any) of the vertex data has been read from the vertex array range by the GPU, so changes to the vertex data after a draw function is called may have undesirable results. The GL_APPLE_fence extension (see Chapter 9, Section 9.2) is typically used to determine whether the GPU has finished reading the vertex data referenced by a particular rendering command, but the **glFinish** function may also be used to ensure that all rendering is complete.

After an application updates the data in the vertex array range, an explicit synchronization can be provoked by calling the **glFlushVertexArrayRangeAPPLE** function,

```
void glFlushVertexArrayRangeAPPLE(GLsizei length,
                                  GLvoid *pointer);
```

The **glFlushVertexArrayRangeAPPLE** function ensures that any previous changes made to the data in the range specified by the *length* and *pointer* parameters are visible to the GPU.

When the vertex array range is enabled, any array element accessed whose data does not lie in the region of memory established as the vertex array range causes an undefined vertex to be generated. Also, there may be a limit on the maximum array element index that can be used when the vertex array range is enabled, and exceeding this limit may generate an undefined vertex. The maximum array element index supported by the implementation is retrieved by calling the **glGetIntegerv** function with *pname* parameter GL_MAX_VERTEX_ARRAY_RANGE_ELEMENT_APPLE.

NEW FUNCTIONS

■ **glVertexArrayRangeAPPLE**—Specify the vertex array range.

Prototype

```
void glVertexArrayRangeAPPLE(GLsizei length,
                             GLvoid *pointer);
```

Parameters

length   Specifies the length of the vertex array range, in bytes.

pointer   Specifies a pointer to the beginning of the vertex array range.

Description

The **glVertexArrayRangeAPPLE** function establishes the vertex array range according to the values of the *length* and *pointer* parameters.

If the *length* parameter is 0 or the *pointer* parameter is null, then any previously established vertex array range is released, and no vertex array range exists upon return. This should always be done before memory used by the vertex array range is released.

Get Functions

glGetIntegerv with *pname* parameter GL_VERTEX_ARRAY_RANGE_LENGTH_APPLE

glGetPointerv with *pname* parameter GL_VERTEX_ARRAY_RANGE_POINTER_APPLE

Errors

GL_INVALID_OPERATION is generated if **glVertexArrayRangeAPPLE** is called between calls to **glBegin** and **glEnd**.

■ **glFlushVertexArrayRangeAPPLE**—Flush the vertex array range.

Prototype

```
void glFlushVertexArrayRangeAPPLE(GLsizei length,
                                  GLvoid *pointer);
```

Parameters

length   Specifies the length of the range to flush, in bytes.

pointer   Specifies a pointer to the beginning of the range to flush.

Description

The **glFlushVertexArrayRangeAPPLE** function performs an explicit synchronization, after which any drawing commands are guaranteed to access the most recently written data in the range of memory specified by the *pointer* and *length* parameters.

Errors

GL_INVALID_OPERATION is generated if **glFlushVertexArrayRangeAPPLE** is called between calls to **glBegin** and **glEnd**.

■ **glVertexArrayParameteriAPPLE**—Specify a vertex array parameter.

Prototype

```
void glVertexArrayParameteriAPPLE(GLenum pname,
                                  GLint param);
```

Parameters

pname   Specifies a vertex array parameter. Must be GL_VERTEX_ARRAY_ STORAGE_HINT_APPLE.

param   Specifies the value of the vertex array parameter. May be GL_STORAGE_ CACHED_APPLE or GL_STORAGE_SHARED_APPLE.

Description

The **glVertexArrayParameteriAPPLE** function can be used by an application to specify a storage hint for the vertex array range. When the *pname* parameter is GL_VERTEX_ARRAY_STORAGE_HINT_APPLE, the *param* parameter may be one of the following values:

GL_STORAGE_CACHED_APPLE
                      Data in the vertex array range is static and should be cached to fast memory if possible.

GL_STORAGE_SHARED_APPLE
                      Data in the vertex array range may be dynamically changed.

Get Functions

glGetIntegerv with *pname* parameter GL_VERTEX_ARRAY_STORAGE_HINT_APPLE

Errors

GL_INVALID_ENUM is generated if *pname* is not an accepted value.

EXTENDED FUNCTIONS

■ **glEnableClientState, glDisableClientState**—Extended to enable/disable the vertex array range.

Prototypes

```
void glEnableClientState(GLenum array);
void glDisableClientState(GLenum array);
```

Extended Parameters

array   Specifies an array to enable or disable. May be GL_VERTEX_ARRAY_ RANGE_APPLE.

Description

The **glEnableClientState** and **glDisableClientState** functions are used to enable or disable client array state. The vertex array range is enabled or disabled by passing the value GL_VERTEX_ARRAY_RANGE_APPLE to the *array* parameter.

■ **glIsEnabled**—Extended to return whether the vertex array range is enabled.

Prototype

```
GLboolean glIsEnabled(GLenum cap);
```

Extended Parameters

cap   Specifies an OpenGL capability. May be GL_VERTEX_ARRAY_RANGE_ APPLE.

Description

Whether the vertex array range is enabled is determined by calling the **glIsEnabled** function with *cap* parameter GL_VERTEX_ARRAY_RANGE_APPLE.

■ **glGetIntegerv**—Extended to allow retrieval of vertex array range state.

Prototype

```
void glGetIntegerv(GLenum pname, GLint *params);
```

Extended Parameters

pname   Specifies the parameter to be returned. May be one of the values listed in Description.

Description

The **glGetIntegerv** function can be used to retrieve state related to the vertex array range. The *pname* parameter may be one of the following values:

GL_VERTEX_ARRAY_RANGE_LENGTH_APPLE
> The length of the vertex array range is returned. The initial value is 0.

GL_VERTEX_ARRAY_STORAGE_HINT_APPLE
> The vertex array range storage hint is returned. The initial value is GL_STORAGE_SHARED_APPLE.

GL_MAX_VERTEX_ARRAY_RANGE_ELEMENT_APPLE
> The maximum index of any array element accessed inside the vertex array range supported by the implementation is returned. This is always at least 65535.

■ **glGetPointerv**—Extended to allow retrieval of the vertex array range pointer.

Prototype

> void **glGetPointerv**(GLenum *pname*, GLvoid **pointer*);

Extended Parameters

pname   Specifies the array pointer to be returned. May be GL_VERTEX_ARRAY_RANGE_POINTER_APPLE.

Description

The **glGetPointerv** function can be used to retrieve the pointer to the vertex array range that was previously specified using the **glVertexArrayRangeAPPLE** function. When the *pname* parameter is GL_VERTEX_ARRAY_RANGE_POINTER_APPLE, the pointer to the vertex array range is returned in the *pointer* parameter. The initial value is a null pointer.

SYNCHRONIZATION

IN THIS CHAPTER

9.1   **GL_NV_fence**

OpenGL version required	OpenGL 1.1
Dependencies	—
Promotions	—
Related extensions	GL_NV_vertex_array_range

DISCUSSION

Unextended OpenGL provides a single mechanism, the **glFinish** function, that can be used to synchronize operations between the CPU and GPU. The **glFinish** function is not very flexible, however, and always blocks until all previously issued OpenGL commands have been completed. The GL_NV_fence extension provides a mechanism by which a *fence* can be placed into the command stream. A fence can be asynchronously tested to determine whether all preceding commands have been completed, or an application can choose to block until a particular fence is processed by the GPU. Fences are typically used to synchronize access to resources that are shared between the CPU and the GPU, such as the memory used by a vertex array range (see Chapter 8, Section 8.6).

Fence Objects

Fences follow the named object convention that is used elsewhere in OpenGL for such things as texture objects and program objects. Previously unused names for fence objects are allocated by calling the **glGenFencesNV** function,

```
void glGenFencesNV(GLsizei n,
                   GLuint *fences);
```

This function generates *n* names and writes them to the array pointed to by the *fences* parameter. The names generated are marked as used, but the associated fence objects are not actually created until the first time a new name is passed to the **glSetFenceNV** function.

Fence objects are deleted and the associated names are freed by calling the **glDeleteFencesNV** function,

```
void glDeleteFencesNV(GLsizei n,
                      const GLuint *fences);
```

Any of the *n* names passed to this function in the array pointed to by the *fences* parameter that do not refer to existing fence objects are silently ignored. Once a fence object is deleted, its name is marked as unused. The **glIsFenceNV** function,

```
GLboolean glIsFenceNV(GLuint fence);
```

can be used to determine whether a particular name specified by the *fence* parameter refers to an existing fence object.

A fence object encapsulates a Boolean status that is initially GL_FALSE when **glSetFenceNV** is called. A fence object also contains a condition value that determines when the status is changed to GL_TRUE.

Fence Operation

A fence is placed into the OpenGL command stream by calling the **glSetFenceNV** function,

```
void glSetFenceNV(GLuint fence,
                  GLenum condition);
```

with a *fence* parameter specifying a new fence object name or the name of a previously created fence object. A fence object is created when its associated name is first passed to the **glSetFenceNV** function. Placing a fence in the command stream sets its status to GL_FALSE and updates its condition to the value specified by the *condition* parameter. Once the condition is satisfied, the status of the fence object is changed to GL_TRUE. The only condition supported by the GL_NV_fence extension is GL_ALL_COMPLETED_NV, and this condition requires that all commands issued before the fence was set must be completed before the fence's status is changed to GL_TRUE.

The status of a fence object that was previously set using the **glSetFenceNV** function can be retrieved by calling the **glTestFenceNV** function,

```
GLboolean glTestFenceNV(GLuint fence);
```

with a *fence* parameter specifying the fence object to test. The return value is GL_TRUE if the fence's condition has been satisfied and GL_FALSE otherwise. The **glTestFenceNV** function always returns immediately.

An application can block until a fence object's status becomes GL_TRUE by calling the **glFinishFenceNV** function,

> void **glFinishFenceNV**(GLuint *fence*);

with a *fence* parameter specifying the fence object upon which to wait. The **glFinish-FenceNV** function does not return until the fence object's condition is satisfied.

Parameters pertaining to a particular fence object can be retrieved by calling the **glGet-FenceivNV** function,

> void **glGetFenceivNV**(GLuint *fence*,
> GLenum *pname*,
> GLint **params*);

with a *fence* parameter specifying the fence object to query. The *pname* parameter must be GL_FENCE_STATUS_NV or GL_FENCE_CONDITION_NV, indicating whether the status of the fence object or the condition established by the **glSetFenceNV** function is returned in the *params* parameter, respectively.

NEW FUNCTIONS

■ **glGenFencesNV**—Generate fence names.

Prototype

> void **glGenFencesNV**(GLsizei *n*,
> GLuint **fences*);

Parameters

n   Specifies the number of fence names to generate.

fences   Specifies a pointer to an array that receives the generated fence names.

Description

The **glGenFencesNV** function returns a set of *n* unused fence names in the array pointed to by the *fences* parameter. Each of the returned names is reserved with respect to fence name generation, but does not represent an existing fence object until the first time the name is passed to the **glSetFenceNV** function.

Fence objects are deleted and the associated fence names are freed by calling the **glDelete-FencesNV** function.

Get Functions

glIsFenceNV

Errors

GL_INVALID_VALUE is generated if *n* is negative.

■ **glDeleteFencesNV**—Delete named fences.

Prototype

```
void glDeleteFencesNV(GLsizei n,
                      const GLuint *fences);
```

Parameters

n   Specifies the number of fences to delete.

fences   Specifies a pointer to an array of fence names to be deleted.

Description

The **glDeleteFencesNV** function deletes the *n* fence objects contained in the array pointer to by the *fences* parameter. When a fence object is deleted, it becomes nonexistent, and its name becomes unused. Deleted fence names may subsequently be returned by the **glGenFencesNV** function. Any unused fence names found in the array pointed to by the *fences* parameter are silently ignored.

Get Functions

glIsFenceNV

Errors

GL_INVALID_VALUE is generated if *n* is negative.

■ **glIsFenceNV**—Determine if a name corresponds to a fence.

Prototype

```
GLboolean glIsFenceNV(GLuint fence);
```

Parameters

fence   Specifies the name of a fence.

Description

The **glIsFenceNV** function returns GL_TRUE if the *fence* parameter names an existing fence object. Otherwise, it returns GL_FALSE.

A fence name generated by the **glGenFencesNV** function does not refer to an existing fence object until a successful call to the **glSetFenceNV** function is made using the fence name.

■ **glSetFenceNV**—Place a fence in the command stream.

Prototype

```
void glSetFenceNV(GLuint fence,
                  GLenum condition);
```

Parameters

fence   Specifies the name of a fence.

condition   Specifies the condition upon which the fence object's state is set to
                 GL_TRUE. Must be GL_ALL_COMPLETED_NV.

Description

The **glSetFenceNV** function places a fence in the command stream and sets the status of
the fence object named by the *fence* parameter to GL_FALSE. The first time that a fence is set
for a particular value of *fence*, the corresponding fence object is created.

Once the condition specified by the *condition* parameter is satisfied, the status of the fence
object is changed to GL_TRUE. The current status of a fence object can be retrieved by calling the **glTestFenceNV** function. The condition GL_ALL_COMPLETED_NV is satisfied when
all commands issued prior to the fence being set have been completed.

Special Considerations

If the **glSetFenceNV** function is called for an existing fence object whose status is
GL_FALSE, then a new fence is placed in the command stream and the previous call to
glSetFenceNV is ignored when the corresponding condition is satisfied.

Get Functions

glTestFenceNV

glGetFenceivNV with *pname* parameter GL_FENCE_STATUS_NV

glGetFenceivNV with *pname* parameter GL_FENCE_CONDITION_NV

Errors

GL_INVALID_ENUM is generated if *condition* is not GL_ALL_COMPLETED_NV.

■ **glTestFenceNV**—Return the status of a fence object.

Prototype

```
GLboolean glTestFenceNV(GLuint fence);
```

Parameters

fence   Specifies the name of a fence object.

Description

The **glTestFenceNV** function returns the status of the fence object named by the *fence* parameter. The status of a fence object is set to GL_FALSE when the **glSetFenceNV** function
is called and is changed to GL_TRUE when its condition is satisfied.

Errors

GL_INVALID_OPERATION is generated if *fence* does not name an existing fence object.

■ **glFinishFenceNV**—Block until a fence finishes.

Prototype

void **glFinishFenceNV**(GLuint *fence*);

Parameters

fence   Specifies the name of a fence object.

Description

The **glFinishFenceNV** function blocks until the status of the fence object named by the *fence* parameter becomes GL_TRUE. For a fence object having the condition GL_ALL_ COMPLETED_NV, the **glFinishFenceNV** function waits until all commands issued before the fence was set using the **glSetFenceNV** function have been completed.

Errors

GL_INVALID_OPERATION is generated if *fence* does not name an existing fence object.

■ **glGetFenceivNV**—Return a fence object parameter.

Prototype

void **glGetFenceivNV**(GLuint *fence*,
                            GLenum *pname*,
                            GLint **params*);

Parameters

fence   Specifies the name of a fence object.

pname   Specifies the fence parameter to return. May be GL_FENCE_STATUS_NV or GL_FENCE_CONDITION_NV.

params   Specifies a pointer to a location in memory that receives the fence parameter.

Description

The **glGetFenceivNV** function retrieves a *fence* parameter for the fence object named by the *fence* parameter. The *pname* parameter may be one of the following values:

GL_FENCE_STATUS_NV

        The Boolean status of the fence object is returned. Querying this value is equivalent to calling the **glTestFenceNV** function. The status of a fence object is set to GL_FALSE when the **glSetFenceNV** function is called and is changed to GL_TRUE when its condition is satisfied.

GL_FENCE_CONDITION_NV

        The condition set for the fence object by the **glSetFenceNV** function is returned.

Errors

GL_INVALID_OPERATION is generated if *fence* does not name an existing fence object.

9.2   **GL_APPLE_fence**

OpenGL version required	OpenGL 1.1
Dependencies	—
Promotions	—
Related extensions	GL_APPLE_vertex_array_range

DISCUSSION

The GL_APPLE_fence extension is nearly identical to the GL_NV_fence extension and provides a mechanism by which a fence can be placed into the command stream. The primary difference is that the **glSetFenceAPPLE** function does not take a *condition* parameter specifying the condition upon which a fence's status is changed to GL_TRUE. Under this extension, the status of a fence always becomes GL_TRUE when all commands issued prior to the fence being placed into the command stream have been completed.

Fence Objects

Fences follow the named object convention that is used elsewhere in OpenGL for such things as texture objects and program objects. Previously unused names for fence objects are allocated by calling the **glGenFencesAPPLE** function,

```
void glGenFencesAPPLE(GLsizei n,
                      GLuint *fences);
```

This function generates *n* names and writes them to the array pointed to by the *fences* parameter. The names generated are marked as used, but the associated fence objects are not actually created until the first time a new name is passed to the **glSetFenceAPPLE** function. Fence objects are deleted and the associated names are freed by calling the **glDelete-FencesAPPLE** function,

```
void glDeleteFencesAPPLE(GLsizei n,
                         const GLuint *fences);
```

Any of the *n* names passed to this function in the array pointed to by the *fences* parameter that do not refer to existing fence objects are silently ignored. Once a fence object is deleted, its name is marked as unused. The **glIsFenceAPPLE** function,

```
GLboolean glIsFenceAPPLE(GLuint fence);
```

can be used to determine whether a particular name specified by the *fence* parameter refers to an existing fence object.

A fence object encapsulates a Boolean status that is initially GL_FALSE when **glSet-FenceAPPLE** is called.

Fence Operation

A fence is placed into the OpenGL command stream by calling the **glSetFenceAPPLE** function,

> void **glSetFenceAPPLE**(GLuint *fence*);

with a *fence* parameter specifying a new fence object name or the name of a previously created fence object. A fence object is created when its associated name is first passed to the **glSetFenceAPPLE** function. Placing a fence in the command stream sets its status to GL_FALSE. Once all commands issued before the fence was set have been completed, the status of the fence object is changed to GL_TRUE.

The status of fence object that was previously set using the **glSetFenceAPPLE** function can be retrieved by calling the **glTestFenceAPPLE** function,

> GLboolean **glTestFenceAPPLE**(GLuint *fence*);

with a *fence* parameter specifying the fence object to test. The return value is GL_TRUE if all commands issued prior to the fence's placement in the command stream have been completed and GL_FALSE otherwise. The **glTestFenceAPPLE** function always returns immediately.

An application can block until a fence object's status becomes GL_TRUE by calling the **glFinishFenceAPPLE** function,

> void **glFinishFenceAPPLE**(GLuint *fence*);

with a *fence* parameter specifying the fence object upon which to wait. The **glFinishFenceNV** function does not return until all commands issued prior to the fence's placement in the command stream have been completed.

NEW FUNCTIONS

■ **glGenFencesAPPLE**—Generate fence names.

Prototype

> void **glGenFencesAPPLE**(GLsizei *n*,
>   GLuint **fences*);

Parameters

n   Specifies the number of fence names to generate.

fences   Specifies a pointer to an array that receives the generated fence names.

Description

The **glGenFencesAPPLE** function returns a set of *n* unused fence names in the array pointed to by the *fences* parameter. Each of the returned names is reserved with respect to fence name generation, but does not represent an existing fence object until the first time the name is passed to the **glSetFenceAPPLE** function.

Fence objects are deleted and the associated fence names are freed by calling the **glDelete-FencesAPPLE** function.

Get Functions

glIsFenceAPPLE

Errors

GL_INVALID_VALUE is generated if *n* is negative.

■ **glDeleteFencesAPPLE**—Delete named fences.

Prototype

```
void glDeleteFencesAPPLE(GLsizei n,
                         const GLuint *fences);
```

Parameters

n   Specifies the number of fences to delete.

fences   Specifies a pointer to an array of fence names to be deleted.

Description

The **glDeleteFencesAPPLE** function deletes the *n* fence objects contained in the array pointed to by the *fences* parameter. When a fence object is deleted, it becomes nonexistent, and its name becomes unused. Deleted fence names may subsequently be returned by the **glGenFencesAPPLE** function. Any unused fence names found in the array pointed to by the *fences* parameter are silently ignored.

Get Functions

glIsFenceAPPLE

Errors

GL_INVALID_VALUE is generated if *n* is negative.

■ **glIsFenceAPPLE**—Determine if a name corresponds to a fence.

Prototype

```
GLboolean glIsFenceAPPLE(GLuint fence);
```

Parameters

fence   Specifies the name of a fence.

Description

The **glIsFenceAPPLE** function returns GL_TRUE if the *fence* parameter names an existing fence object. Otherwise, it returns GL_FALSE.

A fence name generated by the **glGenFencesAPPLE** function does not refer to an existing fence object until a successful call to the **glSetFenceAPPLE** function is made using the fence name.

■ **glSetFenceAPPLE**—Place a fence in the command stream.

Prototype

```
void glSetFenceAPPLE(GLuint fence);
```

Parameters

fence   Specifies the name of a fence.

Description

The **glSetFenceAPPLE** function places a fence in the command stream and sets the status of the fence object named by the *fence* parameter to GL_FALSE. The first time that a fence is set for a particular value of *fence*, the corresponding fence object is created.

Once all commands issued prior to the fence being set have completed, the status of the fence object is changed to GL_TRUE. The current status of a fence object can be retrieved by calling the **glTestFenceAPPLE** function.

Special Considerations

If the **glSetFenceAPPLE** function is called for an existing fence object whose status is GL_FALSE, then a new fence is placed in the command stream, and the previous call to **glSetFenceAPPLE** is ignored when all preceding commands are completed.

Get Functions

glTestFenceAPPLE

■ **glTestFenceAPPLE**—Return the status of a fence object.

Prototype

```
GLboolean glTestFenceAPPLE(GLuint fence);
```

Parameters

fence   Specifies the name of a fence object.

Description

The **glTestFenceAPPLE** function returns the status of the fence object named by the *fence* parameter. The status of a fence object is set to GL_FALSE when the **glSetFenceAPPLE** function is called and is changed to GL_TRUE when commands issued prior to the fence being set have been completed.

Errors

GL_INVALID_OPERATION is generated if *fence* does not name an existing fence object.

■ **glFinishFenceAPPLE**—Block until a fence finishes.

Prototype

```
void glFinishFenceAPPLE(GLuint fence);
```

Parameters

fence   Specifies the name of a fence object.

Description

The **glFinishFenceAPPLE** function blocks until the status of the fence object named by the *fence* parameter becomes GL_TRUE. The **glFinishFenceNV** function waits until all commands issued prior to the fence being set using the **glSetFenceAPPLE** function have been completed.

Errors

GL_INVALID_OPERATION is generated if *fence* does not name an existing fence object.

CHAPTER **10**

LIGHTING

IN THIS CHAPTER

10.1   GL_EXT_separate_specular_color

OpenGL version required	OpenGL 1.1
Dependencies	—
Promotions	Promoted to a core feature in OpenGL 1.2
Related extensions	—

DISCUSSION

When lighting is enabled, OpenGL calculates a color for each vertex that is the sum of a diffuse term (which includes the ambient and emission contributions) and a specular term. This color is interpolated across the face of a primitive and fed into the texture environment where it is normally modulated by a texture color. It is usually desired, however, that the specular contribution to the lighting color not be affected by texturing, but instead added after textures have been applied. The GL_EXT_separate_specular_color extension splits the single color calculated at each vertex into two colors and allows an application to choose whether the specular term is added before or after the texture environment is applied.

When the GL_EXT_separate_specular_color extension is available and lighting is enabled, OpenGL calculates two colors at each vertex, a primary color $\mathbf{C}_{pri}$ and a secondary color $\mathbf{C}_{sec}$. What lighting terms are assigned to these colors depends on the value of a color control parameter that is set by calling the **glLightModeli** function with *pname* parameter

GL_LIGHT_MODEL_COLOR_CONTROL_EXT. If the color control parameter is GL_SINGLE_COLOR_EXT (the initial value), then the primary and secondary colors are given by

$$\mathbf{C}_{pri} = \mathbf{E}_{mat} + \mathbf{A}_{mat}\mathbf{A}_{scene}$$

$$+ \sum_{i=0}^{n-1}(att_i)(spot_i)\left[\mathbf{A}_{mat}\mathbf{A}_i + (\mathbf{N}\cdot\mathbf{L}_i)\mathbf{D}_{mat}\mathbf{D}_i + (\mathbf{N}\cdot\mathbf{L}_i > 0)(\mathbf{N}\cdot\mathbf{H}_i)^r\mathbf{S}_{mat}\mathbf{S}_i\right] \quad (10.1.1)$$

and if the color control parameter is GL_SEPARATE_SPECULAR_COLOR_EXT, then the primary and secondary colors are given by

$$\mathbf{C}_{pri} = \mathbf{E}_{mat} + \mathbf{A}_{mat}\mathbf{A}_{scene}$$

$$+ \sum_{i=0}^{n-1}(att_i)(spot_i)\left[\mathbf{A}_{mat}\mathbf{A}_i + (\mathbf{N}\cdot\mathbf{L}_i)\mathbf{D}_{mat}\mathbf{D}_i\right]$$

$$\mathbf{C}_{sec} = \sum_{i=0}^{n-1}(att_i)(spot_i)(\mathbf{N}\cdot\mathbf{L}_i > 0)(\mathbf{N}\cdot\mathbf{H}_i)^r\mathbf{S}_{mat}\mathbf{S}_i. \quad (10.1.2)$$

The meanings of the values used in these equations are summarized in Table 10.1.1. All dot products are clamped to a minimum value of 0.0.

TABLE 10.1.1 Meanings of the Values Appearing in the Equations Used to Calculate the Primary and Secondary Colors

$\mathbf{A}_{mat}$	The material ambient color.
$\mathbf{E}_{mat}$	The material emission color.
$\mathbf{D}_{mat}$	The material diffuse color.
$\mathbf{S}_{mat}$	The material specular color.
r	The material shininess, also known as the specular exponent.
$\mathbf{A}_{scene}$	The scene ambient light color.
n	The number of enabled lights.
att_i	The attenuation factor for light i.
$spot_i$	The spot effect factor for light i.
$\mathbf{A}_i$	The ambient color for light i.
$\mathbf{D}_i$	The diffuse color for light i.
$\mathbf{S}_i$	The specular color for light i.
$\mathbf{L}_i$	The unit direction vector pointing from the vertex being lit to light i.
$\mathbf{H}_i$	The unit halfway vector for the vertex being lit corresponding to light i.
$\mathbf{N}$	The vertex's normal vector.
$(\mathbf{N}\cdot\mathbf{L}_i > 0)$	A Boolean value indicating whether the vertex's normal vector points toward light i. Evaluates to 1.0 if true and 0.0 if false.

Both the primary color and secondary color are interpolated across the face of a primitive during rasterization. For each fragment, the primary color is passed into the texture environment, and the secondary color is subsequently added to the result of texture application.

EXTENDED FUNCTIONS

■ **glLightModeli**—Extended to control separate specular color.

Prototype

    void **glLightModeli**(GLenum *pname*, GLint *param*);

Extended Parameters

pname   Specifies a lighting model parameter. May be GL_LIGHT_MODEL_COLOR_CONTROL_EXT.

param   Specifies the parameter value. When *pname* is GL_LIGHT_MODEL_COLOR_CONTROL_EXT, this must be GL_SINGLE_COLOR_EXT or GL_SEPARATE_SPECULAR_COLOR_EXT.

Description

The color control parameter is specified by calling the **glLightModeli** function with *pname* parameter GL_LIGHT_MODEL_COLOR_CONTROL_EXT. If the *param* parameter is GL_SINGLE_COLOR_EXT, then the diffuse and specular terms of the lighting equation are added and assigned to the primary color, as in Equation (10.1.1). If the *param* parameter is GL_SEPARATE_SPECULAR_COLOR_EXT, then the diffuse and specular terms are separately assigned to the primary color and secondary color, as in Equation (10.1.2). The initial value is GL_SINGLE_COLOR_EXT.

■ **glGetIntegerv**—Extended to retrieve separate specular color state.

Prototype

    void **glGetIntegerv**(GLenum *pname*, GLint **params*);

Extended Parameters

pname   Specifies the parameter to be returned. May be GL_LIGHT_MODEL_COLOR_CONTROL_EXT.

Description

The value of the color control parameter can be retrieved by calling the **glGetIntegerv** function with *pname* parameter GL_LIGHT_MODEL_COLOR_CONTROL_EXT.

10.2 GL_EXT_secondary_color

OpenGL version required	OpenGL 1.1
Dependencies	Requires GL_EXT_separate_specular_color
Promotions	Promoted to a core feature in OpenGL 1.4
Related extensions	—

DISCUSSION

The GL_EXT_secondary_color extension allows the explicit specification of a per-vertex secondary color that is used when lighting is disabled. The secondary color is interpolated across the face of a primitive and may be added to the color resulting from texture environment application.

The secondary color is implemented as a new vertex attribute whose current value is specified using the **glSecondaryColor3{bsifdubusui}[v]EXT** function. Secondary colors are always specified with three components representing the red, green, and blue channels. The **glSecondaryColor3{bsifdubusui}[v]EXT** function is useful for specifying per-vertex secondary colors one at a time within a block delimited by calls to **glBegin** and **glEnd**. The current secondary color is retrieved by calling the **glGet** function with *pname* parameter GL_CURRENT_SECONDARY_COLOR_EXT.

Secondary colors may also be specified as an array. A secondary color array is specified by calling the **glSecondaryColorPointerEXT** function,

```
void glSecondaryColorPointerEXT(GLint size,
                                GLenum type,
                                GLsizei stride,
                                const GLvoid *pointer);
```

The *size* parameter specifies the number of components per color and must always be 3. (This parameter exists to allow for future extensions that may allow an alpha component to be specified for secondary colors.) The *type* parameter specifies the data type of elements in the array, and the *stride* parameter specifies the byte offset from one color to the next. As with all other arrays, a stride value of 0 indicates that the colors are tightly packed in the array. The *pointer* parameter specifies the location where the secondary color array begins in memory.

The current parameters pertaining to the secondary color array are retrieved by calling the **glGetIntegerv** function with *pname* parameter GL_SECONDARY_COLOR_SIZE_EXT, GL_SECONDARY_COLOR_ARRAY_TYPE_EXT, or GL_SECONDARY_COLOR_ARRAY_STRIDE_EXT. The current pointer to the secondary color array is retrieved by calling the **glGet-Pointerv** function with *pname* parameter GL_SECONDARY_COLOR_ARRAY_POINTER_EXT.

The secondary color array is enabled and disabled by calling the **glEnableClientState** and **glDisableClientState** functions with *array* parameter GL_SECONDARY_COLOR_ARRAY_EXT. The secondary color array is initially disabled.

Whether the secondary color is added to the color resulting from the application of the texture environment is controlled by calling the **glEnable** or **glDisable** function with *cap* parameter GL_COLOR_SUM_EXT. The color sum is initially disabled, in which case the secondary color is ignored during rasterization.

The GL_EXT_secondary_color extension interacts with the required GL_EXT_separate_specular_color extension in the following way: If lighting is enabled and the value of the color control parameter GL_LIGHT_MODEL_COLOR_CONTROL_EXT is GL_SEPARATE_SPECULAR_COLOR_EXT, then it is as if the color sum operation is implicitly enabled, regardless of the state of GL_COLOR_SUM_EXT, and the secondary color is added to the output of texture environment application.

NEW FUNCTIONS

- **glSecondaryColor3{bsifdubusui}[v]EXT**—Set the current secondary color.

Prototypes

```
void glSecondaryColor3bEXT(GLbyte red,
                           GLbyte green,
                           GLbyte blue);
void glSecondaryColor3sEXT(GLshort red,
                           GLshort green,
                           GLshort blue);
void glSecondaryColor3iEXT(GLint red,
                           GLint green,
                           GLint blue);
void glSecondaryColor3fEXT(GLfloat red,
                           GLfloat green,
                           GLfloat blue);
void glSecondaryColor3dEXT(GLdouble red,
                           GLdouble green,
                           GLdouble blue);
void glSecondaryColor3ubEXT(GLubyte red,
                            GLubyte green,
                            GLubyte blue);
void glSecondaryColor3usEXT(GLushort red,
                            GLushort green,
                            GLushort blue);
void glSecondaryColor3uiEXT(GLuint red,
                            GLuint green,
                            GLuint blue);
```

Parameters

red, green, blue   Specify new red, green, and blue color components for the current secondary color.

Prototypes

```
void glSecondaryColor3bvEXT(const GLbyte *coords);
void glSecondaryColor3svEXT(const GLshort *coords);
void glSecondaryColor3ivEXT(const GLint *coords);
void glSecondaryColor3fvEXT(const GLfloat *coords);
```

```
void glSecondaryColor3dvEXT(const GLdouble *coords);
void glSecondaryColor3ubvEXT(const GLubyte *coords);
void glSecondaryColor3usvEXT(const GLushort *coords);
void glSecondaryColor3uivEXT(const GLuint *coords);
```

Parameters

coords   Specifies a pointer to an array containing the new red, green, and blue color components for the current secondary color.

Description

The **glSecondaryColor3{bsifdubusui}[v]EXT** function sets the current secondary color. The secondary color is initially (0,0,0,0).

Special Considerations

The current secondary color can be updated at any time. In particular, **glSecondary-Color3{bsifdubusui}[v]EXT** can be called between calls to **glBegin** and **glEnd**.

Get Functions

glGet with *pname* parameter GL_CURRENT_SECONDARY_COLOR_EXT

■ **glSecondaryColorPointerEXT**—Define an array of secondary colors.

Prototype

```
void glSecondaryColorPointerEXT(GLint size,
                                GLenum type,
                                GLsizei stride,
                                const GLvoid *pointer);
```

Parameters

size   Specifies the number of components per color. Must be 3.

type   Specifies the data type of each color component in the array. The symbolic constants GL_BYTE, GL_UNSIGNED_BYTE, GL_SHORT, GL_UNSIGNED_SHORT, GL_INT, GL_UNSIGNED_INT, GL_FLOAT, and GL_DOUBLE are accepted.

stride   Specifies the byte offset between consecutive colors. A value of 0 indicates that the colors are tightly packed in the array.

pointer   Specifies a pointer to the first component of the first color in the array.

Description

The **glSecondaryColorPointerEXT** function specifies the location and data format of the secondary color array. The *size* parameter specifies the number of components per color and must always be 3. The *type* parameter specifies the data type of each color component in the array, and the *stride* parameter specifies the byte offset from one color to the next. The *pointer* parameter specifies the location of the secondary color array in memory.

The secondary color array is enabled and disabled by calling the **glEnableClientState** and **glDisableClientState** functions with *array* parameter GL_SECONDARY_COLOR_ARRAY_EXT. Initially, the secondary color array is disabled.

Special Considerations

The **glSecondaryColorPointerEXT** function may not be called between calls to **glBegin** and **glEnd**, but an error may not be generated if it is. In this case, the operation is undefined.

Secondary color array parameters are client-side state, and are saved and restored using the **glPushClientAttrib** and **glPopClientAttrib** functions.

Get Functions

glGetIntegerv with *pname* parameter GL_SECONDARY_COLOR_ARRAY_SIZE_EXT

glGetIntegerv with *pname* parameter GL_SECONDARY_COLOR_ARRAY_TYPE_EXT

glGetIntegerv with *pname* parameter GL_SECONDARY_COLOR_ARRAY_STRIDE_EXT

glGetPointerv with *pname* parameter GL_SECONDARY_COLOR_ARRAY_POINTER_EXT

Errors

GL_INVALID_VALUE is generated if *size* is not 3.

GL_INVALID_ENUM is generated if *type* is not an accepted value.

GL_INVALID_VALUE is generated if *stride* is negative.

EXTENDED FUNCTIONS

■ **glEnable, glDisable**—Extended to enable/disable color sum.

Prototypes

```
void glEnable(GLenum cap);
void glDisable(GLenum cap);
```

Extended Parameters

cap   Specifies a GL capability. To enable or disable color sum, this should be GL_COLOR_SUM_EXT.

Description

Color sum is enabled and disabled by passing the value GL_COLOR_SUM_EXT to the **glEnable** and **glDisable** functions. Color sum is initially disabled.

■ **glEnableClientState, glDisableClientState**—Extended to enable/disable the secondary color array.

Prototypes

```
void glEnableClientState(GLenum array);
void glDisableClientState(GLenum array);
```

Extended Parameters

array   Specifies an array to enable or disable. May be GL_SECONDARY_COLOR_ ARRAY_EXT.

Description

The **glEnableClientState** and **glDisableClientState** functions enable or disable arrays stored in client space. The secondary color array is enabled or disabled by passing the value GL_SECONDARY_COLOR_ARRAY_EXT to the *array* parameter.

■ **glIsEnabled**—Extended to return whether the color sum operation or the secondary color array is enabled.

Prototype

```
GLboolean glIsEnabled(GLenum cap);
```

Extended Parameters

cap   Specifies an OpenGL capability. May be GL_COLOR_SUM_EXT or GL_SECONDARY_COLOR_ARRAY_EXT.

Description

The **glIsEnabled** function can be called to determine whether secondary color functionality is enabled. The *cap* parameter may be one of the following values:

GL_COLOR_SUM_EXT
              The return value indicates whether color sum is enabled.

GL_SECONDARY_COLOR_ARRAY_EXT
              The return value indicates whether the secondary color array is enabled.

■ **glGetIntegerv, glGetFloatv, glGetDoublev**—Extended to retrieve the current secondary color.

Prototypes

```
void glGetIntegerv(GLenum pname, GLint *params);
void glGetFloatv(GLenum pname, GLfloat *params);
void glGetDoublev(GLenum pname, GLdouble *params);
```

Extended Parameters

pname   Specifies the parameter to be returned. To retrieve the current secondary color, this should be GL_CURRENT_SECONDARY_COLOR_EXT.

Description

Calling the **glGetIntegerv**, **glGetFloatv**, or **glGetDoublev** function with *pname* parameter GL_CURRENT_SECONDARY_COLOR_EXT returns the current secondary color in the array pointed to by the *params* parameter. Three components representing the red, green, and blue channels of the secondary color are always returned.

- **glGetIntegerv**—Extended to retrieve secondary color array state.

Prototype

    void **glGetIntegerv**(GLenum *pname*, GLint **params*);

Extended Parameters

pname   Specifies the parameter to be returned. May be GL_SECONDARY_COLOR_
                ARRAY_SIZE_EXT,   GL_SECONDARY_COLOR_ARRAY_TYPE_EXT,   or
                GL_SECONDARY_COLOR_ARRAY_STRIDE_EXT.

Description

The **glGetIntegerv** function can be used to retrieve state related to the secondary color array that was previously specified using the **glSecondaryColorPointerEXT** function. The *pname* parameter may be one of the following values:

GL_SECONDARY_COLOR_ARRAY_SIZE_EXT
                The number of components used by each element of the secondary color array is returned. This value is always 3.

GL_SECONDARY_COLOR_ARRAY_TYPE_EXT
                The data type of the secondary color array is returned. The initial value is GL_FLOAT.

GL_SECONDARY_COLOR_ARRAY_STRIDE_EXT
                The stride of the secondary color array is returned. The initial value is 0.

- **glGetPointerv**—Extended to retrieve the secondary color array pointer.

Prototype

    void **glGetPointerv**(GLenum *pname*, GLvoid ***pointer*);

Extended Parameters

pname   Specifies the array pointer to be returned. May be GL_SECONDARY_
                COLOR_ARRAY_POINTER_EXT.

Description

The **glGetPointerv** function can be used to retrieve the pointer to the secondary color array that was previously specified using the **glSecondaryColorPointerEXT** function.

When the *pname* parameter is GL_SECONDARY_COLOR_ARRAY_POINTER_EXT, the pointer to the secondary color array is returned in the *pointer* parameter. The initial value is a null pointer.

10.3   GL_EXT_rescale_normal

OpenGL version required	OpenGL 1.1
Dependencies	—
Promotions	Promoted to a core feature in OpenGL 1.2
Related extensions	—

DISCUSSION

When normal vectors are passed to OpenGL, they are transformed by the inverse transpose of the model-view matrix. If the model-view matrix contains a scale, then the length of each normal vector is modified as it is transformed into eye space. Thus, even if normal vectors having unit length are passed to OpenGL, this property may not be preserved before they are used in the lighting equation. Unextended OpenGL provides a normalization mode controlled by the GL_NORMALIZE capability. When enabled, this mode forces all normal vectors to unit length after transformation. The GL_EXT_rescale_normal extension provides another mode that multiplies each normal vector by a scaling factor derived from the model-view matrix. When the model-view matrix is known to contain a uniform scale, using this new mode may allow some implementations to adjust normal vectors to unit length more efficiently than they could through renormalization.

Normal vector rescaling is enabled and disabled by calling the **glEnable** and **glDisable** functions with *cap* parameter GL_RESCALE_NORMAL_EXT. When normal rescaling is enabled, normal vectors are multiplied by a factor f after transformation to eye space, where f is derived from the model-view matrix **M** as follows:

$$f = \frac{1}{\sqrt{\left(M_{31}^{-1}\right)^2 + \left(M_{32}^{-1}\right)^2 + \left(M_{33}^{-1}\right)^2}} \qquad (10.3.1)$$

That is, f is equal to the reciprocal of the magnitude of the third row of the inverse of the model-view matrix. The entire transformation from a model-space normal vector **N** to an eye-space normal vector **N'** is then given by

$$\mathbf{N'} = f\left(\mathbf{M}^{-1}\right)^{\mathrm{T}} \mathbf{N}. \qquad (10.3.2)$$

If normalization is also enabled in addition to normal rescaling, then the transformed normal vector **N'** is normalized before being used in the lighting equation. Under normal circumstances (i.e., the model-view matrix is invertible), using normalization causes normal rescaling to have no effect, since any scale factor is removed by the normalization operation.

EXTENDED FUNCTIONS

■ **glEnable, glDisable, glIsEnabled**—Extended to enable/disable normal rescaling.

Prototypes

```
void glEnable(GLenum cap);
void glDisable(GLenum cap);
GLboolean glIsEnabled(GLenum cap);
```

Extended Parameters

cap   Specifies a GL capability. To enable or disable normal rescaling, or to query whether normal rescaling is enabled, this should be GL_RESCALE_NORMAL_EXT.

Description

Normal rescaling is enabled and disabled by passing the value GL_RESCALE_NORMAL_EXT to the **glEnable** and **glDisable** functions. Calling the **glIsEnabled** function with *cap* parameter GL_RESCALE_NORMAL_EXT returns a value indicating whether normal rescaling is enabled.

10.4   GL_NV_light_max_exponent

OpenGL version required	OpenGL 1.1
Dependencies	—
Promotions	—
Related extensions	—

DISCUSSION

Unextended OpenGL limits both the material shininess and spot light exponent to a maximum value of 128. The GL_NV_light_max_exponent extension allows an implementation to support larger exponents.

The maximum material shininess supported by an implementation is retrieved by calling the **glGetIntegerv** function with *pname* parameter GL_MAX_SHININESS_NV. Any value between zero and this maximum value may be passed to the *param* parameter of the **glMaterial{if}[v]** function when the *pname* parameter is GL_SHININESS.

The maximum spot light exponent supported by an implementation is retrieved by calling the **glGetIntegerv** function with *pname* parameter GL_MAX_SPOT_EXPONENT_NV. Any value between zero and this maximum value may be passed to the *param* parameter of the **glLight{if}[v]** function when the *pname* parameter is GL_SPOT_EXPONENT.

EXTENDED FUNCTIONS

■ **glGetIntegerv**—Extended to retrieve maximum values for specular shininess and spot exponent.

Prototypes

```
void glGetIntegerv(GLenum pname, GLint *params);
```

Extended Parameters

pname   Specifies the parameter to be returned. May be GL_MAX_SHININESS_NV or GL_MAX_SPOT_EXPONENT_NV.

Description

The **glGetIntegerv** function can be used to retrieve maximum values for exponents used during lighting calculations. The *pname* parameter may be one of the following values:

GL_MAX_SHININESS_NV

The largest specular shininess value that may be specified with the **glMaterial{if}[v]** function is returned.

GL_MAX_SPOT_EXPONENT_NV

The largest spot light exponent value that may be specified with the **glLight{if}[v]** function is returned.

FOG

11.1   **GL_EXT_fog_coord**

OpenGL version required	OpenGL 1.1
Dependencies	—
Promotions	—
Related extensions	—

DISCUSSION

Unextended OpenGL always uses the distance from the camera to a fragment (or the fragment's absolute depth) when calculating the fog factor. The GL_EXT_fog_coord extension allows specification of a per-vertex fog coordinate that is interpolated across the face of a primitive and fed into the fog factor calculation during rasterization.

OpenGL calculates the fog factor *f* using one of the following three formulas, depending on the current value of GL_FOG_MODE.

$$f = \frac{e-c}{e-s} \tag{11.1.1}$$

$$f = \exp(-dc) \tag{11.1.2}$$

$$f = \exp(-d^2 c^2) \tag{11.1.3}$$

The value of *c* in these three formulas is the fog coordinate and ordinarily represents the distance from the camera to a fragment. When the GL_EXT_fog_coord extension is available, an arbitrary fog coordinate may be specified for each vertex. If the value of GL_FOG_MODE is GL_LINEAR, then Equation (11.1.1) is used to calculate the fog factor, where *s* and *e* are the values of GL_FOG_START and GL_FOG_END. If the value of GL_FOG_MODE is GL_EXP or GL_EXP2, then Equation (11.1.2) or (11.1.3) is used to calculate the fog factor, respectively, where *d* is the value of GL_FOG_DENSITY.

A new single-component vertex attribute, the *fog coordinate*, is introduced and has a current value that is set using the **glFogCoord{fd}[v]EXT** function. The fog coordinate is always specified as either a single-precision or double-precision floating-point value. The **glFogCoord{fd}[v]EXT** function is useful for specifying per-vertex fog coordinates one at a time within a block delimited by calls to **glBegin** and **glEnd**. The current fog coordinate is retrieved by calling the **glGetFloatv** or **glGetDoublev** function with *pname* parameter GL_CURRENT_FOG_COORDINATE_EXT.

Fog coordinates may also be specified as an array. A fog coordinate array is specified by calling the **glFogCoordPointerEXT** function,

```
void glFogCoordPointerEXT(GLenum type,
                          GLsizei stride,
                          const GLvoid *pointer);
```

The *type* parameter specifies the data type of elements in the array and can be GL_FLOAT or GL_DOUBLE. The *stride* parameter specifies the byte offset from one fog coordinate to the next. As with all other arrays, a stride value of 0 indicates that the fog coordinates are tightly packed in the array. The *pointer* parameter specifies the location where the fog coordinate array begins in memory.

The current parameters pertaining to the fog coordinate array are retrieved by calling the **glGetIntegerv** function with *pname* parameter GL_FOG_COORDINATE_ARRAY_TYPE_EXT or GL_FOG_COORDINATE_ARRAY_STRIDE_EXT. The current pointer to the fog coordinate array is retrieved by calling the **glGetPointerv** function with *pname* parameter GL_FOG_COORDINATE_ARRAY_POINTER_EXT.

The fog coordinate array is enabled and disabled by calling the **glEnableClientState** and **glDisableClientState** functions with *array* parameter GL_FOG_COORDINATE_ARRAY_EXT. The fog coordinate array is initially disabled.

Whether OpenGL uses the interpolated fog coordinate or the conventional distance from camera when calculating the fog factor *f* is controlled by calling the **glFogi** function with *pname* parameter GL_FOG_COORDINATE_SOURCE_EXT. Specifying GL_FOG_COORDINATE_EXT as the *param* parameter indicates that the interpolated per-vertex fog coordinate should be used as the value of *c* in Equations (11.1.1), (11.1.2), and (11.1.3). Specifying GL_FRAGMENT_DEPTH_EXT as the *param* parameter indicates that the fragment's distance from the camera should be used as the value of *c* as it is in unextended OpenGL.

NEW FUNCTIONS

- **glFogCoord{fd}[v]EXT**—Specify current fog coordinate.

Prototypes

```
void glFogCoordfEXT(float coord);
void glFogCoorddEXT(double coord);
```

Parameters

coord   Specifies the new current fog coordinate.

Prototypes

```
void glFogCoordfvEXT(const float *coord);
void glFogCoorddvEXT(const double *coord);
```

Parameters

coord   Specifies a pointer to the new current fog coordinate.

Description

The **glFogCoord{fd}[v]EXT** function sets the current fog coordinate. The fog coordinate is initially 0.0.

Special Considerations

The current fog coordinate can be updated at any time. In particular, **glFogCoord-{fd}[v]EXT** can be called between calls to **glBegin** and **glEnd**.

Get Functions

glGet with *pname* parameter GL_CURRENT_FOG_COORDINATE_EXT

■ **glFogCoordPointerEXT**—Specify fog coordinate array.

Prototypes

```
void glFogCoordPointerEXT(GLenum type,
                          GLsizei stride,
                          const GLvoid *pointer);
```

Parameters

type   Specifies the data type of each element in the array. The symbolic constants GL_FLOAT and GL_DOUBLE are accepted.

stride   Specifies the byte offset between consecutive fog coordinates. A value of 0 indicates that the fog coordinates are tightly packed in the array.

pointer   Specifies a pointer to the first element in the array.

Description

The **glFogCoordPointerEXT** function specifies the location and data format of the fog coordinate array. The *type* parameter specifies the data type of each element of the array, and the *stride* parameter specifies the byte offset from one element to the next. The *pointer* parameter specifies the location of the fog coordinate array in memory.

The fog coordinate array is enabled and disabled by calling the **glEnableClientState** and **glDisableClientState** functions with *array* parameter GL_FOG_COORDINATE_ARRAY_ EXT. Initially, the fog coordinate array is disabled.

Special Considerations

The **glFogCoordPointerEXT** function may not be called between calls to **glBegin** and **glEnd**, but an error may not be generated if it is. In this case, the operation is undefined.

Fog coordinate array parameters are client-side state, and are saved and restored using the **glPushClientAttrib** and **glPopClientAttrib** functions.

Get Functions

glGetIntegerv with *pname* parameter GL_FOG_COORDINATE_ARRAY_TYPE_EXT

glGetIntegerv with *pname* parameter GL_FOG_COORDINATE_ARRAY_STRIDE_EXT

glGetPointerv with *pname* parameter GL_FOG_COORDINATE_ARRAY_POINTER_EXT

Errors

GL_INVALID_ENUM is generated if *type* is not GL_FLOAT or GL_DOUBLE.

GL_INVALID_VALUE is generated if *stride* is negative.

EXTENDED FUNCTIONS

■ **glFogi**—Extended to allow specification of the fog coordinate source.

Prototype

    void **glFogi**(GLenum *pname*, GLint *param*);

Extended Parameters

pname   Specifies the symbolic name of a fog parameter. May be GL_FOG_ COORDINATE_SOURCE_EXT.

param   Specifies the value of the fog parameter. When *pname* is GL_FOG_ COORDINATE_SOURCE_EXT, this must be GL_FRAGMENT_DEPTH_EXT or GL_FOG_COORDINATE_EXT. The initial value is GL_FRAGMENT_DEPTH_ EXT.

Description

The **glFogi** function is used to set the fog coordinate source. When the fog coordinate source is GL_FRAGMENT_DEPTH_EXT (the initial value), the fog coordinate used during rasterization is derived from the depth of each fragment, just as it is in unextended OpenGL. When the fog coordinate source is set to GL_FOG_COORDINATE_EXT, the fog coordinate used during rasterization is the interpolated value of the fog coordinate specified at each vertex.

■ **glEnableClientState, glDisableClientState**—Extended to enable/disable the fog coordinate array.

Prototypes

```
void glEnableClientState(GLenum array);
void glDisableClientState(GLenum array);
```

Extended Parameters

array   Specifies an array to enable or disable. May be GL_FOG_COORDINATE_ ARRAY_EXT.

Description

The **glEnableClientState** and **glDisableClientState** functions enable or disable arrays stored in client space. The fog coordinate array is enabled or disabled by passing the value GL_FOG_COORDINATE_ARRAY_EXT to the *array* parameter.

■ **glIsEnabled**—Extended to return whether the fog coordinate array is enabled.

Prototype

```
GLboolean glIsEnabled(GLenum cap);
```

Extended Parameters

cap   Specifies an OpenGL capability. May be GL_FOG_COORDINATE_ARRAY_ EXT.

Description

Whether the fog coordinate array is enabled is determined by calling the **glIsEnabled** function with *cap* parameter GL_FOG_COORDINATE_ARRAY_EXT.

■ **glGetFloatv, glGetDoublev**—Extended to allow retrieval of the current fog coordinate.

Prototypes

```
void glGetFloatv(GLenum pname, GLfloat *params);
void glGetDoublev(GLenum pname, GLdouble *params);
```

Extended Parameters

pname   Specifies the parameter to be returned. To retrieve the current fog coordinate, this should be GL_CURRENT_FOG_COORDINATE_EXT.

Description

Calling the **glGetFloatv** or **glGetDoublev** function with *pname* parameter GL_CURRENT_ FOG_COORDINATE_EXT returns the current fog coordinate in the *params* parameter as either a single-precision or double-precision floating-point value, respectively.

■ **glGetIntegerv**—Extended to allow retrieval of fog coordinate array state.

Prototype

    void **glGetIntegerv**(GLenum *pname*, GLint **params*);

Extended Parameters

pname   Specifies the parameter to be returned. May be GL_FOG_COORDINATE_
                 ARRAY_TYPE_EXT, or GL_FOG_COORDINATE_ARRAY_STRIDE_EXT.

Description

The **glGetIntegerv** function can be used to retrieve state related to the fog coordinate
array that was previously specified using the **glFogCoordPointerEXT** function. The *pname*
parameter may be one of the following values:

GL_FOG_COORDINATE_ARRAY_TYPE_EXT
                 The data type of the fog coordinate array is returned. The initial value is
                 GL_FLOAT.

GL_FOG_COORDINATE_ARRAY_STRIDE_EXT
                 The stride of the fog coordinate array is returned. The initial value is 0.

■ **glGetPointerv**—Extended to allow retrieval of the fog coordinate array pointer.

Prototype

    void **glGetPointerv**(GLenum *pname*, GLvoid ***pointer*);

Extended Parameters

pname   Specifies the array pointer to be returned. May be GL_FOG_COORDINATE_
                 ARRAY_POINTER_EXT.

Description

The **glGetPointerv** function can be used to retrieve the pointer to the fog coordinate array
that was previously specified using the **glFogCoordPointerEXT** function. When the *pname*
parameter is GL_FOG_COORDINATE_ARRAY_POINTER_EXT, the pointer to the fog coordinate
array is returned in the *pointer* parameter. The initial value is a null pointer.

11.2 GL_NV_fog_distance

OpenGL version required	OpenGL 1.1
Dependencies	—
Promotions	—
Related extensions	—

DISCUSSION

During rasterization, the OpenGL specification allows implementations to determine the fog distance for a fragment by calculating the true Euclidean distance between the fragment and the camera, or by approximating this value with the fragment's depth relative to the camera plane, as shown in Figure 11.2.1. The GL_NV_fog_distance extension gives applications control over which method is used.

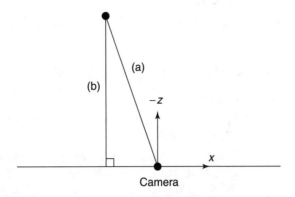

FIGURE 11.2.1   An implementation may choose to determine the fog distance by (a) calculating the true Euclidean distance between a fragment and the camera or (b) by approximating the true distance with the fragment's depth relative to the camera plane.

The fog distance mode is specified by calling the **glFogi** function with *pname* parameter GL_FOG_DISTANCE_MODE_NV. The *param* parameter specifies one of three possible fog distance modes. Let $\langle x_{eye}, y_{eye}, z_{eye} \rangle$ be the eye-space position of a fragment. If *param* is GL_EYE_PLANE_ABSOLUTE_NV, then the fog distance c is given by

$$c = \left| z_{eye} \right|.$$

If *param* is GL_EYE_PLANE, then the fog distance is given by

$$c = z_{eye}.$$

If *param* is GL_EYE_RADIAL_NV, then the fog distance is given by

$$c = \sqrt{x_{eye}^2 + y_{eye}^2 + z_{eye}^2}\,.$$

The value of c is then used to calculate the fog factor using Equation (11.1.1), (11.1.2), or (11.1.3). The current value of the fog distance mode can be retrieved by calling the **glGetIntegerv** function with *pname* parameter GL_FOG_DISTANCE_MODE_NV.

Implementations are free to calculate the fog distance c only at each vertex and then interpolate the values across the face of a primitive, or they may calculate the fog distance for each individual fragment.

The fog distance mode is ignored if the GL_EXT_fog_coord extension is available and the value of GL_FOG_COORDINATE_SOURCE_EXT is GL_FOG_COORDINATE_EXT, because the fog coordinate c is explicitly specified by the application.

EXTENDED FUNCTIONS

■ **glFogi**—Extended to allow specification of the fog distance mode.

Prototype

```
void glFogi(GLenum pname, GLint param);
```

Extended Parameters

pname   Specifies the symbolic name of a fog parameter. May be GL_FOG_DISTANCE_MODE_NV.

param   Specifies the value of the fog parameter. When *pname* is GL_FOG_DISTANCE_MODE_NV, this must be GL_EYE_PLANE_ABSOLUTE_NV, GL_EYE_PLANE, or GL_EYE_RADIAL_NV. The initial value is implementation-dependent.

Description

The fog distance mode is specified by calling the **glFogi** function with *pname* parameter GL_FOG_DISTANCE_MODE_NV. The *param* parameter specifies the fog distance mode and may be one of the following values:

GL_EYE_PLANE_ABSOLUTE_NV

The fog distance is equal to the absolute value of the eye-space z coordinate.

GL_EYE_PLANE

The fog distance is equal to the signed eye-space z coordinate. This results in values that are always negative for visible fragments.

GL_EYE_RADIAL_NV

The fog distance is equal to the Euclidean distance to the camera given by the magnitude of a fragment's eye-space position.

■ **glGetIntegerv**—Extended to allow retrieval of the fog distance mode.

Prototype

```
void glGetIntegerv(GLenum pname, GLint *params);
```

Extended Parameters

pname   Specifies the parameter to be returned. May be GL_FOG_DISTANCE_
                   MODE_NV.

Description

The current value of the fog distance mode can be retrieved by calling the **glGetIntegerv**
function with *pname* parameter GL_FOG_DISTANCE_MODE_NV.

STENCIL OPERATIONS

IN THIS CHAPTER

12.1   **GL_EXT_stencil_wrap**

OpenGL version required	OpenGL 1.1
Dependencies	—
Promotions	—
Related extensions	—

DISCUSSION

Unextended OpenGL provides two stencil operations, GL_INCR and GL_DECR, that increment and decrement the values in the stencil buffer. These operations clamp to the largest and smallest representable values, which may not always be the desired behavior. The GL_EXT_stencil_wrap extension provides two new stencil operations, GL_INCR_WRAP_EXT and GL_DECR_WRAP_EXT, that increment and decrement stencil values and wrap around when the largest and smallest values are exceeded.

The GL_INCR_WRAP_EXT and GL_DECR_WRAP_EXT constants may be passed as any parameter to the **glStencilOp** function. When the GL_INCR_WRAP_EXT operation is performed, the value in the stencil buffer is incremented. If the value in the stencil buffer is $2^n - 1$, where n is the number of bits used by the stencil buffer, then the new value written to the stencil buffer is 0. When the GL_DECR_WRAP_EXT operation is performed, the value in the stencil buffer is decremented. If the value in the stencil buffer is 0, then the new value written to the stencil buffer is $2^n - 1$. The number of bits n used by the stencil buffer can be queried by calling the **glGetIntegerv** function with *pname* parameter GL_STENCIL_BITS.

EXTENDED FUNCTIONS

■ **glStencilOp, glStencilOpSeparateATI**—Extended to support stencil wrap modes.

Prototypes

```
void glStencilOp(GLenum fail, GLenum zfail, GLenum zpass);
void glStencilOpSeparateATI(GLenum face, GLenum fail, GLenum zfail,
    GLenum zpass);
```

Extended Parameters

fail   Specifies the action to take when the stencil test fails. May be GL_INCR_WRAP_EXT or GL_DECR_WRAP_EXT.

zfail   Specifies the action to take when the stencil test passes but the depth test fails. May be GL_INCR_WRAP_EXT or GL_DECR_WRAP_EXT.

zpass   Specifies the action to take when the stencil test passes and the depth test passes. May be GL_INCR_WRAP_EXT or GL_DECR_WRAP_EXT.

Description

Any of the three operations that can be performed based on the outcome of the stencil and depth tests may be GL_INCR_WRAP_EXT or GL_DECR_WRAP_EXT. When these modes are used, incrementing the largest representable value produces zero, and decrementing zero produces the largest representable value.

12.2 GL_EXT_stencil_two_side

OpenGL version required	OpenGL 1.1
Dependencies	—
Promotions	—
Related extensions	—

DISCUSSION

It is often the case that different stencil operations must be performed for front-facing and back-facing polygons in order to achieve a desired effect. Using unextended OpenGL, this would require that geometry be passed through the rendering pipeline twice, once to render front-facing polygons using a certain stencil operation and again to render back-facing polygons using a different stencil operation. The GL_EXT_stencil_two_side extension doubles the stencil state maintained by OpenGL and provides independent stencil operations for front-facing and back-facing polygons, allowing a single rendering call to be made. This can result in a significant performance increase in situations for which vertex processing is the limiting factor.

When two-sided stencil testing is enabled in addition to the standard stencil test, two sets of stencil state are applied during rasterization. One set is applied to front-facing polygons, and another set is applied to back-facing polygons. Two-sided stencil testing is enabled and disabled by calling the **glEnable** and **glDisable** functions with *cap* parameter GL_STENCIL_TEST_TWO_SIDE_EXT. Initially, two-sided stencil testing is disabled, and the stencil operations behave as they would under unextended OpenGL. Two sets of stencil state are still maintained, but the front-facing stencil state is applied to all polygons when two-sided stencil testing is disabled.

Two-sided stencil state is specified using a mechanism that is analogous to the active texture unit introduced by the GL_ARB_multitexture extension. An active stencil face is specified by calling the **glActiveStencilFaceEXT** function,

> void **glActiveStencilFaceEXT**(GLenum *face*);

The *face* parameter passed to this function can be either GL_FRONT or GL_BACK and selects the currently active stencil face. Subsequent calls to the **glStencilOp**, **glStencilFunc**, and **glStencilMask** functions and queries made to stencil state through the **glGet-Integerv** function always apply to the active stencil face regardless of whether two-sided stencil testing is enabled. The initially active stencil face is GL_FRONT.

When two-sided stencil testing is enabled, primitives that do not produce polygonal geometry, such as points and lines, always use the front-facing stencil state. However, if the polygon mode is not GL_FILL, points or lines rendered at polygon boundaries still use the stencil state determined by the polygon's facing. When clearing the stencil buffer, the front-facing stencil mask is always applied.

If the stencil test is disabled, then the state of the two-sided stencil test has no effect during rasterization.

USEFUL TIPS

How can I use two-sided stencil operations to render stencil shadow volumes?

Using unextended OpenGL, a stencil shadow volume is typically rendered by enabling face culling and making two passes, each using a different face-culling mode and stencil operation. This is demonstrated in Listing 12.2.1. When the GL_EXT_stencil_two_side extension is present, the two passes can be combined as shown in Listing 12.2.2.

LISTING 12.2.1 The following code shows the conventional method used to render a stencil shadow volume. Two rendering passes are made. The first renders only front-facing polygons using an incrementing stencil operation, and the second renders only back-facing polygons using a decrementing stencil operation. The RenderShadowVolume() function makes whatever calls are needed to render the shadow volume geometry.

```
glEnable(GL_CULL_FACE);
glEnable(GL_DEPTH_TEST);
glEnable(GL_STENCIL_TEST);

// Disable writes to color and depth buffers
```

```
glColorMask(GL_FALSE, GL_FALSE, GL_FALSE, GL_FALSE);
glDepthMask(GL_FALSE);

glStencilMask(~0);
glStencilFunc(GL_ALWAYS, 0, ~0);

// First pass:
// Increment stencil value for front-facing polygons
// when fragments pass the depth test
glCullFace(GL_BACK);
glStencilOp(GL_KEEP, GL_KEEP, GL_INCR_WRAP_EXT);

RenderShadowVolume();

// Second pass:
// Decrement stencil value for front-facing polygons
// when fragments pass the depth test
glCullFace(GL_FRONT);
glStencilOp(GL_KEEP, GL_KEEP, GL_DECR_WRAP_EXT);

RenderShadowVolume();
```

LISTING 12.2.2   The following code shows how a stencil shadow volume might be rendered using the GL_EXT_stencil_two_side extension. Stencil operations are specified for both front-facing and back-facing polygons, and a single rendering pass is made. The RenderShadowVolume() function makes whatever calls are needed to render the shadow volume geometry.

```
glDisable(GL_CULL_FACE);
glEnable(GL_DEPTH_TEST);
glEnable(GL_STENCIL_TEST);
glEnable(GL_STENCIL_TEST_TWO_SIDE_EXT);

// Disable writes to color and depth buffers
glColorMask(GL_FALSE, GL_FALSE, GL_FALSE, GL_FALSE);
glDepthMask(GL_FALSE);

// Set front-facing stencil state
glActiveStencilFaceEXT(GL_FRONT);
glStencilMask(~0);
glStencilFunc(GL_ALWAYS, 0, ~0);
glStencilOp(GL_KEEP, GL_KEEP, GL_INCR_WRAP_EXT);

// Set back-facing stencil state
glActiveStencilFaceEXT(GL_BACK);
glStencilMask(~0);
glStencilFunc(GL_ALWAYS, 0, ~0);
```

```
glStencilOp(GL_KEEP, GL_KEEP, GL_DECR_WRAP_EXT);

// Perform single rendering pass
RenderShadowVolume();
```

NEW FUNCTIONS

■ **glActiveStencilFaceEXT**—Select the active stencil face.

Prototype

```
void glActiveStencilFaceEXT(GLenum face);
```

Parameters

face   Specifies the active stencil face. Must be GL_FRONT or GL_BACK. The initial value is GL_FRONT.

Description

The **glActiveStencilFaceEXT** function sets the currently active stencil face. Subsequent modifications to the stencil state made through calls to the **glStencilOp**, **glStencilFunc**, and **glStencilMask** functions apply to the currently active stencil face. Also, stencil state queries made using the **glGetIntegerv** function return values corresponding to the currently active stencil face.

Get Functions

glGetIntegerv with *pname* parameter GL_ACTIVE_STENCIL_FACE_EXT

EXTENDED FUNCTIONS

■ **glEnable**, **glDisable**, **glIsEnabled**—Extended to enable/disable two-sided stencil testing.

Prototypes

```
void glEnable(GLenum cap);
void glDisable(GLenum cap);
GLboolean glIsEnabled(GLenum cap);
```

Extended Parameters

cap   Specifies a GL capability. To enable or disable two-sided stencil testing, or to query whether two-sided stencil testing is enabled, this should be GL_STENCIL_TEST_TWO_SIDE_EXT.

Description

Two-sided stencil testing is enabled and disabled by passing the value GL_STENCIL_TEST_TWO_SIDE_EXT to the **glEnable** and **glDisable** functions. Calling the **glIsEnabled** function with the parameter GL_STENCIL_TEST_TWO_SIDE_EXT returns a value indicating whether two-sided stencil testing is enabled.

- **glGetIntegerv**—Extended to allow retrieval of the currently active stencil face.

Prototype

```
void glGetIntegerv(GLenum pname, GLint *params);
```

Extended Parameters

pname   Specifies the parameter to be returned. May be GL_ACTIVE_STENCIL_FACE_EXT.

Description

The currently active stencil face is retrieved by calling the **glGetIntegerv** function with *pname* parameter GL_ACTIVE_STENCIL_FACE_EXT. The return value is always GL_FRONT or GL_BACK. The initial value is GL_FRONT.

12.3 GL_ATI_separate_stencil

OpenGL version required	OpenGL 1.1
Dependencies	—
Promotions	—
Related extensions	—

DISCUSSION

It is often the case that different stencil operations must be performed for front-facing and back-facing polygons in order to achieve a desired effect. Using unextended OpenGL, this would require that geometry be passed through the rendering pipeline twice, once to render front-facing polygons using a certain stencil operation and again to render back-facing polygons using a different stencil operation. The GL_ATI_separate_stencil extension provides independent stencil tests and stencil operations for front-facing and back-facing polygons, allowing a single rendering call to be made. This can result in a significant performance increase in situations for which vertex processing is the limiting factor.

When the GL_ATI_separate_stencil extension is present, two stencil tests and two sets of stencil operations are maintained, one for front-facing polygons and the other for back-facing polygons. In contrast to the GL_EXT_stencil_two_side extension, separate stencil tests and operations do not need to be enabled, but are *always* applied. This does not cause a problem for applications unaware of the extension, however, since the standard functions **glStencilFunc** and **glStencilOp** set the stencil state for both front-facing and back-facing polygons, simultaneously. Another difference between the GL_ATI_separate_stencil and GL_EXT_stencil_two_side extensions is that only one stencil reference value, stencil value mask, and stencil write mask exist and apply to both front-facing and back-facing polygons.

Separate stencil tests are specified by calling the **glStencilFuncSeparateATI** function,

```
void glStencilFuncSeparateATI(GLenum frontfunc,
                              GLenum backfunc,
                              GLint ref,
                              GLuint mask);
```

The *frontfunc* and *backfunc* parameters specify the stencil tests that are applied to front-facing and back-facing polygons, respectively. The *ref* and *mask* parameters are interpreted exactly as they are for the **glStencilFunc** function and specify the stencil reference value and stencil value mask. Calling the standard **glStencilFunc** function sets both the front-facing and back-facing stencil tests to the same value specified by the *func* parameter.

Separate stencil operations are specified by calling the **glStencilOpSeparateATI** function,

```
void glStencilOpSeparateATI(GLenum face,
                            GLenum fail,
                            GLenum zfail,
                            GLenum zpass);
```

The *face* parameter indicates whether the specified operations should be applied to front-facing polygons or back-facing polygons. Calling the standard **glStencilOp** function sets the stencil operations for both front-facing and back-facing polygons to the same values.

Primitives that do not produce polygonal geometry, such as points and lines, always use the front-facing stencil state.

USEFUL TIPS

How can I use separate stencil operations to render stencil shadow volumes?

Using unextended OpenGL, a stencil shadow volume is typically rendered by enabling face culling and making two passes, each using a different face-culling mode and stencil operation. This is demonstrated in Listing 12.2.1 for the GL_NV_stencil_two_side extension. When the GL_ATI_separate_stencil extension is present, the two passes can be combined, as shown in Listing 12.3.1.

LISTING 12.3.1   The following code shows how a stencil shadow volume might be rendered using the GL_ATI_separate_stencil extension. Stencil operations are specified for both front-facing and back-facing polygons, and a single rendering pass is made. The RenderShadowVolume() function makes whatever calls are needed to render the shadow volume geometry.

```
glDisable(GL_CULL_FACE);
glEnable(GL_DEPTH_TEST);
glEnable(GL_STENCIL_TEST);
```

```
// Disable writes to color and depth buffers
glColorMask(GL_FALSE, GL_FALSE, GL_FALSE, GL_FALSE);
glDepthMask(GL_FALSE);

glStencilMask(~0);
glStencilFunc(GL_ALWAYS, 0, ~0);

// Set front-facing stencil state
glStencilOpSeparateATI(GL_FRONT, GL_KEEP,
    GL_KEEP, GL_INCR_WRAP_EXT);

// Set back-facing stencil state
glStencilOpSeparateATI(GL_BACK, GL_KEEP,
    GL_KEEP, GL_DECR_WRAP_EXT);

// Perform single rendering pass
RenderShadowVolume();
```

NEW FUNCTIONS

■ **glStencilFuncSeparateATI**—Specify separate front-facing and back-facing stencil functions.

Prototype

```
void glStencilFuncSeparateATI(GLenum frontfunc,
                              GLenum backfunc,
                              GLint ref,
                              GLuint mask);
```

Parameters

frontfunc   Specifies the stencil test function for front-facing polygons. Accepted values are the same as those accepted by the *func* parameter of the **glStencilFunc** function. The initial value is GL_ALWAYS.

backfunc   Specifies the stencil test function for back-facing polygons. Accepted values are the same as those accepted by the *func* parameter of the **glStencilFunc** function. The initial value is GL_ALWAYS.

ref   Specifies the reference value for both front-facing and back-facing stencil tests. This value is clamped to the range, where n is the number of bits used by the stencil buffer. The initial value is 0.

mask   Specifies a mask that is ANDed with both the reference value and values in the stencil buffer when the stencil test is performed. The initial value consists of all 1s.

Description

The **glStencilFuncSeparateATI** function specifies separate stencil tests for front-facing and back-facing polygons. The *frontfunc* parameter specifies the stencil test that is applied when front-facing polygons are rasterized, and the *backfunc* parameter specifies the stencil test that is applied when back-facing polygons are rasterized. The *ref* and *mask* parameters apply to both front-facing and back-facing polygons.

Special Considerations

Calling the **glStencilFunc** function with a particular value for the *func* parameter is equivalent to calling the **glStencilFuncSeparateATI** function with the same values for both the *frontfunc* and *backfunc* parameters.

Get Functions

glGetIntegerv with *pname* parameter GL_STENCIL_BACK_FUNC_ATI

Errors

GL_INVALID_ENUM is generated if *frontfunc* or *backfunc* is not an accepted value.

GL_INVALID_OPERATION is generated if **glStencilFuncSeparateATI** is called between calls to **glBegin** and **glEnd**.

■ **glStencilOpSeparateATI**—Specify stencil operations for either front-facing or back-facing polygons.

Prototype

```
void glStencilOpSeparateATI(GLenum face,
                            GLenum fail,
                            GLenum zfail,
                            GLenum zpass);
```

Parameters

face	Specifies a facing to which the stencil operations apply. Must be GL_FRONT, GL_BACK, or GL_FRONT_AND_BACK.
fail	Specifies the operation to perform when the stencil test fails. Accepted values are the same as those accepted by the **glStencilOp** function.
zfail	Specifies the operation to perform when the stencil test passes but the depth test fails. Accepted values are the same as those accepted by the **glStencilOp** function.
zpass	Specifies the operation to perform when both the stencil test and depth test pass. Accepted values are the same as those accepted by the **glStencilOp** function.

Description

The **glStencilOpSeparateATI** function allows independent specification of stencil operations for front-facing and back-facing polygons. When the *face* parameter is GL_FRONT, the stencil operations specified by the *fail*, *zfail*, and *zpass* parameters apply only to front-facing polygons. When the *face* parameter is GL_BACK, the stencil operations apply only to back-facing polygons. When the *face* parameter is GL_FRONT_AND_BACK, the stencil operations apply to both front-facing and back-facing polygons.

Special Considerations

Calling the **glStencilOp** function is equivalent to calling the **glStencilOpSeparateATI** function with *face* parameter GL_FRONT_AND_BACK.

If the GL_EXT_stencil_wrap extension is available, then the values GL_INCR_WRAP_EXT and GL_DECR_WRAP_EXT are accepted by the *fail*, *zfail*, and *zpass* parameters.

Get Functions

glGetIntegerv with *pname* parameter GL_STENCIL_BACK_FAIL_ATI

glGetIntegerv with *pname* parameter GL_STENCIL_BACK_PASS_DEPTH_FAIL_ATI

glGetIntegerv with *pname* parameter GL_STENCIL_BACK_PASS_DEPTH_PASS_ATI

Errors

GL_INVALID_ENUM is generated if *face* is not GL_FRONT, GL_BACK, or GL_FRONT_AND_BACK.

GL_INVALID_ENUM is generated if *fail*, *zfail*, or *zpass* is not an accepted value.

GL_INVALID_OPERATION is generated if **glStencilFuncSeparateATI** is called between calls to **glBegin** and **glEnd**.

EXTENDED FUNCTIONS

■ **glGetIntegerv**—Extended to allow retrieval of back-facing stencil state.

Prototype

```
void glGetIntegerv(GLenum pname, GLint *params);
```

Extended Parameters

pname   Specifies the parameter to be returned. May be one of the values listed in Description.

Description

Separate stencil state for back-facing polygons can be retrieved using the **glGetIntegerv** function. The *pname* parameter may be one of the following values:

GL_STENCIL_BACK_FUNC_ATI
                    The stencil function for back-facing polygons is returned.

GL_STENCIL_BACK_FAIL_ATI
                    The stencil operation performed for back-facing polygons when the stencil test fails is returned.

GL_STENCIL_BACK_PASS_DEPTH_FAIL_ATI

>   The stencil operation performed for back-facing polygons when the stencil test passes but the depth test fails is returned.

GL_STENCIL_BACK_PASS_DEPTH_PASS_ATI

>   The stencil operation performed for back-facing polygons when both the stencil test and depth test pass is returned.

CHAPTER **13**

SHADOW MAPPING

IN THIS CHAPTER

13.1   GL_ARB_depth_texture

13.2   GL_ARB_shadow

13.3   GL_ARB_shadow_ambient

13.4   GL_EXT_shadow_funcs

13.1 GL_ARB_depth_texture

OpenGL version required	OpenGL 1.1
Dependencies	—
Promotions	Promoted to a core feature in OpenGL 1.4
Related extensions	GL_ARB_shadow

DISCUSSION

The GL_ARB_depth_texture extension allows a one- or two-dimensional texture to contain depth values. A texture containing depth values is commonly used in conjunction with the GL_ARB_shadow extension (see Section 13.2) to perform shadow mapping.

A depth texture is loaded by specifying one of the internal formats listed in Table 13.1.1 when calling the **glTexImage{12}D** or **glCopyTexImage{12}D** function. When specifying a depth texture image using the **glTexImage{12}D** function, the *format* parameter must be GL_DEPTH_COMPONENT. When specifying a depth texture image using the **glCopyTex-Image{12}D** function, depth values are copied directly from the depth buffer.

TABLE 13.1.1 Depth texture internal formats. Sized internal formats specify how many bits should be used to store each depth component.

Internal Format	Base Internal Format	Depth Bits
GL_DEPTH_COMPONENT	GL_DEPTH_COMPONENT	
GL_DEPTH_COMPONENT16_ARB	GL_DEPTH_COMPONENT	16
GL_DEPTH_COMPONENT24_ARB	GL_DEPTH_COMPONENT	24
GL_DEPTH_COMPONENT32_ARB	GL_DEPTH_COMPONENT	32

The **glTexSubImage{12}D** function may be called to update a subimage of a depth texture, in which case the *format* parameter must be GL_DEPTH_COMPONENT. If the *format* parameter is GL_DEPTH_COMPONENT and the texture being updated is does not have a base internal format of GL_DEPTH_COMPONENT, then the error GL_INVALID_OPERATION is generated.

A depth texture subimage may also be updated using the **glCopyTexSubImage{12}D** function. When a texture's base internal format is GL_DEPTH_COMPONENT, values are copied from the depth buffer. Calling the **glCopyTexSubImage{12}D** function to update a depth texture when there is no depth buffer generates the error GL_INVALID_OPERATION.

If a depth texture is used for ordinary color texturing, then the depth value stored at each texel is interpreted as luminance by default. An application can specify that each depth value be interpreted as a luminance value, an intensity value, or an alpha value by calling the **glTexParameteri** function with *pname* parameter GL_DEPTH_TEXTURE_MODE_ARB. The desired interpretation is specified by passing GL_LUMINANCE, GL_INTENSITY, or GL_ALPHA to the *param* parameter.

EXTENDED FUNCTIONS

- **glTexImage1D, glTexImage2D**—Extended to support depth internal formats.

Prototypes

```
void glTexImage1D(GLenum target, GLint level, GLint internalFormat,
    GLsizei width, GLint border, GLenum format, GLenum type,
    const GLvoid *pixels);
void glTexImage2D(GLenum target, GLint level, GLint internalFormat,
    GLsizei width, GLsizei height, GLint border, GLenum format,
    GLenum type, const GLvoid *pixels);
```

Extended Parameters

internalFormat   Specifies the internal format of the texture. May be GL_DEPTH_COMPONENT, GL_DEPTH_COMPONENT16_ARB, GL_DEPTH_COMPONENT24_ARB, or GL_DEPTH_COMPONENT32_ARB.

format   Specifies the format of the pixel data. If *internalFormat* specifies a depth texture, then this parameter must be GL_DEPTH_COMPONENT.

Description

The **glTexImage1D** and **glTexImage2D** functions are used to load depth texture images. When the *internalFormat* parameter specifies a depth format, the *format* parameter must be GL_DEPTH_COMPONENT, and the pixel data pointed to by the *pixels* parameter is interpreted as depth values.

Special Considerations

If the GL_NV_packed_depth_stencil extension (see Chapter 16, Section 16.5) is supported, then the *format* parameter may be GL_DEPTH_STENCIL_NV (in which case the *type* parameter must be GL_UNSIGNED_INT_24_8_NV). The stencil index component of the pixel data is ignored when the texture image is loaded.

Errors

GL_INVALID_OPERATION is generated if *internalFormat* specifies a depth format and *format* is not GL_DEPTH_COMPONENT.

GL_INVALID_OPERATION is generated if *format* is GL_DEPTH_COMPONENT and *internalFormat* does not specify a depth format.

■ **glCopyTexImage1D**, **glCopyTexImage2D**—Extended to support depth internal formats.

Prototypes

```
void glCopyTexImage1D(GLenum target, GLint level, GLenum internalFormat,
    GLint x,  GLint y, GLsizei width, GLint border);
void glCopyTexImage2D(GLenum target, GLint level, GLenum internalFormat,
    GLint x, GLint y, GLsizei width, GLsizei height, GLint border);
```

Extended Parameters

internalFormat   Specifies the internal format of the texture. May be GL_DEPTH_COMPONENT, GL_DEPTH_COMPONENT16_ARB, GL_DEPTH_COMPONENT24_ARB, or GL_DEPTH_COMPONENT32_ARB.

Description

The **glCopyTexImage1D** and **glCopyTexImage2D** functions can be used to copy depth values from the depth buffer into a texture. When the *internalFormat* parameter specifies a depth format, values are copied from the depth buffer instead of the color buffer.

Errors

GL_INVALID_OPERATION is generated if *internalFormat* specifies a depth format and there is no depth buffer.

- **glTexParameteri**—Extended to allow depth texture mode specification.

Prototype

```
void glTexParameteri(GLenum target, GLenum pname, GLint param);
```

Extended Parameters

pname   Specifies the symbolic name of a texture parameter. May be GL_DEPTH_TEXTURE_MODE_ARB.

param   Specifies the value of the texture parameter. When *pname* is GL_DEPTH_TEXTURE_MODE_ARB, this must be GL_LUMINANCE, GL_INTENSITY, or GL_ALPHA.

Description

The **glGetTexParameteri** function is used to set the depth texture mode for a texture containing depth values. The depth texture mode determines how depth values are interpreted when the texture is used as a color image. When the *pname* parameter is GL_DEPTH_TEXTURE_MODE_ARB, the *param* parameter specifies whether each depth value is interpreted as a luminance value, an intensity value, or an alpha value. The initial value is GL_LUMINANCE.

Errors

GL_INVALID_ENUM is generated if *pname* is GL_DEPTH_TEXTURE_MODE_ARB and *param* is not an accepted value.

- **glGetTexParameteriv**—Extended to return the current depth texture mode.

Prototype

```
void glGetTexParameteriv(GLenum target, GLenum pname,
    GLint *params);
```

Extended Parameters

pname   Specifies the symbolic name of a texture parameter. May be GL_DEPTH_TEXTURE_MODE_ARB.

Description

The **glGetTexParameteriv** function can be used to retrieve the current depth texture mode. When the *pname* parameter is GL_DEPTH_TEXTURE_MODE_ARB, the current depth texture mode is returned in the *params* parameter.

- **glGetTexLevelParameteriv**—Extended to return the internal storage resolution of a depth texture.

Prototype

```
void glGetTexParameteriv(GLenum target, GLint level, GLenum pname,
```

```
GLint *params);
```

Extended Parameters

pname   Specifies the symbolic name of a texture parameter. May be GL_
                 TEXTURE_DEPTH_SIZE_ARB.

Description

The internal storage resolution of the depth component of a texture image is retrieved by
calling the **glGetTexLevelParameteriv** function with *pname* GL_TEXTURE_DEPTH_
SIZE_ARB. If a texture does not contain depth values, then 0 is returned.

13.2 GL_ARB_shadow

OpenGL version required	OpenGL 1.1
Dependencies	Requires GL_ARB_depth_texture
Promotions	Promoted to a core feature in OpenGL 1.4
Related extensions	GL_ARB_shadow_ambient GL_EXT_shadow_funcs

DISCUSSION

The GL_ARB_shadow extension provides a mechanism through which the interpolated *r*
texture coordinate may be compared against the value fetched from a depth texture during
rasterization. The result of the comparison is a value that can be used to modulate lighting
calculations in a shadow-mapping algorithm.

The texture *r*-coordinate comparison mode for a depth texture is set by calling the
glTexParameteri function with *pname* parameter GL_TEXTURE_COMPARE_MODE_ARB.
Initially, the comparison mode is GL_NONE, meaning that the depth values in the texture
image are directly interpreted as luminance values, intensity values, or alpha values (depending on the current setting of the depth texture mode). If the *r*-coordinate comparison
mode is changed to GL_COMPARE_R_TO_TEXTURE_ARB, then the interpolated *r* texture coordinate, after being clamped to the range [0,1], is compared against the depth value fetched
from the texture at each fragment. The result of the comparison produces a value of 0.0 or
1.0 that replaces the depth value and is interpreted as a luminance value, an intensity value,
or an alpha value, as indicated by the depth texture mode. The comparison is not applied if
the texture does not contain depth values.

The result of the texture *r*-coordinate comparison depends on the current comparison
function. The comparison function may be GL_LEQUAL or GL_GEQUAL, and is specified by
calling the **glTexParameteri** function with *pname* parameter GL_TEXTURE_COMPARE_
FUNC_ARB. Let *d* represent the depth value fetched from the texture for a particular fragment, and let *r* be the clamped value of the interpolated *r* texture coordinate corresponding
to the fragment. If the comparison function is GL_LEQUAL (the initial value), then the result
of the comparison is 1.0 if $r \leq d$ and 0.0 otherwise. If the comparison function is GL_GEQUAL,

then the result of the comparison is 1.0 if $r \geq d$ and 0.0 otherwise. Values between 0.0 and 1.0 may be produced by texel filtering and represent a weighted average of comparison results.

EXTENDED FUNCTIONS

■ **glTexParameteri**—Extended to allow texture compare mode and function specification.

Prototype

```
void glTexParameteri(GLenum target, GLenum pname, GLint param);
```

Extended Parameters

pname   Specifies the symbolic name of a texture parameter. May be `GL_TEXTURE_COMPARE_MODE_ARB` or `GL_TEXTURE_COMPARE_FUNC_ARB`.

param   Specifies the value of the texture parameter. When *pname* is `GL_TEXTURE_COMPARE_MODE_ARB`, this must be `GL_NONE` or `GL_COMPARE_R_TO_TEXTURE_ARB`. When *pname* is `GL_TEXTURE_COMPARE_FUNC_ARB`, this must be `GL_LEQUAL` or `GL_GEQUAL`.

Description

The **glTexParameteri** function is used to specify the texture *r*-coordinate comparison mode and the associated comparison function. The *pname* parameter may be one of the following values:

`GL_TEXTURE_COMPARE_MODE_ARB`

The *param* parameter specifies the texture *r*-coordinate comparison mode. The value `GL_COMPARE_R_TO_TEXTURE_ARB` enables the replacement of the texture color based on the comparison of the *r* coordinate and the depth value in the texture, and the value `GL_NONE` disables the comparison. The initial value is `GL_NONE`.

`GL_TEXTURE_COMPARE_FUNC_ARB`

The *param* parameter specifies the texture *r*-coordinate comparison function. Accepted values are `GL_LEQUAL` and `GL_GEQUAL`. The initial value is `GL_LEQUAL`.

■ **glGetTexParameteriv**—Extended to return the current texture compare mode and function.

Prototype

```
void glGetTexParameteriv(GLenum target, GLenum pname,
    GLint *params);
```

Extended Parameters

pname Specifies the symbolic name of a texture parameter. May be GL_TEXTURE_COMPARE_MODE_ARB or GL_TEXTURE_COMPARE_FUNC_ARB.

Description

The **glGetTexParameteriv** function can be used to retrieve the texture *r*-coordinate comparison mode and associated comparison function. The *pname* parameter may be one of the following values:

GL_TEXTURE_COMPARE_MODE_ARB

The texture *r*-coordinate comparison mode is returned.

GL_TEXTURE_COMPARE_FUNC_ARB

The texture *r*-coordinate comparison function is returned.

13.3 GL_ARB_shadow_ambient

OpenGL version required	OpenGL 1.1
Dependencies	Requires GL_ARB_shadow
Promotions	—
Related extensions	—

DISCUSSION

The GL_ARB_shadow extension (see Section 13.2) defines a mechanism through which the interpolated *r* texture coordinate may be compared against the value fetched from a depth texture during rasterization. When the comparison fails, the value 0.0 is produced. The GL_ARB_shadow_ambient extension allows an application to specify an arbitrary value to be produced when the texture *r*-coordinate comparison fails.

The value produced when the texture *r*-coordinate comparison fails is specified by calling the **glTexParameterf** function with *pname* GL_TEXTURE_COMPARE_FAIL_VALUE_ARB. The *param* parameter specifies the comparison failure value, which is initially 0.0.

EXTENDED FUNCTIONS

■ **glTexParameterf**—Extended to allow texture *r*-coordinate comparison failure value specification.

Prototype

```
void glTexParameterf(GLenum target, GLenum pname, GLfloat param);
```

Extended Parameters

pname Specifies the symbolic name of a texture parameter. May be GL_TEXTURE_COMPARE_FAIL_VALUE_ARB.

param   Specifies the value of the texture parameter. When *pname* is GL_
                       TEXTURE_COMPARE_FAIL_VALUE_ARB, this should be a floating-point
                       value between 0.0 and 1.0.

Description

The **glTexParameterf** function is used to specify the value produced when the texture
r-coordinate comparison fails. When the *pname* parameter is GL_TEXTURE_COMPARE_
FAIL_VALUE_ARB, the *param* parameter specifies the comparison failure result value. The
initial value is 0.0.

- **glGetTexParameterfv**—Extended to return the current texture *r*-coordinate comparison failure value.

Prototype

```
void glGetTexParameterfv(GLenum target, GLenum pname,
    GLfloat *params);
```

Extended Parameters

pname   Specifies the symbolic name of a texture parameter. May be GL_
                       TEXTURE_COMPARE_FAIL_VALUE_ARB.

Description

The **glGetTexParameterfv** function can be used to retrieve the value produced when the
texture *r*-coordinate comparison fails. When the *pname* parameter is GL_TEXTURE_
COMPARE_FAIL_VALUE_ARB, the comparison failure result value is returned in the *params*
parameter.

13.4   GL_EXT_shadow_funcs

OpenGL version required	OpenGL 1.1
Dependencies	Requires GL_ARB_shadow
Promotions	—
Related extensions	—

DISCUSSION

The GL_ARB_shadow extension (see Section 13.2) only allows the texture *r*-coordinate comparison mode to be GL_LEQUAL or GL_GEQUAL. The GL_EXT_shadow_funcs extension allows any of the standard OpenGL comparison functions to be used for shadow mapping comparisons.

The texture *r*-coordinate comparison function is specified by calling the **glTex-Parameteri** function with *pname* parameter GL_TEXTURE_COMPARE_FUNC_ARB. The *param* parameter specifies the comparison function and may be any of the values listed in Table 13.4.1. The result produced by each comparison mode is summarized in the table.

TABLE 13.4.1 Texture *r*-coordinate comparison results. The value *d* is the depth value fetched from the texture for a particular fragment, and *r* is the clamped value of the interpolated *r* texture coordinate corresponding to the fragment. The result *d'* replaces the value fetched from the depth texture.

Comparison Function	*Result*
GL_LEQUAL	$d' = \begin{cases} 1.0, & \text{if } r \le d \\ 0.0, & \text{if } r > d \end{cases}$
GL_GEQUAL	$d' = \begin{cases} 1.0, & \text{if } r \ge d \\ 0.0, & \text{if } r < d \end{cases}$
GL_LESS	$d' = \begin{cases} 1.0, & \text{if } r < d \\ 0.0, & \text{if } r \ge d \end{cases}$
GL_GREATER	$d' = \begin{cases} 1.0, & \text{if } r > d \\ 0.0, & \text{if } r \le d \end{cases}$
GL_EQUAL	$d' = \begin{cases} 1.0, & \text{if } r = d \\ 0.0, & \text{if } r \ne d \end{cases}$
GL_NOTEQUAL	$d' = \begin{cases} 1.0, & \text{if } r \ne d \\ 0.0, & \text{if } r = d \end{cases}$
GL_ALWAYS	$d' = 1.0$
GL_NEVER	$d' = 0.0$

IMPLEMENTATION NOTES

- On Nvidia GeForce3 hardware, only one texture comparison mode and its complement may be used across all texture units. For instance, the comparison modes GL_LEQUAL and GL_GREATER may be used on different texture units, but using GL_LEQUAL on one unit and any mode other than GL_LEQUAL or GL_GREATER on another unit is not accelerated.

EXTENDED FUNCTIONS

- **glTexParameteri**—Extended to allow the full set of texture compare functions.

Prototype

```
void glTexParameteri(GLenum target, GLenum pname, GLint param);
```

Extended Parameters

param   Specifies the value of the texture parameter. When *pname* is
                        GL_TEXTURE_COMPARE_FUNC_ARB, this must be GL_LEQUAL,
                        GL_GEQUAL, GL_LESS, GL_GREATER, GL_EQUAL, GL_NOTEQUAL,
                        GL_ALWAYS, or GL_NEVER.

Description

The **glTexParameteri** function is used to specify the current texture *r*-coordinate comparison function. When the *pname* parameter is GL_TEXTURE_COMPARE_FUNC_ARB, the *param* parameter specifies the comparison function. The initial value is GL_LEQUAL.

OCCLUSION CULLING

IN THIS CHAPTER

14.1   **GL_HP_occlusion_test**

OpenGL version required	OpenGL 1.1
Dependencies	—
Promotions	—
Related extensions	The GL_NV_occlusion_query extension offers more flexible occlusion query functionality and can provide superior performance. If available, it should be used instead of the GL_HP_occlusion_test extension.

DISCUSSION

The GL_HP_occlusion_test extension provides a mechanism through which it may be possible to determine whether a complex geometrical model is completely occluded by other objects in a scene lying closer to the camera. The general idea is that a simple bounding volume that encloses a complex model can be rendered with writes to the color and depth buffers disabled. If no fragment of the bounding volume passes the depth test, then it is known that no fragment of the enclosed model can be visible.

An occlusion test produces a single Boolean value indicating whether one or more fragments have passed the depth test. An occlusion test is begun by calling the **glEnable** function with *cap* parameter GL_OCCLUSION_TEST_HP and is ended by calling the **glDisable** function with the same parameter value. The result of an occlusion test is queried by calling the **glGetBooleanv** function with *pname* parameter GL_OCCLUSION_TEST_RESULT_ HP. The initial value of the occlusion test result is GL_FALSE, and it is reset to GL_FALSE any time the value is retrieved using any variant of the **glGet** function. The occlusion test result is set to GL_TRUE whenever a fragment passes the depth test while GL_OCCLUSION_TEST_HP is enabled.

In a typical usage of the GL_HP_occlusion_test extension, an application would first disable writes to the color and depth buffers while leaving the depth test enabled. Second, the occlusion test is enabled. After rendering a simple bounding volume for an object (of course, with any complex shading operations disabled), the occlusion test is disabled. After re-enabling writes to the color and depth buffers, the result of the occlusion test is queried, and if GL_TRUE, the more complex model is rendered. This procedure is demonstrated in Listing 14.1.1.

LISTING 14.1.1   The following code demonstrates a typical usage of the GL_HP_occlusion_test extension.

```
GLboolean result;

// Disable writes to the color and depth buffers
glColorMask(GL_FALSE, GL_FALSE, GL_FALSE, GL_FALSE);
glDepthMask(GL_FALSE);

// Enable depth test (if not already enabled)
glEnable(GL_DEPTH_TEST);

// Enable occlusion test
glEnable(GL_OCCLUSION_TEST_HP);

// Render bounding volume at this point

// Disable occlusion test
glDisable(GL_OCCLUSION_TEST_HP);

// Re-enable writes to the color and depth buffers
glColorMask(GL_TRUE, GL_TRUE, GL_TRUE, GL_TRUE);
glDepthMask(GL_TRUE);

// Retrieve the result of the occlusion test
glGetBooleanv(GL_OCCLUSION_TEST_RESULT_HP, &result);

if (result)
{
    // Render complex geometry here
}
```

It should be noted that querying the result of the occlusion test can stall the rendering pipeline and should be performed as late as possible. A stall may be avoided by rendering some additional unrelated geometry between the end of the occlusion test and the retrieval of the occlusion test result.

Occlusion testing is performed independently of any other rendering state, so it is not required that writes to the color and depth buffers are disabled. However, it is expected that under normal circumstances it is not desired that the image is modified by rendering the bounding volume used to perform the occlusion test.

EXTENDED FUNCTIONS

■ **glEnable, glDisable, glIsEnabled**—Extended to enable/disable occlusion testing.

Prototypes

```
void glEnable(GLenum cap);
void glDisable(GLenum cap);
GLboolean glIsEnabled(GLenum cap);
```

Extended Parameters

cap   Specifies a GL capability. To enable or disable occlusion testing, or to query whether occlusion testing is enabled, this should be GL_OCCLUSION_TEST_HP.

Description

Occlusion testing is enabled and disabled by calling the **glEnable** and **glDisable** functions. When the occlusion test is enabled, any rendered fragments passing the depth test cause the value of GL_OCCLUSION_TEST_RESULT_HP to be set to GL_TRUE.

■ **glGetBooleanv**—Extended to retrieve the result of an occlusion test.

Prototypes

```
void glGetBooleanv(GLenum pname, GLboolean *params);
```

Extended Parameters

pname   Specifies the parameter to be returned. May be GL_OCCLUSION_TEST_RESULT_HP.

Description

The result of an occlusion test is queried by calling the **glGetBooleanv** function with *pname* parameter GL_OCCLUSION_TEST_RESULT_HP. The occlusion test result is initially GL_FALSE and is always reset to GL_FALSE when its value is queried. The occlusion test result is set to GL_TRUE when any rendered fragments pass the depth test while GL_OCCLUSION_TEST_HP is enabled.

14.2   GL_NV_occlusion_query

OpenGL version required	OpenGL 1.1
Dependencies	Requires GL_HP_occlusion_test
Promotions	—
Related extensions	Although this extension requires the GL_HP_occlusion_test extension, there is no direct dependence, and 'occlusion queries' may be performed without actually enabling the 'occlusion test' provided by the GL_HP_occlusion_test extension.

DISCUSSION

The GL_NV_occlusion_query extension expands the functionality provided by the GL_HP_occlusion_test extension in two ways. First, multiple occlusion queries can be issued before the result of any one is retrieved, allowing better parallelism between CPU and GPU processing time. Second, a count of the number of pixels that passed the depth test is maintained instead of a Boolean result indicating whether *any* pixels passed the depth test.

The intended usage is the same as that for the GL_HP_occlusion_test extension. By using an occlusion query, it may be possible to determine that a complex geometrical model is completely occluded by other objects in a scene lying closer to the camera. If a bounding volume enclosing a complex model produces no fragments passing the depth test, then the model does not need to be rendered. Since occlusion queries return the actual number of pixels that passed the depth test, occlusion queries may also be used to select a level of detail. A model might be rendered at a lower level of detail or not at all if the number of fragments of the bounding volume passing the depth test falls below a certain threshold.

Occlusion Query Objects

Occlusion queries follow the named object convention that is used elsewhere in OpenGL for such things as texture objects and program objects. Previously unused names for occlusion query objects are allocated by calling the **glGenOcclusionQueriesNV** function,

```
void glGenOcclusionQueriesNV(GLsizei n,
                             GLuint *ids);
```

This function generates *n* names and writes them to the array pointed to by the *ids* parameter. The names generated are marked as used, but the associated occlusion query objects are not actually created until the first time a new name is passed to the **glBeginOcclusionQueryNV** function.

Occlusion query objects are deleted, and the associated names are freed by calling the **glDeleteOcclusionQueriesNV** function,

```
void glDeleteOcclusionQueriesNV(GLsizei n,
                                const GLuint *ids);
```

Any of the *n* names passed to this function in the array pointed to *ids* parameter that do not refer to existing occlusion query objects are silently ignored. Once an occlusion query object is deleted, its name is marked as unused. The **glIsOcclusionQueryNV** function,

```
GLboolean glIsOcclusionQueryNV(GLuint id);
```

can be used to determine whether a particular name specified by the *id* parameter refers to an existing occlusion query object.

An occlusion query object encapsulates an integer pixel counter that is incremented for each fragment that passes the depth test when the occlusion query is active. The number of bits used by the pixel counter can be retrieved by calling the **glGetIntegerv** function with *pname* parameter GL_PIXEL_COUNTER_BITS_NV. All implementations are required to supply pixel counters that are at least 24 bits in size.

Performing Occlusion Queries

An occlusion query is begun by calling the **glBeginOcclusionQueryNV** function,

```
void glBeginOcclusionQueryNV(GLuint id);
```

with an *id* parameter specifying a new occlusion query object name or the name of a previously created occlusion query object. An occlusion query object is created when its associated name is first passed to the **glBeginOcclusionQueryNV** function. Beginning an occlusion query resets the occlusion query object's pixel counter to zero. Subsequent rendering operations increment an internal pixel counter whenever a fragment passes the depth test. In a multisampling situation, the pixel counter is incremented by the number of samples whose coverage bit is set. Otherwise, the pixel counter is incremented by one. The value of the internal pixel counter is copied to the active occlusion query object when the occlusion query is ended.

An occlusion query is ended by calling the **glEndOcclusionQueryNV** function,

```
void glEndOcclusionQueryNV(void);
```

The number of pixels that passed the depth test during the occlusion query can then be retrieved by calling the **glGetOcclusionQueryuivNV** function,

```
void glGetOcclusionQueryuivNV(GLuint id,
                              GLenum pname,
                              GLuint *params);
```

with *pname* parameter GL_PIXEL_COUNT_NV. Since the GPU renders asynchronously, the driver may have to wait for the GPU to finish rendering the geometry that was submitted during an occlusion query before it can return the pixel count. To determine whether the pixel count is available for a particular occlusion query object, the **glGetOcclusion-Query{iui}vNV** function can be called with *pname* parameter GL_PIXEL_COUNT_AVAILABLE_NV. Such a call immediately returns a Boolean value indicating whether a call to **glGetOcclusionQuery{iui}vNV** with *pname* parameter GL_PIXEL_COUNT_NV would return without waiting. If the pixel count availability is polled, a call to the **glFlush** function should first be made to ensure that all rendering commands are processed by the GPU. Otherwise, querying the pixel count availability may perpetually return GL_FALSE under implementations that buffer drawing commands.

Only one occlusion query may be active at any one time, so calling **glBegin-OcclusionQueryNV** a second time without an intervening call to the **glEndOcclusion-QueryNV** function generates a GL_INVALID_OPERATION error. The name of the currently active occlusion query object can be retrieved by calling the **glGetIntegerv** function with *pname* parameter GL_CURRENT_OCCLUSION_QUERY_ID_NV. If no occlusion query is active, then this call returns 0.

USEFUL TIPS

How would a typical usage of multiple occlusion queries be implemented?

A typical application would render several bounding volumes and perform a separate occlusion query operation for each one. Later, the result of each occlusion query could be tested to determine whether the more complex geometry enclosed by each bounding volume should be rendered. This procedure is shown in Listing 14.2.1.

LISTING 14.2.1   The following code demonstrates a typical usage of the GL_NV_occlusion_query extension.

```
GLuint    occlusionName[numQueries];

glGenOcclusionQueriesNV(numQueries, occlusionName);

// Disable writes to the color and depth buffers
glColorMask(GL_FALSE, GL_FALSE, GL_FALSE, GL_FALSE);
glDepthMask(GL_FALSE);

// Enable depth test (if not already enabled)
glEnable(GL_DEPTH_TEST);

for (int i = 0; i < numQueries; i++)
{
    glBeginOcclusionQueryNV(occlusionName[i]);
    // Render ith bounding volume
    glEndOcclusionQueryNV();
}

// Re-enable writes to the color and depth buffers
glColorMask(GL_TRUE, GL_TRUE, GL_TRUE, GL_TRUE);
glDepthMask(GL_TRUE);
```

```
    // Perform additional rendering at this point

    for (int i = 0; i < numQueries; i++)
    {
        GLuint    pixelCount;

        glGetOcclusionQueryuivNV(occlusionName[i],
            GL_PIXEL_COUNT_NV, &pixelCount);

        if (pixelCount > 0)
        {
            // Render complex geometry here
        }
    }
```

NEW FUNCTIONS

■ **glGenOcclusionQueriesNV**—Generate occlusion query names.

Prototype

```
void glGenOcclusionQueriesNV(GLsizei n,
                             GLuint *ids);
```

Parameters

n   Specifies the number of occlusion query names to generate.

ids   Specifies a pointer to an array that receives the generated occlusion query names.

Description

The **glGenOcclusionQueriesNV** function returns a set of *n* unused occlusion query names in the array pointed to by the *ids* parameter. Each of the returned names is reserved with respect to occlusion query name generation, but does not represent an existing occlusion query object until the first time the name is passed to the **glBeginOcclusionQueryNV** function.

Occlusion query objects are deleted and the associated occlusion query names are freed by calling the **glDeleteOcclusionQueriesNV** function.

Get Functions

glIsOcclusionQuery

Errors

GL_INVALID_VALUE is generated if *n* is negative.

GL_INVALID_OPERATION is generated if **glGenOcclusionQueriesNV** is called while there is an active occlusion query.

GL_INVALID_OPERATION is generated if **glGenOcclusionQueriesNV** is called between calls to **glBegin** and **glEnd**.

■ **glDeleteOcclusionQueriesNV**—Delete named occlusion queries.

Prototype

```
void glDeleteOcclusionQueriesNV(GLsizei n,
                                 const GLuint *ids);
```

Parameters

n   Specifies the number of occlusion queries to delete.

ids   Specifies a pointer to an array of occlusion query names to be deleted.

Description

The **glDeleteOcclusionQueriesNV** function deletes the *n* occlusion query objects contained in the array pointed to by the *ids* parameter. When an occlusion query object is deleted, it becomes nonexistent, and its name becomes unused. Deleted occlusion query names may subsequently be returned by the **glGenOcclusionQueriesNV** function. Any unused occlusion query names found in the array pointed to by the *ids* parameter are silently ignored.

Get Functions

glIsOcclusionQuery

Errors

GL_INVALID_VALUE is generated if *n* is negative.

GL_INVALID_OPERATION is generated if **glDeleteOcclusionQueriesNV** is called while there is an active occlusion query.

GL_INVALID_OPERATION is generated if **glDeleteOcclusionQueriesNV** is called between calls to **glBegin** and **glEnd**.

■ **glIsOcclusionQueryNV**—Determine if a name corresponds to an occlusion query.

Prototype

```
GLboolean glIsOcclusionQueryNV(GLuint id);
```

Parameters

id   Specifies the name of an occlusion query.

Description

The **glIsOcclusionQueryNV** function returns GL_TRUE if the *id* parameter names an existing occlusion query object. Otherwise, it returns GL_FALSE.

An occlusion query name generated by the **glGenOcclusionQueriesNV** function does not refer to an existing occlusion query object until a successful call to the **glBeginOcclusion-QueryNV** function is made using the occlusion query name.

■ **glBeginOcclusionQueryNV**—Begin an occlusion query.

Prototype

    void **glBeginOcclusionQueryNV**(GLuint *id*);

Parameters

id   Specifies the name of the occlusion query to begin.

Description

The **glBeginOcclusionQueryNV** function begins an occlusion query operation. The *id* parameter names the occlusion query object whose pixel count is updated when the occlusion query is ended. The first time an occlusion query is begun for a particular value of *id*, the corresponding occlusion query object is created.

After **glBeginOcclusionQueryNV** has been called, the occlusion query mechanism is in the active state. The name of the currently active occlusion query can be retrieved by calling the **glGetIntegerv** function with *pname* parameter GL_CURRENT_OCCLUSION_QUERY_ ID_NV.

Get Functions

glGetIntegerv with *pname* parameter GL_CURRENT_OCCLUSION_QUERY_ID_NV

Errors

GL_INVALID_OPERATION is generated if **glBeginOcclusionQueryNV** is called while there is an active occlusion query.

GL_INVALID_OPERATION is generated if **glBeginOcclusionQueryNV** is called between calls to **glBegin** and **glEnd**.

■ **glEndOcclusionQueryNV**—End the active occlusion query.

Prototype

    void **glEndOcclusionQueryNV**(void);

Description

The **glEndOcclusionQueryNV** function ends the active occlusion query operation. The internal pixel counter is copied into the occlusion query object associated with the occlusion query by the **glBeginOcclusionQueryNV** function. This value can later be retrieved by calling the **glGetOcclusionQuery{iui}vNV** function.

After **glEndOcclusionQueryNV** has been called, the occlusion query mechanism is in the inactive state.

Errors

GL_INVALID_OPERATION is generated if **glEndOcclusionQueryNV** is called and there is not an active occlusion query.

GL_INVALID_OPERATION is generated if **glEndOcclusionQueryNV** is called between calls to **glBegin** and **glEnd**.

■ **glGetOcclusionQuery{iui}vNV**—Retrieve occlusion query state.

Prototypes

```
void glGetOcclusionQueryivNV(GLuint id,
                                GLenum pname,
                                GLint *params);
void glGetOcclusionQueryuivNV(GLuint id,
                                GLenum pname,
                                GLuint *params);
```

Parameters

id	Specifies the name of an occlusion query.
pname	Specifies the symbolic name of an occlusion query value to retrieve. Must be GL_PIXEL_COUNT_NV or GL_PIXEL_COUNT_AVAILABLE_NV.
params	Specifies a pointer to an array that receives the occlusion query value.

Description

The **glGetOcclusionQuery{iui}vNV** function returns state associated with the occlusion query object specified by the *id* parameter. The *pname* parameter specifies what state should be returned and can be one of the following values:

GL_PIXEL_COUNT_NV

> The pixel count stored in the occlusion query object is returned at the location specified by the *params* parameter. Retrieving this state may cause the driver to block until the data is available from the GPU.

GL_PIXEL_COUNT_AVAILABLE_NV

> A Boolean value indicating whether the occlusion query's pixel count is immediately available is returned at the location specified by the *params* parameter. Retrieving this value never causes the driver to block.

Special Considerations

Before calling the **glGetOcclusionQuery{iui}vNV** function with *pname* parameter GL_PIXEL_COUNT_AVAILABLE_NV, a **glFlush** call should be issued to ensure that all drawing commands have been passed to the GPU. Otherwise, it is possible for implementations that buffer commands to perpetually return GL_FALSE, and polling for pixel count availability would result in an infinite loop.

Errors

GL_INVALID_ENUM is generated if *pname* is not an accepted value.

GL_INVALID_OPERATION is generated if *id* names the currently active occlusion query.

EXTENDED FUNCTIONS

■ **glGetIntegerv**—Extended to retrieve general occlusion query state.

Prototype

>   void **glGetIntegerv**(GLenum *pname*, GLint **params*);

Extended Parameters

pname   Specifies the parameter to be returned. May be GL_PIXEL_COUNTER_
                 BITS_NV or GL_CURRENT_OCCLUSION_QUERY_ID_NV.

Description

Various state values related to occlusion queries can be retrieved by calling the **glGet-Integerv** function. The *pname* parameter may be one of the following values:

GL_PIXEL_COUNTER_BITS_NV
>   The number of bits used by the occlusion query pixel counter is returned.
>   This value is always at least 24.

GL_CURRENT_OCCLUSION_QUERY_ID_NV
>   The name of the currently active occlusion query is returned. If no oc-
>   clusion query is active (which is also the initial state), then the return
>   value is 0.

POINT RENDERING

15.1 **GL_ARB_point_parameters**

OpenGL version required	OpenGL 1.1
Dependencies	—
Promotions	Previously GL_EXT_point_parameters
Related extensions	—

DISCUSSION

When rendering a set of points, conventional OpenGL uses the size specified by the **glPointSize** function for every point. The GL_ARB_point_parameters extension adds new controls that enable point sizes to be based upon their distances from the camera. When multisampling is available, this extension also provides a mechanism for fading a point out when its size falls below a programmable threshold.

When the GL_ARB_point_parameters extension is present, the size of each point rendered is calculated using the formula

$$derived\_size = clamp\left(size\sqrt{\frac{1}{a+bd+cd^2}} \right), \qquad (15.1.1)$$

where *size* is the point size specified using the **glPointSize** function, and *d* is the eye-space distance from the camera to the point's vertex position. The coefficients *a*, *b*, and *c* are specified by calling the **glPointParameterfvARB** function,

```
void glPointParameterfvARB(GLenum pname,
                           const GLfloat *params);
```

with *pname* parameter GL_POINT_DISTANCE_ATTENUATION_ARB. The initial values $a = 0$, $b = 0$, and $c = 0$ produce the same behavior as unextended OpenGL.

The *clamp* function in Equation (15.1.1) clamps the point size to the current values of GL_POINT_SIZE_MIN_ARB and GL_POINT_SIZE_MAX_ARB. These limits are specified using the **glPointParameterf[v]ARB** function and are initially set to a minimum size of 0.0 and a maximum size corresponding to the largest non-antialiased point size supported by the implementation.

When multisampling is enabled, a point's alpha value may be faded out when the value of *derived_size* falls below a certain threshold. In this case, the width of a point is given by

$$fade = \begin{cases} derived\_size, & \text{if } derived\_size \geq threshold; \\ threshold, & \text{otherwise.} \end{cases} \qquad (15.1.2)$$

and the alpha value is multiplied by the factor *fade* given by

$$fade = \begin{cases} 1, & \text{if } derived\_size \geq threshold; \\ \left(\dfrac{derived\_size}{threshold}\right)^2, & \text{otherwise.} \end{cases} \qquad (15.1.3)$$

The value of *threshold* is specified by calling the **glPointParameterf[v]ARB** function with *pname* parameter GL_POINT_FADE_THRESHOLD_ARB, and its initial value is 1.0.

NEW FUNCTIONS

■ **glPointParameterf[v]ARB**—Specify point parameters.

Prototype

```
void glPointParameterfARB(GLenum pname,
                          GLfloat param);
```

Parameters

pname   Specifies a symbol constant for a point parameter. May be GL_POINT_ SIZE_MIN_ARB, GL_POINT_SIZE_MAX_ARB, or GL_POINT_FADE_ THRESHOLD_ARB.

param   Specifies the value of the point parameter. Must be a single, nonnegative floating-point value.

Prototype

```
void glPointParameterfvARB(GLenum pname,
                           const GLfloat *params);
```

Parameters

pname   Specifies a symbol constant for a point parameter. May be GL_POINT_ SIZE_MIN_ARB, GL_POINT_SIZE_MAX_ARB, GL_POINT_FADE_ THRESHOLD_ARB, or GL_POINT_DISTANCE_ATTENUATION_ARB.

params   Specifies a pointer to the value of the point parameter.

Description

The **glPointParameterf[v]ARB** function is used to set point parameters.

GL_POINT_SIZE_MIN_ARB

> The *param* or *params* parameter specifies the minimum allowable point size. If the minimum size is set to a value greater than the maximum size, then any rendered point sizes are undefined. The initial value is 0.0.

GL_POINT_SIZE_MAX_ARB

> The *param* or *params* parameter specifies the maximum allowable point size. If the maximum size is set to a value less than the minimum size, then any rendered point sizes are undefined. The initial value corresponds to the largest point size supported by the implementation.

GL_POINT_FADE_THRESHOLD_ARB

> The *param* or *params* parameter specifies the point size for which smaller points fade out instead of shrinking when multisampling is enabled. The initial value is 1.0.

GL_POINT_DISTANCE_ATTENUATION_ARB

> The *params* parameter points to an array of three values that specify the a, b, and c coefficients used in the distance attenuation function for point sizes. The initial values are $a = 0$, $b = 0$, and $c = 0$.

Get Functions

glGetFloatv with *pname* parameter GL_POINT_SIZE_MIN_ARB

glGetFloatv with *pname* parameter GL_POINT_SIZE_MAX_ARB

glGetFloatv with *pname* parameter GL_POINT_FADE_THRESHOLD_ARB

glGetFloatv with *pname* parameter GL_POINT_DISTANCE_ATTENUATION_ARB

Errors

GL_INVALID_VALUE is generated if *pname* is GL_POINT_SIZE_MIN_ARB, GL_POINT_SIZE_MAX_ARB, or GL_POINT_FADE_THRESHOLD_ARB, and the value specified by the *param* or *params* parameter is less than zero.

EXTENDED FUNCTIONS

■ **glGetFloatv**—Extended to retrieve point parameters.

Prototype

```
void glGetFloatv(GLenum pname, GLfloat *params);
```

Extended Parameters

pname   Specifies the parameter to be returned. May be GL_POINT_SIZE_MIN_
                  ARB, GL_POINT_SIZE_MAX_ARB, GL_POINT_FADE_THRESHOLD_SIZE_
                  ARB, or GL_POINT_DISTANCE_ATTENUATION_ARB.

Description

The current values of each point parameter can be retrieved by calling the **glGetFloatv**
function. If the *pname* parameter is GL_POINT_SIZE_MIN_ARB, GL_POINT_SIZE_MAX_ARB,
or GL_POINT_FADE_THRESHOLD_SIZE_ARB, then a single value is returned in the array
pointed to by the *params* parameter. If the *pname* parameter is GL_POINT_DISTANCE_
ATTENUATION_ARB, then three values are returned corresponding to the *a*, *b*, and *c* coefficients used in the distance attenuation function for point sizes.

15.2   GL_NV_point_sprite

OpenGL version required	OpenGL 1.1
Dependencies	Requires GL_ARB_point_parameters
Promotions	—
Related extensions	—

DISCUSSION

When rendered using conventional OpenGL functionality, points are restricted to a round
shape and a single color. Many applications, especially those employing particle systems,
need to render points having a specific texture map applied to them. To achieve this, the
points are typically rendered using the GL_QUADS primitive instead of GL_POINTS, but this
requires four times the geometrical data and extra computation on the part of the application. The GL_NV_point_sprite extension provides a way to apply a texture map to points
specified with a single vertex position.

Points sprites are enabled by calling the **glEnable** function with *cap* parameter
GL_POINT_SPRITE_NV. When point sprites are enabled, the point antialiasing state corresponding to the value of GL_POINT_SMOOTH is ignored, and points can be drawn with a texture map that fills the viewport area that they occupy. To control whether texture
coordinates vary across the area of a point, each texture unit has a coordinate replacement
state that is enabled or disabled using the **glTexEnv{if}[v]** function. Making the function
call

```
glTexEnvi(GL_POINT_SPRITE_NV, GL_COORD_REPLACE_NV, GL_TRUE);
```

enables texture coordinate replacement for the currently active texture unit. This causes the
s and *t* texture coordinates to be interpolated from 0 to 1 across the area of each point rendered, as shown in Figure 15.2.1. The exact formula used to calculate texture coordinates is

$$s = \frac{1}{2} + \frac{x_f - x_w + \frac{1}{2}}{size}$$

$$t = \frac{1}{2} + \frac{y_f - y_w + \frac{1}{2}}{size} \tag{15.2.1}$$

where x_f and y_f are the integral window coordinates of a fragment within the point, x_w and y_w are the floating-point window coordinates of the point's center, and *size* is the point's size. When texture coordinate replacement is disabled for a particular texture unit, the same texture coordinates are used for every fragment within the entire point.

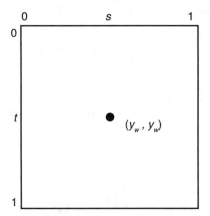

FIGURE 15.2.1   The texture coordinates for a point sprite are interpolated from 0 to 1, right to left, and top to bottom for each texture unit whose value of GL_COORD_REPLACE_NV is GL_TRUE.

When rendering point sprites, it may be useful to animate the texture map by using a 3D texture and varying the *r* texture coordinate. The GL_NV_point_sprite extension provides a global setting that controls the value of the *r* texture coordinate for all texture units. When GL_COORD_REPLACE_NV for a particular texture unit is GL_TRUE, the *r* texture coordinate may be forced to zero, may be a copy of the *s* texture coordinate supplied with the vertex, or may be passed through unaltered. The mode affecting the *r* texture coordinate is set using the **glPointParameteriNV** function,

```
void glPointParameteriNV(GLenum pname,
                         GLint param);
```

with *pname* parameter GL_POINT_SPRITE_R_MODE_NV.

USEFUL TIPS

How do I calculate point sizes corresponding to particles having known radii in 3D coordinate space?

Since a point's size is measured in pixels, we must take into account the size of the window into which the point is rendered as well as the projected radius of the point. Suppose we have a particle of radius r lying at a distance z from the plane of the camera, as shown in Figure 15.2.2. We need to know the radius of the point after it has been projected onto the image plane. The image plane lies at a distance e from the camera and contains points whose eye-space x coordinates range from -1 to 1. The distance e is the focal length of the camera and is related to the horizontal field of view angle α by the equation

$$e = \frac{1}{\tan\left(\alpha/2\right)}.\qquad(15.2.2)$$

(Using the value e, the values passed to the *left* and *right* parameters of the **glFrustum** function are $\pm n/e$, where n is the distance to the near clip plane.) The projected radius r' is simply given by

$$r' = \frac{e}{z}r.\qquad(15.2.3)$$

The diameter, in pixels, of the corresponding point is given by twice the projected radius r' multiplied by half the width of the window. Thus, the point size is given by

$$size = \frac{ew}{z}r,\qquad(15.2.4)$$

where w is the width of the window.

IMPLEMENTATION NOTES

- On Nvidia GeForce3 hardware, point sprites are accelerated only if the value of GL_POINT_SPRITE_R_MODE_NV is GL_ZERO (the default), and texture coordinate replacement is enabled *only* for texture unit 3. Thus, a typical usage of this extension should enable GL_TEXTURE_2D for texture unit 3 and disable texturing for units 0, 1, and 2.

- On ATI Radeon 8000 series hardware, point sprites are accelerated only if the value of GL_POINT_SPRITE_R_MODE_NV is GL_ZERO (the default).

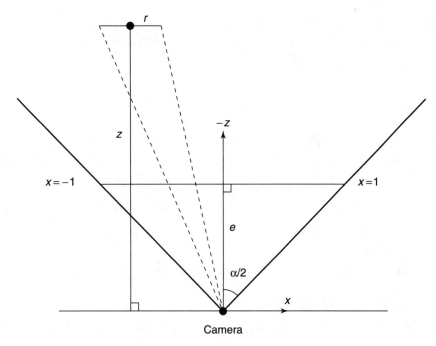

FIGURE 15.2.2 A point's size is calculated by first projecting the particle onto the image plane and then scaling by the size of the window.

NEW FUNCTIONS

■ **glPointParameteri[v]NV**—Specify point parameters.

Prototype

```
void glPointParameteriNV(GLenum pname,
                         GLint param);
```

Parameters

pname   Specifies the symbolic name of a point parameter. Must be GL_POINT_SPRITE_R_MODE_NV.

param   Specifies the value of the point parameter. Must be GL_ZERO, GL_S, or GL_R.

Prototype

```
void glPointParameterivNV(GLenum pname,
                          const GLint *params);
```

Parameters

pname   Specifies the symbolic name of a point parameter. Must be `GL_POINT_SPRITE_R_MODE_NV`.

params   Specifies a pointer to the value of the point parameter. The value pointed to must be `GL_ZERO`, `GL_S`, or `GL_R`.

Description

The **glPointParameteri[v]NV** function is used to set the *r* texture coordinate generation mode. If the value of `GL_POINT_SPRITE_R_MODE_NV` is `GL_ZERO`, then the *r* texture coordinate is always zero. If the value of `GL_POINT_SPRITE_R_MODE_NV` is `GL_S` or `GL_R`, then the *r* texture coordinate is set to the value of the *s* or *r* texture coordinate, respectively, before coordinate replacement takes place. The initial value of `GL_POINT_SPRITE_R_MODE_NV` is `GL_ZERO`.

Get Functions

glGetIntegerv with *pname* parameter `GL_POINT_SPRITE_R_MODE_NV`

EXTENDED FUNCTIONS

■ **glEnable**, **glDisable**, **glIsEnabled**—Extended to enable/disable point sprites.

Prototypes

```
void glEnable(GLenum cap);
void glDisable(GLenum cap);
GLboolean glIsEnabled(GLenum cap);
```

Extended Parameters

cap   Specifies a GL capability. To enable or disable point sprites, or to query whether point sprites are enabled, this should be `GL_POINT_SPRITE_NV`.

Description

Point sprites are enabled and disabled by passing the value `GL_POINT_SPRITE_NV` to the **glEnable** and **glDisable** functions. Calling the **glIsEnabled** function with the parameter `GL_POINT_SPRITE_NV` returns a value indicating whether point sprites are enabled.

■ **glTexEnvi**—Extended to specify per-texture-unit coordinate replacement.

Prototypes

```
void glTexEnvi(GLenum target, GLenum pname, GLint param);
```

Extended Parameters

target   Specifies a texture environment. To specify texture coordinate replacement state for the active texture unit, this should be `GL_POINT_SPRITE_NV`.

pname   Specifies a texture environment parameter. When the *target* parameter is GL_POINT_SPRITE_NV, the *pname* parameter must be GL_COORD_REPLACE_NV.

Description

Texture coordinate replacement is enabled or disabled for the currently active texture unit by calling the **glTexEnvi** function. When the *target* parameter is GL_POINT_SPRITE_NV and the *pname* parameter is GL_COORD_REPLACE_NV, the value of the *param* parameter or the value pointed to by the *params* parameter can be GL_TRUE or GL_FALSE. Specifying GL_TRUE enables the *r* texture coordinate replacement mode corresponding to the value of GL_POINT_SPRITE_R_MODE_NV, and specifying GL_FALSE disables coordinate replacement. The initial value of GL_COORD_REPLACE_NV for each texture unit is GL_FALSE.

■ **glGetTexEnviv**—Extended to retrieve per-texture-unit coordinate replacement.

Prototypes

> void **glGetTexEnviv**(GLenum *target*, GLenum *pname*, GLint **params*);

Extended Parameters

target   Specifies a texture environment. To retrieve texture coordinate replacement state for the active texture unit, this should be GL_POINT_SPRITE_NV.

pname   Specifies a texture environment parameter. When the *target* parameter is GL_POINT_SPRITE_NV, the *pname* parameter must be GL_COORD_REPLACE_NV.

Description

The value of GL_COORD_REPLACE_NV corresponding to the currently active texture unit is retrieved by calling the **glGetTexEnviv** function.

■ **glGetFloatv**—Extended to retrieve the point sprite *r* texture coordinate mode.

Prototypes

> void **glGetFloatv**(GLenum *pname*, GLfloat **params*);

Extended Parameters

pname   Specifies the parameter to be returned. May be GL_POINT_SPRITE_R_MODE_NV.

Description

The current value of GL_POINT_SPRITE_R_MODE_NV is retrieved by calling the **glGetFloatv** function.

PIXEL FORMATS

16.1   GL_EXT_bgra

OpenGL version required	OpenGL 1.1
Dependencies	—
Promotions	Promoted to a core feature in OpenGL 1.2
Related extensions	`GL_EXT_abgr`

DISCUSSION

Unextended OpenGL requires that pixel data consisting of red, green, blue, and alpha components be stored in client memory with the components for each pixel occurring in that order. Some windowing systems normally store the same components in the order blue, green, red, alpha. In order to allow the same images to be shared between OpenGL and these windowing systems, the `GL_EXT_bgra` extension defines new pixel storage formats.

Any function that operates on pixel data may have the symbolic constant `GL_BGR_EXT` or `GL_BGRA_EXT` specified as its *format* parameter. These specify that three-component pixel data is stored using the component order B, G, R; and four-component pixel data is stored using the component order B, G, R, A.

EXTENDED FUNCTIONS

- **`glDrawPixels`, `glReadPixels`, `glTexImage1D`, `glTexImage2D`, `glTexImage3D-EXT`, `glTexSubImage1D`, `glTexSubImage2D`, `glTexSubImage3DEXT`, `glGetTexImage`**— Extended to allow BGRA formats.

Prototypes

```
void glDrawPixels(GLsizei width, GLsizei height, GLenum format,
    GLenum type, const GLvoid *pixels);
void glReadPixels(GLint x, GLint y, GLsizei width, GLsizei height,
    GLenum format, GLenum type, GLvoid *pixels);
void glTexImage1D(GLenum target, GLint level, GLint internalFormat,
    GLsizei width, GLint border, GLenum format, GLenum type,
    const GLvoid *pixels);
void glTexImage2D(GLenum target, GLint level, GLint internalFormat,
    GLsizei width, GLsizei height, GLint border, GLenum format,
    GLenum type, const GLvoid *pixels);
void glTexImage3DEXT(GLenum target, GLint level,
    GLenum internalFormat, GLsizei width, GLsizei height,
    GLsizei depth, GLint border, GLenum format, GLenum type,
    const GLvoid *pixels);
void glTexSubImage1D(GLenum target, GLint level, GLint xoffset,
    GLsizei width, GLenum format, GLenum type, const GLvoid *pixels);
void glTexSubImage2D(GLenum target, GLint level, GLint xoffset,
    GLint yoffset, GLsizei width, GLsizei height, GLenum format,
    GLenum type, const GLvoid *pixels);
void glTexSubImage3DEXT(GLenum target, GLint level, GLint xoffset,
    GLint yoffset, GLint zoffset, GLsizei width, GLsizei height,
    GLsizei depth, GLenum format, GLenum type, const  GLvoid *pixels);
void glGetTexImage(GLenum target, GLint level, GLenum format,
    GLenum type, GLvoid *pixels);
```

Extended Parameters

format　　　　Specifies the format of the pixel data pointed to by the *pixels* parameter.
May be GL_BGR_EXT or GL_BGRA_EXT.

Description

When the GL_EXT_bgra extension is supported, RGB or RGBA pixel data may be stored
with its components in the order B, G, R, A. This is specified by passing the symbolic constant GL_BGR_EXT or GL_BGRA_EXT to the *format* parameter of any function that operates
on pixel data.

16.2　GL_EXT_abgr

OpenGL version required	OpenGL 1.1
Dependencies	—
Promotions	—
Related extensions	GL_EXT_bgra

DISCUSSION

Unextended OpenGL requires that pixel data consisting of red, green, blue, and alpha components be stored in client memory with the components for each pixel occurring in that order. Some windowing systems normally store the same components in the order alpha, blue, green, red. In order to allow the same images to be shared between OpenGL and these windowing systems, the GL_EXT_abgr extension defines new pixel storage formats.

Any function that operates on pixel data may have the symbolic constant GL_ABGR_EXT specified as its *format* parameter. This specifies that four-component pixel data is stored using the component order A, B, G, R.

EXTENDED FUNCTIONS

■ **glDrawPixels, glReadPixels, glTexImage1D, glTexImage2D, glTexImage3-DEXT, glTexSubImage1D, glTexSubImage2D, glTexSubImage3DEXT, glGetTexImage**— Extended to allow ABGR format.

Prototypes

```
void glTexImage1D(GLenum target, GLint level, GLint internalFormat,
    GLsizei width, GLint border, GLenum format, GLenum type,
    const GLvoid *pixels);
void glTexImage2D(GLenum target, GLint level, GLint internalFormat,
    GLsizei width, GLsizei height, GLint border, GLenum format,
    GLenum type, const GLvoid *pixels);
void glTexImage3DEXT(GLenum target, GLint level, GLenum internalFormat,
    GLsizei width, GLsizei height, GLsizei depth, GLint border,
    GLenum format, GLenum type, const GLvoid *pixels);
void glTexSubImage1D(GLenum target, GLint level, GLint xoffset,
    GLsizei width, GLenum format, GLenum type,
    const GLvoid *pixels);
void glTexSubImage2D(GLenum target, GLint level, GLint xoffset,
    GLint yoffset, GLsizei width, GLsizei height, GLenum format,
    GLenum type, const GLvoid *pixels);
void glTexSubImage3DEXT(GLenum target, GLint level, GLint xoffset,
    GLint yoffset, GLint zoffset, GLsizei width, GLsizei height,
    GLsizei depth, GLenum format, GLenum type, const GLvoid *pixels);
void glGetTexImage(GLenum target, GLint level, GLenum format,
    GLenum type, GLvoid *pixels);
```

Extended Parameters

format   Specifies the format of the pixel data pointed to by the *pixels* parameter. May be GL_ABGR_EXT.

Description

When the GL_EXT_abgr extension is supported, RGBA pixel data may be stored with its components in the order A, B, G, R. This is specified by passing the symbolic constant GL_ABGR_EXT to the *format* parameter of any function that operates on pixel data.

16.3   GL_EXT_packed_pixels

OpenGL version required	OpenGL 1.1
Dependencies	—
Promotions	Promoted to a core feature in OpenGL 1.2
Related extensions	—

DISCUSSION

The GL_EXT_packed_pixels extension provides new pixel types that allow multiple components to be packed into a single unsigned byte, unsigned short, or unsigned integer. The packed pixel types introduced by this extension are summarized in Table 16.3.1, and the exact bit layout of each type is shown in Figure 16.3.1.

TABLE 16.3.1   Packed Pixel Types and the Number of Components Implicitly Required by Each Type

Packed Pixel Type	Components	Pixel Size
GL_UNSIGNED_BYTE_3_3_2_EXT	3	1 byte
GL_UNSIGNED_SHORT_4_4_4_4_EXT	4	2 bytes
GL_UNSIGNED_SHORT_5_5_5_1_EXT	4	2 bytes
GL_UNSIGNED_INT_8_8_8_8_EXT	4	4 bytes
GL_UNSIGNED_INT_10_10_10_2_EXT	4	4 bytes

A packed pixel type may be passed to the *type* parameter of any function that operates on pixel data. Each type implicitly requires a specific number of components and must be used with a pixel format that matches it. For example, the GL_UNSIGNED_BYTE_3_3_2_EXT pixel type may only be used with a three-component pixel format, such as GL_RGB; and the GL_UNSIGNED_SHORT_4_4_4_4_EXT pixel may only be used with a four-component pixel format, such as GL_RGBA.

A packed pixel is treated as a single unit by the pixel-packing and pixel-unpacking operations in OpenGL. In particular, if GL_PACK_SWAP_BYTES or GL_UNPACK_SWAP_BYTES is true when pixel data is packed or unpacked in client memory, then the bytes occupied by the entire pixel as a whole are swapped instead of the bytes occupied by each component, because the components do not necessarily occupy whole bytes.

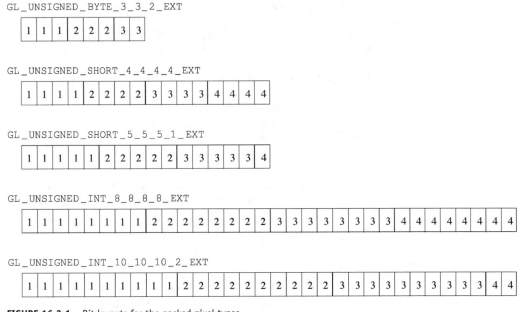

FIGURE 16.3.1 Bit layouts for the packed pixel types.

When an n-bit component of a packed pixel is converted to a floating-point, it is divided by $2^n - 1$ to scale it to the range [0,1]. When a floating-point component is converted to an n-bit packed pixel component, it is multiplied by $2^n - 1$.

EXTENDED FUNCTIONS

■ **glDrawPixels, glReadPixels, glTexImage1D, glTexImage2D, glTexImage3-DEXT, glTexSubImage1D, glTexSubImage2D, glTexSubImage3DEXT, glGetTexImage**—Extended to allow packed pixel types.

Prototypes

```
void glDrawPixels(GLsizei width, GLsizei height, GLenum format,
    GLenum type, const GLvoid *pixels);
void glReadPixels(GLint x, GLint y, GLsizei width, GLsizei height,
    GLenum format, GLenum type, GLvoid *pixels);
void glTexImage1D(GLenum target, GLint level, GLint internalFormat,
    GLsizei width, GLint border, GLenum format, GLenum type,
    const GLvoid *pixels);
void glTexImage2D(GLenum target, GLint level, GLint internalFormat,
    GLsizei width, GLsizei height, GLint border, GLenum format,
    GLenum type, const GLvoid *pixels);
void glTexImage3DEXT(GLenum target, GLint level, GLenum internalFormat,
    GLsizei width, GLsizei height, GLsizei depth, GLint border,
    GLenum format, GLenum type, const GLvoid *pixels);
```

```
void glTexSubImage1D(GLenum target, GLint level, GLint xoffset,
    GLsizei width, GLenum format, GLenum type, const GLvoid *pixels);
void glTexSubImage2D(GLenum target, GLint level, GLint xoffset,
    GLint yoffset, GLsizei width, GLsizei height, GLenum format,
    GLenum type, const GLvoid *pixels);
void glTexSubImage3DEXT(GLenum target, GLint level, GLint xoffset,
    GLint yoffset, GLint zoffset, GLsizei width, GLsizei height,
    GLsizei depth, GLenum format, GLenum type, const GLvoid *pixels);
void glGetTexImage(GLenum target, GLint level, GLenum format,
    GLenum type, GLvoid *pixels);
```

Extended Parameters

type   Specifies the data type for the pixel data pointed to by the *pixels* parameter. May be GL_UNSIGNED_BYTE_3_3_2_EXT, GL_UNSIGNED_SHORT_4_4_4_4_EXT, GL_UNSIGNED_SHORT_5_5_5_1_EXT, GL_UNSIGNED_INT_8_8_8_8_EXT, or GL_UNSIGNED_INT_10_10_10_2_EXT.

Description

When the GL_EXT_packed_pixels extension is supported, any function that operates on pixel data accepts the packed pixel types as the *type* parameter. The number of components specified by the *format* parameter must match the number of components implicitly required by the packed pixel type.

Errors

GL_INVALID_OPERATION is generated if *type* is GL_UNSIGNED_BYTE_3_3_2_EXT and the number of components specified by *format* is not 3.

GL_INVALID_OPERATION is generated if *type* is GL_UNSIGNED_SHORT_4_4_4_4_EXT, GL_UNSIGNED_SHORT_5_5_5_1_EXT, GL_UNSIGNED_INT_8_8_8_8_EXT, or GL_UNSIGNED_INT_10_10_10_2_EXT, and the number of components specified by *format* is not 4.

16.4   GL_APPLE_packed_pixels

OpenGL version required	OpenGL 1.1
Dependencies	—
Promotions	—
Related extensions	—

DISCUSSION

The GL_EXT_packed_pixels extension provides new pixel types that allow multiple components to be packed into a single unsigned byte, unsigned short, or unsigned integer. The packed pixel types introduced by this extension are summarized in Table 16.4.1, and the exact bit layout of each type is shown in Figure 16.4.1.

TABLE 16.4.1   Packed Pixel Types and the Number of Components Implicitly Required by Each Type

Packed Pixel Type	Components	Pixel Size
GL_UNSIGNED_BYTE_3_3_2_APPLE	3	1 byte
GL_UNSIGNED_BYTE_2_3_3_REV_APPLE	3	1 byte
GL_UNSIGNED_SHORT_5_6_5_APPLE	3	2 bytes
GL_UNSIGNED_SHORT_5_6_5_REV_APPLE	3	2 bytes
GL_UNSIGNED_SHORT_4_4_4_4_APPLE	4	2 bytes
GL_UNSIGNED_SHORT_4_4_4_4_REV_APPLE	4	2 bytes
GL_UNSIGNED_SHORT_5_5_5_1_APPLE	4	2 bytes
GL_UNSIGNED_SHORT_1_5_5_5_REV_APPLE	4	2 bytes
GL_UNSIGNED_INT_8_8_8_8_APPLE	4	4 bytes
GL_UNSIGNED_INT_8_8_8_8_REV_APPLE	4	4 bytes
GL_UNSIGNED_INT_10_10_10_2_APPLE	4	4 bytes
GL_UNSIGNED_INT_2_10_10_10_REV_APPLE	4	4 bytes

A packed pixel type may be passed to the *type* parameter of any function that operates on pixel data. Each type implicitly requires a specific number of components and must be used with a pixel format that matches it. For example, the GL_UNSIGNED_BYTE_ 3_3_2_APPLE pixel type may only be used with a three-component pixel format, such as GL_RGB; and the GL_UNSIGNED_SHORT_4_4_4_4_APPLE pixel may only be used with a four-component pixel format, such as GL_RGBA.

A packed pixel is treated as a single unit by the pixel-packing and pixel-unpacking operations in OpenGL. In particular, if GL_PACK_SWAP_BYTES or GL_UNPACK_SWAP_BYTES is true when pixel data is packed or unpacked in client memory, then the bytes occupied by the entire pixel as a whole are swapped instead of the bytes occupied by each component, because the components do not necessarily occupy whole bytes.

When an n-bit component of a packed pixel is converted to floating-point, it is divided by $2^n - 1$ to scale it to the range [1]. When a floating-point component is converted to an n-bit packed pixel component, it is multiplied by $2^n - 1$.

GL_UNSIGNED_BYTE_3_3_2_APPLE

1	1	1	2	2	2	3	3

GL_UNSIGNED_BYTE_2_3_3_REV_APPLE

3	3	2	2	2	1	1	1

GL_UNSIGNED_SHORT_5_6_5_APPLE

1	1	1	1	1	2	2	2	2	2	2	3	3	3	3	3

GL_UNSIGNED_SHORT_5_6_5_REV_APPLE

3	3	3	3	3	2	2	2	2	2	2	1	1	1	1	1

GL_UNSIGNED_SHORT_4_4_4_4_APPLE

1	1	1	1	2	2	2	2	3	3	3	3	4	4	4	4

GL_UNSIGNED_SHORT_4_4_4_4_REV_APPLE

4	4	4	4	3	3	3	3	2	2	2	2	1	1	1	1

GL_UNSIGNED_SHORT_5_5_5_1_APPLE

1	1	1	1	1	2	2	2	2	2	3	3	3	3	3	4

GL_UNSIGNED_SHORT_1_5_5_5_REV_APPLE

4	3	3	3	3	3	2	2	2	2	2	1	1	1	1	1

GL_UNSIGNED_INT_8_8_8_8_APPLE

1	1	1	1	1	1	1	1	2	2	2	2	2	2	2	2	3	3	3	3	3	3	3	3	4	4	4	4	4	4	4	4

GL_UNSIGNED_INT_8_8_8_8_REV_APPLE

4	4	4	4	4	4	4	4	3	3	3	3	3	3	3	3	2	2	2	2	2	2	2	2	1	1	1	1	1	1	1	1

GL_UNSIGNED_INT_10_10_10_2_APPLE

1	1	1	1	1	1	1	1	1	1	2	2	2	2	2	2	2	2	2	2	3	3	3	3	3	3	3	3	3	3	4	4

GL_UNSIGNED_INT_2_10_10_10_REV_APPLE

4	4	3	3	3	3	3	3	3	3	3	3	2	2	2	2	2	2	2	2	2	2	1	1	1	1	1	1	1	1	1	1

FIGURE 16.4.1 Bit layouts for the packed pixel types.

EXTENDED FUNCTIONS

■ **glDrawPixels, glReadPixels, glTexImage1D, glTexImage2D, glTexImage3-
DEXT, glTexSubImage1D, glTexSubImage2D, glTexSubImage3DEXT, glGetTexImage**—Extended to allow packed pixel types.

Prototypes

```
void glDrawPixels(GLsizei width, GLsizei height, GLenum format,
    GLenum type, const GLvoid *pixels);
void glReadPixels(GLint x, GLint y, GLsizei width, GLsizei height,
    GLenum format, GLenum type, GLvoid *pixels);
void glTexImage1D(GLenum target, GLint level, GLint internalFormat,
    GLsizei width, GLint border, GLenum format, GLenum type,
    const GLvoid *pixels);
void glTexImage2D(GLenum target, GLint level, GLint internalFormat,
    GLsizei width, GLsizei height, GLint border, GLenum format,
    GLenum type, const GLvoid *pixels);
void glTexImage3DEXT(GLenum target, GLint level, GLenum internalFormat,
    GLsizei width, GLsizei height, GLsizei depth, GLint border,
    GLenum format, GLenum type, const GLvoid *pixels);
void glTexSubImage1D(GLenum target, GLint level, GLint xoffset,
    GLsizei width, GLenum format, GLenum type, const GLvoid *pixels);
void glTexSubImage2D(GLenum target, GLint level, GLint xoffset,
    GLint yoffset, GLsizei width, GLsizei height, GLenum format,
    GLenum type, const GLvoid *pixels);
void glTexSubImage3DEXT(GLenum target, GLint level, GLint xoffset,
    GLint yoffset, GLint zoffset, GLsizei width, GLsizei height,
    GLsizei depth, GLenum format, GLenum type, const GLvoid *pixels);
void glGetTexImage(GLenum target, GLint level, GLenum format,
    GLenum type, GLvoid *pixels);
```

Extended Parameters

type　　　　　Specifies the data type for the pixel data pointed to by the *pixels* parameter. May be any of the values listed in Table 16.4.1.

Description

When the GL_APPLE_packed_pixels extension is supported, any function that operates
on pixel data accepts the packed pixel types as the *type* parameter. The number of components specified by the *format* parameter must match the number of components implicitly
required by the packed pixel type.

Errors

GL_INVALID_OPERATION is generated if *type* implicitly requires a different number of components than that specified by *format*.

16.5   GL_NV_packed_depth_stencil

OpenGL version required	OpenGL 1.1
Dependencies	—
Promotions	—
Related extensions	—

DISCUSSION

Most implementations store depth and stencil buffers in the same region of memory using an interleaved format containing 24 bits of depth information and 8 bits of stencil information. The GL_NV_packed_depth_stencil extension allows an application to access the depth and stencil data for each pixel as a two-component unit. This provides significant performance advantages to applications that wish to draw to or read from the depth and stencil buffers by facilitating the combination of such accesses into a single operation.

This extension introduces the pixel format GL_DEPTH_STENCIL_NV and the pixel data type GL_UNSIGNED_INT_24_8_NV. These symbolic constants must always be used together and specify that pixel data is composed of units containing a 24-bit depth component and a 8-bit stencil component. The exact bit layout of this pixel format is shown in Figure 16.5.1.

GL _ DEPTH _ STENCIL _ 24 _ 8 _ NV

FIGURE 16.5.1   Bit layout of the depth stencil pixel type. Bits labeled D contain the depth value, and bits labeled S contain the stencil index.

The packed depth stencil format may be passed to the **glDrawPixels** function to draw to both the depth buffer and stencil buffer simultaneously. Depth and stencil information can be read in a single operation by passing the packed depth stencil format to the **glReadPixels** function. The **glCopyPixels** function can be used to copy both depth and stencil data within the frame buffer.

If the GL_ARB_depth_texture extension (see Chapter 13, Section 13.1) is supported, then the packed depth stencil format may be used with functions that operate on texture image data. If packed depth stencil pixels are loaded as a texture image having a base internal format GL_DEPTH_COMPONENT, then the stencil index information is ignored.

EXTENDED FUNCTIONS

■ **glDrawPixels**—Extended to allow packed depth stencil format.

Prototypes

```
void glDrawPixels(GLsizei width, GLsizei height, GLenum format,
    GLenum type, const GLvoid *pixels);
```

Extended Parameters

format   Specifies the format of the pixel data pointed to by the *pixels* parameter. May be GL_DEPTH_STENCIL_NV.

type   Specifies the data type for the pixel data pointed to by the *pixels* parameter. May be GL_UNSIGNED_INT_24_8_NV.

Description

The **glDrawPixels** function can be used to write packed depth stencil data to the depth buffer and stencil buffer simultaneously. When the *format* parameter is GL_DEPTH_STENCIL_NV, the *type* parameter must be GL_UNSIGNED_INT_24_8_NV. These values indicate that the pixel data pointed to by the *pixels* parameter contains 24 bits of depth information and 8 bits of stencil information. The depth component is transformed as if the *format* parameter was GL_DEPTH_COMPONENT, and the stencil index is transformed as if the *format* parameter was GL_STENCIL_INDEX. Only the pixel ownership test, scissor test, depth write mask, and stencil write mask are performed. Other per-fragment operations are skipped, and the color buffer is unaffected.

Errors

GL_INVALID_ENUM is generated if *format* is GL_DEPTH_STENCIL_NV and *type* is not GL_UNSIGNED_INT_24_8_NV.

GL_INVALID_OPERATION is generated if *type* is GL_UNSIGNED_INT_24_8_NV and *format* is not GL_DEPTH_STENCIL_NV.

GL_INVALID_OPERATION is generated if *format* is GL_DEPTH_STENCIL_NV, and there is not both a depth buffer and a stencil buffer.

■ **glReadPixels**—Extended to allow packed depth stencil format.

Prototypes

```
void glReadPixels(GLint x, GLint y, GLsizei width, GLsizei height,
    GLenum format, GLenum type, GLvoid *pixels);
```

Extended Parameters

format   Specifies the format of the pixel data returned in the *pixels* parameter. May be GL_DEPTH_STENCIL_NV.

type   Specifies the data type for the pixel data returned in the *pixels* parameter. May be GL_UNSIGNED_INT_24_8_NV.

Description

The **glReadPixels** function can be used to read packed depth stencil data from the depth buffer and stencil buffer simultaneously. When the *format* parameter is GL_DEPTH_STENCIL_NV, the *type* parameter must be GL_UNSIGNED_INT_24_8_NV. These values indicate that the pixel data returned should be stored at the location specified by the *pixels* parameter using 24 bits of depth information and 8 bits of stencil information. The depth component is transformed as if the *format* parameter was GL_DEPTH_COMPONENT, and the stencil index is transformed as if the *format* parameter was GL_STENCIL_INDEX.

Errors

GL_INVALID_ENUM is generated if *format* is GL_DEPTH_STENCIL_NV and *type* is not GL_UN-SIGNED_INT_24_8_NV.

GL_INVALID_OPERATION is generated if *type* is GL_UNSIGNED_INT_24_8_NV and *format* is not GL_DEPTH_STENCIL_NV.

GL_INVALID_OPERATION is generated if *format* is GL_DEPTH_STENCIL_NV, and there is not both a depth buffer and a stencil buffer.

■ **glCopyPixels**—Extended to allow packed depth stencil format.

Prototype

```
void glCopyPixels(GLint x, GLint y, GLsizei width, GLsizei height,
    GLenum type);
```

Extended Parameters

type   Specifies whether color values, depth values, or stencil values are copied. May be GL_DEPTH_STENCIL_NV.

Description

The **glCopyPixels** function can be used to copy pixels in both the depth buffer and stencil buffer, simultaneously. These values indicate that the pixel data pointed to by the *pixels* parameter contains 24 bits of depth information and 8 bits of stencil information. The depth component is transformed as if the *format* parameter was GL_DEPTH_COMPONENT, and the stencil index is transformed as if the *format* parameter was GL_STENCIL_INDEX. Only the pixel ownership test, scissor test, depth write mask, and stencil write mask are performed. Other per-fragment operations are skipped, and the color buffer is unaffected.

Errors

GL_INVALID_OPERATION is generated if *format* is GL_DEPTH_STENCIL_NV, and there is not both a depth buffer and a stencil buffer.

■ **glTexImage1D, glTexImage2D, glTexImage3DEXT, glTexSubImage1D, glTex-SubImage2D, glTexSubImage3DEXT, glGetTexImage**—Extended to allow packed depth stencil format.

Prototypes

```
void glTexImage1D(GLenum target, GLint level, GLint internalFormat,
    GLsizei width, GLint border, GLenum format, GLenum type,
    const GLvoid *pixels);
```

```
void glTexImage2D(GLenum target, GLint level, GLint internalFormat,
    GLsizei width, GLsizei height, GLint border, GLenum format,
    GLenum type, const GLvoid *pixels);
void glTexImage3DEXT(GLenum target, GLint level, GLenum internalFormat,
    GLsizei width, GLsizei height, GLsizei depth, GLint border,
    GLenum format, GLenum type, const GLvoid *pixels);
void glTexSubImage1D(GLenum target, GLint level, GLint xoffset,
    GLsizei width, GLenum format, GLenum type, const GLvoid *pixels);
void glTexSubImage2D(GLenum target, GLint level, GLint xoffset,
    GLint yoffset, GLsizei width, GLsizei height, GLenum format,
    GLenum type, const GLvoid *pixels);
void glTexSubImage3DEXT(GLenum target, GLint level, GLint xoffset,
    GLint yoffset, GLint zoffset, GLsizei width, GLsizei height,
    GLsizei depth, GLenum format, GLenum type, const GLvoid *pixels);
void glGetTexImage(GLenum target, GLint level, GLenum format,
    GLenum type, GLvoid *pixels);
```

Extended Parameters

format   Specifies the format of the pixel data pointed to by the *pixels* parameter.
                 May be GL_DEPTH_STENCIL_NV.

type   Specifies the data type for the pixel data pointed to by the *pixels* parameter. May be GL_UNSIGNED_INT_24_8_NV.

Description

When the GL_ARB_depth_texture extension is supported and the base internal format corresponding to a texture image is GL_DEPTH_COMPONENT, then the *format* and *type* parameters may be GL_DEPTH_STENCIL_NV and GL_UNSIGNED_INT_24_8_NV, respectively. These values indicate that the pixel data pointed to by the *pixels* parameter contains 24 bits of depth information and 8 bits of stencil information. The depth component is transformed as if the *format* parameter was GL_DEPTH_COMPONENT, and the stencil index is ignored.

■ **glGetTexImage**—Extended to allow packed depth stencil format.

Prototypes

```
void glGetTexImage(GLenum target, GLint level, GLenum format,
    GLenum type, GLvoid *pixels);
```

Extended Parameters

format   Specifies the format of the pixel data returned in the *pixels* parameter.
                 May be GL_DEPTH_STENCIL_NV.

type   Specifies the data type for the pixel data returned in the *pixels* parameter.
                 May be GL_UNSIGNED_INT_24_8_NV.

Description

When the GL_ARB_depth_texture extension is supported and the base internal format corresponding to a texture image is GL_DEPTH_COMPONENT, then the *format* and *type* parameters may be GL_DEPTH_STENCIL_NV and GL_UNSIGNED_INT_24_8_NV, respectively. These values indicate that the pixel data returned should be stored at the location specified by the *pixels* parameter using 24 bits of depth information and 8 bits of stencil information. The stencil index portion of the returned pixel data is undefined.

MISCELLANEOUS

IN THIS CHAPTER

17.1 GL_ARB_transpose_matrix

OpenGL version required	OpenGL 1.1
Dependencies	—
Promotions	Promoted to a core feature in OpenGL 1.3
Related extensions	—

DISCUSSION

OpenGL normally expects a matrix to be stored in column-major order. A 16-entry matrix *m* operates on a 4D vector **V** to produce a transformed vector **V′** as follows:

$$\mathbf{V}' = \begin{bmatrix} m[0] & m[4] & m[8] & m[12] \\ m[1] & m[5] & m[9] & m[13] \\ m[2] & m[6] & m[10] & m[14] \\ m[3] & m[7] & m[11] & m[15] \end{bmatrix} \begin{bmatrix} V_x \\ V_y \\ V_z \\ V_w \end{bmatrix} \tag{17.1.1}$$

The notation *m*[*i*] represents the *i*th entry in the array corresponding to the matrix *m*. Some applications store matrices in row-major order so that a vector **V** is transformed as follows:

$$\mathbf{V'} = \begin{bmatrix} m[0] & m[1] & m[2] & m[3] \\ m[4] & m[5] & m[6] & m[7] \\ m[8] & m[9] & m[10] & m[11] \\ m[12] & m[13] & m[14] & m[15] \end{bmatrix} \begin{bmatrix} V_x \\ V_y \\ V_z \\ V_w \end{bmatrix} \tag{17.1.2}$$

The matrix in Equation (17.1.2) is the transpose of the matrix of the matrix in Equation (17.1.1). The GL_ARB_transpose_matrix extension allows applications to specify matrices in transposed form.

A matrix may be loaded in transposed form or, equivalently, with its entries stored in row-major order by calling the **glLoadTransposeMatrix{fd}ARB** function,

```
void glLoadTransposeMatrixfARB(const GLfloat m[16]);
void glLoadTransposeMatrixdARB(const GLdouble m[16]);
```

The 16 entries of the array specified by the m parameter replace the current matrix. (The current matrix is specified using the **glMatrixMode** function.)

The current matrix may be multiplied by the transpose of another matrix by calling the **glMultTransposeMatrix{fd}ARB** function,

```
void glMultTransposeMatrixfARB(const GLfloat m[16]);
void glMultTransposeMatrixdARB(const GLdouble m[16]);
```

The current matrix is post-multiplied by the matrix consisting of the 16 entries of the array specified by the m parameter.

The transpose of a matrix can be retrieved by calling the **glGetFloatv** or **glGet-Doublev** function with *pname* parameter GL_TRANSPOSE_MODELVIEW_MATRIX_ARB, GL_TRANSPOSE_PROJECTION_MATRIX_ARB, GL_TRANSPOSE_TEXTURE_MATRIX_ARB, or GL_TRANSPOSE_COLOR_MATRIX_ARB.

NEW FUNCTIONS

■ **glLoadTransposeMatrix{fd}ARB**—Replace the current matrix with the transpose of the specified matrix.

Prototypes

```
void glLoadTransposeMatrixfARB(const GLfloat m[16]);
void glLoadTransposeMatrixdARB(const GLdouble m[16]);
```

Parameters

m Specifies a pointer to the 16 entries of the matrix stored in row-major order.

Description

The **glLoadTransposeMatrix{fd}ARB** function replaces the current matrix with the matrix whose entries are specified by the *m* parameter. The entries of the new matrix are assumed to be stored in row-major order, as opposed to the column-major order expected by the **glLoadMatrix{fd}** function.

The current matrix corresponds to the one set using the **glMatrixMode** function.

Get Functions

glGet with argument GL_TRANSPOSE_MODELVIEW_MATRIX_ARB

glGet with argument GL_TRANSPOSE_PROJECTION_MATRIX_ARB

glGet with argument GL_TRANSPOSE_TEXTURE_MATRIX_ARB

glGet with argument GL_TRANSPOSE_COLOR_MATRIX_ARB

Errors

GL_INVALID_OPERATION is generated if **glLoadTransposeMatrix{fd}ARB** is called between calls to **glBegin** and **glEnd**.

■ **glMultTransposeMatrix{fd}ARB**—Multiply the current matrix by the transpose of the specified matrix.

Prototypes

```
void glMultTransposeMatrixfARB(const GLfloat m[16]);
void glMultTransposeMatrixdARB(const GLdouble m[16]);
```

Parameters

m   Specifies a pointer to the 16 entries of the matrix stored in row-major order.

Description

The **glMultTransposeMatrix{fd}ARB** function multiplies the current matrix by the matrix whose entries are specified by the *m* parameter. The entries of the new matrix are assumed to be stored in row-major order, as opposed to the column-major order expected by the **glMultMatrix{fd}** function.

The current matrix corresponds to the one set using the **glMatrixMode** function.

Errors

GL_INVALID_OPERATION is generated if **glMultTransposeMatrix{fd}ARB** is called between calls to **glBegin** and **glEnd**.

EXTENDED FUNCTIONS

- **glGetFloatv, glGetDoublev**—Extended to retrieve the transpose of a matrix.

Prototypes

```
void glGetFloatv(GLenum pname, GLfloat *params);
void glGetDoublev(GLenum pname, GLdouble *params);
```

Extended Parameters

pname   Specifies the parameter to be returned. May be GL_TRANSPOSE_
MODELVIEW_MATRIX_ARB, GL_TRANSPOSE_PROJECTION_MATRIX_ARB,
GL_TRANSPOSE_TEXTURE_MATRIX_ARB, or GL_TRANSPOSE_COLOR_
MATRIX_ARB.

Description

The **glGetFloatv** and **glGetDoublev** functions can be used to retrieve matrices and have their entries stored in row-major order. This is equivalent to retrieving the transpose of a matrix with its entries stored in column-major order. The *pname* parameter may be one of the following values:

GL_TRANSPOSE_MODELVIEW_MATRIX_ARB
    Return the transpose of the modelview matrix.

GL_TRANSPOSE_PROJECTION_MATRIX_ARB
    Return the transpose of the projection matrix.

GL_TRANSPOSE_TEXTURE_MATRIX_ARB
    Return the transpose of the texture matrix.

GL_TRANSPOSE_COLOR_MATRIX_ARB
    Return the transpose of the color matrix (if the imaging subset is supported).

17.2   GL_NV_depth_clamp

OpenGL version required	OpenGL 1.1
Dependencies	—
Promotions	—
Related extensions	—

DISCUSSION

The GL_NV_depth_clamp extension provides a mode in which the near and far clip planes are disabled and window-space depth values are clamped to the range [0,1]. This allows geometry that extends outside the near and far clip planes to be rendered without its depth values exceeding the range of the depth buffer. The four side clip planes still clip geometry normally.

Depth clamping is enabled and disabled by calling the **glEnable** and **glDisable** functions with *cap* parameter GL_DEPTH_CLAMP_NV. When depth clamping is enabled, geometric primitives are not clipped against the near and far clip planes, and all depth values are clamped to the range [0,1] immediately before the depth test occurs.

Normally, the near clip plane guards against rendering fragments whose clip-space w coordinate is not a positive value. When depth clamping is enabled, any fragment for which $w \leq 0$ is discarded. If using the standard perspective projection matrix, this means that only fragments lying in front of the camera are rendered.

EXTENDED FUNCTIONS

- **glEnable, glDisable, glIsEnabled**—Extended to enable/disable depth clamping.

Prototypes

```
void glEnable(GLenum cap);
void glDisable(GLenum cap);
GLboolean glIsEnabled(GLenum cap);
```

Extended Parameters

cap   Specifies a GL capability. To enable or disable depth clamping, or to query whether depth clamping is enabled, this should be GL_DEPTH_CLAMP_NV.

Description

Depth clamping is enabled and disabled by passing the value GL_DEPTH_CLAMP_NV to the **glEnable** and **glDisable** functions. Calling the **glIsEnabled** function with *cap* parameter GL_DEPTH_CLAMP_NV returns a value indicating whether depth clamping is enabled.

17.3   GL_NV_depth_bounds_test

OpenGL version required	OpenGL 1.1
Dependencies	—
Promotions	—
Related extensions	—

DISCUSSION

The GL_NV_depth_bounds_test extension introduces a new per-fragment test that logically occurs after the scissor test and before the alpha test. The depth bounds test, when enabled, compares the depth value stored in the depth buffer against an application-defined range. If the depth value falls outside this range, then the fragment is discarded. The fragment's own depth value is *not* considered during the depth bounds test. The depth bounds test operates on the value already existing in the depth buffer.

The depth bounds test is enabled and disabled by calling the **glEnable** and **glDisable** functions with *pname* parameter GL_DEPTH_BOUNDS_TEST_NV. When the depth bounds test is disabled (the initial state), it is as if the depth bounds test always passes.

The range against which depth values are compared by the depth bounds test is specified by calling the **glDepthBoundsNV** function,

```
void glDepthBoundsNV(GLclampd zmin,
                     GLclampd zmax);
```

The *zmin* and *zmax* parameters specify minimum and maximum window-space depth values that may be stored in the depth buffer for the depth bounds test to pass. The value of *zmin* must not be greater than the value of *zmax*. In window space, depth values range from 0.0 to 1.0, and this is the initial range to which the depth bounds test is applied. If the depth bounds test is enabled during rasterization, the value *z* in the depth buffer is read for each fragment and compared against the values specified by *zmin* and *zmax*. If *z* < *zmin* or *z* < *zmax*, then the corresponding fragment is discarded.

USEFUL TIPS

How can I use the depth bounds test to improve performance when rendering a lighting pass or a shadow volume for an attenuated light source?

Suppose that an attenuated light source exists at the eye-space position **L**, and it has a range *r*, as shown in Figure 17.3.1. The region of space that can be illuminated by the light source extends in the *z*-direction from $L_z + r$ to $L_z - r$. (Recall that the negative *z*-axis points in the view direction in eye space.) Any geometry that falls outside this range at a particular fragment location cannot be illuminated by the light source, so we wish to eliminate unnecessary lighting calculations and stencil operations in these cases.

Before we can apply the depth bounds test, we need to transform the range $[L_z + r, L_z - r]$ into window space minimum and maximum depth values d_{min} and d_{max}. To achieve this, we first transform into homogeneous clip space, then perform the perspective division, and finally apply the linear mapping to window space. To transform a single eye-space depth value z_e into homogeneous clip space, we observe how the projection matrix **P** transforms a vector $\langle 0,0,z_e,1 \rangle$:

$$\mathbf{P}\begin{bmatrix} 0 \\ 0 \\ z_e \\ 1 \end{bmatrix} = \begin{bmatrix} P_{11} & P_{12} & P_{13} & P_{14} \\ P_{21} & P_{22} & P_{23} & P_{24} \\ P_{31} & P_{32} & P_{33} & P_{34} \\ P_{41} & P_{42} & P_{43} & P_{44} \end{bmatrix}\begin{bmatrix} 0 \\ 0 \\ z_e \\ 1 \end{bmatrix} = \begin{bmatrix} P_{13}z_e + P_{14} \\ P_{23}z_e + P_{24} \\ P_{33}z_e + P_{34} \\ P_{43}z_e + P_{44} \end{bmatrix}. \tag{17.3.1}$$

After applying the perspective divide, the value z_d in normalized device coordinates is given by

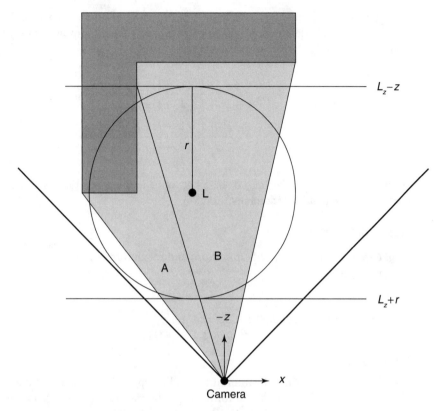

FIGURE 17.3.1 An attenuated light source centered at the eye-space position **L** and having range r can only illuminate geometry lying in the eye-space depth range $[L_z + r, L_z - r]$. The depth bounds test passes in region A and fails in region B.

$$z_d = \frac{P_{33} z_e + P_{34}}{P_{43} z_e + P_{44}}. \tag{17.3.2}$$

Let n and f be the window-space depth values to which the near and far planes are mapped (as specified using the **glDepthRange** function). A value z_d in normalized device coordinates is remapped to the value z_w in window space using the formula

$$z_w = \frac{f - n}{2} z_d + \frac{f + n}{2}. \tag{17.3.3}$$

(The values of n and f are ordinarily 0.0 and 1.0, respectively.) Substituting the value of z_d given in Equation (17.3.2), we have

$$z_w = \frac{f - n}{2} \left(\frac{P_{33} z_e + P_{34}}{P_{43} z_e + P_{44}} \right) + \frac{f + n}{2}. \tag{17.3.4}$$

Thus, given an eye-space depth range $[L_z + r, L_z - r]$, a projection matrix $\mathbf{P}$, and values n and f that determine the depth range mapping, we calculate the minimum and maximum depth bounds d_{min} and d_{max} to test against as follows.

$$d_{min} = \frac{f-n}{2}\left[\frac{P_{33}\left(L_z + r\right) + P_{34}}{P_{43}\left(L_z + r\right) + P_{44}}\right] + \frac{f+n}{2}$$

$$d_{max} = \frac{f-n}{2}\left[\frac{P_{33}\left(L_z - r\right) + P_{34}}{P_{43}\left(L_z - r\right) + P_{44}}\right] + \frac{f+n}{2} \qquad (17.3.5)$$

It does not matter whether d_{min} or d_{max} falls outside the range [0,1], since the values are clamped by the **glDepthBoundsNV** function.

NEW FUNCTIONS

■ **glDepthBoundsNV**—Specify minimum and maximum depth values used in the depth bounds test.

Prototype

```
void glDepthBoundsNV(GLclampd zmin,
                     GLclampd zmax);
```

Parameters

zmin   Specifies the minimum window-space depth value that may be stored in the depth buffer for the depth bounds test to pass. This value is clamped to the range [0,1]. The initial value is 0.0.

zmax   Specifies the maximum window-space depth value that may be stored in the depth buffer for the depth bounds test to pass. This value is clamped to the range [0,1]. The initial value is 1.0.

Description

The **glDepthBoundsNV** function sets the bounds used in the depth bounds test. When the depth bounds test is enabled, the *zmin* and *zmax* parameters specify the minimum and maximum window-space depth values that may be stored in the depth buffer for the depth bounds test to pass. A fragment is discarded when the value in the depth buffer falls outside this range.

Get Functions

glGetFloatv with *pname* parameter GL_DEPTH_BOUNDS_NV

Errors

GL_INVALID_VALUE is generated if *zmin* is greater than *zmax*.

EXTENDED FUNCTIONS

■ **glEnable, glDisable, glIsEnabled**—Extended to enable/disable the depth bounds test.

Prototypes

```
void glEnable(GLenum cap);
void glDisable(GLenum cap);
GLboolean glIsEnabled(GLenum cap);
```

Extended Parameters

cap   Specifies a GL capability. To enable or disable the depth bounds test, or to query whether the depth bounds test is enabled, this should be GL_DEPTH_BOUNDS_TEST_NV.

Description

The depth bounds test is enabled and disabled by passing the value GL_DEPTH_BOUNDS_TEST_NV to the **glEnable** and **glDisable** functions. Calling the **glIsEnabled** function with *cap* parameter GL_DEPTH_BOUNDS_TEST_NV returns a value indicating whether the depth bounds test is enabled.

■ **glGetFloatv**—Extended to allow retrieval of the depth bounds.

Prototype

```
void glGetFloatv(GLenum pname, GLfloat *params);
```

Extended Parameters

pname   Specifies the parameter to be returned. May be GL_DEPTH_BOUNDS_NV.

Description

The **glGetFloatv** function can be used to retrieve the current values of the depth bounds. When the *pname* parameter is GL_DEPTH_BOUNDS_NV, two values are returned in the array pointed to by the *params* parameter representing the minimum and maximum window-space depth values that may be stored in the depth buffer for the depth bounds test to pass.

17.4 GL_NV_primitive_restart

OpenGL version required	OpenGL 1.1
Dependencies	—
Promotions	—
Related extensions	—

DISCUSSION

The `GL_NV_primitive_restart` extension provides a mechanism through which multiple primitives may be rendered using a single set of indexed arrays. The application specifies a special index value that triggers a 'primitive restart' and renders indexed arrays using a function such as **glDrawElements**. When a primitive restart occurs, the index that triggered the restart is ignored, and a new primitive (of type GL_TRIANGLE_FAN, GL_TRIANGLE_STRIP, etc.) is begun with the next index. The index value used to trigger a primitive restart can be any arbitrary, unsigned integer.

Primitive restart is enabled and disabled by calling the **glEnableClientState** and **glDisableClientState** functions with *array* parameter GL_PRIMITIVE_RESTART_NV. The index that triggers a primitive restart is specified by calling the **glPrimitiveRestartIndexNV** function,

```
void glPrimitiveRestartIndexNV(GLuint index);
```

The index specified by the *index* parameter subsequently causes a new primitive to start whenever it is encountered during rendering.

For full orthogonality, the function **glPrimitiveRestartNV** is also defined by the GL_NV_primitive_restart extension and may only be called between calls to **glBegin** and **glEnd**. Calling the **glPrimitiveRestartNV** function,

```
void glPrimitiveRestartNV(void);
```

is equivalent to calling **glEnd** and then calling **glBegin** with the same *mode* parameter that was specified by the previous call to **glBegin**, effectively starting a new primitive of the same type. Applications should not expect any significant performance gain by using the **glPrimitiveRestartNV** function.

NEW FUNCTIONS

■ **glPrimitiveRestartNV**—Restart the current primitive.

Prototype

```
void glPrimitiveRestartNV(void);
```

Description

The **glPrimitiveRestartNV** function triggers a primitive restart. Calling **glPrimitiveRestartNV** is equivalent to calling **glEnd** and then calling **glBegin** with the same *mode* parameter that was previously specified.

Errors

GL_INVALID_OPERATION is generated if **glPrimitiveRestartNV** is called outside calls to **glBegin** and **glEnd**.

■ **glPrimitiveRestartIndexNV**—Specify the index that triggers a primitive restart.

Prototype

```
void glPrimitiveRestartIndexNV(GLuint index);
```

Parameters

index   Specifies the index that triggers a primitive restart. The initial value is 0.

Description

The **glPrimitiveRestartIndexNV** function is used to specify the index that triggers a primitive restart. When primitive restart is enabled and an indexed primitive is being drawn, an occurrence of the index value specified by the *index* parameter triggers a primitive restart.

Get Functions

glGetIntegerv with *pname* parameter GL_PRIMITIVE_RESTART_INDEX_NV

Errors

GL_INVALID_OPERATION is generated if **glPrimitiveRestartIndexNV** is called between calls to **glBegin** and **glEnd**.

EXTENDED FUNCTIONS

■ **glEnableClientState, glDisableClientState**—Extended to enable/disable primitive restarts.

Prototypes

```
void glEnableClientState(GLenum array);
void glDisableClientState(GLenum array);
```

Extended Parameters

array   Specifies a capability to enable or disable. May be GL_PRIMITIVE_RESTART_NV.

Description

The **glEnableClientState** and **glDisableClientState** functions enable or disable capabilities maintained by the client. Primitive restarts are enabled or disabled by passing the value GL_PRIMITIVE_RESTART_NV to the *array* parameter.

■ **glIsEnabled**—Extended to return whether primitive restarts are enabled.

Prototype

```
GLboolean glIsEnabled(GLenum cap);
```

Extended Parameters

cap   Specifies an OpenGL capability. May be GL_PRIMITIVE_RESTART_NV.

Description

Whether primitive restarts are enabled is determined by calling the **glIsEnabled** function with *cap* parameter GL_PRIMITIVE_RESTART_NV.

■ **glGetIntegerv**—Extended to allow retrieval of the primitive restart index.

Prototype

```
void glGetIntegerv(GLenum pname, GLint *params);
```

Extended Parameters

pname   Specifies the parameter to be returned. May be GL_PRIMITIVE_
                 RESTART_INDEX_NV.

Description

The **glGetIntegerv** function can be used to retrieve the primitive restart index that was previously specified using the **glPrimitiveRestartIndexNV** function. When the *pname* parameter is GL_PRIMITIVE_RESTART_INDEX_NV, the primitive restart index is returned in the *params* parameter.

17.5 GL_NV_half_float

OpenGL version required	OpenGL 1.1
Dependencies	—
Promotions	—
Related extensions	—

DISCUSSION

The GL_NV_half_float extension provides a half-precision floating-point data type that can be used when specifying vertex data or pixel data. Called a *half float* or just a *half*, this new data type is represented by a 16-bit quantity that is similar in structure to the standard 32-bit IEEE floating-point representation.

A half float value is represented by a 16-bit quantity whose bit usage is shown in Figure 17.5.1. A half float possesses a 10-bit mantissa M, a 5-bit biased exponent E, and a sign bit S. As with the 32-bit IEEE format, special interpretations of a 16-bit half float quantity exist for the minimum and maximum exponent representations. All possible types of values that a half float may attain are summarized in Table 17.5.1.

FIGURE 17.5.1   A half float is represented by a 10-bit mantissa *M*, a 5-bit exponent *E*, and a sign bit *S*. The sign occupies the most significant bit of the 16-bit quantity, and the mantissa extends to the least significant bit.

TABLE 17.5.1   Half float representations. Each possible interpretation can be positive or negative, depending on the value of the sign bit. In comparisons, +0.0 and −0.0 are considered equivalent.

Exponent E	Mantissa M	Interpretation
$E = 0$	$M = 0$	0.0
$E = 0$	$M \neq 0$	Denormalized value $(M/2^{10}) \times 2^{-14}$
$0 < E < 31$	Any	$(1 + M/2^{10}) \times 2^{E-15}$
$E = 31$	$M = 0$	Infinity
$E = 31$	$M \neq 0$	Not a Number (NAN)

Several new immediate-mode functions have been defined to allow specification of vertex data with half float components. The names of these functions are suffixed with the letter "h" to denote the half float data type. The following new functions are defined by the `GL_NV_half_float` extension:

- `glVertex{234}h[v]NV`
- `glNormal3h[v]NV`
- `glColor{34}h[v]NV`
- `glTexCoord{1234}h[v]NV`
- `glMultiTexCoord{1234}h[v]NV`
- `glFogCoordh[v]NV`
- `glSecondaryColor3h[v]NV`
- `glVertexWeighth[v]NV`
- `glVertexAttrib{1234}h[v]NV`
- `glVertexAttribs{1234}hvNV`

Some of these functions may only be available if other extensions to which they pertain are supported.

Arrays of vertex data may also be specified using the half float data type by passing the constant `GL_HALF_FLOAT_NV` to the *type* parameter of any array pointer specification function (e.g., **glNormalPointer**). In particular, the following functions accept the half float data type.

- **glVertexPointer**
- **glNormalPointer**
- **glColorPointer**
- **glTexCoordPointer**
- **glFogCoordPointerEXT**
- **glSecondaryColorPointerEXT**
- **glVertexWeightPointerEXT**
- **glVertexAttribPointerNV**

The half float data type may also be used when transferring pixel data to or from OpenGL. In particular, the *type* parameter passed to any of the following functions may be GL_HALF_FLOAT_NV.

- **glDrawPixels**
- **glReadPixels**
- **glTexImage1D**
- **glTexImage2D**
- **glTexImage3DEXT**
- **glTexSubImage1D**
- **glTexSubImage2D**
- **glTexSubImage3DEXT**
- **glGetTexImage**

When a pixel image containing half float component types is converted to fixed-point, each component is clamped to the range [0,1].

NEW FUNCTIONS

- **glVertex{234}h[v]NV**—Specify a vertex with half float components.

Prototypes

```
void glVertex2hNV(GLhalf x,
                  GLhalf y);
void glVertex3hNV(GLhalf x,
                  GLhalf y,
                  GLhalf z);
void glVertex4hNV(GLhalf x,
                  GLhalf y,
                  GLhalf z,
                  GLhalf w);
```

Parameters

x, y, z, w   Specify the *x*, *y*, *z*, and *w* components of a vertex.

Prototypes

```
void glVertex2hvNV(const GLhalf *v);
void glVertex3hvNV(const GLhalf *v);
void glVertex4hvNV(const GLhalf *v);
```

Parameters

v   Specifies a pointer to an array of two, three, or four elements containing the components of a vertex.

Description

The **glVertex{234}h[v]NV** function specifies vertex coordinates as half float values.

■ **glNormal3h[v]NV**—Set the current normal with half float components.

Prototype

```
void glNormal3hNV(GLhalf x,
                  GLhalf y,
                  GLhalf z);
```

Parameters

x, y, z   Specify the *x*, *y*, and *z* components of the current normal.

Prototype

```
void glNormal3hvNV(const GLhalf *v);
```

Parameters

v   Specifies a pointer to an array containing a three-component normal.

Description

The **glNormal3h[v]NV** function specifies the components of the current normal as half float values.

Get Functions

glGetFloatv with *pname* parameter GL_CURRENT_NORMAL

■ **glColor{34}h[v]NV**—Set the current color with half float components.

Prototypes

```
void glColor3hNV(GLhalf red,
                 GLhalf green,
                 GLhalf blue);
```

```
void glColor4hNV(GLhalf red,
                 GLhalf green,
                 GLhalf blue,
                 GLhalf alpha);
```

Parameters

red, green, blue, alpha   Specify the red, green, blue, and alpha components of the current color.

Prototypes

```
void glColor3hvNV(const GLhalf *v);
void glColor4hvNV(const GLhalf *v);
```

Parameters

v   Specifies a pointer to an array containing the new current color components.

Description

The **glColor{34}h[v]NV** function specifies the components of the current color as half float values.

Get Functions

glGet with *pname* parameter GL_CURRENT_COLOR

■ **glTexCoord{1234}h[v]NV**—Set the current texture coordinates with half float components.

Prototypes

```
void glTexCoord1hNV(GLhalf s);
void glTexCoord2hNV(GLhalf s,
                    GLhalf t);
void glTexCoord3hNV(GLhalf s,
                    GLhalf t,
                    GLhalf r);
void glTexCoord4hNV(GLhalf s,
                    GLhalf t,
                    GLhalf r,
                    GLhalf q);
```

Parameters

s, t, r, q   Specify the current *s*, *t*, *r*, and *q* texture coordinates.

Prototypes

```
void glTexCoord1hvNV(const GLhalf *v);
void glTexCoord2hvNV(const GLhalf *v);
void glTexCoord3hvNV(const GLhalf *v);
void glTexCoord4hvNV(const GLhalf *v);
```

Parameters

v   Specifies a pointer to an array containing the new current texture coordinates.

Description

The **glTexCoord{1234}h[v]NV** function specifies the components of the current texture coordinates as half float values.

Get Functions

glGet with *pname* parameter GL_CURRENT_TEXTURE_COORDS

■ **glMultiTexCoord{1234}h[v]NV**—Set the current texture coordinates for a particular texture unit with half float components.

Prototypes

```
void glMultiTexCoord1hNV(GLenum texture,
                         GLhalf s);
void glMultiTexCoord2hNV(GLenum texture,
                         GLhalf s,
                         GLhalf t);
void glMultiTexCoord3hNV(GLenum texture,
                         GLhalf s,
                         GLhalf t,
                         GLhalf r);
void glMultiTexCoord4hNV(GLenum texture,
                         GLhalf s,
                         GLhalf t,
                         GLhalf r,
                         GLhalf q);
```

Parameters

texture   Specifies the texture unit for which texture coordinates are being set. Must be GL_TEXTURE*i*_ARB, where *i* is in the range 0 to GL_MAX_TEXTURE_UNITS_ARB − 1.

s, t, r, q   Specify the current *s*, *t*, *r*, and *q* texture coordinates.

Prototypes

```
void glMultiTexCoord1hvNV(GLenum texture,
                          const GLhalf *v);
void glMultiTexCoord2hvNV(GLenum texture,
                          const GLhalf *v);
void glMultiTexCoord3hvNV(GLenum texture,
                          const GLhalf *v);
void glMultiTexCoord4hvNV(GLenum texture,
                          const GLhalf *v);
```

Parameters

texture   Specifies the texture unit for which texture coordinates are being set. Must be GL_TEXTURE*i*_ARB, where *i* is in the range 0 to GL_MAX_ TEXTURE_UNITS_ARB − 1.

v   Specifies a pointer to an array containing the new current texture coordinates.

Description

The **glMultiTexCoord{1234}h[v]NV** function specifies the components of the current texture coordinates associated with the texture unit specified by the *texture* parameter as half float values.

Special Considerations

This function is only available if the GL_ARB_multitexture extension is supported. Also, see the **glMultiTexCoord{1234}{sifd}[v]ARB** function described in Chapter 3, Section 3.1.

Get Functions

glGet with *pname* parameter GL_CURRENT_TEXTURE_COORDS

■ **glFogCoordh[v]NV**—Set current fog coordinate as a half float value.

Prototype

    void **glFogCoordhNV**(GLhalf *fog*);

Parameters

fog   Specifies the new current fog coordinate.

Prototype

    void **glFogCoordhvNV**(const GLhalf **fog*);

Parameters

fog   Specifies a pointer to an array containing the new current fog coordinate.

Description

The **glFogCoordh[v]NV** function specifies the current fog coordinate as a half float value.

Special Considerations

This function is only available if the GL_EXT_fog_coord extension is supported. Also, see the **glFogCoord{fd}[v]EXT** function described in Chapter 11, Section 11.1.

Get Functions

glGet with *pname* parameter GL_CURRENT_FOG_COORDINATE_EXT

- **glSecondaryColor3h[v]NV**—Specify the current secondary color with half float components.

Prototype

```
void glSecondaryColor3hNV(GLhalf red,
                          GLhalf green,
                          GLhalf blue);
```

Parameters

red, green, blue   Specify new red, green, and blue color components for the current secondary color.

Prototype

```
void glSecondaryColor3hvNV(const GLhalf *v);
```

Parameters

v   Specifies a pointer to an array containing the current secondary color.

Description

The **glSecondaryColor3h[v]NV** function specifies the components of the current secondary color as half float values.

Special Considerations

This function is only available if the GL_EXT_secondary_color extension is supported. Also, see the **glSecondaryColor3{bsifdubusui}[v]EXT** function described in Chapter 10, Section 10.2.

Get Functions

glGet with *pname* parameter GL_CURRENT_SECONDARY_COLOR_EXT

- **glVertexWeighth[v]NV**—Specify the current vertex weight as a half float value.

Prototype

```
void glVertexWeighthNV(GLhalf weight);
```

Parameters

weight   Specifies the current vertex weight.

Prototype

```
void glVertexWeighthvNV(const GLhalf *weight);
```

Parameters

weight   Specifies a pointer to an array containing the current vertex weight.

Description

The **glVertexWeighth[v]NV** function specifies the current vertex weight as a half float value.

Special Considerations

This function is only available if the GL_EXT_vertex_weighting extension is supported. Also, see the **glVertexWeightf[v]EXT** function described in Chapter 7, Section 7.1.

Get Functions

glGetFloatv with *pname* parameter GL_CURRENT_VERTEX_WEIGHT_EXT

■ **glVertexAttrib{1234}h[v]NV**—Specify a vertex attribute with half float omponents.

Prototypes

```
void glVertexAttrib1hNV(GLuint index,
                        GLhalf x);
void glVertexAttrib2hNV(GLuint index,
                        GLhalf x,
                        GLhalf y);
void glVertexAttrib3hNV(GLuint index,
                        GLhalf x,
                        GLhalf y,
                        GLhalf z);
void glVertexAttrib4hNV(GLuint index,
                        GLhalf x,
                        GLhalf y,
                        GLhalf z,
                        GLhalf w);
```

Parameters

index   Specifies the index of a vertex attribute. Must be in the range 0 to 15.

x, y, z, w   Specify the components of the vertex attribute.

Prototypes

```
void glVertexAttrib1hvNV(GLuint index,
                         const GLhalf *v);
void glVertexAttrib2hvNV(GLuint index,
                         const GLhalf *v);
void glVertexAttrib3hvNV(GLuint index,
                         const GLhalf *v);
void glVertexAttrib4hvNV(GLuint index,
                         const GLhalf *v);
```

Parameters

index   Specifies the index of a vertex attribute. Must be in the range 0 to 15.

v   Specifies a pointer to the array containing the vertex attribute
                     components.

Description

The **glVertexAttrib{1234}h[v]NV** function specifies the components of the current vertex attribute whose index is specified by the *index* parameter as half float values.

Special Considerations

This function is only available if the GL_NV_vertex_program extension is supported. Also, see the **glVertexAttrib{1234}{ubsfd}[v]NV** function described in Chapter 18, Section 18.2.

Get Functions

glGetVertexAttrib{fd}vNV with *pname* parameter GL_CURRENT_ATTRIB_NV

■ **glVertexAttribs{1234}hvNV**—Specify multiple vertex attributes with half float components.

Prototypes

```
void glVertexAttribs1hvNV(GLuint index,
                          GLsizei n,
                          const GLhalf *v);
void glVertexAttribs2hvNV(GLuint index,
                          GLsizei n,
                          const GLhalf *v);
void glVertexAttribs3hvNV(GLuint index,
                          GLsizei n,
                          const GLhalf *v);
void glVertexAttribs4hvNV(GLuint index,
                          GLsizei n,
                          const GLhalf *v);
```

Parameters

index   Specifies the first index of a set of contiguous vertex attributes. Must be
                     in the range 0 to 15.

n   Specifies the number of vertex attributes to be updated.

v   Specifies a pointer to an array of vertex attributes.

Description

The **glVertexAttribs{1234}hvNV** function specifies the values of multiple vertex attributes beginning with the index specified by the *index* parameter. The *n* parameter specifies how many vertex attributes to update, and the *v* parameter points to an array containing a new set of coordinates for each one stored as half float values.

Special Considerations

This function is only available if the GL_NV_vertex_program extension is supported. Also, see the **glVertexAttribs{1234}{ubsfd}vNV** function described in Chapter 18, Section 18.2.

Get Functions

glGetVertexAttrib{fd}vNV with *pname* parameter GL_CURRENT_ATTRIB_NV

EXTENDED FUNCTIONS

■ **glVertexPointer, glNormalPointer, glColorPointer, glTexCoordPointer, glFogCoordPointerEXT, glSecondaryColorPointerEXT, glVertexWeight-PointerEXT, glVertexAttribPointerNV**—Extended to allow half float data type.

Prototypes

```
void glVertexPointer(GLint size, GLenum type, GLsizei stride,
    const GLvoid *pointer);
void glNormalPointer(GLenum type, GLsizei stride,
    const GLvoid *pointer);
void glColorPointer(GLint size, GLenum type, GLsizei stride,
    const GLvoid *pointer);
void glTexCoordPointer(GLint size, GLenum type, GLsizei stride,
    const GLvoid *pointer);
void glFogCoordPointerEXT(GLenum type, GLsizei stride,
    const GLvoid *pointer);
void glSecondaryColorPointerEXT(GLint size, GLenum type,
    GLsizei stride, const GLvoid *pointer);
void glVertexWeightPointerEXT(GLint size, GLenum type, GLsizei stride,
    const GLvoid *pointer);
void glVertexAttribPointerNV(GLuint index, GLint size, GLenum type,
    GLsizei stride, const GLvoid *pointer);
```

Extended Parameters

type   Specifies the data type of each coordinate in the array. May be GL_HALF_FLOAT_NV.

Description

When the GL_NV_half_float extension is supported, all arrays may be specified with a half float data type.

Get Functions

glGetIntegerv with *pname* parameter GL_VERTEX_ARRAY_TYPE

glGetIntegerv with *pname* parameter GL_NORMAL_ARRAY_TYPE

glGetIntegerv with *pname* parameter GL_COLOR_ARRAY_TYPE

glGetIntegerv with *pname* parameter GL_TEXTURE_COORD_ARRAY_TYPE

glGetIntegerv with *pname* parameter GL_FOG_COORD_ARRAY_TYPE_EXT

glGetIntegerv with *pname* parameter GL_SECONDARY_COLOR_ARRAY_TYPE_EXT

glGetIntegerv with *pname* parameter GL_VERTEX_WEIGHT_ARRAY_TYPE_EXT

glGetVertexAttribivNV with *pname* parameter GL_ATTRIB_ARRAY_TYPE_NV

■ **glDrawPixels, glReadPixels, glTexImage1D, glTexImage2D, glTexImage-3DEXT, glTexSubImage1D, glTexSubImage2D, glTexSubImage3DEXT, glGetTexImage**—Extended to allow half float data type.

Prototypes

```
void glDrawPixels(GLsizei width, GLsizei height, GLenum format,
    GLenum type, const GLvoid *pixels);
void glReadPixels(GLint x, GLint y, GLsizei width, GLsizei height,
    GLenum format, GLenum type, GLvoid *pixels);
void glTexImage1D(GLenum target, GLint level, GLint internalFormat,
    GLsizei width, GLint border, GLenum format, GLenum type,
    const GLvoid *pixels);
void glTexImage2D(GLenum target, GLint level, GLint internalFormat,
    GLsizei width, GLsizei height, GLint border, GLenum format,
    GLenum type, const GLvoid *pixels);
void glTexImage3DEXT(GLenum target, GLint level, GLint internalFormat,
    GLsizei width, GLsizei height, GLsizei depth, GLint border,
    GLenum format, GLenum type, const GLvoid *pixels);
void glTexSubImage1D(GLenum target, GLint level, GLint xoffset,
    GLsizei width, GLenum format, GLenum type, const GLvoid *pixels);
void glTexSubImage2D(GLenum target, GLint level, GLint xoffset,
    GLint yoffset, GLsizei width, GLsizei height, GLenum format,
    GLenum type, const GLvoid *pixels);
void glTexSubImage3DEXT(GLenum target, GLint level, GLint xoffset,
    GLint yoffset, GLint zoffset, GLsizei width, GLsizei height,
    GLsizei depth, GLenum format, GLenum type, const GLvoid *pixels);
void glGetTexImage(GLenum target, GLint level, GLenum format,
    GLenum type, GLvoid *pixels);
```

Extended Parameters

type   Specifies the data type for the pixel data pointed to by the *pixels* parameter. May be GL_HALF_FLOAT_NV.

Description

When the GL_NV_half_float extension is supported, pixel data may be stored using half float components. This is specified by passing the symbolic constant GL_HALF_FLOAT_NV to the *type* parameter of any function that operates on pixel data.

CHAPTER 18

VERTEX PROGRAMS

IN THIS CHAPTER

18.1   GL_ARB_vertex_program
18.2   GL_NV_vertex_program
18.3   GL_NV_vertex_program1_1
18.4   GL_NV_vertex_program2

18.1   GL_ARB_vertex_program

OpenGL version required	OpenGL 1.3
Dependencies	—
Promotions	—
Related extensions	GL_ARB_fragment_program

DISCUSSION

The GL_ARB_vertex_program extension provides fully general programmability for per-vertex calculations including vertex coordinate transformation, lighting, and texture coordinate generation. Conventional per-vertex calculations can be replaced by assembly-like source code that an implementation compiles into a *vertex program*.

Vertex programs provide an interface for directly accessing generalized transform and lighting hardware. Vertex programs are enabled and disabled by calling the **glEnable** and **glDisable** functions with *cap* parameter GL_VERTEX_PROGRAM_ARB. When vertex programs are enabled, the following conventional per-vertex calculations are not performed automatically by OpenGL, but need to be handled by the vertex program itself.

- Vertex coordinate transformation from object space to homogeneous clip space.
- Calculation of primary and secondary colors for vertex lighting.

- Normal vector rescaling and normalization.
- Normalization of evaluated normal vectors using `GL_AUTO_NORMAL`.
- Texture coordinate generation.
- Texture matrix application.
- Fog distance calculation.
- Point size attenuation.
- Vertex weighting.

Vertex programs do not subsume the following functionality, which is still performed by OpenGL when vertex programs are enabled.

- Primitive assembly.
- Face culling.
- View frustum clipping.
- Perspective division by the *w* coordinate.
- Viewport and depth range transformations.
- Clamping primary and secondary colors to [0,1].
- Evaluator calculations (except `GL_AUTO_NORMAL`).

In vertex program mode, user clipping planes are not supported unless a special position-invariant option is utilized. Primitives are only clipped to the six planes of the view frustum without this option.

Vertex programs have access to only a single vertex at a time. The information that a vertex program receives as inputs for each vertex includes conventional types of data, such as the vertex's object-space position, its associated normal vector, primary and secondary colors, and texture coordinates, as well as user-defined generic per-vertex attributes.

Vertex programs have access to a large bank of constant parameter registers that do not change from one vertex to another. These parameters can be used to pass any necessary constant data to a vertex program. For example, material colors and texture generation coefficients would be stored in the parameter registers.

After performing its calculations, a vertex program writes its outputs to a set of result registers, which include types of data such as the vertex's homogeneous clip-space position, primary and secondary colors, and texture coordinates. These outputs are then interpolated across the face of a primitive during the rasterization process and passed to the fragment-processing portion of the graphics pipeline.

Program Structure

A vertex program is specified as a text string containing a series of statements. The text string must begin with the character sequence `!!ARBvp1.0`, with no preceding whitespace, to indicate that the program conforms to the version 1.0 ARB vertex program syntax. The end of the vertex program is indicated by the three-character sequence `END`. The exact syntax specification for version 1.0 ARB vertex programs is given in Appendix A, Section A.1.

A vertex program statement can be either a naming statement or an instruction statement. A naming statement associates an identifier with some kind of data, such as a vertex attribute, a program parameter, or a temporary register. An instruction statement operates on input registers that may or may not be associated with previously named identifiers and stores its result in a temporary register, address register, or output register. Every statement is terminated with a semicolon.

A vertex program instruction consists of a three-character mnemonic followed by a destination register and up to three source operands delimited by commas. The example shown in Listing 18.1.1 performs four dot products to transform a vertex's position into homogeneous clip space and copies the vertex's primary color and texture coordinates to the output registers. The symbol # denotes the beginning of a comment that extends to the end of the line on which it appears.

LISTING 18.1.1 The following vertex program transforms the vertex position from model space to homogeneous clip space, and copies the primary color and texture coordinates to the output registers.

```
!!ARBvp1.0

# Transform vertex position into clip space
DP4     result.position.x, state.matrix.mvp.row[0],
        vertex.position;
DP4     result.position.y, state.matrix.mvp.row[1],
        vertex.position;
DP4     result.position.z, state.matrix.mvp.row[2],
        vertex.position;
DP4     result.position.w, state.matrix.mvp.row[3],
        vertex.position;

# Pass through primary color and texture coordinates
MOV     result.color, vertex.color;
MOV     result.texcoord[0], vertex.texcoord[0];

END
```

The vertex program shown in Listing 18.1.1 does not contain any naming statements, but instead accesses vertex attributes and OpenGL state directly in the instruction statements. The same vertex program could be written in the manner shown in Listing 18.1.2. In this version of the program, the vertex attributes, OpenGL state, and result registers are first bound to identifiers that are used throughout the remainder of the program. The naming statements and instruction statements used in this vertex program are described in the sections that follow.

LISTING 18.1.2 The following vertex program transforms the vertex position from model space to homogeneous clip space and copies the primary color and texture coordinates to the output registers. At the beginning of the program, vertex attributes and OpenGL state values are bound to identifiers that are used throughout the remainder of the program.

```
!!ARBvp1.0

ATTRIB     position = vertex.position;
ATTRIB     color = vertex.color;
ATTRIB     texcoord = vertex.texcoord[0];

PARAM      mvp[4] = state.matrix.mvp;

OUTPUT     hpos = result.position;
OUTPUT     col0 = result.color;
OUTPUT     tex0 = result.texcoord[0];

# Transform vertex position into clip space
DP4     hpos.x, mvp[0], position;
DP4     hpos.y, mvp[1], position;
DP4     hpos.z, mvp[2], position;
DP4     hpos.w, mvp[3], position;

# Pass through primary color and texture coordinates
MOV     col0, color;
MOV     tex0, texcoord;

END
```

All registers manipulated by a vertex program are treated as vectors consisting of four floating-point components: x, y, z, and w. Some instructions require a scalar operand, in which case a vector component must be selected from the source register by appending .x, .y, .z, or .w. For example, the following line calculates the reciprocal of the z component of the operand vector.

```
RCP     temp, vector.z;
```

Operand Modification

In a vertex program instruction statement, any source operand may have an optional negation operation as well as an arbitrary swizzle operation applied to it. Prepending an operand name with a minus sign negates each of its components before it is used by an instruction. For example, the following line subtracts the contents operand b from operand a and places the result in the register associated with the sub identifier.

```
ADD     sub, a, -b;
```

The swizzle operation allows components of a source operand to be reordered or duplicated arbitrarily. Swizzling is denoted by appending a period and a sequence of four letters from the set {x, y, z, w} to an identifier. The four letters define a remapping of the components of a register that are passed to the instruction as one of its source operands. As an example, the following line reads the components of the operand vector in reverse order and stores them in the register reverse.

```
MOV    reverse, vector.wzyx;
```

Omitting the swizzle suffix is equivalent to using the suffix .xyzw.

Components may be duplicated in the swizzle suffix. For example, the following line moves the x component of vector into the x and y components of temp and moves the y component of vector into the z and w components of temp. The z and w components of vector are ignored.

```
MOV    temp, vector.xxyy;
```

A shorthand notation exists for duplicating a single component of a register to all four components of a source operand. Appending an identifier with a period and a single letter is equivalent to using the same letter four times in a row. For example, the following line moves the x component of vector into all four components of temp.

```
MOV    temp, vector.x;
```

This notation is also necessary for denoting the scalar operand required by instructions such as the RCP (reciprocal) instruction.

Destination Masking
A write mask may be applied to the destination register and controls which components of the destination are updated with an instruction's result. A write mask is denoted by appending a period followed by up to four *unique* letters from the set {x, y, z, w} to an identifier in the natural component order. For example, the following line moves the contents of the x component of vector into the x component of temp, but does not alter the y, z, or w components of temp.

```
MOV    temp.x, vector;
```

The following line adds the x and y components of vector and stores the result in the x and w components of temp without affecting the y and z components of temp.

```
ADD    temp.xw, vector.x, vector.y;
```

Omitting the write mask is equivalent to specifying the write mask .xyzw.

Constant Declarations
Vertex programs support embedded constants that may be scalar floating-point quantities or four-component vector quantities. The notation used to specify floating-point constants is identical to that used by the C language.

An embedded scalar constant is specified by simply inserting a signed floating-point number into a location where an identifier would normally be used. A scalar constant is equivalent to a vector constant whose four components are all the same value. The following line adds 2.5 to each component of the operand a.

```
ADD     temp, a, 2.5;
```

An embedded vector constant is represented by a comma-delimited list of one to four floating-point numbers enclosed in braces. For example, the following line adds a different value to each of the components of a:

```
ADD     temp, a, {1.0, 2.0, 3.0, 4.0};
```

If fewer than four components are specified, then the y, z, and w components are filled with 0.0, 0.0, and 1.0, respectively, as needed. For example, the vector constant {3.0, 2.0} is equivalent to the vector constant {3.0, 2.0, 0.0, 1.0}.

If more than four unique scalar floating-point constants are used in a single instruction, some implementations may need to generate additional instructions to perform the operation.

Vertex Attributes

An identifier is bound to a vertex attribute using the ATTRIB statement. The vertex attributes that can be bound are listed in Table 18.1.1. As an example, the following line binds the vertex position to the identifier position.

```
ATTRIB position = vertex.position;
```

After this declaration, instructions that refer to the position identifier as a source operand read the current vertex position.

TABLE 18.1.1   Vertex Attribute Bindings

Attribute Binding	Component Usage	Underlying State
vertex.position	(x,y,z,w)	Object-space position
vertex.weight	(w,w,w,w)	Vertex weights 0–3
vertex.weight[n]	(w,w,w,w)	Vertex weights $n–(n+3)$
vertex.normal	$(x,y,z,1)$	Normal vector
vertex.color	(r,g,b,a)	Primary color
vertex.color.primary	(r,g,b,a)	Primary color
vertex.color.secondary	(r,g,b,a)	Secondary color
vertex.fogcoord	$(f,0,0,1)$	Fog coordinate
vertex.texcoord	(s,t,r,q)	Texture coordinates, unit 0

TABLE 18.1.1   *Continued*

Attribute Binding	Component Usage	Underlying State
vertex.texcoord[n]	(s,t,r,q)	Texture coordinates, unit n
vertex.matrixindex	(i,i,i,i)	Vertex matrix indices 0–3
vertex.matrixindex[n]	(i,i,i,i)	Vertex matrix indices n–$(n+3)$
vertex.attrib[n]	(w,y,z,w)	Generic vertex attribute n

The vertex.attrib[n] binding corresponds to the generic vertex attribute n. Conventional OpenGL vertex attributes are aliased onto the generic vertex attributes, and only one of each pair may be used within a vertex program. Table 18.1.2 lists each conventional OpenGL attribute and its associated generic vertex attribute. Attempting to bind both vertex attributes in any single row of the table results in an ill-formed program that will fail to load.

TABLE 18.1.2   Invalid Vertex Binding Pairs

Conventional Attribute Binding	Generic Attribute Binding
vertex.position	vertex.attrib[0]
vertex.weight	vertex.attrib[1]
vertex.weight[0]	vertex.attrib[1]
vertex.normal	vertex.attrib[2]
vertex.color	vertex.attrib[3]
vertex.color.primary	vertex.attrib[3]
vertex.color.secondary	vertex.attrib[4]
vertex.fogcoord	vertex.attrib[5]
vertex.texcoord	vertex.attrib[8]
vertex.texcoord[0]	vertex.attrib[8]
vertex.texcoord[1]	vertex.attrib[9]
vertex.texcoord[2]	vertex.attrib[10]
vertex.texcoord[3]	vertex.attrib[11]
vertex.texcoord[4]	vertex.attrib[12]
vertex.texcoord[5]	vertex.attrib[13]
vertex.texcoord[6]	vertex.attrib[14]
vertex.texcoord[7]	vertex.attrib[15]
vertex.texcoord[n]	vertex.attrib[8+n]

When rendering, the current value of any vertex attribute can be specified using the **glVertexAttrib{1234}{bsiubusuifd}[v]ARB** function. This function takes an index to a vertex attribute register and up to four components to store in the register. If fewer than four components are specified, then any missing y, z, and w components are set to 0, 0, and 1, respectively. Calling the **glVertexAttrib{1234}{bsiubusuifd}[v]ARB** function with *index* parameter 0 functions like the **glVertex{234}{sifd}[v]** function and must occur between calls to **glBegin** and **glEnd**. Updating vertex attribute 0 causes all other vertex attributes to be associated with the current vertex and invokes the current vertex program. Any other vertex attribute can be updated at any time in the same respect that, for example, the current normal or color would be updated.

When the **glVertexAttrib{1234}{bsiubusuifd}[v]ARB** function specifies fixed-point values, they are converted directly to floating-point values without any range remapping. The **glVertexAttrib4N{bsiubusui}[v]ARB** function is provided to allow an application to specify fixed-point vertex attributes that should be remapped. When using this function, unsigned values are remapped to the range [0,1], and signed values are remapped to the range [−1,1].

Vertex attribute arrays can also be used just as one can specify a conventional vertex array, normal array, and so forth. A vertex attribute array is specified by calling the **glVertexAttribPointerARB** function,

```
void glVertexAttribPointerARB(GLuint index,
                              GLint size,
                              GLenum type,
                              GLboolean normalized,
                              GLsizei stride,
                              const GLvoid *pointer);
```

with the *index* parameter set to the index of the vertex attribute to affect. The *size*, *type*, *stride*, and *pointer* parameters have the same meanings as they do for the conventional counterparts **glVertexPointer**, **glNormalPointer**, etc. The *normalized* parameter indicates whether the values in an array specified with a fixed-point data type are normalized to the range [0,1] (for unsigned types) or the range [−1,1] (for signed types) when they are converted to floating-point. If *normalized* is GL_FALSE, then fixed-point values are not remapped to a normalized range, but are directly converted to floating-point.

Vertex attribute arrays are enabled and disabled by calling the **glEnableVertexAttribArrayARB** and **glDisableVertexAttribArrayARB** functions,

```
void glEnableVertexAttribArrayARB(GLuint index);

void glDisableVertexAttribArrayARB(GLuint index);
```

with the *index* parameter set to the index of a vertex attribute array.

State pertaining to a vertex attribute is retrieved by calling the **glGetVertexAttrib{ifd}vARB** function,

```
void glGetVertexAttrib{ifd}vARB(GLuint index,
                                GLenum pname,
                                T *params);
```

with the *index* parameter set to the index of the vertex attribute to query. (The type T represents GLint, GLfloat, or GLdouble.) The *pname* parameter may be one of the values listed in Table 18.1.3.

TABLE 18.1.3   State Pertaining to Vertex Attributes that Can be Retrieved Using the **glGetVertexAttrib{ifd}vARB** Function

State	Description
GL_VERTEX_ATTRIB_ARRAY_ENABLED_ARB	A Boolean value indicating whether the vertex attribute array is currently enabled.
GL_VERTEX_ATTRIB_ARRAY_SIZE_ARB	The size of the vertex attribute array.
GL_VERTEX_ATTRIB_ARRAY_TYPE_ARB	The data type of the vertex attribute array.
GL_VERTEX_ATTRIB_ARRAY_NORMALIZED_ARB	A Boolean value indicating whether the data in the vertex attribute array is normalized.
GL_VERTEX_ATTRIB_ARRAY_STRIDE_ARB	The stride for the vertex attribute array.
GL_CURRENT_VERTEX_ATTRIB_ARB	The current four-component vertex attribute value.

The pointer to a vertex attribute array is retrieved by calling the **glGetVertexAttrib-PointervARB** function,

```
void glGetVertexAttribPointervARB(GLuint index,
                                  GLenum pname,
                                  GLvoid **pointer);
```

with the *index* parameter set to the index of the vertex attribute array to query. The *pname* parameter must be GL_VERTEX_ATTRIB_POINTER_ARB.

The number of generic vertex attributes supported by an implementation is retrieved by calling the **glGetIntegerv** function with *pname* parameter GL_MAX_VERTEX_ATTRIBS_ARB. The value of the *index* parameter passed to the **glVertexAttrib{1234}-{bsiubusuifd}[v]ARB**, **glVertexAttrib4N{bsiubusui}[v]ARB**, and **glVertex-AttribPointerARB** functions must be less than this limit.

Program Parameters

Vertex programs have access to a set of program parameters that fall into the following three categories:

- **Program environment parameters.** These are global constants that are shared by all vertex programs.
- **Program local parameters.** These are local constants that are private to a single vertex program.
- **OpenGL state.** This includes state such as matrices, lighting materials, and texture coordinate generation parameters.

A vertex program may also declare a floating-point scalar or vector constant either explicitly in a naming statement or implicitly in an instruction statement.

An identifier is bound to a constant value, a program environment parameter, a program local parameter, or a particular OpenGL state using the PARAM statement. A constant vector value is declared by assigning a comma-delimited list of one to four floating-point values enclosed in braces to an identifier. For example, the following line binds the constant vector $\langle 1.0, 2.0, 3.0, 4.0 \rangle$ to the name const.

```
PARAM const = {1.0, 2.0, 3.0, 4.0};
```

If fewer than four components are specified, then the y, z, and w components are filled with 0.0, 0.0, and 1.0, respectively. A scalar constant is declared by simply assigning a floating-point value to an identifier. The following line binds the value $-\pi$ to the name negPi.

```
PARAM negPi = -3.14159;
```

Assigning a scalar value to an identifier is equivalent to assigning a vector to the identifier with the same value for all four components.

Table 18.1.4 lists the names of the program environment parameters and program local parameters that can be bound. A single program environment parameter is bound to the name coef by the following line:

```
PARAM coef = program.env[0];
```

Arrays may also be declared that bind multiple contiguous program parameters to the same identifier. This is done by using the notation [a..b] to specify a range of parameter indices. For example, the following line binds program environment parameters 0 through 3 to the array identifier coef.

```
PARAM coef[4] = program.env[0..3];
```

The size of the array may be omitted, in which case it is deduced from the number of parameters to which the identifier is bound.

TABLE 18.1.4 Program Parameter Bindings

Parameter Binding	Component Usage	Underlying State
program.env[a]	(x,y,z,w)	Program environment parameter a
program.env[a..b]	(x,y,z,w)	The array of program environment parameters a through b
program.local[a]	(x,y,z,w)	Program local parameter a
program.local[a..b]	(x,y,z,w)	The array of program local parameters a through b

Constant data is loaded into a program environment parameter by calling the **gl-ProgramEnvParameter4{fd}[v]ARB** function,

```
void glProgramEnvParameter4{fd}ARB(GLenum target,
                                    GLuint index,
                                    T x,
                                    T y,
                                    T z,
                                    T w);


void glProgramEnvParameter4{fd}vARB(GLenum target,
                                     GLuint index,
                                     const T *params);
```

with *target* parameter GL_VERTEX_PROGRAM_ARB. (The type T represents GLfloat or GLdouble.) The *index* parameter specifies which program environment parameter to load and must be less than the value returned by the **glGetProgramivARB** function when called with *pname* parameter GL_MAX_PROGRAM_ENV_PARAMETERS_ARB.

Constant data is loaded into a program local parameter by calling the **glProgram-LocalParameter4{fd}[v]ARB** function,

```
void glProgramLocalParameter4{fd}ARB(GLenum target,
                                      GLuint index,
                                      T x,
                                      T y,
                                      T z,
                                      T w);


void glProgramLocalParameter4{fd}vARB(GLenum target,
                                       GLuint index,
                                       const T *params);
```

with *target* parameter GL_VERTEX_PROGRAM_ARB. The *index* parameter specifies which program local parameter to load and must be less than the value returned by the **glGet-ProgramivARB** function when called with *pname* parameter GL_MAX_PROGRAM_LOCAL_PARAMETERS_ARB. When a program local parameter is specified, it applies only to the currently bound vertex program.

An identifier can be bound to material property states by using the PARAM statement with one of the names listed in Table 18.1.5. Material properties for both front-facing and back-facing primitives are available, and are distinguished by using the state.material.front prefix or the state.material.back prefix. If the .front or .back component is omitted, the front-facing state is selected.

TABLE 18.1.5   Material Property Bindings

Material Binding	*Component Usage*	*Underlying State*
state.material.ambient	(r,g,b,a)	Front ambient material color
state.material.diffuse	(r,g,b,a)	Front diffuse material color
state.material.specular	(r,g,b,a)	Front specular material color
state.material.emission	(r,g,b,a)	Front emission material color
state.material.shininess	$(s,0,0,1)$	Front specular material shininess
state.material.front.ambient	(r,g,b,a)	Front ambient material color
state.material.front.diffuse	(r,g,b,a)	Front diffuse material color
state.material.front.specular	(r,g,b,a)	Front specular material color
state.material.front.emission	(r,g,b,a)	Front emission material color
state.material.front.shininess	$(s,0,0,1)$	Front specular material shininess
state.material.back.ambient	(r,g,b,a)	Back ambient material color
state.material.back.diffuse	(r,g,b,a)	Back diffuse material color
state.material.back.specular	(r,g,b,a)	Back specular material color
state.material.back.emission	(r,g,b,a)	Back emission material color
state.material.back.shininess	$(s,0,0,1)$	Back specular material shininess

An identifier can be bound to state for a particular light or for the current light model by using the PARAM statement with one of the names listed in Table 18.1.6. Those states that begin with the prefix state.light[n] refer to states associated with light *n*.

TABLE 18.1.6   Light Property Bindings

Light Binding	Component Usage	Underlying State
state.light[n] .ambient	(r,g,b,a)	Light n ambient color
state.light[n] .diffuse	(r,g,b,a)	Light n diffuse color
state.light[n] .specular	(r,g,b,a)	Light n specular color
state.light[n] .position	(x,y,z,w)	Light n position
state.light[n] .attenuation	(k_o,k_l,k_q,e)	Light n attenuation constants k_o, k_l, and k_q and spotlight exponent e
state.light[n].spot .direction	$(d_x,d_y,d_z,\cos\alpha)$	Light n spotlight direction **d** and cosine of spotlight cutoff angle α
state.light[n].half	$(H_x,H_y,H_z,1)$	Light n infinite halfway vector **H**.
state.lightmodel .ambient	(r,g,b,a)	Light model ambient color
state.lightmodel .scenecolor	(r,g,b,a)	Light model front scene color
state.lightmodel .front.scenecolor	(r,g,b,a)	Light model front scene color
state.lightmodel .back.scenecolor	(r,g,b,a)	Light model back scene color
state.lightprod[n] .ambient	(r,g,b,a)	Light n product of light ambient color and front material ambient color
state.lightprod[n] .diffuse	(r,g,b,a)	Light n product of light diffuse color and front material diffuse color
state.lightprod[n] .specular	(r,g,b,a)	Light n product of light specular color and front material specular color
state.lightprod[n] .front.ambient	(r,g,b,a)	Light n product of light ambient color and front material ambient color
state.lightprod[n] .front.diffuse	(r,g,b,a)	Light n product of light diffuse color and front material diffuse color
state.lightprod[n] .front.specular	(r,g,b,a)	Light n product of light specular color and front material specular color
state.lightprod[n] .back.ambient	(r,g,b,a)	Light n product of light ambient color and back material ambient color

(continues)

TABLE 18.1.6   *Continued*

Light Binding	Component Usage	Underlying State
`state.lightprod[n]` `.back.diffuse`	(r,g,b,a)	Light *n* product of light diffuse color and back material diffuse color
`state.lightprod[n]` `.back.specular`	(r,g,b,a)	Light *n* product of light specular color and back material specular color

For convenience and efficiency, it is possible to bind to precomputed quantities that are used in the lighting equation. The `state.light[n].half` state refers to the halfway vector for light *n* and a viewer at infinity. The 3D halfway vector **H** is given by

$$H = \frac{P + \langle 0,0,1 \rangle}{\| P + \langle 0,0,1 \rangle \|}, \tag{18.1.1}$$

where **P** is the 3D vector whose *x*, *y*, and *z* coordinates are the eye-space position of the infinite light.

The front-facing and back-facing scene colors C_{scene} represented by the states having the `.scenecolor` suffix are given by

$$C_{scene} = A_{lightmodel} A_{material} + E_{material}, \tag{18.1.2}$$

where $A_{lightmodel}$ is the light model ambient color, $A_{material}$ is the material ambient color, and $E_{material}$ is the material emission color.

The states whose names begin with `state.lightprod[n]` represent the front-facing and back-facing products of the light and material ambient, diffuse, and specular colors.

An identifier can be bound to a texture coordinate generation plane by using the PARAM statement with one of the names listed in Table 18.1.7. State names beginning with `state.texgen[n].eye` represent eye-space planes for texture unit *n*. State names beginning with `state.texgen[n].object` represent object-space planes for texture unit *n*.

TABLE 18.1.7   Texture Coordinate Generation Bindings

Texture Generation Binding	Component Usage	Underlying State
`state.texgen[n].eye.s`	(a,b,c,d)	Texture generation eye-space linear plane, *s* coordinate, unit *n*
`state.texgen[n].eye.t`	(a,b,c,d)	Texture generation eye-space linear plane, *t* coordinate, unit *n*
`state.texgen[n].eye.r`	(a,b,c,d)	Texture generation eye-space linear plane, *r* coordinate, unit *n*

TABLE 18.1.7 *Continued*

Texture Generation Binding	Component Usage	Underlying State
`state.texgen[n].eye.q`	(a,b,c,d)	Texture generation eye-space linear plane, q coordinate, unit n
`state.texgen[n].object.s`	(a,b,c,d)	Texture generation object-space linear plane, s coordinate, unit n
`state.texgen[n].object.t`	(a,b,c,d)	Texture generation object-space linear plane, t coordinate, unit n
`state.texgen[n].object.r`	(a,b,c,d)	Texture generation object-space linear plane, r coordinate, unit n
`state.texgen[n].object.q`	(a,b,c,d)	Texture generation object-space linear plane, q coordinate, unit n

An identifier can be bound to a fog property by using the PARAM statement with one of the names listed in Table 18.1.8. The `state.fog.color` state represents the fog color. The components of the `state.fog.params` state each have different meanings. The x component represents the fog density, the y and z components represent the start and end distance for linear fog, and the w component contains the reciprocal of the difference between the linear start and end distances.

TABLE 18.1.8 Fog Property Bindings

Fog Binding	Component Usage	Undelying State
`state.fog.color`	(r,g,b,a)	Fog color
`state.fog.params`	$\left(d,s,e,\dfrac{1}{e-s} \right)$	Fog density d, linear start distance s, linear end distance e, and reciprocal of $e-s$

An identifier can be bound to a user-defined clipping plane by using the PARAM statement with the name listed in Table 18.1.9.

TABLE 18.1.9 Clip Plane Property Bindings

Clip Plane Binding	Component Usage	Underlying State
`state.clip[n].plane`	(x,y,z,w)	Clip plane n

An identifier can be bound to a point property by using the PARAM statement with one of the names listed in Table 18.1.10.

TABLE 18.1.10   Point Property Bindings

Point Binding	Component Usage	Underlying State
state.point.size	(s, s_{min}, s_{max}, f)	Point size s, minimum and maximum sizes s_{min} and s_{max}, and fade threshold f
state.point.attenuation	$(a, b, c, 1)$	Point size attenuation constants

An identifier can be bound to a matrix by using the PARAM statement with one of the names listed in Table 18.1.11. The state.matrix.mvp state represents the product of the modelview and projection matrices that transforms vertex positions from object space directly into homogeneous clip space. Since matrices consist of four row vectors, an identifier must be declared as an array if it is bound to the entire matrix. For example, the following line binds the projection matrix to the identifier proj.

```
PARAM proj[] = state.matrix.projection;
```

Subsequent references to proj[0], proj[1], proj[2], and proj[3] represent the rows of the projection matrix. An identifier can be bound to a single row of a matrix by appending the suffix .row[n] to the matrix's name, where $0 \leq n \leq 3$. For example, the following line binds the first row of the modelview matrix to the identifier mv.

```
PARAM mv = state.matrix.modelview.row[0];
```

It is also possible to bind an identifier to fewer than all four rows of a matrix. This is accomplished by appending the suffix .row[a..b] to the matrix's name, where $0 \leq a \leq b \leq 3$. The following line binds the second and third rows of the modelview matrix to the identifier mv23.

```
PARAM mv23[] = state.matrix.modelview.row[1..2];
```

The identifier mv23 is an array with two entries. The expression mv23[0] refers to the second row of the modelview matrix, and the expression mv23[1] refers to the third row.

TABLE 18.1.11   Matrix Property Bindings

Matrix Binding	Underlying State
state.matrix.modelview	Modelview matrix 0
state.matrix.modelview[n]	Modelview matrix n
state.matrix.projection	Projection matrix
state.matrix.mvp	Modelview-projection matrix product
state.matrix.texture	Texture matrix, unit 0

TABLE 18.1.11 *Continued*

Matrix Binding	Underlying State
state.matrix.texture[n]	Texture matrix, unit n
state.matrix.palette[n]	Modelview palette matrix n
state.matrix.program[n]	Program matrix n

The program matrices represented by the array state.matrix.program[] refer to a set of generic matrices defined by the GL_ARB_vertex_program extension that may be used by an application for any purpose. The number of generic program matrices supported by an implementation, which is always at least 8, is retrieved by calling the **glGetIntegerv** function with *pname* parameter GL_MAX_PROGRAM_MATRICES_ARB. The program matrices are manipulated by setting the current matrix mode to GL_MATRIX*i*_ARB using the **glMatrixMode** function, where *i* is in the range 0 to GL_MAX_PROGRAM_MATRICES_ARB − 1. Subsequent matrix-related functions, such as **glLoadMatrix{fd}**, apply to the *i*th program matrix stack. The maximum depth of all program matrix stacks supported by an implementation is retrieved by passing GL_MAX_PROGRAM_MATRIX_STACK_DEPTH_ARB to **glGetIntegerv**.

The GL_ARB_vertex_program extension defines three constants that can be passed to the *pname* parameter of the **glGet** functions to retrieve information about the current matrix stack. The constant GL_CURRENT_MATRIX_ARB is used to retrieve the 16 entries of the matrix associated with the current matrix mode. The constant GL_TRANSPOSE_CURRENT_MATRIX_ARB retrieves the same matrix, but in transposed order. Finally, the constant GL_CURRENT_MATRIX_STACK_DEPTH_ARB is used to retrieve the number of matrices on the matrix stack associated with the current matrix mode.

Vertex Results

An identifier is bound to a vertex result register by using the OUTPUT statement with one of the names listed in Table 18.1.12. Identifiers bound to vertex result registers may only appear as a destination register for an instruction. If a vertex program does not utilize the position-invariant option, it must write to the result.position register.

TABLE 18.1.12 Vertex result bindings. Components labeled * are unused.

Vertex Result Binding	Component Usage	Description
result.position	(x,y,z,w)	Homogeneous clip-space position
result.color	(r,g,b,a)	Front-facing primary color
result.color.primary	(r,g,b,a)	Front-facing primary color

(continues)

TABLE 18.1.12   *Continued*

Vertex Result Binding	Component Usage	Description
result.color.secondary	(r,g,b,a)	Front-facing secondary color
result.color.front	(r,g,b,a)	Front-facing primary color
result.color.front.primary	(r,g,b,a)	Front-facing primary color
result.color.front.secondary	(r,g,b,a)	Front-facing secondary color
result.color.back	(r,g,b,a)	Back-facing primary color
result.color.back.primary	(r,g,b,a)	Back-facing primary color
result.color.back.secondary	(r,g,b,a)	Back-facing secondary color
result.fogcoord	(f,*,*,*)	Fog coordinate f
result.pointsize	(s,*,*,*)	Point size s
result.texcoord	(s,t,r,q)	Texture coordinates, unit 0
result.texcoord[n]	(s,t,r,q)	Texture coordinates, unit n

The back-facing primary and secondary colors represented by the result registers beginning with result.color.back are applied to back-facing polygons only when two-sided vertex program mode is enabled. Two-sided vertex program mode is enabled and disabled by calling the **glEnable** and **glDisable** functions with *cap* parameter GL_VERTEX_PROGRAM_TWO_SIDE_ARB. When two-sided vertex program mode is disabled (the initial state), the front-facing colors are always selected for both front-facing and back-facing polygons.

The point size written to the result.pointsize register is utilized during rasterization only if point-size vertex program mode is enabled. Point-size vertex program mode is enabled and disabled by calling the **glEnable** and **glDisable** functions with *cap* parameter GL_VERTEX_PROGRAM_POINT_SIZE_ARB. When point-size vertex program mode is disabled (the initial state), or the result.pointsize register is not written by a vertex program, a vertex's point size is determined by the current values of the point parameters.

Temporary Registers

Temporary registers are allocated by using the TEMP statement. The TEMP statement is followed by a comma-delimited list of identifiers, each of which becomes a general purpose read/write variable. For example, the following line declares temporary registers temp1 and temp2.

```
TEMP    temp1, temp2;
```

The maximum number of temporary registers that may be declared is determined by calling the **glGetProgramivARB** function with *pname* parameter GL_MAX_PROGRAM_TEMPORARIES_ARB. Temporary registers have undefined contents at the beginning of vertex program execution, and their final values are ignored.

Address Registers

Program parameters may be accessed using a relative offset from the contents of an address register. Address registers are allocated by using the ADDRESS statement. The ADDRESS statement has the same syntax as the TEMP statement, but declares a list of address registers. For example, the following line declares a single address register named addr.

```
ADDRESS     addr;
```

The maximum number of address registers that may be declared is determined by calling the **glGetProgramivARB** function with *pname* parameter GL_MAX_PROGRAM_ADDRESS_ REGISTERS_ARB. The initial contents of an address register are undefined.

An address register is loaded by using the ARL (address register load) instruction. In version 1.0 ARB vertex programs, only the x component of an address register may be accessed. A member of an array of program parameters associated with the identifier array can be accessed with the runtime-computed contents of an address register associated with the identifier addr using the notation array[addr.x+n], where n is an optional constant in the range −64 to 63. If the value addr.x+n is negative or exceeds the size of the array, then the result is undefined.

As an example, suppose a temporary register temp, an address register addr, and an array of program parameters, array, has been declared as follows:

```
TEMP        temp;
ADDRESS     addr;
PARAM       array[] = program.env[0..15];
```

Suppose that the result of some calculation has been placed in the register temp, and that the program wishes to use this result as an offset into the program parameters associated with array. Such an action can be achieved using the following code:

```
ARL     addr.x, temp.z;
MOV     result.color, array[addr.x+8];
```

In this example, the MOV instruction reads the value in the program parameter register associated with the array identifier at the offset given by 8 plus the value of the z component of the temp register. The ARL instruction converts the floating-point operand to an integer by rounding toward negative infinity.

Aliases

An alias may be declared for any identifier by using the ALIAS statement. The ALIAS statement simply establishes that one identifier has the same meaning as another, previously declared identifier. For example, the following code declares a temporary register named R0 and then declares an alias for it named N_dot_L. Either name, when used later in the program, refers to the same temporary register.

```
TEMP        R0;
ALIAS       N_dot_L = R0;
```

Program Resource Limits

An implementation is expected to execute vertex programs in hardware, but may also provide a software path that supports a greater number of instructions, registers, or program parameters. An application can retrieve the maximum vertex program limits imposed by a particular implementation by calling the **glGetProgramivARB** function,

```
void glGetProgramivARB(GLenum target,
                       GLenum pname,
                       GLint *params);
```

with *target* parameter GL_VERTEX_PROGRAM_ARB. The *pname* parameter specifies which value to return and may be any of the values listed in Table 18.1.13. The native limits that can be queried represent the resource limits beneath which a vertex program is guaranteed to be executed in hardware. If a vertex program exceeds the native limits, but not the absolute limits, then an application can expect lower performance, because the vertex program is probably being executed in software.

TABLE 18.1.13 Symbolic constants representing implementation-dependent vertex program resource limits. The native limits represent the maximum number of each resource that can be used in order to ensure that a vertex program is capable of being executed in hardware. The Min Value represents the minimum requirements for any vertex program implementation.

Constant Representing Absolute Limit	Constant Representing Native Limit	Description	Min Value
GL_MAX_PROGRAM_ INSTRUCTIONS_ARB	GL_MAX_PROGRAM_ NATIVE_INSTRUCTIONS_ARB	The maximum number of instructions.	128
GL_MAX_PROGRAM_ ATTRIBS_ARB	GL_MAX_PROGRAM_ NATIVE_ATTRIBS_ARB	The maximum number of vertex attributes declared.	16
GL_MAX_PROGRAM_ PARAMETERS_ARB	GL_MAX_PROGRAM_ NATIVE_PARAMETERS_ARB	The maximum of the sum of the numbers of program environment parameters, program local parameters, and OpenGL state parameters declared.	96
GL_MAX_PROGRAM_ TEMPORARIES_ARB	GL_MAX_PROGRAM_ NATIVE_TEMPORARIES_ARB	The maximum number of temporary registers declared.	12
GL_MAX_PROGRAM_ ADDRESS_REGISTERS_ARB	GL_MAX_PROGRAM_ NATIVE_ADDRESS_REGISTERS_ARB	The maximum number of address registers declared.	1

The **glGetProgramivARB** function is also used to retrieve the numbers of different types of resources used by the currently bound vertex program. Table 18.1.14 lists the resources that can be queried. Separate queries are provided to allow retrieval of the native resource counts used by the implementation after it compiles a vertex program. The native resources used may be greater than the number of instructions, registers, parameters, and so forth declared in a vertex program, because certain hardware implementations may have to emulate some instructions by using multiple native instructions and extra temporary registers. The symbolic constant GL_PROGRAM_UNDER_NATIVE_LIMITS_ARB can be passed to the *pname* parameter of the **glGetProgramivARB** function to determine whether the currently bound vertex program falls within the hardware limits of the implementation.

TABLE 18.1.14 Symbolic constants representing the resources consumed by a vertex program. The native resources represent the number of each type of resource used by the implementation to execute the vertex program in hardware.

Constant Representing Resource Usage	*Constant Representing Native Resource Usage*	*Description*
GL_PROGRAM_ INSTRUCTIONS_ARB	GL_PROGRAM_ NATIVE_INSTRUCTIONS_ARB	The number of instructions used.
GL_PROGRAM_ ATTRIBS_ARB	GL_PROGRAM_ NATIVE_ATTRIBS_ARB	The number of vertex attributes used.
GL_PROGRAM_ PARAMETERS_ARB	GL_PROGRAM_ NATIVE_PARAMETERS_ARB	The sum of the numbers of program environment parameters, program local parameters, and OpenGL state parameters used.
GL_PROGRAM_ TEMPORARIES_ARB	GL_PROGRAM_ NATIVE_TEMPORARIES_ARB	The number of temporary registers used.
GL_PROGRAM_ ADDRESS_REGISTERS_ARB	GL_PROGRAM_ NATIVE_ADDRESS_REGISTERS_ARB	The number of address registers used.

Instruction Set

There are 27 vertex program instructions. The operation performed by each instruction and the corresponding types of input operands and output results are listed in Table 18.1.15.

TABLE 18.1.15 Vertex program instructions. The letter "v" indicates a vector result or operand, and the letter "s" indicates a scalar operand. The vector $\langle s,s,s,s \rangle$ represents a single scalar result that is replicated to all four components of the result vector.

Instruction	Output Result	Input Operands	Operation
ABS	v	v	Absolute value
ADD	v	v, v	Add
ARL	address	s	Address register load
DP3	$\langle s,s,s,s \rangle$	v, v	3D dot product
DP4	$\langle s,s,s,s \rangle$	v, v	4D dot product
DPH	$\langle s,s,s,s \rangle$	v, v	Homogeneous dot product
DST	v	v, v	Distance vector
EX2	$\langle s,s,s,s \rangle$	s	Exponential base 2
EXP	v	s	Approximate exponential base 2
FLR	v	v	Floor
FRC	v	v	Fraction
LG2	$\langle s,s,s,s \rangle$	s	Logarithm base 2
LIT	v	v	Light coefficients
LOG	v	s	Approximate logarithm base 2
MAD	v	v, v, v	Multiply-add
MAX	v	v, v	Maximum
MIN	v	v, v	Minimum
MOV	v	v	Move
MUL	v	v, v	Multiply
POW	$\langle s,s,s,s \rangle$	s, s	Exponentiate
RCP	$\langle s,s,s,s \rangle$	s	Reciprocal
RSQ	$\langle s,s,s,s \rangle$	s	Reciprocal square root
SGE	v	v, v	Set on greater than or equal to
SLT	v	v, v	Set on less than
SUB	v	v, v	Subtract
SWZ	v	v	Extended swizzle
XPD	v	v, v	Cross product

Each of the vertex program instructions is described in detail below. Included with each instruction is pseudocode that demonstrates the instruction's exact effect. The types vec-tor and scalar are used to hold four-component vector quantities and one-component scalar quantities, respectively. When loading data from a register, the pseudocode makes use of the functions `VectorLoad` and `ScalarLoad` to apply the swizzle and negate operations to each operand. In the definitions of these functions, which follow, the `.swiz[n]` field used with the `source` parameter denotes the *n*th component of the source vector after swizzling. The `.comp` field used with the `source` parameter denotes the scalar component selected using the single-component suffix in the vertex program. The value of `negate` is true if the program specifies that the source operand is negated, and false otherwise.

```
vector VectorLoad(vector source)
{
    vector    operand;

    operand.x = source.swiz[0];
    operand.y = source.swiz[1];
    operand.z = source.swiz[2];
    operand.w = source.swiz[3];
    if (negate)
    {
        operand.x = -operand.x;
        operand.y = -operand.y;
        operand.z = -operand.z;
        operand.w = -operand.w;
    }

    return (operand);
}

scalar ScalarLoad(vector source)
{
    scalar    operand;

    operand = source.comp;
    if (negate) operand = -operand;

    return (operand);
}
```

When a vector result is written to a destination register, the pseudocode makes use of the `WriteDest` function to apply the write mask. In the definition of this function, which follows, each of the components of `mask` is true if writing is enabled for the corresponding component of the destination register, and false if writing is disabled.

```
vector WriteDest(vector dest, vector result)
{
    if (mask.x) dest.x = result.x;
    if (mask.y) dest.y = result.y;
    if (mask.z) dest.z = result.z;
```

```
        if (mask.w) dest.w = result.w;

        return (dest);
    }
```

The exact effect of each vertex program instruction follows. The local variable r is used in most of the pseudocode listings and always denotes a temporary vector quantity.

ABS—Absolute value

```
    ABS     result, op0;
```

The ABS instruction performs a componentwise absolute value operation on a single operand.

```
    vector v0 = VectorLoad(op0);
    r.x = fabs(v0.x);
    r.y = fabs(v0.y);
    r.z = fabs(v0.z);
    r.w = fabs(v0.w);
    result = WriteDest(result, r);
```

ADD—Add

```
    ADD     result, op0, op1;
```

The ADD instruction performs a componentwise addition of two operands.

```
    vector v0 = VectorLoad(op0);
    vector v1 = VectorLoad(op1);
    r.x = v0.x + v1.x;
    r.y = v0.y + v1.y;
    r.z = v0.z + v1.z;
    r.w = v0.w + v1.w;
    result = WriteDest(result, r);
```

The addition operation satisfies the following rules:

1. $x + y = y + x$ for all x and y.
2. $x + 0.0 = x$ for all x.

ARL—Address register load

```
    ARL     result.x, op0;
```

The ARL instruction loads the address register with a scalar signed integer.

```
    result.x = floor(ScalarLoad(op0));
```

DP3—Three-component dot product

```
DP3     result, op0, op1;
```

The DP3 instruction performs a three-component dot product between two operands and replicates the result to all four components of the destination.

```
vector v0 = VectorLoad(op0);
vector v1 = VectorLoad(op1);
scalar dot = v0.x * v1.x + v0.y + v1.y + v0.z * v1.z;
r.x = dot;
r.y = dot;
r.z = dot;
r.w = dot;
result = WriteDest(result, r);
```

DP4—Four-component dot product

```
DP4     result, op0, op1;
```

The DP4 instruction performs a four-component dot product between two operands and replicates the result to all four components of the destination.

```
vector v0 = VectorLoad(op0);
vector v1 = VectorLoad(op1);
scalar dot = v0.x * v1.x + v0.y + v1.y
            + v0.z * v1.z + v0.w * v1.w;
r.x = dot;
r.y = dot;
r.z = dot;
r.w = dot;
result = WriteDest(result, r);
```

DPH—Homogeneous dot product

```
DPH     result, op0, op1;
```

The DPH instruction performs a three-component dot product between two operands and adds the *w* component of the second operand. The result is replicated to all four components of the destination.

```
vector v0 = VectorLoad(op0);
vector v1 = VectorLoad(op1);
scalar dot = v0.x * v1.x + v0.y + v1.y
            + v0.z * v1.z + v1.w;
r.x = dot;
r.y = dot;
r.z = dot;
r.w = dot;
result = WriteDest(result, r);
```

The DPH instruction may be emulated by two native instructions on some implementations.

DST—Distance vector

```
DST     result, op0, op1;
```

The DST instruction takes two operands and produces a vector that is useful for attenuation calculations. Given a distance d, the first operand should be formatted as $\langle *,d^2,d^2,* \rangle$ and the second operation should be formatted as $\langle *,1/d,*,1/d \rangle$, where * indicates that the operand's component is not used. The result of the DST instruction is the vector $\langle 1,d,d^2,1/d \rangle$.

```
vector v0 = VectorLoad(op0);
vector v1 = VectorLoad(op1);
r.x = 1.0;
r.y = v0.y * v1.y;
r.z = v0.z;
r.w = v1.w;
result = WriteDest(result, r);
```

EX2—Exponential base 2

```
EX2     result, op0;
```

The EX2 instruction calculates an approximation to 2^p for a single scalar operand p and replicates the result to all four components of the destination.

```
scalar e = ApproxExp2(ScalarLoad(op0));
r.x = e;
r.y = e;
r.z = e;
r.w = e;
result = WriteDest(result, r);
```

The EX2 instruction may be emulated using several native instructions on some implementations. This can be avoided, at the possible cost of precision, by using the EXP instruction.

EXP—Approximate exponential base 2

```
EXP     result, op0;
```

The EXP instruction calculates a rough approximation to 2^p for a single scalar operand p. The result of the exponentiation is returned in the z component of the destination.

```
scalar s0 = ScalarLoad(op0);
r.x = pow(2, floor(s0));
r.y = s0 - floor(s0);
r.z = RoughApproxExp2(s0);
```

```
r.w = 1.0;
result = WriteDest(result, r);
```

The `RoughApproxExp2` function satisfies the precision requirement

$$\left| \text{RoughApproxExp2}(x) - 2^x \right| < \begin{cases} 2^{-11}, & \text{if } 0 \le x < 1; \\ 2^{-11} \cdot 2^{\lfloor x \rfloor}, & \text{otherwise.} \end{cases}$$

FLR—Floor

```
FLR     result, op0;
```

The `FLR` instruction performs a componentwise floor operation on a single operand.

```
vector v0 = VectorLoad(op0);
r.x = floor(v0.x);
r.y = floor(v0.y);
r.z = floor(v0.z);
r.w = floor(v0.w);
result = WriteDest(result, r);
```

The `FLR` instruction may be emulated by multiple native instructions on some implementations.

FRC—Fraction

```
FRC     result, op0;
```

The `FRC` instruction performs a componentwise fraction operation on a single operand. The fraction operation is equivalent to subtracting the floor of the operand from the operand itself.

```
vector v0 = VectorLoad(op0);
r.x = v0.x - floor(v0.x);
r.y = v0.y - floor(v0.y);
r.z = v0.z - floor(v0.z);
r.w = v0.w - floor(v0.w);
result = WriteDest(result, r);
```

The `FRC` instruction may be emulated by multiple native instructions on some implementations.

LG2—Logarithm base 2

```
LG2     result, op0;
```

The `LG2` instruction calculates an approximation to $\log_2(p)$ for a single scalar operand p and replicates the result to all four components of the destination.

```
scalar l = ApproxLog2(ScalarLoad(op0));
r.x = l;
r.y = l;
r.z = l;
r.w = l;
result = WriteDest(result, r);
```

The `LG2` instruction may be emulated using several native instructions on some implementations. This can be avoided, at the possible cost of precision, by using the `LOG` instruction.

LIT—Light coefficients

```
LIT     result, op0;
```

The `LIT` instruction takes a single operand and produces a coefficient vector that is useful for lighting calculations. The operand is assumed to be formatted as $\langle \mathbf{N} \cdot \mathbf{L}, \mathbf{N} \cdot \mathbf{H}, *, m \rangle$ where $\mathbf{N} \cdot \mathbf{L}$ is the diffuse dot product, $\mathbf{N} \cdot \mathbf{H}$ is the specular dot product, m is the specular exponent, and * indicates that the z component is unused. The result of the `LIT` instruction is the vector $\langle 1.0, \mathbf{N} \cdot \mathbf{L}, (\mathbf{N} \cdot \mathbf{H})^m, 1.0 \rangle$, where $\mathbf{N} \cdot \mathbf{L}$ and $\mathbf{N} \cdot \mathbf{H}$ are clamped to 0.0, and the z component is set to 0.0 if $\mathbf{N} \cdot \mathbf{L} \leq 0$. The specular exponent m is clamped to the range $[-128, 128]$.

```
vector v0 = VectorLoad(op0);
if (v0.x < 0.0) v0.x = 0.0;
if (v0.y < 0.0) v0.y = 0.0;
if (v0.w < -128.0 + epsilon) v0.w = -128.0 + epsilon;
else if (v0.w > 128.0 - epsilon) v0.w = 128.0 - epsilon;
r.x = 1.0;
r.y = v0.x;
r.z = (v0.x > 0.0) ? RoughApproxPow(v0.y, v0.w) : 0.0;
r.w = 1.0;
result = WriteDest(result, r);
```

The `RoughApproxPow` function is defined in terms of the rough base-2 exponential and logarithm functions implemented by the `EXP` and `LOG` instructions. Thus,

```
RoughApproxPow(b, e) = RoughApproxExp2(e * RoughApproxLog2(b))
```

and the precision of the `RoughApproxPow` function is limited by the precision of the `RoughApproxExp2` and `RoughApproxLog2` functions.

LOG—Approximate logarithm base 2

```
LOG     result, op0;
```

The `LOG` instruction calculates a rough approximation to $\log_2(p)$ for a single scalar operand p. The result of the operation is returned in the z component of the destination.

```
scalar s0 = fabs(ScalarLoad(op0));
r.x = floor(log2(s0));
r.y = s0 * pow(2, -floor(log2(s0)));
r.z = RoughApproxLog2(s0);
r.w = 1.0;
result = WriteDest(result, r);
```

The `RoughApproxLog2` function satisfies the precision requirement

$$\left| \text{RoughApproxLog2}(x) - \log_2 x \right| < 2^{-11}.$$

MAD—Multiply-add

```
MAD     result, op0, op1, op2;
```

The `MAD` instruction performs a componentwise multiplication and addition of three operands.

```
vector v0 = VectorLoad(op0);
vector v1 = VectorLoad(op1);
vector v2 = VectorLoad(op2);
r.x = v0.x * v1.x + v2.x;
r.y = v0.y * v1.y + v2.y;
r.z = v0.z * v1.z + v2.z;
r.w = v0.w * v1.w + v2.w;
result = WriteDest(result, r);
```

The multiplication and addition operations are subject to the same rules described for the `MUL` and `ADD` instructions.

MAX—Maximum

```
MAX     result, op0, op1;
```

The `MAX` instruction performs a componentwise maximum operation between two operands.

```
vector v0 = VectorLoad(op0);
vector v1 = VectorLoad(op1);
r.x = (v0.x > v1.x) ? v0.x : v1.x;
r.y = (v0.y > v1.y) ? v0.y : v1.y;
r.z = (v0.z > v1.z) ? v0.z : v1.z;
r.w = (v0.w > v1.w) ? v0.w : v1.w;
result = WriteDest(result, r);
```

MIN–Minimum

```
MIN     result, op0, op1;
```

The `MIN` instruction performs a componentwise minimum operation between two operands.

```
vector v0 = VectorLoad(op0);
vector v1 = VectorLoad(op1);
r.x = (v0.x > v1.x) ? v1.x : v0.x;
r.y = (v0.y > v1.y) ? v1.y : v0.y;
r.z = (v0.z > v1.z) ? v1.z : v0.z;
r.w = (v0.w > v1.w) ? v1.w : v0.w;
result = WriteDest(result, r);
```

MOV–Move

```
MOV     result, op0;
```

The `MOV` instruction copies a single operand to the destination.

```
vector v0 = VectorLoad(op0);
result = WriteDest(result, v0);
```

MUL–Multiply

```
MUL     result, op0, op1;
```

The `MUL` instruction performs a componentwise multiplication of two operands.

```
vector v0 = VectorLoad(op0);
vector v1 = VectorLoad(op1);
r.x = v0.x * v1.x;
r.y = v0.y * v1.y;
r.z = v0.z * v1.z;
r.w = v0.w * v1.w;
result = WriteDest(result, r);
```

The multiplication operation satisfies the following rules:

1. $xy = yx$ for all x and y.
2. $x \cdot 1.0 = x$ for all x.
3. $x \cdot \pm 0.0 = \pm 0.0$ for all x, with the possible exceptions of $\pm INF$ and $\pm NAN$.

POW–Exponentiate

```
POW     result, op0, op1;
```

The `POW` instruction calculates an approximation to b^e for two scalar operands b and e, and replicates the result to all four components of the destination.

```
scalar s0 = ScalarLoad(op0);
scalar s1 = ScalarLoad(op1);
scalar p = ApproxPow(op0, op1);
r.x = p;
r.y = p;
r.z = p;
r.w = p;
result = WriteDest(result, r);
```

The ApproxPow function may be implemented using the base-2 exponentiation and logarithm functions defined by the EX2 and LG2 functions. Thus,

```
ApproxPow(b, e) = ApproxExp2(e * ApproxLog2(b)).
```

It may not be possible to correctly raise a negative base to an integer power, since a logarithm is involved.

RCP–Reciprocal

```
RCP     result, op0;
```

The RCP instruction approximates the reciprocal of a single scalar operand and replicates the result to all four components of the destination.

```
scalar s0 = ScalarLoad(op0);
scalar recip = ApproxRecip(s0);
r.x = recip;
r.y = recip;
r.z = recip;
r.w = recip;
result = WriteDest(result, r);
```

The reciprocation operation satisfies the following rule:

$$\text{ApproxRecip}(+1.0) = +1.0$$

RSQ–Reciprocal square root

```
RSQ     result, op0;
```

The RSQ instruction approximates the reciprocal square root of the absolute value of a single scalar operand and replicates the result to all four components of the destination.

```
scalar s0 = fabs(ScalarLoad(op0));
scalar rsqrt = ApproxRSQRT(s0);
r.x = rsqrt;
r.y = rsqrt;
r.z = rsqrt;
```

```
r.w = rsqrt;
result = WriteDest(result, r);
```

SGE—Set on greater than or equal to

```
SGE     result, op0, op1;
```

The SGE instruction performs a componentwise comparison between two operands. Each component of the result vector is set to 1.0 if the corresponding component of the first operand is greater than or equal to the corresponding component of the second operand, and is set to 0.0 otherwise.

```
vector v0 = VectorLoad(op0);
vector v1 = VectorLoad(op1);
r.x = (v0.x >= v1.x) ? 1.0 : 0.0;
r.y = (v0.y >= v1.y) ? 1.0 : 0.0;
r.z = (v0.z >= v1.z) ? 1.0 : 0.0;
r.w = (v0.w >= v1.w) ? 1.0 : 0.0;
result = WriteDest(result, r);
```

SLT—Set on less than

```
SLT     result, op0, op1;
```

The SLT instruction performs a componentwise comparison between two operands. Each component of the result vector is set to 1.0 if the corresponding component of the first operand is less than the corresponding component of the second operand, and is set to 0.0 otherwise.

```
vector v0 = VectorLoad(op0);
vector v1 = VectorLoad(op1);
r.x = (v0.x < v1.x) ? 1.0 : 0.0;
r.y = (v0.y < v1.y) ? 1.0 : 0.0;
r.z = (v0.z < v1.z) ? 1.0 : 0.0;
r.w = (v0.w < v1.w) ? 1.0 : 0.0;
result = WriteDest(result, r);
```

SUB—Subtract

```
SUB     result, op0, op1;
```

The SUB instruction performs a componentwise subtraction of two operands.

```
vector v0 = VectorLoad(op0);
vector v1 = VectorLoad(op1);
r.x = v0.x - v1.x;
r.y = v0.y - v1.y;
r.z = v0.z - v1.z;
r.w = v0.w - v1.w;
result = WriteDest(result, r);
```

SWZ—Extended swizzle

```
SWZ     result, op0, xswiz, yswiz, zswiz, wswiz;
```

The SWZ instruction performs an extended swizzle operation on a single operand. Each component of the result is determined by selecting any component of the operand, the constant 0, or the constant 1, and optionally negating it. The following pseudocode describes the swizzle operation for a single component. The op parameter represents the source operand, the select enumerant represents the component selection where ZERO, ONE, X, Y, Z, and W correspond to the characters "0", "1", "x", "y", "z", and "w" used in the program string, and the negate parameter indicates whether the component is negated.

```
float SwizzleComp(vector op, enum select, bool negate)
{
    float result;

    switch (select)
    {
        case ZERO:      result = 0.0; break;
        case ONE:       result = 1.0; break;
        case X:         result = op.x; break;
        case Y:         result = op.y; break;
        case Z:         result = op.z; break;
        case W:         result = op.w; break;
    }

    if (negate) result = -result;
    return (result);
}
```

The entire extended swizzle is then performed as follows, where *k*Select and *k*Negate represent the swizzle selection and optional negation for each component of the source operand.

```
r.x = SwizzleComp(op0, xSelect, xNegate);
r.y = SwizzleComp(op0, ySelect, yNegate);
r.z = SwizzleComp(op0, zSelect, zNegate);
r.w = SwizzleComp(op0, wSelect, wNegate);
result = WriteDest(result, r);
```

The SWZ instruction may be emulated using two native instructions and a program parameter register on some implementations.

XPD—Cross product

```
XPD     result, op0, op1;
```

The XPD instruction calculates the three-component cross product between two operands. The result is a three-component vector that is stored in the x, y, and z components of the destination. The w component of the destination is undefined.

```
vector v0 = VectorLoad(op0);
vector v1 = VectorLoad(op1);
r.x = v0.y * v1.z - v0.z * v1.y;
r.y = v0.z * v1.x - v0.x * v1.z;
r.z = v0.x * v1.y - v0.y * v1.x;
result = WriteDest(result, r);
```

The XPD instruction may be emulated using two native instructions on some implementations.

Position-Invariant Programs

Vertex programs that transform a vertex position from object space to homogeneous clip space are not guaranteed to produce exactly the same viewport coordinates as does the conventional vertex transformation pipeline. As a consequence, any multipass rendering algorithm that uses vertex programs for any passes must use vertex programs for all passes even though the needed functionality for some passes may be achievable using conventional vertex transformations. Otherwise, undesirable depth-buffering artifacts can appear.

In order to facilitate the mixture of passes using vertex programs and passes using conventional OpenGL transformations, a position-invariant option exists. A vertex program is designated a position-invariant vertex program by inserting the following line before any vertex program instructions:

```
OPTION    ARB_position_invariant;
```

When the position-invariant option is present, a vertex program may *not* write a homogeneous clip-space position to the output register result.position, because the driver will insert the calculation itself using the same process that it uses for conventional vertex transformations. To provide space for the driver to add this calculation, position-invariant vertex programs are limited to four fewer instructions than the number returned by the **glGetProgramivARB** function with *pname* parameter GL_MAX_NATIVE_PROGRAM_INSTRUCTIONS_ARB.

Program Management

Vertex programs follow the named object convention that is used elsewhere in OpenGL for such things as texture objects. A vertex program is identified by a name taken from the set of unsigned integers. Previously unused names for vertex program objects are allocated by calling the **glGenProgramsARB** function,

```
void glGenProgramsARB(GLsizei n,
                      GLuint *programs);
```

This function generates *n* names and writes them to the array pointed to by the *programs* parameter. The names generated are marked as used, but the associated vertex program objects are not actually created until the first time a new name is passed to the **glBindProgramARB** function.

Vertex program objects are deleted and the associated names are freed by calling the **glDeleteProgramsARB** function,

```
void glDeleteProgramsARB(GLsizei n,
                          const GLuint *programs);
```

Any of the *n* names passed to this function in the array pointed to by the *programs* parameter that do not refer to existing vertex program objects are silently ignored. Once a vertex program object is deleted, its name is marked as unused. The **glIsProgramARB** function,

```
GLboolean glIsProgramARB(GLuint program);
```

can be used to determine whether a particular name specified by the *program* parameter refers to an existing vertex program object.

A vertex program object is bound to the vertex program target by calling the **glBind-ProgramARB** function,

```
void glBindProgramARB(GLenum target,
                       GLuint program);
```

with *target* parameter GL_VERTEX_PROGRAM_ARB. The *program* parameter specifies the name of the vertex program object. The first time that a program is bound for a particular name, a vertex program object is created for that name. A program string for the currently bound vertex program object is loaded by calling the **glProgramStringARB** function,

```
void glProgramStringARB(GLenum target,
                         GLenum format,
                         GLsizei len,
                         const GLvoid *string);
```

with *target* parameter GL_VERTEX_PROGRAM_ARB. The *format* parameter specifies the character set of the program string and must be GL_PROGRAM_FORMAT_ASCII_ARB. The *len* parameter specifies the length of the program string pointed to by the *string* parameter. A program string may be loaded for the same vertex program object multiple times.

When vertex program mode is enabled (by calling **glEnable** with *cap* parameter GL_VERTEX_PROGRAM_ARB), the currently bound vertex program is invoked for every vertex passed to OpenGL.

USEFUL TIPS

How do I transform a vertex position from object space to homogeneous clip space?

A 4D vector is transformed from object space to homogeneous clip space by multiplying it by the product of the modelview and projection matrices. This product is accessible through the state.matrix.mvp state parameter. The following code outputs the homogenous clip-space position in the result.position vertex result register.

```
PARAM     transform[] = state.matrix.mvp;
ATTRIB    object_position = vertex.position;
OUTPUT    out = result.position;

DP4    out.x, transform[0], object_position;
DP4    out.y, transform[1], object_position;
DP4    out.z, transform[2], object_position;
DP4    out.w, transform[3], object_position;
```

How do I normalize a 3D vector?

A 3D vector can be normalized by multiplying it by the reciprocal of its magnitude. The square of the magnitude of a 3D vector is obtained by using a DP3 instruction to calculate the dot product of the vector with itself. The following code normalizes the 3D vector stored in vec.

```
# Normalize <vec.x, vec.y, vec.z>

DP3    tmp, vec, vec;
RSQ    tmp, tmp.x;
MUL    vec.xyz, vec, tmp;
```

How do I perform a set on greater than or a set on less than or equal to?

Since $x > y$ if and only if $-x < -y$, the SLT instruction can be used with negated operands to implement a 'set on greater than' (SGT) instruction. Similarly, since $x \leq y$ if and only if $-x \geq -y$, the SGE instruction can be used with negated operands to implement a 'set on less than or equal to' (SLE) instruction. These are demonstrated in the following code.

```
# SGT gt, vec1, vec2;
# SLE le, vec1, vec2;

SLT    gt, -vec1, -vec2;
SGE    le, -vec1, -vec2;
```

How do I refine a reciprocal approximation using Newton-Raphson iteration?

Given an approximation r to the reciprocal of x, a refined approximation r' is given by the formula

$$r' = r(2 - xr). \tag{18.1.3}$$

The following code calculates the approximate reciprocal of vec.x and then performs a single Newton-Raphson iteration.

```
# constant.x = 2.0
# recip = 1.0 / vec.x
```

```
RCP    recip, vec.x;
MAD    tmp, vec.x, -recip, constant.x;
MUL    recip, tmp, recip;
```

How do I refine a reciprocal square root approximation using Newton-Raphson iteration?

Given an approximation r to the reciprocal square root of x, a refined approximation r' is given by the formula

$$r' = \frac{1}{2}r(3 - xr^2).$$

(18.1.4)

The following code calculates the approximate reciprocal square root of `vec.x` and then performs a single Newton-Raphson iteration.

```
# constant = <0.5, 3.0, 0.0, 0.0>
# rsqrt = 1.0 / sqrt(vec.x)

RSQ    rsqrt, vec.x;
MUL    tmp, rsqrt, rsqrt;
MAD    tmp, vec.x, -tmp, constant.y;
MUL    rsqrt, tmp, rsqrt;
MUL    rsqrt, rsqrt, constant.x;
```

NEW FUNCTIONS

■ **glProgramStringARB**—Specify a program string.

Prototype

```
void glProgramStringARB(GLenum target,
                        GLenum format,
                        GLsizei len,
                        const GLvoid *string);
```

Parameters

target   Specifies the target program. Must be GL_VERTEX_PROGRAM_ARB.

format   Specifies the character set of the program string. Must be GL_
               PROGRAM_FORMAT_ASCII_ARB.

len   Specifies the length of the program string.

string   Specifies a pointer to the program string. This string does not need to be
               null-terminated.

Description

The **glProgramStringARB** function loads the program string for the program currently bound to the target specified by the *target* parameter. The character set of the program string is specified by the *format* parameter and currently can only be GL_PROGRAM_FORMAT_ ASCII_ARB. The length of the program string is passed to the *len* parameter.

At the time **glProgramStringARB** is called, the program string is parsed and checked for syntactic validity. If the program fails to load because it contains an error, the error GL_ INVALID_OPERATION is generated.

The values of GL_PROGRAM_ERROR_POSITION_ARB and GL_PROGRAM_ERROR_STRING_ARB are always updated when **glProgramStringARB** is called. If a program loads successfully, the error position is set to −1, but the error string may still contain warning messages. If a program fails to load, the error position is set to the byte offset within the program at which the error occurred. If a program generates an error that can be detected only after the entire program string is interpreted, then the error position is set to the length of the program string. The error position can be retrieved by calling the **glGetIntegerv** function with *pname* parameter GL_PROGRAM_ERROR_POSITION_ARB. The error string contains a description of the error that occurred and can be retrieved by calling the **glGetString** function with *pname* parameter GL_PROGRAM_ERROR_STRING_ARB.

Special Considerations

The **glProgramStringARB** function is also defined by the GL_ARB_fragment_program extension.

Get Functions

glGetProgramStringARB

glGetProgramivARB with *pname* parameter GL_PROGRAM_LENGTH_ARB

glGetProgramivARB with *pname* parameter GL_PROGRAM_FORMAT_ARB

glGetIntegerv with *pname* parameter GL_PROGRAM_ERROR_POSITION_ARB

glGetString with *pname* parameter GL_PROGRAM_ERROR_STRING_ARB

Errors

GL_INVALID_OPERATION is generated if the program string violates the syntactic or semantic rules of the target program.

■ **glGenProgramsARB**—Generate program names.

Prototype

```
void glGenProgramsARB(GLsizei n,
                      GLuint *programs);
```

Parameters

n	Specifies the number of program names to generate.
programs	Specifies a pointer to an array that receives the generated program names.

Description

The **glGenProgramsARB** function returns a set of *n* unused program names in the array pointed to by the *programs* parameter. Each of the returned names is reserved with respect to program name generation, but does not represent an existing program object until it is bound to a program target using the **glBindProgramARB** function.

Programs are deleted and the associated program names are freed by calling the **glDeleteProgramsARB** function.

Special Considerations

The **glGenProgramsARB** function is also defined by the GL_ARB_fragment_program extension.

Get Functions

glIsProgramARB

Errors

GL_INVALID_VALUE is generated if *n* is negative.

■ **glDeleteProgramsARB**—Delete named programs.

Prototype

```
void glDeleteProgramsARB(GLsizei n,
                         const GLuint *programs);
```

Parameters

n   Specifies the number of programs to delete.

programs   Specifies a pointer to an array of program names to be deleted.

Description

The **glDeleteProgramsARB** function deletes the *n* programs contained in the array pointer to by the *programs* parameter. When a program object is deleted, it becomes nonexistent, and its name becomes unused. Deleted program names may subsequently be returned by the **glGenProgramsARB** function. Any unused program names found in the array pointed to by the *programs* parameter are silently ignored.

If a vertex program is deleted when it is the currently bound program, it is as if the **glBindProgramARB** function had been called with *program* parameter 0.

Special Considerations

The **glDeleteProgramsARB** function is also defined by the GL_ARB_fragment_program extension.

Get Functions

glIsProgramARB

Errors

GL_INVALID_VALUE is generated if *n* is negative.

■ **glBindProgramARB**—Bind a named program to a program target.

Prototype

```
void glBindProgramARB(GLenum target,
                      GLuint program);
```

Parameters

target   Specifies the target to which the program is bound. Must be GL_
                  VERTEX_PROGRAM_ARB.

program   Specifies the name of the program to bind.

Description

The **glBindProgramARB** function sets the current vertex program that is invoked for every vertex. If a previously nonexistent program is bound, then it becomes existent at the time that **glBindProgramARB** is called, and its program string is initially empty. A program may subsequently be loaded for the newly created program object by calling the **glProgram-StringARB** function.

Program 0 is implicitly bound if the currently bound vertex program is deleted by the **glDeleteProgramsARB** function.

Special Considerations

The **glBindProgramARB** function is also defined by the GL_ARB_fragment_program extension.

Get Functions

glGetProgramivARB with *pname* parameter GL_PROGRAM_BINDING_ARB

Errors

GL_INVALID_OPERATION is generated if *program* is the name of a program whose target does not match *target*.

■ **glIsProgramARB**—Determine if a name corresponds to a program.

Prototype

```
GLboolean glIsProgramARB(GLuint program);
```

Parameters

program   Specifies the name of a program.

Description

The **glIsProgramARB** function returns GL_TRUE if the *program* parameter names an existing program. Otherwise, it returns GL_FALSE.

A program name generated by the **glGenProgramsARB** function does not refer to an existing program until it is bound using the **glBindProgramARB** function.

Special Considerations

The **glIsProgramARB** function is also defined by the GL_ARB_fragment_program extension.

■ **glProgramEnvParameter4{fd}[v]ARB**—Specify a program environment parameter.

Prototypes

```
void glProgramEnvParameter4fARB(GLenum target,
                                GLuint index,
                                GLfloat x,
                                GLfloat y,
                                GLfloat z,
                                GLfloat w);
void glProgramEnvParameter4dARB(GLenum target,
                                GLuint index,
                                GLdouble x,
                                GLdouble y,
                                GLdouble z,
                                GLdouble w);
```

Parameters

target	Specifies the target program. Must be GL_VERTEX_PROGRAM_ARB.
index	Specifies the index of a program environment parameter. Must be in the range 0 to GL_MAX_PROGRAM_ENV_PARAMETERS_ARB − 1.
x, y, z, w	Specify the components of the program environment parameter.

Prototypes

```
void glProgramEnvParameter4fvARB(GLenum target,
                                 GLuint index,
                                 const GLfloat *params);
void glProgramEnvParameter4dvARB(GLenum target,
                                 GLuint index,
                                 const GLdouble *params);
```

Parameters

target	Specifies the target program. Must be GL_VERTEX_PROGRAM_ARB.
index	Specifies the index of a program environment parameter. Must be in the range 0 to GL_MAX_PROGRAM_ENV_PARAMETERS_ARB − 1.

params   Specifies a pointer to an array containing the four-component program environment parameter.

Description

The **glProgramEnvParameter4{fd}[v]ARB** function specifies a four-component, floating-point vector for the program environment parameter specified by *index*. Program environment parameters are shared by all vertex programs.

Special Considerations

The **glProgramEnvParameter4{fd}[v]ARB** function is also defined by the GL_ARB_ fragment_program extension.

Get Functions

glGetProgramEnvParameter{fd}vARB

glGetProgramivARB with *pname* parameter GL_MAX_PROGRAM_ENV_PARAMETERS_ARB

Errors

GL_INVALID_VALUE is generated if *index* is greater than or equal to the value of GL_MAX_PROGRAM_ENV_PARAMETERS_ARB corresponding to the program target specified by *target*.

■ **glProgramLocalParameter4{fd}[v]ARB**—Specify a program local parameter.

Prototypes

```
void glProgramLocalParameter4fARB(GLenum target,
                                  GLuint index,
                                  GLfloat x,
                                  GLfloat y,
                                  GLfloat z,
                                  GLfloat w);
void glProgramLocalParameter4dARB(GLenum target,
                                  GLuint index,
                                  GLdouble x,
                                  GLdouble y,
                                  GLdouble z,
                                  GLdouble w);
```

Parameters

target   Specifies the target program. Must be GL_VERTEX_PROGRAM_ARB.

index   Specifies the index of a program local parameter. Must be in the range 0 to GL_MAX_PROGRAM_LOCAL_PARAMETERS_ARB − 1.

x, y, z, w   Specify the components of the program local parameter.

Prototypes

```
void glProgramLocalParameter4fvARB(GLenum target,
                                   GLuint index,
                                   const GLfloat *params);
void glProgramLocalParameter4dvARB(GLenum target,
                                   GLuint index,
                                   const GLdouble *params);
```

Parameters

target	Specifies the target program. Must be GL_VERTEX_PROGRAM_ARB.
index	Specifies the index of a program local parameter. Must be in the range 0 to GL_MAX_PROGRAM_LOCAL_PARAMETERS_ARB − 1.
params	Specifies a pointer to an array containing the four-component program local parameter.

Description

The **glProgramLocalParameter4{fd}[v]ARB** function specifies a four-component, floating-point vector for the program local parameter specified by *index*. When program local parameters are specified, they are applied to the currently bound vertex program object.

Special Considerations

The **glProgramLocalParameter4{fd}[v]ARB** function is also defined by the GL_ARB_fragment_program and GL_NV_fragment_program extensions.

Get Functions

glGetProgramLocalParameter{fd}vARB

glGetProgramivARB with *pname* parameter GL_MAX_PROGRAM_LOCAL_PARAMETERS_ARB

Errors

GL_INVALID_VALUE is generated if *index* is greater than or equal to the value of GL_MAX_PROGRAM_LOCAL_PARAMETERS_ARB corresponding to the program target specified by *target*.

■ **glGetProgramEnvParameter{fd}vARB**—Return a program environment parameter.

Prototypes

```
void glGetProgramEnvParameterfvARB(GLenum target,
                                   GLuint index,
                                   GLfloat *params);
void glGetProgramEnvParameterdvARB(GLenum target,
                                   GLuint index,
                                   GLdouble *params);
```

Parameters

target   Specifies the target program. Must be `GL_VERTEX_PROGRAM_ARB`.

index   Specifies the index of a program environment parameter. Must be in the range 0 to `GL_MAX_PROGRAM_ENV_PARAMETERS_ARB` − 1.

params   Specifies a pointer to an array that receives the four-component program environment parameter.

Description

The `glGetProgramEnvParameter{fd}vARB` function returns the current value of the program environment parameter specified by *index*. The four floating-point values are written to the array pointed to by the *params* parameter.

Special Considerations

The `glGetProgramEnvParameter{fd}vARB` function is also defined by the `GL_ARB_fragment_program` extension.

Errors

`GL_INVALID_VALUE` is generated if *index* is greater than or equal to the value of `GL_MAX_PROGRAM_ENV_PARAMETERS_ARB` corresponding to the program target specified by *target*.

■ `glGetProgramLocalParameter{fd}vARB`—Return a program local parameter.

Prototypes

```
void glGetProgramLocalParameterfvARB(GLenum target,
                                     GLuint index,
                                     GLfloat *params);
void glGetProgramLocalParameterdvARB(GLenum target,
                                     GLuint index,
                                     GLdouble *params);
```

Parameters

target   Specifies the target program. Must be `GL_VERTEX_PROGRAM_ARB`.

index   Specifies the index of a program local parameter. Must be in the range 0 to `GL_MAX_PROGRAM_LOCAL_PARAMETERS_ARB` − 1.

params   Specifies a pointer to an array that receives the four-component program local parameter.

Description

The `glGetProgramLocalParameter{fd}vARB` function returns the current value of the program local parameter specified by *index* associated with the currently bound vertex program object. The four floating-point values are written to the array pointed to by the *params* parameter.

Special Considerations

The **glGetProgramLocalParameter{fd}vARB** function is also defined by the GL_ARB_fragment_program and GL_NV_fragment_program extensions.

Errors

GL_INVALID_VALUE is generated if *index* is greater than or equal to the value of GL_MAX_PROGRAM_LOCAL_PARAMETERS_ARB corresponding to the program target specified by *target*.

■ **glGetProgramivARB**—Return program state.

Prototype

```
void glGetProgramivARB(GLenum target,
                       GLenum pname,
                       GLint *params);
```

Parameters

target	Specifies the target program. Must be GL_VERTEX_PROGRAM_ARB.
pname	Specifies the symbolic name of a program value to be queried. Accepted values are listed in Description.
params	Specifies a pointer to an array that receives the queried value.

Description

The **glGetProgramivARB** function returns information about the currently bound vertex program or about implementation-dependent program limits. The *pname* parameter specifies what information to retrieve and may be one of the following values:

GL_PROGRAM_LENGTH_ARB

> The length of the program string for the program object currently bound to *target* is returned. This is useful for determining the size of the buffer needed for a call to the **glGetProgramStringARB** function.

GL_PROGRAM_FORMAT_ARB

> The character set of the program string for the program object currently bound to *target* is returned.

GL_PROGRAM_BINDING_ARB

> The name of the program currently bound to *target* is returned. This is initially 0.

GL_MAX_PROGRAM_INSTRUCTIONS_ARB

> The maximum number of program instructions allowed by the implementation for the vertex program target is returned. This is always at least 128.

`GL_MAX_PROGRAM_ATTRIBS_ARB`

> The maximum number of program attributes allowed by the implementation for the vertex program target is returned. This is always at least 16.

`GL_MAX_PROGRAM_PARAMETERS_ARB`

> The maximum number of program parameters allowed by the implementation for the vertex program target is returned. This value pertains to the sum of the program environment parameters, program local parameters, and any constants defined within a particular program. This is always at least 96.

`GL_MAX_PROGRAM_ENV_PARAMETERS_ARB`

> The maximum number of program environment parameters allowed by the implementation for the vertex program target is returned.

`GL_MAX_PROGRAM_LOCAL_PARAMETERS_ARB`

> The maximum number of program local parameters allowed by the implementation for the vertex program target is returned.

`GL_MAX_PROGRAM_TEMPORARIES_ARB`

> The maximum number of program temporary registers allowed by the implementation for the vertex program target is returned. This is always at least 12.

`GL_MAX_PROGRAM_ADDRESS_REGISTERS_ARB`

> The maximum number of program address registers allowed by the implementation for the vertex program target is returned. This may be as small as 1.

`GL_PROGRAM_INSTRUCTIONS_ARB`

> The number of program instructions used by the program object currently bound to *target* is returned.

`GL_PROGRAM_ATTRIBS_ARB`

> The number of program attributes used by the program object currently bound to *target* is returned.

`GL_PROGRAM_PARAMETERS_ARB`

> The number of program parameters used by the program object currently bound to *target* is returned. This value includes the sum of the program environment parameters, program local parameters, and any constants defined within the program.

`GL_PROGRAM_TEMPORARIES_ARB`

> The number of program temporary registers used by the program object currently bound to *target* is returned.

`GL_PROGRAM_ADDRESS_REGISTERS_ARB`

> The number of program address registers used by the program object currently bound to *target* is returned.

GL_MAX_PROGRAM_NATIVE_INSTRUCTIONS_ARB

> The maximum number of native program instructions allowed by the implementation for the vertex program target is returned.

GL_MAX_PROGRAM_NATIVE_ATTRIBS_ARB

> The maximum number of native program attributes allowed by the implementation for the vertex program target is returned.

GL_MAX_PROGRAM_NATIVE_PARAMETERS_ARB

> The maximum number of native program parameters allowed by the implementation for the vertex program target is returned. This value pertains to the sum of the program environment parameters, program local parameters, and any constants defined within a particular program.

GL_MAX_PROGRAM_NATIVE_TEMPORARIES_ARB

> The maximum number of native program temporary registers allowed by the implementation for the vertex program target is returned.

GL_MAX_PROGRAM_NATIVE_ADDRESS_REGISTERS_ARB

> The maximum number of native program address registers allowed by the implementation for the vertex program target is returned.

GL_PROGRAM_NATIVE_INSTRUCTIONS_ARB

> The number of native program instructions used by the program object currently bound to *target* is returned. This value reflects any implementation-dependent scheduling and optimization algorithms that are applied to the program when it is loaded.

GL_PROGRAM_NATIVE_ATTRIBS_ARB

> The number of native program attributes used by the program object currently bound to *target* is returned. This value reflects any implementation-dependent scheduling and optimization algorithms that are applied to the program when it is loaded.

GL_PROGRAM_NATIVE_PARAMETERS_ARB

> The number of native program parameters used by the program object currently bound to *target* is returned. This value includes the sum of the program environment parameters, program local parameters, and any constants defined within the program. This value also reflects any implementation-dependent scheduling and optimization algorithms that are applied to the program when it is loaded.

GL_PROGRAM_NATIVE_TEMPORARIES_ARB

> The number of native program temporary registers used by the program object currently bound to *target* is returned. This value reflects any implementation-dependent scheduling and optimization algorithms that are applied to the program when it is loaded.

GL_PROGRAM_NATIVE_ADDRESS_REGISTERS_ARB

> The number of native program address registers used by the program object currently bound to *target* is returned. This value reflects any

implementation-dependent scheduling and optimization algorithms that
are applied to the program when it is loaded.

GL_PROGRAM_UNDER_NATIVE_LIMITS_ARB
If the resources used by the program object currently bound to *target* fall
within the native limits set by the implementation, then the value
GL_TRUE is returned. If the native resource limits are exceeded, the value
GL_FALSE is returned.

Special Considerations

The **glGetProgramivARB** function is also defined by the GL_ARB_fragment_program
extension.

■ **glGetProgramStringARB**—Return a program string.

Prototype

```
void glGetProgramStringARB(GLenum target,
                           GLenum pname,
                           GLvoid *string);
```

Parameters

target   Specifies the target program. Must be GL_VERTEX_PROGRAM_ARB.

pname   Must be GL_PROGRAM_STRING_ARB.

string   Specifies a pointer to a region of memory that receives the program
                string.

Description

The **glGetProgramStringARB** function returns the program string for the program object
currently bound to the target specified by the *target* parameter. The *string* parameter points
to a buffer that receives the program string. The length of the program string can be determined by calling the **glGetProgramivARB** function with *pname* parameter GL_
PROGRAM_LENGTH_ARB.

Special Considerations

The **glGetProgramStringARB** function is also defined by the GL_ARB_fragment_
program extension.

Get Functions

glGetProgramivARB with *pname* parameter GL_PROGRAM_LENGTH_ARB

■ **glEnableVertexAttribArrayARB**—Enable a vertex attribute array.

Prototype

```
void glEnableVertexAttribArrayARB(GLuint index);
```

Parameters

index   Specifies the index of the vertex attribute array to enable. Must be in the range 0 to GL_MAX_VERTEX_ATTRIBS_ARB − 1.

Description

The **glEnableVertexAttribArrayARB** function enables the generic vertex attribute array corresponding to the *index* parameter. Vertex attribute arrays are disabled using the **glDisableVertexAttribArrayARB** function.

Get Functions

glGetVertexAttrib{ifd}vARB with *pname* parameter GL_VERTEX_ATTRIB_ARRAY_ENABLED_ARB

Errors

GL_INVALID_VALUE is generated if *index* is greater than or equal to GL_MAX_VERTEX_ATTRIBS_ARB.

■ **glDisableVertexAttribArrayARB**—Disable a vertex attribute array.

Prototype

    void **glDisableVertexAttribArrayARB**(GLuint *index*);

Parameters

index   Specifies the index of the vertex attribute array to disable. Must be in the range 0 to GL_MAX_VERTEX_ATTRIBS_ARB − 1.

Description

The **glDisableVertexAttribArrayARB** function disables the generic vertex attribute array corresponding to the *index* parameter. Vertex attribute arrays are enabled using the **glEnableVertexAttribArrayARB** function.

Get Functions

glGetVertexAttrib{ifd}vARB with *pname* parameter GL_VERTEX_ATTRIB_ARRAY_ENABLED_ARB

Errors

GL_INVALID_VALUE is generated if *index* is greater than or equal to GL_MAX_VERTEX_ATTRIBS_ARB.

■ **glVertexAttrib{1234}{bsiubusuifd}[v]ARB**—Specify a vertex attribute.

Prototypes

    void **glVertexAttrib1sARB**(GLuint *index*,
                                 GLshort *x*);

```
void glVertexAttrib1fARB(GLuint index,
                         GLfloat x);
void glVertexAttrib1dARB(GLuint index,
                         GLdouble x);
void glVertexAttrib2sARB(GLuint index,
                         GLshort x,
                         GLshort y);
void glVertexAttrib2fARB(GLuint index,
                         GLfloat x,
                         GLfloat y);
void glVertexAttrib2dARB(GLuint index,
                         GLdouble x,
                         GLdouble y);
void glVertexAttrib3sARB(GLuint index,
                         GLshort x,
                         GLshort y,
                         GLshort z);
void glVertexAttrib3fARB(GLuint index,
                         GLfloat x,
                         GLfloat y,
                         GLfloat z);
void glVertexAttrib3dARB(GLuint index,
                         GLdouble x,
                         GLdouble y,
                         GLdouble z);
void glVertexAttrib4sARB(GLuint index,
                         GLshort x,
                         GLshort y,
                         GLshort z,
                         GLshort w);
void glVertexAttrib4fARB(GLuint index,
                         GLfloat x,
                         GLfloat y,
                         GLfloat z,
                         GLfloat w);
void glVertexAttrib4dARB(GLuint index,
                         GLdouble x,
                         GLdouble y,
                         GLdouble z,
                         GLdouble w);
```

Parameters

index   Specifies the index of a vertex attribute. Must be in the range 0 to `GL_MAX_VERTEX_ATTRIBS_ARB` − 1.

x, y, z, w   Specify the components of the vertex attribute.

Prototypes

```
void glVertexAttrib1svARB(GLuint index,
                          const GLshort *v);
void glVertexAttrib1fvARB(GLuint index,
                          const GLfloat *v);
void glVertexAttrib1dvARB(GLuint index,
                          const GLdouble *v);
void glVertexAttrib2svARB(GLuint index,
                          const GLshort *v);
void glVertexAttrib2fvARB(GLuint index,
                          const GLfloat *v);
void glVertexAttrib2dvARB(GLuint index,
                          const GLdouble *v);
void glVertexAttrib3svARB(GLuint index,
                          const GLshort *v);
void glVertexAttrib3fvARB(GLuint index,
                          const GLfloat *v);
void glVertexAttrib3dvARB(GLuint index,
                          const GLdouble *v);
void glVertexAttrib4bvARB(GLuint index,
                          const GLbyte *v);
void glVertexAttrib4svARB(GLuint index,
                          const GLshort *v);
void glVertexAttrib4ivARB(GLuint index,
                          const GLint *v);
void glVertexAttrib4ubvARB(GLuint index,
                           const GLubyte *v);
void glVertexAttrib4usvARB(GLuint index,
                           const GLushort *v);
void glVertexAttrib4uivARB(GLuint index,
                           const GLuint *v);
void glVertexAttrib4fvARB(GLuint index,
                          const GLfloat *v);
void glVertexAttrib4dvARB(GLuint index,
                          const GLdouble *v);
```

Parameters

index   Specifies the index of a vertex attribute. Must be in the range 0 to
                 GL_MAX_VERTEX_ATTRIBS_ARB − 1.

v   Specifies a pointer to the array containing the vertex attribute
                 components.

Description

The **glVertexAttrib{1234}{bsiubusuifd}[v]ARB** function specifies the current value
of the vertex attribute corresponding to the *index* parameter.

If fewer than four coordinates are specified, the y, z, and w coordinates are implied to be 0, 0, and 1, respectively. Hence, calling the **glVertexAttrib1{bsiubusuifd}[v]ARB** function sets the current vertex attribute to $\langle x,0,0,1 \rangle$, calling the **glVertexAttrib2 {bsiubusuifd}[v]ARB** function sets the current vertex attribute to $\langle x,y,0,1 \rangle$, and calling the **glVertexAttrib3{bsiubusuifd}[v]ARB** function sets the current vertex attribute to $\langle x,y,z,1 \rangle$.

Calling the **glVertexAttrib{1234}{bsiubusuifd}[v]ARB** function with *index* parameter 0 invokes the currently bound vertex program.

Get Functions

glGetVertexAttrib{ifd}vARB with *pname* parameter GL_CURRENT_VERTEX_ATTRIB_ ARB

Errors

GL_INVALID_VALUE is generated if *index* is greater than or equal to GL_MAX_VERTEX_ ATTRIBS_ARB.

■ **glVertexAttrib4N{bsiubusui}[v]ARB**—Specify a normalized vertex attribute.

Prototype

```
void glVertexAttrib4NubARB(GLuint index,
                           GLubyte x,
                           GLubyte y,
                           GLubyte z,
                           GLubyte w);
```

Parameters

index   Specifies the index of a vertex attribute. Must be in the range 0 to GL_MAX_VERTEX_ATTRIBS_ARB − 1.

x, y, z, w   Specify the components of the vertex attribute.

Prototypes

```
void glVertexAttrib4NbvARB(GLuint index,
                           const GLbyte *v);
void glVertexAttrib4NsvARB(GLuint index,
                           const GLshort *v);
void glVertexAttrib4NivARB(GLuint index,
                           const GLint *v);
void glVertexAttrib4NubvARB(GLuint index,
                            const GLubyte *v);
void glVertexAttrib4NusvARB(GLuint index,
                            const GLushort *v);
void glVertexAttrib4NuivARB(GLuint index,
                            const GLuint *v);
```

Parameters

index   Specifies the index of a vertex attribute. Must be in the range 0 to
               GL_MAX_VERTEX_ATTRIBS_ARB − 1.

v   Specifies a pointer to the array containing the vertex attribute components.

Description

The **glVertexAttrib4N{bsiubusui}[v]ARB** function specifies the current value of the
vertex attribute corresponding to the *index* parameter. Signed integer values are mapped to
the range [−1,1], and unsigned integer values are mapped to the range [0,1].

Calling the **glVertexAttrib4N{bsiubusui}[v]ARB** function with *index* parameter 0 invokes the currently bound vertex program.

Get Functions

glGetVertexAttrib{ifd}vARB with *pname* parameter GL_CURRENT_VERTEX_ATTRIB_
ARB

Errors

GL_INVALID_VALUE is generated if *index* is greater than or equal to GL_MAX_VERTEX_
ATTRIBS_ARB.

■ **glVertexAttribPointerARB**—Specify a vertex attribute array.

Prototype

```
void glVertexAttribPointerARB(GLuint index,
                             GLint size,
                             GLenum type,
                             GLboolean normalized,
                             GLsizei stride,
                             const GLvoid *pointer);
```

Parameters

index   Specifies the index of a vertex attribute. Must be in the range 0 to
               GL_MAX_VERTEX_ATTRIBS_ARB − 1.

size   Specifies the number of components per entry. Must be 1, 2, 3, or 4.

type   Specifies the data type of each attribute component in the array. Accepted
               values are GL_BYTE, GL_UNSIGNED_BYTE, GL_SHORT, GL_UNSIGNED_
               SHORT, GL_INT, GL_UNSIGNED_INT, GL_FLOAT, and GL_DOUBLE.

normalized   Specifies a Boolean flag indicating whether fixed-point values are
               normalized.

stride   Specifies the byte offset between consecutive entries in the array. A value
               of 0 indicates that the entries are tightly packed in the array.

pointer   Specifies a pointer to the first component of the first entry in the array.

Description

The **glVertexAttribPointerARB** function specifies the location and the data format of an array of vertex attribute components that are used by a vertex program. The index of the vertex attribute array is specified by the *index* parameter. The *size* parameter specifies the number of components per vertex attribute, and the *type* parameter specifies the data type of the components. The *stride* parameter specifies the offset from one vertex attribute to the next. A stride of 0 is interpreted to mean that the offset from one vertex attribute to the next is the size of the vertex attribute itself—that is, the vertex attributes are tightly packed together in the array. The *normalized* parameter indicates whether fixed-point data is normalized. If *normalized* is GL_TRUE, then signed integer values are mapped to the range [−1.1], and unsigned integer values are mapped to the range [0,1]. If *normalized* is GL_FALSE, then fixed-point values are converted directly to floating-point values.

Vertex attribute arrays are enabled and disabled by calling the **glEnableVertexAttrib-ArrayARB** and **glDisableVertexAttribArrayARB** functions.

The values of the *size*, *type*, *normalized*, and *stride* parameters can be retrieved by calling the **glGetVertexAttribivARB** function, and the value of the *pointer* parameter can be retrieved by calling the **glGetVertexAttribPointervARB** function.

Get Functions

glGetVertexAttribPointervARB with *pname* parameter GL_VERTEX_ATTRIB_ARRAY_POINTER_ARB

glGetVertexAttribivARB with *pname* parameter GL_VERTEX_ATTRIB_ARRAY_SIZE_ARB

glGetVertexAttribivARB with *pname* parameter GL_VERTEX_ATTRIB_ARRAY_TYPE_ARB

glGetVertexAttribivARB with *pname* parameter GL_VERTEX_ATTRIB_ARRAY_NORMALIZED_ARB

glGetVertexAttribivARB with *pname* parameter GL_VERTEX_ATTRIB_ARRAY_STRIDE_ARB

Errors

GL_INVALID_VALUE is generated if *index* is greater than or equal to GL_MAX_VERTEX_ATTRIBS_ARB.

GL_INVALID_VALUE is generated if *size* is not 1, 2, 3, or 4.

GL_INVALID_VALUE is generated if *stride* is negative.

■ **glGetVertexAttrib{ifd}vARB**—Return vertex attribute state.

Prototypes

```
void glGetVertexAttribivARB(GLuint index,
                            GLenum pname,
                            GLint *params);
void glGetVertexAttribfvARB(GLuint index,
                            GLenum pname,
                            GLfloat *params);
void glGetVertexAttribdvARB(GLuint index,
                            GLenum pname,
                            GLdouble *params);
```

Parameters

index   Specifies the index of a vertex attribute. Must be in the range 0 to GL_
              MAX_VERTEX_ATTRIBS_ARB − 1.

pname   Specifies the symbolic name of the state to query. Accepted values are
              GL_VERTEX_ATTRIB_ARRAY_ENABLED_ARB, GL_VERTEX_ATTRIB_
              ARRAY_SIZE_ARB, GL_VERTEX_ATTRIB_ARRAY_TYPE_ARB, GL_VERTEX_
              ATTRIB_ARRAY_NORMALIZED_ARB, GL_VERTEX_ATTRIB_ARRAY_
              STRIDE_ARB, and GL_CURRENT_VERTEX_ATTRIB_ARB.

params   Specifies a pointer to an array that receives the queried state.

Description

The **glGetVertexAttrib{ifd}vARB** function returns information about the vertex attribute specified by the *index* parameter. The *pname* parameter specifies what information
to retrieve and may be one of the following values:

GL_VERTEX_ATTRIB_ARRAY_ENABLED_ARB
              A Boolean value indicating whether the vertex attribute array corre-
              sponding to the *index* parameter is currently enabled is returned in
              params.

GL_VERTEX_ATTRIB_ARRAY_SIZE_ARB
              The size of the vertex attribute array is returned in *params*. This corre-
              sponds to the value of the *size* parameter passed to the **glVertex-
              AttribPointerARB** function.

GL_VERTEX_ATTRIB_ARRAY_TYPE_ARB
              The data type of the vertex attribute array is returned in *params*. This cor-
              responds to the value of the *type* parameter passed to the **glVertex-
              AttribPointerARB** function.

GL_VERTEX_ATTRIB_ARRAY_NORMALIZED_ARB
              A Boolean value indicating whether the data in the vertex attribute array is
              normalized is returned in *params*. This corresponds to the value of the *nor-
              malized* parameter passed to the **glVertexAttribPointerARB** function.

GL_VERTEX_ATTRIB_ARRAY_STRIDE_ARB

> The stride for the vertex attribute array is returned in *params*. This corresponds to the value of the *stride* parameter passed to the **glVertexAttribPointerARB** function.

GL_CURRENT_VERTEX_ATTRIB_ARB

> The current four-component vertex attribute value is returned in the *params* array.

Errors

GL_INVALID_VALUE is generated if *index* is greater than or equal to GL_MAX_VERTEX_ATTRIBS_ARB.

GL_INVALID_OPERATION is generated if *pname* is GL_CURRENT_VERTEX_ATTRIB_ARB and *index* is 0.

■ **glGetVertexAttribPointervARB**—Return the pointer to a vertex attribute array.

Prototype

```
void glGetVertexAttribPointervARB(GLuint index,
                                  GLenum pname,
                                  GLvoid **pointer);
```

Parameters

index   Specifies the index of a vertex attribute. Must be in the range 0 to GL_MAX_VERTEX_ATTRIBS_ARB − 1.

pname   Must be GL_VERTEX_ARRAY_ATTRIB_POINTER_ARB.

pointer   Specifies a pointer to a location that receives the vertex attribute array pointer.

Description

The **glGetVertexAttribPointervARB** function returns the current pointer to the vertex attribute array specified by the *index* parameter. The array pointer, as specified by the **glVertexAttribPointerARB** function, is returned in the *pointer* parameter.

Errors

GL_INVALID_VALUE is generated if *index* is greater than or equal to GL_MAX_VERTEX_ATTRIBS_ARB.

EXTENDED FUNCTIONS

■ **glEnable**, **glDisable**, **glIsEnabled**—Extended to enable/disable vertex program capabilities.

Prototypes

```
void glEnable(GLenum cap);
void glDisable(GLenum cap);
GLboolean glIsEnabled(GLenum cap);
```

Extended Parameters

cap   Specifies a GL capability. May be one of the values listed in Description.

Description

The **glEnable** and **glDisable** functions are used to enable and disable vertex program capabilities. The *cap* parameter may be one of the following values:

GL_VERTEX_PROGRAM_ARB

If enabled, the currently bound vertex program is invoked for each vertex.

GL_VERTEX_PROGRAM_POINT_SIZE_ARB

If enabled, the value written to the result.pointsize register specifies the point size. Otherwise, point sizes are determined by the current point parameters.

GL_VERTEX_PROGRAM_TWO_SIDE_ARB

If enabled, front-facing colors or back-facing colors are selected based on whether a polygon is front-facing or back-facing. Otherwise, front-facing colors are always selected.

■ **glMatrixMode**—Extended to support generic program matrices.

Prototype

```
void glMatrixMode(GLenum mode);
```

Extended Parameters

mode   Specifies the matrix stack to which subsequent matrix operations apply. May be GL_MATRIX*i*_ARB, where *i* is in the range 0 to GL_MAX_ PROGRAM_MATRICES_ARB − 1.

Description

The **glMatrixMode** function sets the current matrix mode. Generic program matrix stack *i* is made current by specifying GL_MATRIX*i*_ARB as the *mode* parameter.

■ **glGetIntegerv**—Extended to allow retrieval of vertex program state.

Prototype

```
void glGetIntegerv(GLenum pname, GLint *params);
```

Extended Parameters

pname   Specifies the parameter to be returned. May be one of the values listed in Description.

Description

The **glGetIntegerv** function can be used to retrieve various state related to vertex programs. The *pname* parameter may be one of the following values:

GL_PROGRAM_ERROR_POSITION_ARB

        The byte position within the program string at which an error occurred is returned.

GL_CURRENT_MATRIX_ARB

        The 16 entries of the current matrix (as specified by the **glMatrixMode** function) are returned and stored in column-major order.

GL_TRANSPOSE_CURRENT_MATRIX_ARB

        The 16 entries of the current matrix (as specified by the **glMatrixMode** function) are returned and stored in row-major order.

GL_CURRENT_MATRIX_STACK_DEPTH_ARB

        The current depth of the current matrix stack (as specified by the **glMatrixMode** function) is returned.

GL_MAX_VERTEX_ATTRIBS_ARB

        The maximum number of vertex attribute arrays supported by the implementation is returned. This is always at least 16.

GL_MAX_PROGRAM_MATRICES_ARB

        The maximum number of generic program matrices supported by the implementation is returned. This is always at least 8.

GL_MAX_PROGRAM_MATRIX_STACK_DEPTH_ARB

        The maximum stack depth for the generic program matrices GL_MATRIX*i*_NV is returned. This may be as small as 1.

■ **glGetString**—Extended to allow retrieval of the program error string.

Prototype

```
const GLubyte *glGetString(GLenum name);
```

Extended Parameters

name   Specifies the string to return. May be GL_PROGRAM_ERROR_STRING_ARB.

Description

The **glGetString** function can be used to retrieve the program error string after an unsuccessful call to the **glProgramStringARB** function. If no error occurs when a program is loaded, the error string may still contain warning messages.

18.2   GL_NV_vertex_program

OpenGL version required	OpenGL 1.2.1
Dependencies	Requires `GL_ARB_multitexture`
Promotions	—

Related extensions	`GL_NV_vertex_program1_1`
	`GL_NV_vertex_program2`
	`GL_NV_fragment_program`

DISCUSSION

The `GL_NV_vertex_program` extension provides fully general programmability for per-vertex calculations including vertex coordinate transformation, lighting, and texture coordinate generation. Conventional per-vertex calculations can be replaced by assembly-like source code that an implementation compiles into a *vertex program*.

Vertex programs provide an interface for directly accessing generalized transform and lighting hardware. Vertex programs are enabled and disabled by calling the **glEnable** and **glDisable** functions with *cap* parameter `GL_VERTEX_PROGRAM_NV`. When vertex programs are enabled, the following conventional per-vertex calculations are not performed automatically by OpenGL, but need to be handled by the vertex program itself.

- Vertex coordinate transformation from object space to homogeneous clip space.

- Calculation of primary and secondary colors for vertex lighting.

- Normal vector rescaling and normalization.

- Normalization of evaluated normal vectors using `GL_AUTO_NORMAL`.

- Texture coordinate generation.

- Texture matrix application.

- Fog distance calculation.

- Point size attenuation.

- Vertex weighting.

Vertex programs do not subsume the following functionality, which is still performed by OpenGL when vertex programs are enabled.

- Primitive assembly.

- Face culling.

- View frustum clipping.

- Perspective division by the *w* coordinate.

- Viewport and depth range transformations.

- Clamping primary and secondary colors to [0,1].

- Evaluator calculations (except `GL_AUTO_NORMAL`).

In vertex program mode under the GL_NV_vertex_program extension, user clipping planes are not supported. Primitives are only clipped to the six planes of the view frustum. User clipping plane functionality is added by the GL_NV_vertex_program2 extension.

Vertex programs have access to only a single vertex at a time. The information that a vertex program receives as inputs for each vertex includes conventional types of data, such as the vertex's object-space position, its associated normal vector, primary and secondary colors, and texture coordinates, as well as user-defined generic per-vertex attributes.

Vertex programs have access to a large bank of constant parameter registers that do not change from one vertex to another. These parameters can be used to pass any necessary constant data to a vertex program. For example, material colors and texture generation coefficients would be stored in the parameter registers.

After performing its calculations, a vertex program writes its outputs to a set of result registers that includes types of data such as the vertex's homogeneous clip-space position, primary and secondary colors, and texture coordinates. These outputs are then interpolated across the face of a primitive during the rasterization process and passed to the fragment-processing portion of the graphics pipeline.

Program Structure

Vertex programs are passed to the GL as a text string containing a list of up to 128 instructions. The text string must begin with the character sequence !!VP1.0, with no preceding whitespace, to indicate that the program conforms to the version 1.0 vertex program syntax. (The GL_NV_vertex_program1_1 extension and the GL_NV_vertex_program2 extension define versions 1.1 and 2.0 vertex program syntaxes.) The end of the vertex program is indicated by the three-character sequence END. The exact syntax specification for version 1.0 vertex programs is given in Appendix A, Section A.2.

A vertex program instruction consists of a three-character mnemonic followed by a destination register and up to three source operands delimited by commas. Every instruction is terminated with a semicolon. The example shown in Listing 18.2.1 performs four dot products to transform a vertex's position into homogeneous clip space and copies the vertex's primary color and texture coordinates to the output registers. The symbol # denotes the beginning of a comment that extends to the end of the line on which it appears.

LISTING 18.2.1   The following vertex program transforms the vertex position from model space to homogeneous clip space and copies the primary color and texture coordinates to the output registers.

```
!!VP1.0

# Transform vertex position into clip space
# c[0] - c[3] contain the modelview-projection matrix
DP4     o[HPOS].x, c[0], v[OPOS];
DP4     o[HPOS].y, c[1], v[OPOS];
DP4     o[HPOS].z, c[2], v[OPOS];
DP4     o[HPOS].w, c[3], v[OPOS];
```

```
# Pass through primary color and texture coordinates
MOV     o[COL0], v[COL0];
MOV     o[TEX0], v[TEX0];

END
```

All registers manipulated by a vertex program are treated as vectors consisting of the four floating-point components x, y, z, and w. Some instructions require a scalar operand, in which case a vector component must be selected from the source register by appending .x, .y, .z, or .w. For example, the following line calculates the reciprocal of the z component of the temporary register R1.

```
RCP     R0, R1.z;
```

Operand Modification

In a vertex program instruction statement, any source operand may have an optional negation operation as well as an arbitrary swizzle operation applied to it at no additional performance cost. Prepending a register name with a minus sign negates each of its components before it is used by an instruction. For example, the following line subtracts the contents of temporary register R2 from temporary register R1 and stores the result in temporary register R0.

```
ADD     R0, R1, -R2;
```

The swizzle operation allows components of a source operand to be reordered or duplicated arbitrarily. Swizzling is denoted by appending a period and a sequence of four letters from the set {x, y, z, w} to a register name. The four letters define a remapping of the components of a register that are passed to the instruction as one of its source operands. As an example, the following line reads the components of temporary register R1 in reverse order and stores them in temporary register R0.

```
MOV     R0, R1.wzyx;
```

Omitting the swizzle suffix is equivalent to using the suffix .xyzw.

Components may be duplicated in the swizzle suffix. For example, the following line moves the x component of R1 into the x and y components of R0, and moves the y component of R1 into the z and w components of R0. The z and w components of R1 are ignored.

```
MOV     R0, R1.xxyy;
```

A shorthand notation exists for duplicating a single component of a register to all four components of a source operand. Appending a register name with a period and a single letter is equivalent to using the same letter four times in a row. For example, the following line moves the x component of R1 into all four components of R0.

```
MOV     R0, R1.x;
```

This notation is also necessary for denoting the scalar operand required by instructions such as the RCP (reciprocal) instruction.

Destination Masking

A write mask may be applied to the destination register and controls which components of the destination are updated with an instruction's result. A write mask is denoted by appending a period followed by up to four *unique* letters from the set {x, y, z, w} to a register name in the natural component order. For example, the following line moves the contents of the x component of R1 into the x component of R0, but does not alter the y, z, or w components of R0.

```
MOV     R0.x, R1;
```

The following line adds the x and y components of R1, and stores the result in the x and w components of R0 without affecting the y and z components of R0.

```
ADD     R0.xw, R1.x, R1.y;
```

Omitting the write mask is equivalent to specifying the write mask .xyzw.

Register Set

The register set available to vertex programs consists of 16 read-only vertex attribute registers, 15 write-only vertex result registers, 96 read-only program parameter registers, 12 general purpose temporary registers, and one address register. With the exception of the address register, every register consists of four floating-point components labeled x, y, z, and w.

Vertex Attribute Registers

Per-vertex data is passed into a vertex program through a set of 16 vertex attribute registers. A vertex attribute register is denoted within a vertex program by the lowercase letter v followed by a number in the range 0 to 15 inside brackets. For example, vertex attribute register 6 is denoted by v[6]. Vertex attributes are read-only and cannot be specified as the destination register for any instruction. A single instruction may not access more than one unique vertex attribute register, although the same vertex attribute register may be used for multiple source operands.

Vertex attribute 0 always represents the object-space vertex position, but the other 15 vertex attributes have no required semantic meanings and may be used for any purpose deemed suitable. However, many of the vertex attributes have corresponding conventional semantic meanings. As shown in Table 18.2.1, four-character mnemonics may be used in place of the register number for vertex attribute registers that correspond to conventional per-vertex data. For example, v[OPOS] can be used to denote the object-space vertex position instead of v[0].

TABLE 18.2.1 Vertex Attribute Registers

Vertex Attribute Index	Attribute Mnemonic	Conventional Semantic Meaning
0	v[OPOS]	Vertex position
1	v[WGHT]	Vertex weights
2	v[NRML]	Normal
3	v[COL0]	Primary color
4	v[COL1]	Secondary color
5	v[FOGC]	Fog coordinate
6		None
7		None
8	v[TEX0]	Texture 0 coordinates
9	v[TEX1]	Texture 1 coordinates
10	v[TEX2]	Texture 2 coordinates
11	v[TEX3]	Texture 3 coordinates
12	v[TEX4]	Texture 4 coordinates
13	v[TEX5]	Texture 5 coordinates
14	v[TEX6]	Texture 6 coordinates
15	v[TEX7]	Texture 7 coordinates

When rendering, the current value of any vertex attribute can be specified using the **glVertexAttrib{1234}{ubsfd}[v]NV** function. This function takes an index to a vertex attribute register and up to four components to store in the register. If fewer than four components are specified, then any missing y, z, and w components are set to 0, 0, and 1, respectively. Calling the **glVertexAttrib{1234}{ubsfd}[v]NV** function with *index* parameter 0 functions like the **glVertex{234}{sifd}[v]** function and must occur between calls to **glBegin** and **glEnd**. Updating vertex attribute 0 causes all other vertex attributes to be associated with the current vertex and invokes the current vertex program. Any other vertex attribute can be updated at any time in the same respect that, for example, the current normal or color would be updated.

A set of functions named **glVertexAttribs{1234}{ubsfd}vNV** is provided to allow updating of multiple vertex attributes at once. These functions update a contiguous range of vertex attributes and, if the range begins at attribute 0, invoke the current vertex program.

Vertex attribute arrays can also be used just as one can specify a conventional vertex array, normal array, and so forth. A vertex attribute array is specified by calling the **glVertexAttribPointerNV** function,

```
void glVertexAttribPointerNV(GLuint index,
                             GLint size,
                             GLenum type,
                             GLsizei stride,
                             const void *pointer);
```

with the *index* parameter set to the index of the vertex attribute to affect. The *size*, *type*, *stride*, and *pointer* parameters have the same meanings as they do for the conventional counterparts **glVertexPointer**, **glNormalPointer**, and so forth. A vertex attribute array is enabled and disabled by calling the **glEnableClientState** and **glDisable-ClientState** functions with the *array* parameter set to GL_VERTEX_ATTRIB_ARRAY*i*_NV, where $0 \le i \le 15$.

For convenience, conventional per-vertex state is aliased onto the new vertex attribute registers. Table 18.2.2 lists the vertex attribute registers that are updated by conventional per-vertex functions, such as **glVertex{234}{sifd}[v]** and **glNormal3{bsifd}**. Updating a vertex attribute using a conventional function is equivalent to calling **glVertex-Attrib{1234}{ubsfd}[v]NV** with the corresponding attribute index.

When vertex programs are enabled, conventional arrays are still recognized and fed into the appropriate vertex attribute registers. If both a conventional array and its corresponding vertex attribute array are enabled, the vertex attribute array takes precedence.

TABLE 18.2.2   Conventional Vertex Attribute Aliasing

Vertex Attribute	Conventional Command	Component Mapping
v[OPOS]	Vertex	$\langle x,y,z,w \rangle$
v[WGHT]	VertexWeightEXT	$\langle x,0,0,1 \rangle$
v[NRML]	Normal	$\langle x,y,z,1 \rangle$
v[COL0]	Color	$\langle r,g,b,a \rangle$
v[COL1]	SecondaryColorEXT	$\langle r,g,b,1 \rangle$
v[FOGC]	FogCoordEXT	$\langle f,0,0,1 \rangle$
v[TEX0]	MultiTexCoordARB	$\langle s,t,r,q \rangle$
v[TEX1]	MultiTexCoordARB	$\langle s,t,r,q \rangle$
v[TEX2]	MultiTexCoordARB	$\langle s,t,r,q \rangle$
v[TEX3]	MultiTexCoordARB	$\langle s,t,r,q \rangle$
v[TEX4]	MultiTexCoordARB	$\langle s,t,r,q \rangle$
v[TEX5]	MultiTexCoordARB	$\langle s,t,r,q \rangle$
v[TEX6]	MultiTexCoordARB	$\langle s,t,r,q \rangle$
v[TEX7]	MultiTexCoordARB	$\langle s,t,r,q \rangle$

Vertex Result Registers

Vertex programs write their results to the set of 14 vertex result registers listed in Table 18.2.3. A vertex result register is denoted by the lowercase letter o followed by a four-character mnemonic inside brackets. The vertex result registers are write-only and may not appear as source operands in a vertex program. A vertex program must always write to the HPOS (homogeneous position) result register, or the program is ill-formed.

TABLE 18.2.3 Vertex result registers. Components labeled * are unused.

Result Register	Description	Component Interpretation
o[HPOS]	Homogeneous clip-space position	$\langle x,y,z,w\rangle$
o[COL0]	Primary color (front facing)	$\langle r,g,b,a\rangle$
o[COL1]	Secondary color (front facing)	$\langle r,g,b,a\rangle$
o[BFC0]	Back-facing primary color	$\langle r,g,b,a\rangle$
o[BFC1]	Back-facing secondary color	$\langle r,g,b,a\rangle$
o[FOGC]	Fog coordinate	$\langle f,^*,^*,^*\rangle$
o[PSIZ]	Point size	$\langle p,^*,^*,^*\rangle$
o[TEX0]	Texture 0 coordinates	$\langle s,t,r,q\rangle$
o[TEX1]	Texture 1 coordinates	$\langle s,t,r,q\rangle$
o[TEX2]	Texture 2 coordinates	$\langle s,t,r,q\rangle$
o[TEX3]	Texture 3 coordinates	$\langle s,t,r,q\rangle$
o[TEX4]	Texture 4 coordinates	$\langle s,t,r,q\rangle$
o[TEX5]	Texture 5 coordinates	$\langle s,t,r,q\rangle$
o[TEX6]	Texture 6 coordinates	$\langle s,t,r,q\rangle$
o[TEX7]	Texture 7 coordinates	$\langle s,t,r,q\rangle$

The back-facing primary and secondary colors represented by the result registers o[BFC0] and o[BFC1] are applied to back-facing polygons only when two-sided vertex program mode is enabled. Two-sided vertex program mode is enabled and disabled by calling the **glEnable** and **glDisable** functions with *cap* parameter GL_VERTEX_PROGRAM_TWO_SIDE_NV. When two-sided vertex program mode is disabled (the initial state), the front-facing colors are always selected for both front-facing and back-facing polygons.

The point size written to the o[PSIZ] register is utilized during rasterization only if point-size vertex program mode is enabled. Point-size vertex program mode is enabled and disabled by calling the **glEnable** and **glDisable** functions with *cap* parameter GL_VERTEX_PROGRAM_POINT_SIZE_NV. When point-size vertex program mode is disabled (the initial state), or the o[PSIZ] register is not written by a vertex program, a vertex's point size is determined by the current values of the point parameters.

Program Parameter Registers

Vertex programs have access to a set of 96 program parameter registers. Program parameter registers are read-only and may not appear as a destination register in a vertex program. A program parameter register is denoted by a lowercase letter c followed by a number in the range 0 to 95 inside brackets. A single instruction may not access more than one unique program parameter register, although the same program parameter register may be used for multiple source operands.

Constant data is loaded into a single program parameter register by calling the **glProgramParameter4{fd}[v]NV** function,

```
void glProgramParameter4{fd}NV(GLenum target,
                               GLuint index,
                               T x,
                               T y,
                               T z,
                               T w);

void glProgramParameter4{fd}vNV(GLenum target,
                                GLuint index,
                                const T *params);
```

with *target* parameter GL_VERTEX_PROGRAM_NV. (The type T represents GLfloat or GLdouble.) The *index* parameter specifies which program parameter to load. The parameter value specified by the **glProgramParameter4{fd}[v]NV** function is accessed within the vertex program using the notation c[*i*], where *i* corresponds to the *index* parameter.

Data for multiple contiguous program parameter registers can be loaded at the same time by calling the **glProgramParameters4{fd}vNV** function,

```
void glProgramParameters4{fd}vNV(GLenum target,
                                 GLuint index,
                                 GLuint num,
                                 const T *params);
```

with *target* parameter GL_VERTEX_PROGRAM_NV. The *index* parameter specifies the first program parameter to load, and the *num* parameter specifies the number of program parameters that are loaded.

Temporary Registers

A temporary register is denoted within a vertex program by the uppercase letter R followed by a number in the range 0 to 11. Temporary registers are private to each vertex program invocation and are initialized to $\langle 0,0,0,0 \rangle$ each time a program begins execution. The set of 12 temporary registers may be read or written for any purpose, and their final values at the end of a program's execution have no effect.

Address Register

The program parameter registers may also be accessed using a relative offset from the contents of the address register. The address register is denoted by A0.x, indicating the x component of the vector A0. The address register has only one component in version 1.0 vertex programs, but the GL_NV_vertex_program2 extension expands the number of components to four. The address register is loaded using the ARL (address register load) instruction, and a program parameter register can be accessed with the runtime-computed contents of the address register using the notation c[A0.x+n], where n is an optional constant in the range −64 to 63.

Instruction Set

There are 17 vertex program instructions. The operation performed by each instruction and the corresponding types of input operands and output results are listed in Table 18.2.4.

TABLE 18.2.4 Vertex program instructions. The letter "v" indicates a vector result or operand, and the letter "s" indicates a scalar operand. The vector ⟨s,s,s,s⟩ represents a single scalar result that is replicated to all four components of the result vector.

Instruction	Output Result	Input Operands	Operation
ADD	v	v, v	Add
ARL	address	s	Address register load
DP3	⟨s,s,s,s⟩	v, v	3D dot product
DP4	⟨s,s,s,s⟩	v, v	4D dot product
DST	v	v, v	Distance vector
EXP	v	s	Approximate exponential base 2
LIT	v	v	Light coefficients
LOG	v	s	Approximate logarithm base 2
MAD	v	v, v, v	Multiply-add
MAX	v	v, v	Maximum
MIN	v	v, v	Minimum
MOV	v	v	Move
MUL	v	v, v	Multiply
RCP	⟨s,s,s,s⟩	s	Reciprocal
RSQ	⟨s,s,s,s⟩	s	Reciprocal square root
SGE	v	v, v	Set on greater than or equal to
SLT	v	v, v	Set on less than

Each of the vertex program instructions is described in detail below. Included with each instruction is pseudocode that demonstrates the instruction's exact effect. The types vector and scalar are used to hold four-component vector quantities and one-component scalar quantities, respectively. When loading data from a register, the pseudocode makes use of the functions `VectorLoad` and `ScalarLoad` to apply the swizzle and negate operations to each operand. In the definitions of these functions, which follow, the `.swiz[n]` field used with the `source` parameter denotes the *n*th component of the source vector after swizzling. The `.comp` field used with the `source` parameter denotes the scalar component selected using the single component suffix in the vertex program. The value of `negate` is true if the program specifies that the source operand is negated, and is false otherwise.

```
vector VectorLoad(vector source)
{
    vector    operand;

    operand.x = source.swiz[0];
    operand.y = source.swiz[1];
    operand.z = source.swiz[2];
    operand.w = source.swiz[3];
    if (negate)
    {
        operand.x = -operand.x;
        operand.y = -operand.y;
        operand.z = -operand.z;
        operand.w = -operand.w;
    }

    return (operand);
}

scalar ScalarLoad(vector source)
{
    scalar    operand;

    operand = source.comp;
    if (negate) operand = -operand;

    return (operand);
}
```

When a vector result is written to a destination register, the pseudocode makes use of the `WriteDest` function to apply the write mask. In the definition of this function that follows, each of the components of `mask` is true if writing is enabled for the corresponding component of the destination register, and is false if writing is disabled.

```
vector WriteDest(vector dest, vector result)
{
    if (mask.x) dest.x = result.x;
    if (mask.y) dest.y = result.y;
    if (mask.z) dest.z = result.z;
    if (mask.w) dest.w = result.w;
```

```
    return (dest);
}
```

The exact effect of each vertex program instruction follows. The local variable r is used in most of the pseudocode listings and always denotes a temporary vector quantity.

ADD—Add

```
ADD     result, op0, op1;
```

The ADD instruction performs a componentwise addition of two operands.

```
vector v0 = VectorLoad(op0);
vector v1 = VectorLoad(op1);
r.x = v0.x + v1.x;
r.y = v0.y + v1.y;
r.z = v0.z + v1.z;
r.w = v0.w + v1.w;
result = WriteDest(result, r);
```

The addition operation satisfies the following rules:

1. $x + y = y + x$ for all x and y.
2. $x + 0.0 = x$ for all x.

ARL—Address register load

```
ARL     A0.x, op0;
```

The ARL instruction loads the address register with a scalar signed integer.

```
A0.x = floor(ScalarLoad(op0));
```

DP3—Three-component dot product

```
DP3     result, op0, op1;
```

The DP3 instruction performs a three-component dot product between two operands and replicates the result to all four components of the destination.

```
vector v0 = VectorLoad(op0);
vector v1 = VectorLoad(op1);
scalar dot = v0.x * v1.x + v0.y + v1.y + v0.z * v1.z;
r.x = dot;
r.y = dot;
r.z = dot;
r.w = dot;
result = WriteDest(result, r);
```

DP4—Four-component dot product

```
DP4     result, op0, op1;
```

The DP4 instruction performs a four-component dot product between two operands and replicates the result to all four components of the destination.

```
vector v0 = VectorLoad(op0);
vector v1 = VectorLoad(op1);
scalar dot = v0.x * v1.x + v0.y + v1.y
               + v0.z * v1.z + v0.w * v1.w;
r.x = dot;
r.y = dot;
r.z = dot;
r.w = dot;
result = WriteDest(result, r);
```

DST—Distance vector

```
DST     result, op0, op1;
```

The DST instruction takes two operands and produces a vector that is useful for attenuation calculations. Given a distance d, the first operand should be formatted as $\langle *,d^2,d^2,* \rangle$, and the second operation should be formatted as $\langle *,1/d,*,1/d \rangle$, where * indicates that the operand's component is not used. The result of the DST instruction is the vector $\langle 1,d,d^2,1/d \rangle$.

```
vector v0 = VectorLoad(op0);
vector v1 = VectorLoad(op1);
r.x = 1.0;
r.y = v0.y * v1.y;
r.z = v0.z;
r.w = v1.w;
result = WriteDest(result, r);
```

EXP—Approximate exponential base 2

```
EXP     result, op0;
```

The EXP instruction calculates a rough approximation to 2^p for a single scalar operand p. The result of the exponentiation is returned in the z component of the destination.

```
scalar s0 = ScalarLoad(op0);
r.x = pow(2, floor(s0));
r.y = s0 - floor(s0);
r.z = RoughApproxExp2(s0);
r.w = 1.0;
result = WriteDest(result, r);
```

The RoughApproxExp2 function satisfies the precision requirement

$$\left|\text{RoughApproxExp2}(x) - 2^x\right| < \begin{cases} 2^{-11}, & \text{if } 0 \le x < 1; \\ 2^{-11} \cdot 2^{\lfloor x \rfloor}, & \text{otherwise.} \end{cases}$$

LIT—Light coefficients

```
LIT     result, op0;
```

The LIT instruction takes a single operand and produces a coefficient vector that is useful for lighting calculations. The operand is assumed to be formatted as $\langle N \cdot L, N \cdot H, *, m \rangle$, where $N \cdot L$ is the diffuse dot product, $N \cdot H$ is the specular dot product, m is the specular exponent, and $*$ indicates that the z component is unused. The result of the LIT instruction is the vector $\langle 1.0, N \cdot L, (N \cdot H)^m, 1.0 \rangle$, where $N \cdot L$ and $N \cdot H$ are clamped to 0.0 and the z component is set to 0.0 if $N \cdot L \le 0$. The specular exponent m is clamped to the range $[-128, 128]$.

```
vector v0 = VectorLoad(op0);
if (v0.x < 0.0) v0.x = 0.0;
if (v0.y < 0.0) v0.y = 0.0;
if (v0.w < -128.0 + epsilon) v0.w = -128.0 + epsilon;
else if (v0.w > 128.0 - epsilon) v0.w = 128.0 - epsilon;
r.x = 1.0;
r.y = v0.x;
r.z = (v0.x > 0.0) ? RoughApproxPow(v0.y, v0.w) : 0.0;
r.w = 1.0;
result = WriteDest(result, r);
```

The RoughApproxPow function is defined in terms of the rough base-2 exponential and logarithm functions implemented by the EXP and LOG instructions. Thus,

```
RoughApproxPow(b, e) = RoughApproxExp2(e * RoughApproxLog2(b))
```

and the precision of the RoughApproxPow function is limited by the precision of the RoughApproxExp2 and RoughApproxLog2 functions.

LOG—Approximate logarithm base 2

```
LOG     result, op0;
```

The LOG instruction calculates a rough approximation to $\log_2(p)$ for a single scalar operand p. The result of the operation is returned in the z component of the destination.

```
scalar s0 = fabs(ScalarLoad(op0));
r.x = floor(log2(s0));
r.y = s0 * pow(2, -floor(log2(s0)));
r.z = RoughApproxLog2(s0);
r.w = 1.0;
result = WriteDest(result, r);
```

The RoughApproxLog2 function satisfies the precision requirement

$$\left|\text{RoughApproxLog2}(x) - \log_2 x\right| < 2^{-11}.$$

MAD—Multiply-add

```
MAD     result, op0, op1, op2;
```

The MAD instruction performs a componentwise multiplication and addition of three operands.

```
vector v0 = VectorLoad(op0);
vector v1 = VectorLoad(op1);
vector v2 = VectorLoad(op2);
r.x = v0.x * v1.x + v2.x;
r.y = v0.y * v1.y + v2.y;
r.z = v0.z * v1.z + v2.z;
r.w = v0.w * v1.w + v2.w;
result = WriteDest(result, r);
```

The multiplication and addition operations are subject to the same rules described for the MUL and ADD instructions.

MAX—Maximum

```
MAX     result, op0, op1;
```

The MAX instruction performs a componentwise maximum operation between two operands.

```
vector v0 = VectorLoad(op0);
vector v1 = VectorLoad(op1);
r.x = (v0.x > v1.x) ? v0.x : v1.x;
r.y = (v0.y > v1.y) ? v0.y : v1.y;
r.z = (v0.z > v1.z) ? v0.z : v1.z;
r.w = (v0.w > v1.w) ? v0.w : v1.w;
result = WriteDest(result, r);
```

MIN—Minimum

```
MIN     result, op0, op1;
```

The MIN instruction performs a componentwise minimum operation between two operands.

```
vector v0 = VectorLoad(op0);
vector v1 = VectorLoad(op1);
```

```
r.x = (v0.x > v1.x) ? v1.x : v0.x;
r.y = (v0.y > v1.y) ? v1.y : v0.y;
r.z = (v0.z > v1.z) ? v1.z : v0.z;
r.w = (v0.w > v1.w) ? v1.w : v0.w;
result = WriteDest(result, r);
```

MOV—Move

```
MOV     result, op0;
```

The MOV instruction copies a single operand to the destination.

```
vector v0 = VectorLoad(op0);
result = WriteDest(result, v0);
```

MUL—Multiply

```
MUL     result, op0, op1;
```

The MUL instruction performs a componentwise multiplication of two operands.

```
vector v0 = VectorLoad(op0);
vector v1 = VectorLoad(op1);
r.x = v0.x * v1.x;
r.y = v0.y * v1.y;
r.z = v0.z * v1.z;
r.w = v0.w * v1.w;
result = WriteDest(result, r);
```

The multiplication operation satisfies the following rules:

1. $xy = yx$ for all x and y.
2. $x \cdot 1.0 = x$ for all x.
3. $x \cdot \pm 0.0 = \pm 0.0$ for all x, with the possible exceptions of $\pm$INF and $\pm$NAN.

RCP—Reciprocal

```
RCP     result, op0;
```

The RCP instruction approximates the reciprocal of a single scalar operand and replicates the result to all four components of the destination.

```
scalar s0 = ScalarLoad(op0);
scalar recip = ApproxRecip(s0);
r.x = recip;
r.y = recip;
```

```
r.z = recip;
r.w = recip;
result = WriteDest(result, r);
```

The `ApproxRecip` function satisfies the precision requirement

$$\left| \texttt{ApproxRecip}(x) - \frac{1}{x} \right| < 2^{-22}$$

for values of x satisfying $1.0 \leq x \leq 2.0$. The reciprocation operation also satisfies the following rule:

$$\texttt{ApproxRecip}(+1.0) = +1.0$$

RSQ—Reciprocal square root

```
RSQ     result, op0;
```

The `RSQ` instruction approximates the reciprocal square root of the absolute value of a single scalar operand and replicates the result to all four components of the destination.

```
scalar s0 = fabs(ScalarLoad(op0));
scalar rsqrt = ApproxRSQRT(s0);
r.x = rsqrt;
r.y = rsqrt;
r.z = rsqrt;
r.w = rsqrt;
result = WriteDest(result, r);
```

The `ApproxRSQRT` function satisfies the precision requirement

$$\left| \texttt{ApproxRSQRT}(x) - \frac{1}{\sqrt{x}} \right| < 2^{-22}$$

for values of x satisfying $1.0 \leq x \leq 4.0$.

SGE—Set on greater than or equal to

```
SGE     result, op0, op1;
```

The `SGE` instruction performs a componentwise comparison between two operands. Each component of the result vector is set to 1.0 if the corresponding component of the first operand is greater than or equal to the corresponding component of the second operand, and is set to 0.0 otherwise.

```
vector v0 = VectorLoad(op0);
vector v1 = VectorLoad(op1);
r.x = (v0.x >= v1.x) ? 1.0 : 0.0;
r.y = (v0.y >= v1.y) ? 1.0 : 0.0;
r.z = (v0.z >= v1.z) ? 1.0 : 0.0;
r.w = (v0.w >= v1.w) ? 1.0 : 0.0;
result = WriteDest(result, r);
```

SLT—Set on less than

```
SLT     result, op0, op1;
```

The SLT instruction performs a componentwise comparison between two operands. Each component of the result vector is set to 1.0 if the corresponding component of the first operand is less than the corresponding component of the second operand, and is set to 0.0 otherwise.

```
vector v0 = VectorLoad(op0);
vector v1 = VectorLoad(op1);
r.x = (v0.x < v1.x) ? 1.0 : 0.0;
r.y = (v0.y < v1.y) ? 1.0 : 0.0;
r.z = (v0.z < v1.z) ? 1.0 : 0.0;
r.w = (v0.w < v1.w) ? 1.0 : 0.0;
result = WriteDest(result, r);
```

Program Management

Vertex programs follow the named object convention that is used elsewhere in OpenGL for such things as texture objects. A vertex program is identified by a name taken from the set of unsigned integers. Previously unused names for vertex program objects are allocated by calling the **glGenProgramsNV** function,

```
void glGenProgramsNV(GLsizei n, GLuint *ids);
```

This function generates *n* names and writes them to the array pointed to by the *ids* parameter. The names generated are marked as used, but the associated vertex program objects are not actually created until the first time a new name is passed to the **glLoadProgramNV** function.

Vertex program objects are deleted and the associated names are freed by calling the **glDeleteProgramsNV** function,

```
void glDeleteProgramsNV(GLsizei n,
                        const GLuint *ids);
```

Any of the *n* names passed to this function in the array pointed to by the *ids* parameter that do not refer to existing vertex program objects are silently ignored. Once a vertex program object is deleted, its name is marked as unused. The **glIsProgramNV** function,

```
GLboolean glIsProgramNV(GLuint id);
```

can be used to determine whether a particular name specified by the *id* parameter refers to an existing vertex program object.

A program string for a particular vertex program object is loaded by calling the **glLoad-ProgramNV** function,

```
void glLoadProgramNV(GLenum target,
                     GLuint id,
                     GLsizei len,
                     const GLubyte *program);
```

with *target* parameter GL_VERTEX_PROGRAM_NV. The *len* parameter specifies the length of the program string pointed to by the *program* parameter. A program string may be loaded for the same vertex program object multiple times.

A vertex program object is bound to the vertex program target by calling the **glBind-ProgramNV** function,

```
void glBindProgramNV(GLenum target,
                     GLuint id);
```

with *target* parameter GL_VERTEX_PROGRAM_NV. The *id* parameter specifies the name of the vertex program object. When vertex program mode is enabled (by calling **glEnable** with *cap* parameter GL_VERTEX_PROGRAM_NV), the current vertex program is invoked for every vertex passed to OpenGL.

Vertex programs may be requested to be loaded into memory that is quickly accessible by the graphics hardware by calling the **glRequestResidentProgramsNV** function,

```
void glRequestResidentProgramsNV(GLsizei n,
                                 const GLuint *ids);
```

The implementation attempts to keep the *n* programs named in the array pointed to by the *ids* parameter in fast memory. One can determine whether vertex programs currently reside in fast memory by calling the **glAreProgramsResidentNV** function,

```
GLboolean glAreProgramsResidentNV(GLsizei n,
                                  const GLuint *ids,
                                  GLboolean *residences);
```

A Boolean value is written to each of the *n* entries of the array pointed to by the *residences* parameter, indicating whether the corresponding vertex program named in the array pointed to by the *ids* parameter is resident in fast memory.

Tracking Matrices

A mechanism is provided that allows a matrix to be automatically updated within a set of four contiguous program parameter registers. Calling the **glTrackMatrixNV** function,

```
void glTrackMatrixNV(GLenum target,
                     GLuint address,
                     GLenum matrix,
                     GLenum transform);
```

with *target* parameter GL_VERTEX_PROGRAM_NV establishes a connection between the particular matrix specified by the *matrix* parameter, such as the current modelview matrix or the current projection matrix, and the four program parameter registers beginning at the address specified by the *address* parameter. (The value of *address* must be a multiple of four.) Furthermore, the matrix that is tracked into the four program parameter registers may have an inverse operation, transpose operation, or both applied to it as specified by the *transform* parameter. The maximum number of matrices that can be simultaneously tracked can be retrieved by calling the **glGetIntegerv** function with *pname* parameter GL_MAX_TRACK_MATRICES_NV.

The values in any program parameter register occupied by a tracking matrix cannot be separately updated. Calling the **glProgramParameter4{fd}[v]NV** function or the **glProgramParameters4{fd}vNV** function to update a program parameter register that currently has a matrix tracked into it results in a GL_INVALID_OPERATION error.

State pertaining to matrix tracking can be retrieved by calling the **glGetTrackMatrixivNV** function,

```
void glGetTrackMatrixivNV(GLenum target,
                          GLuint address,
                          GLenum pname,
                          GLint *params);
```

with *target* parameter GL_VERTEX_PROGRAM_NV. The *address* parameter specifies the first program parameter register to which a matrix is tracked, and the *pname* parameter specifies what matrix tracking parameter to return. If *pname* is GL_TRACK_MATRIX_NV, then the symbolic constant representing the matrix being tracked into the program parameters beginning at *address* is returned. GL_NONE is returned if no matrix is being tracked into the location specified by the *address* parameter. If *pname* is GL_TRACK_MATRIX_TRANSFORM_NV, then the transformation applied to the matrix tracked into the location specified by the *address* parameter is returned. This corresponds to the value of the *transform* parameter passed to the **glTrackMatrixNV** function.

In addition to the standard matrices defined by unextended OpenGL, a set of generic tracking matrices are provided by the GL_NV_vertex_program extension. These matrices are manipulated by setting the matrix mode to GL_MATRIX*i*_NV using the **glMatrixMode** function, where *i* is in the range 0 to GL_MAX_TRACK_MATRICES_NV − 1. Subsequent matrix-related functions, such as **glLoadMatrix{fd}**, apply to the *i*th tracking matrix stack. The maximum depth of all tracking matrix stacks supported by an implementation is retrieved by passing GL_MAX_PROGRAM_MATRIX_STACK_DEPTH_NV to **glGetIntegerv**.

The GL_NV_vertex_program extension defines two constants that can be passed to the *pname* parameter of the **glGet** functions to retrieve information about the current matrix stack. The constant GL_CURRENT_MATRIX_NV is used to retrieve the 16 entries of the

matrix associated with the current matrix mode. The constant GL_CURRENT_MATRIX_
STACK_DEPTH_NV is used to retrieve the number of matrices on the matrix stack associated
with the current matrix mode.

Vertex State Programs

A special type of program called a *vertex state program* can be created and used to perform
operations on the set of program parameter registers. Whereas ordinary vertex programs
are implicitly executed for each vertex, a vertex state program is explicitly executed by calling the **glExecuteProgramNV** function,

```
void glExecuteProgramNV(GLenum target,
                        GLuint id,
                        const GLfloat *params);
```

with *target* parameter GL_VERTEX_STATE_PROGRAM_NV. The *id* parameter specifies the program object to execute and must name a program that was loaded as a vertex state program
using the **glLoadProgramNV** function. In addition to the program parameter registers, vertex state programs may only access vertex attribute register v[0]. The *params* parameter
points to an array containing the four values that are placed in register v[0] when the
vertex state program is executed.

A vertex state program must begin with the character sequence !!VSP1.0, without any
preceding whitespace, instead of the sequence !!VP1.0 required by ordinary vertex programs. Vertex state programs may read and write to any program parameter register,
whereas program parameter registers are read-only for ordinary vertex programs. A vertex
state program must write to at least one program parameter register, or it will fail to load.
Vertex state programs may not write to the vertex result registers.

USEFUL TIPS

How do I perform subtraction?

Subtraction can be performed by simply negating one of the operands to an ADD instruction. The following code subtracts R1 from R0 and stores the result in R2.

```
# Subtract R1 from R0

ADD    R2, R0, -R1;
```

How do I calculate absolute value?

The absolute value of a vector component can be obtained by evaluating the maximum of
the component and its negation. The following code calculates the componentwise absolute values of R0.

```
# R0 = <|R0.x|, |R0.y|, |R0.z|, |R0.w|>

MAX    R0, R0, -R0;
```

How do I calculate a cross product?

The cross product between two vectors can be calculated using a MUL instruction followed by a MAD instruction. The following code calculates the 3D cross product between R0 and R1 and stores the result in the *x*, *y*, and *z* components of R2.

```
#        | i    j    k   |
# R2 =   | R0.x R0.y R0.z |
#        | R1.x R1.y R1.z |


MUL    R2, R0.zxyw, R1.yzxw;
MAD    R2, R0.yzxw, R1.zxyw, -R2;
```

NEW FUNCTIONS

■ **glLoadProgramNV**—Specify a program string.

Prototype

```
void glLoadProgramNV(GLenum target,
                     GLuint id,
                     GLsizei len,
                     const GLubyte *program);
```

Parameters

target Specifies the target program. Must be GL_VERTEX_PROGRAM_NV or GL_VERTEX_STATE_PROGRAM_NV.

id Specifies the name of the program to load. This may not be 0.

len Specifies the length of the program string.

program Specifies a pointer to the program string. This string does not need to be null-terminated.

Description

The **glLoadProgramNV** function loads the program string for the program named by the *id* parameter. The program string is a sequence of ASCII characters whose length is passed into the *len* parameter.

When a program string is loaded for a particular value of *id* for the first time, the value of the *target* parameter is associated with that program. A new program string for the same value of *id* may be loaded at a later time, without having to delete the program using the **glDelete-PorgramsNV** function, as long as the value of *target* remains the same. An attempt to reload a program using a different value of *target* generates a GL_INVALID_OPERATION error.

At the time **glLoadProgramNV** is called, the program string is parsed and checked for syntactic validity. If the program fails to load because it contains an error, the error GL_ INVALID_OPERATION is generated, and the value of GL_PROGRAM_ERROR_POSITION_NV is updated to reflect the position within the program string at which the error occurred. This position can be retrieved by calling the **glGetIntegerv** function.

Special Considerations

Unlike the **glProgramStringARB** function defined by the GL_ARB_vertex_program extension, a program does not need to be bound before the program string is specified, since the **glLoadProgramNV** function takes an explicit program name in the *id* parameter.

The **glLoadProgramNV** function is also defined by the GL_NV_fragment_program extension.

Get Functions

glGetProgramStringNV

glGetProgramivNV with *pname* parameter GL_PROGRAM_LENGTH_NV

glGetIntegerv with *pname* parameter GL_PROGRAM_ERROR_POSITION_NV

Errors

GL_INVALID_OPERATION is generated if the program string violates the syntactic or semantic rules of the target program.

GL_INVALID_VALUE is generated if *id* is 0.

GL_INVALID_OPERATION is generated if *id* corresponds to a program that has already been loaded with a different value for *target*.

■ **glGenProgramsNV**—Generate program names.

Prototype

```
void glGenProgramsNV(GLsizei n,
                     GLuint *ids);
```

Parameters

n   Specifies the number of program names to generate.

ids   Specifies a pointer to an array that receives the generated program names.

Description

The **glGenProgramsNV** function returns a set of *n* unused program names in the array pointed to by the *ids* parameter. Each of the returned names is reserved with respect to program name generation, but does not represent an existing program object until a program string is loaded using the **glLoadProgramNV** function.

Programs are deleted and the associated program names are freed by calling the **glDeleteProgramsNV** function.

Special Considerations

The **glGenProgramsNV** function is also defined by the GL_NV_fragment_program extension.

Get Functions

glIsProgramNV

Errors

GL_INVALID_VALUE is generated if *n* is negative.

■ **glDeleteProgramsNV**—Delete named programs.

Prototype

```
void glDeleteProgramsNV(GLsizei n,
                        const GLuint *ids);
```

Parameters

n   Specifies the number of programs to delete.

ids   Specifies a pointer to an array of program names to be deleted.

Description

The **glDeleteProgramsNV** function deletes the *n* programs contained in the array pointed to by the *ids* parameter. When a program object is deleted, it becomes nonexistent, and its name becomes unused. Deleted program names may subsequently be returned by the **glGenProgramsNV** function. Any unused program names found in the array pointed to by the *ids* parameter are silently ignored.

If a vertex program is deleted when it is the currently bound program, it is as if the **glBind-ProgramNV** function had been called with *id* parameter 0.

Special Considerations

The **glDeleteProgramsNV** function is also defined by the GL_NV_fragment_program extension.

Get Functions

glIsProgramNV

Errors

GL_INVALID_VALUE is generated if *n* is negative.

■ **glBindProgramNV**—Bind a named program to a program target.

Prototype

```
void glBindProgramNV(GLenum target,
                     GLuint id);
```

Parameters

target   Specifies the target to which the program is bound. Must be `GL_VER-`
                      `TEX_PROGRAM_NV`.

id   Specifies the name of the program to bind.

Description

The **glBindProgramNV** function sets the current vertex program that is invoked for every vertex.

Binding to a nonexistent program does not generate an error. In particular, the *id* parameter may be 0. Since program 0 cannot be loaded, however, it is always nonexistent. Program 0 is implicitly bound if the currently bound vertex program is deleted by the **glDelete-ProgramsNV** function.

Special Considerations

The **glBindProgramNV** function is also defined by the `GL_NV_fragment_program` extension.

Get Functions

glGet with *pname* parameter `GL_VERTEX_PROGRAM_BINDING_NV`

Errors

`GL_INVALID_OPERATION` is generated if *id* is the name of a program whose target does not match *target*.

■ **glIsProgramNV**—Determine if a name corresponds to a program.

Prototype

```
GLboolean glIsProgramNV(GLuint id);
```

Parameters

id   Specifies the name of a program.

Description

The **glIsProgramNV** function returns `GL_TRUE` if the *id* parameter names an existing program. Otherwise, it returns `GL_FALSE`.

A program name generated by the **glGenProgramsNV** function does not refer to an existing program until a successful call to the **glLoadProgramNV** function loads a program corresponding to that name.

Special Considerations

The **glIsProgramNV** function is also defined by the `GL_NV_fragment_program` extension.

■ **glRequestResidentProgramsNV**—Request that programs are loaded into fast memory.

Prototype

```
void glRequestResidentProgramsNV(GLsizei n,
                                 const GLuint *ids);
```

Parameters

n	Specifies the number of programs for which to request residency.
ids	Specifies a pointer to an array of program names.

Description

The **glRequestResidentProgramsNV** function requests that the *n* programs contained in the array pointed to by the *ids* parameter be made resident in fast memory accessible by the graphics hardware. It is not guaranteed that all of the programs in the array are made resident. Earlier programs in the array are given higher priority, and programs not appearing in the array that were resident before the call to **glRequestResidentProgramsNV** may become nonresident. The **glAreProgramsResidentNV** function can be called to determine which programs actually became resident.

Any names in the array pointed to by the *ids* parameter that do not refer to existing programs are ignored.

Special Considerations

The **glRequestResidentProgramsNV** function is also defined by the GL_NV_fragment_program extension.

Get Functions

glAreProgramsResidentNV

■ **glAreProgramsResidentNV**—Determine if programs are resident in fast memory.

Prototype

```
GLboolean glAreProgramsResidentNV(GLsizei n,
                                  const GLuint *ids,
                                  GLboolean *residences);
```

Parameters

n	Specifies the number of programs for which to return residency.
ids	Specifies a pointer to an array of program names.
residences	Specifies a pointer to an array in which the program resident status is returned.

Description

The **glAreProgramsResidentNV** function returns an array of Boolean values in the space pointed to by the *residences* parameter indicating whether each corresponding program named in the array pointed to by the *ids* parameter is currently resident. If all of the programs are resident, the function returns true; otherwise, the return value is false. If any of the names in the array pointed to by the *ids* parameter refers to a nonexistent program, then the GL_INVALID_VALUE error is generated.

The residence status of a single program can be retrieved by calling the **glGetProgramivNV** function with *pname* parameter GL_PROGRAM_RESIDENT_NV.

Special Considerations

The **glAreProgramsResidentNV** function is also defined by the GL_NV_fragment_program extension.

Get Functions

glGetProgramivNV with *pname* parameter GL_PROGRAM_RESIDENT_NV

Errors

GL_INVALID_VALUE is generated if any of the program names in the array pointed to by *ids* are 0 or nonexistent.

■ **glExecuteProgramNV**—Execute a state program.

Prototype

```
void glExecuteProgramNV(GLenum target,
                        GLuint id,
                        const GLfloat *params);
```

Parameters

target	Specifies a target program. Must be GL_VERTEX_STATE_PROGRAM_NV.
id	Specifies the name of a program.
params	Specifies an array of four floating-point values that are passed to the program in vertex attribute register 0.

Description

The **glExecuteProgramNV** function executes a vertex state program. The *id* parameter must name a program whose target is GL_VERTEX_STATE_PROGRAM_NV.

The *params* parameter points to an array of four floating-point values that are passed to the vertex state program in vertex attribute register 0. These parameters are accessed inside the state program by referring to register v[0].

Errors

GL_INVALID_OPERATION is generated if *id* refers to a nonexistent or invalid program, or if *id* refers to a program that is not a vertex state program.

■ **glProgramParameter4{fd}[v]NV**—Specify a program parameter.

Prototypes

```
void glProgramParameter4fNV(GLenum target,
                            GLuint index,
                            GLfloat x,
                            GLfloat y,
                            GLfloat z,
                            GLfloat w);
void glProgramParameter4dNV(GLenum target,
                            GLuint index,
                            GLdouble x,
                            GLdouble y,
                            GLdouble z,
                            GLdouble w);
```

Parameters

target	Specifies the target program. Must be GL_VERTEX_PROGRAM_NV.
index	Specifies the index of a program parameter register. Must be in the range 0 to 95.
x, y, z, w	Specify the components of the program parameter.

Prototypes

```
void glProgramParameter4fvNV(GLenum target,
                             GLuint index,
                             const GLfloat *params);
void glProgramParameter4dvNV(GLenum target,
                             GLuint index,
                             const GLdouble *params);
```

Parameters

target	Specifies the target program. Must be GL_VERTEX_PROGRAM_NV.
index	Specifies the index of a program parameter register. Must be in the range 0 to 95.
params	Specifies a pointer to an array containing the four-component program parameter.

Description

The **glProgramParameter4{fd}[v]NV** function loads a four-component floating-point vector into the program parameter register specified by *index*.

Get Functions

glGetProgramParameter{fd}vNV

Errors

GL_INVALID_VALUE is generated if *index* is greater than 95.

GL_INVALID_OPERATION is generated if *index* refers to a program parameter register into which a matrix is currently being tracked.

■ **glProgramParameters4{fd}vNV**—Specify multiple program parameters.

Prototypes

```
void glProgramParameters4fvNV(GLenum target,
                              GLuint index,
                              GLuint num,
                              const GLfloat *params);
void glProgramParameters4dvNV(GLenum target,
                              GLuint index,
                              GLuint num,
                              const GLdouble *params);
```

Parameters

target	Specifies the target program. Must be GL_VERTEX_PROGRAM_NV.
index	Specifies the first index of a set of contiguous program parameter registers. Must be in the range 0 to 95.
num	Specifies the number of program parameter registers to be updated.
params	Specifies a pointer to an array of four-component program parameters.

Description

The **glProgramParameters4{fd}vNV** function loads multiple four-component floating-point vectors into the program parameter registers beginning with *index*. The *num* parameter specifies how many program parameter registers to update, and the *params* parameter points to an array containing $4 \times num$ floating-point values. Calling the **glProgramParameters4{fd}vNV** function is equivalent to the following:

```
for (int i = 0; i < num; i++)
{
    glProgramParameter4{fd}vNV(GL_VERTEX_PROGRAM_NV,
        index + i, params + i * 4);
}
```

Get Functions

glGetProgramParameter{fd}vNV

Errors

`GL_INVALID_VALUE` is generated if *index* + *num* is greater than 96.

`GL_INVALID_OPERATION` is generated if any of the updated registers is one into which a matrix is currently being tracked.

■ **glGetProgramParameter{fd}vNV**—Return a program parameter.

Prototypes

```
void glGetProgramParameterfvNV(GLenum target,
                               GLuint index,
                               GLenum pname,
                               GLfloat *params);
void glGetProgramParameterdvNV(GLenum target,
                               GLuint index,
                               GLenum pname,
                               GLdouble *params);
```

Parameters

target   Specifies the target program. Must be `GL_VERTEX_PROGRAM_NV`.

index   Specifies the index of a program parameter register. Must be in the range 0 to 95.

pname   Must be `GL_PROGRAM_PARAMETER_NV`.

params   Specifies a pointer to an array that receives the four-component program parameter.

Description

The **glGetProgramParameter{fd}vNV** function returns the current value of the program parameter register specified by *index*. The four floating-point values are written to the array pointed to by the *params* parameter.

Errors

`GL_INVALID_VALUE` is generated if *index* is greater than 95.

■ **glTrackMatrixNV**—Track a matrix into program parameter registers.

Prototype

```
void glTrackMatrixNV(GLenum target,
                     GLuint address,
                     GLenum matrix,
                     GLenum transform);
```

Parameters

target   Specifies the target program. Must be `GL_VERTEX_PROGRAM_NV`.

address   Specifies the first of four program parameter registers into which the matrix is tracked. This must be a multiple of four.

matrix   Specifies the matrix to track. Accepted values are GL_NONE, GL_MODELVIEW, GL_PROJECTION, GL_TEXTURE, GL_TEXTURE*i*_ARB (where *i* is in the range 0 to GL_MAX_TEXTURE_UNITS_ARB − 1), GL_COLOR (if the imaging subset is supported), GL_MODELVIEW_PROJECTION_NV, or GL_MATRIX*i*_NV (where *i* is in the range 0 to GL_MAX_TRACK_MATRICES_NV − 1).

transform   Specifies the transform to apply to the tracked matrix. Must be GL_IDENTITY, GL_INVERSE, GL_TRANSPOSE, or GL_INVERSE_TRANSPOSE.

Description

The **glTrackMatrixNV** function establishes a set of four program parameter registers as a region into which a specific OpenGL matrix is tracked. The *address* parameter specifies the first index of the set of four contiguous registers that is affected and must be a multiple of four. The *matrix* parameter specifies which matrix is tracked into the program parameter registers and may be one of the following values:

GL_NONE

Specifies that no matrix should be tracked into the registers beginning at *address*. This clears any previously established matrix tracking for this address.

GL_MODELVIEW

The current modelview matrix is tracked.

GL_PROJECTION

The current projection matrix is tracked.

GL_TEXTURE

The texture matrix for the currently active texture unit is tracked.

GL_TEXTURE*i*_ARB

The texture matrix for texture unit *i* is tracked.

GL_COLOR

The color matrix is tracked (only if the imaging subset is supported).

GL_MODELVIEW_PROJECTION_NV

The product of the modelview and projection matrix is tracked. This matrix transforms vectors from model space directly into homogeneous clip space.

GL_MATRIXi_NV

The *i*th tracking matrix is tracked.

The *transform* parameter specifies how a matrix is transformed before it is stored in the program parameter registers and may be one of the following values:

`GL_IDENTITY_NV`

> The matrix is not transformed.

`GL_INVERSE_NV`

> The inverse of the matrix is tracked.

`GL_TRANSPOSE_NV`

> The transpose of the matrix is tracked.

`GL_INVERSE_TRANSPOSE_NV`

> The inverse transpose of the matrix is tracked.

Tracked matrices are stored row-wise into the four program parameter registers beginning with *address*. Calling the **glProgramParameter4{fd}[v]NV** function or the **glProgram-Parameters4{fd}vNV** function to update a program parameter register that currently has a matrix tracked into it results in a `GL_INVALID_OPERATION` error.

Get Functions

glGetTrackMatrixivNV with *pname* parameter GL_TRACK_MATRIX_NV

glGetTrackMatrixivNV with *pname* parameter GL_TRACK_MATRIX_TRANSFORM_NV

glGetIntegerv with *pname* parameter GL_MAX_TRACK_MATRICES_NV

Errors

GL_INVALID_VALUE is generated if *address* is greater than 95 or is not a multiple of four.

■ **glGetTrackMatrixivNV**—Return track matrix state.

Prototype

```
void glGetTrackMatrixivNV(GLenum target,
                          GLuint address,
                          GLenum pname,
                          GLint *params);
```

Parameters

target   Specifies the target program. Must be GL_VERTEX_PROGRAM_NV.

address   Specifies the first of four program parameter registers into which a matrix is tracked. This must be a multiple of four.

pname   Specifies the symbolic name of a parameter to query. Must be GL_TRACK_MATRIX_NV or GL_TRACK_MATRIX_TRANSFORM_NV.

params   Specifies a pointer to an array that receives the queried state.

Description

The **glGetTrackMatrixivNV** function returns information about the matrix currently being tracked into the program parameter registers beginning with *address*.

If *pname* is GL_TRACK_MATRIX_NV, then a single value is written to *params*, indicating which matrix is currently being tracked. If no matrix is being tracked beginning at *address*, then GL_NONE is returned. If a texture matrix is being tracked, then GL_TEXTURE*i*_ARB is returned, where *i* is the index of the corresponding texture unit. The value GL_TEXTURE is never returned.

If *pname* is GL_TRACK_MATRIX_TRANSFORM_NV, then a single value is written to *params*, indicating what transform is being applied to the tracked matrix. This is one of the four values, GL_IDENTITY_NV, GL_INVERSE_NV, GL_TRANSPOSE_NV, or GL_INVERSE_TRANSPOSE_NV, discussed with the **glTrackMatrixNV** function.

Errors

GL_INVALID_VALUE is generated if *address* is greater than 95 or is not a multiple of four.

■ **glGetProgramivNV**—Return program state.

Prototype

```
void glGetProgramivNV(GLuint id,
                      GLenum pname,
                      GLint *params);
```

Parameters

id	Specifies a program name.
pname	Specifies the symbolic name of a program value to be queried. Must be GL_PROGRAM_TARGET_NV, GL_PROGRAM_LENGTH_NV, or GL_PROGRAM_RESIDENT_NV.
params	Specifies a pointer to an array that receives the queried value.

Description

The **glGetProgramivNV** function returns information about the program named by the *id* parameter. The *pname* parameter specifies what information to retrieve and may be one of the following values:

GL_PROGRAM_TARGET_NV

> The program target is returned. This may be GL_VERTEX_PROGRAM_NV or GL_VERTEX_STATE_PROGRAM_NV.

GL_PROGRAM_LENGTH_NV

> The length of the program string is returned. This is useful for determining the size of the buffer needed for a call to the **glGetProgramStringNV** function.

GL_PROGRAM_RESIDENT_NV

> A Boolean value indicating whether the program is resident in fast memory is returned.

Special Considerations

The **glGetProgramivNV** function is also defined by the GL_NV_fragment_program extension.

Errors

GL_INVALID_OPERATION is generated if *id* does not refer to an existing program.

■ **glGetProgramStringNV**—Return a program string.

Prototype

```
void glGetProgramStringNV(GLuint id,
                          GLenum pname,
                          GLubyte *program);
```

Parameters

id	Specifies a program name.
pname	Specifies the symbolic name of a program value to be queried. Must be GL_PROGRAM_STRING_NV.
program	Specifies a pointer to a region of memory that receives the program string.

Description

The **glGetProgramStringNV** function returns the program string that was previously loaded for the program named by the *id* parameter. The *program* parameter points to a buffer that receives the program string. The length of the program string can be determined by calling the **glGetProgramivNV** function with *pname* parameter GL_PROGRAM_LENGTH_NV.

Special Considerations

The **glGetProgramStringNV** function is also defined by the GL_NV_fragment_program extension.

Get Functions

glGetProgramivNV with *pname* parameter GL_PROGRAM_LENGTH_NV

Errors

GL_INVALID_OPERATION is generated if *id* does not refer to an existing program.

■ **glVertexAttrib{1234}{ubsfd}[v]NV**—Specify a vertex attribute.

Prototypes

```
void glVertexAttrib1sNV(GLuint index,
                        GLshort x);
void glVertexAttrib1fNV(GLuint index,
                        GLfloat x);
```

```
void glVertexAttrib1dNV(GLuint index,
                        GLdouble x);
void glVertexAttrib2sNV(GLuint index,
                        GLshort x,
                        GLshort y);
void glVertexAttrib2fNV(GLuint index,
                        GLfloat x,
                        GLfloat y);
void glVertexAttrib2dNV(GLuint index,
                        GLdouble x,
                        GLdouble y);
void glVertexAttrib3sNV(GLuint index,
                        GLshort x,
                        GLshort y,
                        GLshort z);
void glVertexAttrib3fNV(GLuint index,
                        GLfloat x,
                        GLfloat y,
                        GLfloat z);
void glVertexAttrib3dNV(GLuint index,
                        GLdouble x,
                        GLdouble y,
                        GLdouble z);
void glVertexAttrib4sNV(GLuint index,
                        GLshort x,
                        GLshort y,
                        GLshort z,
                        GLshort w);
void glVertexAttrib4fNV(GLuint index,
                        GLfloat x,
                        GLfloat y,
                        GLfloat z,
                        GLfloat w);
void glVertexAttrib4dNV(GLuint index,
                        GLdouble x,
                        GLdouble y,
                        GLdouble z,
                        GLdouble w);
void glVertexAttrib4ubNV(GLuint index,
                         GLubyte x,
                         GLubyte y,
                         GLubyte z,
                         GLubyte w);
```

Parameters

index   Specifies the index of a vertex attribute. Must be in the range 0 to 15.

x, y, z, w   Specify the components of the vertex attribute.

Prototypes

```
void glVertexAttrib1svNV(GLuint index,
                         const GLshort *v);
void glVertexAttrib1fvNV(GLuint index,
                         const GLfloat *v);
void glVertexAttrib1dvNV(GLuint index,
                         const GLdouble *v);
void glVertexAttrib2svNV(GLuint index,
                         const GLshort *v);
void glVertexAttrib2fvNV(GLuint index,
                         const GLfloat *v);
void glVertexAttrib2dvNV(GLuint index,
                         const GLdouble *v);
void glVertexAttrib3svNV(GLuint index,
                         const GLshort *v);
void glVertexAttrib3fvNV(GLuint index,
                         const GLfloat *v);
void glVertexAttrib3dvNV(GLuint index,
                         const GLdouble *v);
void glVertexAttrib4svNV(GLuint index,
                         const GLshort *v);
void glVertexAttrib4fvNV(GLuint index,
                         const GLfloat *v);
void glVertexAttrib4dvNV(GLuint index,
                         const GLdouble *v);
void glVertexAttrib4ubvNV(GLuint index,
                          const GLubyte *v);
```

Parameters

index   Specifies the index of a vertex attribute. Must be in the range 0 to 15.

v   Specifies a pointer to the array containing the vertex attribute components.

Description

The **glVertexAttrib{1234}{ubsfd}[v]NV** function specifies the current value of the vertex attribute corresponding to the *index* parameter.

If fewer than four coordinates are specified, the y, z, and w coordinates are implied to be 0, 0, and 1, respectively. Hence, calling the **glVertexAttrib1{ubsfd}[v]NV** function sets the current vertex attribute to $\langle x,0,0,1 \rangle$, calling the **glVertexAttrib2{ubsfd}[v]NV** function sets the current vertex attribute to $\langle x,y,0,1 \rangle$, and calling the **glVertexAttrib3-{ubsfd}[v]NV** function sets the current vertex attribute to $\langle x,y,z,1 \rangle$.

Calling the **glVertexAttrib{1234}{ubsfd}[v]NV** function with *index* parameter 0 invokes the currently bound vertex program.

Special Considerations

Any current vertex attribute can be updated at any time. In particular, **glVertex-Attrib{1234}{ubsfd}[v]NV** can be called between calls to **glBegin** and **glEnd**.

Get Functions

glGetVertexAttrib{fd}vNV with *pname* parameter GL_CURRENT_ATTRIB_NV

Errors

GL_INVALID_VALUE is generated if *index* is greater than 15.

■ **glVertexAttribs{1234}{ubsfd}vNV**—Specify multiple vertex attributes.

Prototypes

```
void glVertexAttribs1svNV(GLuint index,
                          GLsizei n,
                          const GLshort *v);
void glVertexAttribs1fvNV(GLuint index,
                          GLsizei n,
                          const GLfloat *v);
void glVertexAttribs1dvNV(GLuint index,
                          GLsizei n,
                          const GLdouble *v);
void glVertexAttribs2svNV(GLuint index,
                          GLsizei n,
                          const GLshort *v);
void glVertexAttribs2fvNV(GLuint index,
                          GLsizei n,
                          const GLfloat *v);
void glVertexAttribs2dvNV(GLuint index,
                          GLsizei n,
                          const GLdouble *v);
void glVertexAttribs3svNV(GLuint index,
                          GLsizei n,
                          const GLshort *v);
void glVertexAttribs3fvNV(GLuint index,
                          GLsizei n,
                          const GLfloat *v);
void glVertexAttribs3dvNV(GLuint index,
                          GLsizei n,
                          const GLdouble *v);
void glVertexAttribs4svNV(GLuint index,
                          GLsizei n,
                          const GLshort *v);
void glVertexAttribs4fvNV(GLuint index,
                          GLsizei n,
                          const GLfloat *v);
```

```
void glVertexAttribs4dvNV(GLuint index,
                          GLsizei n,
                          const GLdouble *v);
void glVertexAttribs4ubvNV(GLuint index,
                           GLsizei n,
                           const GLubyte *v);
```

Parameters

index   Specifies the first index of a set of contiguous vertex attributes. Must be in the range 0 to 15.

n   Specifies the number of vertex attributes to be updated.

v   Specifies a pointer to an array of vertex attributes.

Description

The **glVertexAttribs{1234}{ubsfd}vNV** function specifies the values of multiple vertex attributes beginning with *index*. The *n* parameter specifies how many vertex attributes to update, and the *v* parameter points to an array containing a new set of coordinates for each one. Calling the **glVertexAttribs{1234}{ubsfd}vNV** function is equivalent to the following, where size is 1, 2, 3, or 4. The attributes are specified in reverse order so that vertex attribute 0 would be updated last, causing vertex program invocation after the other attributes have been updated.

```
for (int i = n - 1; i >= 0; i--)
{
    glVertexAttrib{1234}{ubsfd}vNV(index + i,
        v + i * size);
}
```

Get Functions

glGetVertexAttrib{fd}vNV with *pname* parameter GL_CURRENT_ATTRIB_NV

Errors

GL_INVALID_VALUE is generated if *index* + *n* is greater than 16.

■ **glVertexAttribPointerNV**—Specify a vertex attribute array.

Prototype

```
void glVertexAttribPointerNV(GLuint index,
                             GLint size,
                             GLenum type,
                             GLsizei stride,
                             const void *pointer);
```

Parameters

index   Specifies the index of a vertex attribute. Must be in the range 0 to 15.

size	Specifies the number of components per entry. Must be 1, 2, 3, or 4.
type	Specifies the data type of each attribute component in the array. Accepted values are GL_SHORT, GL_FLOAT, and GL_DOUBLE.
	If *size* is 4, then *type* may also be GL_UNSIGNED_BYTE.
stride	Specifies the byte offset between consecutive entries in the array. A value of 0 indicates that the entries are tightly packed in the array.
pointer	Specifies a pointer to the first component of the first entry in the array.

Description

The **glVertexAttribPointerNV** function specifies the location and the data format of an array of vertex attribute components that are used by a vertex program. The index of the vertex attribute array is specified by the *index* parameter. The *size* parameter specifies the number of components per vertex attribute, and the *type* parameter specifies the data type of the components. The *stride* parameter specifies the offset from one vertex attribute to the next. A stride of 0 is interpreted to mean that the offset from one vertex attribute to the next is the size of the vertex attribute itself—that is, the vertex attributes are tightly packed together in the array.

Vertex attribute arrays are enabled and disabled by calling the **glEnableClientState** and **glDisableClientState** functions with *array* parameter GL_VERTEX_ATTRIB_ARRAY*i*_ NV, where *i* corresponds to the index parameter passed to the **glVertexAttribPointerNV** function.

The values of the *size*, *type*, and *stride* parameters can be retrieved by calling the **glGetVertexAttribivNV** function, and the value of the *pointer* parameter can be retrieved by calling the **glGetVertexAttribPointervNV** function.

Get Functions

glGetVertexAttribPointervNV

glGetVertexAttribivNV with *pname* parameter GL_ATTRIB_ARRAY_SIZE_NV

glGetVertexAttribivNV with *pname* parameter GL_ATTRIB_ARRAY_TYPE_NV

glGetVertexAttribivNV with *pname* parameter GL_ATTRIB_ARRAY_STRIDE_NV

Errors

GL_INVALID_VALUE is generated if *index* is greater than 15.

GL_INVALID_VALUE is generated if size is not 1, 2, 3, or 4.

GL_INVALID_OPERATION is generated if *type* is GL_UNSIGNED_BYTE and *size* is not 4.

GL_INVALID_VALUE is generated if *stride* is negative.

■ **glGetVertexAttrib{ifd}vNV**—Return vertex attribute state.

Prototypes

```
void glGetVertexAttribivNV(GLuint index,
                           GLenum pname,
                           GLint *params);
void glGetVertexAttribfvNV(GLuint index,
                           GLenum pname,
                           GLfloat *params);
void glGetVertexAttribdvNV(GLuint index,
                           GLenum pname,
                           GLdouble *params);
```

Parameters

index   Specifies the index of a vertex attribute. Must be in the range 0 to 15.

pname   Specifies the symbolic name of a vertex attribute parameter to query. Accepted values are GL_ATTRIB_ARRAY_SIZE_NV, GL_ATTRIB_ARRAY_TYPE_NV, GL_ATTRIB_ARRAY_STRIDE_NV, and GL_CURRENT_ATTRIB_NV.

params   Specifies a pointer to an array that receives the queried state.

Description

The **glGetVertexAttrib{ifd}vNV** function returns information about the vertex attribute specified by the *index* parameter. The *pname* parameter specifies what information to retrieve and may be one of the following values:

GL_ATTRIB_ARRAY_SIZE_NV

The size of the current vertex attribute array is returned in *params*. This corresponds to the value of the *size* parameter passed to the **glVertexAttribPointerNV** function.

GL_ATTRIB_ARRAY_TYPE_NV

The data type of the current vertex attribute array is returned in *params*. This corresponds to the value of the *type* parameter passed to the **glVertexAttribPointerNV** function.

GL_ATTRIB_ARRAY_STRIDE_NV

The stride for the current vertex attribute array is returned in *params*. This corresponds to the value of the *stride* parameter passed to the **glVertexAttribPointerNV** function.

GL_CURRENT_ATTRIB_NV

The current four-component vertex attribute value is returned in the *params* array.

Errors

GL_INVALID_VALUE is generated if *index* is greater than 15.

GL_INVALID_VALUE is generated if *pname* is GL_CURRENT_ATTRIB_NV and *index* is 0.

■ **glGetVertexAttribPointervNV**—Return a vertex attribute array pointer.

Prototype

```
void glGetVertexAttribPointervNV(GLuint index,
                                 GLenum pname,
                                 void **pointer);
```

Parameters

index   Specifies the index of a vertex attribute. Must be in the range 0 to 15.

pname   Must be GL_ATTRIB_ARRAY_POINTER_NV.

pointer   Specifies a pointer to a location that receives the vertex attribute array pointer.

Description

The **glGetVertexAttribPointervNV** function returns the current pointer to the vertex attribute array specified by the *index* parameter. The array pointer, as specified by the **glVertexAttribPointerNV** function, is returned in the *pointer* parameter.

Errors

GL_INVALID_VALUE is generated if *index* is greater than 15.

EXTENDED FUNCTIONS

■ **glEnable, glDisable**—Extended to enable/disable vertex program capabilities.

Prototypes

```
void glEnable(GLenum cap);
void glDisable(GLenum cap);
```

Extended Parameters

cap   Specifies a GL capability. May be one of the values listed in Description.

Description

The **glEnable** and **glDisable** functions are used to enable and disable vertex program capabilities. The *cap* parameter may be one of the following values:

GL_VERTEX_PROGRAM_NV

If enabled, the currently bound vertex program is invoked for each vertex.

GL_VERTEX_PROGRAM_POINT_SIZE_NV

> If enabled, the value written to the o[PSIZ] register specifies the point size. Otherwise, point sizes are determined by the current point parameters.

GL_VERTEX_PROGRAM_TWO_SIDE_NV

> If enabled, front-facing colors or back-facing colors are selected based on whether a polygon is front-facing or back-facing. Otherwise, front-facing colors are always selected.

GL_MAP1_VERTEX_ATTRIBi_4_NV

> If enabled, calls to the **glEvalCoord1{fd}[v]**, **glEvalMesh1**, and **glEvalPoint1** functions generate coordinates for vertex attribute array *i*.

GL_MAP2_VERTEX_ATTRIBi_4_NV

> If enabled, calls to the **glEvalCoord2{fd}[v]**, **glEvalMesh2**, and **glEvalPoint2** functions generate coordinates for vertex attribute array *i*.

■ **glEnableClientState, glDisableClientState**—Extended to enable/disable vertex attribute arrays.

Prototypes

    void **glEnableClientState**(GLenum *array*);
    void **glDisableClientState**(GLenum *array*);

Extended Parameters

array   Specifies an array to enable or disable. May be GL_VERTEX_ATTRIB_ ARRAY*i*_NV, where $0 \leq i \leq 15$.

Description

The **glEnableClientState** and **glDisableClientState** functions enable or disable arrays stored in client space. Vertex attribute array *i* is enabled or disabled by passing the value GL_VERTEX_ATTRIB_ARRAY*i*_NV to the *array* parameter.

■ **glIsEnabled**—Extended to return whether vertex program capabilities are enabled.

Prototypes

    GLboolean **glIsEnabled**(GLenum *cap*);

Extended Parameters

cap   Specifies a GL capability. May be one of the values listed in Description.

Description

The **glIsEnabled** function can be used to determine whether vertex program capabilities are enabled. The *cap* parameter may be one of the following values:

GL_VERTEX_PROGRAM_NV
>   Indicates whether vertex programs are enabled.

GL_VERTEX_PROGRAM_POINT_SIZE_NV
>   Indicates whether vertex program point size output is enabled.

GL_VERTEX_PROGRAM_TWO_SIDE_NV
>   Indicates whether vertex program two-sided primary and secondary colors are enabled.

GL_MAP1_VERTEX_ATTRIBi_4_NV
>   Indicates whether 1D evaluators for vertex attribute array *i* are enabled.

GL_MAP2_VERTEX_ATTRIBi_4_NV
>   Indicates whether 2D evaluators for vertex attribute array *i* are enabled.

GL_VERTEX_ATTRIB_ARRAYi_NV
>   Indicates whether vertex attribute array *i* is enabled.

■ **glMatrixMode**—Extended to support generic tracking matrices.

Prototype

    void **glMatrixMode**(GLenum *mode*);

Extended Parameters

mode   Specifies the matrix stack to which subsequent matrix operations apply. May be GL_MATRIXi_NV, where *i* is in the range 0 to GL_MAX_TRACK_MATRICES_NV − 1.

Description

The **glMatrixMode** function sets the current matrix mode. Generic tracking matrix stack *i* is made current by specifying GL_MATRIXi_NV as the *mode* parameter.

■ **glMap1{fd}**—Extended to allow definition of evaluators for vertex attributes.

Prototypes

    void **glMap1f**(GLenum *target*, GLfloat *u1*, GLfloat *u2*, GLint *stride*,
        GLint *order*, const GLfloat **points*);
    void **glMap1d**(GLenum *target*, GLfloat *u1*, GLfloat *u2*, GLint *stride*,
        GLint *order*, const GLdouble **points*);

Extended Parameters

target   Specifies the kind of values generated by the evaluator. May be GL_MAP1_VERTEX_ATTRIBi_4_NV, where $0 \leq i \leq 15$.

Description

The **glMap1{fd}** function can be used to specify the evaluator basis for a generic vertex attribute. When the *target* parameter is GL_MAP1_VERTEX_ATTRIBi_4_NV, each control point is four floating-point values representing *x*, *y*, *z*, and *w*. Internal **glVertexAttrib4** commands are generated when the map is evaluated, but the current vertex attribute is not updated.

■ **glMap2{fd}**—Extended to allow definition of evaluators for vertex attributes.

Prototypes

```
void glMap2f(GLenum target, GLfloat u1, GLfloat u2, GLint ustride,
    GLint uorder, GLfloat v1, GLfloat v2, GLint vstride, GLint vorder,
    const GLfloat *points);
void glMap2d(GLenum target, GLfloat u1, GLfloat u2, GLint ustride,
    GLint uorder, GLfloat v1, GLfloat v2, GLint vstride, GLint vorder,
    const GLdouble *points);
```

Extended Parameters

target   Specifies the kind of values generated by the evaluator. May be GL_MAP2_VERTEX_ATTRIB*i*_4_NV, where $0 \leq i \leq 15$.

Description

The **glMap2{fd}** function can be used to specify the evaluator basis for a generic vertex attribute. When the *target* parameter is GL_MAP2_VERTEX_ATTRIB*i*_4_NV, each control point is four floating-point values representing *x*, *y*, *z*, and *w*. Internal **glVertexAttrib4** commands are generated when the map is evaluated, but the current vertex attribute is not updated.

■ **glGetMap{ifd}v**—Extended to allow retrieval of evaluator parameters corresponding to vertex attributes.

Prototypes

```
void glGetMapi(GLenum target, GLenum pname, GLint *params);
void glGetMapf(GLenum target, GLenum pname, GLfloat *params);
void glGetMapd(GLenum target, GLenum pname, GLdouble *params);
```

Extended Parameters

target   Specifies the symbolic name of a map. May be GL_MAP1_VERTEX_ATTRIB*i*_4_NV or GL_MAP2_VERTEX_ATTRIB*i*_4_NV, where $0 \leq i \leq 15$.

Description

The **glGetMap{ifd}v** function can be used to retrieve evaluator parameters corresponding to generic vertex attributes.

■ **glGetIntegerv**—Extended to retrieve vertex program state.

Prototype

```
void glGetIntegerv(GLenum pname, GLint *params);
```

Extended Parameters

pname   Specifies the parameter to be returned. May be one of the values listed in Description.

Description

The **glGetIntegerv** function can be used to retrieve various state related to vertex programs. The *pname* parameter may be one of the following values:

GL_VERTEX_PROGRAM_BINDING_NV

The name of the program currently bound to the vertex program target is returned.

GL_PROGRAM_ERROR_POSITION_NV

The byte position within the program string at which an error occurred is returned.

GL_CURRENT_MATRIX_NV

The 16 entries of the current matrix (as specified by the **glMatrixMode** function) are returned and stored in column-major order.

GL_CURRENT_MATRIX_STACK_DEPTH_NV

The current depth of the current matrix stack (as specified by the **glMatrixMode** function) is returned.

GL_MAX_TRACK_MATRICES_NV

The maximum number of generic tracking matrices supported by the implementation is returned. This is always at least 8.

GL_MAX_TRACK_MATRIX_STACK_DEPTH_NV

The maximum stack depth for the generic tracking matrices GL_MATRIX*i*_NV is returned. This may be as small as 1.

18.3 GL_NV_vertex_program1_1

OpenGL version required	OpenGL 1.2.1
Dependencies	Requires GL_NV_vertex_program
Promotions	—
Related extensions	GL_NV_vertex_program2

Discussion

The GL_NV_vertex_program1_1 extension builds upon the GL_NV_vertex_program extension and defines version 1.1 vertex programs. This extension adds four new vertex program instructions and a mechanism for specifying program options. The exact syntax specification for version 1.1 vertex programs is given in Appendix A, Section A.3. To indicate that a vertex program conforms to the version 1.1 syntax, its text string must begin with the character sequence !!VP1.1, with no preceding whitespace.

Instruction Set

Four new instructions are added in version 1.1 vertex programs and are summarized in Table 18.3.1. The functionality provided by the ABS (absolute value) and SUB (subtract) instructions can be achieved in version 1.0 vertex programs, so these two instructions are only included for better program clarity. The DPH (homogeneous dot product) and RCC (reciprocal clamped) instructions provide new functionality.

TABLE 18.3.1   Vertex program instructions added in version 1.1. The letter "v" indicates a vector result or operand, and the letter "s" indicates a scalar operand. The vector $\langle s,s,s,s \rangle$ represents a single scalar result that is replicated to all four components of the result vector.

Instruction	Output Result	Input Operands	Operation
ABS	v	v, v	Absolute value
DPH	$\langle s,s,s,s \rangle$	v, v	Homogeneous dot product
RCC	$\langle s,s,s,s \rangle$	s	Reciprocal clamped
SUB	v	v, v	Subtract

Each of the new vertex program instructions is described in detail below. Included with each instruction is pseudocode that demonstrates the instruction's exact effect. The data types and function calls used by the pseudocode have the same meaning as they do in the instruction descriptions for the GL_NV_vertex_program extension.

ABS—Absolute value

```
ABS     result, op0;
```

The ABS instruction performs a componentwise absolute value operation on a single operand.

```
vector v0 = VectorLoad(op0);
r.x = fabs(v0.x);
r.y = fabs(v0.y);
r.z = fabs(v0.z);
r.w = fabs(v0.w);
result = WriteDest(result, r);
```

DPH—Homogeneous dot product

```
DPH     result, op0, op1;
```

The DPH instruction performs a three-component dot product between two operands and adds the *w* component of the second operand. The result is replicated to all four components of the destination.

```
vector v0 = VectorLoad(op0);
vector v1 = VectorLoad(op1);
dot = v0.x * v1.x + v0.y + v1.y + v0.z * v1.z + v1.w;
r.x = dot;
r.y = dot;
r.z = dot;
r.w = dot;
result = WriteDest(result, r);
```

RCC—Reciprocal clamped

```
RCC     result, op0;
```

The RCC instruction approximates the reciprocal of a single scalar operand and replicates the result to all four components of the destination. Any component of the result that is +0.0 or positive is clamped to the range $[2^{-64}, 2^{64}]$, and any component of the result that is −0.0 or negative is clamped to the range $[-2^{64}, -2^{-64}]$.

```
scalar s0 = ScalarLoad(op0);
scalar recip = ApproxRecip(s0);
if (Positive(recip))
{
    if (recip > 2^64) recip = 2^64;
    else if (recip < 2^-64) recip = 2^-64;
}
else
{
    if (recip < -(2^64)) recip = -(2^64);
    else if (recip > -(2^-64)) recip = -(2^-64);
}
r.x = recip;
r.y = recip;
r.z = recip;
r.w = recip;
result = WriteDest(result, r);
```

The Positive function returns true for +0.0 or any positive value, and returns false for −0.0 or any negative value. The ApproxRecip function satisfies the precision requirement

$$\left| \texttt{ApproxRecip}(x) - \frac{1}{x} \right| < 2^{-22}$$

for values of x satisfying $1.0 \le x \le 2.0$. The reciprocation operation also satisfies the following rule:

$$\texttt{ApproxRecip}(+1.0) = +1.0$$

SUB—Subtract

```
SUB     result, op0, op1;
```

The SUB instruction performs a componentwise subtraction of two operands.

```
vector v0 = VectorLoad(op0);
vector v1 = VectorLoad(op1);
r.x = v0.x - v1.x;
r.y = v0.y - v1.y;
r.z = v0.z - v1.z;
r.w = v0.w - v1.w;
result = WriteDest(result, r);
```

Position-Invariant Programs

Vertex programs that transform a vertex position from object space to homogeneous clip space are not guaranteed to produce exactly the same viewport coordinates as does the conventional vertex transformation pipeline. As a consequence, any multipass rendering algorithm that uses vertex programs for any passes must use vertex programs for all passes, even though the needed functionality for some passes may be achievable using conventional vertex transformations. Otherwise, undesirable depth-buffering artifacts can appear.

In order to facilitate the mixture of passes using vertex programs and passes using conventional OpenGL transformations, a position-invariant option has been added to version 1.1 vertex programs. A vertex program is designated a position-invariant vertex program by inserting the following line before any vertex program instructions.

```
OPTION    NV_position_invariant;
```

When the position-invariant option is present, a vertex program may *not* write a homogeneous clip-space position to register o[HPOS], because the driver will insert the calculation itself using the same process that it uses for conventional vertex transformations. To provide space for the driver to add this calculation, position-invariant vertex programs are limited to 124 instructions.

Using the position-invariant option introduces the restriction that relative program parameter addressing cannot be used. That is, the address register A0.x may not appear in an expression that accesses a program parameter. This restriction reflects a hardware limitation. The ARL instruction is still valid, but provides no meaningful functionality without relative addressing.

18.4 GL_NV_vertex_program2

OpenGL version required	OpenGL 1.2.1
Dependencies	Requires GL_NV_vertex_program
Promotions	—
Related extensions	—

DISCUSSION

The GL_NV_vertex_program2 extension builds upon the GL_NV_vertex_program and GL_NV_vertex_program1_1 extensions, and defines version 2.0 vertex programs. In addition to supporting all of the functionality provided by version 1.0 and version 1.1 vertex programs, version 2.0 vertex programs provide the following new capabilities:

- Several arithmetic instructions have been added:
  - EX2 and LG2—High-precision exponential and logarithm base 2
  - SIN and COS—Sine and cosine functions
  - FLR and FRC—Floor and fraction operations
  - SEQ, SNE, SGT, and SLE—Set on equal to, not equal to, greater than, and less than or equal to
  - STR and SFL—Set on true and set on false
  - SSG—Set sign
- Instructions can optionally set fields of a four-component condition register.
- Conditional branching is supported through the BRA instruction; the target instruction of a branch may be absolute or may be indexed in a table using an address register.
- Subroutine calls up to four deep are supported using the CAL and RET instructions, both of which can be executed conditionally.
- Writes to destination register components can be masked using a condition register in addition to the static write mask already present in previous versions.
- The absolute value of any source operand may be evaluated in addition to the negation and swizzling operations present in previous versions.
- Programmable clipping is supported through the addition of six vertex result registers named o[CLP0] through o[CLP5].
- The number of temporary registers has been extended to 16.
- The number of program parameter registers has been extended to 256.

- The number of address registers has been extended to two, and all four components of each address register can be used.
- The maximum number of program instructions has been extended to 256.

Program Structure

Version 2.0 vertex programs are passed to the GL as a text string containing a list of up to 256 instructions. The text string must begin with the character sequence !!VP2.0, with no preceding whitespace, to indicate that the program conforms to the version 2.0 vertex program syntax. The end of the vertex program is indicated by the three-character sequence END. The exact syntax specification for version 1.0 vertex programs is given in Appendix A, Section A.4.

Operand Modification

In version 2.0 vertex programs, any source operand may have an absolute value operation applied to it at no additional performance cost. This is denoted within a vertex program by surrounding a register name with vertical bars. For example, the following line adds the absolute value of temporary register R1 to temporary register R2.

```
ADD    R0, |R1|, R2;
```

Negation and swizzle operations may still be applied when an absolute value is evaluated. The following line moves the negation of the absolute value of the components of R1 into R0, in reverse order.

```
MOV    R0, -|R1.wzyx|;
```

Conditional Operations

Every instruction, except the BRA, CAL, and RET instructions, can have the letter C appended to its three-character mnemonic to indicate that its result should update the condition register. Only those condition register fields that correspond to written components of the destination register are modified. For example, the following line moves the x and y components of R1 into R0, and updates the x and y fields of the condition register to reflect the values written into R0.

```
MOVC   R0.xy, R1;
```

Writes to the destination register can be conditionally masked by testing the condition register fields against a particular rule. This masking occurs in addition to the static write mask available in previous vertex program versions. To specify that a conditional mask is to be applied, a condition code is enclosed in parentheses, following the destination register. For example, the following line moves each component from R1 to R0 only if the corresponding field of the condition register is set to the value EQ (equal to zero).

```
MOV    R0 (EQ), R1;
```

Condition register fields can also be swizzled just like any source operand. The following line writes to the x, y, z, and w components of R0 only if the w, z, y, and x fields of the condition register are respectively set to the value EQ.

```
MOV    R0 (EQ.wzyx), R1;
```

Register Set

The register set available to version 2.0 vertex programs consists of 16 read-only vertex attribute registers v[0]–v[15], 21 write-only vertex result registers, 256 read-only program parameter registers c[0]–c[255], 16 general purpose temporary registers R0–R15, two address registers A0 and A1, and a condition code register. Every register, including the address registers and the condition code register, consists of four components labeled x, y, z, and w. In this section, we discuss only the new functionality provided by version 2.0 vertex programs. See Section 18.2 for a description of the registers that are also available in version 1.0 vertex programs.

Vertex Result Registers

Table 18.4.1 lists the complete set of vertex result registers present in version 2.0 vertex programs. In order to facilitate user-programmable clipping, six new vertex result registers have been added and are named o[CLP0] through o[CLP5]. When a user clipping plane is enabled (by calling the **glEnable** function with *cap* parameter GL_CLIP_PLANE*i*, where $0 \le i \le 5$), the x component of the corresponding clip distance result register is interpreted as the distance from the clipping plane. The y, z, and w coordinates are ignored.

TABLE 18.4.1   Vertex result registers. Components labeled * are unused.

Result Register	Description	Component Interpretation
o[HPOS]	Homogeneous clip-space position	$\langle x,y,z,w \rangle$
o[COL0]	Primary color (front facing)	$\langle r,g,b,a \rangle$
o[COL1]	Secondary color (front facing)	$\langle r,g,b,a \rangle$
o[BFC0]	Back-facing primary color	$\langle r,g,b,a \rangle$
o[BFC1]	Back-facing secondary color	$\langle r,g,b,a \rangle$
o[FOGC]	Fog coordinate	$\langle f,^*,^*,^* \rangle$
o[PSIZ]	Point size	$\langle p,^*,^*,^* \rangle$
o[TEX0]	Texture 0 coordinates	$\langle s,t,r,q \rangle$
o[TEX1]	Texture 1 coordinates	$\langle s,t,r,q \rangle$
o[TEX2]	Texture 2 coordinates	$\langle s,t,r,q \rangle$
o[TEX3]	Texture 3 coordinates	$\langle s,t,r,q \rangle$
o[TEX4]	Texture 4 coordinates	$\langle s,t,r,q \rangle$
o[TEX5]	Texture 5 coordinates	$\langle s,t,r,q \rangle$

TABLE 18.4.1 *Continued.*

Result Register	Description	Component Interpretation
o[TEX6]	Texture 6 coordinates	$\langle s,t,r,q \rangle$
o[TEX7]	Texture 7 coordinates	$\langle s,t,r,q \rangle$
o[CLP0]	Clip distance 0	$\langle d,*,*,* \rangle$
o[CLP1]	Clip distance 1	$\langle d,*,*,* \rangle$
o[CLP2]	Clip distance 2	$\langle d,*,*,* \rangle$
o[CLP3]	Clip distance 3	$\langle d,*,*,* \rangle$
o[CLP4]	Clip distance 4	$\langle d,*,*,* \rangle$
o[CLP5]	Clip distance 5	$\langle d,*,*,* \rangle$

Condition Code Register

The four components of the condition code register hold values that reflect the result of the most recent instruction to specify that the condition register is updated (indicated by appending the instruction mnemonic with the letter C). Each field may be one of the four following values determined by the corresponding component of the result:

- EQ—The result is equal to zero
- LT—The result is less than zero
- GT—The result is greater than zero
- UN—The result is ±NAN (not a number)

As an example, suppose that register R1 contains the values {1.0, 0.0, −1.0, NAN}. Then the instruction

```
    MOVC    R0, R1;
```

would place the values {GT, EQ, LT, UN} into the condition code register. A subsequent instruction that uses the conditional mask to update only components of the destination whose corresponding field of the condition code register is GT would only update the x component of the destination. The condition codes may be swizzled, so the instruction

```
    MOV    R2 (GT.xxzw), R0;
```

would update both the x and y components of the destination, but not the z and w components.

Instruction Set

There are 39 vertex program instructions. The operation performed by each instruction and the corresponding types of input operands and output results are listed in Table 18.4.2.

TABLE 18.4.2 Vertex program instructions. The letter "v" indicates a vector result or operand, and the letter "s" indicates a scalar operand. The vector $\langle s,s,s,s \rangle$ represents a single scalar result that is replicated to all four components of the result vector.

Instruction	Output Result	Input Operands	Operation
ABS[C]	v	v	Absolute value
ADD[C]	v	v, v	Add
ARA[C]	address	address	Address register add
ARL[C]	address	v	Address register load
ARR[C]	address	v	Address register load with round
BRA	none	address scalar	Branch
CAL	none	address scalar	Call subroutine
COS[C]	$\langle s,s,s,s \rangle$	s	Cosine
DP3[C]	$\langle s,s,s,s \rangle$	v, v	3D dot product
DP4[C]	$\langle s,s,s,s \rangle$	v, v	4D dot product
DPH[C]	$\langle s,s,s,s \rangle$	v, v	Homogeneous dot product
DST[C]	v	v, v	Distance vector
EX2[C]	$\langle s,s,s,s \rangle$	s	Exponential base 2
EXP[C]	v	s	Approximate exponential base 2
FLR[C]	v	v	Floor
FRC[C]	v	v	Fraction
LG2[C]	$\langle s,s,s,s \rangle$	s	Logarithm base 2
LIT[C]	v	v	Light coefficients
LOG[C]	v	s	Approximate logarithm base 2
MAD[C]	v	v, v, v	Multiply-add
MAX[C]	v	v, v	Maximum
MIN[C]	v	v, v	Minimum
MOV[C]	v	v	Move
MUL[C]	v	v, v	Multiply
RCC[C]	$\langle s,s,s,s \rangle$	s	Reciprocal clamped
RCP[C]	$\langle s,s,s,s \rangle$	s	Reciprocal
RET	none	none	Return from subroutine
RSQ[C]	$\langle s,s,s,s \rangle$	s	Reciprocal square root
SEQ[C]	v	v, v	Set on equal
SFL[C]	v	v, v	Set on false

TABLE 18.4.2 *Continued*

Instruction	Output Result	Input Operands	Operation
SGE[C]	v	v, v	Set on greater than or equal
SGT[C]	v	v, v	Set on greater than
SIN[C]	$\langle s,s,s,s \rangle$	s	Sine
SLE[C]	v	v, v	Set on less than or equal
SLT[C]	v	v, v	Set on less than
SNE[C]	v	v, v	Set on not equal
SSG[C]	v	v	Set sign
STR[C]	v	v, v	Set on true
SUB[C]	v	v, v	Subtract

Each of the vertex program instructions is described in detail below. Included with each instruction is pseudocode that demonstrates the instruction's exact effect. The types `vector` and `scalar` are used to hold four-component vector quantities and one-component scalar quantities, respectively. When loading data from a register, the pseudocode makes use of the functions `VectorLoad` and `ScalarLoad` to apply the swizzle, negate, and absolute operations to each operand. In the definitions of these functions, which follow, the `.swiz[n]` field used with the `source` parameter denotes the *n*th component of the source vector after swizzling. The `.comp` field used with the `source` parameter denotes the scalar component selected using the single component suffix in the vertex program. The value of `absolute` is true if the program specifies that the absolute value of the source operand be taken, and is false otherwise. The value of `negate` is true if the program specifies that the source operand is negated, and is false otherwise.

```
vector VectorLoad(vector source)
{
    vector    operand;

    operand.x = source.swiz[0];
    operand.y = source.swiz[1];
    operand.z = source.swiz[2];
    operand.w = source.swiz[3];
    if (absolute)
    {
        operand.x = fabs(operand.x);
        operand.y = fabs(operand.y);
        operand.z = fabs(operand.z);
        operand.w = fabs(operand.w);
    }
    if (negate)
```

```
    {
        operand.x = -operand.x;
        operand.y = -operand.y;
        operand.z = -operand.z;
        operand.w = -operand.w;
    }

    return (operand);
}

scalar ScalarLoad(vector source)
{
    scalar    operand;

    operand = source.comp;
    if (absolute) operand = fabs(operand);
    if (negate) operand = -operand;

    return (operand);
}
```

When a vector result is written to a destination register, the pseudocode makes use of the `WriteDest` function to apply both the static write mask and the conditional write mask. This function is defined below along with two additional functions, `TestCond` and `GenerateCond`. The `TestCond` function returns true if the field of the condition code register specified by the `field` parameter satisfies the condition specified by the `rule` parameter, and returns false if the condition is not satisfied. The `GenerateCond` function returns the condition code corresponding to the `value` parameter.

For the `WriteDest` function, each of the components of `mask` is true if writing is enabled for the corresponding component of the destination register, and is false if writing is disabled. When writing is enabled for a component, the same component of the condition code register, represented by the `condReg` identifier, may also be updated. The condition code register is updated when an instruction uses the `C` suffix, and this is represented by the Boolean value `updateCond`. The `cond` identifier represents the four-component condition register.

```
    bool TestCond(CondCode field, CondCode rule)
    {
        switch (rule)
        {
            case EQ: return (field == EQ);
            case NE: return (field != EQ);
            case LT: return (field == LT);
            case GT: return (field == GT);
            case LE: return ((field == EQ) || (field == LT));
            case GE: return ((field == EQ) || (field == GT));
            case FL: return (false);
```

```
            case TR: return (true);
        }
    }

    CondCode GenerateCond(scalar value)
    {
        if (value == NAN) return (UN);
        if (value < 0.0) return (LT);
        if (value > 0.0) return (GT);
        return (EQ);
    }

    vector WriteDest(vector dest, vector result)
    {
        if ((mask.x) && (TestCond(cond.swiz[0]))
        {
            dest.x = result.x;
            if (updateCond) condReg.x = GenerateCond(dest.x);
        }
        if ((mask.y) && (TestCond(cond.swiz[1]))
        {
            dest.y = result.y;
            if (updateCond) condReg.y = GenerateCond(dest.y);
        }
        if ((mask.z) && (TestCond(cond.swiz[2]))
        {
            dest.z = result.z;
            if (updateCond) condReg.z = GenerateCond(dest.z);
        }
        if ((mask.w) && (TestCond(cond.swiz[3]))
        {
            dest.w = result.w;
            if (updateCond) condReg.w = GenerateCond(dest.w);
        }

        return (dest);
    }
```

The exact effect of each vertex program instruction follows. The local variable r is used in most of the pseudocode listings and always denotes a temporary vector quantity.

ABS[C]—Absolute value

```
    ABS     result, op0;
```

The ABS instruction performs a componentwise absolute value operation on a single operand.

```
vector v0 = VectorLoad(op0);
r.x = fabs(v0.x);
r.y = fabs(v0.y);
r.z = fabs(v0.z);
r.w = fabs(v0.w);
result = WriteDest(result, r);
```

Since the absolute value of any operand to any instruction can be evaluated at no cost, the ABS instruction is effectively obsolete and exists only for backward compatibility.

ADD[C]–Add

```
ADD     result, op0, op1;
```

The ADD instruction performs a componentwise addition of two operands.

```
vector v0 = VectorLoad(op0);
vector v1 = VectorLoad(op1);
r.x = v0.x + v1.x;
r.y = v0.y + v1.y;
r.z = v0.z + v1.z;
r.w = v0.w + v1.w;
result = WriteDest(result, r);
```

The addition operation satisfies the following rules:

1. $x + y = y + x$ for all x and y.
2. $x + 0.0 = x$ for all x.

ARA[C]–Address register add

```
ARA     result, op0;
```

The ARA instruction adds two pairs of components of a single vector address register operand. The x and z components of the result contain the sum of the x and z components of the operand, and the y and w components of the result contain the sum of the y and w components of the operand. The resulting sums are clamped to the range [−512,511].

```
vector v0 = AddrVectorLoad(op0);
scalar xz = v0.x + v0.z;
scalar yw = v0.y + v0.w;
if (xz > 511) xz = 511;
else if (xz < -512) xz = -512;
if (yw > 511) yw = 511;
else if (yw < -512) yw = -512;
r.x = xz;
r.y = yw;
r.z = xz;
```

```
r.w = yw;
result = WriteDest(result, r);
```

ARL[C]–Address register load

```
ARL     result, op0;
```

The ARL instruction loads an address register with a single vector operand. The floor operation is applied to the components of the operand, and each component is clamped to the range [–512,511].

```
vector v0 = VectorLoad(op0);
r.x = floor(v0.x);
r.y = floor(v0.y);
r.z = floor(v0.z);
r.w = floor(v0.w);
if (r.x > 511) r.x = 511;
else if (r.x < -512) r.x = -512;
if (r.y > 511) r.y = 511;
else if (r.y < -512) r.y = -512;
if (r.z > 511) r.z = 511;
else if (r.z < -512) r.z = -512;
if (r.w > 511) r.w = 511;
else if (r.w < -512) r.w = -512;
result = WriteDest(result, r);
```

ARR[C]–Address register load with round

```
ARR     result, op0;
```

The ARR instruction loads an address register with a single vector operand. A rounding operation is applied to the components of the operand, and each component is clamped to the range [–512,511].

```
vector v0 = VectorLoad(op0);
r.x = round(v0.x);
r.y = round(v0.y);
r.z = round(v0.z);
r.w = round(v0.w);
if (r.x > 511) r.x = 511;
else if (r.x < -512) r.x = -512;
if (r.y > 511) r.y = 511;
else if (r.y < -512) r.y = -512;
if (r.z > 511) r.z = 511;
else if (r.z < -512) r.z = -512;
if (r.w > 511) r.w = 511;
else if (r.w < -512) r.w = -512;
result = WriteDest(result, r);
```

The round(x) function returns the nearest integer to x. In the case that the fractional part of x is exactly 0.5, the round function returns the nearest *even* integer.

BRA—Branch

```
BRA    label (condition);
BRA    [addr + offset] (condition);
```

The BRA instruction conditionally transfers control to a static target or to a target that is dynamically looked up in a branch table. The condition may be omitted, in which case it always evaluates to true.

```
if (TestCond(condition))
{
    if (usesBranchTable)
    {
        scalar index = ScalarLoad(addr) + offset;
        if (index < 0) index = 0;
        else if (index >= branchTableSize)
            index = branchTableSize - 1;
        target = branchTable[index];
    }
    else
    {
        target = label;
    }

    // Transfer control to the target instruction
}
```

In the above pseudocode, usesBranchTable is true if the BRA instruction uses an address register and offset to index into a branch table. branchTable represents the array of branch targets, and branchTableSize is equal to the number of entries in the branch table.

CAL—Call subroutine

```
CAL    label (condition);
CAL    [addr + offset] (condition);
```

The CAL instruction conditionally transfers control to a static target or to a target that is dynamically looked up in a branch table. The address of the instruction immediately following the CAL instruction is pushed onto the call stack so that execution will resume at that location when the balancing RET instruction is executed. The condition may be omitted, in which case it always evaluates to true.

```
if (TestCond(condition))
{
    if (usesBranchTable)
```

```
    {
        scalar index = ScalarLoad(addr) + offset;
        if (index < 0) index = 0;
        else if (index >= branchTableSize)
            index = branchTableSize - 1;
        target = branchTable[index];
    }
    else
    {
        target = label;
    }

    if (callStackDepth < 4)
    {
        callStack[callStackDepth] = nextInstruction;
        callStackDepth++;
    }
    else
    {
        // Terminate program
    }

    // Transfer control to the target instruction
}
```

In the above pseudocode, usesBranchTable is true if the CAL instruction uses an address register and offset to index into a branch table. branchTable represents the array of branch targets, and branchTableSize is equal to the number of entries in the branch table. callStack represents the stack of return addresses, and callStackDepth represents the number of addresses currently residing on the call stack.

COS[C]–Cosine

```
    COS    result, op0;
```

The COS instruction calculates the approximate cosine of a single scalar operand. The angle is measured in radians and is not restricted to the range $[0,2\pi]$. The result is replicated to all four components of the destination.

```
    scalar s0 = ScalarLoad(op0);
    scalar cosine = ApproxCos(s0);
    r.x = cosine;
    r.y = cosine;
    r.z = cosine;
    r.w = cosine;
    result = WriteDest(result, r);
```

The cosine operation satisfies the precision requirement

$$\left|\text{ApproxCos}(x)-\cos x\right|<2^{-22}$$

if the value of x satisfies $0 \le x \le 2\pi$. If x falls outside this range, the error in the approximate typically increases with the absolute value of x.

DP3[C]—Three-component dot product

```
DP3     result, op0, op1;
```

The DP3 instruction performs a three-component dot product between two operands and replicates the result to all four components of the destination.

```
vector v0 = VectorLoad(op0);
vector v1 = VectorLoad(op1);
scalar dot = v0.x * v1.x + v0.y + v1.y + v0.z * v1.z;
r.x = dot;
r.y = dot;
r.z = dot;
r.w = dot;
result = WriteDest(result, r);
```

DP4[C]—Four-component dot product

```
DP4     result, op0, op1;
```

The DP4 instruction performs a four-component dot product between two operands and replicates the result to all four components of the destination.

```
vector v0 = VectorLoad(op0);
vector v1 = VectorLoad(op1);
scalar dot = v0.x * v1.x + v0.y + v1.y
             + v0.z * v1.z + v0.w * v1.w;
r.x = dot;
r.y = dot;
r.z = dot;
r.w = dot;
result = WriteDest(result, r);
```

DPH[C]—Homogeneous dot product

```
DPH     result, op0, op1;
```

The DPH instruction performs a three-component dot product between two operands and adds the *w* component of the second operand. The result is replicated to all four components of the destination.

```
vector v0 = VectorLoad(op0);
vector v1 = VectorLoad(op1);
scalar dot = v0.x * v1.x + v0.y + v1.y
```

```
                    + v0.z * v1.z + v1.w;
    r.x = dot;
    r.y = dot;
    r.z = dot;
    r.w = dot;
    result = WriteDest(result, r);
```

DST[C]–Distance vector

```
    DST    result, op0, op1;
```

The DST instruction takes two operands and produces a vector that is useful for attenuation calculations. Given a distance d, the first operand should be formatted as $\langle *,d^2,d^2,* \rangle$, and the second operation should be formatted as $\langle *,1/d,*,1/d \rangle$, where $*$ indicates that the operand's component is not used. The result of the DST instruction is the vector $\langle 1,d,d^2,1/d \rangle$.

```
    vector v0 = VectorLoad(op0);
    vector v1 = VectorLoad(op1);
    r.x = 1.0;
    r.y = v0.y * v1.y;
    r.z = v0.z;
    r.w = v1.w;
    result = WriteDest(result, r);
```

EX2[C]–Exponential base 2

```
    EX2    result, op0;
```

The EX2 instruction calculates an approximation to 2^p for a single scalar operand p and replicates the result to all four components of the destination.

```
    scalar e = ApproxExp2(ScalarLoad(op0));
    r.x = e;
    r.y = e;
    r.z = e;
    r.w = e;
    result = WriteDest(result, r);
```

The ApproxExp2 function satisfies the precision requirement

$$\left| \text{ApproxExp2}(x) - 2^x \right| < \begin{cases} 2^{-22}, & \text{if } 0 \leq x < 1; \\ 2^{-22} \cdot 2^{\lfloor x \rfloor}, & \text{otherwise.} \end{cases}$$

EXP[C]–Approximate exponential base 2

```
    EXP    result, op0;
```

The EXP instruction calculates a rough approximation to 2^p for a single scalar operand p. The result of the exponentiation is returned in the z component of the destination.

```
scalar s0 = ScalarLoad(op0);
r.x = pow(2, floor(s0));
r.y = s0 - floor(s0);
r.z = RoughApproxExp2(s0);
r.w = 1.0;
result = WriteDest(result, r);
```

The RoughApproxExp2 function satisfies the precision requirement

$$\left| \text{RoughApproxExp2}(x) - 2^x \right| < \begin{cases} 2^{-11}, & \text{if } 0 \le x < 1; \\ 2^{-11} \cdot 2^{\lfloor x \rfloor}, & \text{otherwise.} \end{cases}$$

The EXP instruction is deprecated. It is recommended that the EX2 instruction be used instead.

FLR[C]—Floor

```
FLR     result, op0;
```

The FLR instruction performs a componentwise floor operation on a single operand.

```
vector v0 = VectorLoad(op0);
r.x = floor(v0.x);
r.y = floor(v0.y);
r.z = floor(v0.z);
r.w = floor(v0.w);
result = WriteDest(result, r);
```

FRC[C]—Fraction

```
FRC     result, op0;
```

The FRC instruction performs a componentwise fraction operation on a single operand. The fraction operation is equivalent to subtracting the floor of the operand from the operand itself.

```
vector v0 = VectorLoad(op0);
r.x = v0.x - floor(v0.x);
r.y = v0.y - floor(v0.y);
r.z = v0.z - floor(v0.z);
r.w = v0.w - floor(v0.w);
result = WriteDest(result, r);
```

LG2[C]—Logarithm base 2

```
LG2     result, op0;
```

The LG2 instruction calculates an approximation to $\log_2(p)$ for a single scalar operand p and replicates the result to all four components of the destination.

```
scalar l = ApproxLog2(ScalarLoad(op0));
r.x = l;
r.y = l;
r.z = l;
r.w = l;
result = WriteDest(result, r);
```

The `ApproxLog2` function satisfies the precision requirement

$$\left| \text{ApproxLog2}(x) - \log_2 x \right| < 2^{-22}.$$

LIT[C]—Light coefficients

```
LIT    result, op0;
```

The `LIT` instruction takes a single operand and produces a coefficient vector that is useful for lighting calculations. The operand is assumed to be formatted as $\langle \mathbf{N \cdot L}, \mathbf{N \cdot H}, *, m \rangle$, where $\mathbf{N \cdot L}$ is the diffuse dot product, $\mathbf{N \cdot H}$ is the specular dot product, m is the specular exponent, and $*$ indicates that the z component is unused. The result of the `LIT` instruction is the vector $\langle 1.0, \mathbf{N \cdot L}, (\mathbf{N \cdot H})^m, 1.0 \rangle$, where $\mathbf{N \cdot L}$ and $\mathbf{N \cdot H}$ are clamped to 0.0 and the z component is set to 0.0 if $\mathbf{N \cdot L} \leq 0$. The specular exponent m is clamped to the range $(-128, 128)$.

```
vector v0 = VectorLoad(op0);
if (v0.x < 0.0) v0.x = 0.0;
if (v0.y < 0.0) v0.y = 0.0;
if (v0.w < -128.0 + epsilon) v0.w = -128.0 + epsilon;
else if (v0.w > 128.0 - epsilon) v0.w = 128.0 - epsilon;
r.x = 1.0;
r.y = v0.x;
r.z = (v0.x > 0.0) ? RoughApproxPow(v0.y, v0.w) : 0.0;
r.w = 1.0;
result = WriteDest(result, r);
```

The `RoughApproxPow` function is defined in terms of the rough base-2 exponential and logarithm functions implemented by the `EXP` and `LOG` instructions. Thus,

```
RoughApproxPow(b, e)
    = RoughApproxExp2(e * RoughApproxLog2(b))
```

and the precision of the `RoughApproxPow` function is limited by the precision of the `RoughApproxExp2` and `RoughApproxLog2` functions.

LOG[C]—Approximate logarithm base 2

```
LOG    result, op0;
```

The `LOG` instruction calculates a rough approximation to $\log_2(p)$ for a single scalar operand p. The result of the operation is returned in the z component of the destination.

```
scalar s0 = fabs(ScalarLoad(op0));
r.x = floor(log2(s0));
r.y = s0 * pow(2, -floor(log2(s0)));
r.z = RoughApproxLog2(s0);
r.w = 1.0;
result = WriteDest(result, r);
```

The RoughApproxLog2 function satisfies the precision requirement

$$\left|\text{RoughApproxLog2}(x) - \log_2 x\right| < 2^{-11}.$$

The LOG instruction is deprecated. It is recommended that the LG2 instruction be used instead.

MAD[C]—Multiply-add

```
MAD     result, op0, op1, op2;
```

The MAD instruction performs a componentwise multiplication and addition of three operands.

```
vector v0 = VectorLoad(op0);
vector v1 = VectorLoad(op1);
vector v2 = VectorLoad(op2);
r.x = v0.x * v1.x + v2.x;
r.y = v0.y * v1.y + v2.y;
r.z = v0.z * v1.z + v2.z;
r.w = v0.w * v1.w + v2.w;
result = WriteDest(result, r);
```

The multiplication and addition operations are subject to the same rules described for the MUL and ADD instructions.

MAX[C]—Maximum

```
MAX     result, op0, op1;
```

The MAX instruction performs a componentwise maximum operation between two operands.

```
vector v0 = VectorLoad(op0);
vector v1 = VectorLoad(op1);
r.x = (v0.x > v1.x) ? v0.x : v1.x;
r.y = (v0.y > v1.y) ? v0.y : v1.y;
r.z = (v0.z > v1.z) ? v0.z : v1.z;
r.w = (v0.w > v1.w) ? v0.w : v1.w;
result = WriteDest(result, r);
```

MIN[C]—Minimum

```
MIN     result, op0, op1;
```

The `MIN` instruction performs a componentwise minimum operation between two operands.

```
vector v0 = VectorLoad(op0);
vector v1 = VectorLoad(op1);
r.x = (v0.x > v1.x) ? v1.x : v0.x;
r.y = (v0.y > v1.y) ? v1.y : v0.y;
r.z = (v0.z > v1.z) ? v1.z : v0.z;
r.w = (v0.w > v1.w) ? v1.w : v0.w;
result = WriteDest(result, r);
```

MOV[C]—Move

```
MOV     result, op0;
```

The `MOV` instruction copies a single operand to the destination.

```
vector v0 = VectorLoad(op0);
result = WriteDest(result, v0);
```

MUL[C]—Multiply

```
MUL     result, op0, op1;
```

The `MUL` instruction performs a componentwise multiplication of two operands.

```
vector v0 = VectorLoad(op0);
vector v1 = VectorLoad(op1);
r.x = v0.x * v1.x;
r.y = v0.y * v1.y;
r.z = v0.z * v1.z;
r.w = v0.w * v1.w;
result = WriteDest(result, r);
```

The multiplication operation satisfies the following rules:

1. $xy = yx$ for all x and y.
2. $x \cdot 1.0 = x$ for all x.
3. $x \cdot \pm 0.0 = \pm 0.0$ for all x, with the possible exception of $\pm INF$ and $\pm NAN$.

RCC[C]—Reciprocal clamped

```
RCC     result, op0;
```

The `RCC` instruction approximates the reciprocal of a single scalar operand and replicates the result to all four components of the destination. Any component of the result that is +0.0 or positive is clamped to the range $[2^{-64}, 2^{64}]$, and any component of the result that is −0.0 or negative is clamped to the range $[-2^{64}, -2^{-64}]$.

```
scalar s0 = ScalarLoad(op0);
scalar recip = ApproxRecip(s0);
if (Positive(recip))
{
    if (recip > 2^64) recip = 2^64;
    else if (recip < 2^-64) recip = 2^-64;
}
else
{
    if (recip < -(2^64)) recip = -(2^64);
    else if (recip > -(2^-64)) recip = -(2^-64);
}
r.x = recip;
r.y = recip;
r.z = recip;
r.w = recip;
result = WriteDest(result, r);
```

The `Positive` function returns true for +0.0 or any positive value, and returns false for −0.0 or any negative value. The `ApproxRecip` function satisfies the precision requirement

$$\left| \text{ApproxRecip}(x) - \frac{1}{x} \right| < 2^{-22}$$

for values of x satisfying $1.0 \le x \le 2.0$. The reciprocation operation also satisfies the following rule:

$$\text{ApproxRecip}(+1.0) = +1.0$$

RCP[C]—Reciprocal

```
RCP     result, op0;
```

The RCP instruction approximates the reciprocal of a single scalar operand and replicates the result to all four components of the destination.

```
scalar s0 = ScalarLoad(op0);
scalar recip = ApproxRecip(s0);
r.x = recip;
r.y = recip;
r.z = recip;
r.w = recip;
result = WriteDest(result, r);
```

The `ApproxRecip` function satisfies the precision requirement

$$\left| \text{ApproxRecip}(x) - \frac{1}{x} \right| < 2^{-22}$$

for values of x satisfying $1.0 \leq x \leq 2.0$. The reciprocation operation also satisfies the following rule:

$$\text{ApproxRecip}(+1.0) = +1.0$$

RET–Return from subroutine

```
RET     (condition)
```

The `RET` instruction conditionally transfers control to the instruction following a previous balancing `CAL` instruction by pulling the instruction address off of the call stack. The condition may be omitted, in which case it always evaluates to true.

```
if (TestCond(condition))
{
    if (callStackDepth > 0)
    {
        callStackDepth-;
        target = callStack[callStackDepth];
    }
    else
    {
        // Terminate program
    }

    // Transfer control to target instruction
}
```

In the above pseudocode, `callStack` represents the stack of return addresses, and `callStackDepth` represents the number of addresses currently residing on the call stack.

RSQ[C]–Reciprocal square root

```
RSQ     result, op0;
```

The `RSQ` instruction approximates the reciprocal square root of a single scalar operand and replicates the result to all four components of the destination.

```
scalar s0 = ScalarLoad(op0);
scalar rsqrt = ApproxRSQRT(s0);
r.x = rsqrt;
r.y = rsqrt;
```

```
r.z = rsqrt;
r.w = rsqrt;
result = WriteDest(result, r);
```

The `ApproxRSQRT` function satisfies the precision requirement

$$\left| \mathtt{ApproxRSQRT}(x) - \frac{1}{\sqrt{x}} \right| < 2^{-22}$$

for values of x satisfying $1.0 \leq x \leq 4.0$.

SEQ[C]—Set on equal

```
SEQ     result, op0, op1;
```

The `SEQ` instruction performs a componentwise comparison between two operands. Each component of the result vector is set to 1.0 if the corresponding component of the first operand is equal to the corresponding component of the second operand, and is set to 0.0 otherwise.

```
vector v0 = VectorLoad(op0);
vector v1 = VectorLoad(op1);
r.x = (v0.x == v1.x) ? 1.0 : 0.0;
r.y = (v0.y == v1.y) ? 1.0 : 0.0;
r.z = (v0.z == v1.z) ? 1.0 : 0.0;
r.w = (v0.w == v1.w) ? 1.0 : 0.0;
result = WriteDest(result, r);
```

SFL[C]—Set on false

```
SFL     result, op0, op1;
```

The `SFL` instruction performs a componentwise comparison between two operands, but always evaluates to false. Thus, the values of the operands are ignored, and each component of the result is set to 0.0.

```
r.x = 0.0;
r.y = 0.0;
r.z = 0.0;
r.w = 0.0;
result = WriteDest(result, r);
```

SGE[C]—Set on greater than or equal

```
SGE     result, op0, op1;
```

The `SGE` instruction performs a componentwise comparison between two operands. Each component of the result vector is set to 1.0 if the corresponding component of the first operand is greater than or equal to the corresponding component of the second operand, and is set to 0.0 otherwise.

```
vector v0 = VectorLoad(op0);
vector v1 = VectorLoad(op1);
r.x = (v0.x >= v1.x) ? 1.0 : 0.0;
r.y = (v0.y >= v1.y) ? 1.0 : 0.0;
r.z = (v0.z >= v1.z) ? 1.0 : 0.0;
r.w = (v0.w >= v1.w) ? 1.0 : 0.0;
result = WriteDest(result, r);
```

SGT[C]–Set on greater than

```
SGT     result, op0, op1;
```

The SGT instruction performs a componentwise comparison between two operands. Each component of the result vector is set to 1.0 if the corresponding component of the first operand is greater than the corresponding component of the second operand, and is set to 0.0 otherwise.

```
vector v0 = VectorLoad(op0);
vector v1 = VectorLoad(op1);
r.x = (v0.x > v1.x) ? 1.0 : 0.0;
r.y = (v0.y > v1.y) ? 1.0 : 0.0;
r.z = (v0.z > v1.z) ? 1.0 : 0.0;
r.w = (v0.w > v1.w) ? 1.0 : 0.0;
result = WriteDest(result, r);
```

SIN[C]–Sine

```
SIN     result, op0;
```

The SIN instruction calculates the approximate sine of a single scalar operand. The angle is measured in radians and is not restricted to the range $[0,2\pi]$. The result is replicated to all four components of the destination.

```
scalar s0 = ScalarLoad(op0);
scalar sine = ApproxSin(s0);
r.x = sine;
r.y = sine;
r.z = sine;
r.w = sine;
result = WriteDest(result, r);
```

The sine operation satisfies the precision requirement

$$\left|\text{ApproxSin}(x) - \sin x\right| < 2^{-22}$$

if the value of x satisfies $0 \leq x < 2\pi$. If x falls outside this range, the error in the approximate typically increases with the absolute value of x.

SLE[C]—Set on less than or equal

```
SLE    result, op0, op1;
```

The SLE instruction performs a componentwise comparison between two operands. Each component of the result vector is set to 1.0 if the corresponding component of the first operand is less than or equal to the corresponding component of the second operand, and is set to 0.0 otherwise.

```
vector v0 = VectorLoad(op0);
vector v1 = VectorLoad(op1);
r.x = (v0.x <= v1.x) ? 1.0 : 0.0;
r.y = (v0.y <= v1.y) ? 1.0 : 0.0;
r.z = (v0.z <= v1.z) ? 1.0 : 0.0;
r.w = (v0.w <= v1.w) ? 1.0 : 0.0;
result = WriteDest(result, r);
```

SLT[C]—Set on less than

```
SLT    result, op0, op1;
```

The SLT instruction performs a componentwise comparison between two operands. Each component of the result vector is set to 1.0 if the corresponding component of the first operand is less than the corresponding component of the second operand, and is set to 0.0 otherwise.

```
vector v0 = VectorLoad(op0);
vector v1 = VectorLoad(op1);
r.x = (v0.x < v1.x) ? 1.0 : 0.0;
r.y = (v0.y < v1.y) ? 1.0 : 0.0;
r.z = (v0.z < v1.z) ? 1.0 : 0.0;
r.w = (v0.w < v1.w) ? 1.0 : 0.0;
result = WriteDest(result, r);
```

SNE[C]—Set on not equal

```
SNE    result, op0, op1;
```

The SNE instruction performs a componentwise comparison between two operands. Each component of the result vector is set to 1.0 if the corresponding component of the first operand is not equal to the corresponding component of the second operand, and is set to 0.0 otherwise.

```
vector v0 = VectorLoad(op0);
vector v1 = VectorLoad(op1);
r.x = (v0.x != v1.x) ? 1.0 : 0.0;
```

```
r.y = (v0.y != v1.y) ? 1.0 : 0.0;
r.z = (v0.z != v1.z) ? 1.0 : 0.0;
r.w = (v0.w != v1.w) ? 1.0 : 0.0;
result = WriteDest(result, r);
```

SSG[C]—Set sign

```
SSG     result, op0;
```

The SSG instruction generates a result vector containing the signs of each component of a single operand. A component of the result is set to 1.0 if the corresponding component of the operand is greater than zero, 0.0 if the corresponding component of the operand is equal to zero, and −1.0 if the corresponding component of the operand is less than zero.

```
float GetSign(float f)
{
    if (f > 0.0) return (1.0);
    if (f == 0.0) return (0.0);
    if (f < 0.0) return (-1.0);
    return (NAN);
}

vector v0 = VectorLoad(op0);
r.x = GetSign(v0.x);
r.y = GetSign(v0.y);
r.z = GetSign(v0.z);
r.w = GetSign(v0.w);
result = WriteDest(result, r);
```

STR[C]—Set on true

```
STR     result, op0, op1;
```

The STR instruction performs a componentwise comparison between two operands, but always evaluates to true. Thus, the values of the operands are ignored and each component of the result is set to 1.0.

```
r.x = 1.0;
r.y = 1.0;
r.z = 1.0;
r.w = 1.0;
result = WriteDest(result, r);
```

SUB[C]—Subtract

```
SUB     result, op0, op1;
```

The SUB instruction performs a componentwise subtraction of two operands.

```
vector v0 = VectorLoad(op0);
vector v1 = VectorLoad(op1);
r.x = v0.x - v1.x;
r.y = v0.y - v1.y;
r.z = v0.z - v1.z;
r.w = v0.w - v1.w;
result = WriteDest(result, r);
```

FRAGMENT PROGRAMS

IN THIS CHAPTER

19.1   **GL_ARB_fragment_program**

OpenGL version required	OpenGL 1.3
Dependencies	Requires `GL_EXT_texture_lod_bias`
Promotions	—
Related extensions	`GL_ARB_vertex_program`

DISCUSSION

The `GL_ARB_fragment_program` extension provides fully general programmability for per-fragment calculations, subsuming the conventional OpenGL texture environment application, color sum, and fog-blending operation. Conventional per-fragment calculations can be replaced by assembly-like source code that an implementation compiles into a *fragment program*. Fragment programs are able to perform complex per-fragment calculations, including flexible dependent texture accesses, to determine the final fragment color that is generated. Fragment programs may also generate a new depth value that replaces the depth value of a fragment normally generated during rasterization.

Fragment programs provide an interface for directly accessing generalized fragment-processing hardware. Fragment programs are enabled and disabled by calling the **glEnable** and **glDisable** functions with *cap* parameter GL_FRAGMENT_PROGRAM_ARB. When fragment programs are enabled, all conventional texture environment and color sum operations are subsumed, and must be handled by the current fragment program. Fragment programs may choose to apply the fog-blending operation themselves or let OpenGL perform the conventional fog calculation.

Fragment programs do not subsume conventional per-fragment operations that occur after the fog-blending operation, such as the scissor test, alpha test, stencil test, or depth test. An instruction is provided, however, that is able to discard fragments based on arbitrary calculations performed by a fragment program.

Fragment programs have access to only a single fragment at a time. The information that a fragment program receives as inputs for each fragment includes rasterized attributes, such as the fragment's window-space position, primary and secondary colors, and texture coordinates. Fragment programs also have access to a large bank of constant parameter registers that do not change from one fragment to another. These parameters can be used to pass any necessary constant data to a fragment program. For example, material colors and fog parameters would be stored in the parameter registers.

After performing its calculations, a fragment program writes a color and/or depth to a pair of result registers. If a new depth coordinate is not written to a result register, the conventionally rasterized depth coordinate is used for the fragment.

Program Structure

A fragment program is specified as a text string containing a series of statements. The text string must begin with the character sequence !!ARBfp1.0, with no preceding whitespace, to indicate that the program conforms to the version 1.0 ARB fragment program syntax. The end of the fragment program is indicated by the three-character sequence END. The exact syntax specification for version 1.0 ARB fragment programs is given in Appendix A, Section A.5.

A fragment program statement can be either a naming statement or an instruction statement. A naming statement associates an identifier with some kind of data, such as a fragment attribute, a program parameter, or a temporary register. An instruction statement operates on input registers that may or may not be associated with previously named identifiers and stores its result in a temporary register or output register. Every statement is terminated with a semicolon.

A fragment program instruction consists of a three-character mnemonic followed by a destination register and up to three source operands delimited by commas. The example shown in Listing 19.1.1 performs a projective texture access into a 2D texture map and modulates the fetched color by the interpolated primary color. The symbol # denotes the beginning of a comment that extends to the end of the line on which it appears.

LISTING 19.1.1   The following fragment program performs a 2D projective texture access using texture image unit 0 and modulates the result by the primary color.

```
!!ARBfp1.0

TEMP    temp;

# Fetch a sample from the 2D texture bound to unit 0
TXP    temp, fragment.texcoord[0], texture[0], 2D;

# Modulate by the primary color
```

```
MUL     result.color, temp, fragment.color;

END
```

The fragment program shown in Listing 19.1.1 contains a single naming statement that declares the temporary register `temp`, but accesses fragment attributes and the color result register directly in the instruction statements. The same fragment program could be written in the manner shown in Listing 19.1.2. In this version of the program, the fragment attributes and the result register are first bound to identifiers that are used in the remainder of the program. The naming statements and instruction statements used in this fragment program are described in the sections that follow.

LISTING 19.1.2 The following fragment program performs a 2D projective texture access using texture image unit 0 and modulates the result by the primary color. At the beginning of the program, fragment attributes and the color result register are bound to identifiers that are used in the remainder of the program.

```
!!ARBfp1.0

ATTRIB     texcoord = texcoord[0];
ATTRIB     color = fragment.color;

OUTPUT     fragColor = result.color;

TEMP       temp;

# Fetch a sample from the 2D texture bound to unit 0
TXP     temp, texcoord, texture[0], 2D;

# Modulate by the primary color
MUL     fragColor, temp, color;

END
```

All registers manipulated by a fragment program are treated as vectors consisting of four floating-point components x, y, z, and w. The components of any vector may also be referred to as r, g, b, and a, representing red, green, blue, and alpha color components. Some instructions require a scalar operand, in which case a vector component must be selected from the source register by appending .x, .y, .z, .w, .r, .g, .b, or .a. For example, the following line calculates the reciprocal of the a component of the operand `color`.

```
RCP     temp, color.a;
```

Operand Modification

In a fragment program instruction statement, any source operand may have an optional negation operation as well as an arbitrary swizzle operation applied to it. Prepending an operand name with a minus sign negates each of its components before it is used by an instruction. For example, the following line subtracts the contents operand b from operand a and places the result in the register associated with the sub identifier.

```
ADD    sub, a, -b;
```

The swizzle operation allows components of a source operand to be reordered or duplicated arbitrarily. Swizzling is denoted by appending a period and a sequence of four letters from one of the sets {x, y, z, w} and {r, g, b, a} to an identifier. The four letters define a remapping of the components of a register that are passed to the instruction as one of its source operands. As an example, the following line reads the components of the operand vector in reverse order and stores them in the register reverse.

```
MOV    reverse, vector.wzyx;
```

Omitting the swizzle suffix is equivalent to using the suffix .xyzw or .rgba.

Components may be duplicated in the swizzle suffix. For example, the following line moves the x component of vector into the x and y components of temp and moves the y component of vector into the z and w components of temp. The z and w components of vector are ignored.

```
MOV    temp, vector.xxyy;
```

A shorthand notation exists for duplicating a single component of a register to all four components of a source operand. Appending an identifier with a period and a single letter is equivalent to using the same letter four times in a row. For example, the following line moves the x component of vector into all four components of temp.

```
MOV    temp, vector.x;
```

This notation is also necessary for denoting the scalar operand required by instructions such as the RCP (reciprocal) instruction.

Destination Masking

A write mask may be applied to the destination register and controls which components of the destination are updated with an instruction's result. A write mask is denoted by appending a period followed by up to four *unique* letters from one of the sets {x, y, z, w} and {r, g, b, a} to an identifier in the natural component order. For example, the following line moves the contents of the x component of vector into the x component of temp, but does not alter the y, z, or w components of temp.

```
MOV    temp.x, vector;
```

The following line adds the r and g components of color and stores the result in the r and a components of temp without affecting the g and b components of temp.

```
ADD     temp.ra, color.r, color.g;
```

Omitting the write mask is equivalent to specifying the write mask .xyzw or .rgba.

Result Saturation

Any fragment program instruction may be suffixed with the sequence _SAT to indicate that any components written to the destination register should saturate in the range [0.0,1.0]. For example, the following line multiplies operands a and b, clamps the result to the range [0.0,1.0], and stores it in temp.

```
MUL_SAT    temp, a, b;
```

The saturate suffix may be used with instructions that access textures, but some implementations may need to insert extra instructions to perform the complete operation.

Constant Declarations

Fragment programs support embedded constants that may be scalar floating-point quantities or four-component vector quantities. The notation used to specify floating-point constants is identical to that used by the C language.

An embedded scalar constant is specified by simply inserting a signed floating-point number into a location where an identifier would normally be used. A scalar constant is equivalent to a vector constant whose four components are all the same value. The following line adds 2.5 to each component of the operand a.

```
ADD     temp, a, 2.5;
```

An embedded vector constant is represented by a comma-delimited list of one to four floating-point numbers enclosed in braces. For example, the following line adds a different value to each of the components of a.

```
ADD     temp, a, {1.0, 2.0, 3.0, 4.0};
```

If fewer than four components are specified, then the y, z, and w components are filled with 0.0, 0.0, and 1.0, respectively, as needed. For example, the vector constant {3.0, 2.0} is equivalent to the vector constant {3.0, 2.0, 0.0, 1.0}.

If more than four unique scalar floating-point constants are used in a single instruction, some implementations may need to generate additional instructions to perform the operation.

Fragment Attributes

An identifier is bound to a fragment attribute using the ATTRIB statement. The fragment attributes that can be bound are listed in Table 19.1.1. As an example, the following line binds the fragment primary color to the identifier primColor.

```
ATTRIB primColor = fragment.color.primary;
```

After this declaration, instructions that refer to the `primColor` identifier as a source operand read the current primary color.

TABLE 19.1.1 Fragment Attribute Bindings

Attribute Binding	Component Usage	Underlying State
`fragment.color`	(r,g,b,a)	Primary color
`fragment.color.primary`	(r,g,b,a)	Primary color
`fragment.color.secondary`	(r,g,b,a)	Secondary color
`fragment.texcoord`	(s,t,r,q)	Texture coordinates, unit 0
`fragment.texcoord[n]`	(s,t,r,q)	Texture coordinates, unit n
`fragment.fogcoord`	$(f,0,0,1)$	Fog coordinate
`fragment.position`	$(x,y,z,1/w)$	Window-space position

The `fragment.fogcoord` binding corresponds to the interpolated fog coordinate. If vertex programs are being used (see Chapter 18), the fog coordinate is interpolated among the values generated at each vertex. Otherwise, if the `GL_EXT_fog_coord` extension is supported (see Chapter 11, Section 11.1), the fog coordinate depends on the current value of `GL_FOG_COORDINATE_SOURCE_EXT`. If the fog coordinate source is `GL_FRAGMENT_DEPTH_EXT`, or the `GL_EXT_fog_coord` extension is not supported, then the fog coordinate is the depth of the fragment. If the fog coordinate source is `GL_FOG_COORDINATE_EXT`, then the fog coordinate is interpolated among the values assigned to each vertex.

The `fragment.position` binding corresponds to the window-space position of the fragment. The x and y components represent the window position of the fragment and fall into the range specified by the **glViewport** function. The z component represents the window depth of the fragment and falls into the range specified by the **glDepthRange** function. The w component contains the reciprocal of the clip-space *w* coordinate corresponding to the fragment.

Program Parameters

Fragment programs have access to a set of program parameters that fall into the following three categories.

- **Program environment parameters.** These are global constants that are shared by all fragment programs.
- **Program local parameters.** These are local constants that are private to a single fragment program.
- **OpenGL state.** This includes state such as matrices, lighting materials, and texture environment colors.

A fragment program may also declare a floating-point scalar or vector constant either explicitly in a naming statement or implicitly in an instruction statement.

An identifier is bound to a constant value, a program environment parameter, a program local parameter, or a particular OpenGL state using the PARAM statement. A constant vector value is declared by assigning a comma-delimited list of one to four floating-point values enclosed in braces to an identifier. For example, the following line binds the constant vector $\langle 1.0, 2.0, 3.0, 4.0 \rangle$ to the name const.

```
PARAM const = {1.0, 2.0, 3.0, 4.0};
```

If fewer than four components are specified, then the y, z, and w components are filled with 0.0, 0.0, and 1.0, respectively, as needed. A scalar constant is declared by simply assigning a floating-point value to an identifier. The following line binds the value $-\pi$ to the name negPi.

```
PARAM negPi = -3.14159;
```

Assigning a scalar value to an identifier is equivalent to assigning a vector to the identifier with the same value for all four components.

Table 19.1.2 lists the names of the program environment parameters and program local parameters that can be bound. A single program environment parameter is bound to the name coef by the following line:

```
PARAM coef = program.env[0];
```

Arrays may also be declared that bind multiple contiguous program parameters to the same identifier. This is done by using the notation [a..b] to specify a range of parameter indices. For example, the following line binds program environment parameters 0 through 3 to the array identifier coef.

```
PARAM coef[4] = program.env[0..3];
```

The size of the array may be omitted, in which case it is deduced from the number of parameters to which the identifier is bound.

TABLE 19.1.2 Program Parameter Bindings

Parameter Binding	Component Usage	Underlying State
program.env[a]	(x,y,z,w)	Program environment parameter a
program.env[a..b]	(x,y,z,w)	The array of program environment parameters a through b
program.local[a]	(x,y,z,w)	Program local parameter a
program.local[a..b]	(x,y,z,w)	The array of program local parameters a through b

Constant data is loaded into a program environment parameter by calling the **gl-ProgramEnvParameter4{fd}[v]ARB** function,

> void **glProgramEnvParameter4{fd}ARB**(GLenum *target*,
>   GLuint *index*,
>   T *x*,
>   T *y*,
>   T *z*,
>   T *w*);

> void **glProgramEnvParameter4{fd}vARB**(GLenum *target*,
>   GLuint *index*,
>   const T *params*);

with *target* parameter GL_FRAGMENT_PROGRAM_ARB. (The type T represents GLfloat or GLdouble.) The *index* parameter specifies which program environment parameter to load and must be less than the value returned by the **glGetProgramivARB** function when called with *pname* parameter GL_MAX_PROGRAM_ENV_PARAMETERS_ARB.

Constant data is loaded into a program local parameter by calling the **glProgram-LocalParameter4{fd}[v]ARB** function,

> void **glProgramLocalParameter4{fd}ARB**(GLenum *target*,
>   GLuint *index*,
>   T *x*,
>   T *y*,
>   T *z*,
>   T *w*);

> void **glProgramLocalParameter4{fd}vARB**(GLenum *target*,
>   GLuint *index*,
>   const T *params*);

with *target* parameter GL_FRAGMENT_PROGRAM_ARB. The *index* parameter specifies which program local parameter to load and must be less than the value returned by the **glGet-ProgramivARB** function when called with *pname* parameter GL_MAX_PROGRAM_LOCAL_PARAMETERS_ARB. When a program local parameter is specified, it applies only to the currently bound fragment program.

An identifier can be bound to material property states by using the PARAM statement with one of the names listed in Table 19.1.3. Material properties for both front-facing and back-facing primitives are available, and are distinguished by using the state.material.front prefix or the state.material.back prefix. If the .front or .back component is omitted, the front-facing state is selected.

TABLE 19.1.3 Material Property Bindings

Material Binding	Component Usage	Underlying State
state.material.ambient	(r,g,b,a)	Front ambient material color
state.material.diffuse	(r,g,b,a)	Front diffuse material color
state.material.specular	(r,g,b,a)	Front specular material color
state.material.emission	(r,g,b,a)	Front emission material color
state.material.shininess	(s,0,0,1)	Front specular material shininess
state.material.front.ambient	(r,g,b,a)	Front ambient material color
state.material.front.diffuse	(r,g,b,a)	Front diffuse material color
state.material.front.specular	(r,g,b,a)	Front specular material color
state.material.front.emission	(r,g,b,a)	Front emission material color
state.material.front.shininess	(s,0,0,1)	Front specular material shininess
state.material.back.ambient	(r,g,b,a)	Back ambient material color
state.material.back.diffuse	(r,g,b,a)	Back diffuse material color
state.material.back.specular	(r,g,b,a)	Back specular material color
state.material.back.emission	(r,g,b,a)	Back emission material color
state.material.back.shininess	(s,0,0,1)	Back specular material shininess

An identifier can be bound to state for a particular light or for the current light model by using the PARAM statement with one of the names listed in Table 19.1.4. Those states that begin with the prefix state.light[n] refer to states associated with light n.

TABLE 19.1.4 Light Property Bindings

Light Binding	Component Usage	Underlying State
state.light[n].ambient	(r,g,b,a)	Light n ambient color
state.light[n].diffuse	(r,g,b,a)	Light n diffuse color
state.light[n].specular	(r,g,b,a)	Light n specular color
state.light[n].position	(x,y,z,w)	Light n position
state.light[n].attenuation	(k_c,k_b,k_q,e)	Light n attenuation constants k_c, k_b, and k_q and spotlight exponent e.

(continues)

TABLE 19.1.4   *Continued*

Light Binding	Component Usage	Underlying State
`state.light[n].spot.direction`	$(d_x, d_y, d_z, \cos \alpha)$	Light n spotlight direction **d** and cosine of spotlight cutoff angle α.
`state.light[n].half`	$(H_x, H_y, H_z, 1)$	Light n infinite halfway vector **H**.
`state.lightmodel.ambient`	(r, g, b, a)	Light model ambient color
`state.lightmodel.scenecolor`	(r, g, b, a)	Light model front scene color
`state.lightmodel.front .scenecolor`	(r, g, b, a)	Light model front scene color
`state.lightmodel.back .scenecolor`	(r, g, b, a)	Light model back scene color
`state.lightprod[n].ambient`	(r, g, b, a)	Light n product of light ambient color and front material ambient color
`state.lightprod[n].diffuse`	(r, g, b, a)	Light n product of light diffuse color and front material diffuse color
`state.lightprod[n].specular`	(r, g, b, a)	Light n product of light specular color and front material specular color
`state.lightprod[n].front .ambient`	(r, g, b, a)	Light n product of light ambient color and front material ambient color
`state.lightprod[n].front .diffuse`	(r, g, b, a)	Light n product of light diffuse color and front material diffuse color
`state.lightprod[n].front .specular`	(r, g, b, a)	Light n product of light specular color and front material specular color
`state.lightprod[n].back.ambient`	(r, g, b, a)	Light n product of light ambient color and back material ambient color
`state.lightprod[n].back .diffuse`	(r, g, b, a)	Light n product of light diffuse color and back material diffuse color
`state.lightprod[n].back .specular`	(r, g, b, a)	Light n product of light specular color and back material specular color

For convenience and efficiency, it is possible to bind to precomputed quantities that are used in the lighting equation. The `state.light[n].half` state refers to the halfway vector for light n and a viewer at infinity. The 3D halfway vector **H** is given by

$$\mathbf{H} = \frac{\mathbf{P} + \langle 0,0,1 \rangle}{\| \mathbf{P} + \langle 0,0,1 \rangle \|}, \tag{19.1.1}$$

where **P** is the 3D vector whose x, y, and z coordinates are the eye-space position of the infinite light.

The front-facing and back-facing scene colors $\mathbf{C}_{\text{scene}}$ represented by the states having the `.scenecolor` suffix are given by

$$\mathbf{C}_{\text{scene}} = \mathbf{A}_{\text{lightmodel}} \mathbf{A}_{\text{material}} + \mathbf{E}_{\text{material}}, \tag{19.1.2}$$

where $\mathbf{A}_{\text{lightmodel}}$ is the light model ambient color, $\mathbf{A}_{\text{material}}$ is the material ambient color, and $\mathbf{E}_{\text{material}}$ is the material emission color.

The states whose names begin with `state.lightprod[n]` represent the front-facing and back-facing products of the light and material ambient, diffuse, and specular colors.

An identifier can be bound to a texture environment constant color by using the PARAM statement with one of the names listed in Table 19.1.5. The `state.texenv[n].color` state represents the texture environment constant color associated with texture unit n.

TABLE 19.1.5   Texture Environment Bindings

Texture Environment Binding	Component Usage	Underlying State
state.texenv.color	(r,g,b,a)	Texture environment constant color, unit 0
state.texenv[n].color	(r,g,b,a)	Texture environment constant color, unit n

An identifier can be bound to a fog property by using the PARAM statement with one of the names listed in Table 19.1.6. The `state.fog.color` state represents the fog color. The components of the `state.fog.params` state each have different meanings. The x component represents the fog density, the y and z components represent the start and end distance for linear fog, and the w component contains the reciprocal of the difference between the linear start and end distances.

TABLE 19.1.6   Fog Property Bindings

Fog Binding	Component Usage	Underlying State
`state.fog.color`	(r,g,b,a)	Fog color
`state.fog.params`	$\left(d,s,e,\dfrac{1}{e-s}\right)$	Fog density d, linear start distance s, linear end distance e, and reciprocal of $e-s$

An identifier can be bound to the depth range state by using the PARAM statement with the name listed in Table 19.1.7. The x and y component represent the near and far depth range values n and f, and the z component contains the difference $f-n$. The w component always contains the value 1.0.

TABLE 19.1.7   Depth Range Property Bindings

Clip Plane Binding	Component Usage	Underlying State
`state.depth.range`	$(n,f,f-n,1)$	Depth range near value n, far value f, and difference $f-n$.

An identifier can be bound to a matrix by using the PARAM statement with one of the names listed in Table 19.1.8. The `state.matrix.mvp` state represents the product of the modelview and projection matrices that transforms vertex positions from object space directly into homogeneous clip space. Since matrices consist of four row vectors, an identifier must be declared as an array if it is bound to the entire matrix. For example, the following line binds the projection matrix to the identifier `proj`.

```
PARAM proj[] = state.matrix.projection;
```

Subsequent references to `proj[0]`, `proj[1]`, `proj[2]`, and `proj[3]` represent the rows of the projection matrix. An identifier can be bound to a single row of a matrix by appending the suffix `.row[n]` to the matrix's name, where $0 \le n \le 3$. For example, the following line binds the first row of the modelview matrix to the identifier `mv`.

```
PARAM mv = state.matrix.modelview.row[0];
```

It is also possible to bind an identifier to fewer than all four rows of a matrix. This is accomplished by appending the suffix `.row[a..b]` to the matrix's name, where $0 \le a \le b \le 3$. The following line binds the second and third rows of the modelview matrix to the identifier `mv23`.

```
PARAM mv23[] = state.matrix.modelview.row[1..2];
```

The identifier mv23 is an array with two entries. The expression mv23[0] refers to the second row of the modelview matrix, and the expression mv23[1] refers to the third row.

TABLE 19.1.8 Matrix Property Bindings

Matrix Binding	Underlying State
state.matrix.modelview	Modelview matrix 0
state.matrix.modelview[n]	Modelview matrix n
state.matrix.projection	Projection matrix
state.matrix.mvp	Modelview projection matrix product
state.matrix.texture	Texture matrix, unit 0
state.matrix.texture[n]	Texture matrix, unit n
state.matrix.palette[n]	Modelview palette matrix n
state.matrix.program[n]	Program matrix n

The program matrices represented by the array state.matrix.program[] refer to a set of generic matrices defined by the GL_ARB_fragment_program extension that may be used by an application for any purpose. The number of generic program matrices supported by an implementation is retrieved by calling the **glGetIntegerv** function with *pname* parameter GL_MAX_PROGRAM_MATRICES_ARB and is always at least 8. The program matrices are manipulated by setting the current matrix mode to GL_MATRIXi_ARB using the **glMatrix-Mode** function, where i is in the range 0 to GL_MAX_PROGRAM_MATRICES_ARB − 1. Subsequent matrix-related functions, such as **glLoadMatrix{fd}**, apply to the ith program matrix stack. The maximum depth of all program matrix stacks supported by an implementation is retrieved by passing GL_MAX_PROGRAM_MATRIX_STACK_DEPTH_ARB to **glGetIntegerv**.

The GL_ARB_fragment_program extension defines three constants that can be passed to the *pname* parameter of the **glGet** functions to retrieve information about the current matrix stack. The constant GL_CURRENT_MATRIX_ARB is used to retrieve the 16 entries of the matrix associated with the current matrix mode. The constant GL_TRANSPOSE_CURRENT_MATRIX_ARB retrieves the same matrix, but in transposed order. Finally, the constant GL_CURRENT_MATRIX_STACK_DEPTH_ARB is used to retrieve the number of matrices on the matrix stack associated with the current matrix mode.

Fragment Results

An identifier is bound to a fragment result register by using the OUTPUT statement with one of the names listed in Table 19.1.9. Identifiers bound to fragment result registers may only appear as a destination register for an instruction.

TABLE 19.1.9   Fragment result bindings. Components labeled * are unused.

Vertex Result Binding	Component Usage	Description
result.color	(r,g,b,a)	Fragment color
result.depth	$(*,*,d,*)$	Fragment depth

The result.color register represents the final color of the fragment. If this register is not written by a fragment program, then the fragment color is undefined. Note that it may be perfectly valid if, for instance, writes to the color buffer are disabled, and a fragment program writes only to the depth buffer. The components of the final fragment color are clamped to the range [0,1].

The z component of the result.depth register represents the final window-space depth of the fragment. If a fragment program does not write to this register, then the conventionally rasterized depth is assigned to the fragment. The depth written to the result.depth register is clamped to the range [0,1].

Temporary Registers

Temporary registers are allocated by using the TEMP statement. The TEMP statement is followed by a comma-delimited list of identifiers, each of which becomes a general purpose read/write variable. For example, the following line declares temporary registers temp1 and temp2.

```
TEMP    temp1, temp2;
```

The maximum number of temporary registers that may be declared is determined by calling the **glGetProgramivARB** function with *pname* parameter GL_MAX_PROGRAM_TEMPORARIES_ARB. Temporary registers have undefined contents at the beginning of fragment program execution, and their final values are ignored.

Aliases

An alias may be declared for any identifier by using the ALIAS statement. The ALIAS statement simply establishes that one identifier has the same meaning as another, previously declared identifier. For example, the following code declares a temporary register named R0 and then declares an alias for it named N_dot_L. Either name, when used later in the program, refers to the same temporary register.

```
TEMP    R0;
ALIAS   N_dot_L = R0;
```

Program Resource Limits

An implementation is expected to execute fragment programs in hardware, but may also provide a software path that supports a greater number of instructions, registers, or program parameters. An application can retrieve the maximum fragment program limits imposed by a particular implementation by calling the **glGetProgramivARB** function,

```
void glGetProgramivARB(GLenum target,
                       GLenum pname,
                       GLint *params);
```

with *target* parameter GL_FRAGMENT_PROGRAM_ARB. The *pname* parameter specifies which value to return and may be any of the values listed in Table 19.1.10. The native limits that can be queried represent the resource limits beneath which a fragment program is guaranteed to be executed in hardware. If a fragment program exceeds the native limits, but not the absolute limits, then an application can expect lower performance, because the fragment program is probably being executed in software.

TABLE 19.1.10 Symbolic constants representing implementation-dependent fragment program resource limits. The native limits represent the maximum number of each resource that can be used in order to ensure that a fragment program is capable of being executed in hardware. The Min Value represents the minimum requirements for any fragment program implementation.

Constant Representing Absolute Limit	*Constant Representing Native Limit*	*Description*	*Min Value*
GL_MAX_PROGRAM_ INSTRUCTIONS_ARB	GL_MAX_PROGRAM_ NATIVE_ INSTRUCTIONS_ARB	The maximum number of instructions.	72
GL_MAX_PROGRAM_ ALU_INSTRUCTIONS_ ARB	GL_MAX_PROGRAM_ NATIVE_ALU_ INSTRUCTIONS_ARB	The maximum number of ALU instructions.	48
GL_MAX_PROGRAM_ TEX_INSTRUCTIONS_ ARB	GL_MAX_PROGRAM_ NATIVE_TEX_ INSTRUCTIONS_ARB	The maximum number of texture instructions.	24
GL_MAX_PROGRAM_ TEX_INDIRECTIONS_ ARB	GL_MAX_PROGRAM_ NATIVE_TEX_ INDIRECTIONS_ARB	The maximum number of texture indirections.	4
GL_MAX_PROGRAM_ ATTRIBS_ARB	GL_MAX_PROGRAM_ NATIVE_ATTRIBS_ARB	The maximum number of attributes declared.	10
GL_MAX_PROGRAM_ PARAMETERS_ARB	GL_MAX_PROGRAM_ NATIVE_PARAMETERS_ ARB	The maximum of the sum of the numbers of program environment parameters, program local parameters, and OpenGL state parameters declared.	24
GL_MAX_PROGRAM_ TEMPORARIES_ARB	GL_MAX_PROGRAM_ NATIVE_TEMPORARIES_ ARB	The maximum number of temporary registers declared.	16

Separate limits exist for the numbers of Arithmetic-Logic Unit (ALU) instructions and texture instructions that may be issued in a fragment program. The four instructions TEX, TXB, TXP, and KIL are considered to be texture instructions, and all others are ALU instructions.

An implementation may impose a limit on the number of *texture indirections* that may be performed by a fragment program. A texture indirection occurs when a texture instruction depends on the result of a previous ALU instruction. A chain of dependent texture fetches may be encoded in a fragment program by using the result of one texture fetch to calculate coordinates used by a second texture fetch whose result is used to perform a third texture fetch, and so on.

The number of texture indirections in a fragment program is determined as follows. A fragment program begins with a single node in the texture indirection chain. Each instruction is considered part of this node until a texture instruction satisfying at least one of the following conditions is encountered.

- The texture instruction uses as its texture coordinates a temporary register that was previously written in the *current* node.

- The texture instruction writes to a temporary register that was previously written in the *current* node.

When such a texture instruction is encountered, a new node is started that includes the texture instruction and any subsequent instructions occurring before another indirection. Note that when multiple texture instructions depend on results calculated in the previous node, only one indirection occurs.

The **glGetProgramivARB** function is also used to retrieve the numbers of resources used by the currently bound fragment program. Table 19.1.11 lists the resources that can be queried. Separate queries are provided to allow retrieval of the native resource counts used by the implementation after it compiles a fragment program. The native resources used may be greater than the number of instructions, registers, parameters, and so forth declared in a fragment program, because certain hardware implementations may have to emulate some instructions by using multiple native instructions and extra temporary registers. The symbolic constant GL_PROGRAM_UNDER_NATIVE_LIMITS_ARB can be passed to the *pname* parameter of the **glGetProgramivARB** function to determine whether the currently bound fragment program falls within the hardware limits of the implementation.

TABLE 19.1.11 Symbolic constants representing the resources consumed by a fragment program. The native resources represent the number of each type of resource used by the implementation to execute the fragment program in hardware.

Constant Representing Resource Usage	*Constant Representing Native Resource Usage*	*Description*
GL_PROGRAM_ INSTRUCTIONS_ ARB	GL_PROGRAM_ NATIVE_ INSTRUCTIONS_ARB	The number of instructions used.

TABLE 19.1.11 *Continued*

Constant Representing Resource Usage	Constant Representing Native Resource Usage	Description
GL_PROGRAM_ ALU_INSTRUCTIONS_ ARB	GL_PROGRAM_ NATIVE_ALU_ INSTRUCTIONS_ARB	The number of ALU instructions used.
GL_PROGRAM_ TEX_INSTRUCTIONS_ ARB	GL_PROGRAM_ NATIVE_TEX_ INSTRUCTIONS_ARB	The number of texture instructions used.
GL_PROGRAM_ TEX_INDIRECTIONS_ ARB	GL_PROGRAM_ NATIVE_TEX_ INDIRECTIONS_ARB	The number of texture indirections used.
GL_PROGRAM_ ATTRIBS_ARB	GL_PROGRAM_ NATIVE_ATTRIBS_ARB	The number of attributes used.
GL_PROGRAM_ PARAMETERS_ARB	GL_PROGRAM_ NATIVE_PARAMETERS_ARB	The sum of the numbers of program environment parameters, program local parameters, and OpenGL state parameters used.
GL_PROGRAM_ TEMPORARIES_ARB	GL_PROGRAM_ NATIVE_TEMPORARIES_ARB	The number of temporary registers used.

An implementation may be forced to implicitly increase the number of texture indirections in order to natively support certain fragment programs. For example, an implementation may not be able to perform a texture fetch using an arbitrary swizzle of the supplied texture coordinates. In such a case, an ALU instruction would have to be inserted before the texture fetch in order to perform the swizzle operation. The actual number of texture indirections used by a fragment program is retrieved by passing the value GL_PROGRAM_ NATIVE_TEX_INDIRECTIONS_ARB to the *pname* parameter of the **glGetProgramivARB** function.

Texture Units

Under some implementations, the number of texture images that can be accessed may be greater than the number of texture coordinate sets supported. The GL_ARB_multitexture extension defines a single texture unit as a collection of both server-side state and client-side state that includes a texture image set, texture environment parameters, texture coordinate generation parameters, a texture matrix stack, current texture coordinates, and a texture coordinate array. Under the GL_ARB_fragment_program extension, state pertaining to texture images is decoupled from state pertaining to texture coordinates.

The **glGetIntegerv** function can be called with *pname* parameter GL_MAX_TEXTURE_ IMAGE_UNITS_ARB and GL_MAX_TEXTURE_COORDS_ARB to retrieve the number of texture image units and number of texture coordinate sets supported by an implementation. The value returned by **glGetIntegerv** when *pname* is GL_MAX_TEXTURE_UNITS_ARB is no larger than the minimum of the number of texture image units and texture coordinate sets supported.

The value passed to the **glActiveTextureARB** function may be GL_TEXTURE*i*_ARB, where *i* is less than the greater of the number of texture image units supported and the number of texture coordinate sets supported. If the index of the active texture is less than GL_MAX_TEXTURE_IMAGE_UNITS_ARB, then any commands pertaining to texture images or texture environment parameters may be issued. Specifically, the following commands may be issued, and any query to retrieve state specified by these commands is allowable.

- **glTexImage{12}D, glTexImage3DEXT**
- **glTexSubImage{12}D, glTexSubImage3DEXT**
- **glCopyTexImage{12}D**
- **glCopyTexSubImage{12}D, glCopyTexSubImage3DEXT**
- **glCompressedTexImage{123}DARB**
- **glCompressedTexSubImage{123}DARB**
- **glTexEnv{if}[v]**
- **glBindTexture**
- **glEnable, glDisable** with any texture target (e.g., GL_TEXTURE_2D)

If any of the above commands or their associated queries are issued when the index of the active texture is greater than or equal to GL_MAX_TEXTURE_IMAGE_UNITS_ARB, then the error GL_INVALID_OPERATION is generated.

If the index of the active texture is less than GL_MAX_TEXTURE_COORDS_ARB, then any commands pertaining to texture coordinate generation parameters, the texture matrix stack, or the current texture coordinates may be issued. Specifically, the following commands may be issued, and any query to retrieve state specified by these commands is allowable.

- **glMultiTexCoord{1234}{sifd}[v]ARB**
- **glTexGen{ifd}[v]**
- **glEnable, glDisable** with any texture coordinate generation capability
- Any matrix command if the matrix mode is GL_TEXTURE

If any of the above commands or their associated queries are issued when the index of the active texture is greater than or equal to GL_MAX_TEXTURE_COORDS_ARB, then the error GL_INVALID_OPERATION is generated.

The value passed to the **glClientActiveTextureARB** function may be GL_TEXTURE*i*_ARB, where *i* is in the range 0 to GL_MAX_TEXTURE_COORDS_ARB − 1. All client state associated with a conventional texture unit pertains to the texture coordinate set.

Instruction Set

There are 33 vertex program instructions. The operation performed by each instruction and the corresponding types of input operands and output results are listed in Table 19.1.12.

TABLE 19.1.12   Fragment program instructions. The letter "v" indicates a vector result or operand, and the letter "s" indicates a scalar operand. The letter "u" indicates a texture image unit identifier, and the letter "t" indicates a texture target. The vector ⟨s,s,s,s⟩ represents a single scalar result that is replicated to all four components of the result vector. Components labeled * are undefined.

Instruction	Output Result	Input Operands	Operation
ABS[_SAT]	v	v	Absolute value
ADD[_SAT]	v	v, v	Add
CMP[_SAT]	v	v, v, v	Compare
COS[_SAT]	⟨s,s,s,s⟩	s	Cosine
DP3[_SAT]	⟨s,s,s,s⟩	v, v	3D dot product
DP4[_SAT]	⟨s,s,s,s⟩	v, v	4D dot product
DPH[_SAT]	⟨s,s,s,s⟩	v, v	Homogeneous dot product
DST[_SAT]	v	v, v	Distance vector
EX2[_SAT]	⟨s,s,s,s⟩	s	Exponential base 2
FLR[_SAT]	v	v	Floor
FRC[_SAT]	v	v	Fraction
KIL	–	v	Kill fragment
LG2[_SAT]	⟨s,s,s,s⟩	s	Logarithm base 2
LIT[_SAT]	v	v	Light coefficients
LRP[_SAT]	v	v, v, v	Linear interpolation
MAD[_SAT]	v	v, v, v	Multiply-add
MAX[_SAT]	v	v, v	Maximum
MIN[_SAT]	v	v, v	Minimum
MOV[_SAT]	v	v	Move
MUL[_SAT]	v	v, v	Multiply
POW[_SAT]	⟨s,s,s,s⟩	s, s	Exponentiate
RCP[_SAT]	⟨s,s,s,s⟩	s	Reciprocal
RSQ[_SAT]	⟨s,s,s,s⟩	s	Reciprocal square root
SCS[_SAT]	⟨s,s,*,*⟩	s	Sine and cosine

(continues)

TABLE 19.1.12   *Continued*

Instruction	Output Result	Input Operands	Operation
SGE	v	v, v	Set on greater than or equal to
SIN[_SAT]	⟨s,s,s,s⟩	s	Sine
SLT	v	v, v	Set on less than
SUB[_SAT]	v	v, v	Subtract
SWZ[_SAT]	v	v	Extended swizzle
TEX[_SAT]	v	v, u, t	Texture sample
TXB[_SAT]	v	v, u, t	Texture sample with bias
TXP[_SAT]	v	v, u, t	Texture sample with projection
XPD[_SAT]	v	v, v	Cross product

Each of the fragment program instructions is described in detail below. Included with each instruction is pseudocode that demonstrates the instruction's exact effect. The types `vector` and `scalar` are used to hold four-component vector quantities and one-component scalar quantities, respectively. When loading data from a register, the pseudocode makes use of the functions `VectorLoad` and `ScalarLoad` to apply the swizzle and negate operations to each operand. In the definitions of the functions that follow, the `.swiz[n]` field used with the `source` parameter denotes the *n*th component of the source vector after swizzling. The `.comp` field used with the `source` parameter denotes the scalar component selected using the single component suffix in the fragment program. The value of `negate` is true if the program specifies that the source operand is negated, and is false otherwise.

```
vector VectorLoad(vector source)
{
    vector    operand;

    operand.x = source.swiz[0];
    operand.y = source.swiz[1];
    operand.z = source.swiz[2];
    operand.w = source.swiz[3];
    if (negate)
    {
        operand.x = -operand.x;
        operand.y = -operand.y;
        operand.z = -operand.z;
        operand.w = -operand.w;
    }

    return (operand);
}
```

```
scalar ScalarLoad(vector source)
{
    scalar    operand;

    operand = source.comp;
    if (negate) operand = -operand;

    return (operand);
}
```

When a vector result is written to a destination register, the pseudocode makes use of the WriteDest function to apply the write mask. In the definition of this function that follows, each of the components of mask is true if writing is enabled for the corresponding component of the destination register, and is false if writing is disabled. The value of saturate is true if the _SAT suffix is present for the fragment program instruction, and is false otherwise.

```
vector WriteDest(vector dest, vector result)
{
    if (mask.x)
    {
        if (saturate) dest.x = min(max(result.x, 0.0), 1.0);
        else dest.x = result.x;
    }
    if (mask.y)
    {
        if (saturate) dest.y = min(max(result.y, 0.0), 1.0);
        else dest.y = result.y;
    }
    if (mask.z)
    {
        if (saturate) dest.z = min(max(result.z, 0.0), 1.0);
        else dest.z = result.z;
    }
    if (mask.w)
    {
        if (saturate) dest.w = min(max(result.w, 0.0), 1.0);
        else dest.w = result.w;
    }

    return (dest);
}
```

When the instructions TEX, TXB, and TXP perform a texture access, the pseudocode uses the TextureSample function to fetch a filtered texel. This function has the following prototype:

```
vector TextureSample(scalar s, scalar t, scalar r, scalar bias,
    int unit, enum target);
```

The s, t, and r parameters specify the texture coordinates used to sample the texture map. The number of coordinates actually used depends on the texture target, which is specified by the target parameter. The target parameter may be 1D, 2D, 3D, CUBE, or RECT, and indicates what texture target to access. The unit parameter specifies which texture image unit to access. If a texture bound to a particular texture image unit is accessed multiple times during a fragment program, then the value of target must be the same each time, or the program will fail to load. The bias parameter specifies a LOD bias that is added to the texture image unit LOD bias and texture object LOD bias.

The exact effect of each fragment program instruction follows. The local variable r is used in most of the pseudocode listings and always denotes a temporary vector quantity.

ABS[_SAT]–Absolute value

```
ABS     result, op0;
```

The ABS instruction performs a componentwise absolute value operation on a single operand.

```
vector v0 = VectorLoad(op0);
r.x = fabs(v0.x);
r.y = fabs(v0.y);
r.z = fabs(v0.z);
r.w = fabs(v0.w);
result = WriteDest(result, r);
```

ADD[_SAT]–Add

```
ADD     result, op0, op1;
```

The ADD instruction performs a componentwise addition of two operands.

```
vector v0 = VectorLoad(op0);
vector v1 = VectorLoad(op1);
r.x = v0.x + v1.x;
r.y = v0.y + v1.y;
r.z = v0.z + v1.z;
r.w = v0.w + v1.w;
result = WriteDest(result, r);
```

The addition operation satisfies the following rules:

1. $x + y = y + x$ for all x and y.
2. $x + 0.0 = x$ for all x.

CMP[_SAT]—Compare

```
CMP     result, op0, op1, op2;
```

The CMP instruction compares each component of the first operand to zero and selects components from the second or third operand based on the result of the comparison.

```
vector v0 = VectorLoad(op0);
vector v1 = VectorLoad(op1);
vector v2 = VectorLoad(op2);
r.x = (op0.x < 0.0) ? op1.x : op2.x;
r.y = (op0.y < 0.0) ? op1.y : op2.y;
r.z = (op0.z < 0.0) ? op1.z : op2.z;
r.w = (op0.w < 0.0) ? op1.w : op2.w;
result = WriteDest(result, r);
```

COS[_SAT]—Cosine

```
COS     result, op0;
```

The COS instruction approximates the cosine of a single scalar operand and replicates the result to all four components of the destination. The angle is measured in radians and does not need to be in the range $[-\pi,\pi]$.

```
scalar c = ApproxCos(ScalarLoad(op0));
r.x = c;
r.y = c;
r.z = c;
r.w = c;
result = WriteDest(result, r);
```

DP3[_SAT]—Three-component dot product

```
DP3     result, op0, op1;
```

The DP3 instruction performs a three-component dot product between two operands and replicates the result to all four components of the destination.

```
vector v0 = VectorLoad(op0);
vector v1 = VectorLoad(op1);
scalar dot = v0.x * v1.x + v0.y + v1.y + v0.z * v1.z;
r.x = dot;
r.y = dot;
r.z = dot;
r.w = dot;
result = WriteDest(result, r);
```

DP4[_SAT]–Four-component dot product

```
DP4     result, op0, op1;
```

The DP4 instruction performs a four-component dot product between two operands and replicates the result to all four components of the destination.

```
vector v0 = VectorLoad(op0);
vector v1 = VectorLoad(op1);
scalar dot = v0.x * v1.x + v0.y + v1.y
             + v0.z * v1.z + v0.w * v1.w;
r.x = dot;
r.y = dot;
r.z = dot;
r.w = dot;
result = WriteDest(result, r);
```

DPH[_SAT]–Homogeneous dot product

```
DPH     result, op0, op1;
```

The DPH instruction performs a three-component dot product between two operands and adds the *w* component of the second operand. The result is replicated to all four components of the destination.

```
vector v0 = VectorLoad(op0);
vector v1 = VectorLoad(op1);
scalar dot = v0.x * v1.x + v0.y + v1.y
             + v0.z * v1.z + v1.w;
r.x = dot;
r.y = dot;
r.z = dot;
r.w = dot;
result = WriteDest(result, r);
```

The DPH instruction may be emulated by two native instructions on some implementations.

DST[_SAT]–Distance vector

```
DST     result, op0, op1;
```

The DST instruction takes two operands and produces a vector that is useful for attenuation calculations. Given a distance d, the first operand should be formatted as $\langle *, d^2, d^2, * \rangle$, and the second operation should be formatted as $\langle *, 1/d, *, 1/d \rangle$, where * indicates that the operand's component is not used. The result of the DST instruction is the vector $\langle 1, d, d^2, 1/d \rangle$.

```
vector v0 = VectorLoad(op0);
vector v1 = VectorLoad(op1);
```

```
r.x = 1.0;
r.y = v0.y * v1.y;
r.z = v0.z;
r.w = v1.w;
result = WriteDest(result, r);
```

EX2[_SAT]—Exponential base 2

```
EX2    result, op0;
```

The EX2 instruction calculates an approximation to 2^p for a single scalar operand p and replicates the result to all four components of the destination.

```
scalar e = ApproxExp2(ScalarLoad(op0));
r.x = e;
r.y = e;
r.z = e;
r.w = e;
result = WriteDest(result, r);
```

FLR[_SAT]—Floor

```
FLR    result, op0;
```

The FLR instruction performs a componentwise floor operation on a single operand.

```
vector v0 = VectorLoad(op0);
r.x = floor(v0.x);
r.y = floor(v0.y);
r.z = floor(v0.z);
r.w = floor(v0.w);
result = WriteDest(result, r);
```

FRC[_SAT]—Fraction

```
FRC    result, op0;
```

The FRC instruction performs a componentwise fraction operation on a single operand. The fraction operation is equivalent to subtracting the floor of the operand from the operand itself.

```
vector v0 = VectorLoad(op0);
r.x = v0.x - floor(v0.x);
r.y = v0.y - floor(v0.y);
r.z = v0.z - floor(v0.z);
r.w = v0.w - floor(v0.w);
result = WriteDest(result, r);
```

KIL—Kill fragment

```
KIL     op0;
```

The `KIL` instruction compares each of the four components of its operand to zero. If any component is less than zero, then the current fragment is discarded and no further processing occurs. Otherwise, the `KIL` instruction has no effect.

```
vector v0 = VectorLoad(op0);
if ((v0.x < 0.0) || (v0.y < 0.0) || (v0.z < 0.0)
    || (v0.w < 0.0))
{
    // exit
}
```

LG2[_SAT]—Logarithm base 2

```
LG2     result, op0;
```

The `LG2` instruction calculates an approximation to $\log_2(p)$ for a single scalar operand p and replicates the result to all four components of the destination.

```
scalar l = ApproxLog2(ScalarLoad(op0));
r.x = l;
r.y = l;
r.z = l;
r.w = l;
result = WriteDest(result, r);
```

LIT[_SAT]—Light coefficients

```
LIT     result, op0;
```

The `LIT` instruction takes a single operand and produces a coefficient vector that is useful for lighting calculations. The operand is assumed to be formatted as $\langle \mathbf{N} \cdot \mathbf{L}, \mathbf{N} \cdot \mathbf{H}, *, m \rangle$, where $\mathbf{N} \cdot \mathbf{L}$ is the diffuse dot product, $\mathbf{N} \cdot \mathbf{H}$ is the specular dot product, m is the specular exponent, and $*$ indicates that the z component is unused. The result of the `LIT` instruction is the vector $\langle 1.0, \mathbf{N} \cdot \mathbf{L}, (\mathbf{N} \cdot \mathbf{H})^m, 1.0 \rangle$, where $\mathbf{N} \cdot \mathbf{L}$ and $\mathbf{N} \cdot \mathbf{H}$ are clamped to 0.0 and the z component is set to 0.0 if $\mathbf{N} \cdot \mathbf{L} \leq 0$. The specular exponent m is clamped to the range $[-128, 128]$.

```
vector v0 = VectorLoad(op0);
if (v0.x < 0.0) v0.x = 0.0;
if (v0.y < 0.0) v0.y = 0.0;
if (v0.w < -128.0 + epsilon) v0.w = -128.0 + epsilon;
else if (v0.w > 128.0 - epsilon) v0.w = 128.0 - epsilon;
r.x = 1.0;
r.y = v0.x;
r.z = (v0.x > 0.0) ? RoughApproxPow(v0.y, v0.w) : 0.0;
r.w = 1.0;
result = WriteDest(result, r);
```

The RoughApproxPow function may be defined in terms of the base-2 exponential and logarithm functions implemented by the EX2 and LG2 instructions. Thus,

```
RoughApproxPow(b, e) = ApproxExp2(e * ApproxLog2(b))
```

and the precision of the RoughApproxPow function is limited by the precision of the ApproxExp2 and ApproxLog2 functions.

LRP[_SAT]—Linear interpolation

```
LRP     result, op0, op1, op2;
```

The LRP instruction performs componentwise linear interpolation between its second and third operands using its first operand as the blend factor.

```
vector v0 = VectorLoad(op0);
vector v1 = VectorLoad(op1);
vector v2 = VectorLoad(op2);
r.x = v0.x * v1.x + (1.0 - v0.x) * v2.x;
r.y = v0.y * v1.y + (1.0 - v0.y) * v2.y;
r.z = v0.z * v1.z + (1.0 - v0.z) * v2.z;
r.w = v0.w * v1.w + (1.0 - v0.w) * v2.w;
result = WriteDest(result, r);
```

MAD[_SAT]—Multiply-add

```
MAD     result, op0, op1, op2;
```

The MAD instruction performs a componentwise multiplication and addition of three operands.

```
vector v0 = VectorLoad(op0);
vector v1 = VectorLoad(op1);
vector v2 = VectorLoad(op2);
r.x = v0.x * v1.x + v2.x;
r.y = v0.y * v1.y + v2.y;
r.z = v0.z * v1.z + v2.z;
r.w = v0.w * v1.w + v2.w;
result = WriteDest(result, r);
```

The multiplication and addition operations are subject to the same rules described for the MUL and ADD instructions.

MAX[_SAT]—Maximum

```
MAX     result, op0, op1;
```

The MAX instruction performs a componentwise maximum operation between two operands.

```
vector v0 = VectorLoad(op0);
vector v1 = VectorLoad(op1);
r.x = (v0.x > v1.x) ? v0.x : v1.x;
r.y = (v0.y > v1.y) ? v0.y : v1.y;
r.z = (v0.z > v1.z) ? v0.z : v1.z;
r.w = (v0.w > v1.w) ? v0.w : v1.w;
result = WriteDest(result, r);
```

MIN[_SAT]–Minimum

```
MIN    result, op0, op1;
```

The `MIN` instruction performs a componentwise minimum operation between two operands.

```
vector v0 = VectorLoad(op0);
vector v1 = VectorLoad(op1);
r.x = (v0.x > v1.x) ? v1.x : v0.x;
r.y = (v0.y > v1.y) ? v1.y : v0.y;
r.z = (v0.z > v1.z) ? v1.z : v0.z;
r.w = (v0.w > v1.w) ? v1.w : v0.w;
result = WriteDest(result, r);
```

MOV[_SAT]–Move

```
MOV    result, op0;
```

The `MOV` instruction copies a single operand to the destination.

```
vector v0 = VectorLoad(op0);
result = WriteDest(result, v0);
```

MUL[_SAT]–Multiply

```
MUL    result, op0, op1;
```

The `MUL` instruction performs a componentwise multiplication of two operands.

```
vector v0 = VectorLoad(op0);
vector v1 = VectorLoad(op1);
r.x = v0.x * v1.x;
r.y = v0.y * v1.y;
r.z = v0.z * v1.z;
r.w = v0.w * v1.w;
result = WriteDest(result, r);
```

The multiplication operation satisfies the following rules:

1. $xy = yx$ for all x and y.
2. $x \cdot 1.0 = x$ for all x.
3. $x \cdot \pm 0.0 = \pm 0.0$ for all x with the possible exception of $\pm$INF and $\pm$NAN.

POW[_SAT]–Exponentiate

```
POW     result, op0, op1;
```

The POW instruction calculates an approximation to b^e for two scalar operands b and e, and replicates the result to all four components of the destination.

```
scalar s0 = ScalarLoad(op0);
scalar s1 = ScalarLoad(op1);
scalar p = ApproxPow(op0, op1);
r.x = p;
r.y = p;
r.z = p;
r.w = p;
result = WriteDest(result, r);
```

The ApproxPow function may be implemented using the base-2 exponentiation and logarithm functions defined by the EX2 and LG2 functions. Thus,

```
ApproxPow(b, e) = ApproxExp2(e * ApproxLog2(b))
```

and it may not be possible to correctly raise a negative base to an integer power since a logarithm is involved.

RCP[_SAT]–Reciprocal

```
RCP     result, op0;
```

The RCP instruction approximates the reciprocal of a single scalar operand and replicates the result to all four components of the destination.

```
scalar s0 = ScalarLoad(op0);
scalar recip = ApproxRecip(s0);
r.x = recip;
r.y = recip;
r.z = recip;
r.w = recip;
result = WriteDest(result, r);
```

The reciprocation operation satisfies the following rule:

$$\text{ApproxRecip}(+1.0) = +1.0$$

RSQ[_SAT]–Reciprocal square root

```
RSQ     result, op0;
```

The RSQ instruction approximates the reciprocal square root of the absolute value of a single scalar operand and replicates the result to all four components of the destination.

```
scalar s0 = fabs(ScalarLoad(op0));
scalar rsqrt = ApproxRSQRT(s0);
r.x = rsqrt;
r.y = rsqrt;
r.z = rsqrt;
r.w = rsqrt;
result = WriteDest(result, r);
```

SCS[_SAT]–Sine and cosine

```
SCS     result, op0;
```

The SCS instruction approximates the sine and cosine of a single scalar operand. The cosine is stored in the x component of the destination, and the sine is stored in the y component of the destination. The z and w components of the destination are undefined. The angle is measured in radians and must be in the range $[-\pi,\pi]$, or the result is undefined.

```
scalar s0 = ScalarLoad(op0);
r.x = ApproxCos(s0);
r.y = ApproxSin(s0);
result = WriteDest(result, r);
```

SGE–Set on greater than or equal to

```
SGE     result, op0, op1;
```

The SGE instruction performs a componentwise comparison between two operands. Each component of the result vector is set to 1.0 if the corresponding component of the first operand is greater than or equal to the corresponding component of the second operand, and to 0.0 otherwise.

```
vector v0 = VectorLoad(op0);
vector v1 = VectorLoad(op1);
r.x = (v0.x >= v1.x) ? 1.0 : 0.0;
r.y = (v0.y >= v1.y) ? 1.0 : 0.0;
r.z = (v0.z >= v1.z) ? 1.0 : 0.0;
r.w = (v0.w >= v1.w) ? 1.0 : 0.0;
result = WriteDest(result, r);
```

SIN[_SAT]–Sine

```
SIN    result, op0;
```

The SIN instruction approximates the sine of a single scalar operand and replicates the result to all four components of the destination. The angle is measured in radians and does not need to be in the range $[-\pi,\pi]$.

```
scalar s = ApproxSin(ScalarLoad(op0));
r.x = s;
r.y = s;
r.z = s;
r.w = s;
result = WriteDest(result, r);
```

SLT–Set on less than

```
SLT    result, op0, op1;
```

The SLT instruction performs a componentwise comparison between two operands. Each component of the result vector is set to 1.0 if the corresponding component of the first operand is less than the corresponding component of the second operand, and is set to 0.0 otherwise.

```
vector v0 = VectorLoad(op0);
vector v1 = VectorLoad(op1);
r.x = (v0.x < v1.x) ? 1.0 : 0.0;
r.y = (v0.y < v1.y) ? 1.0 : 0.0;
r.z = (v0.z < v1.z) ? 1.0 : 0.0;
r.w = (v0.w < v1.w) ? 1.0 : 0.0;
result = WriteDest(result, r);
```

SUB[_SAT]–Subtract

```
SUB    result, op0, op1;
```

The SUB instruction performs a componentwise subtraction of two operands.

```
vector v0 = VectorLoad(op0);
vector v1 = VectorLoad(op1);
r.x = v0.x - v1.x;
r.y = v0.y - v1.y;
r.z = v0.z - v1.z;
r.w = v0.w - v1.w;
result = WriteDest(result, r);
```

SWZ[_SAT]—Extended swizzle

```
SWZ     result, op0, xswiz, yswiz, zswiz, wswiz;
```

The SWZ instruction performs an extended swizzle operation on a single operand. Each component of the result is determined by selecting any component of the operand, the constant 0, or the constant 1, and optionally negating it. The following pseudocode describes the swizzle operation for a single component. The op parameter represents the source operand, the select enumerant represents the component selection where ZERO, ONE, X, Y, Z, and W correspond to the characters "0", "1", "x", "y", "z", and "w" used in the program string, and the negate parameter indicates whether the component is negated.

```
float SwizzleComp(vector op, enum select, bool negate)
{
    float result;

    switch (select)
    {
        case ZERO:      result = 0.0; break;
        case ONE:       result = 1.0; break;
        case X:         result = op.x; break;
        case Y:         result = op.y; break;
        case Z:         result = op.z; break;
        case W:         result = op.w; break;
    }

    if (negate) result = -result;
    return (result);
}
```

The entire extended swizzle is then performed as follows, where *k*Select and *k*Negate represent the swizzle selection and optional negation for each component of the source operand:

```
r.x = SwizzleComp(op0, xSelect, xNegate);
r.y = SwizzleComp(op0, ySelect, yNegate);
r.z = SwizzleComp(op0, zSelect, zNegate);
r.w = SwizzleComp(op0, wSelect, wNegate);
result = WriteDest(result, r);
```

The SWZ instruction may be emulated using two native instructions and a program parameter register on some implementations.

TEX[_SAT]—Texture sample

```
TEX     result, op0, texture[unit], target;
```

The TEX instruction interprets the x, y, and z components of its operand as $\langle s,t,r, \rangle$ texture coordinates used to sample the texture target given by the target parameter that is bound to the texture image unit given by the unit parameter. The target parameter may be 1D, 2D, 3D, CUBE, or RECT, and the unit parameter must be in the range 0 to GL_MAX_ TEXTURE_IMAGE_UNITS_ARB − 1.

```
vector v0 = VectorLoad(op0);
r = TextureSample(v0.x, v0.y, v0.z, 0.0, unit, target);
result = WriteDest(result, r);
```

If the same texture unit is sampled by a subsequent texture instruction (TEX, TXB, or TXP), then the target parameter must be the same or the fragment program will fail to load.

TXB[_SAT]–Texture sample with bias

```
TXB     result, op0, texture[unit], target;
```

The TXB instruction interprets the x, y, and z components of its operand as $\langle s,t,r,\rangle$ texture coordinates used to sample the texture target given by the target parameter that is bound to the texture image unit given by the unit parameter. The target parameter may be 1D, 2D, 3D, CUBE, or RECT, and the unit parameter must be in the range 0 to GL_MAX_TEXTURE_ IMAGE_UNITS_ARB − 1. The w component of the operand is used as an additional LOD bias.

```
vector v0 = VectorLoad(op0);
r = TextureSample(v0.x, v0.y, v0.z, v0.w, unit, target);
result = WriteDest(result, r);
```

TXP[_SAT]–Texture sample with projection

```
TXP     result, op0, texture[unit], target;
```

The TXP instruction interprets the x, y, z, and w components of its operand as $\langle s,t,r,q\rangle$ texture coordinates used to sample the texture target given by the target parameter that is bound to the texture image unit given by the unit parameter. The target parameter may be 1D, 2D, 3D, CUBE, or RECT, and the unit parameter must be in the range 0 to GL_MAX_TEXTURE_IMAGE_UNITS_ARB − 1. A projection is performed by dividing the s, t, and r coordinates by the q coordinate. If $q \leq 0$, the result is undefined.

```
vector v0 = VectorLoad(op0);
r = TextureSample(v0.x / v0.w, v0.y / v0.w, v0.z / v0.w,
    0.0, unit, target);
result = WriteDest(result, r);
```

XPD[_SAT]–Cross product

```
XPD     result, op0, op1;
```

The XPD instruction calculates the three-component cross product between two operands. The result is a three-component vector that is stored in the x, y, and z components of the destination. The w component of the destination is undefined.

```
vector v0 = VectorLoad(op0);
vector v1 = VectorLoad(op1);
r.x = v0.y * v1.z - v0.z * v1.y;
r.y = v0.z * v1.x - v0.x * v1.z;
r.z = v0.x * v1.y - v0.y * v1.x;
result = WriteDest(result, r);
```

The XPD instruction may be emulated using two native instructions on some implementations.

Fog Application

A fragment program may choose to allow OpenGL to perform the fog-blending operation after the final color is written to the `result.color` register. A fragment program indicates that the implementation should apply linear, exponential, or exponential-squared fog by specifying one of the options listed in Table 19.1.13 before any program instructions. If more than one of these options is specified, then the last one encountered in the program determines the fog mode.

TABLE 19.1.13   Fog options and the corresponding conventional fog modes. The instruction cost represents the reduction in the maximum native instruction limit incurred by using each fog option.

Option	Conventional Fog Mode	Instruction Cost
OPTION ARB_fog_linear;	GL_LINEAR	2
OPTION ARB_fog_exp;	GL_EXP	3
OPTION ARB_fog_exp2;	GL_EXP2	4

In order to allow an implementation to augment the fragment program with the instructions and other resources necessary to perform the fog application, a fragment program specifying one of the fog options is limited to one fewer temporary registers, one fewer fragment attributes, and two fewer program parameters than the maximum native values returned by the **glGetProgramivARB** function. Furthermore, a fragment program is limited to fewer instructions by the number shown in Table 19.1.13 for each fog mode.

Precision Hints

Some implementations may be able to execute fragment program instructions at different precisions. A hint may be specified at the beginning of a fragment program to indicate that a precision/performance trade-off is desired. Specifying the program option

```
OPTION    ARB_precision_hint_fastest;
```

indicates that the fastest fragment program execution time should be favored, at a possible loss of precision. Specifying the program option

```
OPTION    ARB_precision_hint_nicest;
```

indicates that the highest precision calculations should be performed, at a possible performance cost. If more than one of these options is specified, the fragment program will fail to load. These options are ignored by implementations that are able to execute fragment programs at only one level of precision.

Program Management

Fragment programs follow the named object convention that is used elsewhere in OpenGL for such things as texture objects. A fragment program is identified by a name taken from the set of unsigned integers. Previously unused names for fragment program objects are allocated by calling the **glGenProgramsARB** function,

```
void glGenProgramsARB(GLsizei n,
                      GLuint *programs);
```

This function generates *n* names and writes them to the array pointed to by the *programs* parameter. The names generated are marked as used, but the associated fragment program objects are not actually created until the first time a new name is passed to the **glBindProgramARB** function.

Fragment program objects are deleted and the associated names are freed by calling the **glDeleteProgramsARB** function,

```
void glDeleteProgramsARB(GLsizei n,
                         const GLuint *programs);
```

Any of the *n* names passed to this function in the array pointed to by the *programs* parameter that do not refer to existing fragment program objects are silently ignored. Once an fragment program object is deleted, its name is marked as unused. The **glIsProgramARB** function,

```
GLboolean glIsProgramARB(GLuint program);
```

can be used to determine whether a particular name specified by the *program* parameter refers to an existing fragment program object.

A fragment program object is bound to the fragment program target by calling the **glBindProgramARB** function,

```
void glBindProgramARB(GLenum target,
                      GLuint program);
```

with *target* parameter GL_FRAGMENT_PROGRAM_ARB. The *program* parameter specifies the name of the fragment program object. The first time that a program is bound for a particular name, a fragment program object is created for that name. A program string for the currently bound fragment program object is loaded by calling the **glProgramStringARB** function,

```
void glProgramStringARB(GLenum target,
                        GLenum format,
                        GLsizei len,
                        const GLvoid *string);
```

with *target* parameter GL_FRAGMENT_PROGRAM_ARB. The *format* parameter specifies the character set of the program string and must be GL_PROGRAM_FORMAT_ASCII_ARB. The *len* parameter specifies the length of the program string pointed to by the *string* parameter. A program string may be loaded for the same fragment program object multiple times.

When fragment program mode is enabled (by calling **glEnable** with *cap* parameter GL_FRAGMENT_PROGRAM_ARB), the currently bound fragment program is invoked for every fragment generated by OpenGL.

NEW FUNCTIONS

- **glProgramStringARB**—Specify a program string.

Prototype

```
void glProgramStringARB(GLenum target,
                        GLenum format,
                        GLsizei len,
                        const GLvoid *string);
```

Parameters

target	Specifies the target program. Must be GL_FRAGMENT_PROGRAM_ARB.
format	Specifies the character set of the program string. Must be GL_PROGRAM_FORMAT_ASCII_ARB.
len	Specifies the length of the program string.
string	Specifies a pointer to the program string. This string does not need to be null-terminated.

Description

The **glProgramStringARB** function loads the program string for the program currently bound to the target specified by the *target* parameter. The character set of the program string is specified by the *format* parameter and currently can only be GL_PROGRAM_FORMAT_ASCII_ARB. The length of the program string is passed into the *len* parameter.

At the time **glProgramStringARB** is called, the program string is parsed and checked for syntactic validity. If the program fails to load because it contains an error, the error GL_INVALID_OPERATION is generated.

The values of GL_PROGRAM_ERROR_POSITION_ARB and GL_PROGRAM_ERROR_STRING_ARB are always updated when **glProgramStringARB** is called. If a program loads successfully, the error position is set to −1, but the error string may still contain warning messages. If a program fails to load, the error position is set to the byte offset within the program at which the error occurred. If a program generates an error that can be detected only after the entire program string is interpreted, then the error position is set to the length of the program string. The error position can be retrieved by calling the **glGetIntegerv** function with *pname* parameter GL_PROGRAM_ERROR_POSITION_ARB. The error string contains a description of the error that occurred and can be retrieved by calling the **glGetString** function with *pname* parameter GL_PROGRAM_ERROR_STRING_ARB.

Special Considerations

The **glProgramStringARB** function is also defined by the GL_ARB_vertex_program extension.

Get Functions

glGetProgramStringARB

glGetProgramivARB with *pname* parameter GL_PROGRAM_LENGTH_ARB

glGetProgramivARB with *pname* parameter GL_PROGRAM_FORMAT_ARB

glGetIntegerv with *pname* parameter GL_PROGRAM_ERROR_POSITION_ARB

glGetString with *pname* parameter GL_PROGRAM_ERROR_STRING_ARB

Errors

GL_INVALID_OPERATION is generated if the program string violates the syntactic or semantic rules of the target program.

■ **glGenProgramsARB**—Generate program names.

Prototype

```
void glGenProgramsARB(GLsizei n,
                      GLuint *programs);
```

Parameters

n   Specifies the number of program names to generate.

programs   Specifies a pointer to an array that receives the generated program names.

Description

The **glGenProgramsARB** function returns a set of *n* unused program names in the array pointed to by the *programs* parameter. Each of the returned names is reserved with respect to program name generation, but does not represent an existing program object until it is bound to a program target using the **glBindProgramARB** function.

Programs are deleted and the associated program names are freed by calling the **glDeleteProgramsARB** function.

Special Considerations

The **glGenProgramsARB** function is also defined by the GL_ARB_vertex_program extension.

Get Functions

glIsProgramARB

Errors

GL_INVALID_VALUE is generated if *n* is negative.

■ **glDeleteProgramsARB**—Delete named programs.

Prototype

```
void glDeleteProgramsARB(GLsizei n,
                         const GLuint *programs);
```

Parameters

n   Specifies the number of programs to delete.

programs   Specifies a pointer to an array of program names to be deleted.

Description

The **glDeleteProgramsARB** function deletes the *n* programs contained in the array pointed to by the *programs* parameter. When a program object is deleted, it becomes non-existent, and its name becomes unused. Deleted program names may subsequently be returned by the **glGenProgramsARB** function. Any unused program names found in the array pointed to by the *programs* parameter are silently ignored.

If a fragment program is deleted when it is the currently bound program, it is as if the **glBindProgramARB** function had been called with *program* parameter 0.

Special Considerations

The **glDeleteProgramsARB** function is also defined by the GL_ARB_vertex_program extension.

Get Functions

glIsProgramARB

Errors

GL_INVALID_VALUE is generated if *n* is negative.

■ **glBindProgramARB**—Bind a named program to a program target.

Prototype

```
void glBindProgramARB(GLenum target,
                      GLuint program);
```

Parameters

target   Specifies the target to which the program is bound. Must be GL_FRAGMENT_PROGRAM_ARB.

program   Specifies the name of the program to bind.

Description

The **glBindProgramARB** function sets the current fragment program that is invoked for every fragment. If a previously nonexistent program is bound, then it becomes existent at the time that **glBindProgramARB** is called, and its program string is initially empty. A program may subsequently be loaded for the newly created program object by calling the **glProgramStringARB** function.

Program 0 is implicitly bound if the currently bound fragment program is deleted by the **glDeleteProgramsARB** function.

Special Considerations

The **glBindProgramARB** function is also defined by the GL_ARB_vertex_program extension.

Get Functions

glGetProgramivARB with *pname* parameter GL_PROGRAM_BINDING_ARB

Errors

GL_INVALID_OPERATION is generated if *program* is the name of a program whose target does not match *target*.

■ **glIsProgramARB**—Determine if a name corresponds to a program.

Prototype

```
GLboolean glIsProgramARB(GLuint program);
```

Parameters

program   Specifies the name of a program.

Description

The **glIsProgramARB** function returns GL_TRUE if the *program* parameter names an existing program. Otherwise, it returns GL_FALSE.

A program name generated by the **glGenProgramsARB** function does not refer to an existing program until it is bound using the **glBindProgramARB** function.

Special Considerations

The **glIsProgramARB** function is also defined by the GL_ARB_vertex_program extension.

■ **glProgramEnvParameter4{fd}[v]ARB**—Specify a program environment parameter.

Prototypes

```
void glProgramEnvParameter4fARB(GLenum target,
                                GLuint index,
                                GLfloat x,
                                GLfloat y,
                                GLfloat z,
                                GLfloat w);
void glProgramEnvParameter4dARB(GLenum target,
                                GLuint index,
                                GLdouble x,
                                GLdouble y,
                                GLdouble z,
                                GLdouble w);
```

Parameters

target   Specifies the target program. Must be GL_FRAGMENT_PROGRAM_ARB.

index   Specifies the index of a program environment parameter. Must be in the
                 range 0 to GL_MAX_PROGRAM_ENV_PARAMETERS_ARB − 1.

x, y, z, w   Specifies the components of the program environment parameter.

Prototypes

```
void glProgramEnvParameter4fvARB(GLenum target,
                                 GLuint index,
                                 const GLfloat *params);
void glProgramEnvParameter4dvARB(GLenum target,
                                 GLuint index,
                                 const GLdouble *params);
```

Parameters

target   Specifies the target program. Must be GL_FRAGMENT_PROGRAM_ARB.

index   Specifies the index of a program environment parameter. Must be in the
                 range 0 to GL_MAX_PROGRAM_ENV_PARAMETERS_ARB − 1.

params   Specifies a pointer to an array containing the four-component program
                 environment parameter.

Description

The **glProgramEnvParameter4{fd}[v]ARB** function specifies a four-component float-ing-point vector for the program environment parameter specified by *index*. Program en-vironment parameters are shared by all fragment programs.

Special Considerations

The **glProgramEnvParameter4{fd}[v]ARB** function is also defined by the GL_ARB_ vertex_program extension.

Get Functions

glGetProgramEnvParameter{fd}vARB

glGetProgramivARB with *pname* parameter GL_MAX_PROGRAM_ENV_PARAMETERS_ARB

Errors

GL_INVALID_VALUE is generated if *index* is greater than or equal to the value of GL_MAX_ PROGRAM_ENV_PARAMETERS_ARB corresponding to the program target specified by *target*.

■ **glProgramLocalParameter4{fd}[v]ARB**—Specify a program local parameter.

Prototypes

```
void glProgramLocalParameter4fARB(GLenum target,
                                  GLuint index,
                                  GLfloat x,
                                  GLfloat y,
                                  GLfloat z,
                                  GLfloat w);
void glProgramLocalParameter4dARB(GLenum target,
                                  GLuint index,
                                  GLdouble x,
                                  GLdouble y,
                                  GLdouble z,
                                  GLdouble w);
```

Parameters

target   Specifies the target program. Must be GL_FRAGMENT_PROGRAM_ARB.

index   Specifies the index of a program local parameter. Must be in the range 0 to GL_MAX_PROGRAM_LOCAL_PARAMETERS_ARB − 1.

x, y, z, w   Specifies the components of the program local parameter.

Prototypes

```
void glProgramLocalParameter4fvARB(GLenum target,
                                   GLuint index,
                                   const GLfloat *params);
void glProgramLocalParameter4dvARB(GLenum target,
                                   GLuint index,
                                   const GLdouble *params);
```

Parameters

target   Specifies the target program. Must be GL_FRAGMENT_PROGRAM_ARB.

index   Specifies the index of a program local parameter. Must be in the range 0 to GL_MAX_PROGRAM_LOCAL_PARAMETERS_ARB − 1.

params   Specifies a pointer to an array containing the four-component program local parameter.

Description

The **glProgramLocalParameter4{fd}[v]ARB** function specifies a four-component floating-point vector for the program local parameter specified by *index*. When program local parameters are specified, they are applied to the currently bound fragment program object.

Special Considerations

The **glProgramLocalParameter4{fd}[v]ARB** function is also defined by the GL_ARB_vertex_program and GL_NV_fragment_program extensions.

Get Functions

glGetProgramLocalParameter{fd}vARB

glGetProgramivARB with *pname* parameter GL_MAX_PROGRAM_LOCAL_PARAMETERS_ARB

Errors

GL_INVALID_VALUE is generated if *index* is greater than or equal to the value of GL_MAX_PROGRAM_LOCAL_PARAMETERS_ARB corresponding to the program target specified by *target*.

■ **glGetProgramEnvParameter{fd}vARB**—Return a program environment parameter.

Prototypes

```
void glGetProgramEnvParameterfvARB(GLenum target,
                                   GLuint index,
                                   GLfloat *params);
void glGetProgramEnvParameterdvARB(GLenum target,
                                   GLuint index,
                                   GLdouble *params);
```

Parameters

target	Specifies the target program. Must be GL_FRAGMENT_PROGRAM_ARB.
index	Specifies the index of a program environment parameter. Must be in the range 0 to GL_MAX_PROGRAM_ENV_PARAMETERS_ARB − 1.
params	Specifies a pointer to an array that receives the four-component program environment parameter.

Description

The **glGetProgramEnvParameter{fd}vARB** function returns the current value of the program environment parameter specified by *index*. The four floating-point values are written to the array pointed to by the *params* parameter.

Special Considerations

The **glGetProgramEnvParameter{fd}vARB** function is also defined by the GL_ARB_vertex_program extension.

Errors

GL_INVALID_VALUE is generated if *index* is greater than or equal to the value of GL_MAX_ PROGRAM_ENV_PARAMETERS_ARB corresponding to the program target specified by *target*.

■ **glGetProgramLocalParameter{fd}vARB**—Return a program local parameter.

Prototypes

```
void glGetProgramLocalParameterfvARB(GLenum target,
                                     GLuint index,
                                     GLfloat *params);
void glGetProgramLocalParameterdvARB(GLenum target,
                                     GLuint index,
                                     GLdouble *params);
```

Parameters

target   Specifies the target program. Must be GL_FRAGMENT_PROGRAM_ARB.

index   Specifies the index of a program local parameter. Must be in the range 0 to GL_MAX_PROGRAM_LOCAL_PARAMETERS_ARB − 1.

params   Specifies a pointer to an array that receives the four-component program local parameter.

Description

The **glGetProgramLocalParameter{fd}vARB** function returns the current value of the program local parameter specified by *index* associated with the currently bound fragment program object. The four floating-point values are written to the array pointed to by the *params* parameter.

Special Considerations

The **glGetProgramLocalParameter{fd}vARB** function is also defined by the GL_ARB_ vertex_program and GL_NV_fragment_program extensions.

Errors

GL_INVALID_VALUE is generated if *index* is greater than or equal to the value of GL_MAX_ PROGRAM_ENV_PARAMETERS_ARB corresponding to the program target specified by *target*.

■ **glGetProgramivARB**—Return program state.

Prototype

```
void glGetProgramivARB(GLenum target,
                       GLenum pname,
                       GLint *params);
```

Parameters

target   Specifies the target program. Must be GL_FRAGMENT_PROGRAM_ARB.

pname   Specifies the symbolic name of a program value to be queried. Accepted
                     values are listed in Description.

params   Specifies a pointer to an array that receives the queried value.

Description

The **glGetProgramivARB** function returns information about the currently bound fragment program or about implementation-dependent program limits. The *pname* parameter
specifies what information to retrieve and may be one of the following values:

GL_PROGRAM_LENGTH_ARB
                     The length of the program string for the program object currently bound
                     to *target* is returned. This is useful for determining the size of the buffer
                     needed for a call to the **glGetProgramStringARB** function.

GL_PROGRAM_FORMAT_ARB
                     The character set of the program string for the program object currently
                     bound to *target* is returned.

GL_PROGRAM_BINDING_ARB
                     The name of the program currently bound to *target* is returned. This is
                     initially 0.

GL_MAX_PROGRAM_INSTRUCTIONS_ARB
                     The maximum number of program instructions allowed by the imple-
                     mentation for the fragment program target is returned. This is always at
                     least 72.

GL_MAX_PROGRAM_ALU_INSTRUCTIONS_ARB
                     The maximum number of program ALU instructions allowed by the im-
                     plementation for the fragment program target is returned. This is always
                     at least 48.

GL_MAX_PROGRAM_TEX_INSTRUCTIONS_ARB
                     The maximum number of program texture instructions allowed by the
                     implementation for the fragment program target is returned. This is al-
                     ways at least 24.

GL_MAX_PROGRAM_TEX_INDIRECTIONS_ARB
                     The maximum number of texture indirections allowed by the imple-
                     mentation for the fragment program target is returned. This is always at
                     least 4. If an implementation has no limit on the number of texture indi-
                     rections, then this value will be equal to the maximum number of texture
                     instructions.

GL_MAX_PROGRAM_ATTRIBS_ARB
                     The maximum number of program attributes allowed by the implementa-
                     tion for the fragment program target is returned. This is always at least 10.

GL_MAX_PROGRAM_PARAMETERS_ARB

> The maximum number of program parameters allowed by the implementation for the fragment program target is returned. This value pertains to the sum of the program environment parameters, program local parameters, and any constants defined within a particular program. This is always at least 24.

GL_MAX_PROGRAM_ENV_PARAMETERS_ARB

> The maximum number of program environment parameters allowed by the implementation for the fragment program target is returned.

GL_MAX_PROGRAM_LOCAL_PARAMETERS_ARB

> The maximum number of program local parameters allowed by the implementation for the fragment program target is returned.

GL_MAX_PROGRAM_TEMPORARIES_ARB

> The maximum number of program temporary registers allowed by the implementation for the fragment program target is returned. This is always at least 16.

GL_PROGRAM_INSTRUCTIONS_ARB

> The number of program instructions used by the program object currently bound to *target* is returned.

GL_PROGRAM_ALU_INSTRUCTIONS_ARB

> The number of program ALU instructions used by the program object currently bound to *target* is returned.

GL_PROGRAM_TEX_INSTRUCTIONS_ARB

> The number of program texture instructions used by the program object currently bound to *target* is returned.

GL_PROGRAM_TEX_INDIRECTIONS_ARB

> The number of texture indirections used by the program object currently bound to *target* is returned.

GL_PROGRAM_ATTRIBS_ARB

> The number of program attributes used by the program object currently bound to *target* is returned.

GL_PROGRAM_PARAMETERS_ARB

> The number of program parameters used by the program object currently bound to *target* is returned. This value includes the sum of the program environment parameters, program local parameters, and any constants defined within the program.

GL_PROGRAM_TEMPORARIES_ARB

> The number of program temporary registers used by the program object currently bound to *target* is returned.

GL_MAX_PROGRAM_NATIVE_INSTRUCTIONS_ARB

> The maximum number of native program instructions allowed by the implementation for the fragment program target is returned.

GL_MAX_PROGRAM_NATIVE_ALU_INSTRUCTIONS_ARB

> The maximum number of native program ALU instructions allowed by the implementation for the fragment program target is returned.

GL_MAX_PROGRAM_NATIVE_TEX_INSTRUCTIONS_ARB

> The maximum number of native program texture instructions allowed by the implementation for the fragment program target is returned.

GL_MAX_PROGRAM_NATIVE_TEX_INDIRECTIONS_ARB

> The maximum number of native texture indirections allowed by the implementation for the fragment program target is returned.

GL_MAX_PROGRAM_NATIVE_ATTRIBS_ARB

> The maximum number of native program attributes allowed by the implementation for the fragment program target is returned.

GL_MAX_PROGRAM_NATIVE_PARAMETERS_ARB

> The maximum number of native program parameters allowed by the implementation for the fragment program target is returned. This value pertains to the sum of the program environment parameters, program local parameters, and any constants defined within a particular program.

GL_MAX_PROGRAM_NATIVE_TEMPORARIES_ARB

> The maximum number of native program temporary registers allowed by the implementation for the fragment program target is returned.

GL_PROGRAM_NATIVE_INSTRUCTIONS_ARB

> The number of native program instructions used by the program object currently bound to *target* is returned. This value reflects any implementation-dependent scheduling and optimization algorithms that are applied to the program when it is loaded.

GL_PROGRAM_NATIVE_ALU_INSTRUCTIONS_ARB

> The number of native program ALU instructions used by the program object currently bound to *target* is returned. This value reflects any implementation-dependent scheduling and optimization algorithms that are applied to the program when it is loaded.

GL_PROGRAM_NATIVE_TEX_INSTRUCTIONS_ARB

> The number of native program texture instructions used by the program object currently bound to *target* is returned. This value reflects any implementation-dependent scheduling and optimization algorithms that are applied to the program when it is loaded.

GL_PROGRAM_NATIVE_TEX_INDIRECTIONS_ARB

> The number of native texture indirections used by the program object currently bound to *target* is returned. This value reflects any implemen-

tation-dependent scheduling and optimization algorithms that are applied to the program when it is loaded.

GL_PROGRAM_NATIVE_ATTRIBS_ARB

The number of native program attributes used by the program object currently bound to *target* is returned. This value reflects any implementation-dependent scheduling and optimization algorithms that are applied to the program when it is loaded.

GL_PROGRAM_NATIVE_PARAMETERS_ARB

The number of native program parameters used by the program object currently bound to *target* is returned. This value includes the sum of the program environment parameters, program local parameters, and any constants defined within a the program. This value also reflects any implementation-dependent scheduling and optimization algorithms that are applied to the program when it is loaded.

GL_PROGRAM_NATIVE_TEMPORARIES_ARB

The number of native program temporary registers used by the program object currently bound to *target* is returned. This value reflects any implementation-dependent scheduling and optimization algorithms that are applied to the program when it is loaded.

GL_PROGRAM_UNDER_NATIVE_LIMITS_ARB

If the resources used by the program object currently bound to *target* fall within the native limits set by the implementation, then the value GL_TRUE is returned. If the native resource limits are exceeded, the value GL_FALSE is returned.

Special Considerations

The **glGetProgramivARB** function is also defined by the GL_ARB_vertex_program extension.

■ **glGetProgramStringARB**—Return a program string.

Prototype

```
void glGetProgramStringARB(GLenum target,
                           GLenum pname,
                           GLvoid *string);
```

Parameters

target   Specifies the target program. Must be GL_FRAGMENT_PROGRAM_ARB.

pname   Must be GL_PROGRAM_STRING_ARB.

string   Specifies a pointer to a region of memory that receives the program string.

Description

The **glGetProgramStringARB** function returns the program string for the program object currently bound to the target specified by the *target* parameter. The *string* parameter points to a buffer that receives the program string. The length of the program string can be determined by calling the **glGetProgramivARB** function with *pname* parameter GL_PROGRAM_LENGTH_ARB.

Special Considerations

The **glGetProgramStringARB** function is also defined by the GL_ARB_vertex_program extension.

Get Functions

glGetProgramivARB with *pname* parameter GL_PROGRAM_LENGTH_ARB

EXTENDED FUNCTIONS

■ **glEnable, glDisable, glIsEnabled**—Extended to enable/disable fragment programs.

Prototypes

```
void glEnable(GLenum cap);
void glDisable(GLenum cap);
GLboolean glIsEnabled(GLenum cap);
```

Extended Parameters

cap   Specifies a GL capability. To enable or disable fragment programs, or to query whether fragment programs are enabled, this should be GL_FRAGMENT_PROGRAM_ARB.

Description

Fragment programs are enabled and disabled by passing the value GL_FRAGMENT_PROGRAM_ARB to the **glEnable** and **glDisable** functions. Calling the **glIsEnabled** function with the parameter GL_FRAGMENT_PROGRAM_ARB returns a value indicating whether fragment programs are enabled.

■ **glMatrixMode**—Extended to support generic program matrices.

Prototype

```
void glMatrixMode(GLenum mode);
```

Extended Parameters

mode   Specifies the matrix stack to which subsequent matrix operations apply. May be GL_MATRIXi_ARB, where i is in the range 0 to GL_MAX_PROGRAM_MATRICES_ARB − 1.

Description

The **glMatrixMode** function sets the current matrix mode. Generic program matrix stack *i* is made current by specifying GL_MATRIX*i*_ARB as the *mode* parameter.

■ **glGetIntegerv**—Extended to allow retrieval of fragment program state.

Prototype

    void **glGetIntegerv**(GLenum *pname*, GLint **params*);

Extended Parameters

pname   Specifies the parameter to be returned. May be one of the values listed in Description.

Description

The **glGetIntegerv** function can be used to retrieve various state related to fragment programs. The *pname* parameter may be one of the following values:

GL_PROGRAM_ERROR_POSITION_ARB
> The byte position within the program string at which an error occurred is returned.

GL_CURRENT_MATRIX_ARB
> The 16 entries of the current matrix (as specified by the **glMatrixMode** function) are returned and stored in column-major order.

GL_TRANSPOSE_CURRENT_MATRIX_ARB
> The 16 entries of the current matrix (as specified by the **glMatrixMode** function) are returned and stored in row-major order.

GL_CURRENT_MATRIX_STACK_DEPTH_ARB
> The current depth of the current matrix stack (as specified by the **gl-MatrixMode** function) is returned.

GL_MAX_PROGRAM_MATRICES_ARB
> The maximum number of generic program matrices supported by the implementation is returned. This is always at least 8.

GL_MAX_PROGRAM_MATRIX_STACK_DEPTH_ARB
> The maximum stack depth for the generic program matrices GL_MATRIX*i*_NV is returned. This may be as small as 1.

GL_MAX_TEXTURE_COORDS_ARB
> The maximum number of texture coordinate sets supported by the implementation is returned. This is always at least 2.

GL_MAX_TEXTURE_IMAGE_UNITS_ARB
> The maximum number of texture image units supported by the implementation is returned. This is always at least 2.

■ **glGetString**—Extended to allow retrieval of the program error string.

Prototype

```
const GLubyte *glGetString(GLenum name);
```

Extended Parameters

name   Specifies the string to return. May be GL_PROGRAM_ERROR_STRING_ARB.

Description

The **glGetString** function can be used to retrieve the program error string after an un-successful call to the **glProgramStringARB** function. If no error occurs when a program is loaded, the error string may still contain warning messages.

19.2 GL_NV_fragment_program

OpenGL version required	OpenGL 1.2.1
Dependencies	Requires GL_ARB_multitexture
Promotions	—
Related extensions	GL_NV_vertex_program

DISCUSSION

The GL_NV_fragment_program extension provides fully general programmability for per-fragment calculations, subsuming the conventional OpenGL texture environment application, color sum, and fog-blending operation. Conventional per-fragment calculations can be replaced by assembly-like source code that an implementation compiles into a *fragment program*. Fragment programs are able to perform complex per-fragment calculations, including arbitrary dependent texture accesses, to determine the final fragment color that is generated. Fragment programs may also generate a new depth value that replaces the depth value of a fragment normally generated during rasterization.

Fragment programs provide an interface for directly accessing generalized fragment processing hardware, and each program may be one of two varieties. A general fragment program performs all the calculations necessary to determine the final fragment color. However, it may be desirable for some applications to continue using the register combiner environment defined by the GL_NV_register_combiners extension (see Chapter 6, Section 6.1). A register combiner fragment program can calculate up to four texture colors that are subsequently passed to the register combiner environment. Either type of fragment program may replace a fragment's depth.

Fragment programs are enabled and disabled by calling the **glEnable** and **glDisable** functions with *cap* parameter GL_FRAGMENT_PROGRAM_NV. When fragment programs are enabled, all conventional texture environment operations are subsumed and must be handled by the current fragment program. If the fragment program is not a register combiner fragment program, then the color sum and fog-blending operations are also the responsibility of the fragment program.

Fragment programs do not subsume conventional per-fragment operations that occur after the fog-blending operation, such as the scissor test, alpha test, stencil test, or depth test. An instruction is provided, however, that is able to discard fragments based on arbitrary calculations performed by a fragment program.

Fragment programs have access to only a single fragment at a time. The information that a fragment program receives as inputs for each fragment includes rasterized attributes such as the fragment's window-space position, primary and secondary colors, and texture coordinates. Fragment programs also have access to a large bank of constant parameter registers that do not change from one fragment to another. These parameters can be used to pass any necessary constant data to a fragment program. For example, material colors and fog parameters would be stored in the parameter registers.

After performing its calculations, a fragment program writes a color and/or depth to a pair of result registers. If a new depth coordinate is not written to a result register, the conventionally rasterized depth coordinate is used for the fragment.

Program Structure

A fragment program is specified as a text string containing a series of statements that may include up to 1,024 instructions. The text string must begin with the character sequence !!FP1.0 (for general fragment programs) or !!FCP1.0 (for register combiner fragment programs), with no preceding whitespace, to indicate that the program conforms to the version 1.0 fragment program syntax. The end of the fragment program is indicated by the three-character sequence END. The exact syntax specification for version 1.0 fragment programs is given in Appendix A, Section A.6.

A fragment program statement can be either a naming statement or an instruction statement. A naming statement associates an identifier with a constant that is either explicitly defined in the program or a local parameter that can be changed externally. An instruction statement operates on input registers and stores its result in a temporary register or output register. Every statement is terminated with a semicolon.

A fragment program instruction consists of a three-character mnemonic followed by a destination register and up to three source operands delimited by commas. The example shown in Listing 19.2.1 performs a projective texture access into a 2D texture map and modulates the fetched color by the interpolated primary color. The symbol # denotes the beginning of a comment that extends to the end of the line on which it appears.

LISTING 19.2.1 The following fragment program performs a 2D projective texture access using texture image unit 0 and modulates the result by the primary color.

```
!!FP1.0

# Fetch a sample from the 2D texture bound to unit 0
TXP   R0, f[TEX0], TEX0, 2D;
```

```
# Modulate by the primary color
MUL    o[COLR], R0, f[COL0];

END
```

All registers manipulated by a fragment program are treated as vectors consisting of the four floating-point components x, y, z, and w. Some instructions require a scalar operand, in which case a vector component must be selected from the source register by appending .x, .y, .z, or .w. For example, the following line calculates the reciprocal of the z component of the temporary register R1.

```
RCP    R0, R1.z;
```

Operand Modification

In a fragment program instruction statement, any source operand may have an optional negation operation, arbitrary swizzle operation, and absolute value operation applied to it at no additional performance cost. Prepending a register name with a minus sign negates each of its components before it is used by an instruction. For example, the following line subtracts the contents of temporary register R2 from temporary register R1 and stores the result in temporary register R0.

```
ADD    R0, R1, -R2;
```

The swizzle operation allows components of a source operand to be reordered or duplicated arbitrarily. Swizzling is denoted by appending a period and a sequence of four letters from the set {x, y, z, w} to a register name. The four letters define a remapping of the components of a register that are passed to the instruction as one of its source operands. As an example, the following line reads the components of temporary register R1 in reverse order and stores them in temporary register R0.

```
MOV    R0, R1.wzyx;
```

Omitting the swizzle suffix is equivalent to using the suffix .xyzw.

Components may be duplicated in the swizzle suffix. For example, the following line moves the x component of R1 into the x and y components of R0 and moves the y component of R1 into the z and w components of R0. The z and w components of R1 are ignored.

```
MOV    R0, R1.xxyy;
```

A shorthand notation exists for duplicating a single component of a register to all four components of a source operand. Appending a register name with a period and a single letter is equivalent to using the same letter four times in a row. For example, the following line moves the x component of R1 into all four components of R0.

```
MOV    R0, R1.x;
```

This notation is also necessary for denoting the scalar operand required by instructions such as the RCP (reciprocal) instruction.

Any source operand may also have an absolute value operation applied to it. Absolute value is denoted within a fragment program by surrounding a register name with vertical bars. For example, the following line adds the absolute value of temporary register R1 to temporary register R2.

```
ADD     R0, |R1|, R2;
```

Negation and swizzle operations may still be applied when an absolute value is evaluated. The following line moves the negation of the absolute value of the components of R1 into R0 in reverse order.

```
MOV     R0, -|R1.wzyx|;
```

Destination Masking

A write mask may be applied to the destination register and controls which components of the destination are updated with an instruction's result. A write mask is denoted by appending a period followed by up to four *unique* letters from the set {x, y, z, w} to a register name in the natural component order. For example, the following line moves the contents of the x component of R1 into the x component of R0, but does not alter the y, z, or w components of R0.

```
MOV     R0.x, R1;
```

The following line adds the x and y components of R1, and stores the result in the x and w components of R0 without affecting the y and z components of R0.

```
ADD     R0.xw, R1.x, R1.y;
```

Omitting the write mask is equivalent to specifying the write mask .xyzw.

Result Saturation

Any fragment program instruction may be suffixed with the sequence _SAT to indicate that any components written to the destination register should saturate in the range [0.0,1.0]. For example, the following line multiplies operands R0 and R1, clamps the result to the range [0.0,1.0], and stores it in R2.

```
MUL_SAT    R2, R0, R1;
```

Conditional Operations

Every instruction can have the letter C appended to its three-character mnemonic to indicate that its result should update the condition register. Only those condition register fields that correspond to written components of the destination register are modified. For example, the following line moves the x and y components of R1 into R0, and updates the x and y fields of the condition register to reflect the values written into R0.

```
MOVC    R0.xy, R1;
```

Writes to the destination register can be conditionally masked by testing the condition register fields against a particular rule. This masking occurs in addition to the static write mask previously described. To specify that a conditional mask is to be applied, a condition code is enclosed in parentheses and follows the destination register. For example, the following line moves each component from R1 to R0 only if the corresponding field of the condition register is set to the value EQ (equal to zero).

```
MOV     R0 (EQ), R1;
```

Condition register fields can also be swizzled just like any source operand. The following line writes to the x, y, z, and w components of R0 only if the w, z, y, and x fields of the condition register are respectively set to the value EQ.

```
MOV     R0 (EQ.wzyx), R1;
```

Precision Selection

Most fragment program instructions can be executed using more than one level of precision. The letter R, H, or X can be appended to an instruction's three-character mnemonic to indicate that the instruction should be carried out using 32-bit floating-point precision (fp32), 16-bit floating-point precision (fp16), or signed 12-bit fixed-point precision (fx12), respectively. (See the GL_NV_half_float extension described in Chapter 17, Section 17.5 for details about the 16-bit floating-point format.) Using lower precision calculations may increase performance. Not all instructions may use all available precision modes—possible combinations are indicated in Table 19.2.3. If a precision mode is not specified for an instruction, the instruction is carried out at the precision corresponding to the destination register. Any source operands that do not match the instruction's precision are automatically converted to the correct precision at no cost.

Constant Declarations

Fragment programs support both named constants and embedded constants. Either may be a scalar floating-point quantity or a four-component vector quantity. The notation used to specify floating-point constants is identical to that used by the C language. A named constant is declared at the beginning of a program and referred to by its name within instruction statements. An embedded constant is inserted directly into an instruction statement.

An embedded scalar constant is specified by simply inserting a signed floating-point number into a location where a register name would normally be used. A scalar constant is equivalent to a vector constant whose four components are all the same value. The following line adds 2.5 to each component of the register R1.

```
ADD     R0, R1, 2.5;
```

An embedded vector constant is represented by a comma-delimited list of one to four floating-point numbers enclosed in braces. For example, the following line adds a different value to each of the components of R1.

```
ADD    R0, R1, {1.0, 2.0, 3.0, 4.0};
```

If fewer than four components are specified, then the y, z, and w components are filled with 0.0, 0.0, and 1.0, respectively, as needed. For example, the vector constant {3.0, 2.0} is equivalent to the vector constant {3.0, 2.0, 0.0, 1.0}.

At most, four unique floating-point scalars may be used in any one instruction. A compiler will not apply absolute value and negation operations to meet this requirement, so the statement

```
MAD    R0, R1, 2.0, {1.0, 2.0, 3.0, 4.0};
```

is legal because it is equivalent to

```
MAD    R0, R1, {1.0, 2.0, 3.0, 4.0}.y, {1.0, 2.0, 3.0, 4.0};
```

However, a statement such as

```
MAD    R0, R1, -2.0, {1.0, 2.0, 3.0, 4.0};
```

is not allowed and will cause a fragment program to fail to load.

A named constant is defined by using the DEFINE statement to associate a name with a constant scalar or vector quantity. For example, the following line defines the identifier const as the vector [1.0,2.0,3.0,4.0].

```
DEFINE const = {1.0, 2.0, 3.0, 4.0};
```

As with embedded constants, if fewer than four components are specified, then the y, z, and w components are filled with 0.0, 0.0, and 1.0, respectively, as needed. A scalar constant is declared by simply assigning a floating-point value to an identifier. The following line defines the identifier negPi as the value $-\pi$.

```
DEFINE negPi = -3.14159;
```

Assigning a scalar value to an identifier is equivalent to assigning a vector to the identifier with the same value for all four components.

Fragment programs may also declare named local parameters by using the DECLARE statement. The DECLARE statement defines a name that may optionally be initialized using the same syntax as the DEFINE statement. For example, both of the following lines are allowed.

```
DECLARE color;
DECLARE color = 0.5;
```

A name declared by the DECLARE statement without an initializer is assigned the value ⟨0.0,0.0,0.0,0.0⟩ when the fragment program is loaded. The difference between the DEFINE statement and the DECLARE statement is that values associated with names defined by the

DECLARE statement may be externally updated. The value of a named local parameter is specified by calling the **glProgramNamedParameter4{fd}[v]NV** function.

Register Set

The register set available to fragment programs consists of 32 full-precision temporary registers, 64 half-precision temporary registers, 12 read-only fragment attribute registers, at least 64 read-only program parameter registers, 7 write-only fragment result registers, and a condition code register. Every register consists of four components labeled x, y, z, and w.

Fragment Attribute Registers

Per-fragment data is passed into a fragment program through a set of 12 fragment attribute registers. A fragment attribute register is denoted within a fragment program by the lowercase letter f followed by one of the four-character mnemonics listed in Table 19.2.1, inside brackets. Fragment attributes are read-only and cannot be specified as the destination register for any instruction. A single instruction may not access more than one unique fragment attribute register, although the same fragment attribute register may be used for multiple source operands.

TABLE 19.2.1   Fragment Attribute Registers

Attribute Mnemonic	Description	Component Interpretation
f[WPOS]	Window-space position	$(x,y,z,1/w)$
f[COL0]	Primary color	(r,g,b,a)
f[COL1]	Secondary color	(r,g,b,a)
f[FOGC]	Fog coordinate	$(f,0,0,0)$
f[TEX0]	Texture 0 coordinates	(s,t,r,q)
f[TEX1]	Texture 1 coordinates	(s,t,r,q)
f[TEX2]	Texture 2 coordinates	(s,t,r,q)
f[TEX3]	Texture 3 coordinates	(s,t,r,q)
f[TEX4]	Texture 4 coordinates	(s,t,r,q)
f[TEX5]	Texture 5 coordinates	(s,t,r,q)
f[TEX6]	Texture 6 coordinates	(s,t,r,q)
f[TEX7]	Texture 7 coordinates	(s,t,r,q)

The f[WPOS] attribute register corresponds to the window-space position of the fragment. The x and y components represent the window position of the fragment and fall into the range specified by the **glViewport** function. The z component represents the window depth of the fragment and falls into the range specified by the **glDepthRange** function. The w component contains the reciprocal of the clip-space w coordinate corresponding to the fragment.

Fragment Result Registers

Fragment programs write their results to the set of seven fragment result registers listed in Table 19.2.2. A fragment result register is denoted by the lowercase letter o followed by a four-character mnemonic inside brackets. The vertex result registers are write-only and may not appear as source operands in a vertex program. A general fragment program may write to one of the registers o[COLR] or o[COLH], but not both, to specify the final fragment color. General fragment programs may not write to the texture color result registers. Register combiner fragment programs must write to at least one texture color result register, but may not write to either of the final fragment color registers, because that color is determined by the register combiners. Either type of fragment program may write to the o[DEPR] register. If a fragment program does not write to at least one result register, then it will fail to load.

TABLE 19.2.2 Fragment result registers. Components labeled * are unused.

Result Register	Description	Precision	Component Interpretation
o[COLR]	Final fragment color	32-bit	(r,g,b,a)
o[COLH]	Final fragment color	16-bit	(r,g,b,a)
o[TEX0]	Texture 0 color	16-bit	(r,g,b,a)
o[TEX1]	Texture 1 color	16-bit	(r,g,b,a)
o[TEX2]	Texture 2 color	16-bit	(r,g,b,a)
o[TEX3]	Texture 3 color	16-bit	(r,g,b,a)
o[DEPR]	Final fragment depth	32-bit	$(*,*,d,*)$

The z component of the o[DEPR] register represents the final window-space depth of the fragment. If a fragment program does not write to this register, then the conventionally rasterized depth is assigned to the fragment. The depth written to the o[DEPR] register is clamped to the range [0,1].

Program Parameter Registers

Fragment programs have access to a set of at least 64 local program parameter registers. Values in program parameter registers are always stored at full 32-bit precision. The number of local program parameters supported by an implementation is retrieved by calling the **glGetIntegerv** function with *pname* parameter GL_MAX_FRAGMENT_PROGRAM_LOCAL_ PARAMETERS_NV. Program parameter registers are read-only and may not appear as a destination register in a fragment program. A program parameter register is denoted by a lowercase letter p followed by a number in the range 0 to GL_MAX_FRAGMENT_PROGRAM_ LOCAL_PARAMETERS_NV − 1, inside brackets. A single instruction may not access more than one unique program parameter register, although the same program parameter register may be used for multiple source operands.

Constant data is loaded into a single program parameter register by calling the **glProgramLocalParameter4{fd}[v]ARB** function (borrowed from the GL_ARB_fragment_program extension),

```
void glProgramLocalParameter4{fd}ARB(GLenum target,
                                     GLuint index,
                                     T x,
                                     T y,
                                     T z,
                                     T w);

void glProgramLocalParameter4{fd}vARB(GLenum target,
                                      GLuint index,
                                      const T *params);
```

with *target* parameter GL_FRAGMENT_PROGRAM_NV. (The type T represents GLfloat or GLdouble.) The *index* parameter specifies which program parameter to load. The program local parameter applies only to the currently bound fragment program. Each fragment program has its own set of local parameters that are automatically switched in when the program becomes active. The local parameter value specified by the **glProgramLocalParameter4{fd}[v]ARB** function is accessed within the fragment program using the notation p[i], where i corresponds to the *index* parameter.

The value of a named local parameter defined by the DECLARE statement within a fragment program is updated by calling the **glProgramNamedParameter4{fd}[v]NV** function,

```
void glProgramNamedParameter{fd}NV(GLuint id,
                                   GLsizei len,
                                   const GLubyte *name,
                                   T x,
                                   T y,
                                   T z,
                                   T w);

void glProgramNamedParameter{fd}vNV(GLuint id,
                                    GLsizei len,
                                    const GLubyte *name,
                                    const T *params);
```

with *id* parameter specifying the name of a fragment program object. The *len* and *name* parameters specify the name of the local parameter to update. The new values are applied only to the program specified by the *id* parameter. If multiple fragment programs declare the same named local parameter, each must be updated separately.

Temporary Registers

There are a total of 96 temporary registers, but full-precision and half-precision temporary registers, as well as the fragment result registers, occupy the same hardware resources. A full-precision temporary register is denoted within a fragment program by the uppercase letter R followed by a number in the range 0 to 31. A half-precision temporary register is denoted by the uppercase letter H followed by a number in the range 0 to 63. Temporary registers are private to each fragment program invocation and are initialized to $\langle 0,0,0,0 \rangle$ each time a program begins execution. The set of temporary registers may be read or written for any purpose, and their final values at the end of a program's execution have no effect.

The total number of temporary registers used by a fragment program is limited to 64. All writable full-precision registers (R0–R31, o[COLR], and o[DEPR]) count as two temporary registers against this limit, and writable half-precision registers (H0–H63, o[COLH], and o[TEX0]–o[TEX3]) count as one temporary register. In a register combiner fragment program, all four texture color result registers are counted, regardless of whether they are written by the program. Any fragment program that exceeds the temporary register limit will fail to load.

Condition Code Register

The four components of the condition code register hold values that reflect the result of the most recent instruction to specify that the condition register is updated (indicated by appending the instruction mnemonic with the letter C). Each field may be one of the four following values, which are determined by the corresponding component of the result.

- EQ—The result is equal to zero
- LT—The result is less than zero
- GT—The result is greater than zero
- UN—The result is NAN (not a number)

As an example, suppose that register R1 contains the values {1.0, 0.0, −1.0, NAN}. Then the instruction

```
MOVC    R0, R1;
```

would place the values {GT, EQ, LT, UN} into the condition code register. A subsequent instruction that uses the conditional mask to update only components of the destination whose corresponding field of the condition code register is GT would only update the x component of the destination. The condition codes may be swizzled, so the instruction

```
MOV    R2 (GT.xxzw), R0;
```

would update both the x and y components of the destination, but not the z and w components.

Instruction Set

There are 45 fragment program instructions. The operation performed by each instruction and the corresponding types of input operands and output results are listed in Table 19.2.3.

TABLE 19.2.3 Fragment program instructions. The letter "v" indicates a vector result or operand, and the letter "s" indicates a scalar operand. The vector $\langle s,s,s,s \rangle$ represents a single scalar result that is replicated to all four components of the result vector.

Instruction	Output Result	Input Operands	Operation
ADD[RHX][C][_SAT]	v	v, v	Add
COS[RH][C][_SAT]	$\langle s,s,s,s \rangle$	s	Cosine
DDX[RH][C][_SAT]	v	v	Derivative relative to x
DDY[RH][C][_SAT]	v	v	Derivative relative to y
DP3[RHX][C][_SAT]	$\langle s,s,s,s \rangle$	v, v	3D dot product
DP4[RHX][C][_SAT]	$\langle s,s,s,s \rangle$	v, v	4D dot product
DST[RH][C][_SAT]	v	v, v	Distance vector
EX2[RH][C][_SAT]	$\langle s,s,s,s \rangle$	s	Exponential base 2
FLR[RHX][C][_SAT]	v	v	Floor
FRC[RHX][C][_SAT]	v	v	Fraction
KIL	–	–	Kill fragment
LG2[RH][C][_SAT]	$\langle s,s,s,s \rangle$	s	Logarithm base 2
LIT[RH][C][_SAT]	v	v	Light coefficients
LRP[RHX][C][_SAT]	v	v, v, v	Linear interpolation
MAD[RHX][C][_SAT]	v	v, v, v	Multiply-add
MAX[RHX][C][_SAT]	v	v, v	Maximum
MIN[RHX][C][_SAT]	v	v, v	Minimum
MOV[RHX][C][_SAT]	v	v	Move
MUL[RHX][C][_SAT]	v	v, v	Multiply
PK2H	$\langle s,s,s,s \rangle$	v	Pack two half floats
PK2US	$\langle s,s,s,s \rangle$	v	Pack two unsigned shorts
PK4B	$\langle s,s,s,s \rangle$	v	Pack four signed bytes
PK4UB	$\langle s,s,s,s \rangle$	v	Pack four unsigned bytes
POW[RH][C][_SAT]	$\langle s,s,s,s \rangle$	s, s	Exponentiate
RCP[RH][C][_SAT]	$\langle s,s,s,s \rangle$	s	Reciprocal
RFL[RH][C][_SAT]	v	v, v	Reflection vector
RSQ[RH][C][_SAT]	$\langle s,s,s,s \rangle$	s	Reciprocal square root
SEQ[RHX][C]	v	v, v	Set on equal
SFL[RHX][C]	v	v, v	Set on false
SGE[RHX][C]	v	v, v	Set on greater than or equal
SGT[RHX][C]	v	v, v	Set on greater than

TABLE 19.2.3 *Continued*

Instruction	Output Result	Input Operands	Operation
SIN[RH][C][_SAT]	⟨s,s,s,s⟩	s	Sine
SLE[RHX][C]	v	v, v	Set on less than or equal
SLT[RHX][C]	v	v, v	Set on less than
SNE[RHX][C]	v	v, v	Set on not equal
STR[RHX][C]	v	v, v	Set on true
SUB[RHX][C][_SAT]	v	v, v	Subtract
TEX[C][_SAT]	v	v	Texture sample
TXD[C][_SAT]	v	v, v, v	Texture sample with derivatives
TXP[C][_SAT]	v	v	Texture sample with projection
UP2H	v	s	Unpack two half floats
UP2US	v	s	Unpack two unsigned shorts
UP4B	v	s	Unpack two signed bytes
UP4UB	v	s	Unpack two unsigned bytes
X2D[RH][C][_SAT]	v	v, v, v	2D transformation

The TEX, TXD, and TXP instructions each sample a texture map. The values written to the destination register depend on the base internal format in which the texture image is stored. Table 19.2.4 summarizes how texture image components are mapped to the x, y, z, and w components of the destination register.

TABLE 19.2.4 Mapping of Filtered Texel Components to Fragment Program Register Components

Base Internal Format	X	Y	Z	W
GL_ALPHA	0.0	0.0	0.0	A
GL_LUMINANCE	L	L	L	1.0
GL_LUMINANCE_ALPHA	L	L	L	A
GL_INTENSITY	I	I	I	I
GL_RGB	R	G	B	1.0
GL_RGBA	R	G	B	A

(continues)

TABLE 19.2.4 *Continued*

Base Internal Format	X	Y	Z	W
GL_HILO_NV (signed)	HI	LO	$\sqrt{\max\left(1-\text{HI}^2-\text{LO}^2\right)}$	1.0
GL_HILO_NV (unsigned)	HI	LO	1.0	1.0
GL_DSDT_NV	DS	DT	0.0	1.0
GL_DSDT_MAG_NV	DS	DT	MAG	1.0
GL_DSDT_MAG_INTENSITY_NV	DS	DT	MAG	I
GL_FLOAT_R_NV	R	0.0	0.0	1.0
GL_FLOAT_RG_NV	R	G	0.0	1.0
GL_FLOAT_RGB_NV	R	G	B	1.0
GL_FLOAT_RGBA_NV	R	G	B	A

Each of the fragment program instructions is described in detail below. Included with each instruction is pseudocode that demonstrates the instruction's exact effect. The types vector and scalar are used to hold four-component vector quantities and one-component scalar quantities, respectively. When loading data from a register, the pseudocode makes use of the functions VectorLoad and ScalarLoad to apply the swizzle, negate, and absolute value operations to each operand. In the definitions of these functions, which follow, the .swiz[n] field used with the source parameter denotes the nth component of the source vector after swizzling. The .comp field used with the source parameter denotes the scalar component selected using the single component suffix in the vertex program. The value of absolute is true if the program specifies that the absolute value of the source operand be taken, and is false otherwise. The value of negate is true if the program specifies that the source operand is negated, and is false otherwise.

```
vector VectorLoad(vector source)
{
    vector    operand;

    operand.x = source.swiz[0];
    operand.y = source.swiz[1];
    operand.z = source.swiz[2];
    operand.w = source.swiz[3];
    if (absolute)
    {
        operand.x = fabs(operand.x);
        operand.y = fabs(operand.y);
        operand.z = fabs(operand.z);
        operand.w = fabs(operand.w);
    }
    if (negate)
```

```
        {
            operand.x = -operand.x;
            operand.y = -operand.y;
            operand.z = -operand.z;
            operand.w = -operand.w;
        }

        return (operand);
    }

    scalar ScalarLoad(vector source)
    {
        scalar      operand;

        operand = source.comp;
        if (absolute) operand = fabs(operand);
        if (negate) operand = -operand;

        return (operand);
    }
```

When a vector result is written to a destination register, the pseudocode makes use of the
WriteDest function to apply both the static write mask and the conditional write mask.
This function is defined below along with two addition functions, TestCond and GenerateCond. The TestCond function returns true if the field of the condition code register
specified by the field parameter satisfies the condition specified by the rule parameter,
and is false if the condition is not satisfied. The GenerateCond function returns the condition code corresponding to the value parameter.

For the WriteDest function, each of the components of mask is true if writing is enabled
for the corresponding component of the destination register, and is false if writing is disabled. When writing is enabled for a component, the same component of the condition
code register, represented by the condReg identifier, may also be updated. The condition code register is updated when an instruction uses the C suffix, and this is represented
by the Boolean value updateCond. The cond identifier represents the four-component
condition register.

```
    bool TestCond(CondCode field, CondCode rule)
    {
        switch (rule)
        {
            case EQ: return (field == EQ);
            case NE: return (field != EQ);
            case LT: return (field == LT);
            case GT: return (field == GT);
            case LE: return ((field == EQ) || (field == LT));
            case GE: return ((field == EQ) || (field == GT));
            case FL: return (false);
```

```
            case TR: return (true);
        }
    }

    CondCode GenerateCond(scalar value)
    {
        if (value == NAN) return (UN);
        if (value < 0.0) return (LT);
        if (value > 0.0) return (GT);
        return (EQ);
    }

    vector WriteDest(vector dest, vector result)
    {
        if ((mask.x) && (TestCond(cond.swiz[0]))
        {
            dest.x = result.x;
            if (updateCond) condReg.x = GenerateCond(dest.x);
        }
        if ((mask.y) && (TestCond(cond.swiz[1]))
        {
            dest.y = result.y;
            if (updateCond) condReg.y = GenerateCond(dest.y);
        }
        if ((mask.z) && (TestCond(cond.swiz[2]))
        {
            dest.z = result.z;
            if (updateCond) condReg.z = GenerateCond(dest.z);
        }
        if ((mask.w) && (TestCond(cond.swiz[3]))
        {
            dest.w = result.w;
            if (updateCond) condReg.w = GenerateCond(dest.w);
        }

        return (dest);
    }
```

When the instructions TEX and TXP perform a texture access, the pseudocode uses the TextureSample function to fetch a filtered texel. This function has the following prototype:

```
vector TextureSample(scalar s, scalar t, scalar r, enum unit,
    enum target);
```

The s, t, and r parameters specify the texture coordinates used to sample the texture map. The number of coordinates actually used depends on the texture target, which is specified by the target parameter. The target parameter may be 1D, 2D, 3D, CUBE, or RECT, and indicates what texture target to access. The unit parameter specifies which texture image unit to access and must be TEX*i*, where *i* is in the range 0 to GL_MAX_TEXTURE_IMAGE_ UNITS_NV − 1. If a texture bound to a particular texture image unit is accessed multiple times during a fragment program, then the value of target must be the same each time, or the program will fail to load.

When the TXD instruction performs a texture access, the pseudocode uses the Texture- SampleDeriv function to fetch a filtered texel. This function has the following prototype:

```
vector TextureSampleDeriv(scalar s, scalar t, scalar r,
      vector dx, vector dy, enum unit, enum target);
```

The dx and dy arguments explicitly specify the partial derivatives with respect to the window-space *x*- and *y*-directions, and all other arguments have the same meaning as they do for the TextureSample function. The partial derivatives passed to TextureSampleDeriv override the implicitly calculated derivatives that are normally calculated during rasterization to perform texel filtering.

The exact effect of each vertex program instruction follows. The local variable r is used in most of the pseudocode listings and always denotes a temporary vector quantity.

ADD[RHX][C][_SAT]–Add

```
ADD     result, op0, op1;
```

The ADD instruction performs a componentwise addition of two operands.

```
vector v0 = VectorLoad(op0);
vector v1 = VectorLoad(op1);
r.x = v0.x + v1.x;
r.y = v0.y + v1.y;
r.z = v0.z + v1.z;
r.w = v0.w + v1.w;
result = WriteDest(result, r);
```

The addition operation satisfies the following rules:

1. $x + y = y + x$ for all x and y.
2. $x + 0.0 = x$ for all x.

COS[RH][C][_SAT]–Cosine

```
COS     result, op0;
```

The COS instruction calculates the approximate cosine of a single scalar operand. The angle is measured in radians and is not restricted to the range $[0, 2\pi]$. The result is replicated to all four components of the destination.

```
scalar s0 = ScalarLoad(op0);
scalar cosine = ApproxCos(s0);
```

```
r.x = cosine;
r.y = cosine;
r.z = cosine;
r.w = cosine;
result = WriteDest(result, r);
```

The cosine operation satisfies the precision requirement

$$\left|\text{ApproxCos}(x) - \cos x\right| < 2^{-22}$$

if the value of x satisfies $0 \le x < 2\pi$. If x falls outside this range, the error in the approximate typically increases with the absolute value of x.

DDX[RH][C][_SAT]—Derivative relative to x

```
DDX      result, op0;
```

The DDX instruction approximates the partial derivatives of the components of a single vector operand with respect to the x window-space direction.

```
vector v0 = VectorLoad(op0);
r.x = ComputeDerivX(v0.x);
r.y = ComputeDerivX(v0.y);
r.z = ComputeDerivX(v0.z);
r.w = ComputeDerivX(v0.w);
result = WriteDest(result, r);
```

The derivative is calculated at the center of the fragment. The derivative calculation is approximate, so derivatives of derivatives may not yield accurate second derivatives.

DDY[RH][C][_SAT]—Derivative relative to y

```
DDY      result, op0;
```

The DDY instruction approximates the partial derivatives of the components of a single vector operand with respect to the y window-space direction.

```
vector v0 = VectorLoad(op0);
r.x = ComputeDerivY(v0.x);
r.y = ComputeDerivY(v0.y);
r.z = ComputeDerivY(v0.z);
r.w = ComputeDerivY(v0.w);
result = WriteDest(result, r);
```

The derivative is calculated at the center of the fragment. The derivative calculation is approximate, so derivatives of derivatives may not yield accurate second derivatives.

DP3[RHX][C][_SAT]–Three-component dot product

```
DP3     result, op0, op1;
```

The `DP3` instruction performs a three-component dot product between two operands and replicates the result to all four components of the destination.

```
vector v0 = VectorLoad(op0);
vector v1 = VectorLoad(op1);
scalar dot = v0.x * v1.x + v0.y + v1.y + v0.z * v1.z;
r.x = dot;
r.y = dot;
r.z = dot;
r.w = dot;
result = WriteDest(result, r);
```

DP4[RHX][C][_SAT]–Four-component dot product

```
DP4     result, op0, op1;
```

The `DP4` instruction performs a four-component dot product between two operands and replicates the result to all four components of the destination.

```
vector v0 = VectorLoad(op0);
vector v1 = VectorLoad(op1);
scalar dot = v0.x * v1.x + v0.y + v1.y
                + v0.z * v1.z + v0.w * v1.w;
r.x = dot;
r.y = dot;
r.z = dot;
r.w = dot;
result = WriteDest(result, r);
```

DST[RH][C][_SAT]–Distance vector

```
DST     result, op0, op1;
```

The `DST` instruction takes two operands and produces a vector that is useful for attenuation calculations. Given a distance d, the first operand should be formatted as $\langle *,d^2,*,d^2 \rangle$ and the second operation should be formatted as $\langle *,1/d,*,1/d \rangle$, where * indicates that the operand's component is not used. The result of the `DST` instruction is the vector $\langle 1,d,d^2,1/d \rangle$.

```
vector v0 = VectorLoad(op0);
vector v1 = VectorLoad(op1);
r.x = 1.0;
r.y = v0.y * v1.y;
r.z = v0.z;
r.w = v1.w;
result = WriteDest(result, r);
```

EX2[RH][C][_SAT]—Exponential base 2

```
EX2     result, op0;
```

The EX2 instruction calculates an approximation to 2^p for a single scalar operand p and replicates the result to all four components of the destination.

```
scalar e = ApproxExp2(ScalarLoad(op0));
r.x = e;
r.y = e;
r.z = e;
r.w = e;
result = WriteDest(result, r);
```

The ApproxExp2 function satisfies the precision requirement

$$\left|\mathrm{ApproxExp2}(x) - 2^x\right| < \begin{cases} 2^{-22}, & \text{if } 0 \le x < 1; \\ 2^{-22} \cdot 2^{\lfloor x \rfloor}, & \text{otherwise.} \end{cases}$$

FLR[RHX][C][_SAT]—Floor

```
FLR     result, op0;
```

The FLR instruction performs a componentwise floor operation on a single operand.

```
vector v0 = VectorLoad(op0);
r.x = floor(v0.x);
r.y = floor(v0.y);
r.z = floor(v0.z);
r.w = floor(v0.w);
result = WriteDest(result, r);
```

FRC[RHX][C][_SAT]—Fraction

```
FRC     result, op0;
```

The FRC instruction performs a componentwise fraction operation on a single operand. The fraction operation is equivalent to subtracting the floor of the operand from the operand itself.

```
vector v0 = VectorLoad(op0);
r.x = v0.x - floor(v0.x);
r.y = v0.y - floor(v0.y);
r.z = v0.z - floor(v0.z);
r.w = v0.w - floor(v0.w);
result = WriteDest(result, r);
```

KIL–Kill fragment

```
KIL     (cond);
```

The `KIL` instruction tests the four components of the swizzled condition register. If any component tests true, then the current fragment is discarded, and no further processing occurs. Otherwise, the `KIL` instruction has no effect.

```
if ((TestCond(cond.swiz[0])) || (TestCond(cond.swiz[1]))
    || (TestCond(cond.swiz[2])) || (TestCond(cond.swiz[3])))
{
    // exit
}
```

LG2[RH][C][_SAT]–Logarithm base 2

```
LG2     result, op0;
```

The `LG2` instruction calculates an approximation to $\log_2(p)$ for a single scalar operand p and replicates the result to all four components of the destination.

```
scalar l = ApproxLog2(ScalarLoad(op0));
r.x = l;
r.y = l;
r.z = l;
r.w = l;
result = WriteDest(result, r);
```

The `ApproxLog2` function satisfies the precision requirement

$$\left|\text{ApproxLog2}(x) - \log_2 x\right| < 2^{-22}.$$

LIT[RH][C][_SAT]–Light coefficients

```
LIT     result, op0;
```

The `LIT` instruction takes a single operand and produces a coefficient vector that is useful for lighting calculations. The operand is assumed to be formatted as $\langle \mathbf{N}\cdot\mathbf{L},\mathbf{N}\cdot\mathbf{H},*,m\rangle$, where $\mathbf{N}\cdot\mathbf{L}$ is the diffuse dot product, $\mathbf{N}\cdot\mathbf{H}$ is the specular dot product, m is the specular exponent, and $*$ indicates that the z component is unused. The result of the `LIT` instruction is the vector $\langle 1.0, \mathbf{N}\cdot\mathbf{L}, (\mathbf{N}\cdot\mathbf{H})^m, 1.0 \rangle$, where $\mathbf{N}\cdot\mathbf{L}$ and $\mathbf{N}\cdot\mathbf{H}$ are clamped to 0.0, and the z component is set to 0.0 if $\mathbf{N}\cdot\mathbf{L} \leq 0$. The specular exponent m is clamped to the range $[-128,128]$.

```
vector v0 = VectorLoad(op0);
if (v0.x < 0.0) v0.x = 0.0;
if (v0.y < 0.0) v0.y = 0.0;
if (v0.w < -128.0 + epsilon) v0.w = -128.0 + epsilon;
else if (v0.w > 128.0 - epsilon) v0.w = 128.0 - epsilon;
```

```
r.x = 1.0;
r.y = v0.x;
r.z = (v0.x > 0.0) ? RoughApproxPow(v0.y, v0.w) : 0.0;
r.w = 1.0;
result = WriteDest(result, r);
```

The RoughApproxPow function is defined in terms of the base-2 exponential and logarithm functions implemented by the EX2 and LG2 instructions. Thus,

```
RoughApproxPow(b, e) = ApproxExp2(e * ApproxLog2(b))
```

and the precision of the RoughApproxPow function is limited by the precision of the ApproxExp2 and ApproxLog2 functions.

LRP[RHX][C][_SAT]—Linear interpolation

```
LRP     result, op0, op1, op2;
```

The LRP instruction performs componentwise linear interpolation between its second and third operands using its first operand as the blend factor.

```
vector v0 = VectorLoad(op0);
vector v1 = VectorLoad(op1);
vector v2 = VectorLoad(op2);
r.x = v0.x * v1.x + (1.0 - v0.x) * v2.x;
r.y = v0.y * v1.y + (1.0 - v0.y) * v2.y;
r.z = v0.z * v1.z + (1.0 - v0.z) * v2.z;
r.w = v0.w * v1.w + (1.0 - v0.w) * v2.w;
result = WriteDest(result, r);
```

MAD[RHX][C][_SAT]—Multiply-add

```
MAD     result, op0, op1, op2;
```

The MAD instruction performs a componentwise multiplication and addition of three operands.

```
vector v0 = VectorLoad(op0);
vector v1 = VectorLoad(op1);
vector v2 = VectorLoad(op2);
r.x = v0.x * v1.x + v2.x;
r.y = v0.y * v1.y + v2.y;
r.z = v0.z * v1.z + v2.z;
r.w = v0.w * v1.w + v2.w;
result = WriteDest(result, r);
```

The multiplication and addition operations are subject to the same rules described for the MUL and ADD instructions.

MAX[RHX][C][_SAT]—Maximum

```
MAX    result, op0, op1;
```

The MAX instruction performs a componentwise maximum operation between two operands.

```
vector v0 = VectorLoad(op0);
vector v1 = VectorLoad(op1);
r.x = (v0.x > v1.x) ? v0.x : v1.x;
r.y = (v0.y > v1.y) ? v0.y : v1.y;
r.z = (v0.z > v1.z) ? v0.z : v1.z;
r.w = (v0.w > v1.w) ? v0.w : v1.w;
result = WriteDest(result, r);
```

MIN[RHX][C][_SAT]—Minimum

```
MIN    result, op0, op1;
```

The MIN instruction performs a componentwise minimum operation between two operands.

```
vector v0 = VectorLoad(op0);
vector v1 = VectorLoad(op1);
r.x = (v0.x > v1.x) ? v1.x : v0.x;
r.y = (v0.y > v1.y) ? v1.y : v0.y;
r.z = (v0.z > v1.z) ? v1.z : v0.z;
r.w = (v0.w > v1.w) ? v1.w : v0.w;
result = WriteDest(result, r);
```

MOV[RHX][C][_SAT]—Move

```
MOV    result, op0;
```

The MOV instruction copies a single operand to the destination.

```
vector v0 = VectorLoad(op0);
result = WriteDest(result, v0);
```

MUL[RHX][C][_SAT]—Multiply

```
MUL    result, op0, op1;
```

The MUL instruction performs a componentwise multiplication of two operands.

```
vector v0 = VectorLoad(op0);
vector v1 = VectorLoad(op1);
r.x = v0.x * v1.x;
r.y = v0.y * v1.y;
r.z = v0.z * v1.z;
```

```
r.w = v0.w * v1.w;
result = WriteDest(result, r);
```

The multiplication operation satisfies the following rules:

1. $xy = yx$ for all x and y.
2. $x \cdot 1.0 = x$ for all x.
3. $x \cdot \pm 0.0 = \pm 0.0$ for all x with the possible exceptions of $\pm$INF and $\pm$NAN.

PK2H—Pack two half floats

```
PK2H    result, op0;
```

The PK2H instruction converts the x and y components of a single vector operand to 16-bit floating-point values and packs them into a single 32-bit value that is replicated to all four components of the result. The operation performed by the PK2H instruction can be reversed by the UP2H instruction.

```
vector v0 = VectorLoad(op0);
scalar p = ConvertToHalf(v0.x) | (ConvertToHalf(v0.y) << 16);
r.x = p;
r.y = p;
r.z = p;
r.w = p;
result = WriteDest(result, r);
```

The result of the PK2H instruction must be written to a register possessing 32-bit components. Valid destination registers are the 32 temporary registers Ri, the color output register o[COLR], and the depth output register o[DEPR]. Specifying any other destination register will cause a fragment program to fail to load.

PK2US—Pack two unsigned shorts

```
PK2US    result, op0;
```

The PK2US instruction converts the x and y components of a single vector operand to unsigned 16-bit fixed-point values and packs them into a single 32-bit value that is replicated to all four components of the result. The operation performed by the PK2US instruction can be reversed by the UP2US instruction.

```
vector v0 = VectorLoad(op0);
scalar p = ConvertToUS(v0.x) | (ConvertToUS(v0.y) << 16);
r.x = p;
r.y = p;
r.z = p;
r.w = p;
result = WriteDest(result, r);
```

The `ConvertToUS` function in the pseudocode clamps its argument to the range [0.0,1.0], and then converts to fixed-point by linearly mapping 0.0 to 0x0000 and 1.0 to 0xFFFF.

The result of the `PK2US` instruction must be written to a register possessing 32-bit components. Valid destination registers are the 32 temporary registers Ri, the color output register o[COLR], and the depth output register o[DEPR]. Specifying any other destination register will cause a fragment program to fail to load.

PK4B—Pack four signed bytes

```
PK4B      result, op0;
```

The `PK4B` instruction converts the four components of a single vector operand to signed 8-bit fixed-point values and packs them into a single 32-bit value that is replicated to all four components of the result. The operation performed by the `PK4B` instruction can be reversed by the `UP4B` instruction.

```
vector v0 = VectorLoad(op0);
scalar p = ConvertToB(v0.x) | (ConvertToB(v0.y) << 8)
           | (ConvertToB(v0.z) << 16)
           | (ConvertToB(v0.w) << 24);
r.x = p;
r.y = p;
r.z = p;
r.w = p;
result = WriteDest(result, r);
```

The `ConvertToB` function in the pseudocode clamps its argument to the range $\left[-\frac{128}{127}, 1.0\right]$ and then converts to fixed-point by linearly mapping $-\frac{128}{127}$ to 0x00 and 1.0 to 0xFF.

The result of the `PK4B` instruction must be written to a register possessing 32-bit components. Valid destination registers are the 32 temporary registers Ri, the color output register o[COLR], and the depth output register o[DEPR]. Specifying any other destination register will cause a fragment program to fail to load.

PK4UB—Pack four unsigned bytes

```
PK4UB     result, op0;
```

The `PK4UB` instruction converts the four components of a single vector operand to unsigned 8-bit fixed-point values and packs them into a single 32-bit value that is replicated to all four components of the result. The operation performed by the `PK4UB` instruction can be reversed by the `UP4UB` instruction.

```
vector v0 = VectorLoad(op0);
scalar p = ConvertToUB(v0.x) | (ConvertToUB(v0.y) << 8)
           | (ConvertToUB(v0.z) << 16)
           | (ConvertToUB(v0.w) << 24);
```

```
r.x = p;
r.y = p;
r.z = p;
r.w = p;
result = WriteDest(result, r);
```

The `ConvertToUB` function in the pseudocode clamps its argument to the range [0.0,1.0], and then converts to fixed-point by linearly mapping 0.0 to 0x00 and 1.0 to 0xFF.

The result of the PK4UB instruction must be written to a register possessing 32-bit components. Valid destination registers are the 32 temporary registers `Ri`, the color output register `o[COLR]`, and the depth output register `o[DEPR]`. Specifying any other destination register will cause a fragment program to fail to load.

POW[RH][C][_SAT]—Exponentiate

```
POW     result, op0, op1;
```

The POW instruction calculates an approximation to b^e for two scalar operands b and e and replicates the result to all four components of the destination.

```
scalar s0 = ScalarLoad(op0);
scalar s1 = ScalarLoad(op1);
scalar p = ApproxPow(op0, op1);
r.x = p;
r.y = p;
r.z = p;
r.w = p;
result = WriteDest(result, r);
```

The `ApproxPow` function is defined in terms of the base-2 exponentiation and logarithm functions defined by the EX2 and LG2 functions. Thus,

```
ApproxPow(b, e) = ApproxExp2(e * ApproxLog2(b))
```

and it may not be possible to correctly raise a negative base to an integer power, since a logarithm is involved.

RCP[RH][C][_SAT]—Reciprocal

```
RCP     result, op0;
```

The RCP instruction approximates the reciprocal of a single scalar operand and replicates the result to all four components of the destination.

```
scalar s0 = ScalarLoad(op0);
scalar recip = ApproxRecip(s0);
r.x = recip;
```

```
r.y = recip;
r.z = recip;
r.w = recip;
result = WriteDest(result, r);
```

The `ApproxRecip` function satisfies the precision requirement

$$\left|\texttt{ApproxRecip}(x)-\frac{1}{x}\right|<2^{-22}$$

for values of x satisfying $1.0 \leq \times \leq 2.0$. The reciprocation operation also satisfies the following rule:

$$\texttt{ApproxRecip}(+1.0)=+1.0$$

RFL[RH][C][_SAT]–Reflection vector

```
RFL     result, op0, op1;
```

The `RFL` instruction calculates the reflection of its second vector operand about its first vector operand. Both operands are treated as 3D vectors (the w components are ignored). The axis defined by the first operand does not need to have unit length. The reflection of the direction defined by the second operand will have the same length as the original direction (within floating-point precision limits).

```
vector axis = VectorLoad(op0);
vector direction = VectorLoad(op1);
scalar a2 = axis.x * axis.x + axis.y * axis.y
            + axis.z * axis.z;
scalar a_dot_d = axis.x * direction.x
            + axis.y * direction.y
            + axis.z * direction.z;
scalar s = 2.0 * a_dot_d / a2;
r.x = s * axis.x - direction.x;
r.y = s * axis.y - direction.y;
r.z = s * axis.z - direction.z;
result = WriteDest(result, r);
```

The w component may not be enabled in the write mask of the destination register. Attempting to write the w component will cause a fragment program to fail to load.

RSQ[RH][C]–Reciprocal square root

```
RSQ     result, op0;
```

The `RSQ` instruction approximates the reciprocal square root of a single scalar operand and replicates the result to all four components of the destination.

```
scalar s0 = ScalarLoad(op0);
scalar rsqrt = ApproxRSQRT(s0);
r.x = rsqrt;
r.y = rsqrt;
r.z = rsqrt;
r.w = rsqrt;
result = WriteDest(result, r);
```

The `ApproxRSQRT` function satisfies the precision requirement

$$\left| \text{ApproxRSQRT}(x) - \frac{1}{\sqrt{x}} \right| < 2^{-22}$$

for values of x satisfying $1.0 \le x \le 4.0$.

SEQ[RHX][C]—Set on equal

```
SEQ     result, op0, op1;
```

The `SEQ` instruction performs a componentwise comparison between two operands. Each component of the result vector is set to 1.0 if the corresponding component of the first operand is equal to the corresponding component of the second operand, and is set to 0.0 otherwise.

```
vector v0 = VectorLoad(op0);
vector v1 = VectorLoad(op1);
r.x = (v0.x == v1.x) ? 1.0 : 0.0;
r.y = (v0.y == v1.y) ? 1.0 : 0.0;
r.z = (v0.z == v1.z) ? 1.0 : 0.0;
r.w = (v0.w == v1.w) ? 1.0 : 0.0;
result = WriteDest(result, r);
```

SFL[RHX][C]—Set on false

```
SFL     result, op0, op1;
```

The `SFL` instruction performs a componentwise comparison between two operands, but always evaluates to false. Thus, the values of the operands are ignored, and each component of the result is set to 0.0.

```
r.x = 0.0;
r.y = 0.0;
r.z = 0.0;
r.w = 0.0;
result = WriteDest(result, r);
```

SGE[RHX][C]–Set on greater than or equal

```
SGE     result, op0, op1;
```

The SGE instruction performs a componentwise comparison between two operands. Each component of the result vector is set to 1.0 if the corresponding component of the first operand is greater than or equal to the corresponding component of the second operand, and is set to 0.0 otherwise.

```
vector v0 = VectorLoad(op0);
vector v1 = VectorLoad(op1);
r.x = (v0.x >= v1.x) ? 1.0 : 0.0;
r.y = (v0.y >= v1.y) ? 1.0 : 0.0;
r.z = (v0.z >= v1.z) ? 1.0 : 0.0;
r.w = (v0.w >= v1.w) ? 1.0 : 0.0;
result = WriteDest(result, r);
```

SGT[RHX][C]–Set on greater than

```
SGT     result, op0, op1;
```

The SGT instruction performs a componentwise comparison between two operands. Each component of the result vector is set to 1.0 if the corresponding component of the first operand is greater than the corresponding component of the second operand, and is set to 0.0 otherwise.

```
vector v0 = VectorLoad(op0);
vector v1 = VectorLoad(op1);
r.x = (v0.x > v1.x) ? 1.0 : 0.0;
r.y = (v0.y > v1.y) ? 1.0 : 0.0;
r.z = (v0.z > v1.z) ? 1.0 : 0.0;
r.w = (v0.w > v1.w) ? 1.0 : 0.0;
result = WriteDest(result, r);
```

SIN[RH][C]–Sine

```
SIN     result, op0;
```

The SIN instruction calculates the approximate sine of a single scalar operand. The angle is measured in radians and is not restricted to the range $[0,2\pi]$. The result is replicated to all four components of the destination.

```
scalar s0 = ScalarLoad(op0);
scalar sine = ApproxSin(s0);
r.x = sine;
r.y = sine;
r.z = sine;
r.w = sine;
result = WriteDest(result, r);
```

The sine operation satisfies the precision requirement

$$\left|\mathrm{ApproxSin}(x) - \sin x\right| < 2^{-22}$$

if the value of x satisfies $0 \le x < 2\pi$. If x falls outside this range, the error in the approximate typically increases with the absolute value of x.

SLE[RHX][C]—Set on less than or equal

```
SLE     result, op0, op1;
```

The SLE instruction performs a componentwise comparison between two operands. Each component of the result vector is set to 1.0 if the corresponding component of the first operand is less than or equal to the corresponding component of the second operand, and is set to 0.0 otherwise.

```
vector v0 = VectorLoad(op0);
vector v1 = VectorLoad(op1);
r.x = (v0.x <= v1.x) ? 1.0 : 0.0;
r.y = (v0.y <= v1.y) ? 1.0 : 0.0;
r.z = (v0.z <= v1.z) ? 1.0 : 0.0;
r.w = (v0.w <= v1.w) ? 1.0 : 0.0;
result = WriteDest(result, r);
```

SLT[RHX][C]—Set on less than

```
SLT     result, op0, op1;
```

The SLT instruction performs a componentwise comparison between two operands. Each component of the result vector is set to 1.0 if the corresponding component of the first operand is less than the corresponding component of the second operand, and is set to 0.0 otherwise.

```
vector v0 = VectorLoad(op0);
vector v1 = VectorLoad(op1);
r.x = (v0.x < v1.x) ? 1.0 : 0.0;
r.y = (v0.y < v1.y) ? 1.0 : 0.0;
r.z = (v0.z < v1.z) ? 1.0 : 0.0;
r.w = (v0.w < v1.w) ? 1.0 : 0.0;
result = WriteDest(result, r);
```

SNE[RHX][C]—Set on not equal

```
SNE     result, op0, op1;
```

The SNE instruction performs a componentwise comparison between two operands. Each component of the result vector is set to 1.0 if the corresponding component of the first operand is not equal to the corresponding component of the second operand, and is set to 0.0 otherwise.

```
vector v0 = VectorLoad(op0);
vector v1 = VectorLoad(op1);
r.x = (v0.x != v1.x) ? 1.0 : 0.0;
r.y = (v0.y != v1.y) ? 1.0 : 0.0;
r.z = (v0.z != v1.z) ? 1.0 : 0.0;
r.w = (v0.w != v1.w) ? 1.0 : 0.0;
result = WriteDest(result, r);
```

STR[RHX][C]—Set on true

```
STR     result, op0, op1;
```

The STR instruction performs a componentwise comparison between two operands, but always evaluates to true. Thus, the values of the operands are ignored and each component of the result is set to 1.0.

```
r.x = 1.0;
r.y = 1.0;
r.z = 1.0;
r.w = 1.0;
result = WriteDest(result, r);
```

SUB[RHX][C][_SAT]—Subtract

```
SUB     result, op0, op1;
```

The SUB instruction performs a componentwise subtraction of two operands.

```
vector v0 = VectorLoad(op0);
vector v1 = VectorLoad(op1);
r.x = v0.x - v1.x;
r.y = v0.y - v1.y;
r.z = v0.z - v1.z;
r.w = v0.w - v1.w;
result = WriteDest(result, r);
```

TEX[C][_SAT]—Texture sample

```
TEX     result, op0, unit, target;
```

The TEX instruction interprets the x, y, and z components of its operand as $\langle s,t,r \rangle$ texture coordinates used to sample the texture target given by the target parameter that is bound to the texture image unit given by the unit parameter. The target parameter may be 1D, 2D, 3D, CUBE, or RECT, and the unit parameter must be TEXi, where i is in the range 0 to GL_MAX_TEXTURE_IMAGE_UNITS_NV $- 1$.

```
vector v0 = VectorLoad(op0);
r = TextureSample(v0.x, v0.y, v0.z, unit, target);
result = WriteDest(result, r);
```

The mapping of filtered texel components to x, y, z, and w vector components is summarized in Table 19.2.4 for each base internal texture format.

If the same texture unit is sampled by a subsequent texture instruction (TEX, TXD, or TXP), then the target parameter must be the same, or the fragment program will fail to load.

TXD[C][_SAT]–Texture sample with derivatives

```
TXD     result, op0, op1, op2, unit, target;
```

The TXD instruction interprets the x, y, and z components of its first operand as $\langle s,t,r \rangle$ texture coordinates used to sample the texture target given by the target parameter that is bound to the texture image unit given by the unit parameter. The target parameter may be 1D, 2D, 3D, CUBE, or RECT, and the unit parameter must be TEX*i*, where *i* is in the range 0 to GL_MAX_TEXTURE_IMAGE_UNITS_NV − 1.

The partial derivatives used to perform filtering are specified by the second and third operands. The x, y, and z components of the second operand are interpreted as the partial derivatives $\langle \partial s/\partial x, \partial t/\partial x, \partial r/\partial x \rangle$ with respect to the window-space x-direction. The x, y, and z components of the third operand are interpreted as the partial derivatives $\langle \partial s/\partial y, \partial t/\partial y, \partial r/\partial y \rangle$ with respect to the window-space y-direction.

```
vector v0 = VectorLoad(op0);
vector v1 = VectorLoad(op1);
vector v2 = VectorLoad(op2);
r = TextureSampleDeriv(v0.x, v0.y, v0.z, v1, v2,
    unit, target);
result = WriteDest(result, r);
```

The mapping of filtered texel components to x, y, z, and w vector components is summarized in Table 19.2.4 for each base internal texture format.

If the same texture unit is sampled by a subsequent texture instruction (TEX, TXD, or TXP), then the target parameter must be the same, or the fragment program will fail to load.

TXP[C][_SAT]–Texture sample with projection

```
TXP     result, op0, unit, target;
```

The TXP instruction interprets the x, y, z, and w components of its operand as $\langle s,t,r,q \rangle$ texture coordinates used to sample the texture target given by the target parameter that is bound to the texture image unit given by the unit parameter. The target parameter may be 1D, 2D, 3D, CUBE, or RECT, and the unit parameter must be TEX*i*, where *i* is in the range 0 to GL_MAX_TEXTURE_IMAGE_UNITS_NV − 1. Unless the target parameter is CUBE, a projection is performed by dividing the *s*, *t*, and *r* coordinates by the *q* coordinate. If $q \leq 0$, the result is undefined.

```
vector v0 = VectorLoad(op0);
r = TextureSample(v0.x / v0.w, v0.y / v0.w, v0.z / v0.w,
    unit, target);
result = WriteDest(result, r);
```

The mapping of filtered texel components to x, y, z, and w vector components is summarized in Table 19.2.4 for each base internal texture format.

If the same texture unit is sampled by a subsequent texture instruction (TEX, TXD, or TXP), then the target parameter must be the same, or the fragment program will fail to load.

UP2H—Unpack two half floats

```
UP2H     result, op0;
```

The UP2H instruction unpacks two 16-bit floating-point values stored in a single 32-bit scalar operand. The half-float value stored in the lower 16 bits of the operand is written to the x and z components of the result, and the half float stored in the higher 16 bits of the operand is written to the y and w components of the result. The UP2H instruction undoes the operation performed by the PK2H instruction.

```
scalar s0 = ScalarLoad(op0);
scalar x = ConvertFromHalf(s0 & 0xFFFF);
scalar y = ConvertFromHalf((s0 >> 16) & 0xFFFF);
r.x = x;
r.y = y;
r.z = x;
r.w = y;
result = WriteDest(result, r);
```

The logic operations in the pseudocode operate on the raw bits representing the scalar s0.

The operand of the UP2H instruction must be a 32-bit register or program parameter. Otherwise, the fragment program will fail to load.

UP2US—Unpack two unsigned shorts

```
UP2US    result, op0;
```

The UP2US instruction unpacks two unsigned 16-bit fixed-point values stored in a single 32-bit scalar operand and converts them to floating-point. The unsigned short value stored in the lower 16 bits of the operand is written to the x and z components of the result, and the unsigned short stored in the higher 16 bits of the operand is written to the y and w components of the result. The UP2US instruction undoes the operation performed by the PK2US instruction.

```
scalar s0 = ScalarLoad(op0);
scalar x = ConvertFromUS(s0 & 0xFFFF);
scalar y = ConvertFromUS((s0 >> 16) & 0xFFFF);
r.x = x;
r.y = y;
r.z = x;
r.w = y;
result = WriteDest(result, r);
```

The logic operations in the pseudocode operate on the raw bits representing the scalar s0. The ConvertFromUS function converts to floating-point by linearly mapping 0x0000 to 0.0 and 0xFFFF to 1.0.

The operand of the UP2US instruction must be a 32-bit register or program parameter. Otherwise, the fragment program will fail to load.

UP4B—Unpack four signed bytes

```
UP4B    result, op0;
```

The UP4B instruction unpacks four signed 8-bit fixed-point values stored in a single 32-bit scalar operand and converts them to floating-point. The byte value stored in the lowest 8 bits of the operand is written to the x component of the result, and the byte stored in the highest 8 bits of the operand is written to the w component of the result. The UP4B instruction undoes the operation performed by the PK4B instruction.

```
scalar s0 = ScalarLoad(op0);
r.x = ConvertFromB(s0 & 0xFFFF);
r.y = ConvertFromB((s0 >> 8) & 0xFFFF);
r.z = ConvertFromB((s0 >> 16) & 0xFFFF);
r.w = ConvertFromB((s0 >> 24) & 0xFFFF);
result = WriteDest(result, r);
```

The logic operations in the pseudocode operate on the raw bits representing the scalar s0. The ConvertFromB function converts to floating-point by linearly mapping 0x00 to $-\frac{128}{127}$ and 0xFF to 1.0.

The operand of the UP4B instruction must be a 32-bit register or program parameter. Otherwise, the fragment program will fail to load.

UP4UB—Unpack four unsigned bytes

```
UP4UB    result, op0;
```

The UP4UB instruction unpacks four unsigned 8-bit fixed-point values stored in a single 32-bit scalar operand and converts them to floating-point. The unsigned byte value stored in the lowest 8 bits of the operand is written to the x component of the result, and the unsigned byte stored in the highest 8 bits of the operand is written to the w component of the result. The UP4UB instruction undoes the operation performed by the PK4UB instruction.

```
scalar s0 = ScalarLoad(op0);
r.x = ConvertFromUB(s0 & 0xFFFF);
r.y = ConvertFromUB((s0 >> 8) & 0xFFFF);
r.z = ConvertFromUB((s0 >> 16) & 0xFFFF);
r.w = ConvertFromUB((s0 >> 24) & 0xFFFF);
result = WriteDest(result, r);
```

The logic operations in the pseudocode operate on the raw bits representing the scalar s0. The ConvertFromUB function converts to floating-point by linearly mapping 0x00 to 0.0 and 0xFF to 1.0.

The operand of the UP4UB instruction must be a 32-bit register or program parameter. Otherwise, the fragment program will fail to load.

X2D[RH][C][_SAT]—2D transformation

```
X2D     result, op0, op1, op2;
```

The X2D instruction performs the following 2×2 matrix-vector multiplication and 2D vector addition, where vi corresponds to the value of operand opi after swizzling.

$$\begin{bmatrix} x \\ y \end{bmatrix} = \begin{bmatrix} v2.x & v2.y \\ v2.z & v2.w \end{bmatrix} \begin{bmatrix} v1.x \\ v1.y \end{bmatrix} + \begin{bmatrix} v0.x \\ v0.y \end{bmatrix}$$

The value of x is written to the x and z components of the result, and the value of y is written to the y and w components of the result.

```
vector v0 = VectorLoad(op0);
vector v1 = VectorLoad(op1);
vector v2 = VectorLoad(op2);
scalar x = v2.x * v1.x + v2.y * v1.y + v0.x;
scalar y = v2.z * v1.x + v2.w * v1.y + v0.y;
r.x = x;
r.y = y;
r.z = x;
r.w = y;
result = WriteDest(result, r);
```

The X2D instruction can be used to displace texture coordinates in the same manner as the GL_OFFSET_TEXTURE_2D_NV texture shader mode defined by the GL_NV_texture_shader extension (see Chapter 6, Section 6.3).

Program Management

Fragment programs follow the named object convention that is used elsewhere in OpenGL for such things as texture objects. A fragment program is identified by a name taken from the set of unsigned integers. Previously unused names for fragment program objects are allocated by calling the **glGenProgramsNV** function,

```
void glGenProgramsNV(GLsizei n,
                     GLuint *ids);
```

This function generates *n* names and writes them to the array pointed to by the *ids* parameter. The names generated are marked as used, but the associated fragment program objects are not actually created until the first time a new name is passed to the **glLoadProgramNV** function.

Fragment program objects are deleted and the associated names are freed by calling the **glDeleteProgramsNV** function,

```
void glDeleteProgramsNV(GLsizei n,
                        const GLuint *ids);
```

Any of the *n* names passed to this function in the array pointed to by the *ids* parameter that do not refer to existing fragment program objects are silently ignored. Once a fragment program object is deleted, its name is marked as unused. The **glIsProgramNV** function,

```
GLboolean glIsProgramNV(GLuint id);
```

can be used to determine whether a particular name specified by the *id* parameter refers to an existing fragment program object.

A program string for a particular fragment program object is loaded by calling the **glLoadProgramNV** function,

```
void glLoadProgramNV(GLenum target,
                     GLuint id,
                     GLsizei len,
                     const GLubyte *program);
```

with *target* parameter GL_FRAGMENT_PROGRAM_NV. The *len* parameter specifies the length of the program string pointed to by the *program* parameter. A program string may be loaded for the same fragment program object multiple times.

A fragment program object is bound to the fragment program target by calling the **glBindProgramNV** function,

```
void glBindProgramNV(GLenum target,
                     GLuint id);
```

with *target* parameter GL_FRAGMENT_PROGRAM_NV. The *id* parameter specifies the name of the fragment program object. When fragment program mode is enabled (by calling **glEnable** with *cap* parameter GL_FRAGMENT_PROGRAM_NV), the current fragment program is invoked for every fragment generated by OpenGL.

Fragment programs may be requested to be loaded into memory that is quickly accessible by the graphics hardware by calling the **glRequestResidentProgramsNV** function,

```
void glRequestResidentProgramsNV(GLsizei n,
                                 const GLuint *ids);
```

The implementation attempts to keep the *n* programs named in the array pointed to by the *ids* parameter in fast memory. One can determine whether fragment programs currently reside in fast memory by calling the **glAreProgramsResidentNV** function,

```
GLboolean glAreProgramsResidentNV(GLsizei n,
                                  const GLuint *ids,
                                  GLboolean *residences);
```

A Boolean value is written to each of the *n* entries of the array pointed to by the *residences* parameter, indicating whether the corresponding fragment program named in the array pointed to by the *ids* parameter is resident in fast memory.

NEW FUNCTIONS

- **glLoadProgramNV**—Specify a program string.

Prototype

```
void glLoadProgramNV(GLenum target,
                     GLuint id,
                     GLsizei len,
                     const GLubyte *program);
```

Parameters

target	Specifies the target program. Must be GL_FRAGMENT_PROGRAM_NV.
id	Specifies the name of the program to load. This may not be 0.
len	Specifies the length of the program string.
program	Specifies a pointer to the program string. This string does not need to be null-terminated.

Description

The **glLoadProgramNV** function loads the program string for the program named by the *id* parameter. The program string is a sequence of ASCII characters whose length is passed into the *len* parameter.

When a program string is loaded for a particular value of *id* for the first time, the value of the *target* parameter is associated with that program. A new program string for the same value of *id* may be loaded at a later time without having to delete the program using the **glDeleteProgramsNV** function, as long as the value of *target* remains the same. An attempt to reload a program using a different value of *target* generates a GL_INVALID_OPERATION error.

At the time **glLoadProgramNV** is called, the program string is parsed and checked for syntactic validity. If the program fails to load because it contains an error, the error GL_INVALID_OPERATION is generated, and the value of GL_PROGRAM_ERROR_POSITION_NV is updated to reflect the position within the program string at which the error occurred. This position can be retrieved by calling the **glGetIntegerv** function.

Special Considerations

Unlike the **glProgramStringARB** function defined by the GL_ARB_fragment_program extension, a program does not need to be bound before the program string is specified, since the **glLoadProgramNV** function takes an explicit program name in the *id* parameter. The **glLoadProgramNV** function is also defined by the GL_NV_vertex_program extension.

Get Functions

glGetProgramStringNV

glGetProgramivNV with *pname* parameter GL_PROGRAM_LENGTH_NV

glGetIntegerv with *pname* parameter GL_PROGRAM_ERROR_POSITION_NV

Errors

GL_INVALID_OPERATION is generated if the program string violates the syntactic or semantic rules of the target program.

GL_INVALID_VALUE is generated if *id* is 0.

GL_INVALID_OPERATION is generated if *id* corresponds to a program that has already been loaded with a different value for *target*.

■ **glGenProgramsNV**—Generate program names.

Prototype

```
void glGenProgramsNV(GLsizei n,
                     GLuint *ids);
```

Parameters

n	Specifies the number of program names to generate.
ids	Specifies a pointer to an array that receives the generated program's names.

Description

The **glGenProgramsNV** function returns a set of *n* unused program names in the array pointed to by the *ids* parameter. Each of the returned names is reserved with respect to program name generation, but does not represent an existing program object until a program string is loaded using the **glLoadProgramNV** function.

Programs are deleted and the associated program names are freed by calling the **glDeleteProgramsNV** function.

Special Considerations

The **glGenProgramsNV** function is also defined by the GL_NV_vertex_program extension.

Get Functions

glIsProgramNV

Errors

GL_INVALID_VALUE is generated if *n* is negative.

- **glDeleteProgramsNV**—Delete named programs.

Prototype

```
void glDeleteProgramsNV(GLsizei n,
                        const GLuint *ids);
```

Parameters

n   Specifies the number of programs to delete.

ids   Specifies a pointer to an array of program names to be deleted.

Description

The **glDeleteProgramsNV** function deletes the *n* programs contained in the array pointed to by the *ids* parameter. When a program object is deleted, it becomes nonexistent, and its name becomes unused. Deleted program names may subsequently be returned by the **glGenProgramsNV** function. Any unused program names found in the array pointed to by the *ids* parameter are silently ignored.

If a fragment program is deleted when it is the currently bound program, it is as if the **glBindProgramNV** function had been called with *id* parameter 0.

Special Considerations

The **glDeleteProgramsNV** function is also defined by the GL_NV_vertex_program extension.

Get Functions

glIsProgramNV

Errors

GL_INVALID_VALUE is generated if *n* is negative.

- **glBindProgramNV**—Bind a named program to a program target.

Prototype

```
void glBindProgramNV(GLenum target,
                     GLuint id);
```

Parameters

target   Specifies the target to which the program is bound. Must be GL_
           FRAGMENT_PROGRAM_NV.

id   Specifies the name of the program to bind.

Description

The **glBindProgramNV** function sets the current fragment program that is invoked for every fragment.

Binding to a nonexistent program does not generate an error. In particular, the *id* parameter may be 0. Since program 0 cannot be loaded, however, it is always nonexistent. Program 0 is implicitly bound if the currently bound fragment program is deleted by the **glDelete-ProgramsNV** function.

Special Considerations

The **glBindProgramNV** function is also defined by the GL_NV_vertex_program extension.

Get Functions

glGet with *pname* parameter GL_FRAGMENT_PROGRAM_BINDING_NV

Errors

GL_INVALID_OPERATION is generated if *id* is the name of a program whose target does not match *target*.

■ **glIsProgramNV**—Determine if a name corresponds to a program.

Prototype

```
GLboolean glIsProgramNV(GLuint id);
```

Parameters

id   Specifies the name of a program.

Description

The **glIsProgramNV** function returns GL_TRUE if the *id* parameter names an existing program. Otherwise, it returns GL_FALSE.

A program name generated by the **glGenProgramsNV** function does not refer to an existing program until a successful call to the **glLoadProgramNV** function loads a program corresponding to that name.

Special Considerations

The **glIsProgramNV** function is also defined by the GL_NV_vertex_program extension.

■ **glRequestResidentProgramsNV**—Request that programs are loaded into fast memory.

Prototype

```
void glRequestResidentProgramsNV(GLsizei n,
                                 const GLuint *ids);
```

Parameters

n   Specifies the number of programs for which to request residency.

ids   Specifies a pointer to an array of program names.

Description

The **glRequestResidentProgramsNV** function requests that the *n* programs contained in the array pointed to by the *ids* parameter be made resident in fast memory accessible by the graphics hardware. It is not guaranteed that all of the programs in the array are made resident. Earlier programs in the array are given higher priority, and programs not appearing in the array that were resident before the call to **glRequestResidentProgramsNV** may become nonresident. The **glAreProgramsResidentNV** function can be called to determine which programs actually became resident.

Any names in the array pointed to by the *ids* parameter that do not refer to existing programs are ignored.

Special Considerations

The **glRequestResidentProgramsNV** function is also defined by the GL_NV_vertex_ program extension.

Get Functions

glAreProgramsResidentNV

■ **glAreProgramsResidentNV**—Determine if programs are resident in fast memory.

Prototype

```
GLboolean glAreProgramsResidentNV(GLsizei n,
                                  const GLuint *ids,
                                  GLboolean *residences);
```

Parameters

n   Specifies the number of programs for which to return residency.

ids   Specifies a pointer to an array of program names.

residences   Specifies a pointer to an array in which the program resident status is returned.

Description

The **glAreProgramsResidentNV** function returns an array of Boolean values in the space pointed to by the *residences* parameter, indicating whether each corresponding program named in the array pointed to by the *ids* parameter is currently resident. If all of the programs are resident, the function returns true; otherwise, the return value is false. If any of the names in the array pointed to by the *ids* parameter refers to a nonexistent program, then the GL_INVALID_VALUE error is generated.

The residence status of a single program can be retrieved by calling the **glGetProgramivNV** function with *pname* parameter GL_PROGRAM_RESIDENT_NV.

Special Considerations

The **glAreProgramsResidentNV** function is also defined by the GL_NV_vertex_program extension.

Get Functions

glGetProgramivNV with *pname* parameter GL_PROGRAM_RESIDENT_NV

Errors

GL_INVALID_VALUE is generated if any of the program names in the array pointed to by *ids* are 0 or nonexistent.

■ **glProgramNamedParameter{fd}[v]NV**—Specify a named program parameter.

Prototypes

```
void glProgramNamedParameterfNV(GLuint id,
                                GLsizei len,
                                const GLubyte *name,
                                GLfloat x,
                                GLfloat y,
                                GLfloat z,
                                GLfloat w);
void glProgramNamedParameterdNV(GLuint id,
                                GLsizei len,
                                const GLubyte *name,
                                GLdouble x,
                                GLdouble y,
                                GLdouble z,
                                GLdouble w);
```

Parameters

id	Specifies the name of a fragment program.
len	Specifies the length of the name string for the program parameter.
name	Specifies the name string for the program parameter. This string does not need to be null-terminated.
x, y, z, w	Specify the components of the program parameter corresponding to the *name* parameter.

Prototypes

```
void glProgramNamedParameterfvNV(GLuint id,
                                 GLsizei len,
                                 const GLubyte *name,
```

```
                                        const GLfloat *params);
    void glProgramNamedParameterdvNV(GLuint id,
                                     GLsizei len,
                                     const GLubyte *name,
                                     const GLdouble *params);
```

Parameters

id	Specifies the name of a fragment program.
len	Specifies the length of the name of the program parameter.
name	Specifies the name of the program parameter.
params	Specifies a pointer to an array containing the four-component program parameter corresponding to the *name* parameter.

Description

The **glProgramNamedParameter4{fd}[v]NV** function specifies a four-component floating-point vector for the program local parameter corresponding to the *name* parameter in the fragment program specified by the *id* parameter.

Get Functions

glGetProgramNamedParameter{fd}vNV

Errors

GL_INVALID_OPERATION is generated if *id* does not refer to an existing program.

GL_INVALID_VALUE is generated if *len* is 0.

GL_INVALID_VALUE is generated if *name* does not specify the name of a local parameter in the program corresponding to *id*.

■ **glProgramLocalParameter4{fd}[v]ARB**—Specify a program local parameter.

Prototypes

```
    void glProgramLocalParameter4fARB(GLenum target,
                                      GLuint index,
                                      GLfloat x,
                                      GLfloat y,
                                      GLfloat z,
                                      GLfloat w);
    void glProgramLocalParameter4dARB(GLenum target,
                                      GLuint index,
                                      GLdouble x,
                                      GLdouble y,
                                      GLdouble z,
                                      GLdouble w);
```

Parameters

target   Specifies the target program. Must be `GL_FRAGMENT_PROGRAM_NV`.

index   Specifies the index of a program local parameter. Must be in the range 0 to `GL_MAX_FRAGMENT_PROGRAM_LOCAL_PARAMETERS_NV` − 1.

x, y, z, w   Specify the components of the program local parameter.

Prototypes

```
void glProgramLocalParameter4fvARB(GLenum target,
                                   GLuint index,
                                   const GLfloat *params);
void glProgramLocalParameter4dvARB(GLenum target,
                                   GLuint index,
                                   const GLdouble *params);
```

Parameters

target   Specifies the target program. Must be `GL_FRAGMENT_PROGRAM_NV`.

index   Specifies the index of a program local parameter. Must be in the range 0 to `GL_MAX_FRAGMENT_PROGRAM_LOCAL_PARAMETERS_NV` − 1.

params   Specifies a pointer to an array containing the four-component program local parameter.

Description

The **glProgramLocalParameter4{fd}[v]ARB** function specifies a four-component floating-point vector for the program local parameter specified by *index*. When program local parameters are specified, they are applied to the currently bound fragment program object.

Special Considerations

The **glProgramLocalParameter4{fd}[v]ARB** function is also defined by the `GL_ARB_vertex_program` and `GL_ARB_fragment_program` extensions.

Get Functions

glGetProgramLocalParameter{fd}vARB

glGetIntegerv with *pname* parameter `GL_MAX_FRAGMENT_PROGRAM_LOCAL_PARAMETERS_NV`

Errors

`GL_INVALID_VALUE` is generated if *index* is greater than or equal to the value of `GL_MAX_FRAGMENT_PROGRAM_LOCAL_PARAMETERS_NV`.

■ **glGetProgramNamedParameter{fd}vNV**—Specify a named program parameter.

Prototype

```
void glGetProgramNamedParameterfvNV(GLuint id,
```

```
                                          GLsizei len,
                                          const GLubyte *name,
                                          GLfloat *params);
      void glGetProgramNamedParameterdvNV(GLuint id,
                                          GLsizei len,
                                          const GLubyte *name,
                                          GLdouble *params);
```

Parameters

id   Specifies the name of a fragment program.

len   Specifies the length of the name string for the program parameter.

name   Specifies the name string for the program parameter. This string does not
            need to be null-terminated.

params   Specifies a pointer to an array that receives the four-component program
            parameter corresponding to the *name* parameter.

Description

The **glGetProgramNamedParameter{fd}vNV** function returns the current value of the
program local parameter corresponding to the *name* parameter in the fragment program
specified by the *id* parameter. The four floating-point values are written to the array pointed
to by the *params* parameter.

Errors

GL_INVALID_OPERATION is generated if *id* does not refer to an existing program.

GL_INVALID_VALUE is generated if *len* is 0.

GL_INVALID_VALUE is generated if *name* does not specify the name of a local parameter in
the program corresponding to *id*.

■ **glGetProgramLocalParameter{fd}vARB**—Return a program local parameter.

Prototypes

```
      void glGetProgramLocalParameterfvARB(GLenum target,
                                           GLuint index,
                                           GLfloat *params);
      void glGetProgramLocalParameterdvARB(GLenum target,
                                           GLuint index,
                                           GLdouble *params);
```

Parameters

target   Specifies the target program. Must be GL_FRAGMENT_PROGRAM_NV.

index   Specifies the index of a program local parameter. Must be in the range 0
            to GL_MAX_FRAGMENT_PROGRAM_LOCAL_PARAMETERS_NV − 1.

params   Specifies a pointer to an array that receives the four-component program local parameter.

Description

The **glGetProgramLocalParameter{fd}vARB** function returns the current value of the program local parameter specified by *index* associated with the currently bound fragment program object. The four floating-point values are written to the array pointed to by the *params* parameter.

Special Considerations

The **glGetProgramLocalParameter{fd}vARB** function is also defined by the GL_ARB_ fragment_program and GL_ARB_vertex_program extensions.

Errors

GL_INVALID_VALUE is generated if *index* is greater than or equal to the value of GL_MAX_ FRAGMENT_PROGRAM_LOCAL_PARAMETERS_NV.

■ **glGetProgramivNV**—Return program state.

Prototype

```
void glGetProgramivNV(GLuint id,
                      GLenum pname,
                      GLint *params);
```

Parameters

id   Specifies a program name.

pname   Specifies the symbolic name of a program value to be queried. Must be GL_PROGRAM_TARGET_NV, GL_PROGRAM_LENGTH_NV, or GL_PROGRAM_ RESIDENT_NV.

params   Specifies a pointer to an array that receives the queried value.

Description

The **glGetProgramivNV** function returns information about the program named by the *id* parameter. The *pname* parameter specifies what information to retrieve and may be one of the following values:

GL_PROGRAM_TARGET_NV
        The program target is returned. This may be GL_FRAGMENT_PROGRAM_ NV.

GL_PROGRAM_LENGTH_NV
        The length of the program string is returned. This is useful for determining the size of the buffer needed for a call to the **glGetProgramStringNV** function.

GL_PROGRAM_RESIDENT_NV

> A Boolean value indicating whether the program is resident in fast memory is returned.

Special Considerations

The **glGetProgramivNV** function is also defined by the GL_NV_vertex_program extension.

Errors

GL_INVALID_OPERATION is generated if *id* does not refer to an existing program.

■ **glGetProgramStringNV**—Return a program string.

Prototype

```
void glGetProgramStringNV(GLuint id,
                          GLenum pname,
                          GLubyte *program);
```

Parameters

id	Specifies a program name.
pname	Specifies the symbolic name of a program value to be queried. Must be GL_PROGRAM_STRING_NV.
program	Specifies a pointer to a region of memory that receives the program string.

Description

The **glGetProgramStringNV** function returns the program string that was previously loaded for the program named by the *id* parameter. The *program* parameter points to a buffer that receives the program string. The length of the program string can be determined by calling the **glGetProgramivNV** function with *pname* parameter GL_PROGRAM_LENGTH_NV.

Special Considerations

The **glGetProgramStringNV** function is also defined by the GL_NV_vertex_program extension.

Get Functions

glGetProgramivNV with *pname* parameter GL_PROGRAM_LENGTH_NV

Errors

GL_INVALID_OPERATION is generated if *id* does not refer to an existing program.

EXTENDED FUNCTIONS

■ **glEnable, glDisable, glIsEnabled**—Extended to enable/disable fragment programs.

Prototypes

```
void glEnable(GLenum cap);
void glDisable(GLenum cap);
GLboolean glIsEnabled(GLenum cap);
```

Extended Parameters

cap   Specifies a GL capability. To enable or disable fragment programs, or to query whether fragment programs are enabled, this should be GL_FRAGMENT_PROGRAM_NV.

Description

Fragment programs are enabled and disabled by passing the value GL_FRAGMENT_PROGRAM_NV to the **glEnable** and **glDisable** functions. Calling the **glIsEnabled** function with the parameter GL_FRAGMENT_PROGRAM_NV returns a value indicating whether fragment programs are enabled.

■ **glGetIntegerv**—Extended to allow retrieval of fragment program state.

Prototype

```
void glGetIntegerv(GLenum pname, GLint *params);
```

Extended Parameters

pname   Specifies the parameter to be returned. May be one of the values listed in Description.

Description

The **glGetIntegerv** function can be used to retrieve various state related to fragment programs. The *pname* parameter may be one of the following values:

GL_FRAGMENT_PROGRAM_BINDING_NV
    The name of the program currently bound to the fragment program target is returned.

GL_PROGRAM_ERROR_POSITION_NV
    The byte position within the program string at which an error occurred is returned.

GL_MAX_TEXTURE_COORDS_NV
    The maximum number of texture coordinate sets supported by the implementation is returned. This is always at least 2.

GL_MAX_TEXTURE_IMAGE_UNITS_NV

> The maximum number of texture image units supported by the implementation is returned. This is always at least 2.

GL_MAX_FRAGMENT_PROGRAM_LOCAL_PARAMETERS_NV

> The maximum number of fragment program local parameters supported by the implementation is returned. This is always at least 64.

■ **glGetString**—Extended to allow retrieval of the program error string.

Prototype

```
const GLubyte *glGetString(GLenum name);
```

Extended Parameters

name   Specifies the string to return. May be GL_PROGRAM_ERROR_STRING_NV.

Description

The **glGetString** function can be used to retrieve the program error string after an unsuccessful call to the **glLoadProgramNV** function. If no error occurs when a program is loaded, the error string may still contain warning messages.

PROGRAM SYNTAX SPECIFICATIONS

IN THIS APPENDIX:

This appendix contains the formal syntax specifications for every vertex and fragment programming environment discussed in Chapters 18 and 19. The syntactic rules of each programming environment are defined using the Backus-Naur Form (BNF) grammar.

The syntax for integer constants (represented by the `<integer>` rule), floating-point constants (represented by the `<floatConstant>` rule), and identifiers (represented by the `<identifier>` rule) share the following common definitions.

```
<integer>              ::= <integer> <integerDigit>

<integerDigit>         ::= "0" | "1" | "2" | "3" | "4"
                           | "5" | "6" | "7" | "8" | "9"
                           | ""

<floatConstant>        ::= <optionalIntegerPart> <decimalPoint>
                             <fractionPart> <optionalExponentPart>
                           | <integerPart> <optionalDecimalPoint>
                             <exponentPart>
                           | <integerPart> <decimalPoint>
```

```
<integerPart>          ::= <integer>

<optionalIntegerPart>  ::= <integerPart>
                         | ""

<decimalPoint>         ::= "."

<optionalDecimalPoint> ::= <decimalPoint>
                         | ""

<fractionPart>         ::= <integer>

<exponentPart>         ::= <exponentToken> <optionalSign> <integer>

<optionalExponentPart> ::= <exponentPart>
                         | ""

<exponentToken>        ::= "e" | "E"

<optionalSign>         ::= "+" | "-"
                         | ""

<identifier>           ::= <firstIdentifierChar> <identifierSequence>

<identifierSequence>   ::= <identifierSequence> <identifierChar>

<firstIdentifierChar>  ::= uppercase letter "A" through "Z"
                         | lowercase letter "a" through "z"
                         | "_"
                         | "$"

<identifierChar>       ::= <firstIdentifierChar>
                         | <integer>
                         | ""
```

A.1   GL_ARB_vertex_program

The following sequences are reserved keywords and may not be used as identifiers.

ABS	FLR	POW
ADD	FRC	RCP
ADDRESS	LG2	RSQ
ALIAS	LIT	SGE
ARL	LOG	SLT

ATTRIB	MAD	SUB
DP3	MAX	SWZ
DP4	MIN	TEMP
DPH	MOV	XPD
DST	MUL	program
END	OPTION	result
EX2	OUTPUT	state
EXP	PARAM	vertex

A vertex program must begin with the sequence "!!ARBvp1.0", without any preceding whitespace.

```
<program>                ::= "!!ARBvp1.0" <optionSequence>
                             <statementSequence> "END"

<optionSequence>         ::= <optionSequence> <option>
                           | ""

<option>                 ::= "OPTION" <identifier> ";"

<statementSequence>      ::= <statementSequence> <statement>
                           | ""

<statement>              ::= <instruction> ";"
                           | <namingStatement> ";"

<instruction>            ::= <ARL_instruction>
                           | <VECTORop_instruction>
                           | <SCALARop_instruction>
                           | <BINSCop_instruction>
                           | <BINop_instruction>
                           | <TRIop_instruction>
                           | <SWZ_instruction>

<ARL_instruction>        ::= "ARL" <maskedAddrReg> "," <scalarSrcReg>

<VECTORop_instruction>   ::= <VECTORop> <maskedDstReg> ","
                             <swizzleSrcReg>

<VECTORop>               ::= "ABS"
                           | "FLR"
                           | "FRC"
                           | "LIT"
                           | "MOV"
```

```
<SCALARop_instruction> ::= <SCALARop> <maskedDstReg> ","
                             <scalarSrcReg>

<SCALARop>            ::= "EX2"
                         | "EXP"
                         | "LG2"
                         | "LOG"
                         | "RCP"
                         | "RSQ"

<BINSCop_instruction> ::= <BINSCop> <maskedDstReg> "," <scalarSrcReg>
                             "," <scalarSrcReg>

<BINSCop>            ::= "POW"

<BINop_instruction>  ::= <BINop> <maskedDstReg> ","
                             <swizzleSrcReg> "," <swizzleSrcReg>

<BINop>              ::= "ADD"
                         | "DP3"
                         | "DP4"
                         | "DPH"
                         | "DST"
                         | "MAX"
                         | "MIN"
                         | "MUL"
                         | "SGE"
                         | "SLT"
                         | "SUB"
                         | "XPD"

<TRIop_instruction>  ::= <TRIop> <maskedDstReg> ","
                             <swizzleSrcReg> "," <swizzleSrcReg> ","
                           <swizzleSrcReg>

<TRIop>              ::= "MAD"

<SWZ_instruction>    ::= "SWZ" <maskedDstReg> "," <srcReg> ","
                             <extendedSwizzle>

<scalarSrcReg>       ::= <optionalSign> <srcReg> <scalarSuffix>

<swizzleSrcReg>      ::= <optionalSign> <srcReg> <swizzleSuffix>

<maskedDstReg>       ::= <dstReg> <optionalMask>

<maskedAddrReg>      ::= <addrReg> <addrWriteMask>
```

```
<extendedSwizzle>       ::= <extSwizComp> "," <extSwizComp> ","
                            <extSwizComp> "," <extSwizComp>

<extSwizComp>           ::= <optionalSign> <extSwizSel>

<extSwizSel>            ::= "0"
                          | "1"
                          | <component>

<srcReg>                ::= <vertexAttribReg>
                          | <temporaryReg>
                          | <progParamReg>

<dstReg>                ::= <temporaryReg>
                          | <vertexResultReg>

<vertexAttribReg>       ::= <establishedName>
                          | <vtxAttribBinding>

<temporaryReg>          ::= <establishedName>

<progParamReg>          ::= <progParamSingle>
                          | <progParamArray> "[" <progParamArrayMem>
                            "]"
                          | <paramSingleItemUse>

<progParamSingle>       ::= <establishedName>

<progParamArray>        ::= <establishedName>

<progParamArrayMem>     ::= <progParamArrayAbs>
                          | <progParamArrayRel>

<progParamArrayAbs>     ::= <integer>

<progParamArrayRel>     ::= <addrReg> <addrComponent>
                            <addrRegRelOffset>

<addrRegRelOffset>      ::= ""
                          | "+" <addrRegPosOffset>
                          | "-" <addrRegNegOffset>

<addrRegPosOffset>      ::= <integer> from 0 to 63

<addrRegNegOffset>      ::= <integer> from 0 to 64

<vertexResultReg>       ::= <establishedName>
                          | <resultBinding>
```

```
<addrReg>                ::= <establishedName>

<addrComponent>          ::= "." "x"

<addrWriteMask>          ::= "." "x"

<scalarSuffix>           ::= "." <component>

<swizzleSuffix>          ::= ""
                           | "." <component>
                           | "." <component> <component> <component>
                             <component>

<component>              ::= "x"
                           | "y"
                           | "z"
                           | "w"

<optionalMask>           ::= ""
                           | "." "x"
                           | "." "y"
                           | "." "xy"
                           | "." "z"
                           | "." "xz"
                           | "." "yz"
                           | "." "xyz"
                           | "." "w"
                           | "." "xw"
                           | "." "yw"
                           | "." "xyw"
                           | "." "zw"
                           | "." "xzw"
                           | "." "yzw"
                           | "." "xyzw"

<namingStatement>        ::= <ATTRIB_statement>
                           | <PARAM_statement>
                           | <TEMP_statement>
                           | <ADDRESS_statement>
                           | <OUTPUT_statement>
                           | <ALIAS_statement>

<ATTRIB_statement>       ::= "ATTRIB" <establishName> "="
                             <vtxAttribBinding>

<vtxAttribBinding>       ::= "vertex" "." <vtxAttribItem>
```

```
<vtxAttribItem>         ::= "position"
                          | "weight" <vtxOptWeightNum>
                          | "normal"
                          | "color" <optColorType>
                          | "fogcoord"
                          | "texcoord" <optTexCoordNum>
                          | "matrixindex" "[" <vtxWeightNum> "]"
                          | "attrib" "[" <vtxAttribNum> "]"

<vtxAttribNum>          ::= <integer> from 0 to
                              MAX_VERTEX_ATTRIBS_ARB-1

<vtxOptWeightNum>       ::= ""
                          | "[" <vtxWeightNum> "]"

<vtxWeightNum>          ::= <integer> from 0 to MAX_VERTEX_UNITS_ARB-1,
                              must be divisible by four

<PARAM_statement>       ::= <PARAM_singleStmt>
                          | <PARAM_multipleStmt>

<PARAM_singleStmt>      ::= "PARAM" <establishName> <paramSingleInit>

<PARAM_multipleStmt>    ::= "PARAM" <establishName> "[" <optArraySize>
                              "]" <paramMultipleInit>

<optArraySize>          ::= ""
                          | <integer> from 1 to
                              MAX_PROGRAM_PARAMETERS_ARB

<paramSingleInit>       ::= "=" <paramSingleItemDecl>

<paramMultipleInit>     ::= "=" "{" <paramMultInitList> "}"

<paramMultInitList>     ::= <paramMultipleItem>
                          | <paramMultipleItem> ","
                              <paramMultiInitList>

<paramSingleItemDecl>   ::= <stateSingleItem>
                          | <programSingleItem>
                          | <paramConstDecl>

<paramSingleItemUse>    ::= <stateSingleItem>
                          | <programSingleItem>
                          | <paramConstUse>
```

```
<paramMultipleItem>      ::= <stateMultipleItem>
                           | <programMultipleItem>
                           | <paramConstant>

<stateMultipleItem>      ::= <stateSingleItem>
                           | "state" "." <stateMatrixRows>

<stateSingleItem>        ::= "state" "." <stateMaterialItem>
                           | "state" "." <stateLightItem>
                           | "state" "." <stateLightModelItem>
                           | "state" "." <stateLightProdItem>
                           | "state" "." <stateTexGenItem>
                           | "state" "." <stateFogItem>
                           | "state" "." <stateClipPlaneItem>
                           | "state" "." <statePointItem>
                           | "state" "." <stateMatrixRow>

<stateMaterialItem>      ::= "material" <optFaceType> "."
                               <stateMatProperty>

<stateMatProperty>       ::= "ambient"
                           | "diffuse"
                           | "specular"
                           | "emission"
                           | "shininess"

<stateLightItem>         ::= "light" "[" <stateLightNumber> "]" "."
                               <stateLightProperty>

<stateLightProperty>     ::= "ambient"
                           | "diffuse"
                           | "specular"
                           | "position"
                           | "attenuation"
                           | "spot" "." <stateSpotProperty>
                           | "half"

<stateSpotProperty>      ::= "direction"

<stateLightModelItem>    ::= "lightmodel" <stateLModProperty>

<stateLModProperty>      ::= "." "ambient"
                           | <optFaceType> "." "scenecolor"

<stateLightProdItem>     ::= "lightprod" "[" <stateLightNumber> "]"
                               <optFaceType> "." <stateLProdProperty>
```

```
<stateLProdProperty>    ::= "ambient"
                          | "diffuse"
                          | "specular"

<stateLightNumber>      ::= <integer> from 0 to MAX_LIGHTS-1

<stateTexGenItem>       ::= "texgen" <optTexCoordNum> "."
                              <stateTexGenType> "." <stateTexGenCoord>

<stateTexGenType>       ::= "eye"
                          | "object"

<stateTexGenCoord>      ::= "s"
                          | "t"
                          | "r"
                          | "q"

<stateFogItem>          ::= "fog" "." <stateFogProperty>

<stateFogProperty>      ::= "color"
                          | "params"

<stateClipPlaneItem>    ::= "clip" "[" <stateClipPlaneNum> "]" "."
                              "plane"

<stateClipPlaneNum>     ::= <integer> from 0 to MAX_CLIP_PLANES-1

<statePointItem>        ::= "point" "." <statePointProperty>

<statePointProperty>    ::= "size"
                          | "attenuation"

<stateMatrixRow>        ::= <stateMatrixItem> "." "row" "["
                              <stateMatrixRowNum> "]"

<stateMatrixRows>       ::= <stateMatrixItem> <optMatrixRows>

<optMatrixRows>         ::= ""
                          | "." "row" "[" <stateMatrixRowNum> ".."
                              <stateMatrixRowNum> "]"

<stateMatrixItem>       ::= "matrix" "." <stateMatrixName>
                              <stateOptMatModifier>

<stateOptMatModifier>   ::= ""
                          | "." <stateMatModifier>
```

```
<stateMatModifier>        ::= "inverse"
                            | "transpose"
                            | "invtrans"

<stateMatrixRowNum>       ::= <integer> from 0 to 3

<stateMatrixName>         ::= "modelview" <stateOptModMatNum>
                            | "projection"
                            | "mvp"
                            | "texture" <optTexCoordNum>
                            | "palette" "[" <statePaletteMatNum> "]"
                            | "program" "[" <stateProgramMatNum> "]"

<stateOptModMatNum>       ::= ""
                            | "[" <stateModMatNum> "]"

<stateModMatNum>          ::= <integer> from 0 to MAX_VERTEX_UNITS_ARB-1

<statePaletteMatNum>      ::= <integer> from 0 to
                                  MAX_PALETTE_MATRICES_ARB-1

<stateProgramMatNum>      ::= <integer> from 0 to
                                  MAX_PROGRAM_MATRICES_ARB-1

<programSingleItem>       ::= <progEnvParam>
                            | <progLocalParam>

<programMultipleItem>     ::= <progEnvParams>
                            | <progLocalParams>

<progEnvParams>           ::= "program" "." "env" "[" <progEnvParamNums>
                                  "]"

<progEnvParamNums>        ::= <progEnvParamNum>
                            | <progEnvParamNum> ".." <progEnvParamNum>

<progEnvParam>            ::= "program" "." "env" "[" <progEnvParamNum>
                                  "]"

<progLocalParams>         ::= "program" "." "local" "["
                                  <progLocalParamNums> "]"

<progLocalParamNums>      ::= <progLocalParamNum>
                            | <progLocalParamNum> ".."
                                  <progLocalParamNum>

<progLocalParam>          ::= "program" "." "local" "["
                                  <progLocalParamNum> "]"
```

```
<progEnvParamNum>       ::= <integer> from O to
                            MAX_PROGRAM_ENV_PARAMETERS_ARB-1

<progLocalParamNum>     ::= <integer> from O to
                            MAX_PROGRAM_LOCAL_PARAMETERS_ARB-1

<paramConstDecl>        ::= <paramConstScalarDecl>
                          | <paramConstVector>

<paramConstUse>         ::= <paramConstScalarUse>
                          | <paramConstVector>

<paramConstScalarDecl>  ::= <signedFloatConstant>

<paramConstScalarUse>   ::= <floatConstant>

<paramConstVector>      ::= "{" <signedFloatConstant> "}"
                          | "{" <signedFloatConstant> ","
                            <signedFloatConstant> "}"
                          | "{" <signedFloatConstant> ","
                            <signedFloatConstant> ","
                            <signedFloatConstant> "}"
                          | "{" <signedFloatConstant> ","
                            <signedFloatConstant> ","
                            <signedFloatConstant> ","
                            <signedFloatConstant> "}"

<signedFloatConstant>   ::= <optionalSign> <floatConstant>

<optionalSign>          ::= ""
                          | "-"
                          | "+"

<TEMP_statement>        ::= "TEMP" <varNameList>

<ADDRESS_statement>     ::= "ADDRESS" <varNameList>

<varNameList>           ::= <establishName>
                          | <establishName> "," <varNameList>

<OUTPUT_statement>      ::= "OUTPUT" <establishName> "="
                            <resultBinding>

<resultBinding>         ::= "result" "." "position"
                          | "result" "." <resultColBinding>
                          | "result" "." "fogcoord"
                          | "result" "." "pointsize"
                          | "result" "." "texcoord" <optTexCoordNum>
```

```
<resultColBinding>      ::= "color" <optFaceType> <optColorType>

<optFaceType>           ::= ""
                          | "." "front"
                          | "." "back"

<optColorType>          ::= ""
                          | "." "primary"
                          | "." "secondary"

<optTexCoordNum>        ::= ""
                          | "[" <texCoordNum> "]"

<texCoordNum>           ::= <integer> from 0 to MAX_TEXTURE_UNITS-1

<ALIAS_statement>       ::= "ALIAS" <establishName> "="
                              <establishedName>

<establishName>         ::= <identifier>

<establishedName>       ::= <identifier
```

When a vertex program uses the position-invariant option, the following change to the
<resultBinding> rule is effective:

```
<resultBinding>         ::= "result" "." <resultColBinding>
                          | "result" "." "fogcoord"
                          | "result" "." "pointsize"
                          | "result" "." "texcoord" <optTexCoordNum>
```

A.2 GL_NV_vertex_program

A vertex program must begin with the sequence "!!VP1.0", without any preceding whitespace. Vertex state programs must adhere to the more restricted grammar listed at the end
of this section.

```
<program>               ::= "!!VP1.0" <instructionSequence> "END"

<instructionSequence>   ::= <instructionSequence> <instructionLine>
                          | <instructionLine>

<instructionLine>       ::= <instruction> ";"

<instruction>           ::= <ARL-instruction>
                          | <VECTORop-instruction>
                          | <SCALARop-instruction>
```

```
                                  | <BINop-instruction>
                                  | <TRIop-instruction>

<ARL-instruction>        ::= "ARL" <addrReg> "," <scalarSrcReg>

<VECTORop-instruction> ::= <VECTORop> <maskedDstReg> ","
                             <swizzleSrcReg>

<SCALARop-instruction> ::= <SCALARop> <maskedDstReg> ","
                             <scalarSrcReg>

<BINop-instruction>      ::= <BINop> <maskedDstReg> ","
                             <swizzleSrcReg> "," <swizzleSrcReg>

<TRIop-instruction>      ::= <TRIop> <maskedDstReg> ","
                             <swizzleSrcReg> "," <swizzleSrcReg> ","
                             <swizzleSrcReg>

<VECTORop>               ::= "MOV"
                             | "LIT"

<SCALARop>               ::= "RCP"
                             | "RSQ"
                             | "EXP"
                             | "LOG"

<BINop>                  ::= "MUL"
                             | "ADD"
                             | "DP3"
                             | "DP4"
                             | "DST"
                             | "MIN"
                             | "MAX"
                             | "SLT"
                             | "SGE"

<TRIop>                  ::= "MAD"

<scalarSrcReg>           ::= <optionalSign> <srcReg> <scalarSuffix>

<swizzleSrcReg>          ::= <optionalSign> <srcReg> <swizzleSuffix>

<maskedDstReg>           ::= <dstReg> <optionalMask>

<optionalMask>           ::= ""
                             | "." "x"
                             | "." "y"
                             | "." "x" "y"
```

```
                                    | "." "z"
                                    | "." "x" "z"
                                    | "." "y" "z"
                                    | "." "x" "y" "z"
                                    | "." "w"
                                    | "." "x" "w"
                                    | "." "y" "w"
                                    | "." "x" "y" "w"
                                    | "." "z" "w"
                                    | "." "x" "z" "w"
                                    | "." "y" "z" "w"
                                    | "." "x" "y" "z" "w"

<optionalSign>           ::= "-"
                           | ""

<srcReg>                 ::= <vertexAttribReg>
                           | <progParamReg>
                           | <temporaryReg>

<dstReg>                 ::= <temporaryReg>
                           | <vertexResultReg>

<vertexAttribReg>        ::= "v" "[" vertexAttribRegNum "]"

<vertexAttribRegNum>     ::= decimal integer from 0 to 15 inclusive
                           | "OPOS"
                           | "WGHT"
                           | "NRML"
                           | "COL0"
                           | "COL1"
                           | "FOGC"
                           | "TEX0"
                           | "TEX1"
                           | "TEX2"
                           | "TEX3"
                           | "TEX4"
                           | "TEX5"
                           | "TEX6"
                           | "TEX7"

<progParamReg>           ::= <absProgParamReg>
                           | <relProgParamReg>

<absProgParamReg>        ::= "c" "[" <progParamRegNum> "]"

<progParamRegNum>        ::= decimal integer from 0 to 95 inclusive
```

```
<relProgParamReg>       ::= "c" "[" <addrReg> "]"
                          | "c" "[" <addrReg> "+"
                            <progParamPosOffset> "]"
                          | "c" "[" <addrReg> "-"
                            <progParamNegOffset> "]"

<progParamPosOffset>    ::= decimal integer from 0 to 63 inclusive

<progParamNegOffset>    ::= decimal integer from 0 to 64 inclusive

<addrReg>               ::= "A0" "." "x"

<temporaryReg>          ::= "R0"
                          | "R1"
                          | "R2"
                          | "R3"
                          | "R4"
                          | "R5"
                          | "R6"
                          | "R7"
                          | "R8"
                          | "R9"
                          | "R10"
                          | "R11"

<vertexResultReg>       ::= "o" "[" vertexResultRegName "]"

<vertexResultRegName>   ::= "HPOS"
                          | "COL0"
                          | "COL1"
                          | "BFC0"
                          | "BFC1"
                          | "FOGC"
                          | "PSIZ"
                          | "TEX0"
                          | "TEX1"
                          | "TEX2"
                          | "TEX3"
                          | "TEX4"
                          | "TEX5"
                          | "TEX6"
                          | "TEX7"

<scalarSuffix>          ::= "." <component>

<swizzleSuffix>         ::= ""
                          | "." <component>
                          | "." <component> <component> <component>
                            <component>
```

```
<component>              ::= "x"
                          | "y"
                          | "z"
                          | "w"
```

The syntax for vertex state programs is identical to that for ordinary vertex programs, but with the following modifications:

```
<program>               ::= "!!VSP1.0" <instructionSequence> "END"

<dstReg>                ::= <absProgParamReg> | <temporaryReg>

<vertexAttribReg>       ::= "v" "[" "0" "]"
```

A.3   GL_NV_vertex_program1_1

The syntax for the version 1.1 vertex programs defined by the GL_NV_vertex_program1_1 extension is identical to the syntax for the version 1.0 vertex programs defined by the GL_NV_vertex_program extension, but with the following modifications:

```
<program>               ::= "!!VP1.1" <optionSequence>
                                <instructionSequence> "END"

<optionSequence>        ::= <optionSequence> <option>
                          | ""

<option>                ::= "OPTION" "NV_position_invariant" ";"

<SCALARop>              ::= "RCP"
                          | "RSQ"
                          | "EXP"
                          | "LOG"
                          | "RCC"
                          | "ABS"

<BINop>                 ::= "MUL"
                          | "ADD"
                          | "DP3"
                          | "DP4"
                          | "DST"
                          | "MIN"
                          | "MAX"
                          | "SLT"
                          | "SGE"
                          | "DPH"
                          | "SUB"
```

```
<optionalSign>            ::= "-"
                          | "+"
                          | ""
```

When a version 1.1 vertex program uses the position-invariant option, the following additional changes to the version 1.0 syntax are effective:

```
<vertexResultRegName>  ::= "COL0"
                        | "COL1"
                        | "BFC0"
                        | "BFC1"
                        | "FOGC"
                        | "PSIZ"
                        | "TEX0"
                        | "TEX1"
                        | "TEX2"
                        | "TEX3"
                        | "TEX4"
                        | "TEX5"
                        | "TEX6"
                        | "TEX7"

<relProgParamReg>      ::= "c" "[" <addrReg> "]"
```

A.4   GL_NV_vertex_program2

A vertex program must begin with the sequence "!!VP1.0", "!!VP1.1", or "!!VP2.0", without any preceding whitespace.

```
<program>            ::= <vp1-program>
                      | <vp11-program>
                      | <vp2-program>

<vp1-program>        ::= "!!VP1.0" <programBody> "END"

<vp11-program>       ::= "!!VP1.1" <programBody> "END"

<vp2-program>        ::= "!!VP2.0" <programBody> "END"

<programBody>        ::= <optionSequence> <vp2-branchTable>
                          <programText>

<optionSequence>     ::= <option> <optionSequence>
                      | ""
```

```
<option>                ::= "OPTION" <vp11-option> ";"
                          | "OPTION" <vp2-option> ";"

<vp11-option>           ::= "NV_position_invariant"

<vp2-option>            ::= "NV_position_invariant"

<programText>           ::= <programTextItem> <programText>
                          | ""

<programTextItem>       ::= <instruction> ";"
                          | <vp2-instructionLabel>

<instruction>           ::= <ARL-instruction>
                          | <VECTORop-instruction>
                          | <SCALARop-instruction>
                          | <BINop-instruction>
                          | <TRIop-instruction>
                          | <vp2-BRA-instruction>
                          | <vp2-RET-instruction>
                          | <vp2-ARA-instruction>

<ARL-instruction>       ::= <vp1-ARL-instruction>
                          | <vp2-ARL-instruction>

<vp1-ARL-instruction>   ::= "ARL" <maskedAddrReg> "," <scalarSrc>

<vp2-ARL-instruction>   ::= <vp2-ARLop> <maskedAddrReg> ","
                            <vectorSrc>

<vp2-ARLop>             ::= "ARL" | "ARLC" | "ARR" | "ARRC"

<VECTORop-instruction>  ::= <VECTORop> <maskedDstReg> "," <vectorSrc>

<VECTORop>              ::= "LIT"
                          | "MOV"
                          | <vp11-VECTORop>
                          | <vp2-VECTORop>

<vp11-VECTORop>         ::= "ABS"

<vp2-VECTORop>          ::= "ABS" | "ABSC"
                          | "FLR" | "FLRC"
                          | "FRC" | "FRCC"
                          | "LITC"
                          | "MOVC"
                          | "SSG" | "SSGC"
```

```
<SCALARop-instruction> ::= <SCALARop> <maskedDstReg> "," <scalarSrc>

<SCALARop>              ::= "EXP"
                         | "LOG"
                         | "RCP"
                         | "RSQ"
                         | <vp2-SCALARop>

<vp2-SCALARop>         ::= "COS" | "COSC"
                         | "EX2" | "EX2C"
                         | "LG2" | "LG2C"
                         | "EXPC"
                         | "LOGC"
                         | "RCPC"
                         | "RSQC"

<BINop-instruction>    ::= <BINop> <maskedDstReg> "," <vectorSrc> ","
                            <vectorSrc>

<BINop>                ::= "ADD"
                         | "DP3"
                         | "DP4"
                         | "DST"
                         | "MAX"
                         | "MIN"
                         | "MUL"
                         | "SGE"
                         | "SLT"
                         | <vp11-BINop>
                         | <vp2-BINop>

<vp11-BINop>           ::= "DPH"

<vp2-BINop>            ::= "ADDC"
                         | "DP3C"
                         | "DP4C"
                         | "DPH" | "DPHC"
                         | "DSTC"
                         | "MAXC"
                         | "MINC"
                         | "MULC"
                         | "SEQ" | "SEQC"
                         | "SFL" | "SFLC"
                         | "SGEC"
                         | "SGT" | "SGTC"
                         | "SLTC"
                         | "SLE" | "SLEC"
                         | "SNE" | "SNEC"
                         | "STR" | "STRC"
```

```
<TRIop-instruction>    ::= <TRIop> <maskedDstReg> "," <vectorSrc> ","
                           <vectorSrc> "," <vectorSrc>

<TRIop>                ::= "MAD"
                         | <vp2-TRIop>

<vp2-TRIop>            ::= "MADC"

<vp2-BRA-instruction>  ::= <vp2-BRANCHop> <vp2-branchTarget>
                           <vp2-branchCondition>

<vp2-BRANCHop>         ::= "BRA"
                         | "CAL"

<vp2-RET-instruction>  ::= "RET" <vp2-branchCondition>

<vp2-ARA-instruction>  ::= <vp2-ARAop> <maskedAddrReg> ","
                           <addrRegister>

<vp2-ARAop>            ::= "ARA" | "ARAC"

<scalarSrc>            ::= <baseScalarSrc>
                         | <vp2-absScalarSrc>

<vp2-absScalarSrc>     ::= <optionalSign> "|" <baseScalarSrc> "|"

<baseScalarSrc>        ::= <optionalSign> <srcRegister>
                           <scalarSuffix>

<vectorSrc>            ::= <baseVectorSrc>
                         | <vp2-absVectorSrc>

<vp2-absVectorSrc>     ::= <optionalSign> "|" <baseVectorSrc> "|"

<baseVectorSrc>        ::= <optionalSign> <srcRegister>
                           <swizzleSuffix>

<srcRegister>          ::= <vtxAttribRegister>
                         | <progParamRegister>
                         | <tempRegister>

<maskedDstReg>         ::= <dstRegister> <optionalWriteMask>
                           <optionalCCMask>

<dstRegister>          ::= <vtxResultRegister>
                         | <tempRegister>
                         | <vp2-nullRegister>
```

```
<vp2-nullRegister>        ::= "CC"

<vp2-branchCondition>     ::= <optionalCCMask>

<vp2-branchTarget>        ::= <vp2-absoluteBranch>
                            | <vp2-indexedBranch>

<vp2-absoluteBranch>      ::= <vp2-branchLabel>

<vp2-indexedBranch>       ::= "[" <scalarAddr> <vp2-indexedBrOffset> "]"

<vp2-indexedBrOffset>     ::= ""
                            | "+" <vp2-indexedBrBase>

<vp2-indexedBrBase>       ::= decimal integer from 0 to 15 inclusive

<vtxAttribRegister>       ::= "v" "[" <vtxAttribRegNum> "]"

<vtxAttribRegNum>         ::= decimal integer from 0 to 15 inclusive
                            | "OPOS"
                            | "WGHT"
                            | "NRML"
                            | "COL0"
                            | "COL1"
                            | "FOGC"
                            | "TEX0"
                            | "TEX1"
                            | "TEX2"
                            | "TEX3"
                            | "TEX4"
                            | "TEX5"
                            | "TEX6"
                            | "TEX7"

<progParamRegister>       ::= <absProgParamReg>
                            | <relProgParamReg>

<absProgParamReg>         ::= "c" "[" <progParamRegNum> "]"

<progParamRegNum>         ::= <vp1-progParamRegNum>
                            | <vp2-progParamRegNum>

<vp1-progParamRegNum>     ::= decimal integer from 0 to 95 inclusive

<vp2-progParamRegNum>     ::= decimal integer from 0 to 255 inclusive

<relProgParamReg>         ::= "c" "[" <scalarAddr> <relProgParamOffset>
                                "]"
```

```
<relProgParamOffset>     ::= ""
                           | "+" <progParamPosOffset>
                           | "-" <progParamNegOffset>

<progParamPosOffset>     ::= <vp1-progParamPosOff>
                           | <vp2-progParamPosOff>

<vp1-progParamPosOff>    ::= decimal integer from 0 to 63 inclusive

<vp2-progParamPosOff>    ::= decimal integer from 0 to 255 inclusive

<progParamNegOffset>     ::= <vp1-progParamNegOff>
                           | <vp2-progParamNegOff>

<vp1-progParamNegOff>    ::= decimal integer from 0 to 64 inclusive

<vp2-progParamNegOff>    ::= decimal integer from 0 to 256 inclusive

<tempRegister>           ::= "R0" | "R1" | "R2" | "R3" | "R4" | "R5" |
                             "R6" | "R7" | "R8" | "R9" | "R10" | "R11"

<vp2-tempRegister>       ::= "R12" | "R13" | "R14" | "R15"

<vtxResultRegister>      ::= "o" "[" <vtxResultRegName> "]"

<vtxResultRegName>       ::= "HPOS"
                           | "COL0"
                           | "COL1"
                           | "BFC0"
                           | "BFC1"
                           | "FOGC"
                           | "PSIZ"
                           | "TEX0"
                           | "TEX1"
                           | "TEX2"
                           | "TEX3"
                           | "TEX4"
                           | "TEX5"
                           | "TEX6"
                           | "TEX7"

<scalarAddr>             ::= <addrRegister> "." <addrRegisterComp>

<maskedAddrReg>          ::= <addrRegister> <addrWriteMask>

<addrRegister>           ::= "A0"
                           | <vp2-addrRegister>
```

```
<vp2-addrRegister>        ::= "A1"

<addrRegisterComp>        ::= "x"
                            | <vp2-addrRegisterComp>

<vp2-addrRegisterComp> ::= "y"
                            | "z"
                            | "w"

<addrWriteMask>           ::= "." "x"
                            | <vp2-addrWriteMask>

<vp2-addrWriteMask>       ::= ""
                            | "." "y"
                            | "." "x" "y"
                            | "." "z"
                            | "." "x" "z"
                            | "." "y" "z"
                            | "." "x" "y" "z"
                            | "." "w"
                            | "." "x" "w"
                            | "." "y" "w"
                            | "." "x" "y" "w"
                            | "." "z" "w"
                            | "." "x" "z" "w"
                            | "." "y" "z" "w"
                            | "." "x" "y" "z" "w"

<optionalSign>            ::= ""
                            | "-"
                            | <vp2-optionalSign>

<vp2-optionalSign>        ::= "+"

<vp2-instructionLabel> ::= <vp2-branchLabel> ":"

<vp2-branchTable>         ::= ""
                            | "JMPTABLE" "{" <vp2-branchList> "}"

<vp2-branchList>          ::= ""
                            | <vp2-branchLabel>
                            | <vp2-branchLabel> "," <vp2-branchList>

<vp2-branchLabel>         ::= <identifier>

<optionalWriteMask>       ::= ""
                            | "." "x"
                            | "." "y"
```

```
                                    | "." "x" "y"
                                    | "." "z"
                                    | "." "x" "z"
                                    | "." "y" "z"
                                    | "." "x" "y" "z"
                                    | "." "w"
                                    | "." "x" "w"
                                    | "." "y" "w"
                                    | "." "x" "y" "w"
                                    | "." "z" "w"
                                    | "." "x" "z" "w"
                                    | "." "y" "z" "w"
                                    | "." "x" "y" "z" "w"

<optionalCCMask>        ::= ""
                          | <vp2-ccMask>

<vp2-ccMask>            ::= "(" <vp2-ccMaskRule> <swizzleSuffix> ")"

<vp2-ccMaskRule>        ::= "EQ" | "GE" | "GT" | "LE" | "LT" | "NE" |
                            "TR" | "FL"

<scalarSuffix>          ::= "." <component>

<swizzleSuffix>         ::= ""
                          | "." <component>
                          | "." <component> <component> <component>
                            <component>

<component>             ::= "x"
                          | "y"
                          | "z"
                          | "w"
```

A.5   GL_ARB_fragment_program

The following sequences are reserved keywords and may not be used as identifiers.

ABS	EX2_SAT	MUL	SUB_SAT
ABS_SAT	FLR	MUL_SAT	SWZ
ADD	FLR_SAT	OPTION	SWZ_SAT
ADD_SAT	FRC	OUTPUT	TEMP
ALIAS	FRC_SAT	PARAM	TEX
ATTRIB	KIL	POW	TEX_SAT

CMP	LG2	POW_SAT	TXB
CMP_SAT	LG2_SAT	RCP	TXB_SAT
COS	LIT	RCP_SAT	TXP
COS_SAT	LIT_SAT	RSQ	TXP_SAT
DP3	LRP	RSQ_SAT	XPD
DP3_SAT	LRP_SAT	SIN	XPD_SAT
DP4	MAD	SIN_SAT	fragment
DP4_SAT	MAD_SAT	SCS	program
DPH	MAX	SCS_SAT	result
DPH_SAT	MAX_SAT	SGE	state
DST	MIN	SGE_SAT	texture
DST_SAT	MIN_SAT	SLT	
END	MOV	SLT_SAT	
EX2	MOV_SAT	SUB	

A fragment program must begin with the sequence "!!ARBfp1.0", without any preceding whitespace.

```
<program>              ::= "!!ARBfp1.0" <optionSequence>
                           <statementSequence> "END"

<optionSequence>       ::= <optionSequence> <option>
                           | ""

<option>               ::= "OPTION" <identifier> ";"

<statementSequence>    ::= <statementSequence> <statement>
                           | ""

<statement>            ::= <instruction> ";"
                           | <namingStatement> ";"

<instruction>          ::= <ALUInstruction>
                           | <TexInstruction>

<ALUInstruction>       ::= <VECTORop_instruction>
                           | <SCALARop_instruction>
                           | <BINSCop_instruction>
                           | <BINop_instruction>
                           | <TRIop_instruction>
                           | <SWZ_instruction>
```

```
<TexInstruction>        ::= <SAMPLE_instruction>
                          | <KIL_instruction>

<VECTORop_instruction> ::= <VECTORop> <maskedDstReg> ","
                             <vectorSrcReg>

<VECTORop>              ::= "ABS" | "ABS_SAT"
                          | "FLR" | "FLR_SAT"
                          | "FRC" | "FRC_SAT"
                          | "LIT" | "LIT_SAT"
                          | "MOV" | "MOV_SAT"

<SCALARop_instruction> ::= <SCALARop> <maskedDstReg> ","
                             <scalarSrcReg>

<SCALARop>              ::= "COS" | "COS_SAT"
                          | "EX2" | "EX2_SAT"
                          | "LG2" | "LG2_SAT"
                          | "RCP" | "RCP_SAT"
                          | "RSQ" | "RSQ_SAT"
                          | "SIN" | "SIN_SAT"
                          | "SCS" | "SCS_SAT"

<BINSCop_instruction>  ::= <BINSCop> <maskedDstReg>
                             "," <scalarSrcReg>
                             "," <scalarSrcReg>

<BINSCop>              ::= "POW" | "POW_SAT"

<BINop_instruction>    ::= <BINop> <maskedDstReg> "," <vectorSrcReg>
                             "," <vectorSrcReg>

<BINop>                ::= "ADD" | "ADD_SAT"
                          | "DP3" | "DP3_SAT"
                          | "DP4" | "DP4_SAT"
                          | "DPH" | "DPH_SAT"
                          | "DST" | "DST_SAT"
                          | "MAX" | "MAX_SAT"
                          | "MIN" | "MIN_SAT"
                          | "MUL" | "MUL_SAT"
                          | "SGE" | "SGE_SAT"
                          | "SLT" | "SLT_SAT"
                          | "SUB" | "SUB_SAT"
                          | "XPD" | "XPD_SAT"

<TRIop_instruction>    ::= <TRIop> <maskedDstReg> "," <vectorSrcReg>
                             "," <vectorSrcReg> "," <vectorSrcReg>
```

```
<TRIop>                     ::= "CMP" | "CMP_SAT"
                              | "LRP" | "LRP_SAT"
                              | "MAD" | "MAD_SAT"

<SWZ_instruction>           ::= <SWZop> <maskedDstReg> "," <srcReg> ","
                                <extendedSwizzle>

<SWZop>                     ::= "SWZ" | "SWZ_SAT"

<SAMPLE_instruction>        ::= <SAMPLEop> <maskedDstReg> ","
                                <vectorSrcReg> "," <texImageUnit> ","
                                <texTarget>

<SAMPLEop>                  ::= "TEX" | "TEX_SAT"
                              | "TXP" | "TXP_SAT"
                              | "TXB" | "TXB_SAT"

<KIL_instruction>           ::= "KIL" <vectorSrcReg>

<texImageUnit>              ::= "texture" <optTexImageUnitNum>

<texTarget>                 ::= "1D"
                              | "2D"
                              | "3D"
                              | "CUBE"
                              | "RECT"

<optTexImageUnitNum>        ::= ""
                              | "[" <texImageUnitNum> "]"

<texImageUnitNum>           ::= <integer> from 0 to
                                MAX_TEXTURE_IMAGE_UNITS_ARB-1

<scalarSrcReg>              ::= <optionalSign> <srcReg> <scalarSuffix>

<vectorSrcReg>              ::= <optionalSign> <srcReg> <optionalSuffix>

<maskedDstReg>              ::= <dstReg> <optionalMask>

<extendedSwizzle>           ::= <xyzwExtendedSwizzle>
                              | <rgbaExtendedSwizzle>

<xyzwExtendedSwizzle>       ::= <xyzwExtSwizComp> "," <xyzwExtSwizComp> ","
                                <xyzwExtSwizComp> "," <xyzwExtSwizComp>

<rgbaExtendedSwizzle>       ::= <rgbaExtSwizComp> "," <rgbaExtSwizComp>
                                "," <rgbaExtSwizComp>
                                "," <rgbaExtSwizComp>
```

```
<xyzwExtSwizComp>       ::= <optionalSign> <xyzwExtSwizSel>

<rgbaExtSwizComp>       ::= <optionalSign> <rgbaExtSwizSel>

<xyzwExtSwizSel>        ::= "0"
                          | "1"
                          | <xyzwComponent>

<rgbaExtSwizSel>        ::= "0"
                          | "1"
                          | <rgbaComponent>

<srcReg>                ::= <fragmentAttribReg>
                          | <temporaryReg>
                          | <progParamReg>

<dstReg>                ::= <temporaryReg>
                          | <fragmentResultReg>

<fragmentAttribReg>     ::= <establishedName>
                          | <fragAttribBinding>

<temporaryReg>          ::= <establishedName>

<progParamReg>          ::= <progParamSingle>
                          | <progParamArray> "[" <progParamArrayAbs>
                            "]"
                          | <paramSingleItemUse>

<progParamSingle>       ::= <establishedName>

<progParamArray>        ::= <establishedName>

<progParamArrayAbs>     ::= <integer>

<fragmentResultReg>     ::= <establishedName>
                          | <resultBinding>

<scalarSuffix>          ::= "." <component>

<optionalSuffix>        ::= ""
                          | "." <component>
                          | "." <xyzwComponent> <xyzwComponent>
                            <xyzwComponent> <xyzwComponent>
                          | "." <rgbaComponent> <rgbaComponent>
                            <rgbaComponent> <rgbaComponent>

<component>             ::= <xyzwComponent>
                          | <rgbaComponent>
```

```
<xyzwComponent>        ::= "x" | "y" | "z" | "w"

<rgbaComponent>        ::= "r" | "g" | "b" | "a"

<optionalMask>         ::= ""
                         | <xyzwMask>
                         | <rgbaMask>

<xyzwMask>             ::= "." "x"
                         | "." "y"
                         | "." "xy"
                         | "." "z"
                         | "." "xz"
                         | "." "yz"
                         | "." "xyz"
                         | "." "w"
                         | "." "xw"
                         | "." "yw"
                         | "." "xyw"
                         | "." "zw"
                         | "." "xzw"
                         | "." "yzw"
                         | "." "xyzw"

<rgbaMask>             ::= "." "r"
                         | "." "g"
                         | "." "rg"
                         | "." "b"
                         | "." "rb"
                         | "." "gb"
                         | "." "rgb"
                         | "." "a"
                         | "." "ra"
                         | "." "ga"
                         | "." "rga"
                         | "." "ba"
                         | "." "rba"
                         | "." "gba"
                         | "." "rgba"

<namingStatement>      ::= <ATTRIB_statement>
                         | <PARAM_statement>
                         | <TEMP_statement>
                         | <OUTPUT_statement>
                         | <ALIAS_statement>

<ATTRIB_statement>     ::= "ATTRIB" <establishName> "="
                             <fragAttribBinding>
```

```
<fragAttribBinding>      ::= "fragment" "." <fragAttribItem>

<fragAttribItem>         ::= "color" <optColorType>
                           | "texcoord" <optTexCoordNum>
                           | "fogcoord"
                           | "position"

<PARAM_statement>        ::= <PARAM_singleStmt>
                           | <PARAM_multipleStmt>

<PARAM_singleStmt>       ::= "PARAM" <establishName> <paramSingleInit>

<PARAM_multipleStmt>     ::= "PARAM" <establishName> "[" <optArraySize>
                             "]" <paramMultipleInit>

<optArraySize>           ::= ""
                           | <integer> from 1 to
                             MAX_PROGRAM_PARAMETERS_ARB

<paramSingleInit>        ::= "=" <paramSingleItemDecl>

<paramMultipleInit>      ::= "=" "{" <paramMultInitList> "}"

<paramMultInitList>      ::= <paramMultipleItem>
                           | <paramMultipleItem> ","
                             <paramMultInitList>

<paramSingleItemDecl>    ::= <stateSingleItem>
                           | <programSingleItem>
                           | <paramConstDecl>

<paramSingleItemUse>     ::= <stateSingleItem>
                           | <programSingleItem>
                           | <paramConstUse>

<paramMultipleItem>      ::= <stateMultipleItem>
                           | <programMultipleItem>
                           | <paramConstDecl>

<stateMultipleItem>      ::= <stateSingleItem>
                           | "state" "." <stateMatrixRows>

<stateSingleItem>        ::= "state" "." <stateMaterialItem>
                           | "state" "." <stateLightItem>
                           | "state" "." <stateLightModelItem>
                           | "state" "." <stateLightProdItem>
                           | "state" "." <stateTexEnvItem>
                           | "state" "." <stateFogItem>
```

```
                                      | "state" "." <stateDepthItem>
                                      | "state" "." <stateMatrixRow>

<stateMaterialItem>     ::= "material" <optFaceType> "."
                              <stateMatProperty>

<stateMatProperty>      ::= "ambient"
                          | "diffuse"
                          | "specular"
                          | "emission"
                          | "shininess"

<stateLightItem>        ::= "light" "[" <stateLightNumber> "]" "."
                              <stateLightProperty>

<stateLightProperty>    ::= "ambient"
                          | "diffuse"
                          | "specular"
                          | "position"
                          | "attenuation"
                          | "spot" "." <stateSpotProperty>
                          | "half"

<stateSpotProperty>     ::= "direction"

<stateLightModelItem>   ::= "lightmodel" <stateLModProperty>

<stateLModProperty>     ::= "." "ambient"
                          | <optFaceType> "." "scenecolor"

<stateLightProdItem>    ::= "lightprod" "[" <stateLightNumber> "]"
                              <optFaceType> "." <stateLProdProperty>

<stateLProdProperty>    ::= "ambient"
                          | "diffuse"
                          | "specular"

<stateLightNumber>      ::= <integer> from 0 to MAX_LIGHTS-1

<stateTexEnvItem>       ::= "texenv" <optTexCoordNum> "."
                              <stateTexEnvProperty>

<stateTexEnvProperty>   ::= "color"

<stateFogItem>          ::= "fog" "." <stateFogProperty>

<stateFogProperty>      ::= "color"
                          | "params"
```

```
<stateDepthItem>          ::= "depth" "." <stateDepthProperty>

<stateDepthProperty>      ::= "range"

<stateMatrixRow>          ::= <stateMatrixItem> "." "row" "["
                                <stateMatrixRowNum> "]"

<stateMatrixRows>         ::= <stateMatrixItem> <optMatrixRows>

<optMatrixRows>           ::= ""
                            | "." "row" "[" <stateMatrixRowNum> ".."
                              <stateMatrixRowNum> "]"

<stateMatrixItem>         ::= "matrix" . <stateMatrixName>
                                <stateOptMatModifier>

<stateOptMatModifier>     ::= ""
                            | "." <stateMatModifier>

<stateMatModifier>        ::= "inverse"
                            | "transpose"
                            | "invtrans"

<stateMatrixRowNum>       ::= <integer> from 0 to 3

<stateMatrixName>         ::= "modelview" <stateOptModMatNum>
                            | "projection"
                            | "mvp"
                            | "texture" <optTexCoordNum>
                            | "palette" "[" <statePaletteMatNum> "]"
                            | "program" "[" <stateProgramMatNum> "]"

<stateOptModMatNum>       ::= ""
                            | "[" <stateModMatNum> "]"

<stateModMatNum>          ::= <integer> from 0 to MAX_VERTEX_UNITS_ARB-1

<statePaletteMatNum>      ::= <integer> from 0 to
                                MAX_PALETTE_MATRICES_ARB-1

<stateProgramMatNum>      ::= <integer> from 0 to
                                MAX_PROGRAM_MATRICES_ARB-1

<programSingleItem>       ::= <progEnvParam>
                            | <progLocalParam>

<programMultipleItem>     ::= <progEnvParams>
                            | <progLocalParams>
```

```
<progEnvParams>          ::= "program" "." "env" "[" <progEnvParamNums>
                             "]"

<progEnvParamNums>       ::= <progEnvParamNum>
                           | <progEnvParamNum> ".." <progEnvParamNum>

<progEnvParam>           ::= "program" "." "env" "[" <progEnvParamNum>
                             "]"

<progLocalParams>        ::= "program" "." "local" "["
                             <progLocalParamNums> "]"

<progLocalParamNums>     ::= <progLocalParamNum>
                           | <progLocalParamNum> ".."
                             <progLocalParamNum>

<progLocalParam>         ::= "program" "." "local" "["
                             <progLocalParamNum> "]"

<progEnvParamNum>        ::= <integer> from 0 to
                             MAX_PROGRAM_ENV_PARAMETERS_ARB-1

<progLocalParamNum>      ::= <integer> from 0 to
                             MAX_PROGRAM_LOCAL_PARAMETERS_ARB-1

<paramConstDecl>         ::= <paramConstScalarDecl>
                           | <paramConstVector>

<paramConstUse>          ::= <paramConstScalarUse>
                           | <paramConstVector>

<paramConstScalarDecl>   ::= <signedFloatConstant>

<paramConstScalarUse>    ::= <floatConstant>

<paramConstVector>       ::= "{" <signedFloatConstant> "}"
                           | "{" <signedFloatConstant> ","
                             <signedFloatConstant> "}"
                           | "{" <signedFloatConstant> ","
                             <signedFloatConstant> ","
                             <signedFloatConstant> "}"
                           | "{" <signedFloatConstant> ","
                             <signedFloatConstant> ","
                             <signedFloatConstant> ","
                             <signedFloatConstant> "}"

<signedFloatConstant>    ::= <optionalSign> <floatConstant>
```

```
<optionalSign>            ::= ""
                            | "-"
                            | "+"

<TEMP_statement>          ::= "TEMP" <varNameList>

<varNameList>             ::= <establishName>
                            | <establishName> "," <varNameList>

<OUTPUT_statement>        ::= "OUTPUT" <establishName> "="
                                <resultBinding>

<resultBinding>           ::= "result" "." "color"
                            | "result" "." "depth"

<optFaceType>             ::= ""
                            | "." "front"
                            | "." "back"

<optColorType>            ::= ""
                            | "." "primary"
                            | "." "secondary"

<optTexCoordNum>          ::= ""
                            | "[" <texCoordNum> "]"

<texCoordNum>             ::= <integer> from 0 to
                                MAX_TEXTURE_COORDS_ARB-1

<ALIAS_statement>         ::= "ALIAS" <establishName> "="
                                <establishedName>

<establishName>           ::= <identifier>

<establishedName>         ::= <identifier>
```

A.6 GL_NV_fragment_program

A fragment program must begin with the sequence "!!FP1.0" or "!!FCP1.0", without any preceding whitespace.

```
<program>                 ::= <progPrefix> <instructionSequence> "END"

<progPrefix>              ::= <colorProgPrefix>
                            | <combinerProgPrefix>

<colorProgPrefix>         ::= "!!FP1.0"
```

```
<combinerProgPrefix>    ::= "!!FCP1.0"

<instructionSequence>   ::= <instructionSequence>
                              <instructionStatement>
                            | <instructionStatement>

<instructionStatement>  ::= <instruction> ";"
                            | <constantDefinition> ";"
                            | <localDeclaration> ";"

<instruction>           ::= <VECTORop-instruction>
                            | <SCALARop-instruction>
                            | <BINSCop-instruction>
                            | <BINop-instruction>
                            | <TRIop-instruction>
                            | <KILop-instruction>
                            | <TEXop-instruction>
                            | <TXDop-instruction>

<VECTORop-instruction>  ::= <VECTORop> <maskedDstReg> "," <vectorSrc>

<VECTORop>              ::= "DDX"  | "DDX_SAT"
                            | "DDXR"  | "DDXR_SAT"
                            | "DDXH"  | "DDXH_SAT"
                            | "DDXC"  | "DDXC_SAT"
                            | "DDXRC" | "DDXRC_SAT"
                            | "DDXHC" | "DDXHC_SAT"
                            | "DDY"  | "DDY_SAT"
                            | "DDYR"  | "DDYR_SAT"
                            | "DDYH"  | "DDYH_SAT"
                            | "DDYC"  | "DDYC_SAT"
                            | "DDYRC" | "DDYRC_SAT"
                            | "DDYHC" | "DDYHC_SAT"
                            | "FLR"  | "FLR_SAT"
                            | "FLRR"  | "FLRR_SAT"
                            | "FLRH"  | "FLRH_SAT"
                            | "FLRX"  | "FLRX_SAT"
                            | "FLRC"  | "FLRC_SAT"
                            | "FLRRC" | "FLRRC_SAT"
                            | "FLRHC" | "FLRHC_SAT"
                            | "FLRXC" | "FLRXC_SAT"
                            | "FRC"  | "FRC_SAT"
                            | "FRCR"  | "FRCR_SAT"
                            | "FRCH"  | "FRCH_SAT"
                            | "FRCX"  | "FRCX_SAT"
                            | "FRCC"  | "FRCC_SAT"
                            | "FRCRC" | "FRCRC_SAT"
                            | "FRCHC" | "FRCHC_SAT"
```

```
                                  | "FRCXC" | "FRCXC_SAT"
                                  | "LIT" | "LIT_SAT"
                                  | "LITR" | "LITR_SAT"
                                  | "LITH" | "LITH_SAT"
                                  | "LITC" | "LITC_SAT"
                                  | "LITRC" | "LITRC_SAT"
                                  | "LITHC" | "LITHC_SAT"
                                  | "MOV" | "MOV_SAT"
                                  | "MOVR" | "MOVR_SAT"
                                  | "MOVH" | "MOVH_SAT"
                                  | "MOVX" | "MOVX_SAT"
                                  | "MOVC" | "MOVC_SAT"
                                  | "MOVRC" | "MOVRC_SAT"
                                  | "MOVHC" | "MOVHC_SAT"
                                  | "MOVXC" | "MOVXC_SAT"
                                  | "PK2H"
                                  | "PK2US"
                                  | "PK4B"
                                  | "PK4UB"

<SCALARop-instruction> ::= <SCALARop> <maskedDstReg> "," <scalarSrc>

<SCALARop>             ::= "COS" | "COS_SAT"
                                  | "COSR" | "COSR_SAT"
                                  | "COSH" | "COSH_SAT"
                                  | "COSC" | "COSC_SAT"
                                  | "COSRC" | "COSRC_SAT"
                                  | "COSHC" | "COSHC_SAT"
                                  | "EX2" | "EX2_SAT"
                                  | "EX2R" | "EX2R_SAT"
                                  | "EX2H" | "EX2H_SAT"
                                  | "EX2C" | "EX2C_SAT"
                                  | "EX2RC" | "EX2RC_SAT"
                                  | "EX2HC" | "EX2HC_SAT"
                                  | "LG2" | "LG2_SAT"
                                  | "LG2R" | "LG2R_SAT"
                                  | "LG2H" | "LG2H_SAT"
                                  | "LG2C" | "LG2C_SAT"
                                  | "LG2RC" | "LG2RC_SAT"
                                  | "LG2HC" | "LG2HC_SAT"
                                  | "RCP" | "RCP_SAT"
                                  | "RCPR" | "RCPR_SAT"
                                  | "RCPH" | "RCPH_SAT"
                                  | "RCPC" | "RCPC_SAT"
                                  | "RCPRC" | "RCPRC_SAT"
                                  | "RCPHC" | "RCPHC_SAT"
                                  | "RSQ" | "RSQ_SAT"
                                  | "RSQR" | "RSQR_SAT"
```

```
                                    | "RSQH" | "RSQH_SAT"
                                    | "RSQC" | "RSQC_SAT"
                                    | "RSQRC" | "RSQRC_SAT"
                                    | "RSQHC" | "RSQHC_SAT"
                                    | "SIN" | "SIN_SAT"
                                    | "SINR" | "SINR_SAT"
                                    | "SINH" | "SINH_SAT"
                                    | "SINC" | "SINC_SAT"
                                    | "SINRC" | "SINRC_SAT"
                                    | "SINHC" | "SINHC_SAT"
                                    | "UP2H" | "UP2H_SAT"
                                    | "UP2HC" | "UP2HC_SAT"
                                    | "UP2US" | "UP2US_SAT"
                                    | "UP2USC" | "UP2USC_SAT"
                                    | "UP4B" | "UP4B_SAT"
                                    | "UP4BC" | "UP4BC_SAT"
                                    | "UP4UB" | "UP4UB_SAT"
                                    | "UP4UBC" | "UP4UBC_SAT"

<BINSCop-instruction>   ::= <BINSCop> <maskedDstReg> "," <scalarSrc>
                            "," <scalarSrc>

<BINSCop>               ::= "POW" | "POW_SAT"
                            | "POWR" | "POWR_SAT"
                            | "POWH" | "POWH_SAT"
                            | "POWC" | "POWC_SAT"
                            | "POWRC" | "POWRC_SAT"
                            | "POWHC" | "POWHC_SAT"

<BINop-instruction>     ::= <BINop> <maskedDstReg> "," <vectorSrc> ","
                            <vectorSrc>

<BINop>                 ::= "ADD" | "ADD_SAT"
                            | "ADDR" | "ADDR_SAT"
                            | "ADDH" | "ADDH_SAT"
                            | "ADDX" | "ADDX_SAT"
                            | "ADDC" | "ADDC_SAT"
                            | "ADDRC" | "ADDRC_SAT"
                            | "ADDHC" | "ADDHC_SAT"
                            | "ADDXC" | "ADDXC_SAT"
                            | "DP3" | "DP3_SAT"
                            | "DP3R" | "DP3R_SAT"
                            | "DP3H" | "DP3H_SAT"
                            | "DP3X" | "DP3X_SAT"
                            | "DP3C" | "DP3C_SAT"
                            | "DP3RC" | "DP3RC_SAT"
                            | "DP3HC" | "DP3HC_SAT"
                            | "DP3XC" | "DP3XC_SAT"
```

```
|  "DP4"  |  "DP4_SAT"
|  "DP4R"  |  "DP4R_SAT"
|  "DP4H"  |  "DP4H_SAT"
|  "DP4X"  |  "DP4X_SAT"
|  "DP4C"  |  "DP4C_SAT"
|  "DP4RC"  |  "DP4RC_SAT"
|  "DP4HC"  |  "DP4HC_SAT"
|  "DP4XC"  |  "DP4XC_SAT"
|  "DST"  |  "DST_SAT"
|  "DSTR"  |  "DSTR_SAT"
|  "DSTH"  |  "DSTH_SAT"
|  "DSTC"  |  "DSTC_SAT"
|  "DSTRC"  |  "DSTRC_SAT"
|  "DSTHC"  |  "DSTHC_SAT"
|  "MAX"  |  "MAX_SAT"
|  "MAXR"  |  "MAXR_SAT"
|  "MAXH"  |  "MAXH_SAT"
|  "MAXX"  |  "MAXX_SAT"
|  "MAXC"  |  "MAXC_SAT"
|  "MAXRC"  |  "MAXRC_SAT"
|  "MAXHC"  |  "MAXHC_SAT"
|  "MAXXC"  |  "MAXXC_SAT"
|  "MIN"  |  "MIN_SAT"
|  "MINR"  |  "MINR_SAT"
|  "MINH"  |  "MINH_SAT"
|  "MINX"  |  "MINX_SAT"
|  "MINC"  |  "MINC_SAT"
|  "MINRC"  |  "MINRC_SAT"
|  "MINHC"  |  "MINHC_SAT"
|  "MINXC"  |  "MINXC_SAT"
|  "MUL"  |  "MUL_SAT"
|  "MULR"  |  "MULR_SAT"
|  "MULH"  |  "MULH_SAT"
|  "MULX"  |  "MULX_SAT"
|  "MULC"  |  "MULC_SAT"
|  "MULRC"  |  "MULRC_SAT"
|  "MULHC"  |  "MULHC_SAT"
|  "MULXC"  |  "MULXC_SAT"
|  "RFL"  |  "RFL_SAT"
|  "RFLR"  |  "RFLR_SAT"
|  "RFLH"  |  "RFLH_SAT"
|  "RFLC"  |  "RFLC_SAT"
|  "RFLRC"  |  "RFLRC_SAT"
|  "RFLHC"  |  "RFLHC_SAT"
|  "SEQ"  |  "SEQ_SAT"
|  "SEQR"  |  "SEQR_SAT"
|  "SEQH"  |  "SEQH_SAT"
|  "SEQX"  |  "SEQX_SAT"
```

```
| "SEQC"  | "SEQC_SAT"
| "SEQRC"  | "SEQRC_SAT"
| "SEQHC"  | "SEQHC_SAT"
| "SEQXC"  | "SEQXC_SAT"
| "SFL"  | "SFL_SAT"
| "SFLR"  | "SFLR_SAT"
| "SFLH"  | "SFLH_SAT"
| "SFLX"  | "SFLX_SAT"
| "SFLC"  | "SFLC_SAT"
| "SFLRC"  | "SFLRC_SAT"
| "SFLHC"  | "SFLHC_SAT"
| "SFLXC"  | "SFLXC_SAT"
| "SGE"  | "SGE_SAT"
| "SGER"  | "SGER_SAT"
| "SGEH"  | "SGEH_SAT"
| "SGEX"  | "SGEX_SAT"
| "SGEC"  | "SGEC_SAT"
| "SGERC"  | "SGERC_SAT"
| "SGEHC"  | "SGEHC_SAT"
| "SGEXC"  | "SGEXC_SAT"
| "SGT"  | "SGT_SAT"
| "SGTR"  | "SGTR_SAT"
| "SGTH"  | "SGTH_SAT"
| "SGTX"  | "SGTX_SAT"
| "SGTC"  | "SGTC_SAT"
| "SGTRC"  | "SGTRC_SAT"
| "SGTHC"  | "SGTHC_SAT"
| "SGTXC"  | "SGTXC_SAT"
| "SLE"  | "SLE_SAT"
| "SLER"  | "SLER_SAT"
| "SLEH"  | "SLEH_SAT"
| "SLEX"  | "SLEX_SAT"
| "SLEC"  | "SLEC_SAT"
| "SLERC"  | "SLERC_SAT"
| "SLEHC"  | "SLEHC_SAT"
| "SLEXC"  | "SLEXC_SAT"
| "SLT"  | "SLT_SAT"
| "SLTR"  | "SLTR_SAT"
| "SLTH"  | "SLTH_SAT"
| "SLTX"  | "SLTX_SAT"
| "SLTC"  | "SLTC_SAT"
| "SLTRC"  | "SLTRC_SAT"
| "SLTHC"  | "SLTHC_SAT"
| "SLTXC"  | "SLTXC_SAT"
| "SNE"  | "SNE_SAT"
| "SNER"  | "SNER_SAT"
| "SNEH"  | "SNEH_SAT"
| "SNEX"  | "SNEX_SAT"
```

```
                              | "SNEC" | "SNEC_SAT"
                              | "SNERC" | "SNERC_SAT"
                              | "SNEHC" | "SNEHC_SAT"
                              | "SNEXC" | "SNEXC_SAT"
                              | "STR" | "STR_SAT"
                              | "STRR" | "STRR_SAT"
                              | "STRH" | "STRH_SAT"
                              | "STRX" | "STRX_SAT"
                              | "STRC" | "STRC_SAT"
                              | "STRRC" | "STRRC_SAT"
                              | "STRHC" | "STRHC_SAT"
                              | "STRXC" | "STRXC_SAT"
                              | "SUB" | "SUB_SAT"
                              | "SUBR" | "SUBR_SAT"
                              | "SUBH" | "SUBH_SAT"
                              | "SUBX" | "SUBX_SAT"
                              | "SUBC" | "SUBC_SAT"
                              | "SUBRC" | "SUBRC_SAT"
                              | "SUBHC" | "SUBHC_SAT"
                              | "SUBXC" | "SUBXC_SAT"

<TRIop-instruction>    ::= <TRIop> <maskedDstReg> "," <vectorSrc> ","
                           <vectorSrc> "," <vectorSrc>

<TRIop>                ::= "MAD" | "MAD_SAT"
                              | "MADR" | "MADR_SAT"
                              | "MADH" | "MADH_SAT"
                              | "MADX" | "MADX_SAT"
                              | "MADC" | "MADC_SAT"
                              | "MADRC" | "MADRC_SAT"
                              | "MADHC" | "MADHC_SAT"
                              | "MADXC" | "MADXC_SAT"
                              | "LRP" | "LRP_SAT"
                              | "LRPR" | "LRPR_SAT"
                              | "LRPH" | "LRPH_SAT"
                              | "LRPX" | "LRPX_SAT"
                              | "LRPC" | "LRPC_SAT"
                              | "LRPRC" | "LRPRC_SAT"
                              | "LRPHC" | "LRPHC_SAT"
                              | "LRPXC" | "LRPXC_SAT"
                              | "X2D" | "X2D_SAT"
                              | "X2DR" | "X2DR_SAT"
                              | "X2DH" | "X2DH_SAT"
                              | "X2DC" | "X2DC_SAT"
                              | "X2DRC" | "X2DRC_SAT"
                              | "X2DHC" | "X2DHC_SAT"

<KILop-instruction>    ::= <KILop> <ccMask>
```

```
<KILop>                 ::= "KIL"

<TEXop-instruction>     ::= <TEXop> <maskedDstReg> "," <vectorSrc> ","
                            <texImageId>

<TEXop>                 ::= "TEX" | "TEX_SAT"
                            | "TEXC" | "TEXC_SAT"
                            | "TXP" | "TXP_SAT"
                            | "TXPC" | "TXPC_SAT"

<TXDop-instruction>     ::= <TXDop> <maskedDstReg> "," <vectorSrc> ","
                            <vectorSrc> "," <vectorSrc> ","
                            <texImageId>

<TXDop>                 ::= "TXD" | "TXD_SAT"
                            | "TXDC" | "TXDC_SAT"

<scalarSrc>             ::= <absScalarSrc>
                            | <baseScalarSrc>

<absScalarSrc>          ::= <negate> "|" <baseScalarSrc> "|"

<baseScalarSrc>         ::= <signedScalarConstant>
                            | <negate> <namedScalarConstant>
                            | <negate> <vectorConstant> <scalarSuffix>
                            | <negate> <namedLocalParameter>
                              <scalarSuffix>
                            | <negate> <numberedLocal> <scalarSuffix>
                            | <negate> <srcRegister> <scalarSuffix>

<vectorSrc>             ::= <absVectorSrc>
                            | <baseVectorSrc>

<absVectorSrc>          ::= <negate> "|" <baseVectorSrc> "|"

<baseVectorSrc>         ::= <signedScalarConstant>
                            | <negate> <namedScalarConstant>
                            | <negate> <vectorConstant> <scalarSuffix>
                            | <negate> <vectorConstant> <swizzleSuffix>
                            | <negate> <namedLocalParameter>
                              <scalarSuffix>
                            | <negate> <namedLocalParameter>
                              <swizzleSuffix>
                            | <negate> <numberedLocal> <scalarSuffix>
                            | <negate> <numberedLocal> <swizzleSuffix>
                            | <negate> <srcRegister> <scalarSuffix>
                            | <negate> <srcRegister> <swizzleSuffix>
```

```
<maskedDstReg>          ::= <dstRegister> <optionalWriteMask>
                              <optionalCCMask>

<dstRegister>           ::= <fragTempReg>
                          | <fragOutputReg>
                          | "RC"
                          | "HC"

<optionalCCMask>        ::= "(" <ccMask> ")"
                          | ""

<ccMask>                ::= <ccMaskRule> <swizzleSuffix>
                          | <ccMaskRule> <scalarSuffix>

<ccMaskRule>            ::= "EQ" | "GE" | "GT" | "LE" | "LT" | "NE"
                          | "TR" | "FL"

<optionalWriteMask>     ::= ""
                          | "." "x"
                          | "." "y"
                          | "." "x" "y"
                          | "." "z"
                          | "." "x" "z"
                          | "." "y" "z"
                          | "." "x" "y" "z"
                          | "." "w"
                          | "." "x" "w"
                          | "." "y" "w"
                          | "." "x" "y" "w"
                          | "." "z" "w"
                          | "." "x" "z" "w"
                          | "." "y" "z" "w"
                          | "." "x" "y" "z" "w"

<srcRegister>           ::= <fragAttribReg>
                          | <fragTempReg>

<fragAttribReg>         ::= "f" "[" <fragAttribRegId> "]"

<fragAttribRegId>       ::= "WPOS" | "COL0" | "COL1" | "FOGC"
                          | "TEX0" | "TEX1" | "TEX2" | "TEX3"
                          | "TEX4" | "TEX5" | "TEX6" | "TEX7"

<fragTempReg>           ::= <fragF32Reg>
                          | <fragF16Reg>

<fragF32Reg>            ::= "R0" | "R1" | "R2" | "R3"
                          | "R4" | "R5" | "R6" | "R7"
```

```
                                      | "R8"  | "R9"  | "R10" | "R11"
                                      | "R12" | "R13" | "R14" | "R15"
                                      | "R16" | "R17" | "R18" | "R19"
                                      | "R20" | "R21" | "R22" | "R23"
                                      | "R24" | "R25" | "R26" | "R27"
                                      | "R28" | "R29" | "R30" | "R31"

<fragF16Reg>          ::= "H0"  | "H1"  | "H2"  | "H3"
                                      | "H4"  | "H5"  | "H6"  | "H7"
                                      | "H8"  | "H9"  | "H10" | "H11"
                                      | "H12" | "H13" | "H14" | "H15"
                                      | "H16" | "H17" | "H18" | "H19"
                                      | "H20" | "H21" | "H22" | "H23"
                                      | "H24" | "H25" | "H26" | "H27"
                                      | "H28" | "H29" | "H30" | "H31"
                                      | "H32" | "H33" | "H34" | "H35"
                                      | "H36" | "H37" | "H38" | "H39"
                                      | "H40" | "H41" | "H42" | "H43"
                                      | "H44" | "H45" | "H46" | "H47"
                                      | "H48" | "H49" | "H50" | "H51"
                                      | "H52" | "H53" | "H54" | "H55"
                                      | "H56" | "H57" | "H58" | "H59"
                                      | "H60" | "H61" | "H62" | "H63"

<fragOutputReg>       ::= "o" "[" <fragOutputRegName> "]"

<fragOutputRegName>   ::= "COLR" | "COLH" | "DEPR"
                                      | "TEX0" | "TEX1" | "TEX2" | "TEX3"

<numberedLocal>       ::= "p" "[" <localNumber> "]"

<localNumber>         ::= <integer> from 0 to
                                      MAX_FRAGMENT_PROGRAM_LOCAL_PARAMETERS_NV-1

<scalarSuffix>        ::= "." <component>

<swizzleSuffix>       ::= ""
                                      | "." <component> <component> <component>
                                        <component>

<component>           ::= "x" | "y" | "z" | "w"

<texImageId>          ::= <texImageUnit> "," <texImageTarget>

<texImageUnit>        ::= "TEX0"  | "TEX1"  | "TEX2"  | "TEX3"
                                      | "TEX4"  | "TEX5"  | "TEX6"  | "TEX7"
                                      | "TEX8"  | "TEX9"  | "TEX10" | "TEX11"
                                      | "TEX12" | "TEX13" | "TEX14" | "TEX15"
```

```
<texImageTarget>        ::= "1D" | "2D" | "3D" | "CUBE" | "RECT"

<constantDefinition>    ::= "DEFINE" <namedVectorConstant> "="
                              <vectorConstant>
                            | "DEFINE" <namedScalarConstant> "="
                              <scalarConstant>

<localDeclaration>      ::= "DECLARE" <namedLocalParameter>
                              <optionalLocalValue>

<optionalLocalValue>    ::= ""
                            | "=" <vectorConstant>
                            | "=" <scalarConstant>

<vectorConstant>        ::= "{" <vectorConstantList> "}"
                            | <namedVectorConstant>

<vectorConstantList>    ::= <scalarConstant>
                            | <scalarConstant> "," <scalarConstant>
                            | <scalarConstant> "," <scalarConstant> ","
                              <scalarConstant>
                            | <scalarConstant> "," <scalarConstant> ","
                              <scalarConstant> "," <scalarConstant>

<scalarConstant>        ::= <signedScalarConstant>
                            | <namedScalarConstant>

<signedScalarConstant>  ::= <optionalSign> <floatConstant>

<namedScalarConstant>   ::= <identifier>

<namedVectorConstant>   ::= <identifier>

<namedLocalParameter>   ::= <identifier>

<negate>                ::= "-" | "+" | ""

<optionalSign>          ::= "-" | "+" | ""
```

EXTENSION INDEX

FUNCTION INDEX

INDEX